2019
RUGBY
ALMANACK

2019 RUGBY ALMANACK

Edited by Clive Akers, Geoff Miller & Adrian Hill

Cover Photographs
Front: New Zealand Player of the Year, Kendra Cocksedge. *Photosport*
Back: Karl Tu'inukuafe and skipper Kieran Read with the Freedom Cup after the All Blacks' stunning come-from-behind win over South Africa at Pretoria. *Getty*

A catalogue record for this book is available from the National Library of New Zealand.

A Mower Book
Published in 2019 by Upstart Press Ltd
Level 4, 15 Huron Street, Takapuna 0622
Auckland, New Zealand

ISBN 978-1-988516-53-0
© 2019 Text C.A. Akers, G.D. Miller and A.D. Hill
The moral rights of the authors have been asserted.
© 2019 Upstart Press Ltd

All rights reserved. No part of this publication may be reproduced or transmitted in any form or by any means, electronic or mechanical, including photocopying, recording, or any information storage and retrieval system, without permission in writing from the publishers.

Typesetting and design by CVD Limited (www.cvdgraphics.nz)
Printed by Printlink Ltd, Wellington

The editors welcome notification of any errors or omissions.

Please correspond directly with the editors:

Clive Akers
Opiki
RD4
Palmerston North 4474
Phone: 06 329 1822
email: akers@xtra.co.nz

Geoff Miller
8 Whalers Rise
Whalers Gate
New Plymouth 4310
email: rugbystat@xtra.co.nz

Adrian Hill
1/212 Grove Road
Hastings 4122
email: adhill@xtra.co.nz

ACKNOWLEDGEMENTS

The publishers and editors acknowledge the assistance of the New Zealand Rugby Union and appreciate their co-operation and the co-operation of the 26 rugby unions in compiling the *2019 Rugby Almanack*.

KEY

In team record charts

RS	Ranfurly Shield
LC	Sir Brian Lochore Cup
MC	Sir Colin Meads Cup
P	Mitre 10 Cup Premiership
C	Mitre 10 Cup Championship
P/C	Mitre 10 Cup crossover match
H	Mitre 10 Heartland Championship

In individual appearance charts

15	fullback
14	right wing
13	centre
12	second five-eighth
11	left wing
10	first five-eighth
9	halfback
8	number eight
7	open-side flanker
6	blind-side flanker
5	right lock
4	left lock
3	right (tighthead) prop
2	hooker
1	left (loosehead) prop
*	retired injured or substituted
s	substitute
t	includes penalty try

CONTENTS

Editorial 10
Union Directory 13
New Zealand Rugby Union 15
2018 Honours 16
Five Players of the Year 22
Promising Players of the Year 25
New Zealand Representatives 2018 28
All Blacks Management 2018 29
Test Match Records of 2018 New Zealand Representatives 30
France in New Zealand, Investec Rugby Championship & Bledisloe Cup 31
French Barbarians 51
Vista All Blacks Northern Tour of Japan, England, Ireland & Italy 2018 53
U.K. Barbarians 61
New Zealand Under 20 62
Maori All Blacks Tour of the USA, Brazil & Chile 2018 67
New Zealand Universities 69
New Zealand Heartland 71
New Zealand Marist 73
Investec Super Rugby 2018 74
Results from 2018 First-Class Season in New Zealand. 110
National Provincial Championship Winners 116
Mitre 10 Cup 117
Mitre 10 Heartland Championship 121
    The Unions
    Auckland 125
    Bay of Plenty 130
    Buller. 135
    Canterbury 139
    Counties Manukau. 144
    Ngati Porou East Coast 149
    Hawke's Bay. 153
    Horowhenua Kapiti 158
    King Country. 162
    Manawatu 166
    Mid Canterbury. 171
    North Harbour 175
    North Otago 180
    Northland 184
    Otago. 189
    Poverty Bay 194
    South Canterbury 198
    Southland 202
    Taranaki. 206

  Tasman 211
  Thames Valley 216
  Waikato 221
  Wairarapa Bush 225
  Wanganui. 229
  Wellington 233
  West Coast. 238
Ranfurly Shield 2018. 242
Happenings. 245
2018 Season's Statistics 250
Current Player Statistics 254
First-Class Statistics 255
Referees. 258
Sevens Rugby 269
Club Finals 289
Jock Hobbs Memorial National Under 19 Tournament 293
Secondary Schools Rugby 298
Women's Rugby
  The Almanack New Zealand XV 304
  Players of the Year 305
  Season in Review 306
  New Zealand Black Ferns 309
  New Zealand Women's Representatives, 1989–2018 311
  Black Ferns Records. 316
  Results from 2018 First-Class Season in New Zealand 320
  Women's Club Finals. 322
  Farah Palmer Cup 323
  Grand Final Results. 325
  Championship Records 326
  The Unions
    Auckland Storm 327
    Bay of Plenty Volcanix. 331
    Canterbury. 335
    Counties Manukau Heat. 339
    Hawke's Bay Tui 343
    Manawatu Cyclones 347
    North Harbour Hibiscus. 351
    Otago Spirit 355
    Taranaki Whio 359
    Tasman Mako. 363
    Waikato 366
    Wellington Pride. 370
  Women's First-Class Statistics 374
  Women's Rugby Referees 2018. 377
  Women's Sevens Rugby 379

Chronicle of Events	391
International Results 2018	404
The Foreign Legion	409
New Zealand Origin and First-Class Players Capped Overseas, 2018	415
Overseas Players in New Zealand First-Class Rugby 2018	421
Offshore New Zealand Origin Coaches 2018	423
All Blacks Test Match Record	424
All Black Statistics	425
Playing Records of New Zealand Teams	434
Surviving New Zealand Representatives	439
New Zealand Representatives 1884–2018	441
NZR Annual Awards	463
NZ Rugby Foundation	468
Obituaries	469
Amendments	486

EDITORIAL

Rugby was again full of interest on and off the field in 2018. The two flagship teams — the All Blacks and Black Ferns — both ended the year still holding their world number one rankings despite suffering defeat.

The All Blacks retained the Investec Rugby Championship, with a two-point loss to South Africa at Wellington and in the return match at Pretoria having to come from 13–30 behind to win 32–30 with a last-minute converted try. South Africa's performances throughout the year were inconsistent but they obviously raised their game when meeting the All Blacks. A total of 51 players were picked for the five Tests on the Vista Northern Tour, with 19 of them selected only for participation in the Test against Japan and to then return home. The two big games on the tour were something of a struggle. England were defeated by one point, with the hosts having a try disallowed with five minutes left while Ireland deserved their win over the All Blacks, winning in Dublin for the first time. These results were quite interesting, with the All Blacks and South Africa to meet in their opening pool match at the World Cup in less than 12 months and the loser probably to play Ireland in the quarter-finals.

The Black Ferns had comfortable wins over Australia (twice) and the USA and shared the series with France, in France, on their Northern Tour. The French team was a very good one, having performed the Grand Slam in the Women's Six Nations Championship earlier in the year.

Sevens was a huge success story in 2018. Both the men's and women's teams completed a fantastic double, winning gold at the Commonwealth Games on the Gold Coast and again, three months later, at the World Cup in San Francisco. The women also finished runner-up to Australia in the World Rugby Sevens Series despite winning three of the five legs on the circuit while the men finished third in winning one of the ten legs. Such was the dominance of the women's team during the year that the three finalists for World Rugby's Women's Sevens Player of the year were all from the Black Ferns Sevens; ultimately won by Michaela Blyde. The Black Ferns Sevens also became the first New Zealand rugby team to win the Lonsdale Cup, awarded annually by the New Zealand Olympic Committee for best sporting performance in an Olympic/Commonwealth Games sport during the year.

A new initiative by New Zealand Rugby this year was the Ignite7 programme. An open call was made to 18 to 20-year-old men and women anywhere in the country, regardless of whether they played rugby or not, to register their interest in being fast tracked into the New Zealand sevens programme. Over 500 applications were made and 96 were selected to attend a camp and a final day tournament. The talent search produced three men and three women to attend development camps with the national men's and women's teams.

New Zealand dominated the Investec Super Rugby competition, with four of the five teams making the playoffs. The vagaries of the conference system meant the Chiefs, who finished the regular season with the third highest points total across all teams, had to play an away quarter-final. The Crusaders deservedly made it two consecutive titles and New Zealand teams have now won the Investec Super Rugby competition 16 times in its 23 year history.

Domestic rugby saw a return to winning ways for Auckland, taking out the Mitre 10 Cup competition to gain their first title since 2007, their longest ever period between winning titles. Auckland announced there would be free entry to the Final against Canterbury and were rewarded with a crowd of over 20,000. It has been many years since a crowd of that size attended a Mitre 10 Cup game. The Farah Palmer Cup continues to grow, with Taranaki entering a team the Cup expanded to a 12-team competition. Canterbury and Counties Manukau met in the final for the second year in a row and Canterbury won back-to-back titles. The tip of the hat, though, goes to Thames Valley for winning their maiden Heartland Championship title. The Swamp Foxes qualified for the top four for the first time, beat the undefeated defending champions Wanganui at Wanganui in the semi-final, and in the final came from 3–12 down at halftime to defeat favourites South Canterbury 17–12 at Timaru.

The 2018 rugby season may well be remembered as being the year of the woman. In no particular order: Rebecca Mahoney refereed three men's first-class matches and Whiti Timutimu refereed the Ngati Porou East Coast club final. Playing numbers increased more than the men in percentage terms, again. New Zealand won the right to host the 2021 Women's Rugby World Cup. Tonia Cawood became Chair of the Chiefs. Former All Blacks doctor Deb Robinson took a seat on the World Rugby Council. Rikki Swannell was play-by-play commentator for SKY TV in Investec Super Rugby. Kendra Cocksedge won the Kelvin R Tremain Memorial Player of the Year award. The Black Ferns Sevens were New Zealand Team of the Year. The Black Ferns were, at last, rewarded with fulltime contracts and a first ceremony was held to officially award caps to past and present Test players. All these events were firsts for women with the exception of the increased player numbers and winning the Team of the Year award.

The Editors continue to remain bemused by the neglect of the dropped goal as a scoring action in New Zealand first-class rugby. In 2018 there were zero dropped goals recorded in first-class matches in New Zealand. The last time this occurred was in 1917 when only 15 first-class fixtures were played. If it wasn't for Beauden Barrett kicking two dropped goals on the Vista Northern tour there would have been zero kicked in all New Zealand first-class rugby in 2018. Considering defence is much practised, analysed and coached these days, it is surprising to us that the dropped goal is not an option against these well-set defences, particularly post the set pieces. There were three occasions this year when a successful dropped goal would have changed the outcome of the game in the dying moments. In all three instances the team with possession was in the opposition 22 and in front of the posts during the course of play. At Wellington against South Africa, the All Blacks declined a drop kick and lost by two points. In the Mitre 10 Cup Premiership final with scores level, Auckland declined a drop kick and had to go to another 20 minutes of extra time to win it. In the Heartland Lochore Cup final Wairarapa Bush declined a drop kick which would have forced extra time and given them another 20 minutes to win the game. They lost by three points.

Investec Super Rugby could be heading for some kind of revamp from 2021 when the current broadcast deals expire at the end of 2020. We hope so. The current conference system just does not operate a level playing field: (1) Not all teams are met, so stronger teams can be avoided. (2) Separate points tables allow a team with less accumulated points in one conference to make the playoffs ahead of a team in another conference with more points. (3) Each of the conferences are not at the same playing standard. All of these anomalies would be removed if there was a return to a complete round robin of 14, or the current 15, teams. It would also mean at least two fewer games for our players at a time when there are repeated concerns about player welfare and workload. One advantage assisting the competition from 2020 is that the Southern Hemisphere test window will shift from June to July and allow Investec Super Rugby to run through to completion without the current Test break. But with each of the four SANZAAR partners having different agendas, and their own different problems, and with unanimous agreement needed on whatever the final format is, there is no guarantee on change at all.

The decision of New Zealand Rugby in August to buy back the largest shareholding (40 percent) in Super Rugby club the Blues from Bolton Equities Limited was something of an inevitability due to another year of poor on-field performance. As was noted at the time, it was not for financial reasons but due to a disconnect at Board level determined in the annual end of season review. Such stepping in to revive a struggling affiliated entity is, unfortunately, not a new one for the parent body. In the last decade they have had to do so for at least five provincial unions, all for financial reasons.

The semi-professional Mitre 10 Cup competition's third ranking in our structure is fair enough but belies its necessity. The NZR annual report for 2017 showed grants to the 14 Mitre 10 Cup provinces totalled $26.3 million. Three of the provinces made a loss with those grants. If the NZR funding was removed then all 14 provinces would have made a loss. Gate takings and sponsorship just simply do not cover the semi-professional provincial game. In 2006 the All Blacks became removed from the competition due to an expanded (then) Tri-Nations and now the Investec Rugby Championship. In recent years Super Rugby players have been allowed to skip the Mitre 10 Cup to take up short-term contracts overseas, usually in Japan, and return for the following Investec Super Rugby season as part of the battle New Zealand Rugby faces every year to retain its fulltime contracted talent against the greater money on offer overseas. This year players such as Israel Dagg, Elliot Dixon and Matt Todd, all All Blacks, bypassed the 2018 Mitre 10 Cup to play in Japan and will return for the 2019 Investec Super Rugby season. Despite these modern-day realities the competition continues to produce amazing talent and long may it (the competition and the talent) continue even though the patient does need a lot of nursing from New Zealand Rugby.

This edition of the Almanack once again records rugby activity in all 12 months of the year. We have a number of people who provide contributions such as Chris Jansen (Referees), Adam Julian (Schools), John Lea (Overseas Players), Rikki Swannell and Melodie Robinson (Women's Rugby) while Campbell Burnes, Brent Drabble, Lindsay Knight, Ron Palenski and Kelvin 'Kelly' Plummer continue to assist us with valued information, and we thank them all. Overseas colleagues John Blanch (Australia), Gilles Etienne (France), Eddie Grieb (South Africa), Stuart Farmer and John Griffiths (both England) also provide us with support which is appreciated. Again our heartfelt thanks go to New Zealand Rugby and the Provincial Unions who supply us with the information we require and answer our queries.

Clive Akers, Geoff Miller, Adrian Hill
January 2019

UNION DIRECTORY

New Zealand Rugby Union
Auckland office:
4A, 125 The Strand, Parnell, Auckland
Postal: PO Box 2453, Shortland Street,
Auckland 1140
Telephone: 09 300 4995
Wellington office:
New Zealand Rugby House, Level 4,
100 Molesworth Street, Wellington
Postal: PO Box 2172, Wellington 6140
Telephone: 04 499 4995
Fax: 04 499 4224
email: info@nzrugby.co.nz
Websites: www.allblacks.com
www.nzrugby.co.nz

Auckland RU
Office: Eden Park, Walters Rd, Auckland
Postal: PO Box 56-152, Dominion Rd,
Auckland 1446
Telephone: 09 815 4850
Fax: 09 849 5300
email: info@aucklandrugby.co.nz
Website: www.aucklandrugby.co.nz

Bay of Plenty RFU
Office: University of Waikato HP Centre,
52 Blake Street, Mount Maunganui
(since 2016)
Postal: PO Box 4058, Mt Maunganui South 3149
Telephone: 07 574 2037
Fax: 07 574 2046
email: info@boprugby.co.nz
Website: www.boprugby.co.nz

Buller RFU
Office: Craddock Park, Domett Street
Postal: PO Box 361, Westport 7866
Telephone: 03 789 8330
Fax: 03 789 8330
email: andrew@bullerrugby.co.nz
Website: www.bullerrugby.co.nz

Canterbury RFU
Office: Rugby Park, Cnr Malvern and Rutland
Streets, Christchurch (since Dec 2015)
Postal: PO Box 755, Christchurch 8140
Telephone: 03 379 8300
Fax: 03 365 3565
email: info@crfu.co.nz
Website: www.crfu.co.nz

Counties Manukau RFU
Office: Navigation Homes Stadium,
Stadium Drive, Pukekohe
Postal: PO Box 175, Pukekohe 2340
Telephone: 09 237 0033
Fax: 0800 478429
email: admin@steelers.co.nz
Website: www.steelers.co.nz

Hawke's Bay RFU
Office: McLean Park, Latham Street, Napier
Postal: PO Box 201, Napier 4140
Telephone: 06 835 7617
email: admin@hbrugby.co.nz
Website: www.hbmagpies.co.nz

Horowhenua Kapiti RFU
Office: 15-19 Bristol Street, Levin (since 2015)
Postal: PO Box 503, Levin 5540
Telephone: 06 367 8059
email: office@hkrfu.co.nz
Website: www.hkrfu.co.nz

King Country RFU
Office: Cotter St, Te Kuiti
Postal: PO Box 159, Te Kuiti
Telephone: 07 878 7545
email: generalmanager@kingcountryrugby.co.nz

Manawatu RU
Office: Central Energy Trust Arena, Palmerston Nth
Postal: PO Box 1729, Palmerston North 4440
Telephone: 06 357 2633
Fax: 06 354 1670
email: info@manawaturugby.co.nz
Website: www.manawaturugby.co.nz

Mid Canterbury RU
Office: A&P Showgrounds, Brucefield Avenue,
Ashburton
Postal: PO Box 98, Ashburton 7740
Telephone: 03 308 8718
Fax: 03 308 0103
email: admin@midcanterburyrugby.co.nz
Website: www.midcanterburyrugby.co.nz

Ngati Porou East Coast RFU
Office: 187 Waiomatatini Rd, Ruatoria
Postal: PO Box 106, Ruatoria 4032
Telephone: 06 864 8812
Fax: 06 864 8813
email: admin@npec.co.nz
Website: www.npec.co.nz

North Harbour RU
Office: QBE Stadium, Stadium Drive, Albany
Postal: PO Box 300 492, Albany 0752
Telephone: 09 447 2100
Fax: 09 447 2101
email: harbour@harbourrugby.co.nz
Website: www.harbourrugby.co.nz

North Otago RFU
Office: Shop 6a, Thames Arcade,
203 Thames Street, Oamaru
Postal: PO Box 102, Oamaru 9444
Telephone: 03 434 2053
Fax: 03 434 2054
email: admin@northotagorugby.co.nz
Website: www.northotagorugby.co.nz

Northland RU
Office: 50 Kioreroa Rd, Whangarei
Postal: PO Box 584, Whangarei 0140
Telephone: 09 438 4743
Fax: 09 438 9185
email: reception@northlandrugby.co.nz
Website: www.taniwha.co.nz

Otago RFU
Office: Forsyth Barr Stadium, Anzac Avenue, Dunedin
Postal: PO Box 691, Dunedin 9054
Telephone: 03 477 0928
email: orfu@orfu.co.nz
Website: www.orfu.co.nz

Poverty Bay RFU
Office: River Oak Mews
74 Grey St, Gisborne
Postal: PO Box 520, Gisborne 4040
Telephone: 06 868 9968
Fax: 06 868 9954
email: karen@povertybayrugby.co.nz
Website: www.povertybayrugby.co.nz

Rugby Southland
Office: Rugby Park Stadium, Tweed Street, Invercargill
Postal: PO Box 291, Invercargill 9840
Telephone: 03 216 8694
Fax: 03 216 8695
email: reception@rugbysouthland.co.nz
Website: www.rugbysouthland.co.nz

South Canterbury RFU
Office: Alpine Energy Stadium, Church Street, Timaru
Postal: PO Box 787, Timaru 7940
Telephone: 03 688 8653
Fax: 03 688 6179
email: tracy@scrfu.co.nz
Website: www.scrfu.co.nz

Taranaki RFU
Office: Pukekura Raceway, Rogan Street, New Plymouth
Postal: PO Box 5004, New Plymouth 4343
Telephone: 06 759 0167
email: info@trfu.co.nz
Website: www.trfu.co.nz

Tasman RU
Office: Hathaway Terrace, Nelson
Postal: PO Box 7157, Nelson 7042
Telephone: 03 548 7030
Fax: 03 548 8282
email: info@tasmanrugby.co.nz
Website: www.makos.co.nz

Thames Valley RFU
Office: 140a Normanby Rd, Paeroa
Postal: PO Box 245, Paeroa 3640
Telephone: 07 862 6352
Fax: 07 838 1713
email: swampfoxes@tvrfu.co.nz
Website: www.thamesvalleyswampfoxes.co.nz

Waikato RU
Office: FMG Stadium,
128 Seddon Road, Hamilton
Postal: PO Box 9507, Hamilton 3240
Telephone: 07 839 5675
Fax: 07 838 9911
email: admin@mooloo.co.nz
Website: www.mooloo.co.nz

Wairarapa Bush RFU
Office: 149 Dixon St, Masterton
Postal: PO Box 372, Masterton 5840
Telephone: 06 378 8369
email: info@waibush.co.nz
Website: www.waibush.co.nz

Wanganui RFU
Office: 40 Maria Place Extn, Wanganui
Postal: PO Box 4213, Wanganui 4541
Telephone: 06 349 2313
Fax: 06 347 8006
email: info@wanganuirugby.co.nz
Website: www.wanganuirugby.co.nz

Wellington RFU
Office: 191 Thorndon Quay, Wellington (since 2015)
Postal: PO Box 7201, Wellington South 6242
Telephone: 04 389 0020
Fax: 04 389 0889
email: mail@wrfu.co.nz
Website: www.wrfu.co.nz

West Coast RFU
Office: 123 Main South Rd, Greymouth
Postal: PO Box 31, Greymouth 7840
Telephone: 03 768 7822
email: wcrugby@netaccess.co.nz
Website: www.westcoastrfu.co.nz

New Zealand Rugby Museum
326 Main St, Palmerston North
Postal: PO Box 36, Palmerston North 4440
Telephone: 06 358 6947
Fax: 06 358 6947
email: info@rugbymuseum.co.nz
Website: www.rugbymuseum.co.nz

NEW ZEALAND RUGBY UNION

OFFICE BEARERS
2018-2019

Patron
Sir Brian Lochore ONZ, KNZM, OBE

President
M.W. Trapp (*Auckland*)

Vice-president
W.M. Osborne (*Tauranga*)

Chairman
B.G. Impey

Board

Elected members:	A.J. Golightly (*Northland*), J.S. Mitchell (*Canterbury*), S.T. Morris (*Manawatu*) M.P. Robinson (*Taranaki*), Sir Michael Jones KNZM, MNZM (*Auckland*).
Appointed members:	R.P. Dellabarca (*Auckland*), B.G. Impey (*Auckland*), P.N. Kean (*Auckland*).
Maori representative:	Dr F.R. Palmer ONZM (*Manawatu*).

Chief Executive Officer
S.J. Tew

Life Members
R.A. Guy ONZM; E.J. Tonks CBE; R.A. Fisher ONZM;
J.A Sturgeon ONZM, MBE; Sir Brian Lochore ONZ, KNZM, OBE;
A.R. Leslie MNZM; Sir Graham Henry KNZM; R.J. Littlejohn.

NZRU Team Coaches, Selectors

New Zealand:	S.W. Hansen (*coach*), I.D. Foster (*assistant*), G.J. Fox (*selector*).
New Zealand Under 20:	C.A. Philpott (*coach*), D. Hill (*assistant*), W.T.C. Rickards (*assistant*).
New Zealand Maori:	C.R. McMillan (*coach*), J.S. Maddock (*assistant*), R.Q. Randle (*assistant*).
New Zealand Heartland:	C.M. Scanlon (*coach, Buller*), M.P. Rutene (*assistant, Wairarapa Bush*), E.W. Kirton (*selector*).
New Zealand Sevens:	C. Laidlaw (*coach*), T. Cama (*assistant*).
New Zealand Secondary Schools:	B. Mooar (*coach*), S. Moore (*assistant*).
New Zealand Women:	G.M. Moore (*coach*), W. Clarke (*assistant*), J. Haggart (*assistant*).
New Zealand Women's Sevens:	A.M. Bunting (*coach*).

2018 HONOURS
THE ALMANACK NEW ZEALAND XV

Ben Smith
Highlanders

Waisake Naholo   Jack Goodhue   Rieko Ioane
Highlanders   *Crusaders*   *Blues*

Ryan Crotty
Crusaders

Beauden Barrett
Hurricanes

Aaron Smith
Highlanderss

Kieran Read (capt)
Crusaders

Ardie Savea   Samuel Whitelock   Brodie Retallick   Liam Squire
Hurricanes   *Crusaders*   *Chiefs*   *Highlanders*

Owen Franks   Codie Taylor   Karl Tu'inukuafe
Crusaders   *Crusaders*   *Chiefs*

Reserves –
James Parsons (*Blues/North Harbour*), Ofa Tu'ungafasi (*Blues*), Angus Ta'avao (*Chiefs/Taranaki*), Scott Barrett (*Crusaders*), Sam Cane (*Chiefs*), TJ Perenara (*Hurricanes*), Richie Mo'unga (*Crusaders*), Damian McKenzie (*Chiefs*).

COMMENTS

The following comment on leading players is mainly on those who appeared in Super Rugby, being the basis of selection for the majority of the All Blacks tests. Comment on players who appeared in the Mitre 10 Cup is mainly on those who played no, or very little, Super Rugby.

Fullbacks: Ben Smith is still the premier fullback in the country, and it is odd that the best fullback in the country should play the majority of his tests on the wing, when in particular he does not have the top end pace normally associated with the wing position, but that is how the test year panned out. Regardless, he always made good decisions whether in an attacking or defensive position, hardly ever putting a foot wrong. His all-round game was par excellence.

Jordie Barrett was in good form for the Hurricanes prior to the June tests and seemed to be in an alternating pattern with Ben Smith at fullback in the black jersey, but this ceased after the shock loss to South Africa at Wellington where Barrett played fullback.

David Havili gave several polished performances for the Crusaders, again being preferred at fullback ahead of Israel Dagg who was placed on the wing when free from injury.

Twenty-year old Tasman fullback Will Jordan missed the entire Super Rugby season with the Crusaders due to concussion. His brilliant running, particularly on the counter-attack, brought him nine tries in the Mitre 10 Cup, including memorable efforts against Southland and Otago. He does look a future All Black. Chase Tiatia and Jamie-Jerry Taulagi made significant contributions to Bay of Plenty and Hawke's Bay respectively.

Wing three-quarters: There was almost an embarrassment of riches on the wing with a number of standout performers as Solomon Alaimalo, George Bridge, Rieko Ioane, Ben Lam and Waisake Naholo all topping the try scoring for their respective Super Rugby teams.

Naholo's appearances for New Zealand were limited, usually playing only when Ben Smith was fullback. Through no real fault of his own, he appeared in just eight tests as the All Blacks selectors focused on the back three as one entity after the loss at Wellington. Nevertheless, in a season where he was injury free, he displayed his strong running game and finishing ability. Rieko Ioane played the majority of his rugby for the Blues in the midfield, but on the left wing for the All Blacks he showed he was the premier wing in the country, scoring 11 tries in his 11 tests.

Ben Lam shot to prominence in Super Rugby by equalling the Hurricanes season try-scoring record. He had the pace and the strength to hold off defenders, and must have attracted scrutiny from the All Blacks selectors. However, it was George Bridge who gained their pick for the end of year tour, the Crusaders wing being a consistent performer for the Super Rugby champions as he equalled their season try-scoring record. His cameo off the bench against Japan for two tries was an impressive test debut.

Solomon Alaimalo was playing superbly for the Chiefs on the wing, being their most attacking weapon, when he was shifted to fullback for their last six matches. Here he seemed to be even more of a threat to the opposition with his impressive running.

Julian Savea finished the season strongly for the Hurricanes but appeared to have lost a yard of pace, and then left for French club Toulon.

There was a lot of talent on display in the Mitre 10 Cup, but Sevu Reece was the outstanding wing in the competition. The Waikato flyer scored 14 tries, revealing all the pace, finishing and ability to beat a man required for the position.

Others worthy of mention are the Otago pairing of Mitchell Scott and Jona Nareki, Auckland's Salesi Rayasi, Taranaki's Regan Ware and Hawke's Bay's Jonah Lowe, although the last's best position might actually be centre.

Centre three-quarter: Jack Goodhue's form at centre for the Crusaders was compelling as they won back-to-back Super Rugby titles. Making his test debut in the dead rubber third test against France, he retained the first-choice role for the rest of the year apart from when suffering from glandular fever. He exhibited excellent defence, pace and an astute awareness of what was around him with ball in hand.

Anton Lienert-Brown performed well for the Chiefs, and he played the first two tests against France. His next start was in the loss to South Africa at Wellington, in which he was not the only one to have an indifferent game.

Rob Thompson had a wonderful season for the Highlanders, exhibiting the full gamut of making breaks, beating defenders, passing to better-placed support runners and strong tackling. He is unlucky his form of the past two years has not led to All Blacks selection. Before missing the last eight matches due to injury, Matt Proctor was having a good season for the Hurricanes.

This was another position in which there was a good array of talent on display in the Mitre 10 Cup. Waikato's Quinn Tupaea looked an outstanding prospect in his debut season; the 19-year old played with the maturity of one a lot more experienced, and is one of our five promising players of the year.

Canterbury's Braydon Ennor had a good first season in his new position of centre after impressing on the wing last year, while Tasman's Levi Aumua was a hard man to stop and a hard man to get past. Rene Ranger was again something of a talisman for Northland, emphasising the value of experience.

Second five-eighth: Sonny Bill Williams appeared only five times for both the Blues and the All Blacks in 2018 due to injury. The selectors turned to Ryan Crotty and Ngani Laumape in his absence and showed a preference for Crotty for the biggest games. We agree with this assessment, but both candidates provide a contrast in style in the position.

At international level, getting over the advantage line with size and physicality is the tactical style the game is evolving to in this position and Ngani Laumape provided exactly that numerous times for the Hurricanes in Super Rugby. Crotty, without the size and physicality of Laumape, effectively combined with Goodhue in the midfield for the title-winning Crusaders, displaying his usual all-round game of distribution, experience and reliability, which he brought to the All Blacks. Defensively he and Laumape were on a par, with Crotty in the semi-final against the Hurricanes shutting Laumape down with a superb defensive display.

Neither player, though, has the offloading ability in a tackle that Williams can provide and no doubt the All Blacks selectors are hoping to see a lot more of him in 2019.

Charlie Ngatai left for France after Super Rugby. His play for the Chiefs was sublime in 2015-16 but after the long-standing concussion that followed, he sadly never recaptured those heights again.

Tinoai 'TJ' Faiane had three starts for the Blues in Super Rugby, but he was the form second five-eighth in the Mitre 10 Cup for Auckland. He set up tries, found gaps and showed a much-improved defensive ability. He also captained Auckland to the title.

Dwayne Sweeney at 34 years old was a valuable member of the Waikato team, guiding the young backline around him and captaining the team to the Championship title and promotion to the Premiership. Thomas Umaga-Jensen produced some useful performances for Wellington.

First five-eighth: Richie Mo'unga had a brilliant season for the Crusaders as they won their ninth title. He did everything required: kicked for position accurately, ran well on attack, distributed to his outsides at the right time, and goal-kicked reliably. For the All Blacks there were two starts in 2018 which was a good reward for this talented player in his debut test year. Mitchell Hunt was an efficient back-up, also covering fullback, and played every game for the Crusaders.

With the All Blacks selectors endorsement, Damian McKenzie was moved up from fullback to first five-eighth by the Chiefs and shone brightly, being dangerous as ever with ball in hand. His tactical decision making became more authoritative as the season went along, growing into the transformation. For the All Blacks he gave a good exhibition in the 10 jersey against France in the third test. After the All Blacks' loss to South Africa at Wellington, the selectors had a strategic rethink and preferred McKenzie to revert to fullback for them on the end of year tour. Against England he gave a superb display in the rain at Twickenham.

When he performs as he did against Australia at Eden Park, scoring four tries, there is no doubt Beauden Barrett is the best first five-eighth in the country. His invention, speed and uncanny ability to appear in the right place is something he alone has all combined. Although his goal-kicking let him down at Wellington, it won the test against England. For the third consecutive year he was a finalist for World Rugby's Men's Player of the Year award.

Prior to the start of Super Rugby, Lima Sopoaga announced he had signed for English club Wasps and, possibly due to this, his performances for the Highlanders were not as influential as previous years. Stephen Perofeta took over at the Blues after Bryn Gatland started. He had some encouraging moments but at other times seemed to lack a bit of confidence.

There was a number of young players in the Mitre 10 Cup that gave an indication of some ability, namely Auckland's Harry Plummer, Canterbury's Brett Cameron, Waikato's Fletcher Smith and Otago's Josh Ioane. Of the more experienced players Jack Debreczeni and Jackson Garden-Bachop had good moments for Northland and Wellington respectively, while Otere Black missed the whole season for the Blues due to injury, healing in time to turn out for Manawatu.

Halfback: Aaron Smith remains the best halfback in the country, but he did not seem to be on top of his game in the test arena in the latter half of the season. The speed to the ball was still there but the delivery of pass was not instant as we have come to expect, and unusually there were some misfires.

TJ Perenara loses little in comparison to Smith. He always played with confidence, being well involved in the comeback at Pretoria, and gaining a rare start against Australia at Tokyo.

For the champion Crusaders Bryn Hall rendered fine service and held his starting position against competition from Mitchell Drummond. Te Toiroa Tahuriorangi was a surprise selection as third All Blacks halfback for the French series and Rugby Championship, ending the Super Rugby season having played every game for the Chiefs but in a lot less minutes than Brad Weber. Weber made a very successful return from the fractured femur he suffered in last year's Brisbane Tens competition.

Richard Judd and Finlay Christie hardly featured for the Hurricanes in Super Rugby, but they had very good Mitre 10 Cup seasons for their respective Bay of Plenty and Tasman provinces.

Number eight: The All Black captain Kieran Read is again our number eight. He missed the test series against France and most of the Crusaders season while on the comeback from injury. The prominence on attack was not quite there but there was nothing wrong with his defensive prowess.

Akira Ioane was a key performer in both the struggling Blues and champion Auckland teams. He joined the All Blacks squad temporarily during the test series against France so was definitely in the sights of the All Blacks selectors. His non-inclusion in the 51 for the end of year tour is for reasons known only to the selectors.

Jordan Taufua produced a number of barnstorming performances for the Crusaders but missed the final, and the rest of the season, due to a broken arm in the semi-final. This bad luck followed being named in the All Blacks squad for the series against France then having to withdraw due to a calf injury.

Having transferred from the Highlanders, Gareth Evans had his best season in Super Rugby, getting regular game time with the Hurricanes to run into form. His work at the breakdown in gaining valuable turnovers was a feature of his play.

Luke Whitelock had another steady season for the Highlanders and played the three tests against France in the absence of Kieran Read, but he does not have the pace or ball-in-hand attacking game required for regular test selection.

After long service for the Chiefs, and 43 tests for New Zealand, Liam Messam departed for French club Toulon.

Otago's Dylan Nel had an excellent Mitre 10 Cup season, being a strong ball carrier with strong defence. The return of Thomas Waldrom to Wellington from England was not the success anticipated but was compensated for by the performances of Teariki Ben-Nicholas.

Flankers: Ardie Savea really came to the fore in 2018, producing his best ever form for the All Blacks. While his extended game time was due to the horrendous broken neck Sam Cane suffered against South Africa in Pretoria, Savea's form for the Hurricanes and the All Blacks had been top notch all year, well prior to Cane's injury.

Cane took over the captaincy of the Chiefs and this had no lessening of effect on his performance in Super Rugby, being at his tireless best at the breakdown and in the tackle. It is to be hoped that he makes a full recovery and returns to play in 2019.

Dillon Hunt was prominent for the Highlanders, getting through a lot of work, being a constant presence in and around the tackle/ruck area and providing strong support in attack.

Crusaders flanker Matt Todd had an interesting year. In 2017 he was the backup to Sam Cane for the All Blacks but missed selection for this year's French test series, although called in for the third test as injury replacement. It was something of a surprise when he announced he was taking up a short-term contract in Japan to coincide with the Mitre 10 Cup, thus ruling him out of any further All Blacks consideration for the year. Then the injury to Sam Cane prompted the All Blacks selectors to obtain NZR Board approval for dispensation to select Todd for the end of year tour where he appeared in the three major tests.

Despite missing the majority of the Highlanders season, Liam Squire, as the incumbent, was the preferred player at blindside flanker in the tests.

In Squire's absences at the Highlanders, long-serving Elliot Dixon and debutant Shannon

Frizell got more game time than expected. Dixon turned in two or three good performances, but it was Frizell who was a surprise pick for the All Blacks. In the four tests he played he showed enough to indicate a future career of considerable promise, having the size, athleticism and lineout ability for the position. It was a shame injury ruled him out of the end of year tour.

Two other players announced themselves in their debut season of Super Rugby. Luke Jacobson produced several eye-catching displays in the second half of the Chiefs' season with his ball-carrying physicality and work rate on defence. Dalton Papali'i attracted positive attention for the Blues in their dismal season and then was in brilliant form for Auckland in the Mitre 10 Cup, propelling him into the All Blacks for their end of year tour. He could be a loose forward of the highest class.

Brad Shields had a tremendous final year for the Hurricanes before departing for English club Wasps, and with a lot of irony he went on to make his test debut for England. Another to head overseas after Super Rugby was Blues and 81-test All Black Jerome Kaino after a career containing two World Cup winners' medals.

In the Mitre 10 Cup, openside Mitchell Jacobson featured prominently for Waikato and Ethan Blackadder played consistently well on the blindside for Tasman. Canadian international Evan Olmstead made a good impression with Auckland.

Locks: Brodie Retallick and Sam Whitelock are still an A+ pairing for the All Blacks and have been for seven years now. New Zealand has been fortunate to have these two world-class locks appearing at the same time, and their efforts in 2018 in Super Rugby and in the test arena were again immense. But Whitelock did look a bit tired on the end of year tour after a big year captaining the Crusaders to the Super Rugby title and appearing in all but two tests. He played his 100th test in the first test against Australia at Sydney. Retallick had fewer matches in Super Rugby and for New Zealand, due to injury, and did look fresher by comparison at the end of the year. It would be a wise move for their, and the All Blacks', sake if their appearances were to be managed throughout 2019.

Scott Barrett firmly established himself this year as the third best lock in the country with a strong presence in the set pieces and mobility with ball carrying and defence. He was used a lot by the All Blacks as a replacement blindside flanker in the second half of tests to good effect.

There was a gap back to the next group, in which we would place the Highlanders pairing of Jackson Hemopo and Tom Franklin, as well as the Hurricanes Sam Lousi. Vaea Fifita played in fits and starts for the Hurricanes, but we think he is more suited to blindside flanker where he played his best rugby for the Hurricanes in 2017.

Luke Romano was third or fourth choice for the Crusaders but had an outstanding Mitre 10 Cup for Canterbury, deservedly winning the Duane Monkley medal. Injury in the final forced him to withdraw from the test against Japan. The best three young locks on display in the Mitre 10 Cup were Tasman's Pari Pari Parkinson, Waikato's James Tucker and Wellington's James Blackwell.

Props: At loosehead Karl Tu'inukuafe was the find of the year in an amazing rise from a week by week injury cover proposition for the Chiefs through to a finalist for the World Rugby Breakthrough player of the year after 13 test appearances. A strong scrummager, he was getting more involved around the field by the finish of the end of the year tour.

Joe Moody featured in just six tests due to injury, while Ofa Tu'ungafasi showed his value to the All Blacks of being able to play both sides of the scrum, covering the tighthead side during the French series and Rugby Championship and the loosehead side on the end of year tour. Unfortunately, Kane Hames played no rugby at all in 2018 due to the ongoing effects of concussion.

On the tighthead side, Owen Franks retained his premier position and played his 100th test in the second test against Australia at Eden Park. Nepo Laulala made a welcome return from injury to go on the end of year tour after missing all but the opening two games of the Chief's campaign.

Angus Ta'avao was another to start the year as injury cover at the Chiefs on a week by week basis and ended up playing every match of the season due to injuries to the contracted props, making a significant contribution to the efforts of the forwards.

Jeffrey To'omaga-Allen was again a consistent performer for the Hurricanes and passed 100 games during the season.

During 2018 Wyatt Crockett announced his retirement from test rugby, became the first man to play 200 games of Super Rugby in his final season for the Crusaders and was a class act for Tasman in the Mitre 10 Cup.

Reuben O'Neill came to the fore for Taranaki with strong displays on the loosehead side of the scrum and Josh Iosefa-Scott made a big advance at tighthead for Waikato. The experienced Auckland pairing of Sam Prattley and Marcel Renata toiled away in good fashion for the provincial champions.

Hooker: Codie Taylor was easily the best hooker on display in New Zealand during the season. His efforts were world class, displaying all the requirements of accurate throwing into the lineout, quick striking in the scrum, speed and work rate around the field, all to a high standard.

Ricky Riccitelli made full use of the opportunities afforded him in the absence of Dane Coles at the Hurricanes. He started every game, featured prominently in a number of games and was unlucky not to make the All Blacks squad for the French series and the Rugby Championship, although he was called into the squad as injury cover for the third test against France. Taylor and Riccitelli were the form New Zealand hookers in Super Rugby by a distance.

James Parsons gave good service to the Blues, despite their underperforming, and should play his 100th game for the club next year. For North Harbour in 2018 he did play his 100th game.

The Chiefs' Nathan Harris and the Highlanders' Liam Coltman and Ash Dixion are three very similar, reliable performers for their teams.

After a handful of substitute appearances in Super Rugby, Waikato's Samisoni Taukei'aho and Wellington's Asafo Aumua were the leading hooking exponents in the Mitre 10 Cup. The play of former Brumbies hooker Robbie Abel was often at a high standard for Auckland as was Andrew Makalio's for Tasman.

Dane Coles eventually appeared in 2018 with two brief appearances for Wellington in the Mitre 10 Cup after the ACL rupture he suffered against France in November 2017. He immediately became second choice hooker in his long-awaited return to the All Blacks setup on the end of year tour.

FIVE PLAYERS OF THE YEAR

With Brodie Retallick and Sam Whitelock coming together as the All Blacks' lock pairing in 2012, a number of candidates have come into contention since for being the next choice, but none had become permanent. In demonstrating the form he did in 2018 **Scott Kevin Barrett** *(Crusaders/Taranaki)* cemented that third choice position.

As the Crusaders secured their second Super Rugby title in a row, Barrett made the most appearances of the five locks used, appearing in 17 of the 20 matches, three more than Sam Whitelock. He presented a physical presence in the pack, with his carries in the tight-loose, forceful tackling on defence, and lineout work in a measure and quality that was comparable to his more illustrious partner.

With Brodie Retallick out injured, the partnership continued for the June home test series against France, Barrett playing all 240 minutes, his effort in the third test at Dunedin being a standout. The first test at Auckland was notable for his brothers Beauden and Jordie also starting, being the first time in All Blacks' history three brothers have started in the same test.

Appearing in 13 (nine starts) of the All Blacks' 14 tests in 2018, the 1.97-m 111-kg lock showed he could function as a regular starter and has the mobility and versatility for the blindside flanker position. All four of his appearances as a substitute were in this position, enabling a potent lineout trio with Retallick and Whitelock, one that certainly got the better of the England lineout in the much-awaited clash on the end of year tour.

In May he re-signed with NZR, Crusaders and Taranaki to the end of 2020.

Scott Barrett was an Almanack promising player of the year for 2014.

With Aaron Cruden having left New Zealand for French club Montpellier in August 2017, All Blacks coach Steve Hansen opined that a return to the first five-eighths position for **Damian Sinclair McKenzie** *(Chiefs/Waikato)* would give him more opportunities to control a game, the position in which he played for his province Waikato. His 2016 and 2017 seasons for the Chiefs and All Blacks were at fullback due to the presence of Aaron Cruden and Beauden Barrett respectively.

For the Chiefs in 2018, McKenzie duly was the first-choice number 10, and a successful transition it proved as the Chiefs qualified for the quarter-finals. His attacking stats for ball in hand with tries, try assists, line breaks and metres run were all impressive, as was his goal-kicking with 62 goals from 80 attempts (78 per cent).

Given a start for the All Blacks against France in the third test, he was in good control and attacked the line well. But for the end of year tour Steve Hansen preferred McKenzie back at fullback to try to re-energise the back three entity by having playmakers at both first five-eighth and fullback on the field.

Against England in the rain he was safe under the high ball, produced nimble footwork to evade players coming at him in defensive positions, made two breaks from the back, and scored the All Blacks' only try in what was probably the best fullback display in the All Blacks jersey in 2018.

In March he re-signed with NZR/Chiefs/Waikato to the end of 2021.

Damian McKenzie was an Almanack promising player of the year for 2014.

Five Players of the Year

James William Parsons *(Blues/North Harbour)* played his 100th first-class match for North Harbour during 2018, a very significant achievement in modern-day rugby for a Mitre 10 Cup union when careers in the competition are short, with players quick to move overseas when greater financial reward is usually on offer.

Since the advent of the Mitre 10 Cup/Heartland Championship competitions in 2006, Parsons is just the fifth player to have played 100 games for a Mitre 10 Cup union where all 100 games have been from 2006 onwards (see Happenings). Such longevity is invaluable when the average age of Mitre 10 Cup players is 23–24 years old, his experience at hooker, and captaincy, being significant in leading a good forward pack in North Harbour's resurgence of the last three years. He had started the year with consistent form in an otherwise struggling Blues outfit.

Born at Palmerston North on 27 November 1986 and educated at Auckland's King's College from 2000 to 2004, appearing for the first XV in his final year, James Parsons then joined the Takapuna club in 2005.

His first four matches for North Harbour were in 2007, and he has been first-choice hooker for the province since 2009, although injury disrupted his 2009 and 2016 seasons. He assumed the captaincy in 2013 and was handed it again in 2016, with North Harbour winning the Championship to win promotion to the Premiership, and he has retained leadership duties since.

He made his Super Rugby debut with the Blues in 2012, and at the end of the 2018 season has accumulated 91 appearances for the club. He had also captained the team in 2016 and 2017.

On 1 November 2014 Parsons appeared for the UK Barbarians team against Australia at Twickenham, his then Blues coach Sir John Kirwan being the Barbarians coach for the match. On the same day at Chicago against the USA, the All Blacks played the first of four matches on their end of year Northern Hemisphere tour. Hooker Nathan Harris was injured after just 10 minutes and invalided out of the tour. As the All Blacks' next match was at Twickenham seven days later, and Parsons was already there, he was added to the All Blacks' touring party for the remainder of the tour. He closed the year making his test debut with a starting appearance against Scotland on 15 November.

There was one further test appearance against Australia at Wellington in the 2016 Rugby Championship.

In the second half of the All Blacks' season of 2018 openside flanker **Ardie Suetualo Savea** *(Hurricanes/Wellington)* played the best test rugby of his career.

Against Argentina at Buenos Aires he was a late call-up to the unfamiliar position of number eight due to Luke Whitelock's withdrawal on the day of the match, and he responded with a standout performance. In the next match against South Africa at Pretoria, openside flanker incumbent Sam Cane suffered a season-ending injury after 35 minutes and Savea scored the last-minute try to level the scores at 30–30 and give Richie Mo'unga the successful conversion attempt to win the match.

Another standout match against Australia at Tokyo followed, and he was one of the All Blacks' best in the loss to Ireland a week after a similar effort against England in the 16–15 victory in the wet.

In his six appearances in the last seven tests of the year he exhibited the full all-round game for a modern-day loose forward of turnovers won, strong ball carries and tackles made, and any lingering questions as to whether he was strong enough over, or with, the ball or aggressive enough at the tackle were effectively answered.

During the year he was in negotiation with French club Pau for post the 2019 World Cup, but in December he re-signed with NZR to the end of 2021.

Ardie Savea was an Almanack promising player of the year for 2012.

George Zvi Karl Tu'inukuafe *(Chiefs/North Harbour)* had an extraordinary 2018. When the Super Rugby squads were announced on 1 November 2017 the 1.82-m 135-kg loosehead prop was not among them and not considered an unlucky omission. However, Chiefs coach Colin Cooper invited him to pre-Christmas training alongside the squad, having been impressed with his scrummaging for North Harbour in the Mitre 10 Cup. It proved to be an inspired decision.

During the pre-season, loosehead props Mitchell Graham and Kane Hames fell under injury, followed by Atu Moli (opening match) and Aidan Ross (seventh match).

Tu'inukuafe's original pre-Christmas training stint turned into a full-season one for the Chiefs, ending with 16 appearances (nine starts) in their 17 matches as Graham, Hames, Moli and Ross never returned from their injuries. And it did not end there.

The All Blacks squad was named for the three-test series against France on 20 May. Three days later Tim Perry withdrew with injury and Tu'inukuafe was the replacement. His debut off the bench in the first test at Auckland produced an auspicious first act in the black jersey. Running on to the field in the 46th minute for a scrum on the French 22, French put in, the All Blacks shoved the French back five metres and earned a penalty.

It was the first of his 13 test appearances in 2018, missing only the test against Japan. Such was his form in them that he was on the final three shortlist for World Rugby's Breakthrough Player of the Year award.

Karl Tu'inukuafe was born at Auckland on 21 February 1993. He attended Sunnynook School and then Wesley College from 2004 to 2010, appearing in the first XV in his final two years. While there he represented the Counties Manukau under 16 and under 18 teams.

In 2011, his first year out of school, he took employment at a security firm and joined the Karaka club, playing for the under 19 team and the Counties Manukau under 21 team, then the following year appeared for the Karaka club's under 21 team. In 2013 and 2014 he chose not to play any rugby at all. After a visit to the doctor and the need to lose weight he resumed rugby and joined the Takapuna club in 2015, playing for the Premier Two team, and gaining selection in the North Harbour B team, but he did get the chance to make his first-class debut, with a solitary appearance off the bench for North Harbour in the Mitre 10 Cup. From there it was to France for a season with the Narbonne club in the second tier Pro D2 competition.

He returned home for the 2016 New Zealand season and debuted for Takapuna's Premier One team. Seven appearances for North Harbour in the Mitre 10 Cup followed, and 2017 was similar with nine appearances.

Tu'inukuafe will play for the Blues in 2019, having signed a three-year contract in July.

PROMISING PLAYERS OF THE YEAR

Thomas Michael Christie (*Canterbury*) captained the New Zealand Under 20 team in 2018 that won the Oceania Championship and finished fourth at the World Championship. The very promising 1.85-m 103-kg openside flanker was then named in the Canterbury Mitre 10 Cup squad for the first time and appeared in 11 of the 12 matches. Such was his form throughout the year that at the ASB NZ Rugby Awards in December he won the Age Grade Player of the Year award.

Born at Gore on 4 March 1998 he was educated at Beckenham School and Christchurch South Intermediate and then enrolled at Shirley Boys High School in 2011. He was part of the first XV for three years (2013–15), being captain in that last year as Shirley Boys were defeated in the final of the Crusaders Schools championship. He finished the year with selection in the NZ Schools team and winning the Shirley BHS sportsman of the year award for his efforts in rugby, basketball and rowing. Earlier in 2015 he had represented the school at the Maadi Cup rowing regatta.

He entered Canterbury University in 2016 for an engineering degree and played for Canterbury at the Jock Hobbs Memorial National Under 19 tournament which Canterbury won.

In 2017 he made his premier debut for the Christchurch club, made his first-class debut when selected in the New Zealand Under 20 team that won the World Championship in Georgia, captained Canterbury in his second appearance at the Jock Hobbs Memorial National Under 19 tournament and made his Canterbury debut in the Mitre 10 Cup final victory against Tasman when he came on for the last five minutes. He was in the Crusaders Knights 2017 and 2018 teams.

In his debut season at first-class level, **Scott William Gregory** (*Northland*) had the distinction to make two national teams. The 1.84-m 93-kg midfield back gained selection in the New Zealand Under 20 team for both the Oceania and World Championships then debuted for the NZ Sevens team at the Oceania Sevens in Fiji in November, impressing enough to sign a contract for the 2018–19 World Rugby Sevens circuit, ending the year playing in the first two events in Dubai and Cape Town. In between turning out for those two national teams, he debuted for Northland in the Mitre 10 Cup playing in ten of the 11 matches, appearing in both the midfield and left wing positions.

Scott Gregory was born at Whangarei on 7 January 1999 and joined the Hikurangi club at the age of five. Educated at Whangarei Boys' High School he was in the first XV for his final two years (2015–16) and captained the side in 2016. During the final year he played for both the Northland under 18 and Blues under 18 teams, and completed the year winning the 2016 Northland Secondary Schools male sportsman of the year award for his rugby and athletics prowess.

At the 2016 national under 18 athletic championship in Dunedin he won the gold medals in the shot put, discus and hammer throws, and at the national under 20 championship he won gold in the hammer throw, silver in the discus and bronze in the shot put.

In 2017, his first year out of school, he hardly played any rugby all due to a stress fracture in his back but did play for Northland at the Jock Hobbs Memorial National Under 19 tournament in September.

Dalton Reece Papali'i (*Auckland*) had an outstanding first full Mitre 10 Cup campaign for Auckland. The 1.90-m 105-kg openside/blindside flanker was full of hard running and topped the Mitre 10 Cup tackle count with 169 in his nine matches, an average of 18 per match, missing just six. Four days after his 21st birthday he was the only uncapped player selected in the All Blacks' 32-man squad for the end of year tour, which caused him to miss both of Auckland's playoff matches on the way to the province's premiership title. This topped off a year which had begun with seven appearances for the Blues in his debut Super Rugby season.

He was born at Auckland on 11 October 1997 and joined the Pakuranga United club at an early age, being a part of the under 12 and under 13 title winning teams of 2009 and 2010. In 2010 he also represented Auckland East at the annual Roller Mills tournament. At Saint Kentigern College he was in the first XV 2012-15, captaining in his final year. The College won the Auckland 1A title in three of those four years and the National title in 2012 and beaten finalist in 2013. He finished 2015 with selection in the NZ Secondary Schools team.

In 2016 he made his first-class debut when selected in the New Zealand under 20 team for the Oceania and World Championships, captained the Blues under 20 team and captained Auckland at the Jock Hobbs Memorial National Under 19 tournament.

Last year was almost a replica, making the New Zealand under 20 team which won the World Championship, captaining the Blues under 20 team, having his first taste of Mitre 10 Cup rugby with four sporadic appearances as a substitute for Auckland, but ending with a full contract with the Blues for 2018.

Kaleb Richard Trask (*Bay of Plenty*) was an influential part in Bay of Plenty winning the Jock Hobbs Memorial National Under 19 tournament. The 1.80-m 89-kg first five-eighth/fullback was the tournament's top points scorer with 54 and recipient of the DJ Graham Award for player of the tournament. In the 35-30 win over Canterbury in the final, Trask scored 20 points with two tries, two conversions and two penalty goals.

He had already been named in the Steamers' squad for the Mitre 10 Cup, going on to make a total of seven appearances — two before the under 19 tournament and five after — having started the year as a member of the New Zealand under 20 team at the Oceania and World Championships.

Kaleb Trask was born at Rotorua on 27 January 1999 and attended Westbrook Primary school and Rotorua Intermediate before starting at Rotorua Boys' High School in 2012. He had three years in the first XV 2014-16, and in those years was part of the school's two national titles — the 2014 Condor Sevens and the 2015 first XV championship — and represented the Bay of Plenty under 16 and under 18 teams.

Having played for the Kahukura Rugby and Sports club's junior teams in his school years, in 2017 upon leaving school he linked with the Tauranga Sports club and made his premier debut. He made his first appearance at the Jock Hobbs Memorial National Under 19 tournament as Bay of Plenty finished fifth. In 2017 and 2018 he played for the Chiefs under 20 teams.

His grandfather Bruce Trask was a fullback who represented North Otago 1967-68, Bay of Plenty 1969-74 and Hawke's Bay 1975.

As Waikato worked their way to the Mitre 10 Championship title, and promotion back to the Premiership for 2019, a prominent member of the backline was centre **Quinn Puketahinga Claude Tupaea** (*Waikato*). In his debut season at first-class level the 1.87-m 102-kg 19-year-old played in all 12 matches for Waikato, scoring seven tries.

Born at Hamilton on 10 May 1999, he was schooled at Marian Primary and Southwell School before entering Hamilton Boys' High School in 2013. In his three years in the first XV 2015-17, captain in his final year, Hamilton Boys' won the Super Eight title twice, including once shared, were runners up in the 2017 national championship, and won the Condor Sevens in all three years. He concluded 2017 by being named captain of the New Zealand schoolboys team.

Also while at Hamilton Boys he represented the Waikato under 16 (2014), and Chiefs under 18 (2015-17) teams. He also rowed for the school at the Maadi Cup — in 2014 at the under 15 level he was part of the coxed eight, coxed quad sculls and coxed fours first placed teams, and in 2015 part of the under 16 coxed eight which came first.

Leaving school in 2018 he started a plumbing apprenticeship and joined Hamilton Old Boys, making his senior debut. After missing selection in the New Zealand under 20 team he did join the team as injury cover in time for the World Championship semi-final but was not required for either of the final two games.

His father Brent (Counties) and mother Kelly (Northland) all played age-grade representative rugby as have his brothers Tayne and Mason for Waikato.

NEW ZEALAND REPRESENTATIVES 2018

Choosing 35 new All Blacks over the last three years was not a sign of indecision, rather it was a demonstration that no stone would be left unturned in the search for the best squad for Rugby World Cup 2019.

Details of the 11 new All Blacks are:

BRIDGE, George Crispin *born Gisborne, April 1, 1995*
All Blacks #1178 New Zealand Under 20 2015 (3); Canterbury 2016 (8), 2017 (10), 2018 (11); Crusaders 2017 (19), 2018 (18); UK Barbarians 2017 (2); New Zealand 2018 (1).

CAMERON, Brett Donald *born Wanganui, October 4, 1996*
All Blacks # 1181 Canterbury 2017 (11), 2018 (12); Crusaders 2018 (1); New Zealand 2018 (1).

EVANS, Gareth Owen *born Hastings, August 5, 1991*
All Blacks #1179 Otago 2011 (10), 2012 (13), 2013 (9); Highlanders Development XV 2012 (1), 2013 (1); Highlanders 2014 (11), 2015 (14), 2016 (4), 2017 (15); Hawke's Bay 2014 (7), 2015 (1), 2017 (2), 2018 (9); Hurricanes 2018 (16); New Zealand 2018 (1).

FRIZELL, Shannon Michael *born Tongatapu, Tonga, February 11, 1994*
All Blacks #1172 Tasman 2016 (12), 2017 (11), 2018 (1); Highlanders 2018 (14); New Zealand 2018 (4).

HEMOPO Jackson Nikora *born Wanganui, November 14, 1993*
All Blacks #1173 Otago 2012 (2), 2014 (10), 2015 (6); Highlanders 2015 (1), 2017 (9), 2018 (16); Manawatu 2016 (10), 2017 (10), 2018 (2); Maori All Blacks 2017 (2), 2018 (2); New Zealand 2018 (3).

LOMAX, Tyrel Shae *born Canberra, Australia, March 16, 1996*
All Blacks #1180 Rebels 2017 (13); Tasman 2017 (8), 2018 (11); Highlanders 2018 (16); New Zealand 2018 (1); Maori All Blacks 2017 (2), 2018 (2)

PAPALI'I, Dalton Reece *born Auckland, October 11, 1997*
All Blacks #1176 New Zealand Under 20 2016 (4), 2017 (6); Auckland 2017 (6), 2018 (9); Blues 2018 (7); New Zealand 2018 (2)

PROCTOR, Matthew Phillip *born Wellington, October 26, 1992*
All Blacks #1177 New Zealand Under 20 2012 (3); Wellington 2012 (11), 2013 (7), 2014 (6), 2015 (10), 2016 (9), 2018 (9); Hurricanes Development XV (2); Hurricanes 2013 (4), 2014 (9), 2015 (11), 2016 (12), 2017 (7), 2018 (9); Maori All Blacks 2013 (2), 2014 (2), 2015 (2), 2016 (3), 2017 (1), 2018 (2); New Zealand 2018 (1).

TA'AVAO-MATAU, Angus Wilkie Faiumiolemau *born Auckland, March 22, 1990*
All Blacks #1175 New Zealand Under 20 2010 (4); Auckland 2010 (7), 2011 (8), 2012 (11), 2013 (10); Blues 2012 (6), 2013 (16), 2014 (16), 2015 (11); Taranaki 2014 (12), 2015 (10), 2017 (9), 2018 (3); UK Barbarians 2014 (2); Waratahs 2016 (15), 2017 (8); Chiefs 2018 (17); New Zealand 2018 (3)

TAHURIORANGI, Te Toiroa Hohepa *born Rotorua, March 31, 1995*
All Blacks # 1174   New Zealand Under 20 2015 (8); Taranaki 2015 (11), 2016 (10), 2017 (10), 2018 (2); New Zealand Barbarians 2015 (1); Hurricanes 2016 (1), 2017 (10); Maori All Blacks 2017 (1); Chiefs 2018 (17); New Zealand 2018 (3)

TU'INUKUAFE, George Zvi Karl   *born Auckland, February 21, 1993*
All Blacks #1171   North Harbour 2015 (1), 2016 (7), 2017 (9); Chiefs 2018 (16); New Zealand 2018 (13)

ALL BLACKS MANAGEMENT 2018

Head Coach:	Steve Hansen
Assistant Coach (Selector):	Ian Foster
Assistant Coach (Forwards):	Mike Cron
Assistant Coach (Defence):	Scott McLeod
Selector:	Grant Fox
Manager (Business):	Darren Shand
Manager (Leadership):	Gilbert Enoka
Coach (Strength and Conditioning):	Dr Nic Gill
Assistant Coach (Strength and conditioning):	Kim Simperingham
Player Development Manager:	Mike Anthony
Performance Analyst:	Jamie Hamilton
Assistant Performance Analyst:	Hayden Chapman
Doctor:	Dr Tony Page
Physiotherapist:	Peter Gallagher
Physiotherapist (Japan test):	John Roche
Manual Therapist:	George Duncan
Nutritionist:	Katrina Darry
Team Services Manager:	Bianca Thiel
Media Manager:	Joe Locke
Logistics Manager:	James Iversen

TEST MATCH RECORDS OF 2018 NEW ZEALAND REPRESENTATIVES
ALL BLACK CAREER RECORDS TO JANUARY 1, 2019

	Debut	Tests	Starts	Wins	Winning %	Tries	Conversions	Penalty Goals	Dropped Goals	Points
Beauden Barrett	2012	73	43	65	89	32	138	51	2	595
Jordie Barrett	2017	9	7	7	77.8	8	1	–	–	42
Scott Barrett	2016	29	13	23	79.3	3	–	–	–	15
George Bridge	2018	1	–	1	100	2	–	–	–	10
Brett Cameron	2018	1	–	1	100	–	–	–	–	–
Sam Cane	2012	60	41	53	88.3	13	–	–	–	65
Dane Coles	2012	60	44	53	88.3	11	–	–	–	55
Liam Coltman	2016	4	–	3	75	–	–	–	–	–
Ryan Crotty	2013	44	32	38	86.4	9	–	–	–	45
Mitch Drummond	2018	1	–	1	100	–	–	–	–	–
Gareth Evans	2018	1	–	1	100	–	–	–	–	–
Vaea Fifita	2017	9	6	9	100	2	–	–	–	10
Owen Franks	2009	106	96	91	85.9	–	–	–	–	–
Shannon Frizell	2018	4	4	4	100	1	–	–	–	5
Jack Goodhue	2018	7	6	5	71.4	2	–	–	–	10
Nathan Harris	2014	20	1	18	90	2	–	–	–	10
Jackson Hemopo	2018	3	1	3	100	–	–	–	–	–
Dillon Hunt	2018	1	–	1	100	–	–	–	–	–
Rieko Ioane	2016	24	21	20	83.3	22	–	–	–	110
Nepo Laulala	2015	17	10	14	82.4	–	–	–	–	–
Ngani Laumape	2017	10	5	8	80	6	–	–	–	30
Anton Lienert–Brown	2016	33	16	28	84.8	6	–	–	–	30
Tyrel Lomax	2018	1	–	1	100	–	–	–	–	–
Damian McKenzie	2016	23	16	20	87	12	10	–	–	80
Nehe Milner-Skudder	2015	13	13	12	92.3	12	–	–	–	60
Joe Moody	2014	37	30	32	86.5	3	–	–	–	15
Richie Mo'unga	2018	9	2	8	88.9	1	19	3	–	52
Waisake Naholo	2015	26	24	23	88.5	16	–	–	–	80
Dalton Papali'i	2018	2	1	2	100	–	–	–	–	–
TJ Perenara	2014	55	13	48	87.3	11	–	–	–	55
Tim Perry	2018	6	–	5	83.3	–	–	–	–	–
Matt Proctor	2018	1	1	1	100	1	–	–	–	5
Kieran Read	2008	118	111	101	85.6	25	–	–	–	125
Brodie Retallick	2012	75	61	68	90.7	4	–	–	–	20
Ardie Savea	2016	35	11	29	82.9	7	–	–	–	35
Aaron Smith	2012	82	76	71	86.6	16	1	–	–	82
Ben Smith	2009	76	66	68	86.8	33	–	–	–	165
Liam Squire	2016	23	17	19	82.6	4	–	–	–	20
Angus Ta'avao-Matau	2018	3	1	3	100	–	–	–	–	–
Te Toiroa Tahuriorangi	2018	3	1	3	100	1	–	–	–	5
Codie Taylor	2015	41	22	34	82.9	9	–	–	–	45
Matt Todd	2013	17	4	16	94.1	1	–	–	–	5
Karl Tu'inukuafe	2018	13	6	11	84.6	–	–	–	–	–
Patrick Tuipulotu	2014	21	7	18	85.7	3	–	–	–	15
Ofa Tu'ungafasi	2016	26	3	22	84.6	1	–	–	–	5
Luke Whitelock	2013	7	5	7	100	–	–	–	–	–
Samuel Whitelock	2010	108	89	95	88	5	–	–	–	25
Sonny Bill Williams	2010	51	38	47	92.2	11	–	–	–	55

FRANCE IN NEW ZEALAND, INVESTEC RUGBY CHAMPIONSHIP AND BLEDISLOE CUP

	Franchise	Date of Birth	Height	Weight	Test at 1/1/18
B.J. (Beauden) Barrett	Hurricanes	27/5/91	1.87	91	62
J.M. (Jordie) Barrett	Hurricanes	17/2/97	1.96	101	2
S.K. (Scott) Barrett	Crusaders	20/11/93	1.97	111	16
S.J. (Sam) Cane	Chiefs	13/1/92	1.89	106	53
L.J. (Liam) Coltman	Highlanders	25/1/90	1.86	110	1
R.S. (Ryan) Crotty	Crusaders	23/9/88	1.81	94	35
V.T.L. (Vaea) Fifita	Hurricanes	17/6/92	1.96	112	5
O.T. (Owen) Franks	Crusaders	23/12/87	1.85	122	95
S.M. (Shannon) Frizell	Highlanders	11/2/94	1.95	108	–
E.J. (Jack) Goodhue	Crusaders	13/6/95	1.87	98	–
N.P. (Nathan) Harris	Chiefs	8/3/92	1.86	106	11
J.N. (Jackson) Hemopo	Highlanders	14/11/93	1.94	113	–
R.E. (Rieko) Ioane	Blues	18/3/97	1.89	103	13
K.H. (Ngani) Laumape	Hurricanes	24/4/93	1.77	103	4
A.R. (Anton) Lienert-Brown	Chiefs	15/4/95	1.85	96	22
D.S. (Damian) McKenzie	Chiefs	20/4/95	1.75	82	12
N.R. (Nehe) Milner-Skudder	Hurricanes	15/12/90	1.80	90	11
J.P.T. (Joe) Moody	Crusaders	18/9/88	1.88	120	31
R. (Richie) Mo'unga	Crusaders	25/5/94	1.76	88	–
W.R. (Waisake) Naholo	Highlanders	8/5/91	1.86	105	18
T.T.R. (TJ) Perenara	Hurricanes	23/1/92	1.84	90	42
T.G. (Tim) Perry	Crusaders	1/8/88	1.91	118	–
K.J. (Kieran) Read	Crusaders	26/10/85	1.93	111	109
B.A. (Brodie) Retallick	Chiefs	31/5/91	2.04	123	68
A.S. (Ardie) Savea	Hurricanes	14/10/93	1.88	100	22
A.L. (Aaron) Smith	Highlanders	21/11/88	1.71	83	71
B.R. (Ben) Smith	Highlanders	1/6/88	1.86	94	64
L.I.J. (Liam) Squire	Highlanders	20/3/91	1.96	109	15
C.J.D. (Codie) Taylor	Crusaders	31/3/91	1.83	106	29
A.W.F.(Angus) Ta'avao-Matau	Chiefs	22/3/90	1.94	128	–
T.T.H. (Te Toiroa) Tahuriorangi	Chiefs	31/3/95	1.71	83	–
M.B. (Matt) Todd	Crusaders	14/4/88	1.85	103	13
G.Z.K. (Karl) Tu'inukuafe	Chiefs	21/2/93	1.82	135	–
P.T. (Patrick) Tuipulotu	Blues	23/1/93	1.98	120	16
A.O.H.M. (Ofa) Tu'ungafasi	Blues	19/4/92	1.95	122	14
L.C. (Luke) Whitelock	Highlanders	29/1/91	1.90	108	2
S.L. (Samuel) Whitelock	Crusaders	12/10/88	2.02	122	96
S.B. (Sonny Bill) Williams	Blues	3/8/85	1.91	111	46

FRANCE IN NEW ZEALAND, INVESTEC RUGBY CHAMPIONSHIP AND BLEDISLOE CUP 2018 ALL BLACKS APPEARANCES

ALL BLACKS 2018	France 1	France 2	France 3	Australia 1	Australia 2	Argentina 1	South Africa 1	Argentina 2	South Africa 2	TOTALS
J. Barrett	15*	15	s	–	15*	–	15*	–	–	5
B. Smith	14	14	15	15	14	15*	14	15*	15	9
Naholo	–	–	14	14	11	11	–	14	14*	6
Milner-Skudder	–	–	–	–	–	14	–	–	–	1
Ioane	11	11	11	11*	–	–	11	11	11	7
Lienert-Brown	13	13*	–	s	s	s	13*	s	s	8
Goodhue	–	–	13	13	13*	13	s	–	–	5
Crotty	12*	12*	–	12*	–	–	12	13	13	6
Laumape	s	s	–	–	12	12*	–	–	–	4
Williams	–	–	12*	–	–	–	–	12*	12*	3
B. Barrett	10	10*	–	10	10	–	10	10	10	7
McKenzie	s	s	10*	s	s	s	s	–	–	7
Mo'unga	–	–	s	–	–	10	–	s	s	4
A. Smith	9*	9*	9*	9*	9*	–	9*	s	9*	8
Perenara	s	s	s	s	s	9*	s	9*	s	9
Tahuriorangi	–	–	–	–	–	s	–	–	–	1
L. Whitelock	8*	8	8	–	–	s	–	–	–	4
Read	–	–	–	8	8	8*	8	–	8	5
Cane	7*	7*	–	7*	7*	–	7*	7	7*	7
Savea	s	s	7*	s	s	7	s	8	s	9
Todd	–	–	s	–	–	–	–	–	–	1
Squire	6	6*	–	6*	6*	–	6*	–	–	5
Fifita	s	s	–	–	–	–	–	–	–	2
Frizell	–	–	6	–	–	6	–	6*	6*	4
S. Barrett	5	5	5	s	s	5	5	5*	5	9
S. Whitelock	4	4	4*	5	5	4	4	4	4	9
Retallick	–	–	–	4	4	4*	–	–	–	3
Hemopo	–	–	s	–	–	–	–	s	–	2
Tuipulotu	–	–	–	–	–	s	s	s	s	3
Franks	3*	3*	3*	3*	3*	3*	3*	–	3*	8
Tu'ungafasi	s	s	s	–	s	s	s	3*	s	8
Ta'avao-Matau	–	–	–	–	–	–	–	s	–	1
Moody	1*	1*	1*	1*	1*	–	–	–	–	5
Tu'inukuafe	s	s	s	s	s	1*	1*	1*	1*	9
Perry	–	–	–	s	–	s	s	s	s	5
Taylor	2*	2*	2*	2*	2*	2*	2*	2*	2*	9
Harris	s	s	–	s	s	s	–	s	s	7
Coltman	–	–	s	–	–	–	s	–	–	2

INDIVIDUAL SCORING

	Tries	Con	PG	DG	Points		Tries	Con	PG	DG	Points
B. Barrett	6	18	4	–	78	Frizell	1	–	–	–	5
Ioane	10	–	–	–	50	Laumape	1	–	–	–	5
McKenzie	3	10	–	–	35	Lienert-Brown	1	–	–	–	5
Mo'unga	–	9	2	–	24	Milner-Skudder	1	–	–	–	5
J. Barrett	3	–	–	–	15	Read	1	–	–	–	5
Naholo	3	–	–	–	15	Retallick	1	–	–	–	5
Savea	3	–	–	–	15	Squire	1	–	–	–	5
A. Smith	3	–	–	–	`15	Todd	1	–	–	–	5
B. Smith	3	–	–	–	15	Tuipulotu	1	–	–	–	5
Goodhue	2	–	–	–	10						
Moody	2	–	–	–	10	**Totals**	**52**	**37**	**6**	**0**	**352**
Perenara	2	–	–	–	10						
Taylor	2	–	–	–	10	*Opposition scored*	*20*	*17*	*12*	*0*	*170*
S. Barrett	1	–	–	–	5						

FRANCE IN NEW ZEALAND, INVESTEC RUGBY CHAMPIONSHIP AND BLEDISLOE CUP SCORING RECORD 2018   Played 9   Won 8   Lost 1   Points for 352   Points against 170

Date	Opponent	Location	Score	Tries	Con	PG	Referee
June 9	France	Auckland	52–11	Ioane (2), B. Barrett, Taylor, B. Smith, McKenzie, Savea, Laumape	B. Barrett(3)	B. Barrett(2)	L. Pearce *England*
June 16	France	Wellington	26–13	J. Barrett (2), Moody, B. Smith	McKenzie (3)		A. Gardner *Australia*
June 23	France	Dunedin	49–14	Ioane (3), McKenzie (2), B. Smith, Todd	McKenzie (7)		J. Lacey *Ireland*
August 18	Australia	Sydney	38–13	Naholo (2), A. Smith, Goodhue, B. Barrett, Retallick	B. Barrett (4)		J. Peyper *South Africa*
August 25	Australia	Auckland	40–12	B. Barrett (4), Moody, Squire	B. Barrett (5)		W. Barnes *England*
September 8	Argentina	Nelson	46–24	Perenara (2), Milner-Skudder, Read, Frizell, Goodhue	Mo'unga (5)	Mo'unga (2)	P. Gauzere *France*
September 15	South Africa	Wellington	34–36	Ioane (2), J. Barrett, A. Smith, Taylor, Savea	B. Barrett (2)		N. Owens *Wales*
September 29	Argentina	BuenosAires	35–17	Ioane (2), Naholo, Tuipulotu, Lienert-Brown	B. Barrett(4), Mo'unga		J. Lacey *Ireland*
October 6	South Africa	Pretoria	32–30	A. Smith, Ioane, S. Barrett, Savea	Mo'unga (3)	B. Barrett(2)	A. Gardner *Australia*

NEW ZEALAND v FRANCE

Test #567 Eden Park, Auckland June 9, 2018

Won by New Zealand 52–11

NEW ZEALAND

Jordie Barrett

Ben Smith Anton Lienert-Brown Rieko Ioane

Ryan Crotty

Beauden Barrett

Aaron Smith

Luke Whitelock

Sam Cane Scott Barrett Sam Whitelock (capt) Liam Squire

Owen Franks Codie Taylor Joe Moody

Dany Priso Camille Chat Uini Atonio

Kevin Gourdon Paul Gabrillagues Yoann Maestri Judicael Concoriet

Fabien Sanconnie

Morgan Parra

Anthony Belleau

Geoffrey Doumayrou

Remy Grosso Mathieu Basteraud (capt) Teddy Thomas

Maxime Medard

FRANCE

Reserves: New Zealand — Karl Tu'inukuafe (sub Moody 45m), Ofa Tu'ungafasi (sub Franks 58m), Ngani Laumape (sub Crotty 60m), D. McKenzie (sub J. Barrett 60m), A. Savea (sub Cane 63m), N. Harris (sub Taylor 63m), T. Perenara (sub A. Smith 65m), V. Fifita (sub L. Whitelock 72m).

France — Rabah Slimani (sub Atonio 41m), Cyril Baille (sub Priso 54m), Gael Fickou (sub Grosso 58m), Adrien Pelissie (sub Chat 58m), Baptiste Serin (sub Parra 58m), Alexandre Lapandry (sub Cancoriet 60m), Jules Plisson (sub Belleau 60m), Bernard le Roux (sub Gabrillagues 68m).

Referee: Luke Pearce (*England*) *Kick-off:* 7.35pm
Assistant Referees: Angus Gardner (*Australia*) *Attendance:* 46,000
John Lacey (*Ireland*) *Conditions:* excellent
TMO: George Ayoub (*Australia*)

Scorers: New Zealand: *France*
Tries: Ioane (2), B. Barrett, Taylor, B. Smith Try: Grosso
McKenzie, Laumape, Savea Penalties: Parra (2)
Conversions: B. Barrett (3)
Penalties: B. Barrett (2)

Scoring: First half: 6m Grosso try 0-5, 13m B. Barrett penalty goal 3-5, 19m Parra penalty goal 3-8, 21m B. Barrett try 8-8, 35m Parra penalty goal 8-11.

Second half: 47m B. Barrett penalty goal 11-11, 52m Taylor try, B. Barrett conversion 18-11, 55m B. Smith try, B. Barrett conversion 25-11, 61m Ioane try 30-11, 63m McKenzie try 35-11, 66m Laumape try 40-11, 74m Ioane try 45-11, 78m Savea try, B. Barrett conversion 52-11.

Yellow card to Gabrillagues 50m

All Blacks debut Karl Tu'inukuafe

NEW ZEALAND v FRANCE

Test #568 Westpac Trust Stadium, Wellington June 16, 2018
Won by New Zealand 26–13

NEW ZEALAND

Jordie Barrett

Ben Smith Anton Lienert-Brown Rieko Ioane

Ryan Crotty

Beauden Barrett

Aaron Smith

Luke Whitelock

Sam Cane Scott Barrett Sam Whitelock (capt) Liam Squire

Owen Franks Codie Taylor Joe Moody

Dany Priso Camille Chat Uini Atonio

Mathieu Babillot Bernard le Roux Yoann Maestri Kelian Galletier

Kevin Gourdon

Morgan Parra

Anthony Belleau

Geoffrey Doumayrou

Gael Fickou Mathieu Basteraud (capt) Teddy Thomas

Benjamin Fall

FRANCE

Reserves: New Zealand — Damian McKenzie (sub B. Barrett 11m), Ofa Tu'ungafasi (sub Franks 33m), Vaea Fifita (sub Squire 40m), Ardie Savea (sub Cane 43m), Karl Tu'inukuafe (sub Moody 45m), Nathan Harris (sub Taylor 50m), TJ Perenara (sub A. Smith 54m), Ngani Lauampe (sub Lienert-Brown 57m), Lienert-Brown (sub Crotty 71m).

France — Cyril Baille (sub Priso 47m), Cedate Gomes Sa (sub Atonio 47m), Baptiste Serin sub Parra 54m), Pierre Bourgarit (sub Chat 57m), Paul Gabrillagues (sub Maestri 57m), Maxime Medard (sub Doumayrou 61m), Alexandre Lapandry (sub Galletier 64m), Jules Plisson (sub Belleau 71m) .

Referee: Angus Gardner(*Australia*) *Kick-off:* 7.35pm
Assistant Referees: Luke Pearce (*England*) *Attendance:* 34,422
John Lacey (*Ireland*) *Conditions:* Fine, light breeze
TMO: George Ayoub (*Australia*)

Scorers: New Zealand: France
  Tries: J. Barrett (2), Moody, B. Smith *Try:* Gomes Sa
  Conversions: McKenzie (3) *Conversion:* Plisson
    Penalties: Parra (2)

Scoring: First half: 10m Parra penalty goal 0-3, 12m Moody try, McKenzie conversion 7-3, 19m B. Smith try, McKenzie conversion 14-3, 30m Parra penalty goal 14-6, 39m J. Barrett try, McKenzie conversion 21-6.

Second half: 56m J. Barrett try 26-6, 80m Gomes Sa try, Plisson conversion 26-13.

Red card to Fall 11m, later rescinded Yellow card to Perenara 62m

All Blacks retained the Dave Gallaher Cup

NEW ZEALAND v FRANCE
Test #569　　　Forsyth Barr Stadium, Dunedin　　　June 23, 2018
Won by New Zealand 49–14

NEW ZEALAND

Ben Smith

Waisake Naholo　　　Jack Goodhue　　　Rieko Ioane

Sonny Bill Williams

Damian McKenzie

Aaron Smith

Luke Whitelock

Ardie Savea　　　Scott Barrett　　　Sam Whitelock (capt)　　　Shannon Frizell

Owen Franks　　　Codie Taylor　　　Joe Moody

Dany Priso　　　Camille Chat　　　Uini Atonio

Mathieu Babillot　　　Bernard le Roux　　　Yoann Maestri　　　Kelian Galletier

Kevin Gourdon

Morgan Parra (capt)

Anthony Belleau

Wesley Fofana

Gael Fickou　　　Remi Lamerat　　　Teddy Thomas

Benjamin Fall

FRANCE

Reserves: New Zealand — Matt Todd (sub Savea 16m), Jackson Hemopo (temp sub Frizell 21-30m, sub S. Whitelock 69m), Ofa Tu'ungafasi (sub Franks 45m), Jordie Barrett (sub Williams 57m), TJ Perenara (sub A. Smith 63m), Karl Tu'inukuafe (sub Moody 63m), Richie Mo'unga (sub McKenzie 65m), Liam Coltman (sub Taylor 71m).

France — Baptiste Serin (sub Parra 7m), Adrien Pelissie (temp sub Chat 44-48m, sub 63), Maxime Medard (temp sub Fall 47m-59, sub Thomas 59m), Cyril Baille (sub Priso 48m), Sedate Gomes Sa (sub Atonio 50m), Alexandre Lapandry (sub Gourdon 50m), Felix Lambey (sub le Roux 63m), Jules Plisson (sub Lamerat 74m).

Referee: John Lacey (*England*)　　　***Kick-off:*** 7.35pm
Assistant Referees: Angus Gardner (*Australia*)　　　***Attendance:*** 27,807
　　　　　　Graham Cooper (*Australia*)　　　***Conditions:*** excellent
TMO: George Ayoub (*Australia*)

Scorers: New Zealand:　　　　　　　　　　　　　*France*
　Tries: Ioane (3), McKenzie (2), B. Smith, Todd　　*Tries:* Serin, Fofana
　Conversions: McKenzie (7)　　　　　　　　　　　*Conversions:* Belleau (2)

Scoring: First half: 11m Serin try, Belleau conversion 0-7, 15m B. Smith try, McKenzie 7-7, 22m Todd try, McKenzie conversion 14-7, 27m Fofana try, Belleau conversion 14-14, 31m McKenzie try, McKenzie conversion 21-14.

Second half: 46 m McKenzie try, McKenzie conversion 28-14, 52m Ioane try, McKenzie conversion 35-14, 58m Ioane try, McKenzie conversion 42-14, 64m Ioane try, McKenzie conversion 49-14 .

Shannon Frizell and Jackson Hemopo made their All Blacks debut. Jack Goodhue and Richie Mo'unga made their Test match debut .

NEW ZEALAND v AUSTRALIA

Bledisloe Cup
Test #570 ANZ Stadium, Sydney August 18, 2018
Won by New Zealand 38–13

NEW ZEALAND

Ben Smith
Waisake Naholo Jack Goodhue Rieko Ioane
Ryan Crotty
Beauden Barrett
Aaron Smith
Kieran Read (capt)
Sam Cane Sam Whitelock Brodie Rettalick Liam Squire
Owen Franks Codie Taylor Joe Moody

Tom Robertson Tatafu Polota-Nau Sekope Kepu
Michael Hooper (capt) Izack Rodda Adam Coleman Lukhan Tui
David Pocock
Will Genia
Bernard Foley
Kurtley Beale
Marika Koroibete Reece Hodge Dane Haylett-Petty
Israel Folau

AUSTRALIA

Reserves: New Zealand — Anton Lienert-Brown (sub Crotty 12m), Damian McKenzie (sub Ioane 46m, Ben Smith to #11), Tim Perry (sub Moody 53m), Karl Tu'inukuafe (sub Franks 53m), Scott Barrett (sub Squire 58m), TJ Perenara (sub A.Smith 67m), Nathan Harris (sub Taylor 67m), Ardie Savea (sub Cane 67m).

Australia — Jermaine Ainsley (temp sub Kepu 34-40m, sub Robertson 69m), Tolu Latu (sub Polota-Nau 45m), Jack Maddocks (sub Haylett-Petty 53m), Allan Ala'alatoa (sub Kepu 58m), Matt To'omua (sub Folau 63m), Rob Simmons (sub Rodda 64m), Pete Samu (sub Hooper 73m), Nick Phipps (sub Genia 73).

Referee: Jaco Peyper (*South Africa*) *Kick-off:* 7.50pm
Assistant Referees: Wayne Barnes (*England*) *Attendance:* 66,318
Luke Pearce (*England*) *Conditions:* good
TMO: Marius Jonker (*South Africa*)

Scorers: New Zealand: *Australia*
Tries: Naholo (2), A. Smith, Goodhue, Try: Maddocks
B. Barrett, Retallick Conversion: Foley
Conversions: B. Barrett (4) Penalties: Hodge, Foley

Scoring: First half: 9m Hodge penalty goal 0-3, 20m Foley penalty goal 0-6, 38m A. Smith try 5-6.

Second half: 42m Goodhue try, B. Barrett conversion 12-6, 51m B. Barrett try, B. Barrett conversion 19-6, 62m Retallick try, B. Barrett conversion 26-6, 66m Maddocks try, Foley conversion 26-13, 73m Naholo try 31-13, 74m Naholo try, B. Barrett conversion 38-13.

Tim Perry made his Test match debut
Wallaby debutant Jermaine Ainsley is son of Joe McDonnell All Black # 1015

NEW ZEALAND v AUSTRALIA

Bledisloe Cup

Test #571 Eden Park, Auckland August 25, 2018

Won by New Zealand 40–12

NEW ZEALAND

Jordie Barrett

Ben Smith Jack Goodhue Waisake Naholo

Ngani Laumape

Beauden Barrett

Aaron Smith

Kieran Read (capt)

Sam Cane Sam Whitelock Brodie Rettalick Liam Squire

Owen Franks Codie Taylor Joe Moody

Scott Sio Tatafu Polota-Nau Allan Ala'alatoa

Michael Hooper (capt) Izack Rodda Adam Coleman Lukhan Tui

David Pocock

Will Genia

Bernard Foley

Kurtley Beale

Marika Koroibete Reece Hodge Jack Maddocks

Dane Haylett-Petty

AUSTRALIA

Reserves: New Zealand — Ofa Tu'ungafasi (sub Franks 51m), Ardie Savea (sub Cane 52m), Karl Tu'inukuafe (sub Moody 55m), Scott Barrett (sub Squire 55m), Nathan Harris (sub Taylor 55m), TJ Perenara (sub A. Smith 62m), Anton Lienert-Brown (sub Goodhue 62m) Damian McKenzie (sub J. Barrett 66m).

Australia — Tom Robertson (sub Sio 51m), Sekope Kepu (sub Ala'alatoa 51m), Rob Simmons (sub Rodda 51m), Folau Fainga'a (sub Polota-Nau 51m), Matt To'omua (sub Haylett-Petty 64m), Tom Banks (sub Foley 70m), Nick Phipps (sub Genia 70), Pete Samu (sub Hooper 70m).

Referee: Wayne Barnes (*England*) *Kick-off:* 7.35pm
Assistant Referees: Jaco Peyper (*south Africa*) *Attendance:* 48,493
Luke Pearce (*England*) *Conditions:* good
TMO: Marius Jonker (*South Africa*)

Scorers: New Zealand: *Australia*
Tries: B. Barrett (4), Moody, Squire Tries: Genia, Hodge
Conversions: B. Barrett (5) Conversion: Foley

Scoring: First half: 12m B. Barrett try, B. Barrett conversion 7-0, 28m Genia try, Foley conversion 7-7, 37m B. Barrett try, B. Barrett conversion 14-7.

Second half: 42m Moody try, B. Barrett conversion 21-7, 47m Squire try, B. Barrett conversion 28-7, 54m Hodge try 28-12, 61m B. Barrett try, B. Barrett conversion 35-12, 68m B. Barrett try 40-12.

Beauden Barrett first All Black to score four tries on Eden Park. Beauden Barrett was the first first five eighth to score four tries in an international match.

NEW ZEALAND v ARGENTINA

Test #572 Trafalgar Park, Nelson September 8, 2018
Won by New Zealand 46–24

NEW ZEALAND

Ben Smith
Nehe Milner-Skudder Jack Goodhue Waisake Naholo
Ngani Laumape
Richie Mo'unga
TJ Perenara
Kieran Read (capt)
Ardie Savea Scott Barrett Brodie Rettalick Shannon Frizell
Owen Franks Codie Taylor Karl Tu'inukuafe

Nahuel Chaparro Agustin Creevy (capt) Santiago Botta
Marcos Kremer Guido Petti Tomas Lavanini Tomas Lezana
Javier Desio
Martin Landajo
Nicolas Sanchez
Jeronimo de la Fuente
Ramiro Moyano Matias Moroni Bautista Delguy
Emiliano Boffelli

ARGENTINA

Reserves: New Zealand — Anton Lienert-Browni (sub Laumape 4m), Damian McKenzie (temp sub B. Smith 9-19m, sub Naholo 58m), Sam Whitelock (sub Retallick 9m), Ofa Tu'ungafasi (sub Franks 46m), Luke Whitelock (sub Read 57m), Tim Perry (sub Tu'inukuafe 58m), Nathan Harris (sub Taylor 62m), Te Toiroa Tahuriorangi (sub Perenarra 71m).

Argentina — Gaston Cortes (sub Chaparro 50m), Julian Montoya (sub Creevy 50m), Juan Zeiss (sub Botta 57m), Matias Alemanno (sub Petti 58m), Pablo Matero (sub Lezana 62m), Tomas Cubelli (sub Landajo 62m), Juan Mallia (sub Moroni 64m), Bautista Ezcurra.

Referee: Pascal Gauzere (*France*) *Kick-off:* 7.35pm
Assistant Referees: Nigel Owens (*Wales*) *Attendance:* 21,404
Nic Berry (*Australia*) *Conditions:* excellent
TMO: Rowan Kitt (*England*)

Scorers: New Zealand: *Argentina*
  Tries: Perenara (2), Milner-Skudder, Read, *Tries:* Moyano, Sanchez, Boffelli
    Frizell, Goodhue *Conversions:* Sanchez (3)
  Conversions: Mo'unga (5) *Penalty:* Sanchez
  Penalties: Mo'unga (2)

Scoring: First half: 4m Mo'unga penalty goal 3-0, 14m Moyano try, Sanchez conversion 3-7, 17m Milner-Skudder try, Mo'unga conversion 10-7, 29m Perenara try 15-7, 41m Mo'unga penalty goal 18-7.
Second half: 41m Sanchez try, Sanchez conversion 18-14, 48m Read try, Mo'unga conversion 25-14, 55m Sanchez penalty goal 25-17, 57m Perenara try, Mo'unga conversion 32-17, 69m Boffelli try, Sanchez conversion 32-24, 73m Frizell try, Mo'unga conversion 39-24, 79m Goodhue try, Mo'unga conversion 46-24.

Te Toiro Tahuriorangi made his All Blacks debut

This was the first time the All Blacks had played in Nelson

NEW ZEALAND v SOUTH AFRICA

Test #573 Westpac Stadium, Wellington September 15, 2018
Won by South Africa 36–34

NEW ZEALAND

Jordie Barrett

Ben Smith   Anton Lienert-Brown   Rieko Ioane

Ryan Crotty

Beauden Barrett

Aaron Smith

Kieran Read (capt)

Sam Cane   Scott Barrett   Sam Whitelock   Liam Squire

Owen Franks   Codie Taylor   Karl Tu'inukuafe

Steven Kitshoff   Malcolm Marx   Frans Malherbe

Siya Kolisi (capt)   Eben Etzebeth   Franco Mostert   Pieter-Steph du Toit

Warren Whiteley

Faf de Klerk

Handre Pollard

Damian de Allende

Aphiwe Dyantyi   Lukhanyo Am   Jesse Kriel

Willie le Roux

SOUTH AFRICA

Reserves: New Zealand — Ofa Tu'ungafasi (sub Franks 44m), TJ Perenara (sub A. Smith 49m), Patrick Tuipulotu (sub Squire 56m), Jack Goodhue (sub Lienert-Brown 58m), Damian McKenzie (sub J. Barrett 58m), Tim Perry (sub Tu'inukuafe 58m), Ardie Savea (sub Cane 68m), Liam Coltman (sub Taylor 75m).

South Africa — Cheslin Kolbe (sub Am 40m), Elton Jantjies (sub de Allende 47m), Rudolph Snyman (sub Etzebeth 50m), Wilco Louw (sub Malherbe 64m), Francios Louw (sub Kolisi 65m), Tendai Mtawarira (sub Kitshoff 65m), Bongi Mbonambi (sub Marx 68m), Ross Kronje

Referee: Nigel Owens (*Wales*) **Kick-off:** 7.35pm
Assistant Referees: Pascal Gauzere (*France*) **Attendance:** 34,182
  Nic Berry (*Australia*) **Conditions:** good
TMO: Rowan Kitt (*England*)

Scorers: New Zealand:
  Tries: Ioane (2), J. Barrett, A. Smith, Taylor Savea
  Conversions: B. Barrett (2)

South Africa
  Tries: Dyantyi (2), le Roux, Marx, Kolbe
  Conversions: Pollard (4)
  Penalty: Pollard

Scoring: First half: 4m J. Barrett try 5-0, 15m A. Smith try, B. Barrett conversion 12-0, 19m Dyantyi try, Pollard conversion 12-7, 24m le Roux try, Pollard conversion 14-12, 31m Marx try, Pollard conversion 21-12, 37m Ioane try 17-21, 41m Pollard penalty goal 17-24.

Second half: 41m Kolbe try, Pollard conversion 17-31, 51m Ioane try, B. Barrett conversion 24-31, 56m Dyantyi try 24-36, 60m Taylor try 29-36, 73m Savea try 34-36.

Yellow card le Roux at 66m

NEW ZEALAND v ARGENTINA

Test #574   Jose Amalfitani Stadium, Buenos Aires   September 29, 2018
Won by New Zealand 35–17

NEW ZEALAND

Ben Smith
Waisake Naholo   Ryan Crotty   Rieko Ioane
Sonny Bill Williams
Beauden Barrett
TJ Perenara
Ardie Savea
Sam Cane   Scott Barrett   Sam Whitelock (capt)   Shannon Frizell
Ofa Tu'ungafasi   Codie Taylor   Karl Tu'inukuafe

Nahuel Chaparro   Agustin Creevy (capt)   Ramiro Herrera
Marcos Kremer   Guido Petti   Tomas Lavanini   Pablo Matera
Javier Desio
Gonzalo Bertranou
Nicolas Sanchez
Bautista Ezcurra
Matias Moroni   Jeronimo de la Fuente   Bautista Delguy
Emiliano Boffelli

ARGENTINA

Reserves: New Zealand — Patrick Tuipulotu (sub Whitelock 50m), Angus Ta'avao-Matau (sub Tu'ungafasi 51m), Tim Perry (sub Tu'inukuafe 56m), Anton Liebert-Brown (sub Williams 56m), Richie Mo'unga (sub B. Smith 58m, B. Barrett to #15), Nathan Harris (sub Taylor 59m), Aaron Smith (sub Perenara 66m), Jackson Hemopo (sub Frizell 66m).

Argentina — Sebastian Cancelliere (sub Delguy 33m), Tomas Cubelli (sub Bertranou 40m), Julian Montoya (sub Creevy 50m), Matias Alemanno (sub Petti 53m), Santiago Medrano (sub Herrera 53m), Juan Zeiss (sub Chaparro 57m), Matias Orlando (sub Ezcurra 62m), Juan Leguizamon (sub Kremer 70m).

Referee: Mathieu Raynal *(France)*
Assistant Referees: Jaco Peyper *(South Africa)*
Marius van der Westhuizen
(South Africa)
TMO: David Grashof *(England)*

Kick-off: 7.45pm
Attendance: 30,562
Conditions: Remarkably good following torrential rain

Scorers: New Zealand:
   Tries: Ioane (2), Naholo, Tuipulotu, Lienert-Brown
   Conversions: B. Barrett (4), Mo'unga

Argentina
   Tries: Cubelli, Boffelli
   Conversions: Sanchez (2)
   Penalty: Sanchez

Scoring: First half: 5m Sanchez penalty goal 0-3, 7m Ioane try, B. Barrett conversion 7-3, 16m Naholo try, B. Barrett conversion 14-3, 29m Ioane try, B. Barrett conversion 21-3.

Second half: 54m Tuipulotu try, B. Barrett conversion 28-3, 57m Cubelli try, Sanchez conversion 28-10, 67m Boffelli try, Sanchez conversion 28-17, 72m Lienert-Brown try, Mo'unga conversion 35-17.

Yellow card to Williams 36m

Angus Ta'avao-Matau made his All Blacks debut.

NEW ZEALAND v SOUTH AFRICA

Test #575 Loftus Versfeld, Pretoria October 6, 2018
Won by New Zealand 32–30

NEW ZEALAND

Ben Smith
Waisake Naholo   Ryan Crotty   Rieko Ioane
Sonny Bill Williams
Beauden Barrett
Aaron Smith
Kieran Read (capt)
Sam Cane   Scott Barrett   Sam Whitelock   Shannon Frizell
Owen Franks   Codie Taylor   Karl Tu'inukuafe

Steven Kitshoff   Malcolm Marx   Frans Malherbe
Siya Kolisi (capt)   Eben Etzebeth   Franco Mostert   Pieter-Steph du Toit
Francois Louw
Faf de Klerk
Handre Pollard
Damian de Allende
Aphiwe Dyantyi   Jesse Kriel   Cheslin Kolbe
Willie le Roux

SOUTH AFRICA

Reserves: New Zealand — Ardie Savea (sub Cane 35m), Tim Perry (sub Tu'inukuafe 45m), Patrick Tuipulotu (sub Frizell 45m, S. Barrett to #6), Ofa Tu'ungafasi (sub Franks 45m), Richie Mo'unga (sub Naholo 50m, B. Smith to #14, B. Barrett to #15), Anton Lienert-Brown (sub Williams 59m, Crotty to #12), Nathan Harris (sub Taylor 65m), TJ Perenara (sub A. Smith 69m), Tu'inukuafe (temp sub Perry 69-77).

South Africa — Vincent Koch (sub Malherbe 59m), Rudolph Snyman (sub Etzebeth 62m), Damian Willemse (sub le Roux 65m), Sikhumbuzo Notshe (sub Louw 69m), Embrose Papier (sub de Klerk 72m), Bongi Mbonambi (sub Marx 72m), Tendai Mtawarira (sub Kitshoff 73m), Elton Jantjies (sub de Allende 77m)..

Referee: Angus Gardner (*Australia*) **Kick-off:** 3.05pm
Assistant Referees: Jerome Garces (*France*) **Attendance:** 50,116
Matthew Carley (*England*) **Conditions:** good
TMO: Graham Hughes (*England*)

Scorers: New Zealand:
    Tries: A. Smith, Ioane, S. Barrett
    Savea
    Conversions: Mo'unga (3)
    Penalties: B. Barrett (2)

South Africa
    Tries: Kriel, de Allende, Kolbe
    Conversions: Pollard (3)
    Penalties: Pollard (3)

Scoring: First half: 3m Pollard penalty goal 0-3, 12m Pollard penalty goal 0-6, 25m B. Barrett penalty goal 3-6, 35m B. Barrett penalty goal 6-6.

Second half: 43m Kriel try, Pollard conversion 6-13, 47m Pollard penalty goal 6-16, 51m de Allende try, Pollard conversion 6-23, 53m A. Smith try, Mo'unga conversion 13-23, 58m Kolbe try, Pollard conversion 13-30, 61m Ioane try 18-30, 75m S. Barrett try, Mo'unga conversion 25-30, 78m Savea try, Mo'unga conversion 32-30.

This was the 1300th game played by the All Blacks.

Scott Barrett's try brought up 2000 points scored by the All Blacks against South Africa.

SOUTH AFRICA V ARGENTINA

Kings Park Durban August 18, 2018

Won by South Africa 34–21

SOUTH AFRICA

Willie le Roux

Makazole Mapimpi Lukhanyo Am Aphiwe Dyantyi

Andre Esterhuizen

Handre Pollard

Faf de Klerk

Warren Whiteley

Siya Kolisi (capt) Pieter-Steph du Toit Eben Etzebeth Francois Louw

Frans Malherbe Malcolm Marx Tendai Mtawarira

Nahuel Chaparro Agustin Creevy (capt) Juan Figallo

Marcos Kremer Matias Alemanno Guido Petti Pablo Matera

Javier Desio

Gonzalo Bertranou

Nicolas Sanchez

Bautista Ezcurra

Ramiro Moyano Matias Moroni Bautista Delguy

Emiliano Boffelli

ARGENTINA

Reserves: *South Africa* — Steven Kitshoff (sub Mtawarira 51m), Thomas du Toit (sub Malherbe 57m), Marco van Staden (sub Louw 59m), Damian Willemse (sub Esterhuizen 62m), Bongi Mbonambi (sub Marx 64m), Lionel Mapoe (sub Am 74m), Embrose Papier (sub Dyantyi 73m), Marvin Orie.

Argentina — Garcia Botta (sub Chaparro 50m), Tomas Lezana (sub Matera 50m), Tomas Lavanini (sub Alemanno 53m), Santiago Medrano (sub Figallo 62m), Martin Landajo (sub Bertranou 62m), Diego Fortuny (sub Creevy 71m), Gonzalez Iglesias (sub Ezcurra 79m), Juan Mallia.

Referee: Ben O'Keeffe (*New Zealand*)   **Kick-off:** 5.05pm
Assistant Referees: Angus Gardner (*Australia*)   **Attendance:** 26,836
           Andrew Brace (*Ireland*)   **Conditions:** perfect
TMO: Simon McDowell (*Ireland*)

Scorers: *South Africa:*   *Argentina*
     Tries: Dyantyi (2), Mapimpi (2), Am, de Klerk   *Tries:* Sanchez, Matera, Moroni
     Conversions: Pollard (2)   *Conversions:* Sanchez (3)

Scoring: First half: 7m Am try 5-0, 14m Sanchez try, Sanchez conversion 5-7, 26m Matera try, Sanchez conversion 5-14, 31m Dyantyi try 10-14.

Second half: 41m Dyantyi try, Pollard conversion 17-14, 48m Mapimpi try 22-14, 52m Mapimpi try 27-14, 69m de Klerk try, Pollard conversion 34-21.

ARGENTINA V SOUTH AFRICA

Estadio Malvinas Argentinas, Mendoza   August 25, 2018

Won by Argentina 32–19

ARGENTINA

Emiliano Boffelli

Bautista Delguy   Matias Moroni   Ramiro Moyano

Bautista Ezcurra

Nicolas Sanchez

Gonzalo Bertranou

Javier Desio

Marcos Kremer   Tomas Lavanini   Guido Petti   Pablo Matera

Juan Figallo   Agustin Creevy (capt)   Nahuel Chaparro

Tendai Mtawarira   Malcolm Marx   Frans Malherbe

Francios Louw   Eben Etzebeth   Franco Mostert   Siya Kolisi (capt)

Warren Whiteley

Faf de Klerk

Handre Pollard

Andre Esterhuizen

Aphiwe Dyantyi   Lukhanyo Am   Makazole Mapimpi

Willie le Roux

SOUTH AFRICA

Reserves: Argentina — Jeronimo de la Fuente (sub Moyano 57m), Tomas Lezana (sub Matera 59m), Garcia Botta (sub Chaparro 63m), Tomas Cubelli (sub Bertranou 68m), Santiago Medrano (sub Figallo 68m), Matias Alemanno (sub Lavanini 71m), Facundo Bosch (sub Creevy 76m), Juan Mallia (sub Ezcurra 79m).

South Africa — Lionel Mapoe (sub Mapimpi 11m), Steven Kitshoff (sub Mtawarira 42m), Pieter-Steph du Toit (sub Etzebeth 46m), R.G. Snyman (temp sub Whiteley 52-62m), Damian Willemse (sub Esterhuizen 62m), Wilco Louw (sub Malherbe 62m), Bongi Mbonambi (sub Marx 71m), Embrose Papier.

Referee: Angus Gardner (*Australia*)   **Kick-off:** 7.10pm
Assistant Referees: Ben O'Keeffe (*New Zealand*)   **Attendance:** 27,460
                 Andrew Brace (*Ireland*)   **Conditions:** fine
TMO: Simon McDowell (*Ireland*)

Scorers: Argentina
    Tries: Delguy (2), Sanchez, Moyano
    Conversions: Sanchez (3)

South Africa
    Tries: Mapoe (2), Kolisi
    Conversions: Pollard (2)
    Penalty: Sanchez
    Dropped goal: Sanchez

Scoring: First half: 4m Sanchez penalty goal 3-0, 13m Kolisi try, Pollard conversion 3-7, 18m Delguy try, Sanchez conversion 10-7, 22m Delguy try, Sanchez conversion 17-7, 26m Sanchez try, Sanchez conversion 24-7, 36m Sanchez dropped goal 27-7.

Second half: 45m Moyano try 32-7, 47m Mapoe try, Pollard conversion 32-14, 64m Mapoe try 32-19.

Yellow card Etzebeth 24m.

AUSTRALIA V SOUTH AFRICA

Suncorp Stadium, Brisbane September 8, 2018

Won by Australia 23–18

AUSTRALIA

Dane Haylett-Petty
Jack Maddocks   Reece Hodge   Marika Koroibete
Matt Toomua
Kurtley Beale
Will Genia
Pete Samu
Michael Hooper (capt)   Izack Rodda   Rory Arnold   Lukhan Tui
Allan Ala'alatoa   Tatafu Polota-Nau   Scott Sio

Steven Kitshoff   Bongi Mbonambi   Frans Malherbe
Siya Kolisi (capt)   Eben Etzebeth   Franco Mostert   Pieter-Steph du Toit
Warren Whiteley
Faf de Klerk
Elton Jantjies
Damian de Allende
Aphiwe Dyantyi   Jesse Kriel   Makazole Mapimpi
Willie le Roux

SOUTH AFRICA

Reserves: Australia — Folau Fainga'a (sub Polota-Nau 33m), Rob Simmons (sub Rodda 41m), Taniela Tupou (sub Ala'alatoa 47m), Rodda (temp sub Arnold 58-67m), Bernard Foley (sub Maddocks 61m), Tom Banks (sub Hodge 68m), Tom Robertson (sub Sio 69m), Polota-Nau (sub Fainga'a 71m), Hodge (sub Koroibete 75m), Ned Hanigan (sub Arnold 76m). Joe Powell.

South Africa — Cheslin Kolbe (sub Mapimpi 33m), Malcolm Marx (sub Mbonambi 34m), Tendai Mtawarira (sub Kitshoff 57m), Wilco Louw (sub Malherbe 57m), Rudolf Snyman (sub Etzebeth 60m), Francois Louw (sub Whiteley 61m), Handre Pollard (sub Jantjies 64m), Embrose Papier.

Referee: Glen Jackson (*New Zealand*)   *Kick-off:* 8.05pm
Assistant Referees: John Lacey (*Ireland*)   *Attendance:* 27,849
Paul Williams (*New Zealand*)   *Conditions:* wet
TMO: Glenn Newman (*New Zealand*)

Scorers: Australia
  Tries: Hooper, Toomua
  Conversions: Toomua (2)
  Penalties: Toomua (2), Hodge

South Africa
  Tries: Mbonambi, Mapimpi
  Conversion: Jantjies
  Penalties: Jantjies (2)

Scoring: First half: 1m Hooper try, Toomua conversion 7-0, 6m Jantjies penalty goal 7-3, 13m Mbonambi try, Jantjies conversion 7-10, 27m Mapimpi try 7-15, 32m Toomua try, Tommua conversion 14-15, 38m Jantjies penalty goal 14-18, 42m Hodge penalty goal 17-18.

Second half: 54m Toomua penalty goal 20-18, 67m Toomua penalty goal 23-18.

AUSTRALIA V ARGENTINA
Cbus Super Stadium, Gold Coast September 15, 2018
Won by Argentina 23-19
AUSTRALIA

Dane Haylett-Petty

Israel Folau Reece Hodge Marika Koroibete

Matt Toomua

Kurtley Beale

Will Genia

Pete Samu

David Pocock (capt) Izack Rodda Rory Arnold Lukhan Tui
Allan Ala'alatoa Tatafu Polota-Nau Scott Sio

Nahuel Chaparro Agustin Creevy (capt) Santiago Medrano
Marcos Kremer Guido Petti Tomas Lavanini Pablo Matera

Javier Desio

Gonzalo Bertranou

Nicolas Sanchez

Jeronimo de la Fuente

Ramiro Moyano Matias Moroni Bautista Delguy

Emiliano Boffelli

ARGENTINA

Reserves: Australia — Folau Fainga'a (sub Polota-Nau 41m), Ned Hanigan (sub Samu 46m), Adam Coleman (sub Arnold 46m), Bernard Foley (sub Toomua 49m), Taniela Tupou (sub Ala'alatoa 52m), Sekope Kepu (sub Sio 54m), Arnold (sub Rodda 59m), Jack Maddocks (sub Koroibete 70m), Nick Phipps (sub Genia 70m).

Argentina — Bautista Ezcurra (sub Moyano 42m), Julian Montoya (sub Creevy 67m), Santiago Botta (sub Chaparro 67m), Juan Zeiss (sub Medrano 67m), Juan Leguizamon (sub Kremer 67m), Matias Alemanno (sub Petti 71m), Juan Mallia (sub de la Fuente 71m), Martin Landajo.

Referee: John Lacey (*Ireland*) *Kick-off:* 8.00pm
Assistant Referees: Glen Jackson (*New Zealand*) *Attendance:* 16,019
 Paul Williams (*New Zealand*) *Conditions:* very good
TMO: Glenn Newman (*New Zealand*)

Scorers: Australia *Argentina*
 Tries: Folau, Genia, Haylett-Petty *Tries:* Delguy, Sanchez
 Conversions: Toomua (2) *Conversions:* Sanchez (2)
 Penalties: Boffelli (2), Sanchez

Scoring: First half: 4m Boffelli penalty goal 0-3, 10m Genia try, Toomua conversion 7-3, 15m Sanchez try, Sanchez conversion 7-10, 18m Folau try, Toomua conversion 14-10, 35m Delguy try, Sanchez conversion 14-17.

Second half: 47m Sanchez penalty goal 14-20, 54m Haylett-Petty try 19-20, 75m Boffelli penalty goal 19-23.

SOUTH AFRICA V AUSTRALIA

Nelson Mandela Bay Stadium, Port Elizabeth September 29, 2018

Won by South Africa 23–12

SOUTH AFRICA

Willie le Roux

Cheslin Kolbe Jesse Kriel Aphiwe Dyantyi

Andre Esterhuizen

Handre Pollard

Faf de Klerk

Sikhumbuzo Notshe

Pieter-Steph du Toit Franco Mostert Eben Etzebeth Siya Kolisi (capt)

Frans Malherbe Malcolm Marx Tendai Mtawarira

Scott Sio Folau Fainga'a Taniela Tupou

Michael Hooper (capt) Izack Rodda Adam Coleman Ned Hanigan

David Pocock

Will Genia

Kurtley Beale

Matt Toomua

Marika Koroibete Reece Hodge Israel Folau

Dane Haylett-Petty

AUSTRALIA

Reserves: South Africa — Steven Kitshoff (sub Mtawarira 42m), Marco van Staden (sub Notshe 44m), Wilco Louw (sub Malherbe 62m), Bongi Mbonambi (sub Marx 69m), Rudolph Snyman (sub Etzebeth 76m), Embrose Papier, Elton Jantjies, Damian Willemse.

Australia — Jack Maddocks (sub Koroibete 31m), Sekope Kepu (sub Sio 49m), Allan Ala'alatoa (sub Tupou 49m), Bernard Foley (sub Maddocks 58m), Brandon Paenga-Amosa (sub Fainga's 62m), Rob Simmons (sub Coleman 69m), Nick Phipps (sun Genia 69m), Rory Arnold (sub Rodda 69m).

Referee: Jerome Garces (*France*) *Kick-off:* 5.05pm
Assistant Referees: Wayne Barnes (*England*) *Attendance:* 41,332
Matthew Carley (*England*) *Conditions:* fine
TMO: Graham Hughes (*England*)

Scorers: South Africa: *Australia*
Tries: Dyantyi, de Klerk Tries: Hodge, Genia
Conversions: Pollard (2) Conversion: Toomua
Penalties: Pollard (3)

Scoring: First half: 30sec Dyantyi try, Pollard conversion 7-0, 20m de Klerk try, Pollard conversion 14-0, 25m Hodge try 14-5, 28m Genia try, Toomua conversion 14-12, 33m Pollard penalty goal 17-12, 41m Pollard penalty goal 20-12.

Second half: 45m Pollard penalty goal 23-12.

Yellow card to Dyantyi 64m

AUSTRALIA V ARGENTINA

Ernesto Maltearena, Salta   October 8, 2018

Won by Australia 45–34

AUSTRALIA

Dane Haylett-Petty

Israel Folau   Reece Hodge   Marika Koroibete

Kurtley Beale

Bernard Foley

Will Genia

David Pocock

Michael Hooper (capt)   Adam Coleman   Izack Rodda   Ned Hanigan

Taniela Tupou   Folau Fainga'a   Scott Sio

Nahuel Chaparro   Agustin Creevy (capt)   Ramiro Herrera

Marcos Kremer   Guido Petti   Tomas Lavanini   Pablo Matera

Javier Desio

Gonzalo Bertranou

Nicolas Sanchez

Jeronimo de la Fuente

Ramiro Moyano   Matias Orlando   Matias Moroni

Emiliano Boffelli

ARGENTINA

Reserves: Australia — Tolu Latu (sub Fainga'a 41m), Sekope Kepu (sub Sio 41m), Allan Ala'alatoa (sub Tupou 41m), Nick Phipps (sub Genia 65m), Rob Simmons (sub Rodda 65m), Sio (sub Kepu 65m), Matt Toomua (sub Beale 74m), Caleb Timu , Tom Banks

Argentina — Santiago Iglesias (sub Sanchez 28m), Santiago Medrano (sub Herrera 52m), Julian Montoya (sub Creevy 52m), Tomas Cubelli (sub Bertranou 58m), Santiago Botta (sub Chaparro 65m), Juan Leguizamon (sub Kremer 65m), Matias Alemanno (sub Labanini 65m), Sebastian Cancelliere (sub Moroni 70m).

Referee: Jaco Peyper (*South Africa*)   *Kick-off:* 7.40pm
Assistant Referees: Mathieu Raynal (*France*)   *Attendance:* 20,512
                     Marius van der Westhuizen   *Conditions:* cool
                     (*South Africa*)
TMO: David Grashof (*England*)

Scorers: Australia
     Tries: Haylett-Petty (2), Hooper, Rodda, Folau, Pocock
     Conversions: Foley (6)
     Penalty: Foley

Argentina
     Tries: Matera, Boffelli, Orlando, Iglesias
     Conversions: Sanchez (3), Iglesias
     Penalties: Iglesias (2)

Scoring: First half: 1m Matera try, Sanchez conversion 0-7, 4m Boffelli try, Sanchez conversion 0-14, 17m Hooper try, Foley conversion 7-14, 28m Orlando try, Sanchez conversion 7-21, 31m Iglesias try, Iglesias conversion 7-28, 37m Iglesias penalty goal 7-31.

Second half: 44m Rodda try, Foley conversion 14-31, 47m Folau try, Foley conversion 21-31, 50m Haylett-Petty try, Foley conversion 28-31, 60m Iglesias penalty goal 28-34, 63m Pocock try, Foley conversion 35-34, 65m Haylett-Petty try, Foley conversion 42-34, 74m Foley penalty goal 45-34.

Yellow card to Latu 76m

This was a record successful points chase by Australia.

INVESTEC RUGBY CHAMPIONSHIP

Results

August 18	New Zealand	38	Australia	13	at Sydney
August 18	South Africa	34	Argentina	21	at Durban
August 25	New Zealand	40	Australia	12	at Auckland
August 25	Argentina	32	South Africa	19	at Mendoza
September 8	New Zealand	46	Argentina	24	at Nelson
September 8	Australia	23	South Africa	18	at Brisbane
September 15	South Africa	36	New Zealand	34	at Wellington
September 15	Argentina	23	Australia	19	at Gold Coast
September 29	South Africa	23	Australia	12	at Port Elizabeth
September 29	New Zealand	35	Argentina	17	at Buenos Aires
October 6	New Zealand	32	South Africa	30	at Pretoria
October 6	Australia	45	Argentina	34	at Salta

Final Standings

Team	P	W	D	L	For	Against	Bonus	Total
New Zealand	6	5	–	1	225	132	5	25
South Africa	6	3	–	3	160	154	3	15
Australia	6	2	–	4	124	176	1	9
Argentina	6	2	–	4	151	198	0	8

Scoring Distribution

	FOR					AGAINST				
Team	T	C	PG	DG	Pts	T	C	PG	DG	Pts
New Zealand	33	24	4	-	225	16	14	8	-	132
South Africa	21	14	9	-	160	21	14	6	1	154
Australia	16	13	6	-	124	22	18	10	-	176
Argentina	18	17	8	1	151	29	22	3	-	198
TOTALS	**88**	**68**	**27**	**1**	**660**	**88**	**68**	**27**	**1**	**660**

FRENCH BARBARIANS

Following a game by the French Barbarians against the All Blacks on their end-of-year tour in 2017, a French Barbarians team visited New Zealand for the first time in June 2018, playing the Crusaders and Highlanders, albeit without their All Blacks.

CRUSADERS v FRENCH BARBARIANS
AMI Stadium, Christchurch   June 15, 2018
Won by Crusaders 42–26

CRUSADERS

M. Hunt

I. Dagg　　　　T. Fainganuku　　　　J. Macilai (sub C. Makene)

R. Poihipi (sub S. Beard)

M. Delany (sub J. Stratton)

M. Drummond (capt)

E. Blackadder

W. Harmon (sub W. Douglas)　　H. Dalzell (sub L. Romano)　　Q. Strange　　M. Dunshea

M. Ala'alatoa (sub c. King)　　A. Makalio (sub S. Sitiaga)　　D. Brighouse (sub R. Coxon)

A. Tichit (sub Q. Bethune)　　J. Marchand (sub Q. Lespiaucq)　　E. Setiano (sub D. Aldegheri)

F. Cros (capt)　　F. Verhaeghe　　T. Jolmes (sub S. Rebbadj)　　J. Cancoriet (sub Y. Tanga)

B. Pesenti (sub P. Sobela)

A. Bales (sub T. Daubagne)

J. Doussain

P. Fouyssac

D. Camara (sub A. Retiere)　　D. Penaud　　A. Batle

J. Dumora

FRENCH BARBARIANS

Referee: J.J. Doleman

Scorers: Crusaders
   Tries: Hunt 2, Drummond 2, Poihipi, Dagg
   Conversions: Hunt 6

French Barbarians
   Tries: Penau 2, Marchand, Cancoriet
   Conversions: Doussain 3

HIGHLANDERS v FRENCH BARBARIANS
Forsyth Barr Stadium, Dunedin June 22, 2018
Won by Highlanders 29–10

HIGHLANDERS

J. McKay

M. Faddes
(sub J. Ioane)
R. Thompson
T. Li

R. Buckman

L. Sopoaga
(sub T. Umaga-Jensen)

J. Renton
(sub K. Hammington)

E. Dixon
(sub M. Mikaele-Tu'u)

| J. Lentjies | P. Parkinson | A. Ainley | J. Dickson (sub D. Pryor) |

S. Tokolahi
(sub T. Lomax)
A. Dixon (capt)
(sub G. Pleasants-Tate)
A. Seiuli
(sub G. Millar)

Q. Bethune
(sub A. Tichit, sub P. Bourgarit)
Q. Lespiaucq
sub J. Marchand),
S. Taofifenua
(sub E. Setiano)

P. Sobela
F. Verhaeghe
(sub T. Jolmes)
S. Rebbadj
Y. Tanga
(sub J. Cancoriet)

F. Sanconnie
(sub F. Cros)

A. Bales
(sub T. Daubagne)

J. Doussain (capt)

P. Fouyssac

H. Bonneval
D. Penaud
A. Retiere

J. Dumora

FRENCH BARBARIANS

Referee: M.I. Fraser

Scorers: Highlanders
  Tries: Lentjies, McKay, Sopoaga,
  Pleasants-Tate, Thompson
  Conversions: Sopoaga, Ioane

French Barbarians
  Tries: Bonneval
  Conversions: Dumora
  Penalty: Doussain

VISTA ALL BLACKS NORTHERN TOUR OF JAPAN, ENGLAND, IRELAND & ITALY 2018

	Franchise	Date of Birth	Height	Weight	Tests at 1/1/19
A.J. (Ausofa) Aumua	Hurricanes	5/5/97	1.77	110	*
B.J. (Beauden) Barrett	Hurricanes	27/5/91	1.87	91	73
J.M. (Jordie) Barrett	Hurricanes	17/2/97	1.96	101	9
S.K. (Scott) Barrett	Crusaders	20/11/93	1.97	111	29
G.C. (George) Bridge	Crusaders	1/4/95	1.86	96	1
B.D. (Brett) Cameron	Crusaders	4/10/96	1.71	83	1
D.S. (Dane) Coles	Hurricanes	10/12/86	1.84	110	60
L.J. (Liam) Coltman	Highlanders	25/1/90	1.86	110	4
R.S. (Ryan) Crotty	Crusaders	23/9/88	1.81	94	44
M.D. (Mitch) Drummond	Crusaders	15/2/94	1.80	88	1
G.O. (Gareth) Evans	Hurricanes	5/8/91	1.90	106	1
V.T.L. (Vaea) Fifita	Hurricanes	17/6/92	1.96	112	9
O.T. (Owen) Franks	Crusaders	23/12/87	1.85	122	106
E.J. (Jack) Goodhue	Crusaders	13/6/95	1.87	98	7
B.D. (Bryn) Hall	Crusaders	3/2/92	1.89	95	*
N.P. (Nathan) Harris	Chiefs	8/3/92	1.86	106	20
D.K. (David) Havili	Crusaders	23/12/94	1.85	95	3*
J.N. (Jackson) Hemopo	Highlanders	14/11/93	1.94	113	3
D. (Dillon) Hunt	Highlanders	23/2/95	1.89	103	1
R.E. (Rieko) Ioane	Blues	18/3/97	1.89	103	24
N.E. (Nepo) Laulala	Chiefs	11/6/91	1.84	116	17
K.H. (Ngani) Laumape	Hurricanes	24/4/93	1.77	103	10
A.R. (Anton) Lienert-Brown	Chiefs	15/4/95	1.85	96	33
T.S. (Tyrel) Lomax	Highlanders	1/6/96	1.92	127	1
D.S. (Damian) McKenzie	Chiefs	20/4/95	1.75	82	23
N.R. (Nehe) Milner-Skudder	Hurricanes	15/12/90	1.80	90	13
J.P.T. (Joe) Moody	Crusaders	18/9/88	1.88	120	37
R. (Richie) Mo'unga	Crusaders	25/5/94	1.76	88	0
W.R. (Waisake) Naholo	Highlanders	8/5/91	1.86	105	26
R.G. (Reuben) O'Neil	Chiefs	17/2/95	1.83	117	*
D.R. (Dalton) Papali'i	Blues	11/10/97	1.90	105	2
T.T.R. (TJ) Perenara	Hurricanes	23/1/92	1.84	90	55
T.G. (Tim) Perry	Crusaders	1/8/88	1.91	118	6
M.P. (Matt) Proctor	Hurricanes	23/6/89	1.83	94	1
K.J. (Kieran) Read	Crusaders	26/10/85	1.93	111	118
B.A. (Brodie) Retallick	Chiefs	31/5/91	2.04	123	75
A.S. (Ardie) Savea	Hurricanes	14/10/93	1.88	100	35
A.L. (Aaron) Smith	Highlanders	21/11/88	1.71	83	82
B.R. (Ben) Smith	Highlanders	1/6/88	1.86	94	76
L.I.J. (Liam) Squire	Highlanders	20/3/91	1.96	109	23

Name	Team	DOB	Height	Weight	Caps
C.J.D. (Codie) Taylor	Crusaders	31/3/91	1.83	106	41
A.W.F.(Angus) Ta'avao-Matau	Chiefs	22/3/90	1.94	128	3
T.T.H. (Te Toiroa) Tahuriorangi	Chiefs	31/3/95	1.71	83	3
M.B. (Matt) Todd	Crusaders	14/4/88	1.85	103	17
G.Z.K. (Karl) Tu'inukuafe	Chiefs	21/2/93	1.82	135	13
P.T. (Patrick) Tuipulotu	Blues	23/1/93	1.98	120	21
A.O.H.M. (Ofa) Tu'ungafasi	Blues	19/4/92	1.95	122	26
L.C. (Luke) Whitelock	Highlanders	29/1/91	1.90	108	7
S.L. (Samuel) Whitelock	Crusaders	12/10/88	2.02	122	108
S.B. (Sonny Bill) Williams	Blues	3/8/85	1.91	111	51

*= did not play on this tour

VISTA ALL BLACKS NORTHERN TOUR OF JAPAN, ENGLAND, IRELAND & ITALY 2018

INDIVIDUAL SCORING

	Tries	Con	PG	DG	Points		Tries	Con	PG	DG	Points
B. Barrett	2	9	6	2	52	Proctor	1	–	–	–	5
Mo'unga	1	10	1	–	28	Read	1	–	–	–	5
J. Barrett	4	1	–	–	22	B. Smith	1	–	–	–	5
Laumape	4	–	–	–	20	Squire	1	–	–	–	5
McKenzie	4	–	–	–	20	Tahuriorangi	1	–	–	–	5
Bridge	2	–	–	–	10						
Coles	1	–	–	–	5	**Totals**	**26**	**20**	**7**	**2**	**197**
Ioane	1	–	–	–	5						
Naholo	1	–	–	–	5	*Opposition scored*	*10*	*7*	*6*	*1*	*85*
Perenara	1	–	–	–	5						

ALL BLACKS 2018

	Australia	Japan	England	Ireland	Italy	Totals
McKenzie	15*	–	15*	15*	15	4
J. Barrett	–	15	–	–	14	2
Bridge	–	s	–	–	–	1
B. Smith	14	–	14	14	–	3
Milner-Skudder	–	14*	–	–	–	1
Ioane	11	–	11	11	s	4
Naholo	–	11*	–	–	11*	2
Lienert-Brown	s	–	–	s	13	3
Crotty	13*	–	s	12*	–	3
Proctor	–	13	–	–	–	1
Goodhue	–	–	13	13	–	2
Williams	12	–	12*	–	–	2
Laumape	–	12	–	–	12	2
B. Barrett	10	–	10	10	10*	4
Cameron	–	s	–	–	–	1
Mo'unga	s	10	s	s	s	5
Perenara	9*	–	s	s	9*	4
A. Smith	s	–	9*	9*	–	3
Tahuriorangi	–	9*	–	–	s	2
Drummond	–	s	–	–	–	1
Read	8	–	8	8	8	4
L. Whitelock	–	8	–	–	–	1
Savea	7	–	7*	7*	7*	4
Papali'i	–	7*	–	–	s	2
Todd	s	–	s	s	–	3
Squire	6*	–	6*	6*	–	3
Fifita	–	6	–	–	6	2
Evans	–	s	–	–	–	1
Hunt	–	s	–	–	–	1
S. Barrett	5	–	s	s	5*	4
Hemopo	–	5	–	–	–	1
Retallick	s	–	5	4	s	4
S. Whitelock	4*	–	4	5	–	3
Tuipulotu	–	4*	–	–	4	2
Franks	3*	–	3*	3*	–	3
Ta'avao-Matau	–	3*	–	–	s	2
Laulala	s	–	s	s	3*	4
Moody	1*	–	–	–	–	1
Lomax	–	s	–	–	–	1
Perry	–	s	–	–	–	1
Tu'inukuafe	s	–	1*	1*	s	4
Tu'ungafasi	–	1*	s	s	1*	4
Taylor	2*	–	2*	2*	–	3
Harris	s	–	–	–	s	2
Coles	–	2*	s	s	2*	4
Coltman	–	s	–	–	–	1

NEW ZEALAND IN JAPAN, ENGLAND, IRELAND AND ITALY 2018

PLAYED 5　WON 4　LOST 1　POINTS FOR 197　POINTS AGAINST 85

Date	Opponent	Location	Score	Tries	Con	PG	DG	Referee
October 27	Australia	Yokohama	37–20	Squire, Read, B. Barrett, B. Smith, Ioane	B. Barrett (3)	B. Barrett (2)		R. Poite France
November 3	Japan	Tokyo	69–31	Laumape (3), Bridge (2), Coles, Mo'unga, Tahuriorangi, Naholo, Proctor	Mo'unga (7) J. Barrett	Mo'unga		M. Carley England
November 10	England	Twickenham	16–15	McKenzie	B. Barrett (2)		B. Barrett	J. Garces France
November 17	Ireland	Dublin	9–16			B. Barrett (2)	B. Barrett	W. Barnes England
November 24	Italy	Rome	66–3	J. Barrett (4), McKenzie (3), Perenara, Laumape, B. Barrett	B. Barrett (5) Mo'unga (3)			A. Brace Ireland Replaced by P. Gauzere France at 24m

NEW ZEALAND v AUSTRALIA
Bledisloe Cup

Test #576   Nissan Stadium, Yokohama   October 27, 2018
Won by New Zealand 37–20

NEW ZEALAND

Damian McKenzie
Ben Smith   Ryan Crotty   Rieko Ioane
Sonny Bill Williams
Beauden Barrett
TJ Perenara
Kieran Read (capt)
Ardie Savea   Scott Barrett   Sam Whitelock   Liam Squire
Owen Franks   Codie Taylor   Joe Moody

Scott Sio   Folau Fainga'a   Allan Ala'alatoa
Michael Hooper (capt)   Izack Rodda   Rob Simmons   Ned Hanigan
David Pocock
Will Genia
Bernard Foley
Kurtley Beale
Marika Koroibete   Israel Folau   Sefa Naivalu
Dane Haylett-Petty

AUSTRALIA

Reserves: New Zealand — Karl Tu'inukuafe (sub Moody 51m), Nepo Laulala (sub Franks 51m), Brodie Retallick (sub Whitelock 51m), Aaron Smith (sub Perenara 59m), Anton Lienert-Brown (sub Crotty 59m), Matt Todd (sub Squire 67m), Richie Mo'unga (sub McKenzie 67m, B. Barrett to #15), Nathan Harris (sub Taylor 69m).

Australia — Jack Dempsey (sub Hanigan 51m), Tolu Latu (sub Fainga'a 53m), Sekope Kepu (sub Sio 53m), Taniela Tupou (sub Ala'alatoa 53m), Samu Kerevi (sub Naivalu 57m), Rory Arnold (sub Simmons 65m), Nick Phipps (sub Genia 70m), Fainga'a (sub Haylett-Petty *(yellow card)* 70-76m), Tom Banks (sub Koroibete 71m).

Referee: Romain Poite (*France*)   *Kick-off:* 3.00pm
Assistant Referees: Marius van der Westhuizen   *Attendance:* 46,140
(*South Africa*)
Rasta Rasivhenge (*South Africa*)   *Conditions:* soft surface
TMO: Marius Jonker (*South Africa*)

Scorers: New Zealand: *Australia*
   Tries: Squire, Read, B. Barrett, B. Smith, Ioane   *Tries:* Naivalu, Folau
   Conversions: B. Barrett (3)   *Conversions:* Foley (2)
   Penalties: B. Barrett (2)   *Penalties:* Beale, Foley

Scoring: First half: 11m Squire try, B. Barrett conversion 7–0, 20m Beale penalty goal 7–3, 24m B. Barrett penalty goal 10–3, 35m Read try, B. Barrett conversion 17–3, 38m Naivalu try, Foley conversion 17–10.

Second half: 46m Foley penalty goal 17–13, 52m B. Barrett penalty goal 20–13, 58m B. Barrett try, B. Barrett conversion 27–13, 69m B. Smith try 32–13, 75m Folau try, Foley conversion 32–20, 77m Ioane try 37–20.

Yellow card to Latu 67m.

NEW ZEALAND v JAPAN

Test #577 Ajinomoto Stadium, Tokyo November 3, 2018
Won by New Zealand 69–31

NEW ZEALAND

Jordie Barrett

Nehe Milner-Skudder　　Matt Proctor　　Waisake Naholo

Ngani Laumape

Richie Mo'unga

Te Toiroa Tahuriorangi

Luke Whitelock (capt)

Dalton Papali'i　　Jackson Hemopo　　Patrick Tuipulotu　　Vaea Fifita

Angus Ta'avao-Matau　　Dane Coles　　Ofa Tu'ungafasi

Keita Inagaki　　Atsushi Sakate　　Hiroshi Yamashita

Kazuki Himeno　　Samuela Anisi　　Wimpie van der Walt　　Michael Leitch (capt)

Hendrik Tui

Yutaka Nagare

Yu Tamura

Timothy Lafaele

Kenki Fukuoka　　Will Tupou　　Jamie Henry

Ryohei Yamanaka

JAPAN

Reserves: New Zealand — George Bridge (sub Milner-Skudder 40m), Liam Coltman (sub Coles 51m), Tim Perry (sub Tu'ungafasi 53m), Gareth Evans (sub Tuipulotu 53m), Mitch Drummond (sub Tahuriohangi 58m), Tyrel Lomax (sub Ta'avao-Matau 58m), Dillon Hunt (sub Papali'i 58m), Brett Cameron (sub Naholo 70m).

Japan — Fumiaki Tanaka (sub Nagare 48m), Isileli Nakajima (sub van der Walt 48m), Ryoto Nakamura (sub Henry 60m), Uwe Helu (sub Anisi 63m), Yusuke Niwai (sub Sakate 63m), Masataka Mikami (sub Inagaki 63m), Asaeli Valu (sub Yamashita 65m), Rikiya Matsuda (sub Yamanaka 65m).

Referee: Matthew Carley (*England*)　　**Kick-off:** 2.45pm
Assistant Referees: Damon Murphy (*Australia*)　　**Attendance:** 43,751
　　　　　　　　Graham Cooper (*Australia*)　　**Conditions:** Good
TMO: James Leckie (*Ireland*)

Scorers: New Zealand:　　　　　　　　　　　　**Japan**
　　Tries: Laumape (3), Bridge (2), Coles,　　　　*Tries:* Lafaele (2), Anisi, Tui, Henry
　　Mo'unga, Tahuriorangi, Naholo,　　　　　　*Conversions:* Tamura (3)
　　Proctor
　　Conversions: Mo'unga (7), J. Barrett
　　Penalty: Mo'unga

Scoring: First half: 2m Mo'unga penalty goal 3–0, 3m Anisi try, Tamura conversion 3–7, 14m Coles try, Mo'unga conversion 10–7, 18m Mo'unga try, Mo'unga conversion 17–7, 27m Laumape try, Mo'unga conversion 24–7, 32m Tui try, Tamura conversion 24–14, 34m Tahuriorangi try, Mo'unga conversion 31–14, 37m Laumape try, Mo'unga conversion 38–14, 40m Lafaele try 38–19,

Second half: 46m Bridge try, Mo'unga conversion 45–19, 51m Henry try 45–24, 56m Naholo try 50–24, 59m Proctor try, Mo'unga conversion 57–24, 62m Laumape try, J. Barrett conversion 64–24, 66m Bridge try 69–24, 69m Lafaele try, Tamura conversion 69–31.

All Blacks debut for Papali'i, Proctor, Bridge, Evans, Lomax and Cameron.

Test match debut for Drummond and Hunt

NEW ZEALAND v ENGLAND
Hillary Shield

Test #578   Twickenham, London   November 10, 2018

Won by New Zealand 16–15

NEW ZEALAND

Damian McKenzie

Ben Smith   Jack Goodhue   Rieko Ioane

Sonny Bill Williams   Beauden Barrett

Aaron Smith

Kieran Read (capt)

Ardie Savea   Sam Whitelock   Brodie Retallick   Liam Squire

Owen Franks   Codie Taylor   Karl Tu'inukuafe

Ben Moon   Dylan Hartley (co-captain)   Kyle Sinckler

Sam Underhill   Maro Itoje   George Kruis   Brad Shields

Mark Wilson

Ben Youngs

Owen Farrell (co-captain)

Ben Te'o

Jonny May   Henry Slade   Chris Ashton

Elliot Daly

ENGLAND

Reserves: New Zealand — Ryan Crotty (sub Williams 30m), Dane Coles (sub Taylor 43m), Nepo Laulala (sub Franks 43m), Scott Barrett (sub Squire 51m), Ofa Tu'ungafasi (sub Tu'inukuafe 56m), TJ Perenara (sub A. Smith 62m), Richie Mo'unga (sub McKenzie 62m, B. Barrett to #15), Matt Todd (sub Savea 67m).

England — Courtney Lawes (temp sub Shields 26–40m, sub Shields 64m), Jamie George (sub Hartley 40m), Alec Hepburn (sub Moon 57m), Harry Williams (sub Sinckler 57m), Danny Care (sub Youngs 62m), Charlie Ewels (sub Kruis 65m), Jack Nowell (sub Ashton 67m), George Ford (sub Te'o 67m).

Referee: Jerome Garces (*France*)   *Kick-off:* 3.07pm
Assistant Referees: Jaco Peyper (*South Africa*)   *Attendance:* 82,149
    Marius Mitrea (*Italy*)   *Conditions:* steady rain
TMO: Marius Jonker (*South Africa*)

Scorers: New Zealand: *England*
     Try: McKenzie   *Tries:* Ashton, Hartley
     Conversion: B. Barrett   *Conversion:* Farrell
     Penalties: B. Barrett (2)   *Dropped goal:* Farrell
     Dropped goal: B. Barrett

Scoring: First half: 1m Ashton try 0–5, 9m Farrell dropped goal 0–8, 23m Hartley try, Farrell conversion 0–15, 38m McKenzie try, B. Barrett conversion 7–15, 42m B. Barrett penalty goal 10–15.

Second half: 45m B. Barrett dropped goal 13–15, 59m B. Barrett penalty goal 16–15.

NEW ZEALAND v IRELAND

Test #579 Aviva Stadium, Dublin November 17, 2018
Won by Ireland 16–9

NEW ZEALAND

Damian McKenzie
Ben Smith   Jack Goodhue   Rieko Ioane
Ryan Crotty
Beauden Barrett
Aaron Smith
Kieran Read (capt)
Ardie Savea   Sam Whitelock   Brodie Retallick   Liam Squire
Owen Franks   Codie Taylor   Karl Tu'inukuafe

Cian Healy   Rory Best (capt)   Tadhg Furlong
Josh van der Flier   Devin Toner   James Ryan   Peter O'Mahony
C.J. Stander
Kieran Marmion
Johnny Sexton
Bundee Aki
Jacob Stockdale   Garry Ringrose   Keith Earls
Rob Kearney

IRELAND

Reserves: New Zealand — Scott Barrett (sub Squire 31m), Dane Coles (sub Taylor 46m), Ofa Tu'ungafasi (sub Tu'inukuafe 46m), Nepo Laulala (sub Franks 46m), Richie Mo'unga (sub McKenzie 55m, B. Barrett to #15), T.J. Perenara (sub A. Smith 57m), Anton Lienert-Brown (sub Crotty 61m), Matt Todd (sub Savea 73m).

Ireland — Jack McGrath (sub Healy 51m), Luke McGrath (sub Marmion 58m), Iain Henderson (sub Toner 61m), Jordi Murphy (sub O'Mahony 61m), Andrew Porter (sub Furlong 63m), Sean Cronin (sub Best 64m), Jordan Larmour (sub Kearney 65m), Joey Carbery (sub Sexton 76m).

Referee: Wayne Barnes (*England*) *Kick-off:* 7.02pm
Assistant Referees: Mathieu Raynal (*France*) *Attendance:* 52,000
Marius Mitrea (*Italy*) *Conditions:* good surface, no wind
TMO: Rowan Kitt (*England*)

Scorers: New Zealand: *Ireland*
  Penalties: B. Barrett (2)   *Try:* Stockdale
  Dropped goal: B. Barrett   *Conversion:* Sexton
  Penalties: Sexton (3)

Scoring: First half: 10m Sexton penalty goal 0–3, 16m B. Barrett penalty goal 3–3, 26m Sexton penalty goal 3–6, 28m B. Barrett dropped goal 6–6, 38m Sexton penalty goal 6–9.
Second half: 47m Stockdale try, Sexton conversion 6–16, 68m B. Barrett penalty goal 9–16.

NEW ZEALAND v ITALY

Test #580 Stadio Olimpico, Rome November 24, 2018
Won by New Zealand 66–3

NEW ZEALAND

Damian McKenzie

Jordie Barrett Anton Lienert-Brown Waisake Naholo

Ngani Laumape

Beauden Barrett

TJ Perenara

Kieran Read (capt)

Ardie Savea Scott Barrett Patrick Tuipulotu Vaea Fifita

Nepo Laulala Dane Coles Ofa Tu'ungafasi

Andrea Lovotti Leonardo Ghiraldini (capt) Simone Ferrari

Jake Polledri Alessandro Zanni Dean Budd Sebastian Negri

Braam Steyn

Tito Tebaldi

Tommaso Allan

Tommaso Castello

Luca Sperandio Michele Campagnaro Tommaso Benvenuti

Jayden Hayward

ITALY

Reserves: **New Zealand** — Dalton Papali'i (sub Savea 47m), Te Toiroa Tahuriorangi (sub Perenara 50), Richie Mo'unga (sub B. Barrett 50m), Angus Ta'avao-Matau (sub Laulala 53m), Rieko Ioane (sub Naholo 54m), Karl Tu'inukuafe (sub Tu'ungafasi 54m), Nathan Harris (sub Coles 59m), Brodie Retallick (sub S. Barrett 59m).

Italy — Marco Fuser (sub Zanni 37m), Cherif Traore (sub Lovotti 47m), Edoardo Padovani (sub Sperandio 50m), Luca Morisi (sub Allan 54m), Tiziano Pasquali (sub Ferrari 59m), Luca Bigi (sub Ghiraldini 59m), Guglielmo Palazzani (sub Tebaldi 66m), Johan Meyer (sub Negri 70m).

Referee: Andrew Brace (*Ireland*) *Kick-off:* 3.00pm
(sub P. Gauzere 24m)
Assistant Referees: Pascal Gauzere (*France*) *Attendance:* 50,000
Sean Gallagher (*Ireland*) *Conditions:* warm, drizzle, surface slippery
TMO: Andrew McMenemy (*Scotland*)

Scorers: **New Zealand:** **Italy**
Tries: J. Barrett (4), McKenzie (3), Perenara, *Penalty:* Allan
Laumape, B. Barrett
Conversions: B. Barrett (5), Mo'unga (3)

Scoring: First half: 8m Perenara try 5–0, 12m Allan penalty goal 5–3, 17m McKenzie try, B. Barrett conversion 12–3, 27m McKenzie try 17–3, 31m J. Barrett try, B. Barrett conversion 24–3, 41m J. Barrett try, B. Barrett conversion 31–3.

Second half: 43m Laumape try, B. Barrett conversion 38–3, 45m B. Barrett try, B. Barrett conversion 45–3, 52m McKenzie try, Mo'unga conversion 52–3, 72m J. Barrett try, Mo'unga conversion 59–3, 82m J. Barrett ry, Mo'unga conversion 66–3.

Italian players Budd and Hayward had been Promising Players of the Year in the Rugby Almanack 2009.

Jordie Barrett was the first All Black to score four tries in a test against Italy.

U.K. BARBARIANS

The Barbarians club this year played Argentina on 1 December as their 2018 Killik Cup match. Killik & Co have sponsored matches for the Barbarians against international teams since 2009.
Four New Zealanders played, thus gaining a first-class appearance.
Played at Twickenham, the Barbarians win 38–35.

U.K. BARBARIANS 2018

J.M. (Jack) Debreczeni	Northland	15
L.P.C. (Leon) Fukofuka	Auckland	9
S.J. (Jordan) Taufua	Counties Manukau	s
W.W.V. (Wyatt) Crockett (capt)	Tasman	1

Wyatt Crockett, Jackson Hemopo, Dillon Hunt, Tevita Li, Nehe Milner-Skudder, Toni Pulu, and Ricky Riccitelli played for a World XV v Japan at Osaka on 26 October. Both teams used more than 23 players so no first-class appearances are credited.

NEW ZEALAND UNDER 20
WORLD RUGBY U20 CHAMPIONSHIPS

Although there were some magic moments, at no stage did the New Zealand Under 20 team look like a champion in waiting at the World Under 20 Championship, held in France. The greater need is still that the New Zealand Under 20 team proves a good nursery for the All Blacks — which is less apparent in other countries' age group teams in their contribution to their national team. There is no fear that the New Zealand team has faltered in this.

Pool A
May 30	Wales	26	Australia	21	Beziers
	New Zealand	67	Japan	0	Narbonne
June 3	Australia	54	Japan	19	Narbonne
	New Zealand	42	Wales	10	Beziers
June 7	Wales	18	Japan	17	Perpignan
	New Zealand	27	Australia	18	Perpignan

Pool B
May 30	Italy	27	Scotland	26	Beziers
	England	39	Argentina	18	Narbonne
June 3	Argentina	29	Scotland	13	Perpignan
	England	43	Italy	5	Perpignan
June 7	Italy	30	Argentina	36	Beziers
	England	35	Scotland	10	Beziers

Pool C
May 30	South Africa	33	Georgia	27	Perpignan
	France	26	Ireland	24	Perpignan
June 3	France	24	Georgia	12	Beziers
	South Africa	30	Ireland	7	Narbonne
June 7	Georgia	24	Ireland	20	Narbonne
	France	46	South Africa	29	Narbonne

9th place semi-final
June 12	Scotland	45	Ireland	29	Perpignan
	Georgia	24	Japan	20	Perpignan

5th place semi-final
June 12	Argentina	39	Wales	15	Narbonne
	Australia	44	Italy	15	Narbonne

Semi-finals
June 12	England	32	South Africa	31	Narbonne
	France	16	New Zealand	7	Perpignan

11th place playoff
June 17	Ireland	39	Japan	33	Beziers

9th place playoff
June 17	Georgia	39	Scotland	31	Beziers

7th place playoff
June 17	Wales	34	Italy	17	Beziers

5th place playoff
June 17	Australia	41	Argentina	15	Beziers

3rd place playoff

June 17	South Africa	40	New Zealand	30	Beziers

Final

June 17	France	33	England	25	Beziers

NEW ZEALAND UNDER 20, 2018

Player	Union	Date of birth	Height	Weight	Games	Points
J.S. (John) Akau'ola-Laula	Auckland	16/3/98	1.99	111	7	5
S.F.J. (Sione) Asi	Manawatu	3/3/98	1.86	135	7	15
S. (Suetena) Asomua	Counties Manukau	6/7/98	1.85	111	2	–
T.M. (Tom) Christie (capt)	Canterbury	4/3/98	1.85	103	15	45
C.D. (Caleb) Clarke	Auckland	29/3/99	1.87	103	11	40
R.L. (Rob) Cobb	Auckland	8/4/99	1.89	117	5	–
L.O.K.W.T. (Leicester) Fainga'anuku	Tasman	11/10/99	1.88	104	4	25
D.J. (Devan) Flanders	Hawke's Bay	20/7/99	1.92	105	7	5
T.H.T. (Tom) Florence	Taranaki	20/5/98	1.89	103	5	5
S.J. (Scott) Gregory	Northland	7/1/99	1.84	93	6	–
R.D. (Ricky) Jackson	Otago	2/8/98	1.80	100	7	15
V.T. (Vilimoni) Koroi	Otago	11/4/98	1.80	88	5	5
L.E. (Laghlan) McWhannell	Waikato	20/10/98	2.01	112	6	–
T.T.P. (Tevita) Mafileo	Bay of Plenty	4/2/98	1.86	118	7	5
C.R. (Ciarahn) Matoe	Taranaki	16/11/98	1.81	89	5	20
O.M. (Ollie) Norris	Waikato	11/12/99	1.85	110	1	–
X.J.S. (Xavier) Numia	Wellington	29/11/98	1.89	111	3	–
H.R.J. (Harry) Plummer	Auckland	19/6/98	1.84	96	8	110
C.T. (Carlos) Price	Wellington	30/9/98	1.78	80	4	10
B.D. (Billy) Proctor	Wellington	14/5/99	1.87	96	7	10
N.G.J. (Ngatungane) Punivai	Canterbury	30/8/98	1.84	101	3	–
W. (Waimana) Riedlinger-Kapa	Auckland	2/9/98	1.92	106	7	10
J.L. (Jay) Renton	Southland	16/3/98	1.75	84	6	10
X.O'C. (Xavier) Roe	Waikato	13/12/98	1.79	81	6	15
H.C.R. (Hoskins) Sotutu	Auckland	12/7/98	1.92	106	6	–
J.W. (Jamie) Spowart	Tasman	15/5/98	1.80	87	7	25
B.W.N. (Bailyn) Sullivan	Waikato	3/9/98	1.86	95	5	15
T.R. (Tanielu) Tele'a	Auckland	16/9/98	1.87	107	4	10
F.C. (Flynn) Thomas	Southland	23/6/98	1.78	100	8	–
K.R. (Kaleb) Trask	Bay of Plenty	27/1/99	1.80	90	7	17
W.A. (Will) Tremain	Hawke's Bay	30/7/98	1.88	101	7	10
W.A. (Will) Tucker	Canterbury	16/3/98	2.02	111	5	10
Q.P. (Quinn) Tupaea	Waikato	10/5/99	1.82	100	–	–
K. (Kaliopasi) Uluilakepa	Wellington	18/1/99	1.90	145	7	–

Manager: Martyn Vercoe *Head coach:* Craig Philpott
Assistant coaches: David Hill, David Hewett, Willie Rickards

NEW ZEALAND UNDER 20 APPEARANCES AT WORLD RUGBY CHAMPIONSHIP 2018

	Japan	Wales	Australia	France	South Africa	TOTALS
Koroi	15*	15	15	15*	–	4
Punivai	–	–	–	–	15*	1
Spowart	14	s	14	s	s	5
Sullivan	13	14*	–	14	14*	4
Clarke	–	–	11	11	11	3
Fainga'anuku	11	11*	–	–	–	2
Proctor	12*	13*	13	13	13	5
Tele'a	–	12	–	–	–	1
Gregory	s	s	12*	12*	s	5
Trask	10	s	s	s	10	5
Plummer	s	10	10	10	12	5
Roe	9*	9	–	9*	s	4
Renton	s	–	9	s	9*	4
Sotutu	8	–	s	s	8	4
Flanders	–	8	8	8*	6*	4
Christie	7*	7	7	7	7	5
Tremain	s	s	–	s	s	4
Florence	6	6*	–	–	–	2
Riedlinger-Kapa	s	–	6*	6*	5	4
Tucker	5*	5*	s	5	–	4
Akau'ola-Laula	4	s	5*	–	s	4
McWhannell	–	4	4	4	4*	4
Mafileo	3*	s	3*	3*	–	4
Uluilakepa	–	3*	s*	s	3*	4
Numia	1*	–	s	1*	–	3
Cobb	s	1*	1*	–	–	3
Asi	s	s	–	s	s	4
Norris	–	–	–	–	1*	1
Asomua	–	–	–	–	s	1
Thomas	2*	s	2	2*	s	5
Jackson	s	2*	–	s	2*	4

INDIVIDUAL SCORING AT RUGBY WORLD CHAMPIONSHIP

	Tries	Con	PG	DG	Points
Plummer	3	10	7	–	56
Spowart	4	–	–	–	20
Trask	–	6	–	–	12
Christie	2	–	–	–	10
Fainga'anuku	2	–	–	–	10
Roe	2	–	–	–	10
Sullivan	2	–	–	–	10
Koroi	1	–	–	–	5
Clarke	1	–	–	–	5
Proctor	1	–	–	–	5
Renton	1	–	–	–	5
Flanders	1	–	–	–	5
Tucker	1	–	–	–	5
Riedlinger-Kapa	1	–	–	–	5
Akau'ola-Laula	1	–	–	–	5
Mafilo	1	–	–	–	5
Totals	**24**	**16**	**7**	**0**	**173**
Opposition scored	10t	7	6	0	84

NEW ZEALAND UNDER 20 APPEARANCES AT OCEANIA TOURNAMENT 2018

	Tonga	Fiji	Australia	TOTALS
Trask	15	–	10	2
Spowart	–	15	14*	2
Koroi	–	–	15	1
Sullivan	14*	–	–	1
Fainga'anuku	11	–	11	2
Punivai	–	11	s	2
Proctor	13	13	–	2
Tele'a	12	14*	13	3
Gregory	–	s	–	1
Plummer	10*	12	12*	3
Matoe	s	10	s	3
Price	9	–	s	2
Roe	s	9*	–	2
Renton	–	s	9*	2
Flanders	8*	6*	8*	3
Sotutu	s	8*	–	2
Christie	7*	s	7	3
Tremain	s	7	s	3
Florence	6	s	6	3
Akau'ola-Laula	5*	s	s	3
Tucker	–	5*	–	1
McWhannell	4	–	4	2
Riedlinger-Kapa	s	4	5*	3
Uluilakepa	3*	s	s	3
Asomua	–	3*	–	1
Mafileo	s	s	3*	3
Cobb	1*	–	1*	2
Asi	s	1*	s	3
Jackson	2*	s	2*	3
Thomas	s	2*	s	3

INDIVIDUAL SCORING AT OCEANIA TOURNAMENT

	Tries	Con	PG	DG	Points		Tries	Con	PG	DG	Points
Plummer	3	18	1	–	54	Riedlinger-Kapa	1	–	–	–	5
Asi	3	–	–	–	15	Roe	1	–	–	–	5
Christie	3	–	–	–	15	Spowart	1	–	–	–	5
Fainga'anuku	3	–	–	–	15	Sullivan	1	–	–	–	5
Jackson	3	–	–	–	15	Trask	1	–	–	–	5
Tele'a	2	–	–	–	10	Tucker	1	–	–	–	5
Tremain	2	–	–	–	10	Matoe	–	2	–	–	4
penalty try	1	–	–	–	7						
Florence	1	–	–	–	5	**Totals**	**30**	**20**	**1**	**0**	**195**
Price	1	–	–	–	5						
Proctor	1	–	–	–	5	Opposition scored	6	5	1	0	43
Renton	1	–	–	–	5						

NEW ZEALAND UNDER 20 TEAM RECORD 2018

Played 8   Won 6   Lost 2   Points for 368   Points against 127

Date	Opponent	Location	Score	Tries	Con	PG	Referee
April 27	Tonga (OT)	Gold Coast	97–0	Fainga'anuku (2), Jackson, Christie, Florence, Trask, penalty try, Plummer, Sullivan, Tele'a, Asi, Price, Riedlinger-Kapa, Tremain, Proctor	Plummer (8) Matoe (2)		J. Quinn (Australia)
May 1	Fiji (OT)	Gold Coast	55–15	Plummer (2), Asi (2), Roe, Tremain, Tucker, Tele'a, Spowart	Plummer (5)		D. Murphy (Australia)
May 5	Australia (OT)	Gold Coast	43–28	Jackson (2), Christie (2), Renton, Fainga'anuku	Plummer (5)	Plummer	D. Murphy (Australia)
May 30	Japan (WR)	Beziers	67–10	Spowart (3), Fainga'anuku (2), Koroi, Sullivan, Roe, Tucker, Akau'ola-Laula, Christie	Trask (6)		A. Piardi
June 3	Wales (WR)	Beziers	42–10	Proctor, Sullivan, Christie, Mafileo, Roe	Plummer (4)	Plummer (3)	L. Cayre (France)
June 7	Australia (WR)	Perpignan	27–18	Plummer, Flanders, Spowart	Plummer (3)	Plummer (2)	K. Dickson (England)
June 12	France (WR)	Perpignan	7–15	Plummer	Plummer		K. Dickson (England)
June 17	South Africa (WR)	Beziers	30–40	Renton, Plummer, Riedlinger-Kapa, Clarke	Plummer (2)	Plummer (2)	L. Cayre (France)

MAORI ALL BLACKS TOUR OF USA, BRAZIL & CHILE 2018

	Province	Date of Birth	Height	Weight	Games to 1/1/19
R. (Robert) Abel	Auckland	4/7/89	1.83	110	3
O.W. (Otere) Black	Manawatu	4/5/95	1.84	86	7
A.L. (Ash) Dixon (capt)	Hawke's Bay	1/9/88	1.80	103	14
C.I. (Chris) Eves	North Harbour	11/12/87	1.88	118	13
B.D. (Bryn) Hall	North Harbour	3/2/92	1.83	93	3
W.K. (Billy) Harmon	Canterbury	23/12/94	1.87	104	3
J.N. (Jackson) Hemopo	Manawatu	14/11/93	1.94	113	4
A.L. (Akira) Ioane	Auckland	16/6/95	1.94	113	11
J.R. (Josh) Ioane	Otago	11/7/95	1.78	92	2
M.R. (Mitch) Karpik	Bay or Plenty	2/6/95	1.86	103	3
M.R.T. (Matt) Lansdown	Waikato	2/4/97	1.84	99	8
T.S. (Tyrel) Lomax	Tasman	1/6/96	1.92	127	4
J.H. (Jonah) Lowe	Hawke's Bay	9/5/96	1.84	92	3
H.M. (Hoani) Matenga	Bay or Plenty	13/4/87	1.93	103	1
B. (Ben) May	Hawke's Bay	13/10/82	1.93	124	15
S.J. (Sam) Nock	Northland	18/6/96	1.75	85	1
P.P.M. (Paripari) Parkinson	Tasman	12/9/96	2.04	119	3
R.J. (Reed) Prinsep	Canterbury	17/2/93	1.92	109	5
M.P. (Matt) Proctor	Wellington	23/6/89	1.83	94	12
M.T. (Marcel) Renata	Auckland	24/2/94	1.89	118	10
J.L. (Jonathan) Ruru	Auckland	2/2/93	1.84	94	3
S.T. (Shaun) Stevenson	North Harbour	14/11/96	1.92	96	5
R. (Rob) Thompson	Manawatu	2/8/91	1.84	103	6
T.T. (Tei) Walden	Taranaki	25/5/97	1.82	94	4
I.E.T. (Isaia) Walker–Leawere	Wellington	16/4/97	1.97	119	3
R.E. (Regan) Ware	Taranaki	7/8/94	1.87	101	1
B.M. (Brad) Weber	Hawke's Bay	17/1/91	1.72	75	8
R.G. (Ross) Wright	Northland	25/8/86	1.80	113	4

Coach: Clayton McMillan
Assistant Coaches: Joe Maddock, Roger Randle
Kaumatua: Luke Crawford
Manager: Tony Ward
Tour Manager: Matt Sexton
Trainer: Simon Thomas
Analyst: Jayson Ross
Doctor: Ra Durie
Physio: Ash Draper
Assistant Physio: Adam Letts

INDIVIDUAL SCORING

	Tries	Con	PG	DG	Points
Black	–	17	–	–	34
Karpik	4	–	–	–	20
Dixon	3	–	–	–	15
Hemopo	3	–	–	–	15
Lowe	3	–	–	–	15
Walker-Leawere	3	–	–	–	15
J. Ioane	1	4	–	–	13
Hall	2	–	–	–	10
Nock	2	–	–	–	10
May	1	–	–	–	5
Stevenson	1	–	–	–	5
Thompson	1	–	–	–	5
Ware	1	–	–	–	5
Totals	**25**	**21**	**–**	**–**	**167**
Opposition scored	3	2	2	–	25

MAORI ALL BLACKS 2018

	USA	Brazil	Chile	Totals
Stevenson	15	11	14	3
Lansdown	s	15	11	2
Lowe	14	14	s	3
Ware	11	–	–	1
Proctor	–	s	13	2
Thompson	13	13	12	3
Walden	12	12	s	3
J. Ioane	s	s	15	3
Black	10	10	10	3
Weber	9	–	–	1
Ruru	s	9	–	2
Hall	–	s	9	2
Nock	–	–	s	1
A. Ioane	8	8	8	3
Matenga	s	–	–	1
Karpik	7	s	7	3
Harmon	s	7	s	3
Prinsep	6	6	6	3
Parkinson	5	5	5	3
Walker-Leawere	4	4	s	3
Hemopo	–	s	4	2
May	3	1	–	2
Renata	s	3	s	3
Lomax	–	s	3	2
Eves	1	s	s	3
Wright	s	–	1	2
Dixon	2	2	2	3
Abel	s	s	s	3

MAORI ALL BLACKS 2018

PLAYED 3 WON 3 POINTS FOR 167 POINTS AGAINST 25

Date	Opponent	Location	Score	Tries	Con	PG	DG	Referee
November 3	USA	Chicago	59–22	Walker-Leawere (2), Ware, Karpik, Dixon, May, Thompson, Lowe, Stevenson	Black (5) J. Ioane(2)	–	–	K. Dickson
November 10	Brazil	Sao Paulo	35–3	Dixon (2), Walker-Leawere, Hemopo, Lowe	Black (5)	–	–	F. Anselmi
November 17	Chile	Santiago	73–0	Karpik (3), Hall (2), Nock (2), Hemopo (2), Lowe, J. Ioane	Black (7) J. Ioane(2)	–	–	P. de Luca

NEW ZEALAND UNIVERSITIES

With the ongoing sponsorship by ANZCO and Nissui, since 2003, New Zealand Universities made a four-match tour to Japan and Singapore. Results were:
April 28, v Kyushu, at Kumamoto, won 58–31 (not first-class)
May 3, v Kansai Universities, at Kyoto, won 47–33 (not first-class)
May 6, v Kanto Universities, at Tokyo, won 34–17
May 9, v Singapore XV, Singapore, won 52–7 (not first-class)

v KANTO UNIVERSITIES
Chichibunomiya Stadium, Tokyo   May 6, 2018
Won 34–17

		Caleb Makene		
Taylor Haugh		Josh Timu		Te Rangatira Waitokia
	Hamish Northcott			
			Tyrone Elkington-MacDonald	
		Henry Saker		
		Teariki Ben-Nicholas		
Damien Scott	Hamish Dalzell		Ben Morris	William Mangos
Pouri Rakete-Stones		Nick Werahiko (capt)		Chris Gawler

Reserves: Maile Koloto (sub Makene 38th min), Trent Lawn (sub Werahiko h/t), Hauwai McGahan (sub Scott 56th min), Oliver McCowan (sub Morris 56th-67th), Rakete-Stones 78th min), Antonio Mikaele-Tu'u (sub Northcott 67th min), Justin Sangster (sub Dalzell 67th min), Connor McLeod (sub Saker 70th min), Kilipati Lea (sub Gawler 73rd min).

Scorers:
Tries: Ben-Nicholas (2), Timu, Mangos, Koloto, Haugh
Conversions: Elkington-MacDonald (2)

Referee: Rui Shimizu (Japan)

Before the team assembled original selections Tyler Campbell (*Waikato University*), Lyndon Dunshea (*Auckland University*), Kurt Eklund (*Auckland University*), and Te Wehi Wright (*Old Boys University*) withdrew and replaced by George Stratton, Justin Sangster, Trent Lawn and Maile Koloto respectively. Kirk Tufuga joined the team when Brett Cameron returned home injured after the match v Kyushu. Reece Brosnan joined the team when Josh Timu returned home after the match v Kanto Universities.

Manager: P.R. (Peter) Magson (*Lincoln*)
Coach: B.P. (Brendon) Timmins (*Otago*)
Assistant Coach: S.J. (Simon) Forrest (*Otago*)
Doctor: S.J. (Stephen) Williams (*Otago*)
Physio: J.D. (Jonathon) Moyle (*Auckland*)

		Date of Birth	Height	Weight
TG (Teariki) Ben-Nicholas	Old Boys University	18/07/1995	194	109
RS (Reece) Brosnan	Massey University	20/12/1995	183	88
BD (Brett) Cameron	Lincoln University	04/10/1996	175	83
HA (Hamish) Dalzell	Lincoln University	16/01/1996	201	114
TD (Tyrone) Elkington-MacDonald	Auckland University	29/04/1991	179	93
CM (Chris) Gawler	Lincoln University	14/12/1993	187	114
NWK (Nick) Grogan	Massey University	04/04/1993	183	108
TC (Taylor) Haugh	Otago University	03/12/1997	180	82
MT (Maile) Koloto	Old Boys University	19/05/1997	191	98
TBF (Trent) Lawn	Canterbury University	06/09/1997	–	–
SKK (Kilipati) Lea	Otago University	10/01/1998	186	108
CL (Caleb) Makene	Lincoln University	20/04/1996	178	85
WK (William) Mangos	Old Boys University	26/03/1992	193	110
OJ (Oliver) McCowan	Canterbury University	18/05/1996	185	112
HP (Hauwai) McGahan	North Harbour Marist	15/05/1997	185	100
CPA (Connor) McLeod	Otago University	29/06/1997	173	72
AMW (Antonio) Mikaele-Tu'u	Waikato University	06/11/1997	186	98
BJ (Ben) Morris	Lincoln University	01/03/1997	196	102
HC (Hamish) Northcott	Massey University	06/08/1992	183	93
PG (Pouri) Rakete-Stones	Napier Pirates	17/06/1997	182	115
HM (Henry) Saker	Auckland University	21/05/1997	175	77
JT (Justin) Sangster	Waikato University	30/11/1996	198	110
DA (Damien) Scott	Napier Pirates	31/01/1996	189	97
GE (George) Stratton	Lincoln University	12/10/1996	183	87
JC (Josh) Timu	Otago University	09/07/1997	182	91
KMS (Kirk) Tufuga	Massey University	04/01/1991	187	102
TRW (Te Rangitira) Waitokia	Massey University	11/04/1996	180	84
NAJ (Nick) Werahiko (capt)	Lincoln University	04/08/1993	183	105

NEW ZEALAND HEARTLAND

The New Zealand Heartland team had a two match programme in 2018, a match against a Vanua XV from Fiji and the annual match with NZ Marist for the MacRae Cup.

The Vanua XV was selected from players in the Vodafone Vanua Championship, the Fiji B division provincial competition.

James Lash extended his record points scoring aggregate for the Heartland team to 95. Ngati Porou East Coast was the only Heartland union not represented in the squad.

	Union	Date of Birth	Height	Weight	Games for NZ Heartland XV as at 24/10/2018 *
A.J. (Alex) Bradley (capt)	Thames Valley	30/09/1981	1.88	123	0
S.A. (Scott) Cameron	Horowhenua Kapiti	02/08/1987	1.83	120	4
C.W. (Carl) Carmichael	King Country	16/03/1985	1.85	112	3
D.R. (Dean) Church	King Country	08/09/1989	1.80	85	0
C.D. (Craig) Clare	Wanganui	19/08/1984	1.84	93	1
C.J. (Cameron) Crowley	Wanganui	30/11/1989	1.80	90	5
R.K. (Ralph) Darling	North Otago	21/08/1986	1.78	115	12
J.W.P.R. (James) Goodger	Wairarapa Bush	27/05/1988	1.92	93	3
C.J. (Campbell) Hart	Wanganui	11/10/1991	1.94	107	0
S.F. (Sione) Holani	West Coast	18/04/1986	1.75	102	0
Meli Kolinisau	North Otago	20/03/1995	1.76	128	1
S.S. (Seta) Koroitamana	Mid Canterbury	01/06/1995	1.84	100	1
A.D. (Aaron) Lahmert	Horowhenua Kapiti	17/02/1991	1.82	100	1
J.J. (James) Lash	Buller	16/01/1990	1.70	78	6
S.M. (Sam) McCahon	Thames Valley	20/04/1993	1.78	98	0
Callum McDonald	Poverty Bay	24/06/1991	1.90	99	0
G.F. (Glen) McIntyre	Thames Valley	30/10/1990	1.83	112	0
P.B. (Peni) Nabainivalu	Wanganui	06/03/1987	1.82	97	3
W.E. (Willie) Paia'aua	Horowhenua Kapiti	24/12/1992	1.73	90	4
V.J. (Veikoso) Poloniati	South Canterbury	27/08/1995	1.97	121	0
B.D. (Brett) Ranga	Thames Valley	19/01/1991	1.91	107	0
A.P. (Andrew) Stephens	Buller	18/04/1981	1.82	94	11
T.K. (Troy) Tauwhare	West Coast	12/01/1990	1.85	108	2
A.M. (Alex) Thrupp	King Country	15/08/1996	1.87	98	0
W.A. (Willie) Wright	South Canterbury	30/04/1992	1.75	87	1

* *The naming of the team.*
Original selections Shaun Hill (Thames Valley), Simon Lilicama (North Otago) and Nick Strachan (South Canterbury) withdrew after selection and replaced by Sam McCahon, Wille Paia'aua and Callum McDonald respectively.

Coach: C.A. (Craig) Scanlon (Buller)
Assistant coach: M.P. (Mark) Rutene (Horowhenua Kapiti)
Manager: G.I. (Gavin) Hodder (Wairarapa Bush)
Physiotherapist: P.J. (Philippa) Masoe (North Otago)
Doctor: P.J. (Patrick) McHugh (Poverty Bay)

NEW ZEALAND HEARTLAND, 2018

	Vanua XV	NZ Marist	TOTALS
Clare	15	15	2
Church	14*	s	2
Crowley	11	11	2
Paia'aua	s	14*	2
Nabainivalu	13	13	2
Holani	12*	12*	2
Thrupp	s	–	1
McCahon	–	s	1
Lash	10	10	2
Wright	9*	9*	2
Stephens	s	s	2
Bradley (capt)	8*	8	2
Lahmert	s	–	1
Koroitamana	7	7*	2
McDonald	–	s	1
Ranga	6	4	2
Poloniati	5*	5*	2
Hart	4	6	2
Goodger	s	s	2
Cameron	3*	3*	2
Carmichael	1*	1*	2
Darling	s	s	2
Kolinisau	s	s	2
Tauwhare	2*	2*	2
McIntyre	s	s	2

INDIVIDUAL SCORING

	Tries	Con	PG	DG	Points
Lash	1	9	2	–	29
Bradley	4	1	–	–	22
Nabainivalu	3	–	–	–	15
Clare	2	–	–	–	10
Paia'aua	2	–	–	–	10
Wright	1	–	–	–	5
McIntyre	1	–	–	–	5
Hart	1	–	–	–	5
Holani	1	–	–	–	5
Totals	**16**	**10**	**2**	**0**	**106**
Opposition scored	3	2	0	0	19

NEW ZEALAND HEARTLAND, 2018

PLAYED 2　WON 2　POINTS FOR 106　POINTS AGAINST 19

Date	Opponent	Location	Score	Tries	Con	PG	DG	Referee
November 1	Vanua XV	Taupo	60–0	Bradley (3), Nabainivalu (2), Wright, McIntyre, Clare, Hart	Lash (6)	Lash		M.C.J. Winter
November 4	NZ Marist (MacRae Cup)	Taupo	46–19	Paia'aua (2), Lash, Clare, Holani, Nabainivalu, Bradley	Lash (3), Bradley	Lash		P.M. Williams

NEW ZEALAND MARIST

In their annual encounter with the NZ Heartland team, NZ Marist included 11 players who had appeared in the Mitre 10 Cup or Heartland Championship in 2018.

v NEW ZEALAND HEARTLAND

Owen Delany Park, Taupo   4 November, 2018

Lost 19–46

Zac Saunders
Celtic Timaru

Ben Werthmuller   Timo Vaiusu   Leethan Rawiri
OB Marist, Palm. Nth   *Hastings RS*   *Marist, Whakatane*

Star Timu
Hastings RS

Chase Tiatia (capt)
Hutt OB Marist/Rangatau

Zac Donaldson
OB Marist, Napier

Sione Tuipulotu
Marist, Ardmore

Savelio Ropati   Daymon Leasuasu   Ben Fotheringham   Hannon Brighouse
Marist, Ardmore   *Marist, Ardmore*   *Marist, Invercargill*   *Napier OB Marist*

Aleki Vuki   James O'Reilly   Shaun Stodart
Hastings RS   *Hutt OB Marist*   *Marist, Invercargill*

Reserves: Saia Paese Napier OB Marist (*sub Vaiusu 34-37 min, Saunders 50 min*), Richie Tuivanuavou Marist St Michaels, Rotorua (*sub Tuipulotu 39 min*), Sam Madams Marist, Wanganui (*sub Fotheringham (h/t)*), Michael Sosene-Feagai Marist, Ardmore/Mt Wellington (*sub O'Reilly h/t*), Siaosi Nginingini Marist, Ardmore (*sub Donaldson h/t*), Finau Dyer Marist St Michaels, Rotorua (*sub Stodart 50 min*), Josiah Tavita-Metcalfe Hastings RS (*sub Vuki 50 min*), Josiah Bogileka Marist, Wanganui (*sub Rawiri 60 min*).

Scorers:
Tries: Stodart, Vaiusu, Tuivanuavou
Conversions: Tiatia (2)

Referee: : Paul Williams

Original selection Sanalio Taunauta (*Marist, Hamilton*) withdrew after selection and replaced by Finau Dyer.

Co-Coaches: Shaun Breen (*Timaru*), Dion Waller (*Wellington*)
Manager: Chris Back (*Wanganui*)
Assistant Manager: Paul Teddy (*Napier*)
Physio: Kerry Williamson (*Napier*)

INVESTEC SUPER RUGBY 2018

The eventual front-runners quickly identified themselves, but this did not detract from the interest of the competition. As expected, the Sunwolves were stone-cold last, but the tries scored for and against for teams ranked two to 14 were remarkably close. Eleven of the 15 teams scored more than 50 tries and all teams scored 36 or more. Last year the least scored was 23. This year that team, the Reds, scored 49 tries – their second most ever. A contributor to the try scoring was the general reluctance to kick penalty goals in favour of field position. A record low of four penalty goals were kicked by the Lions in the round robin phase. Apparently, it was not all innocence as there were 17 penalty tries conceded – with the Hurricanes and Brumbies being the only teams with a clean sheet. A few years back penalty tries were awarded as punishment for foul play, now they are punishment for the incompetence of an inferior scrum. There were nearly 100 cards issued – more than we would like to see for foul or, rather, dangerous play. There appeared to be an increased number for technical infringements. Remarkably, the high-flying Lions conceded only one card and the Hurricanes just three.

There was the usual criticism of the conference system, but the team ranked second (Lions) and the team ranked third (Waratahs) were also the second and third top try-scoring teams. It was unusual that the only team to fail to score in a match (Waratahs v Lions in Sydney) was also the team to record the highest score in a match (77 points Waratahs v Sunwolves in Sydney).

BLUES

The highlight for the Blues was an early season away win at Johannesburg against last year's, and as it turned out this year's' runner-up team, the Lions. Two close losses to the Chiefs was the best result on the local scene. Coming second to last for the second consecutive year and the third time in the competition's history leaves them in an uncomfortable situation. There must always be signs of encouragement, and among them were the Blues scored 50 tries – their sixth most in the competition's 23-year history. A record home team concession of 63 points on Eden Park occurred against the Sharks. Although both teams scored six tries, poor discipline led to the Sharks kicking seven penalty goals.

Although he scored almost as many tries as the outside backs combined, Reiko Ioane did not convince in midfield. Akira Ioane was New Zealand's top forward try scorer. If he had maintained close to his early season form of seven tries in his first seven matches, he would have been hard for the All Blacks selectors to ignore. Stephen Perofeta is a talented first five-eighth but must quickly develop more leadership skills. Having to go beyond the wider training group to cover for injuries was not uncommon this year, but having to introduce players to first-class rugby at this level begs questions. Jerome Kaino, who began his career with the Blues 15 years earlier, played his last season.

CHIEFS

One more win would have seen the Chiefs second on the points table and in a home playoff. On reflection, narrow losses to both the Sharks and Jaguares suggests that should have happened. The 64 tries scored is the second most ever for the Chiefs, but a record 52 tries conceded is less flattering. The 49 conversions kicked is the 11th most by any team in the 23 years of Super Rugby. A Chiefs record winning margin against the Sunwolves almost passed unnoticed.

Damian McKenzie continues to be a crowd pleaser. His ability to score points and his goal-kicking smile never fails to please. His resilience amazes. He has missed just four games in four seasons. Three of those games have been compulsory stand-downs at the request of the All Blacks selectors. Solomon Alaimalo, in his second year, played in every game and is already recognised as hot property. Anton Lienert-Brown hasn't attracted the headlines, but his teammates appreciate the value he adds to every game. The skills and leadership of Charlie Ngatai will be missed. The same will be said of Liam Messam who retires as the second most capped Super Rugby player to date. Brodie Retallick continues to be a colossus and was second equal top try-scorer with six. Alarm bells were ringing earlier in the season as the attrition of props, including three All Blacks, continued to rise. Never was the expression 'one door closes – another door opens' more apt. Angus Ta'avao, unwanted at the end of last year, returned and played some of the best rugby of his life, featuring in all 17 games and starting in the last 15. He became a popular choice for the All Blacks squad in June. Karl Tu'inukuafe, virtually unheard of in February, became an automatic choice for the All Blacks.

HURRICANES

Last year's semi-finals spot seemed a long way away as the Hurricanes were narrowly beaten first game up to South Africa's lowest-ranked team. Normal order was restored with 10 consecutive, mostly comfortable, victories. Finishing their round robin with four losses out of five was not anticipated. A one-point win in the quarter-final led to a second consecutive semi-final loss.

Ben Lam, who had earlier scored just two tries in a Super Rugby career beginning in 2012, scored a Investec Super Rugby record of 16 tries this year. His strong running proved unstoppable. Ngani Laumape joined with Lam in becoming the first two Hurricanes players to score four tries in a Super Rugby match. A late rush of try-scoring saw Julian Savea leave for France with his name among the top try-scorers in Super Rugby. Jordie Barrett alternated between midfield and fullback and, while never letting anyone down, his development in either position hesitated. A burden that comes from being 'World Rugby Player of the Year' is that the public expect magic every time you touch the ball. Couple this with extra attention from the opposition, then every flaw is magnified a thousand fold. The next generation of first five-eighths are still a long way behind the genius of Beauden Barrett. The 48 tries scored by TJ Perenara is a career record for a halfback in Super Rugby.

Captain Brad Shields will be missed as he continues to seek an alternative path in international rugby. Playing Vaea Fifita at lock damaged his All Blacks aspirations. Former Highlander Gareth Evans excelled at number eight. Perhaps some time off the bench might have been Ricky Riccitelli's thoughts about being selected along with two All Blacks hookers. Fate had other ideas as he was the only New Zealand hooker to start every game. Former Chiefs and Wallaby prop Toby Smith started more games in the front row than did any other prop.

CRUSADERS

Having won the Investec Super Rugby title on nine occasions and being a runner-up on four further occasions means that the Crusaders have played in the finals in 13 of a possible 23 years. Reaching team highs of most points (691), most tries (96), and most conversions (75) and a team low of 19 penalty goals suggests that this team will be long remembered. Although a record number of players were used, on most occasions it seemed that the Crusaders were a class above.

The season started promisingly with a pair of 45 points, which was followed by a swing down to earth with a pair of local losses, which was in turn followed by 16 consecutive victories. George Bridge equalled Rico Gear's Crusaders record of 15 tries in a season to confirm he is a star on the rise. Jack Goodhue's good form saw him secure a place at international level. The Fijian family from Taranaki of Seta Tamanivalu and Manasa Mataele kept the scoreboard ticking over. There is some public concern at the frequency of head knocks received by outstanding midfielder Ryan Crotty. Richie Mo'unga had his best season to date. Mitchell Hunt was an able deputy. Halfbacks Mitchell Drummond and Bryn Hall mixed and matched effectively.

Kieran Read's absence through injury gave opportunities to Jordan Taufua to be a regular starter at number eight. Opportunities he took full advantage of to confirm his standing as one of the best number eights in the country. Matt Todd continued to deliver excellence at openside flanker. Unwanted at the start of the season, Heiden Bedwell-Curtis was called in as injury cover and quickly became an indispensable part of the loose forward trio. Having access to three All Black locks meant that the lineouts were never found wanting. Injuries dictated the make-up of the front row. Michael Alaalatoa was the most used, playing in 19 games. The personal highlight of the year was Wyatt Crockett attaining 200 Super Rugby caps to finish with a figure that will rarely be equalled. Another feature was the plucking from retirement of Chris King to fill a Crusaders propping crisis. As a pair of hookers, Codie Taylor and Andrew Makalio would take some beating.

HIGHLANDERS

Beginning the season with three consecutive wins, including a defeat of the reigning champions and conceding just one bonus point, was a great start. A Highlanders record 66 tries suggests success, but in fact the season seemed to stutter along as the points for of 489 and points against of 485 tells us. Fifth-equal Championship points from a pool that included two games each against the three NZ teams ranked above them meant they were expected to work hard.

Ben Smith led the team from fullback. While only scoring in two matches, his skill at turning defence into attack was instrumental in the scoring of many more tries. He should be the first Highlander to pass 150 appearances next year. Leading try scorer Waisake Naholo, with 10, created a new Highlanders career record of 41 tries. Rob Thompson, starting in all but one game, was a powerhouse in midfield. Lima Sopoaga, who started in every game, established a new Highlanders points-scoring record of 892 before departing for overseas. Aaron Smith continues to build an impressive CV. Kayne Hammington could always be depended on to provide energy at the end of the match.

The forward pack may have initially looked modest, but it was to contain seven All Blacks by mid-year. Luke Whitelock delivered a consistently good game. Liam Squire was a powerful blindside flanker when available. It was a surprise to see Elliot Dixon used sparingly, mostly from the bench. This was because of Dillon Hunt developing into a very good openside flanker. Just four starts and 10 from the bench was sufficient to propel Shannon Frizell into the All Blacks. Mind you, scoring three tries in your second start does draw attention. Tom Franklin was in outstanding form at lock, but it was his locking partner Jackson Hemopo who debuted for the All Blacks. Selected on promise, Tyrel Lomax became the regular tighthead prop. Daniel Lienert-Brown with 17 appearances (13 starts) and Aki Seiuli 18 games (5 starts) saw to it that the loosehead position was never found wanting. There was always maturity and wisdom from those chosen to hook.

ALMANACK NEW ZEALAND RUGBY SUPER XV

Ben Smith
Highlanders

George Bridge   Anton Lienert-Brown   Ben Lam
Crusaders   *Chiefs*   *Hurricanes*

Ryan Crotty
Crusaders

Richie Mo'unga
Crusaders

Aaron Smith
Highlanders

Akira Ioane
Blues

Matt Todd   Brodie Retallick   Samuel Whitelock   Jordan Taufua
Crusaders   *Chiefs*   *Crusaders*   *Crusaders*

Angus Ta'avao-Matau   Ricky Riccitelli   Karl Tu'inukuafe
Chiefs   *Hurricanes*   *Chiefs*

Reserves: Codie Taylor (*Crusaders*), Tim Perry (*Crusaders*), Owen Franks (*Crusaders*), Scott Barrett (*Crusaders*), Sam Cane (*Chiefs*), TJ Perenara (*Hurricanes*), Damian McKenzie (*Chiefs*), Solomona Alaimalo (*Chiefs*).

SUPER RUGBY STANDINGS

Final standings after round robin:

	P	W	D	L	B³	B⁷	Pts	FOR T	C	PG	DG	Pts	AGAINST T	C	PG	DG	Pts
Crusaders	16	14	–	2	7	–	63	77²	60	11	–	542	39¹	25	16	–	295
Lions	16	9	–	7	6	4	46	77³	58	4	–	519	55¹	46	22	–	435
Waratahs	16	9	1	6	4	2	44	74	62	21	–	557	59¹	38	24	–	445
Hurricanes	16	11	–	5	5	2	51	66	48	16	–	474	43	31	22	–	343
Chiefs	16	11	–	5	3	2	49	60²	45	23	–	463	48²	32	20	–	368
Highlanders	16	10	–	6	3	1	44	59	41	20	–	437	57¹	46	22	–	445
Jaguares	16	9	–	7	2	–	38	51²	36	26	–	409	55¹	42	19	–	418
Sharks	16	7	1	8	2	4	36	49	45	34	–	437	57¹	46	21	–	442
Rebels	16	7	–	9	5	3	36	57¹	39	25	–	440	60¹	48	21	–	461
Brumbies	16	7	–	9	2	4	34	56	34	15	–	393	52	42	26	–	422
Stormers	16	6	–	10	–	5	29	46¹	37	28	–	390	56²	41	18	1	423
Bulls	16	6	–	10	2	3	29	59²	47	16	–	441	66²	51	22	–	502
Reds	16	6	–	10	1	3	28	49¹	32	26	–	389	66²	46	25	–	501
Blues	16	4	–	12	2	4	22	50¹	30	22	–	378	66¹	51	25	–	509
Sunwolves	16	3	–	13	–	2	14	48²	38	27	1	404	99¹	67	11	–	664
TOTALS								878	652	314	1	6673	878	652	314	1	6673

Points: 4 points for a win
2 points for a draw
B³ =bonus points for three tries or more than opponent
B⁷ =bonus points for a seven point or less loss

Superscript indicates number of penalty tries that count for seven points

PREVIOUS WINNERS

1996	Auckland Blues	2007	Bulls
1997	Auckland Blues	2008	Crusaders
1998	Crusaders	2009	Bulls
1999	Crusaders	2010	Bulls
2000	Crusaders	2011	Reds
2001	Brumbies	2012	Chiefs
2002	Crusaders	2013	Chiefs
2003	Blues	2014	Waratahs
2004	Brumbies	2015	Highlanders
2005	Crusaders	2017	Crusaders
2006	Crusaders	2018	Crusaders

SUPER RUGBY RECORDS
(S12 and S14 records have been rolled forward)

BY THE TEAMS

	BEST IN 2018	**RECORD**
Season totals		
Points	691 Crusaders	691 Crusaders *2018*
Tries	96 Crusaders	97 Hurricanes 2017
Conversions	75 Crusaders	75 Crusaders *2018*
Penalty goals	35 Sharks	76 Sharks *2014*
Dropped goals	1 Sunwolves	11 Bulls *2009*
	1 Lions	
Match totals		
Points	77 by Waratahs v Sunwolves	96 by Crusaders v Waratahs *2002*
Tries	12 by Waratahs v Sunwolves	14 by Crusaders v Waratahs *2002*
		by Cheetahs v Sunwolves *2016*
		by Lions v Sunwolves *2017*
Conversions	8 by Chiefs v Sunwolves	13 by Crusaders v Waratahs *2002*
Penalty goals	7 by Sharks v Blues	9 by Hurricanes v Blues *2010*
	by Sunwolves v Reds	
Dropped goals	1 by Sunwolves v Stormers	4 by Bulls v Crusaders *2009*
	by Lions v Jaguares	

BY THE PLAYERS

	BEST IN 2018	**RECORD**
Season totals		
Points	223 B.T. Foley (Waratahs)	263 M. Steyn (Bulls) *2010*
Tries	16 M.B. Lam (Hurricanes	16 M.B. Lam (Hurricanes) *2018*
Match totals		
Points	38 R.J. du Preez (Sharks v Blues)	50 G.E. Lawless (Natal v Highlanders) *1997*
Tries	4 M.B. Lam	4 on 17 occasions
	(Hurricanes v Rebels)	
	4 K. H Laumape	
	(Hurricanes v Blues)	
	4 M. Tambwe	
	(Lions v Stormers)	
Conversions	8 D.S. McKenzie	A.P. Mehrtens
	(Chiefs v Sunwolves)	(Crusaders v Waratahs) *2002*
Penalty goals	7 R.J. du Preez (Sharks v Blues)	9 E.T. Jantjies
	H.J. Parker (Sunwolves v Reds)	(Lions v Cheetahs) *2012*
Dropped goals	1 on two occasions	4 M. Steyn (Bulls v Crusaders) *2009*
Career records		
Points	1708 D.W. Carter (Crusaders)	
Tries	59 D.C. Howlett (Blues/	
	Hurricanes/Highlanders)	
Games	202 W.W.V. Crockett (Crusaders)	

MOST GAMES

Games	Player	Teams
202	W.W.V. Crockett	Crusaders
178	L.J. Messam	Chiefs
177	S.T. Moore	Reds / Brumbies
175	K.F. Mealamu	Blues / Chiefs
164	G.B. Smith	Brumbies / Reds
162	N.C. Sharpe	Reds / Force
160	M.A. Nonu	Hurricanes / Highlanders / Blues
156	J.A. Strauss	Cheetahs/Bulls
155	S.U.T. Polota-Nau	Force / Waratahs
153	A.M. Ellis	Crusaders
150	C.R. Flynn	Crusaders
150	T. Mtawarira	Sharks

MOST POINTS

Points	Player	Team	Games	Tries	Conv	PG	DG
1708	D.W. Carter	Crusaders	141	36	287	307	11
1449	M. Steyn	Bulls	123	13	242	275	25
1120	B.J. Barrett	Hurricanes	113	31	214	176	1
1037	S.A. Mortlock	Brumbies	138	55	162	146	-
990	A.P. Mehrtens	Crusaders	87	13	134	202	17

MOST TRIES

Tries	Player	Teams
59	D.C. Howlett	Blues / Highlanders / Hurricanes
58	C.S. Ralph	Chiefs / Crusaders
57	J.W.C. Roff	Brumbies
56	C.M. Cullen	Hurricanes
56	B.G. Habana	Bulls / Stormers
55	S.A. Mortlock	Brumbies
53	M.A. Nonu	Hurricanes / Blues / Highlanders
52	S.J. Savea	Hurricanes

SUPER RUGBY 2018 RESULTS

Date	Winning Team				Venue
February					
17	Stormers	28	Jaguares	20	Cape Town
17	Lions	26	Sharks	19	Johannesburg
23	Highlanders	41	Blues	34	Dunedin
23	Rebels	45	Reds	19	Melbourne
24	Brumbies	32	Sunwolves	25	Tokyo
24	Crusaders	45	Chiefs	23	Christchurch
24	Waratahs	34	Stormers	27	Sydney
24	Lions	47	Jaguares	27	Johannesburg
24	Bulls	21	Hurricanes	19	Pretoria
March					
2	Chiefs	27	Blues	21	Auckland
2	Reds	18	Brumbies	10	Brisbane
3	Crusaders	45	Stormers	28	Christchurch
3	Rebels	37	Sunwolves	17	Tokyo
3	Sharks	24	Waratahs	24	Durban
3	Lions	49	Bulls	35	Pretoria
3	Hurricanes	34	Jaguares	9	Buenos Aires
9	Highlanders	33	Stormers	15	Dunedin
9	Rebels	33	Brumbies	10	Melbourne
10	Hurricanes	29	Crusaders	19	Wellington
10	Reds	20	Bulls	14	Brisbane
10	Sharks	50	Sunwolves	22	Durban
10	Blues	38	Lions	35	Johannesburg
10	Jaguares	38	Waratahs	28	Buenos Aires
16	Chiefs	41	Bulls	28	Hamilton
17	Highlanders	25	Crusaders	17	Dunedin
17	Brumbies	24	Sharks	17	Canberra
17	Stormers	37	Blues	20	Cape Town
17	Lions	40	Sunwolves	38	Johannesburg
17	Reds	18	Jaguares	7	Buenos Aires
18	Waratahs	51	Rebels	27	Sydney
23	Crusaders	33	Bulls	14	Christchurch
23	Rebels	46	Sharks	14	Melbourne
24	Chiefs	61	Sunwolves	10	Tokyo
24	Hurricanes	29	Highlanders	12	Wellington

24	Stormers	25	Reds	18	Cape Town
24	Jaguares	49	Lions	35	Buenos Aires
30	Chiefs	27	Highlanders	22	Hamilton
30	Hurricanes	50	Rebels	19	Melbourne
31	Sharks	63	Blues	40	Auckland
31	Waratahs	24	Brumbies	17	Canberra
31	Bulls	33	Stormers	23	Pretoria
April					
1	Crusaders	14	Lions	8	Johannesburg
6	Hurricanes	38	Sharks	37	Napier
7	Waratahs	50	Sunwolves	29	Tokyo
7	Chiefs	21	Blues	19	Hamilton
7	Brumbies	45	Reds	21	Canberra
7	Lions	52	Stormers	31	Johannesburg
7	Crusaders	40	Jaguares	14	Buenos Aires
13	Hurricanes	25	Chiefs	13	Wellington
14	Blues	24	Sunwolves	10	Tokyo
14	Jaguares	25	Rebels	22	Melbourne
14	Highlanders	43	Brumbies	17	Dunedin
14	Waratahs	37	Reds	16	Sydney
14	Bulls	40	Sharks	10	Durban
20	Highlanders	34	Blues	16	Auckland
20	Lions	29	Waratahs	0	Sydney
21	Crusaders	33	Sunwolves	11	Christchurch
21	Chiefs	36	Reds	12	Brisbane
21	Bulls	28	Rebels	10	Pretoria
21	Sharks	24	Stormers	17	Durban
22	Jaguares	25	Brumbies	20	Canberra
27	Hurricanes	43	Sunwolves	15	Wellington
27	Stormers	34	Rebels	18	Cape Town
28	Reds	27	Lions	22	Brisbane
28	Jaguares	20	Blues	13	Auckland
28	Crusaders	21	Brumbies	8	Canberra
28	Highlanders	29	Bulls	28	Pretoria
May					
4	Jaguares	23	Chiefs	19	Rotorua
4	Crusaders	55	Rebels	10	Melbourne

5	Blues	24	Waratahs	21	Sydney
5	Hurricanes	28	Lions	19	Wellington
5	Stormers	29	Bulls	17	Cape Town
5	Sharks	38	Highlanders	12	Durban
11	Hurricanes	36	Blues	15	Auckland
12	Sunwolves	63	Reds	28	Tokyo
12	Crusaders	31	Waratahs	29	Christchurch
12	Highlanders	39	Lions	27	Dunedin
12	Rebels	27	Brumbies	24	Canberra
12	Chiefs	15	Stormers	9	Cape Town
12	Bulls	39	Sharks	33	Pretoria
18	Hurricanes	38	Reds	34	Wellington
19	Sunwolves	26	Stormers	23	Hong Kong
19	Crusaders	32	Blues	24	Auckland
19	Waratahs	41	Highlanders	12	Sydney
19	Sharks	28	Chiefs	24	Durban
19	Lions	42	Brumbies	24	Johannesburg
19	Jaguares	54	Bulls	24	Buenos Aires
25	Crusaders	24	Hurricanes	13	Christchurch
25	Rebels	40	Sunwolves	13	Melbourne
25	Jaguares	29	Sharks	13	Buenos Aires
26	Chiefs	39	Waratahs	27	Hamilton
26	Highlanders	18	Reds	15	Brisbane
26	Brumbies	38	Bulls	28	Pretoria
26	Lions	26	Stormers	23	Cape Town

June

1	Highlanders	30	Hurricanes	14	Dunedin
2	Rebels	20	Blues	10	Auckland
2	Crusaders	34	Chiefs	20	Hamilton
2	Waratahs	52	Reds	41	Brisbane
3	Brumbies	41	Sunwolves	31	Canberra
29	Blues	39	Reds	16	Auckland
29	Waratahs	31	Rebels	26	Melbourne
30	Chiefs	45	Highlanders	22	Suva (Fiji)
30	Brumbies	24	Hurricanes	12	Canberra
30	Sunwolves	42	Bulls	37	Singapore
30	Sharks	31	Lions	24	Durban

| 30 | Jaguares | 25 | Stormers | 14 | Buenos Aires |

July

6	Crusaders	45	Highlanders	22	Christchurch
6	Reds	37	Rebels	23	Brisbane
7	Chiefs	24	Brumbies	19	Hamilton
7	Hurricanes	42	Blues	24	Wellington
7	Waratahs	77	Sunwolves	25	Sydney
7	Bulls	43	Jaguares	34	Pretoria
7	Stormers	27	Sharks	16	Cape Town
13	Chiefs	28	Hurricanes	24	Hamilton
13	Reds	48	Sunwolves	27	Brisbane
14	Highlanders	43	Rebels	37	Dunedin
14	Crusaders	54	Blues	17	Christchurch
14	Brumbies	40	Waratahs	31	Sydney
14	Lions	38	Bulls	12	Johannesburg
14	Sharks	20	Jaguares	10	Durban

Quarter-finals

20	Hurricanes	32	Chiefs	31	Wellington
21	Crusaders	40	Sharks	10	Christchurch
21	Waratahs	30	Highlanders	23	Sydney
21	Lions	40	Jaguares	23	Johannesburg

Semi-finals

| 29 | Crusaders | 30 | Hurricanes | 12 | Christchurch |
| 29 | Lions | 44 | Waratahs | 26 | Johannesburg |

Final
August

| 4 | Crusaders | 37 | Lions | 18 | Christchurch |

QUARTER FINALS
At Wellington July 20
Hurricanes 32 Perenara 2, J. Savea, Lam tries; B. Barrett 2, J. Barrett conversions; B. Barrett 2 penalty goals defeated **Chiefs 31** Weber, Lienert-Brown, D. McKenzie, Boshier tries; D. McKenzie 3, Ngatai conversions; D. McKenzie penalty goal. Referee: G. Jackson (*New Zealand*).

At Christchurch July 22
Crusaders 40 Hall, Havili, Todd, Ennor, Samu tries; Mo'unga 3 conversions; Mo'unga 3 penalty goals defeated **Sharks 10** van Wyk try; R. du Preez conversion; R. du Preez penalty goal. Referee: M. Fraser (*New Zealand*).

At Sydney July 21
Waratahs 30 Foley 2, Folau tries; Foley 3 conversions; Foley 3 penalty goals defeated **Highlanders 23** Naholo, Thompson tries; Sopoaga 2 conversions; Sopoaga 3 penalty goals. Referee: A. Gardner (*Australia*).

At Johannesburg July 21
Lions 40 Combrink, Vorster, Marx, A. Coetzee tries; Jantjies 4 conversions; Jantjies 3 penalty goals, Jantjies dropped goal defeated **Jaguares 23** Delguy, Matero tries; Sanchez 2 conversions; Sanchez 3 penalty goals. Referee: J. Peyper (*South Africa*).

SEMI-FINALS
At Christchurch July 28
Crusaders 30 Mo'unga, Bridge, Havili, Ennor tries; Mo'unga 2 conversions; Mo'unga 2 penalty goals defeated **Hurricanes 12** Lam, J. Savea tries; B. Barrett conversion. Referee: J. Peyper (*South Africa*).

At Johannesburg July 28
Lions 44 Marx 2, K. Smith 2, Combrink, Skosan tries; Jantjies 4 conversions; Jantjies 2 penalty goals defeated **Waratahs 26** Hanigan, Folau, Robertson, Gordon tries; Foley 3 conversions. Referee: G. Jackson (*New Zealand*).

FINAL
At Christchurch August 4
Crusaders 37 Tamanivalu, Havili, Drummond, Barrett tries; Mo'unga 4 conversions; Mo'unga 3 penalty goals defeated **Lions 18** Brink, Marx tries; Jantjies conversion; Jantjies 2 penalty goals. Referee: A. Gardner (*Australia*)

BLUES

Postal address: Box 77 012 Mt Albert,
Auckland 1350
Telephone: (09) 846 5425
Email: info@theblues.co.nz
Home venues: Eden Park, Auckland; North Harbour Stadium, Albany
Colours: Royal and navy blue.

Played 312, Won 161, Lost 145, Drew 6

	Tries	Conv	Pen	DG	Points
For	996	673	650	11	8311
Against	859	597	713	26	7710

RECORDS — TEAM

Most points in a game	74	v Stormers, 1998
Most points in a season	513	1997
Biggest winning margin	53	60–7 v Hurricanes, 2002
Most tries in a game	11	v Stormers, 1998
Most tries in a season	70	1996

RECORDS — INDIVIDUAL

Most points in a game	29	G.W. Anscombe, v Bulls, 2012
Most points in a season	180	A.R. Cashmore, 1998
Most points in a career	619	A.R. Cashmore
Most tries in a game	4	J. Vidiri, v Bulls, 2000; D.C. Howlett, v Hurricanes 2002; J.M. Muliaina, v Bulls, 2002
Most tries in a season	12	D.C. Howlett, 2003
Most tries in a career	55	D.C. Howlett
Most conversions in a game	7	A.R. Cashmore, v Stormers, 1998; A.R. Cashmore, v Bulls, 2000; C.J. Spencer, v Bulls, 2002
Most conversions in a season	34	A.R. Cashmore, 1998
Most conversions in a career	120	C.J. Spencer
Most penalty goals in a game	6	A.R. Cashmore, v Chiefs, 1998; A.R. Cashmore, v Hurricanes, 1999; J.A. Arlidge, v Bulls, 2001; S.A. Brett, v Bulls, 2010; C.M. Noakes, v Stormers, 2013
Most penalty goals in a season	34	A.R. Cashmore, 1999
Most penalty goals in a career	114	A.R. Cashmore
Most dropped goals in a game	1	on 11 occasions
Most dropped goals in a season	2	O. Ai'i, 2000
Most dropped goals in a career	3	C.J. Spencer
Most games	164	K.F. Mealamu

Player	Union	Date of birth	Height	Weight	Blues Games	Blues Points
L.C.A. (Leni) Apisai	Wellington	8/3/96	1.81	108	7	–
C.D. (Caleb) Clarke	Auckland	29/3/99	1.87	103	5	5
M.W.V. (Michael) Collins	Otago	3/6/93	1.86	99	27	25
G.E. (Gerrard) Cowley-Tuioti	North Harbour	16/6/92	1.96	110	30	15
M.D. (Matt) Duffie	North Harbour	16/8/90	1.92	95	36	50
L. (Lyndon) Dunshea	Auckland	18/12/91	1.94	112	2	–
T.J. (Tinoai) Faiane	Auckland	24/10/95	1.84	93	16	–
B.E.C. (Bryn) Gatland	North Harbour	5/10/95	1.78	88	15	60
B.T. (Blake) Gibson	Auckland	19/4/95	1.86	102	30	10
J.K. (Josh) Goodhue	Northland	13/6/95	1.99	115	6	–
S.T. (Sione) Havili	Tasman	25/1/98	1.85	104	1	–
T.R.T. (Terrence) Hepetema	Bay of Plenty	3/1/92	1.82	99	2	5
A.T.O.A. (Alex) Hodgman	Canterbury	16/7/93	1.90	119	12	–
J.S.C. (Jordan) Hyland	Northland	3/10/89	1.88	101	3	10
A.L. (Akira) Ioane	Auckland	16/6/95	1.94	113	49	65
R.E. (Rieko) Ioane	Auckland	18/3/97	1.88	103	35	115
J. (Jerome) Kaino	Auckland	6/4/83	1.96	105	139	70
A.I. (Antonio) Kiri Kiri	Manawatu	17/12/91	1.87	105	3	–
D.J.P. (Daniel) Kirkpatrick	Auckland	28/8/88	1.81	90	11	–
O.N.T. (Orbyn) Leger	Counties Manukau	13/3/97	1.84	90	7	5
S.T. (Sione) Mafileo	North Harbour	14/4/93	1.78	128	34	–
P.P. (Pauliasi) Manu	Counties Manukau	23/12/87	1.84	113	33	5
T. (Tumua) Manu	Auckland	18/4/93	1.83	97	4	15
M. (Matiaha) Martin	Counties Manukau	3/6/92	1.99	112	4	–
G. (George) Moala	Auckland	5/11/90	1.88	99	74	110
M.G. (Matt) Moulds	Northland	15/5/91	1.88	108	24	10
M.H. (Melani) Nanai	Auckland	3/8/93	1.92	95	48	80
B.P. (Ben) Nee-Nee	Auckland	12/5/93	2.00	115	8	–
S.J. (Sam) Nock	Northland	18/6/96	1.78	85	17	–
D.R. (Dalton) Papali'i	Auckland	11/10/97	1.90	105	7	5
J.W. (James) Parsons	North Harbour	27/11/86	1.85	108	91	45
S. (Stephen) Perofeta	Taranaki	12/3/97	1.81	85	17	108
J.W.L. (Jacob) Pierce	North Harbour	10/9/97	2.02	112	2	–
G.I. (Glenn) Preston	North Harbour	11/4/92	1.93	105	1	–
K.A. (Kara) Pryor	Northland	2/4/91	1.89	104	23	15
A.W. (Augustine) Pulu (capt)	Counties Manukau	4/1/90	1.80	90	24	5
J.L. (Jonathan) Ruru	Otago	2/3/93	1.83	94	13	5
S.N. (Scott) Scrafton	Auckland	18/4/93	2.00	114	15	15
M. (Mike) Tamoaieta	North Harbour	7/7/95	1.75	102	10	–
M.V.U. (Murphy) Taramai	North Harbour	17/8/92	1.86	100	19	5
J.V. (Jordan) Trainor	Auckland	31/1/96	1.87	86	2	–
T.R. (Tamati) Tua	Northland	26/11/97	1.91	98	1	–
P.T. (Patrick) Tuipulotu	Auckland	23/1/93	1.98	120	53	40
S.J. (Jimmy) Tupou	Counties Manukau	8/8/92	1.96	109	16	5
A.O.H.M. (Ofa) Tu'ungafasi	Auckland	19/4/92	1.95	129	69	5
S.B. (Sonny Bill) Williams	Counties Manukau	3/8/85	1.91	108	12	5
R.G. (Ross) Wright	Northland	25/8/86	1.80	113	12	–

Manager: Richard Fry
Coach: Tana Umaga
Assistant coaches: Dave Ellis, Steve Jackson, Alistair Rogers

BLUES 2018

	Highlanders	Chiefs	Lions	Stormers	Sharks	Chiefs	Sunwolves	Highlanders	Jaguares	Waratahs	Hurricanes	Crusaders	Rebels	Reds	Hurricanes	Crusaders	TOTALS
Collins	15	s	15	15	15	15	15	–	–	–	–	s	15	13	13	13	12
Duffie	14	14	14	14	–	14	11	s	15	15	15	15	14	15	15	15	15
Nanai	s	15	11	11	11	–	–	–	–	–	s	14	–	14	14	14	10
Trainor	–	–	–	–	14	–	–	–	–	–	–	–	–	–	–	–	1
Hyland	–	–	–	–	–	–	14	14	14	–	–	–	–	–	–	–	3
T. Manu	–	–	–	–	–	–	s	11	14	–	–	11	–	–	–	–	4
Clarke	–	–	–	–	–	–	–	–	–	11	11	–	–	11	11	11	5
R. Ioane	11	11	13	13	12	13	12	11	12	12	14	11	–	12	12	12	15
Tua	–	–	–	–	–	–	–	–	–	–	–	–	–	–	–	s	1
Moala	13	13	–	s	13	11	–	–	–	–	–	–	–	–	–	–	5
Leger	–	–	–	–	–	13	13	13	13	13	13	13	–	–	–	–	7
Williams	12	–	12	12	–	–	–	–	–	12	12	–	–	–	–	–	5
Faiane	–	12	–	–	s	12	s	12	–	–	–	–	s	s	s	–	8
Hepetema	–	–	–	–	–	–	–	–	–	s	–	–	12	–	–	–	2
Kirkpatrick	s	–	–	–	–	–	–	s	s	s	–	–	–	–	–	–	4
Gatland	10	10	10	10	s	s	s	10	–	–	–	–	s	s	–	s	11
Perofeta	–	–	s	s	10	10	10	15	10	10	10	10	10	10	10	10	14
Pulu	9	9	–	–	–	–	–	s	9	9	9	9	–	9	9	9	9
Ruru	s	–	s	s	s	9	9	9	9	s	s	s	s	s	–	–	13
Nock	–	s	9	9	9	–	s	s	–	–	–	–	9	s	s	–	9
A. Ioane	8	8	8	8	8	8	8	8	8	8	8	8	8	8	8	8	16
Taramai	7	7	s	7	–	–	s	–	s	7	–	–	–	s	s	s	11
Kiri Kiri	s	–	7	7	–	–	–	–	–	–	–	–	–	–	–	–	3
Pryor	–	–	–	–	s	7	7	7	7	–	–	–	–	–	–	–	5
Papali'i	–	–	–	–	–	s	s	6	6	7	–	7	7	–	–	–	7
Gibson	–	–	–	–	–	–	–	–	–	–	–	–	–	7	7	7	3
Kaino	–	s	6	6	6	–	–	–	6	6	6	6	6	6	6	6	12
Preston	6	–	–	–	–	–	–	–	–	–	–	–	–	–	–	–	1
Tupou	–	6	s	s	s	s	6	5	–	–	–	–	–	–	–	–	7
Havili	–	–	–	–	–	–	–	–	–	–	–	s	–	–	–	–	1
Scrafton	5	5	s	–	–	–	–	–	–	–	–	–	–	–	–	–	3
Goodhue	–	–	–	–	5	5	5	–	5	–	–	–	–	–	–	–	4
Martin	–	–	–	–	–	–	–	–	–	–	5	5	5	5	–	–	4
Cowley-Tuioti	4	s	5	5	–	s	–	–	4	5	5	4	4	4	4	4	13
Tuipulotu	s	4	4	4	4	4	4	4	–	4	4	–	–	–	–	–	10
Nee-Nee	–	–	–	–	–	–	s	s	s	–	s	s	s	–	s	5	8
Pierce	–	–	–	–	–	–	–	–	–	–	–	–	–	s	–	s	2
Tu'ungafasi	3	3	3	3	–	3	3	–	–	–	3	3	3	3	3	3	12
Tamoaieta	s	s	s	s	3	s	s	3	s	s	–	–	–	–	–	–	10
Mafileo	–	–	–	–	s	–	–	s	3	3	s	s	s	s	s	s	10
Hodgman	1	s	1	–	–	–	–	–	–	–	–	–	1	1	1	1	7
P. Manu	s	1	s	1	1	1	1	1	s	1	s	1	s	s	s	s	16
Wright	–	–	s	s	s	s	s	s	s	1	1	s	–	–	s	s	12
Dunshea	–	–	–	–	–	–	–	s	–	s	–	–	–	–	–	–	2
Parsons	2	2	2	2	2	2	2	2	2	2	–	–	–	–	–	–	12
Apisai	s	s	–	s	s	–	–	s	–	–	–	s	s	–	–	–	7
Moulds	–	–	–	–	–	s	s	s	–	s	s	s	2	2	2	2	10

BLUES INDIVIDUAL SCORING

	Tries	Con	PG	DG	Points
Perofeta	2	21	15	–	97
R. Ioane	10	–	–	–	50
Gatland	2	9	7	–	49
A. Ioane	8	–	–	–	40
Collins	3	–	–	–	15
Duffie	3	–	–	–	15
T. Manu	3	–	–	–	15
Nanai	3	–	–	–	15
Hyland	2	–	–	–	10
penalty try	1	–	–	–	7
Clarke	1	–	–	–	5
Hepetema	1	–	–	–	5
Leger	1	–	–	–	5
Moala	1	–	–	–	5

	Tries	Con	PG	DG	Points
Moulds	1	–	–	–	5
Papali'i	1	–	–	–	5
Parsons	1	–	–	–	5
Pulu	1	–	–	–	5
Ruru	1	–	–	–	5
Taramai	1	–	–	–	5
Tuipulotu	1	–	–	–	5
Tupou	1	–	–	–	5
Tu'ungafasi	1	–	–	–	5
Totals	**50**	**30**	**22**	**0**	**378**
Opposition scored	66	51	25	0	509

BLUES TEAM RECORD 2018

Played 16 Won 4 Lost 12 Points for 378 Points against 509

Date	Opponent	Location	Score	Tries	Con	PG	DG	Referee
February 23	Highlanders	Dunedin	34–41	A. Ioane (2), Gatland, Duffie	Gatland (4)	Gatland (2)		J. Nutbrown
March 2	Chiefs	Auckland	21–27	Pulu, A.Ioane, Gatland	Gatland (3)			B. O'Keeffe
March 10	Lions	Johannesburg	38–35	R. Ioane (2), A. Ioane, Tupou, Taramai	Perofeta (4) Gatland	Gatland		N. Berry (Australia)
March 17	Stormers	Cape Town	20–37	A. Ioane, Collins, R. Ioane	Perofeta	Gatland		N. Berry (Australia)
March 31	Sharks	Auckland	40–63	Collins, A. Ioane, Tuipulotu, Perofeta, R. Ioane, Moala	Perofeta (4) Gatland			N. Briant
April 7	Chiefs	Hamilton	19–21	Parsons	Perofeta	Perofeta (4)		P. Williams
April 14	Sunwolves	Tokyo	24–10	Hyland (2), A. Ioane, Papali'i	Perofeta (2)			N. Briant
April 20	Highlanders	Auckland	16–34	Ruru, T. Manu		Gatland (2)		M. van der Westhuizen (South Africa)
April 28	Jaguares	Auckland	13–20	T. Manu, Duffie		Perofeta		P. Williams
May 5	Waratahs	Sydney	24–21	R. Ioane, T. Manu	Perofeta	Perofeta (4)		J. Peyper (South Africa)
May 11	Hurricanes	Auckland	15–36	Leger, Tu'ungafasi	Perofeta	Perofeta		J. Peyper (South Africa) subP. Williams
May 19	Crusaders	Auckland	24–32	R. Ioane (2), Duffie, Collins	Perofeta (2)			G. Jackson
June 2	Rebels	Auckland	10–20	Hepetema	Perofeta	Perofeta		N. Briant
June 29	Reds	Auckland	39–16	Nanai, R. Ioane, Moulds, Perofeta, Clarke	Perofeta	Perofeta (3) Gatland		E. Seconds (South Africa)
July 7	Hurricanes	Wellington	24–42	R. Ioane (2), A. Ioane	Perofeta (3)	Perofeta		B. O'Keeffe
July 14	Crusaders	Christchurch	17–54	Nanai (2), penalty try				F. Anselmi (Argentina)

CHIEFS

Postal address: Box 4292, Hamilton East 3247
Telephone: (07) 853 0231
Email: admin@chiefs.co.nz
Home venues: Waikato Stadium, Hamilton;
International Stadium, Rotorua
Colours: Black base with yellow and red. Black shorts

Played 315, Won 171, Lost 136 ,Drew 8

	Tries	Conv	Pen	DG	Points
For	945	685	703	8	8232
Against	850	605	733	23	7732

RECORDS — TEAM

Most points in a game	72	v Lions, 2010
Most points in a season	560	2016
Biggest winning margin	51	(61-10) v Sunwolves 2018
Most tries in a game	9	v Force, 2007
	9	v Blues, 2009
	9	v Lions, 2010
	9	v Force 2016
	9	v Sunwolves 2018
Most tries in a season	76	2016

RECORDS — INDIVIDUAL

Most points in a game	32	S.R. Donald, v Lions, 2010
Most points in a season	251	A.W. Cruden, 2012
Most points in a career	875	S.R. Donald
Most tries in a game	4	S.W. Sivivatu, v Blues, 2009
	4	A.T. Tikoirotuma, v Blues 2012
	4	C.J. Ngatai v Force 2016
Most tries in a season	12	R.Q. Randle, 2002
Most tries in a career	42	S.W. Sivivatu
Most conversions in a game	9	S.R. Donald, v Lions, 2010
Most conversions in a season	43	A.W. Cruden, 2012
	43	D.S. McKenzie 2016
Most conversions in a career	151	S.R. Donald
Most penalty goals in a game	6	G.W. Jackson, v Reds, 2001
	6	S.R. Donald, v Crusaders, 2007
Most penalty goals in a season	50	A.W. Cruden, 2012
Most penalty goals in a career	153	S.R. Donald
Most dropped goals in a game	1	on eight occasions
Most dropped goals in a season	2	I.D. Foster, 1996
Most dropped goals in a career	2	I.D. Foster
	2	G.W. Jackson
Most games	178	L.J. Messam

Player	Union	Date of birth	Height	Weight	Chiefs Games	Chiefs Points
S. (Solomona) Alaimalo	Northland	27/12/95	1.95	99	26	50
M.G. (Michael) Allardice	Hawke's Bay	19/10/91	2.00	115	34	–
T.J. (Tyler) Ardron	Bay of Plenty	16/10/91	1.94	110	10	15
D.J. (Dominic) Bird	Canterbury	9/4/91	2.06	119	29	15
L.S. (Lachlan) Boshier	Taranaki	16/11/94	1.91	106	30	25
M. (Mitchell) Brown	Taranaki	15/8/93	1.94	110	21	10
S.J. (Sam) Cane (co capt)	Bay of Plenty	13/1/92	1.89	105	106	70
J.F. (Johnny) Fa'auli	Taranaki	13/9/95	1.80	100	18	15
T.J. (Tiaan) Falcon	Hawke's Bay	19/6/97	1.81	90	3	–
N.P. (Nathan) Harris	Bay of Plenty	8/3/92	1.86	110	44	35
L.B. (Luke) Jacobson	Waikato	20/4/97	1.91	107	13	15
M.R. (Mitchell) Karpik	Bay of Plenty	2/6/95	1.86	103	13	5
S.S.V. (Sosefo) Kautai	Waikato	16/8/96	1.89	133	5	–
L.E. (Luteru) Laulala	Counties Manukau	30/5/95	1.86	94	1	–
N.E. (Nepo) Laulala	Canterbury	6/11/91	1.84	116	17	–
A.R. (Anton) Lienert-Brown	Waikato	15/4/95	1.87	103	54	20
D.S. (Damian) McKenzie	Waikato	20/4/95	1.75	81	65	539
M.R. (Marty) McKenzie	Taranaki	14/8/923	1.83	85	20	44
M.E.S. (Matt) Matich	Northland	10/7/91	1.86	106	2	–
L.J. (Liam) Messam	Waikato	25/3/84	1.90	109	178	160
A. (Atu) Moli	Waikato	12/6/95	1.89	125	29	10
A.P. (Alex) Nankivell	Tasman	25/10/96	1.88	98	9	–
C.J. (Charlie) Ngatai (co capt)	Taranaki	17/8/90	1.86	100	56	97
D.P.T.K. (Declan) O'Donnell	Taranaki	28/11/90	1.88	94	2	–
J.W.Z. (Jesse) Parete	Bay of Plenty	20/4/93	1.96	110	9	5
L.J. (Liam) Polwart	Bay of Plenty	2/4/95	1.85	107	20	10
S.M.J. (Sam) Prattley	Auckland	16/1/90	1.94	113	10	–
T.H. (Toni) Pulu	Counties Manukau	28/11/89	1.84	93	32	70
B.A. (Brodie) Retallick	Hawke's Bay	31/5/91	2.04	121	98	70
A.(Aidan) Ross	Bay of Plenty	25/10/95	1.89	111	13	–
T.J.A. (Taleni) Seu	Auckland	26/12/93	1.98	110	34	15
P-G (Pita) Sowakula	Taranaki	10/10/94	1.95	110	7	–
S.T. (Shaun) Stevenson	North Harbour	14/11/96	1.93	95	33	30
B.W.M. (Bailyn) Sullivan	Waikato	3/9/98	1.87	93	1	–
A.(Angus) Ta'avao	Taranaki	22/3/90	1.94	124	17	–
T.T.H. (Te Toiroa) Tahuriorangi	Taranaki	31/3/95	1.73	84	17	–
J.A. (Jonathan) Taumateine	Counties Manukau	28/9/96	1.77	82	9	–
S.F. (Samisoni) Taukei'aho	Waikato	8/8/97	1.83	115	9	5
J.R. (Jeff) Thwaites	Bay of Plenty	22/11/92	1.90	115	10	–
G.Z.K. (Karl) Tu'inukuafe	North Harbour	21/2/93	1.82	135	16	5
S.T. (Sean) Wainui	Taranaki	23/10/95	1.92	104	14	30
B.M. (Brad) Weber	Hawke's Bay	17/1/91	1.75	75	51	50

Manager: Nikita Hall
Coach: Colin Cooper
Assistant coaches: Andrew Strawbridge, Neil Barnes, Carl Hoeft, Tabai Matson

Investec Super Rugby 2018

CHIEFS 2018	Crusaders	Blues	Bulls	Sunwolves	Highlanders	Blues	Hurricanes	Reds	Jaguares	Stormers	Sharks	Waratahs	Crusaders	Highlanders	Brumbies	Hurricanes	Hurricanes	TOTALS
Ngatai	15	–	–	s	–	15	15	15	15	13	12	12	12	12	–	12		12
M. McKenzie	s	–	s	15	–	s	s	s	–	s	10	–	–	s	s	10	–	11
Stevenson	14	–	–	–	–	–	–	–	–	s	15	s	s	s	11	11	11	9
L. Laulala	–	–	–	–	–	–	–	–	–	s	–	–	–	–	–	–	–	1
Wainui	s	14	14	s	11	11	14	14	–	–	14	11	11	11	13	–	14	14
Pulu	–	–	–	14	14	–	–	14	14	s	14	14	14	14	14	–		11
Alaimalo	11	11	11	11	15	15	11	11	11	11	11	15	15	15	15	15	15	17
O'Donnell	–	s	s	–	–	–	–	–	–	–	–	–	–	–	–	–	–	2
Sullivan	–	–	–	s	–	–	–	–	–	–	–	–	–	–	–	–	–	1
Lienert-Brown	13	13	13	13	13	13	13	13	13	13	–	13	13	13	–	13	13	15
Fa'auli	12	12	12	12	12	12	12	12	–	12	12	–	–	–	s	12	–	12
Nankivell	–	–	–	–	–	s	s	s	12	–	–	–	–	–	–	s	–	5
D. McKenzie	10	15	15	10	10	10	10	10	10	10	–	10	10	10	10	–	10	15
Falcon	–	10	10	–	–	–	–	–	–	–	–	–	–	–	–	s	–	3
Weber	9	9	9	s	9	–	–	s	s	9	9	9	9	9	9	9	9	15
Tahuriorangi	s	s	s	9	s	9	9	9	9	s	s	s	s	s	s	s	s	17
Taumateine	–	–	–	–	–	s	s	–	–	–	–	–	–	–	–	–	–	2
Seu	8	8	–	8	8	–	8	–	–	–	–	–	–	–	–	–	–	5
Messam	s	6	8	s	6	s	s	s	7	7	7	8	8	8	8	s	8	17
Sowakula	–	–	–	–	s	8	–	8	8	s	8	–	s	–	–	–	–	7
Parete	–	–	–	–	–	–	–	–	s	s	s	s	s	s	s	8	s	9
Cane	7	–	7	7	7	7	7	7	–	–	–	–	–	7	7	–	7	11
Karpik	–	–	–	s	–	–	–	–	–	–	–	7	7	s	–	7	s	6
Boshier	s	s	6	6	s	6	6	6	–	–	–	–	–	–	s	6	6	11
Brown	6	4	5	–	–	–	–	–	–	–	–	–	–	–	–	–	–	3
Jacobson	–	s	s	–	–	s	s	s	6	6	6	6	6	6	6	s	–	13
Matich	–	–	–	–	–	–	–	–	–	–	s	s	–	–	–	–	–	2
Bird	5	–	–	–	–	–	–	–	–	–	–	–	–	–	–	–	–	1
Allardice	–	5	s	–	–	–	5	–	4	5	5	5	5	4	4	5	5	12
Ardron	–	s	–	5	5	5	–	5	5	8	4	–	–	5	5	–	–	10
Retallick	4	–	4	4	4	4	4	4	s	4	–	4	4	–	–	4	4	13
N. Laulala	3	3	–	–	–	–	–	–	–	–	–	–	–	–	–	–	–	2
Ta'avao	s	s	3	3	3	3	3	3	3	3	3	3	3	3	3	3	3	17
Thwaites	–	–	–	s	–	s	s	s	s	s	s	–	s	s	–	–	–	10
Ross	1	1	1	1	1	1	1	–	–	–	–	–	–	–	–	–	–	7
Moli	s	–	–	–	–	–	–	–	–	–	–	–	–	–	–	–	–	1
Tu'inukuafe	–	s	s	s	s	s	s	1	1	1	1	1	1	1	1	s	1	16
Prattley	–	–	–	–	–	–	s	s	s	s	s	s	s	s	1	s		10
Kautai	–	–	–	–	–	–	–	–	–	–	–	–	–	–	–	s	–	1
Harris	2	2	2	2	2	2	–	s	2	–	2	2	–	2	–	2		13
Polwart	s	s	s	s	s	s	s	2	2	–	2	–	s	2	–	2	s	14
Taukei'aho	–	–	–	–	–	–	s	–	s	s	s	–	s	s	s	–	–	7

CHIEFS INDIVIDUAL SCORING

	Tries	Con	PG	DG	Points		Tries	Con	PG	DG	Points
D. McKenzie	6	39	23	–	177	Cane	2	–	–	–	10
Alaimalo	8	–	–	–	40	Fa'auli	2	–	–	–	10
Retallick	6	–	–	–	30	Polwart	2	–	–	–	10
Wainui	6	–	–	–	30	Brown	1	–	–	–	5
M. McKenzie	–	9	1	–	21	Karpik	1	–	–	–	5
Harris	4	–	–	–	20	Parete	1	–	–	–	5
Pulu	4	–	–	–	20	Seu	1	–	–	–	5
Ardron	3	–	–	–	15	Taukei'aho	1	–	–	–	5
Jacobson	3	–	–	–	15	Tu'inukuafe	1	–	–	–	5
Lienert-Brown	3	–	–	–	15						
Weber	3	–	–	–	15	**Totals**	**64**	**49**	**24**	**0**	**494**
penalty tries	2	–	–	–	14						
Ngatai	2	1	–	–	12	Opposition scored	52	35	22	0	400
Boshier	2	–	–	–	10						

CHIEFS TEAM RECORD 2018

Played 17 Won 11 Lost 6 Points for 494 Points against 400

Date	Opponent	Location	Score	Tries	Con	PG	DG	Referee
February 24	Crusaders	Christchurch	23–45	Cane, Alaimalo	D. McKenzie (2)	D. McKenzie (3)		B. O'Keeffe
March 2	Blues	Auckland	27–21	Seu, Wainui, Cane, Weber	D. McKenzie (2)	D. McKenzie		B. O'Keeffe
March 16	Bulls	Hamilton	41–28	Retallick (2), Fa'auli, Brown, Alaimalo, Lienert-Brown	D. McKenzie (4)	D. McKenzie		S. Kubo (Japan)
March 24	Sunwolves	Tokyo	61–10	Alaimalo (2), D. McKenzie (2), Ardron, Retallick, Harris, Polwart, Wainui	D. McKenzie (8)			W. Houston (Australia)
March 30	Highlanders	Hamilton	27–22	Alaimalo, Harris, Wainui	D. McKenzie (3)	D. McKenzie (2)		G. Jackson
April 7	Blues	Hamilton	21–19	Wainui, penalty try		D. McKenzie (3)		P. Williams
April 13	Hurricanes	Wellington	13–25	Boshier	D. McKenzie	D. McKenzie (2)		J. Nutbrown
April 21	Reds	Brisbane	36–12	Ardron, Ngatai, Retallick, Polwart, Tauke'iaho	D. McKenzie (2) M. McKenzie (2)	D. McKenzie		J. Peyper (South Africa)
May 4	Jaguares	Rotorua	19–23	Parete	D. McKenzie	D. McKenzie (4)		M. Fraser
May 12	Stormers	Cape Town	15–9	Lienert-Brown, penalty try		D. McKenzie		M. Fraser
May 19	Sharks	Durban	24–28	Ardron, Ngatai, Alaimalo	M. McKenzie (3)	M. McKenzie		M. Fraser
May 26	Waratahs	Hamilton	39–27	Pulu (2), D. McKenzie (2), Retallick, Harris	D. McKenzie (3)	D. McKenzie		G. Jackson
June 2	Crusaders	Hamilton	20–34	Jacobson (2), Wainui	D. McKenzie	D. McKenzie		N. Berry (Australia)
June 29	Highlanders	Suva	45–22	Pulu (2), Alaimalo, Tu'inukuafe, Jacobson, Wainui	D. McKenzie (6)	D. McKenzie		P. Williams
July 7	Brumbies	Hamilton	24–19	Harris, D. McKenzie, Fa'auli	D. McKenzie (3)	D. McKenzie		R. Rasivhenge (South Africa)
July 13	Hurricanes	Hamilton	28–24	Retallick, Weber, Alaimalo, Karpik	M. McKenzie (4)			M. Fraser
July 20	Hurricanes (Quarter-final)	Wellington	31–32	Weber, Lienert-Brown, D. McKenzie, Boshier	D. McKenzie (3) Ngatai	D. McKenzie		G. Jackson

HURRICANES

Postal address: Box 7201, Wellington
Telephone: (04) 389 0020
Email: mail@hurricanes.co.nz
Home venues: Westpac Stadium Wellington; McLean Park, Napier; FMG Stadium, Palmerston North
Colours: Yellow and black.

Played 316, Won 177, Lost 134, Drew 5

	Tries	Conv	Pen	DG	Points
For	1023	719	656	5	8536
Against	837	577	730	24	7601

RECORDS — TEAM

Most points in a game	83	v Sunwolves 2017
Most points in a season	691	2017
Biggest winning margin	66	83-17 v Sunwolves 2017
Most tries in a game	13	v Sunwolves 2017
Most tries in a season	101	2017

RECORDS — INDIVIDUAL

Most points in a game	30	D.E. Holwell v Highlanders, 2001
Most points in a season	223	B.J. Barrett, 2016
Most points in a career	1120	B.J. Barrett
Most tries in a game	4	M.B. Lam v Rebels 2018
	4	K.H. Laumape v Blues 2018
Most tries in a season	16	K.H. Laumape, 2017
	16	M.B. Lam 2018
Most tries in a career	56	C.M. Cullen
Most conversions in a game	9	B.J. Barrett v Rebels, 2012
		O.W. Black v Sunwolves, 2017
Most conversions in a season	50	B.J. Barrett, 2016
Most conversions in a career	214	B.J. Barrett
Most penalty goals in a game	7	J.B. Cameron v Blues, 1996
	7	D.E. Holwell v Highlanders, 2001
Most penalty goals in a season	40	B.J. Barrett, 2014
Most penalty goals in a career	178	B.J. Barrett
Most dropped goals in a game	1	by five players
Most dropped goals in a season	1	by five players
Most dropped goals in a career	1	by five players
Most games	126	M.A. Nonu
	126	C.G. Smith

Investec Super Rugby 2018

Player	Union	Date of birth	Height	Weight	Hurricanes Games	Hurricanes Points
F.P. (Fraser) Armstrong	Manawatu	18/4/92	1.93	127	9	–
V.T. (Vince) Aso	Auckland	5/1/95	1.86	98	41	105
A.J. (Asafo) Aumua	Wellington	5/5/97	1.77	108	4	–
B.J. (Beauden) Barrett	Taranaki	27/5/91	1.86	92	113	1120
J.M. (Jordie) Barrett	Taranaki	15/2/97	1.96	96	34	200
J.P. (Jamie) Booth	Manawatu	14/1/94	1.71	92	11	–
F.T. (Finlay) Christie	Tasman	13/9/95	1.77	84	6	5
M.I. (Murray) Douglas	Northland	27/10/89	2.00	114	7	–
G.O. (Gareth) Evans	Hawke's Bay	5/8/91	1.90	107	16	10
C.I. (Chris) Eves	North Harbour	11/12/87	1.87	123	79	10
M.J. (Michael) Fatialofa	Auckland	14/9/92	1.98	113	37	10
A.F. (Alex) Fidow	Wellington	19/8/97	1.87	137	1	–
V.T.L. (Vaea) Fifita	Wellington	17/6/92	1.96	112	45	35
J.K. (Jackson) Garden-Bachop	Wellington	3/10/94	1.83	99	4	3
W.T. (Wes) Goosen	Wellington	20/10/95	1.78	92	24	60
S.T. (Sam) Henwood	Counties Manukau	28/3/91	1.86	109	6	–
R.P. (Richard) Judd	Bay of Plenty	18/5/92	1.80	88	3	–
M.B. (Ben) Lam	Wellington	9/6/91	1.94	106	23	85
K.H. (Ngani) Laumape	Manawatu	24/4/93	1.77	103	45	145
S.T. (Sam) Lousi	Wellington	20/7/91	1.97	122	28	10
J.H. (Jonah) Lowe	Hawke's Bay	9/5/96	1.84	92	1	–
B. (Ben) May	Hawke's Bay	13/10/82	1.94	119	79	10
N.R. (Nehe) Milner-Skudder	Manawatu	15/12/90	1.82	90	36	40
J.P. (James) O'Reilly	Bay of Plenty	19/11/94	1.82	103	11	–
T.T.R. (TJ) Perenara	Wellington	23/1/92	1.84	94	111	240
R.J. (Reed) Prinsep	Canterbury	17/2/93	1.92	108	28	15
M.P. (Matt) Proctor	Wellington	26/10/92	1.80	90	52	55
M.T. (Marcel) Renata	Auckland	24/2/94	1.89	118	2	–
J.R. (Ricky) Riccitelli	Taranaki	3/2/95	1.92	110	45	15
A.S. (Ardie) Savea	Wellington	14/10/93	1.88	100	75	85
S.J. (Julian) Savea	Wellington	7/8/90	1.90	103	121	260
B.D.F. (Brad) Shields (capt)	Wellington	2/4/91	1.93	111	104	50
T.J. (Toby) Smith	Waikato	10/10/88	1.90	112	13	–
B.N. (Blade) Thomson	Taranaki	4/12/90	1.98	107	51	55
J.L. (Jeff) To'omaga-Allen	Wellington	19/11/90	1.92	125	102	25
P. (Peter) Umaga-Jensen	Wellington	31/12/97	1.87	95	1	–
N.B. (Nathan) Vella	Canterbury	10/2/90	1.83	106	1	–
I.E.T. (Isaia) Walker-Leawere	Wellington	16/4/97	1.87	127	1	–
I.T. (Ihaia) West	Hawke's Bay	16/1/92	1.75	85	14	22

Manager: Tony Ward
Coach: Chris Boyd
Assistant coaches: John Plumtree, Jason Holland, Richard Watt, Dan Cron

HURRICANES 2018

	Bulls	Jaguares	Crusaders	Highlanders	Rebels	Sharks	Chiefs	Sunwolves	Lions	Blues	Reds	Crusaders	Highlanders	Brumbies	Blues	Chiefs	Chiefs	Crusaders	TOTALS
J. Barrett	–	15	15	15	15	15	15	15	–	s	15	13	13	13	15	15	13	13	16
Milner-Skudder	–	–	–	–	–	–	–	s	15	15	14	15	15	14	14	15	15	–	11
J. Savea	14	14	14	14	14	14	–	14	14	14	s	14	14	14	11	s	14	14	17
Lam	s	11	11	11	11	11	11	11	11	11	11	11	11	11	s	11	11	11	18
Aso	13	s	s	s	13	13	14	12	s	–	–	–	–	–	–	–	–	–	9
Proctor	15	13	13	13	–	–	13	13	13	13	13	–	–	–	–	–	–	–	9
Goosen	11	–	–	–	s	s	s	–	–	–	–	–	s	s	13	13	s	s	10
Laumape	12	12	12	12	12	12	12	–	12	12	–	12	12	12	12	12	12	12	16
Umaga-Jensen	–	–	–	–	–	–	–	–	–	–	12	–	–	–	–	–	–	–	1
Lowe	–	–	–	–	–	–	–	–	–	–	–	s	–	–	–	–	–	–	1
B. Barrett	s	10	10	10	10	–	10	10	10	10	10	10	10	–	10	10	10	10	16
West	10	–	–	s	s	10	s	–	s	s	–	s	s	s	s	s	s	s	14
Garden-Bachop	–	s	–	–	–	–	–	s	–	–	–	s	–	10	–	–	–	–	4
Perenara	9	9	9	9	9	9	–	–	–	s	9	9	9	9	9	9	9	9	15
Booth	s	s	–	–	s	s	9	s	s	–	–	–	–	–	s	s	–	s	11
Judd	–	–	s	s	–	–	s	–	–	–	–	–	–	–	–	–	–	–	3
Christie	–	–	–	–	–	–	–	9	9	9	–	s	s	–	–	s	–	–	6
Evans	8	8	8	8	8	8	8	s	8	8	–	–	8	8	s	s	7	7	16
Thomson	s	s	s	–	–	–	–	–	–	s	8	8	s	s	8	8	8	8	12
A. Savea	7	7	7	7	–	–	–	7	7	7	7	7	7	–	–	–	–	–	10
Henwood	–	–	–	–	7	7	7	–	–	–	–	–	–	7	7	7	–	–	6
Shields	6	6	6	6	6	6	6	6	6	6	s	6	6	–	6	6	6	6	17
Prinsep	–	–	–	s	s	s	s	8	s	–	6	s	–	6	–	s	s	s	12
Lousi	5	5	5	5	5	5	–	s	s	5	5	5	5	5	5	5	5	5	17
Walker-Leawere	–	–	–	–	–	–	–	–	–	–	–	–	–	s	–	–	–	–	1
Fifita	4	4	4	–	4	s	4	–	4	4	4	–	–	–	4	–	s	s	12
Douglas	s	–	–	4	–	–	s	5	–	–	s	s	s	–	–	–	–	–	7
Fatialofa	–	–	s	s	s	4	5	4	5	s	–	4	4	4	s	4	4	4	15
May	3	3	3	3	3	s	s	3	–	s	s	s	s	–	3	s	s	s	16
To'omaga-Allen	–	–	–	s	s	3	3	s	3	3	3	3	3	s	3	3	3	3	15
Armstrong	s	s	s	s	s	–	–	s	–	–	–	–	–	–	s	–	–	s	9
Smith	1	–	–	–	–	–	1	1	1	1	1	1	1	1	1	1	1	1	13
Eves	s	1	1	1	1	1	s	s	s	s	s	s	s	–	s	s	–	–	16
Fidow	–	s	–	–	–	–	–	–	–	–	–	–	–	–	–	–	–	–	1
Renata	–	–	s	–	–	–	–	–	–	–	–	–	–	s	–	–	–	–	2
Riccitelli	2	2	2	2	2	2	2	2	2	2	2	2	2	2	2	2	2	2	18
O'Reilly	s	–	–	–	–	–	–	s	s	s	–	–	s	s	s	s	s	s	10
Aumua	–	–	s	s	s	s	–	–	–	–	–	–	–	–	–	–	–	–	4
Vella	–	–	–	–	–	–	–	–	–	–	–	s	–	–	–	–	–	–	1

HURRICANES INDIVIDUAL SCORING

	Tries	Con	PG	DG	Points
B. Barrett	6	34	8	–	122
Lam	16	–	–	–	80
J. Barrett	3	13	5	–	56
Laumape	9	–	–	–	45
J. Savea	6	–	–	–	30
Aso	5	–	–	–	25
West	–	5	4	–	22
Perenara	4	–	–	–	20
Proctor	3	–	–	–	15
Thomson	3	–	–	–	15
Evans	2	–	–	–	10
Goosen	2	–	–	–	10
Lousi	2	–	–	–	10
Prinsep	2	–	–	–	10
Riccitelli	2	–	–	–	10
Christie	1	–	–	–	5
Eves	1	–	–	–	5
May	1	–	–	–	5
Milner-Skudder	1	–	–	–	5
A. Savea	1	–	–	–	5
Shields	1	–	–	–	5
To'omaga-Allen	1	–	–	–	5
Garden-Bachop	–	–	1	–	3
Totals	**72**	**52**	**18**	**0**	**518**
Opposition scored	51	37	25	0	404

HURRICANES TEAM RECORD 2018

PLAYED 18　WON 12　LOST 6　POINTS FOR 518　POINTS AGAINST 404

Date	Opponent	Location	Score	Tries	Con	PG	DG	Referee
February 24	Bulls	Pretoria	19–21	Riccitelli, Goosen, B. Barrett	West (2)			R. Rasivhenge (South Africa)
March 3	Jaguares	Buenos Aires	34–9	Lam, Laumape, Proctor, Aso, Thomson	B. Barrett (3)	Garden-Bachop		N. Briant
March 10	Crusaders	Wellington	29–19	Eves, Perenara, Lam, Proctor	B. Barrett (3)	J. Barrett		B. Pickerill
March 24	Highlanders	Wellington	29–12	Lam (2), B. Barrett, Aso	B. Barrett (3)	J. Barrett		M. Fraser
March 30	Rebels	Melbourne	50–19	Lam (4), B. Barrett, Evans, Laumape	B. Barrett (3)	B. Barrett (3)		A. Gardner (Australia)
April 6	Sharks	Napier	38–37	Laumape (2), J. Barrett, Aso	West (3)	West (4)		N. Berry (Australia)
April 13	Chiefs	Wellington	25–13	Lam, B. Barrett, Laumape	J. Barrett (2)	J. Barrett (2)		J. Nutbrown
April 27	Sunwolves	Wellington	43–15	Aso (2), J. Savea, Christie, Prinsep, J. Barrett, Shields	B. Barrett (3) J. Barrett			J. Nutbrown
May 5	Lions	Wellington	28–19	Lam (3), A. Savea	B. Barrett (4)			N. Berry (Australia)
May 11	Blues	Auckland	36–15	Riccitelli, Evans, Milner-Skudder, Lousi, Proctor	B. Barrett (4)	B. Barrett		J. Peyper (South Africa) sub P. Williams
May 18	Reds	Wellington	38–34	Lam (2), B. Barrett, Thomson, Lousi	B. Barrett (5)	B. Barrett		B. O'Keeffe
May 25	Crusaders	Christchurch	13–24	Prinsep	B. Barrett	J. Barrett B. Barrett		A. Gardner (Australia)
June 1	Highlanders	Dunedin	14–30	J. Barrett, To'omaga-Allen	B. Barrett (2)			B. O'Keeffe
June 30	Brumbies	Canberra	12–24	Perenara, J. Savea	J. Barrett			N. Briant
July 7	Blues	Wellington	42–24	Laumape (4), J. Savea, B. Barrett	J. Barrett (6)			B. O'Keeffe
July 13	Chiefs	Hamilton	24–28	Goosen, Thomson, May, J. Savea	J. Barrett (2)			M. Fraser
July 20	Chiefs (Quarter-final)	Wellington	32–31	Perenara (2), J. Savea, Lam	B. Barrett (2) J. Barrett	B. Barrett (2)		G. Jackson
July 28	Crusaders (Semi-final)	Christchurch	12–30	J. Savea, Lam	B. Barrett			J. Peyper (South Africa)

CRUSADERS

Postal address: Box 755, Christchurch
Telephone: (03) 379 8300
Email: chantelle.tehaara@crusaders.co.nz
Home venue: AMI Stadium, Addington, Christchurch
Colours: Red and black.

Played 338, Won 235, Lost 97, Drew 6

	Tries	Conv	Pen	DG	Points
For	1168	819	865	46	10,217
Against	793	562	688	28	7239

RECORDS — TEAM

Most points in a game	96	v Waratahs, 2002
Most points in a season	691	2018
Biggest winning margin	77	96–19 v Waratahs, 2002
Most tries in a game	14	v Waratahs, 2002
Most tries in a season	96	2018

RECORDS — INDIVIDUAL

Most points in a game	31	T.J. Taylor, v Stormers, 2012
Most points in a season	221	D.W. Carter, 2006
Most points in a career	1708	D.W. Carter
Most tries in a game	4	C.S. Ralph, v Waratahs, 2002
	4	S.D. Maitland, v Brumbies, 2011
Most tries in a season	15	R.L. Gear, 2005
	15	G.C. Bridge 2018
Most tries in a career	52	C.S. Ralph
Most conversions in a game	13	A.P. Mehrtens, v Waratahs, 2002
Most conversions in a season	38	D.W. Carter, 2006
	38	R. Mo'unga 2018
Most conversions in a career	287	D.W. Carter
Most penalty goals in a game	8	T.J. Taylor, v Stormers, 2012
Most penalty goals in a season	46	C.R. Slade, 2014
Most penalty goals in a career	307	D.W. Carter
Most dropped goals in a game	3	A.P. Mehrtens, v Highlanders, 1998
Most dropped goals in a season	4	A.P. Mehrtens, 1998, 1999, 2002
Most dropped goals in a career	17	A.P. Mehrtens
Most games	203	W.W.V. Crockett

Investec Super Rugby 2018

Player	Union	Date of birth	Height	Weight	Crusaders Games	Crusaders Points
M.S. (Michael) Ala'alatoa	Manawatu	28/8/91	1.90	136	53	15
H.M. (Harrison) Allen	Canterbury	7/5/97	1.83	110	2	–
S.G. (Sam) Anderson-Heather	Otago	15/2/88	1.85	109	1	–
S.K. (Scott) Barrett	Taranaki	20/11/93	1.98	116	53	45
T.E.S. (Tim) Bateman	Canterbury	3/6/87	1.82	91	48	40
S. (Sam) Beard	Canterbury	3/5/90	1.83	94	1	–
H.K. (Heiden) Bedwell-Curtis	Manawatu	25/6/91	1.88	104	21	20
E.J. (Ethan) Blackadder	Tasman	22/3/95	1.91	107	4	–
G.C. (George) Bridge	Canterbury	1/4/95	1.85	96	37	115
D.I.M. (Donald) Brighouse	Otago	29/3/93	1.80	119	6	–
B.D. (Brett) Cameron	Canterbury	4/10/96	1.71	83	1	–
R.C. (Ryan) Coxon	Tasman	30/9/97	1.83	118	1	–
W.W.V. (Wyatt) Crockett	Canterbury	24/1/83	1.93	116	203	55
R.S. (Ryan) Crotty	Canterbury	23/9/88	1.81	96	137	115
I.J.A. (Israel) Dagg	Hawke's Bay	6/6/88	1.86	96	89	140
H.A. (Hamish) Dalzell	Canterbury	16/1/96	2.01	110	1	–
M.P. (Mike) Delany	Bay of Plenty	15/6/82	1.78	86	6	14
W.H. (Whetu) Douglas	–	18/4/94	1.90	109	7	15
M.D. (Mitchell) Drummond	Canterbury	15/12/94	1.80	86	66	70
M.T.W. (Mitchell) Dunshea	Canterbury	18/11/95	1.96	114	4	–
B.M. (Braydon) Ennor	Canterbury	16/7/97	1.87	93	8	15
L.T. (Tima) Fainga'anuku	Tasman	26/4/97	1.88	103	2	–
O.T. (Owen) Franks	Canterbury	23/1/87	1.85	121	146	10
B.C.J. (Ben) Funnell	Canterbury	6/6/90	1.80	109	82	35
E.J. (Jack) Goodhue	Northland	13/6/95	1.86	98	30	45
B.D. (Bryn) Hall	North Harbour	3/2/92	1.83	89	36	50
W.K. (Billy) Harmon	Canterbury	23/12/94	1.87	104	5	5
D.K. (David) Havili	Tasman	23/12/94	1.84	95	59	82
M.J. (Mitchell) Hunt	Tasman	19/6/95	1.79	88	39	134
O.G.J.T. (Oliver) Jager	Canterbury	5/7/95	1.92	120	10	–
C.C. (Chris) King	Canterbury	30/4/81	1.86	116	25	5
J. (Jone) Macilai	Northland	27/8/90	1.78	97	16	35
A.(Andrew) Makalio	Tasman	22/1/92	1.82	122	18	15
C.I. (Caleb) Makene	Canterbury	20/4/96	1.79	84	1	–
M.M.B.T. (Manasa) Mataele	Taranaki	27/11/96	1.85	100	21	70
J.P.T. (Joe) Moody	Canterbury	16/9/88	1.88	120	67	10
R. (Richie) Mo'unga	Canterbury	25/5/94	1.76	86	42	465
T.G. (Tim) Perry	Tasman	1/8/88	1.88	122	23	5
R. H. (Rameka) Poihipi	Canterbury	14/10/98	1.88	101	1	5
K.J. (Kieran) Read	Counties Manukau	26/10/85	1.93	110	145	135
L. (Luke) Romano	Canterbury	16/2/86	1.59	120	112	40
P. (Pete) Samu	Tasman	17/12/91	1.85	101	33	45
T.B. (Tom) Sanders	Canterbury	5/2/94	1.91	109	4	–
S.P. (Seb) Siataga	Bay of Plenty	27/1/93	1.81	107	2	–
Q.J. (Quinten) Strange	Tasman	21/8/96	1.99	112	19	5
J. (Jack) Stratton	Canterbury	21/8/94	1.85	92	2	5
S. (Seta) Tamanivalu	Taranaki	23/1/92	1.89	108	33	75
J. (Jordan) Taufua	Counties Manukau	29/1/92	1.85	110	82	55
C.J. (Codie) Taylor	Canterbury	31/3/91	1.83	111	68	55
M.B. (Matt) Todd	Canterbury	24/3/88	1.85	105	125	130
S.L. (Samuel) Whitelock (capt)	Canterbury	12/10/88	2.03	120	132	40

Manager: Angus Gardiner **Coach:** Scott Robertson
Assistant coaches: Brad Mooar, Jason Ryan, Ronan O'Gara

CRUSADERS 2018

Player	Chiefs	Stormers	Hurricanes	Highlanders	Bulls	Lions	Jaguares	Sunwolves	Brumbies	Rebels	Waratahs	Blues	Hurricanes	Chiefs	Fr. Barbarians	Highlanders	Blues	Sharks	Hurricanes	Lions	TOTAL
Havili	15	15	15	15	15	15	15	–	15	15	–	15	15	12	–	15	–	15	15	15	16
Tamanivalu	14	14	14	14	–	14	–	s	11	14	14	14	14	13	–	14	14	14	14	14	17
Dagg	–	–	–	–	–	–	14	14	–	–	–	–	–	15	14	–	15	–	–	–	5
Bridge	11	11	11	11	11	11	11	15	–	11	15	11	11	–	11	–	11	11	11	11	18
Mataele	s	s	s	s	14	s	14	11	s	s	11	s	–	–	–	s	–	–	–	–	13
Ennor	–	–	–	–	s	–	s	–	–	–	s	–	s	–	–	–	s	s	s	s	8
Macilai	–	–	–	–	–	–	–	–	–	–	–	–	–	14	11	–	–	–	–	–	2
Makene	–	–	–	–	–	–	–	–	–	–	–	–	–	–	s	–	–	–	–	–	1
Goodhue	13	13	13	13	13	13	–	–	–	13	13	13	13	–	–	13	13	13	13	13	15
Fainga'anuku	–	–	–	–	–	–	–	–	–	–	–	–	–	s	13	–	–	–	–	–	2
Crotty	12	12	12	–	12	12	12	12	12	12	–	12	–	–	–	12	12	12	12	12	15
Bateman	–	–	–	12	–	–	13	13	13	–	12	–	12	–	–	–	–	–	–	–	6
Poihipi	–	–	–	–	–	–	–	–	–	–	–	–	–	12	–	–	–	–	–	–	1
Beard	–	–	–	–	–	–	–	–	–	–	–	–	–	–	s	–	–	–	–	–	1
Mo'unga	10	10	–	–	–	–	–	–	10	10	10	10	10	–	10	10	10	10	10	10	12
Hunt	s	s	10	10	10	10	10	s	s	s	s	s	s	s	15	s	s	s	s	s	20
Delany	–	–	s	–	–	s	s	10	10	–	–	–	–	–	10	–	–	–	–	–	6
Cameron	–	–	–	–	s	–	–	–	–	–	–	–	–	–	–	–	–	–	–	–	1
Hall	9	9	9	s	–	9	9	–	9	s	9	9	9	9	–	9	s	9	9	9	18
Drummond	s	s	s	9	9	s	s	9	s	9	s	s	s	s	9	s	9	s	s	s	20
Stratton	–	–	–	–	–	–	s	–	–	–	–	–	–	–	s	–	–	–	–	–	2
Taufua	8	8	8	8	8	8	–	–	8	8	8	8	–	–	–	s	6	6	6	–	14
Read	–	–	–	–	–	–	–	–	–	–	–	–	–	–	–	8	8	8	8	8	5
Todd	7	–	7	7	–	7	7	7	7	7	7	7	7	7	–	7	7	7	7	7	17
Harmon	s	7	s	–	7	–	–	–	–	–	–	–	–	–	7	–	–	–	–	–	5
Douglas	–	–	–	–	–	–	–	–	–	–	–	–	–	–	s	–	–	–	–	–	1
Samu	6	6	–	–	–	–	s	s	s	6	6	s	6	s	–	–	s	s	s	s	14
Bedwell-Curtis	–	s	6	6	6	6	8	–	6	s	s	6	8	8	–	6	–	–	–	6	14
Sanders	–	–	–	–	s	s	6	8	–	–	–	–	–	–	–	–	–	–	–	–	4
Blackadder	–	–	–	–	–	–	–	6	–	–	–	–	s	6	8	–	–	–	–	–	4
Dunshea	–	–	–	–	–	–	–	–	s	–	s	–	–	–	6	–	–	–	–	–	3
Whitelock	5	5	5	–	5	5	5	–	5	5	5	–	–	–	–	5	5	5	5	5	14
Strange	–	–	–	s	s	s	s	5	s	–	–	5	5	5	4	s	4	–	–	–	12
Dalzell	–	–	–	–	–	–	–	–	–	–	–	–	–	–	5	–	–	–	–	–	1
Barrett	s	4	4	5	4	4	–	4	4	4	4	4	4	4	–	4	–	4	4	4	17
Romano	4	s	s	4	–	–	4	s	–	–	–	–	s	s	s	–	s	s	s	s	13
Ala'alatoa	3	3	3	3	3	3	3	–	s	s	3	s	3	3	3	s	3	s	s	s	19
Franks	–	–	–	–	–	–	3	3	3	–	3	–	–	–	–	3	–	3	3	3	8
Jager	s	s	s	s	s	–	–	–	–	–	–	–	–	–	–	–	–	–	–	–	5
Allen	–	–	–	–	–	–	s	–	–	–	–	–	–	–	–	–	–	–	–	–	2
Brighouse	–	–	–	–	–	s	–	–	–	s	–	s	s	1	–	s	–	–	–	–	6
Crockett	1	1	1	1	s	s	–	s	1	s	1	s	1	s	–	s	s	s	s	–	15
King	s	s	s	s	–	s	s	s	–	–	–	s	–	s	–	s	–	–	–	–	9
Perry	–	–	–	–	1	1	1	1	–	–	1	–	–	–	–	1	1	s	–	s	10
Moody	–	–	–	–	–	–	–	–	1	–	–	1	–	1	–	1	–	–	1	1	5
Coxon	–	–	–	–	–	–	–	–	–	–	–	–	–	–	s	–	–	–	–	–	1
Taylor	2	2	2	2	2	2	2	–	2	s	2	2	2	–	–	s	–	2	2	2	17
Funnell	s	–	s	s	s	s	s	2	–	–	–	–	–	–	–	–	–	–	–	–	7
Makalio	–	s	–	–	–	–	s	s	s	2	s	s	s	s	2	2	s	–	s	–	13
Siataga	–	–	–	–	–	–	–	–	–	–	–	–	–	–	s	–	–	–	s	–	2
Anderson-Heather	–	–	–	–	–	–	–	–	–	–	–	–	–	–	–	–	–	s	–	–	1

CRUSADERS INDIVIDUAL SCORING

	Tries	Con	PG	DG	Points		Tries	Con	PG	DG	Points
Mo'unga	4	38	18	–	150	Bedwell-Curtis	2	–	–	–	10
Hunt	3	29	1	–	76	Makalio	2	–	–	–	10
Bridge	15	–	–	–	75	Samu	2	–	–	–	10
Mataele	8	–	–	–	40	Taufua	2	–	–	–	10
Goodhue	6	–	–	–	30	Bateman	1	–	–	–	5
Hall	6	–	–	–	30	Crockett	1	–	–	–	5
Tamanivalu	5	–	–	–	25	Dagg	1	–	–	–	5
Todd	5	–	–	–	25	Harmon	1	–	–	–	5
Havili	4	1	–	–	22	Moody	1	–	–	–	5
Barrett	4	–	–	–	20	Poihipi	1	–	–	–	5
Crotty	3	–	–	–	15	Romano	1	–	–	–	5
Drummond	3	–	–	–	15	Strange	1	–	–	–	5
Ennor	3	–	–	–	15	Stratton	1	–	–	–	5
Taylor	3	–	–	–	15						
Whitelock	3	–	–	–	15	**Totals**	**96**	**75**	**19**	**0**	**691**
Delany	–	7	–	–	14						
penalty tries	2	–	–	–	14	Opposition scored	48	31	19	0	361
Alaalatoa	2	–	–	–	10						

CRUSADERS TEAM RECORD 2018

Played 20 Won 18 Lost 2 Points for 691 Points against 361

Date	Opponent	Location	Score	Tries	Con	PG	DG	Referee
February 24	Chiefs	Christchurch	45–23	Todd, Mo'unga, Taufua, Whitelock, penalty try, Bridge, Mataele	Mo'unga (3) Havili			B. O'Keeffe
March 3	Stormers	Christchurch	45–28	Bridge (2), Taylor, Harmon, Hall, Tamanivalu, Mo'unga	Mo'unga (5)			N. Berry *(Australia)*
March 10	Hurricanes	Wellington	19–29	Mataele, Taufua, Alaalatoa	Hunt (2)			B. Pickerill
March 17	Highlanders	Dunedin	17–25	Bridge, Hall	Hunt (2)	Hunt		N. Briant
March 25	Bulls	Christchurch	33–14	Goodhue (2), Barrett, Taylor, Bridge	Hunt (4)			F. Anselmi *(Argentina)*
April 1	Lions	Johannesburg	14–8	Whitelock, Goodhue	Hunt (2)			J. Peyper *(South Africa)*
April 7	Jaguares	Buenos Aires	40–14	Bridge (2), Mataele (2), Hunt, Crotty	Hunt (4) Delany			M. van der Westhuizen *(South Africa)*
April 21	Sunwolves	Christchurch	33–11	Crotty (2), Todd, Mataele, Stratton	Delany (3) Hunt			B. Pickerill
April 28	Brumbies	Canberra	21–8	Matale (2), Bateman	Delany (3)			J. Peyper *(South Africa)*
May 4	Rebels	Melbourne	55–10	Makalio (2), Tamanivalu, Goodhue, Samu, Hall, Crockett, Mataele	Hunt (4) Mo'unga (2)	Mo'unga		N. Briant
May 12	Waratahs	Christchurch	31–29	Moody, Taylor, Ennor, Tamanivalu, penalty try	Mo'unga (2)			B. O'Keeffe
May 19	Blues	Auckland	32–24	Bridge, Strange, Todd, Hall	Mo'unga (3)	Mo'unga (2)		G. Jackson
May 25	Hurricanes	Christchurch	24–13	Barrett, Alaalatoa, Bedwell-Curtis	Mo'unga (3)	Mo'unga		A. Gardner *(Australia)*
June 2	Chiefs	Hamilton	34–20	Bedwell-Curtis, Todd, Bridge, Romano	Mo'unga (3) Hunt	Mo'unga (2)		N. Berry *(Australia)*
June 15	French Barbarians	Christchurch	42–26	Hunt (2), Drummond (2), Dagg, Poihipi	Hunt (6)			J. Doleman
July 6	Highlanders	Christchurch	45–22	Bridge (2), Havili, Barrett, Mo'unga	Mo'unga (4)	Mo'unga (4)		B. Pickerill
July 14	Blues	Christchurch	54–17	Bridge (3), Goodhue (2), Tamanivalu, Whitelock, Hall	Mo'unga (4) Hunt (3)			F. Anselmi *(Argentina)*
July 21	Sharks (Quarter-final)	Christchurch	40–10	Hall, Havili, Todd, Ennor, Samu	Mo'unga (3)	Mo'unga (3)		M. Fraser
July 28	Hurricanes (Semi-final)	Christchurch	30–12	Mo'unga, Bridge, Havili, Ennor	Mo'unga (2)	Mo'unga (2)		J. Peyper *(South Africa)*
August 4	Lions (Final)	Christchurch	37–18	Tamanivalu, Havili, Drummond, Barrett	Mo'unga (4)	Mo'unga (3)		A. Gardner *(Australia)*

HIGHLANDERS

Postal address: Box 6070, Dunedin 9059
Telephone: (03) 479 9280
Email: contactus@highlanders.net.nz
Home venues: Forsyth Barr Stadium, Dunedin;
Rugby Park Stadium, Invercargill
Colours: Blue with gold and maroon.

Played 315, Won 158, Lost 155, Drew 2

	Tries	Conv	Pen	DG	Points
For	868	599	731	27	7814
Against	898	646	660	15	7811

RECORDS — TEAM

Most points in a game	65	v Bulls, 1999
Most points in a season	530	2015
Biggest winning margin	49	55-6 v Force 2017
Most tries in a game	9	v Bulls, 1999
Most tries in a season	64	2017

RECORDS — INDIVIDUAL

Most points in a game	28	B.A. Blair, v Sharks, 2005
Most points in a season	191	L.Z. Sopoaga, 2015
Most points in a career	892	L.Z. Sopoaga
Most tries in a game	3	on 11 occasions
Most tries in a season	13	W.R. Naholo, 2015
Most tries in a career	41	W.R. Naholo
Most conversions in a game	7	T.E. Brown, v Bulls, 1999
Most conversions in a season	41	L.Z. Sopoaga 2018
Most conversions in a career	163	L.Z. Sopoaga
Most penalty goals in a game	8	W.C. Walker, v Chiefs, 2003
Most penalty goals in a season	34	T.E. Brown, 2000
Most penalty goals in a career	180	T.E. Brown
Most dropped goals in a game	1	on twenty seven occasions
Most dropped goals in a season	3	L.Z. Sopoaga, 2015
Most dropped goals in a career	6	T.E. Brown
Most games	144	B.R. Smith

Player	Union	Date of birth	Height	Weight	Highlanders Games	Highlanders Points
A.N. (Alex) Ainley	Tasman	16/7/81	1.97	109	40	–
R.J. (Richard) Buckman	Hawke's Bay	27/5/89	1.84	95	47	55
L.J. (Liam) Coltman	Otago	25/1/90	1.85	112	87	20
J.M. (Josh) Dickson	Otago	2/1/94	2.00	109	5	–
A.L. (Ash) Dixon (co capt)	Hawke's Bay	1/9/88	1.82	105	58	10
E.C. (Elliot) Dixon	Southland	4/9/89	1.93	110	93	60
M.A. (Matt) Faddes	Otago	6/11/91	1.85	94	36	80
T.S.G. (Tom) Franklin	Bay of Plenty	11/8/90	2.00	113	71	10
S.M. (Shannon) Frizell	Tasman	11/2/94	1.95	108	14	25
K.W. (Kayne) Hammington	Manawatu	24/9/90	1.70	75	27	15
J.N. (Jackson) Hemopo	Manawatu	14/11/93	1.94	113	26	–
D. (Dillon) Hunt	Otago	23/2/95	1.89	103	26	20
J.R. (Josh) Ioane	Otago	11/7/95	1.76	85	9	2
J.A.R. (James) Lentjes	Otago	16/1/91	1.88	104	23	10
D.P. (Daniel) Lienert-Brown	Canterbury	9/2/93	1.84	112	61	15
T. (Tevita) Li	North Harbour	23/3/95	1.82	95	26	40
T.S. (Tyrell) Lomax	Tasman	1/6/96	1.92	127	16	10
J.A. (Josh) McKay	Canterbury	10/10/97	1.83	92	3	5
M.E.R. (Marino) Mikaele-Tu'u	Hawke's Bay	6/11/97	1.93	114	6	–
G.P. (Guy) Millar	Southland	23/4/92	1.86	117	6	–
T. (Tevita) Nabura	Counties Manukau	28/6/92	1.92	107	3	–
W.R. (Waisake) Naholo	Taranaki	8/5/91	1.86	96	54	205
P.P.M. (Paripari) Parkinson	Tasman	12/9/96	2.04	119	2	–
G.W. (Greg) Pleasants-Tate	Auckland	12/5/91	1.82	112	18	20
D.J. (Dan) Pryor	Northland	14/4/88	1.90	104	35	30
J.D. (Josh) Renton	Otago	25/5/94	1.74	81	8	–
A. (Aki) Seiuli	Otago	22/12/92	1.84	116	40	15
A.L. (Aaron) Smith	Manawatu	21/10/88	1.71	83	124	120
B.R. (Ben) Smith (co capt)	Otago	1/6/86	1.86	94	144	185
F.H. (Fletcher) Smith	Otago	1/3/95	1.80	88	16	34
L.Z. (Lima) Sopoaga	Southland	3/2/91	1.77	91	92	892
L.I.J. (Liam) Squire	Tasman	20/3/91	1.95	113	30	35
R. (Robert) Thompson	Canterbury	29/8/91	1.84	103	37	55
S.F. (Siate) Tokolahi	Canterbury	16/3/92	1.84	116	26	5
P.F. (Sio) Tompkinson	Otago	27/5/96	1.82	94	6	10
K.E. (Kalolo) Tuiloma	Counties Manukau	24/6/90	1.93	151	10	–
T.N.M. (Thomas) Umaga-Jensen	Wellington	31/12/97	1.87	95	2	–
T.T. (Tei) Walden	Otago	25/5/93	1.82	94	25	40
L.C. (Luke) Whitelock	Canterbury	29/1/91	1.94	112	39	15

Manager: Paul McLaughlan
Coach: Aaron Mauger
Assistant coaches: Mark Hammett, Glen Delaney

HIGHLANDERS 2018	Blues	Stormers	Crusaders	Hurricanes	Chiefs	Brumbies	Blues	Bulls	Sharks	Lions	Waratahs	Reds	Hurricanes	Fr. Barbarians	Chiefs	Crusaders	Rebels	Waratahs	TOTALS
B. Smith	15	15	15	15	15	15	14	15	15	15	–	15	–	15	15	–	15		15
McKay	–	–	–	–	–	–	–	–	–	–	15	–	15	–	–	–	s	–	3
Naholo	14	14	14	14	14	14	14	–	14	14	14	14	–	14	14	14	14		16
Li	11	–	11	11	11	11	11	11	–	–	s	11	11	11	11	–	11	11	14
Nabura	–	11	–	–	–	–	–	–	–	11	11	–	–	–	–	–	–	–	3
Faddes	–	s	s	s	13	s	s	–	s	–	–	–	–	14	–	–	s		9
Thompson	13	13	13	13	12	13	13	13	13	13	13	13	13	13	13	13	–	13	17
Umaga-Jensen	–	–	–	–	–	–	–	–	–	–	–	–	–	–	s	–	–	13	2
Tomkinson	–	–	–	–	s	–	–	s	11	s	12	–	–	–	–	–	–	–	5
Walden	12	12	12	12	–	12	12	12	12	12	–	12	12	–	12	12	12	12	15
Buckman	–	–	–	–	–	–	–	–	–	–	s	s	12	s	11	–	–		5
Sopoaga	10	10	10	10	10	10	10	10	10	10	10	10	10	10	10	10	10	10	18
F. Smith	s	–	s	s	–	s	s	s	15	–	–	–	–	–	–	–	–	–	6
Ioane	–	–	–	s	–	–	–	–	–	s	s	s	–	s	s	s	s	15	9
A. Smith	9	9	9	9	9	9	s	9	9	–	9	s	9	–	9	9	–	9	15
Hammington	s	–	s	s	–	s	9	s	s	9	s	9	–	s	s	s	9	–	14
Renton	–	–	–	–	–	–	–	–	–	s	–	–	–	9	–	–	s	–	3
Whitelock	8	8	8	8	8	8	8	8	8	8	8	–	8	–	8	8	–	8	15
Hunt	7	7	7	7	7	7	7	7	7	–	7	7	7	–	7	–	s	–	14
Lentjes	–	–	–	–	–	–	–	s	–	7	–	6	–	7	–	7	7	7	7
Pryor	s	–	–	–	–	–	–	–	–	–	–	–	s	–	–	–	–	–	2
Squire	6	6	6	–	–	–	–	–	–	–	–	s	6	–	6	8	6	–	8
E. Dixon	s	–	s	6	6	s	6	s	6	6	–	s	8	6	s	–	s		15
Mikaele-Tu'u	–	s	–	–	–	–	–	–	–	s	s	8	–	s	–	–	–	–	6
Frizell	–	s	s	s	6	6	s	6	–	s	–	s	–	s	s	6	s		14
Franklin	5	5	5	5	s	5	5	5	5	5	5	5	–	5	5	s	s		17
Dickson	–	–	–	–	5	–	–	–	–	s	–	s	–	6	–	–	–	–	4
Hemopo	4	4	4	4	4	4	4	–	4	4	4	–	4	s	4	5	4		16
Ainley	–	–	–	–	s	s	s	4	4	–	–	–	4	s	–	4	–	–	8
Parkinson	–	–	–	–	–	–	–	–	–	–	–	–	–	5	–	4	–	–	2
Tokolahi	3	3	3	s	3	3	3	–	–	–	–	–	–	3	3	–	–	–	9
Lomax	s	s	–	3	s	–	s	3	3	3	3	3	s	s	s	3	3	3	16
Tuiloma	–	–	s	–	–	–	s	–	s	s	s	s	3	–	–	–	s		10
Lienert-Brown	1	1	s	1	1	1	1	1	s	1	1	1	–	1	s	s	1		17
Seilui	s	s	1	s	s	s	s	s	1	s	s	s	1	s	1	1	s		18
Millar	–	–	–	–	–	–	–	–	–	–	–	–	–	s	–	s	–	–	2
A. Dixon	2	–	s	s	2	s	2	s	s	s	2	2	2	2	s	–	s		16
Coltman	s	2	2	2	–	2	s	2	2	2	s	–	s	–	s	2	?	2	15
Pleasants-Tate	–	s	–	–	s	–	–	–	–	–	–	s	–	s	–	–	s	–	5

HIGHLANDERS INDIVIDUAL SCORING

	Tries	Con	PG	DG	Points		Tries	Con	PG	DG	Points
Sopoaga	4	41	21	–	165	Squire	2	–	–	–	10
Naholo	10	–	–	–	50	Whitelock	2	–	–	–	10
Walden	7	–	–	–	35	A. Dixon	1	–	–	–	5
Frizell	5	–	–	–	25	Franklin	1	–	–	–	5
Li	4	–	–	–	20	Lentjes	1	–	–	–	5
A. Smith	4	–	–	–	20	McKay	1	–	–	–	5
F. Smith	2	2	2	–	20	Seiuli	1	–	–	–	5
Thompson	4	–	–	–	20	Tokolahi	1	–	–	–	5
B. Smith	3	1	–	–	17	Tompkinson	1	–	–	–	5
Coltman	2	–	–	–	10	Ioane	–	1	–	–	2
E. Dixon	2	–	–	–	10						
Hammington	2	–	–	–	10	**Totals**	**66**	**45**	**23**	**0**	**489**
Hunt	2	–	–	–	10						
Lomax	2	–	–	–	10	Opposition scored	61	50	26	0	485
Pleasants-Tate	2	–	–	–	10						

HIGHLANDERS TEAM RECORD 2018

Played 18 Won 11 Lost 7 Points for 489 Points against 485

Date	Opponent	Location	Score	Tries	Con	PG	DG	Referee
February 23	Blues	Dunedin	41–34	Thompson (2), Walden (2), Tokolahi	Sopoaga (5)	Sopoaga, F. Smith		J. Nutbrown
March 9	Stormers	Dunedin	33–15	A. Smith (2), Squire, Naholo, Whitelock	Sopoaga (4)			G. Jackson
March 17	Crusaders	Dunedin	25–17	Coltman, Sopoaga, E. Dixon	Sopoaga (2)	Sopoaga (2)		N. Briant
March 24	Hurricanes	Wellington	12–29	Naholo (2)	Sopoaga			M. Fraser
March 30	Chiefs	Hamilton	22–27	Naholo, Li, Tompkinson	F. Smith (2)	F. Smith		G. Jackson
April 14	Brumbies	Dunedin	43–17	B. Smith (2), Sopoaga, Naholo, Frizell, F. Smith	Sopoaga (4)	Sopoaga		B. O'Keeffe
April 20	Blues	Auckland	34–16	Frizell (3), Hunt, Hammington	Sopoaga (3)	Sopoaga		M. van der Westhuizen (South Africa)
April 28	Bulls	Pretoria	29–28	A. Smith, F. Smith	Sopoaga (2)	Sopoaga (5)		G. Jackson
May 5	Sharks	Durban	12–38	Hunt, Walden	Sopoaga			M. van der Westhuizen (South Africa)
May 12	Lions	Dunedin	39–27	Sopoaga, Coltman, Whitelock, Naholo, Walden	Sopoaga (4)	Sopoaga (2)		A. Gardner (Australia)
May 19	Waratahs	Sydney	12–41	E. Dixon, A. Dixon	Sopoaga			B. Pickerill
May 26	Reds	Brisbane	18–15	Li, Squire	Sopoaga	Sopoaga (2)		R. Rasivhenge (South Africa)
June 1	Hurricanes	Dunedin	30–14	Li, A. Smith, Lomax, Naholo	Sopoaga (2)	Sopoaga (2)		B. O'Keeffe
June 22	French Barbarians	Invercargill	29–10	Lentjes, McKay, Sopoaga, Pleasants-Tate, Thompson	Sopoaga, Ioane			M. Fraser
June 30	Chiefs	Suva	22–45	Walden (2), Seiuli, Frizell	Sopoaga			P. Williams
July 6	Crusaders	Christchurch	22–45	Lomax, B. Smith, Naholo	Sopoaga (2)	Sopoaga		B. Pickerill
July 14	Rebels	Dunedin	43–37	Naholo, Hammington, Walden, Li, Pleasants-Tate, Franklin	Sopoaga (5)	Sopoaga		G. Jackson
July 21	Waratahs (Quarter-final)	Sydney	23–30	Naholo, Thompson	Sopoaga (2)	Sopoaga (3)		A. Gardner (Australia)

RESULTS FROM 2018 FIRST-CLASS SEASON

Key:
- RC — SANZAAR Rugby Championship
- W20 — World Rugby Under 20 Championship
- OJC — Oceania Rugby Junior Championship
- S15 — SANZAAR Super 15
- RS — Ranfurly Shield
- P — Mitre 10 Cup Premiership
- C — Mitre 10 Cup Championship
- P/C — Crossover match between teams from ITM Cup Premiership and Championship divisions.
- H — Heartland Championship
- MC — Meads Cup
- LC — Lochore Cup
- qf — Quarter-final
- sf — Semi-final
- f — Final
- ★ — not first-class

Winning team listed first

January

Day	Date	Type	Match				Venue
Sat–Sun	13–14	★	National Sevens				Rotorua
Fri–Sun	26–28	★	Round Three 2017–2018 World Rugby Sevens Series				Sydney, Australia

February

Day	Date	Type	Match				Venue
Sat–Sun	3–4	★	Round Four 2017–2018 World Rugby Sevens Series				Hamilton, New Zealand
Fri	23	S15	Highlanders	41	Blues	34	Dunedin
Sat	24	S15	Crusaders	45	Chiefs	23	Christchurch
	24	S15	Bulls	21	Hurricanes	19	Pretoria

March

Day	Date	Type	Match				Venue
Fri	2	S15	Chiefs	27	Blues	21	Auckland
Fri–Sun	2–4	★	Round Five 2017–2018 World Rugby Sevens Series				Las Vegas, USA
Sat	3	S15	Crusaders	45	Stormers	28	Christchurch
	3	S15	Hurricanes	34	Jaguares	9	Buenos Aires
Fri	9	S15	Highlanders	33	Stormers	15	Dunedin
Sat	10	S15	Hurricanes	29	Crusaders	19	Wellington
	10	S15	Blues	38	Lions	35	Johannesburg
Sat–Sun	10–11	★	Round Six 2017–2018 World Rugby Sevens Series				Vancouver, Canada
Fri	16	S15	Chiefs	41	Bulls	28	Hamilton
Sat	17	S15	Highlanders	25	Crusaders	17	Dunedin
	17	S15	Stormers	37	Blues	20	Cape Town
Fri	23	S15	Crusaders	33	Bulls	14	Christchurch
Sat	24	S15	Chiefs	61	Sunwolves	10	Tokyo
	24	S15	Hurricanes	29	Highlanders	12	Wellington
Fri	30	S15	Chiefs	27	Highlanders	22	Hamilton
	30	S15	Hurricanes	50	Rebels	19	Melbourne
Sat	31	S15	Sharks	63	Blues	40	Auckland

Results from 2018 First-Class Season in New Zealand

April

Day	Date	Comp	Team	Score	Opponent	Score	Venue
Sun	1	S15	Crusaders	14	Lions	8	Johannesburg
Fri	6	S15	Hurricanes	38	Sharks	37	Napier
Fri–Sun	6–8	*	Round Seven 2017–2018 World Rugby Sevens Series				Causeway Bay, Hong Kong
Sat	7	S15	Chiefs	21	Blues	19	Hamilton
	7	S15	Crusaders	40	Jaguares	14	Buenos Aires
Fri–Sun	13–15	*	Commonwealth Games Sevens				Robina, Gold Coast
Fri	13	S15	Hurricanes	25	Chiefs	13	Wellington
Sat	14	S15	Blues	24	Sunwolves	10	Tokyo
	14	S15	Highlanders	43	Brumbies	17	Dunedin
Fri	20	S15	Highlanders	34	Blues	16	Auckland
Sat	21	S15	Crusaders	33	Sunwolves	11	Christchurch
	21	S15	Chiefs	36	Reds	12	Brisbane
Fri	27	O20	New Zealand Under 20	97	Tonga Under 20	0	Gold Coast
	27	S15	Hurricanes	43	Sunwolves	15	Wellington
Sat–Sun	28–29	*	Round Eight 2017–2018 World Rugby Sevens Series				Kalang, Singapore
Sat	28	S15	Jaguares	20	Blues	13	Auckland
	28	S15	Crusaders	21	Brumbies	8	Canberra
	28	S15	Highlanders	29	Bulls	28	Pretoria

May

Day	Date	Comp	Team	Score	Opponent	Score	Venue
Tues	1	O20	New Zealand Under 20	55	Fiji Under 20	15	Gold Coast
Fri	4	S15	Jaguares	23	Chiefs	19	Rotorua
	4	S15	Crusaders	55	Rebels	10	Melbourne
Sat	5	S15	Hurricanes	28	Lions	19	Wellington
	5	O20	New Zealand Under 20	43	Australia Under 20	28	Gold Coast
	5	S15	Blues	24	Waratahs	21	Sydney
	5	S15	Sharks	38	Highlanders	12	Durban
Sun	6		New Zealand Universities	34	Kanto Universities	17	Tokyo
Fri	11	S15	Hurricanes	36	Blues	15	Auckland
Sat	12	S15	Crusaders	31	Waratahs	29	Christchurch
	12	S15	Highlanders	39	Lions	27	Dunedin
	12	S15	Chiefs	15	Stormers	9	Cape Town
Fri	18	S15	Hurricanes	38	Reds	34	Wellington
Sat	19	S15	Crusaders	32	Blues	24	Auckland
	19	S15	Waratahs	41	Highlanders	12	Sydney
	19	S15	Sharks	28	Chiefs	24	Durban
Fri	25	S15	Crusaders	24	Hurricanes	13	Christchurch
Sat	26	S15	Chiefs	39	Waratahs	27	Hamilton
	26	S15	Highlanders	18	Reds	15	Brisbane
Wed	30	W20	New Zealand Under 20	67	Japan Under 20	0	Narbonne

June

Day	Date	Comp	Team	Score	Opponent	Score	Venue
Fri	1	S15	Highlanders	30	Hurricanes	15	Dunedin
Sat	2		Poverty Bay	58	Ngati Porou East Coast	18	Tolaga Bay
	2	S15	Rebels	20	Blues	10	Auckland
	2	S15	Crusaders	34	Chiefs	20	Hamilton
Sat–Sun	2–3	*	Round Nine 2017–2018 World Rugby Sevens Series				London, England

111

Day	Date	Comp	Team	Score	Opponent	Score	Venue
Sun	3	W20	New Zealand Under 20	42	Wales Under 20	10	Beziers
Thurs	7	W20	New Zealand Under 20	27	Australia Under 20	18	Perpignan
Sat	9		New Zealand	52	France	11	Auckland
Sat–Sun	9–10	*	Round Ten 2017–2018 World Rugby Sevens Series				Paris, France
Tues	12	W20 sf	France Under 20	16	New Zealand Under 20	7	Perpignan
Fri	15		Crusaders	42	French Barbarians	26	Christchurch
Sat	16		New Zealand	26	France	13	Wellington
Sun	17	W20 3–4	South Africa Under 20	42	New Zealand Under 20	30	Beziers
Fri	22		Highlanders	29	French Barbarians	10	Invercargill
Sat	23		New Zealand	49	France	14	Dunedin
Fri	29	S15	Blues	39	Reds	16	Auckland
Sat	30	S15	Chiefs	45	Highlanders	22	Suva
	30	S15	Brumbies	24	Hurricanes	12	Canberra
July							
Fri	6	S15	Crusaders	45	Highlanders	22	Christchurch
Sat	7	S15	Chiefs	24	Brumbies	19	Hamilton
	7	S15	Hurricanes	42	Blues	24	Wellington
Fri	13	S15	Chiefs	28	Hurricanes	24	Hamilton
Sat	14	S15	Highlanders	43	Rebels	37	Dunedin
	14	S15	Crusaders	54	Blues	17	Christchurch
Fri	20	S15 qf	Hurricanes	32	Chiefs	31	Wellington
Fri–Sun	20–22	*	World Cup Sevens				San Francisco, USA
Sat	21	S15 qf	Crusaders	40	Sharks	10	Christchurch
	21	S15 qf	Waratahs	30	Highlanders	23	Sydney
Sat	28	RS	Taranaki	78	Poverty Bay	0	Tikorangi
	28	S15 sf	Crusaders	30	Hurricanes	12	Christchurch
August							
Sat	4	RS	Taranaki	33	Wanganui	10	Hawera
	4	S15 f	Crusaders	37	Lions	18	Christchurch
Thurs	16	P/C	North Harbour	21	Northland	20	Albany
Fri	17	P	Tasman	25	Canterbury	17	Blenheim
Sat	18	C	Manawatu	24	Waikato	19	Palmerston North
	18	P	Auckland	23	Counties Manukau	19	Auckland
	18	P/C	Bay of Plenty	30	Taranaki	10	Rotorua
	18	RC	New Zealand	38	Australia	13	Sydney
Sun	19	P/C	Wellington	34	Otago	16	Wellington
	19	C	Hawke's Bay	31	Southland	10	Invercargill
Thurs	23	P/C	Bay of Plenty	22	Counties Manukau	17	Pukekohe
Fri	24	C	Hawke's Bay	31	Otago	25	Dunedin
	24	P/C RS	Taranaki	41	Manawatu	21	New Plymouth
Sat	25	H	West Coast	27	Thames Valley	25	Te Aroha
	25	P	Canterbury	27	Wellington	20	Christchurch
	25	H	Mid Canterbury	30	Horowhenua Kapiti	24	Foxton
	25	H	King Country	75	Ngati Porou East Coast	17	Te Kuiti
	25	H	North Otago	30	Buller	24	Oamaru
	25	H	Poverty Bay	27	Wairarapa Bush	22	Gisborne
	25	H	Wanganui	21	South Canterbury	10	Wanganui
	25	P/C	North Harbour	29	Waikato	28	Hamilton

Results from 2018 First-Class Season in New Zealand

	25	RC	New Zealand	40	Australia	12	Auckland
Sun	26	P/C	Tasman	45	Southland	24	Blenheim
	26	P/C	Auckland	28	Northland	12	Whangarei
Wed	29	P	Taranaki	26	Counties Manukau	19	Pukekohe
Thurs	30	P/C	Auckland	35	Waikato	17	Auckland
Fri	31	P/C	Wellington	52	Southland	7	Wellington
September							
Sat	1	H	Thames Valley	44	Wairarapa Bush	32	Masterton
	1	H	Wanganui	33	West Coast	21	Greymouth
	1	P/C	Canterbury	31	Bay of Plenty	19	Tauranga
	1	H	King Country	30	Buller	28	Westport
	1	H	North Otago	34	Mid Canterbury	33	Ashburton
	1	H	Horowhenua Kapiti	46	Ngati Porou East Coast	8	Ruatoria
	1	H	South Canterbury	40	Poverty Bay	11	Timaru
	1	C	Otago	50	Manawatu	17	Palmerston North
	1	P	Tasman	32	North Harbour	20	Albany
Sun	2	P/C	Counties Manukau	29	Hawke's Bay	25	Napier
	2	P/C	Northland	18	Taranaki	17	Whangarei
Wed	5	P/C	Waikato	43	Wellington	31	Hamilton
Thurs	6	P/C	Canterbury	34	Manawatu	23	Christchurch
Fri	7	C	Otago	27	Northland	23	Dunedin
	7	P	Auckland	36	Tasman	10	Auckland
Sat	8	H	Thames Valley	43	Buller	22	Westport
	8	P/C	Counties Manukau	43	Southland	26	Invercargill
	8	H	Wairarapa Bush	26	Ngati Porou East Coast	5	Ruatoria
	8	H	King Country	22	North Otago	18	Taumarunui
	8	H	Mid Canterbury	36	West Coast	29	Ashburton
	8	H	Wanganui	53	Poverty Bay	0	Gisborne
	8	C	Hawke's Bay	29	Bay of Plenty	28	Napier
	8	RC	New Zealand	46	Argentina	24	Nelson
Sun	9	H	South Canterbury	52	Horowhenua Kapiti	29	Wellington
	9	P	Wellington	35	North Harbour	23	Wellington
	9	P/C RS	Waikato	33	Taranaki	19	New Plymouth
Wed	12	P	Canterbury	31	North Harbour	21	Albany
Thurs	13	C RS	Waikato	42	Hawke's Bay	22	Hamilton
Fri	14	C	Northland	49	Manawatu	19	Whangarei
	14	P	Tasman	53	Taranaki	17	Nelson
Sat	15	H	King Country	37	Thames Valley	29	Te Aroha
	15	P	Wellington	53	Counties Manukau	12	Pukekohe
	15	H	Horowhenua Kapiti	27	North Otago	24	Oamaru
	15	H	South Canterbury	100	Ngati Porou East Coast	7	Timaru
	15	H	Wanganui	30	Mid Canterbury	12	Wanganui
	15	H	Wairarapa Bush	61	Buller	29	Masterton
	15	H	West Coast	31	Poverty Bay	30	Greymouth
	15	C	Otago	43	Southland	24	Invercargill
	15	RC	South Africa	36	New Zealand	34	Wellington
Sun	16	P/C	North Harbour	32	Bay of Plenty	20	Albany
	16	P	Auckland	34	Canterbury	29	Christchurch
Wed	19	P/C	Tasman	29	Manawatu	19	Palmerston North
Thurs	20	C	Northland	26	Southland	10	Invercargill

Day	Date	Type	Team	Score	Team	Score	Venue
Fri	21	C	Waikato	54	Bay of Plenty	21	Rotorua
Sat	22	H	Thames Valley	43	North Otago	21	Te Aroha
	22	H	West Coast	34	Buller	28	Westport
	22	H	Poverty Bay	26	Ngati Porou East Coast	19	Ruatoria
	22	H	Horowhenua Kapiti	37	Wairarapa Bush	21	Levin
	22	H	Wanganui	36	King Country	19	Te Kuiti
	22	H	South Canterbury	41	Mid Canterbury	10	Timaru
	22	P/C	North Harbour	51	Hawke's Bay	34	Napier
	22	P/C	Canterbury	47	Otago	25	Dunedin
	22	P	Auckland	31	Taranaki	30	New Plymouth
Sun	23	P	Tasman	21	Counties Manukau	19	Nelson
	23	P/C	Wellington	49	Manawatu	7	Palmerston North
Wed	26	C	Hawke's Bay	55	Northland	41	Napier
Thurs	27	C	Manawatu	17	Bay of Plenty	15	Rotorua
Fri	28	P/C	Otago	31	Auckland	26	Auckland
Sat	29	H	Horowhenua Kapiti	36	King Country	30	Paraparaumu
	29	H	Mid Canterbury	56	Ngati Porou East Coast	7	Ashburton
	29	H	North Otago	40	West Coast	19	Oamaru
	29	H	Thames Valley	37	Poverty Bay	34	Gisborne
	29	H	Wanganui	45	Buller	14	Wanganui
	29	H	Wairarapa Bush	27	South Canterbury	24	Masterton
	29	C RS	Waikato	42	Southland	11	Hamilton
	29	P	North Harbour	55	Taranaki	26	New Plymouth
	29	P	Tasman	28	Wellington	22	Wellington
	29	RC	New Zealand	35	Argentina	17	Buenos Aires
Sun	30	P/C	Canterbury	49	Hawke's Bay	24	Christchurch
	30	P/C	Northland	24	Counties Manukau	20	Pukekohe

October

Day	Date	Type	Team	Score	Team	Score	Venue
Wed	3	C	Otago	45	Bay of Plenty	34	Dunedin
Thurs	4	P	Auckland	29	Wellington	24	Wellington
Fri	5	C	Hawke's Bay	45	Manawatu	17	Napier
Sat	6	H	Buller	37	Mid Canterbury	19	Westport
	6	H	Wairarapa Bush	23	West Coast	5	Greymouth
	6	H	Thames Valley	29	Horowhenua Kapiti	27	Te Aroha
	6	H	Wanganui	56	East Coast	10	Tolaga Bay
	6	H	King Country	59	Poverty Bay	38	Taupo
	6	H	South Canterbury	41	North Otago	22	Oamaru
	6	C	Waikato	71	Northland	28	Whangarei
	6	P	North Harbour	36	Counties Manukau	26	Albany
	6	P	Canterbury	41	Taranaki	7	Christchurch
	6	RC	New Zealand	32	South Africa	30	Pretoria
Sun	7	C	Bay of Plenty	26	Southland	22	Invercargill
	7	P/C	Tasman	47	Otago	21	Dunedin
Wed	10	P/C	Auckland	56	Southland	8	Invercargill
Thurs	11	P/C	Tasman	29	Hawke's Bay	0	Nelson
Fri	12	P	Wellington	34	Taranaki	10	New Plymouth
Sat	13	H	West Coast	62	Ngati Porou East Coast	26	Greymouth
	13	H	King Country	31	Mid Canterbury	29	Ashburton
	13	H	Buller	41	Poverty Bay	27	Gisborne
	13	H	South Canterbury	33	Thames Valley	24	Timaru

Results from 2018 First-Class Season in New Zealand

	13	H	Wanganui	57	Horowhenua Kapiti	27	Wanganui
	13	H	North Otago	24	Wairarapa Bush	0	Masterton
	13	C	Bay of Plenty	38	Northland	35	Tauranga
	13	C RS	Otago	23	Waikato	19	Hamilton
	13	P	Canterbury	19	Counties Manukau	14	Pukekohe
Sun	14	P	Auckland	45	North Harbour	29	Auckland
	14	C	Manawatu	38	Southland	26	Palmerston North
Fri	19	P sf	Canterbury	21	Tasman	16	Nelson
Sat	20	LC sf	Wairarapa Bush	30	North Otago	21	Masterton
	20	LC sf	Horowhenua Kapiti	34	Mid Canterbury	24	Levin
	20	MC sf	Thames Valley	17	Wanganui	7	Wanganui
	20	MC sf	South Canterbury	58	King Country	21	Timaru
	20	C sf	Waikato	48	Northland	26	Hamilton
	20	P sf	Auckland	38	Wellington	17	Auckland
	20	C sf	Otago	20	Hawke's Bay	19	Dunedin
Fri	26	C f	Waikato	35	Otago	13	Hamilton
Sat	27	MC f	Thames Valley	17	South Canterbury	12	Timaru
	27	P f	Auckland	40 aet	Canterbury	33 aet	Auckland
	27		New Zealand	37	Australia	20	Tokyo
Sun	28	LC f	Horowhenua Kapiti	26	Wairarapa Bush	23	Levin
November							
Thurs	1		NZ Heartland	60	Vanua XV	0	Taupo
Sat	3		New Zealand	69	Japan	31	Tokyo
	3		NZ Maori	59	USA	22	Chicago
Sun	4		NZ Heartland	46	NZ Marist	19	Taupo
Fri–Sat	9–10	*	Oceania Sevens				Suva, Fiji
Sat	10		New Zealand	16	England	15	London
	10		NZ Maori	35	Brazil	3	Sao Paulo
Sat	17		Ireland	16	New Zealand	9	Dublin
	17		NZ Maori	73	Chile	0	Santiago
Sat	24		New Zealand	66	Italy	3	Rome
Fri–Sat	30–1	*	Round One 2018–2019 World Rugby Sevens				Dubai
December							
Sat	1		UK Barbarians	38	Argentina	35	London
Sat–Sun	8–9	*	Round Two 2018–2019 World Rugby Sevens				Cape Town
Sat–Sun	15–16	*	National Sevens				Tauranga

229 first-class matches

NATIONAL PROVINCIAL CHAMPIONSHIP WINNERS

	First Division	Second Division (North)	Second Division (South)
1976	Bay of Plenty	Taranaki	South Canterbury
1977	Canterbury	North Auckland	South Canterbury
1978	Wellington	Bay of Plenty	Marlborough
1979	Counties	Hawke's Bay	Marlborough
1980	Manawatu	Waikato	Mid Canterbury
1981	Wellington	Wairarapa Bush	South Canterbury
1982	Auckland	Taranaki	Southland
1983	Canterbury	Taranaki	Mid Canterbury
1984	Auckland	Taranaki	Southland

	First Division	Second Division	Third Division
1985	Auckland	Taranaki	North Harbour
1986	Wellington	Waikato	South Canterbury
1987	Auckland	North Harbour	Poverty Bay
1988	Auckland	Hawke's Bay	Thames Valley
1989	Auckland	Southland	Wanganui
1990	Auckland	Hawke's Bay	Thames Valley
1991	Otago	King Country	South Canterbury
1992	Waikato	Taranaki	Nelson Bays
1993	Auckland	Counties	Horowhenua
1994	Auckland	Southland	Mid Canterbury
1995	Auckland	Taranaki	Thames Valley
1996	Auckland	Southland	Wanganui
1997	Canterbury	Northland	Marlborough
1998	Otago	Central Vikings	Mid Canterbury
1999	Auckland	Nelson Bays	East Coast
2000	Wellington	Bay of Plenty	East Coast
2001	Canterbury	Hawke's Bay	South Canterbury
2002	Auckland	Hawke's Bay	North Otago
2003	Auckland	Hawke's Bay	Wanganui
2004	Canterbury	Nelson Bays	Poverty Bay
2005	Auckland	Hawke's Bay	Wairarapa Bush

	Air New Zealand Cup	Meads Cup	Lochore Cup
2006	Waikato	Wairarapa Bush	Poverty Bay
2007	Auckland	North Otago	Poverty Bay
2008	Canterbury	Wanganui	Poverty Bay
2009	Canterbury	Wanganui	North Otago

	ITM Cup		
2010	Canterbury	North Otago	Wairarapa Bush

	ITM Premiership	ITM Championship	Meads Cup	Lochore Cup
2011	Canterbury	Hawke's Bay	Wanganui	Poverty Bay
2012	Canterbury	Counties Manukau	East Coast	Buller
2013	Canterbury	Tasman	Mid Canterbury	South Canterbury
2014	Taranaki	Manawatu	Mid Canterbury	Wanganui
2015	Canterbury	Hawke's Bay	Wanganui	King Country

	MITRE 10 CUP		MITRE 10 HEARTLAND CHAMPIONSHIP	
	Premiership	Championship	Meads Cup	Lochore Cup
2016	Canterbury	North Harbour	Wanganui	North Otago
2017	Canterbury	Wellington	Wanganui	Mid-Canterbury
2018	Auckland	Waikato	Thames Valley	Horowhenua Kapiti

MITRE 10 CUP

Auckland was crowned national champion for the 17th time, having to go to extra time against Canterbury in the Premiership final for their first title since 2007. The union announced entry would be free to Eden Park for the final, and attracted a crowd of over 20,000.

Taranaki was relegated to the Championship for 2019, while Counties Manukau survived with the same number of wins as Taranaki — two — by virtue of four more bonus points. In the eight years of the Premiership/Championship split, the two wins by Counties Manukau is the lowest number of games won by a team while still retaining their Premiership status.

Waikato returned to the Premiership at their first attempt by defeating Otago in the Championship final at Hamilton, just 13 days after having lost the Ranfurly Shield to Otago at Hamilton.

The 594 tries scored in the 76 matches played was a new record tally, edging past last year's 590 tries. The 436 conversions was also a new record, passing last year's 426 conversions. The tally of 139 penalty goals kicked is the second lowest tally ever recorded, only the 136 penalty goals kicked in the 1979 first division (55 matches) is lower. For the first time ever there were zero dropped goals kicked.

ROUND ROBIN

Each team played all six other teams in their division plus crossover matches against four teams in the other division for a total of ten matches.

	P	W	D	L	B[4]	B[7]	Pts	T	C	PG	DG	Total	T	C	PG	DG	Total
								\multicolumn{5}{c}{FOR}	\multicolumn{5}{c}{AGAINST}
PREMIERSHIP DIVISION																	
Auckland	10	9	0	1	9	1	46	50	36	7	0	343	30	19	7	0	209
Tasman	10	9	0	1	7	0	43	44	33	11	0	319	27	21	6	0	195
Canterbury	10	8	0	2	8	1	41	46[2]	35	7	0	325	28	21	10	0	212
Wellington	10	6	0	4	7	3	34	53	31	9	0	354	26	18	12	0	202
North Harbour	10	6	0	4	6	0	30	42[2]	29	15	0	317	40[1]	31	11	0	297
Counties Manukau	10	2	0	8	3	6	17	33[1]	21	3	0	218	39[2]	23	10	0	275
Taranaki	10	2	0	8	3	2	13	26	20	11	0	203	48	34	9	0	335
CHAMPIONSHIP DIVISION																	
Waikato	10	6	0	4	7	3	34	55[1]	44	1	0	368	35[1]	21	8	0	243
Otago	10	6	0	4	4	1	29	41	31	13	0	306	43[1]	32	7	0	302
Hawke's Bay	10	5	0	5	7	1	28	43	30	7	0	296	42	36	13	0	321
Northland	10	4	0	6	5	3	24	36	30	12	0	276	44[1]	30	8	0	306
Bay of Plenty	10	4	0	6	3	2	21	34[1]	24	11	0	253	40[1]	33	8	0	292
Manawatu	10	3	0	7	2	0	14	28	22	6	0	202	53	34	8	0	357
Southland	10	0	0	10	3	1	4	23	16	7	0	168	59	49	3	0	402
TOTALS								554	402	120	0	3948	554	402	120	0	3948

B[4] bonus points for four or more tries in a match. B[7] bonus points for loss by seven or fewer points.
[1] includes one penalty try (7 points) [2] includes two penalty tries (14 points)

PLAYOFF SUMMARY

In the semi-finals, the top qualifier was home to the fourth-placed qualifier and the second-placed qualifier was home to the third-place qualifier. In the final, the highest qualifier of the two participants played at home.

PREMIERSHIP

Semi-finals: Canterbury 21 (2t, c, 3pg) v Tasman 16 (t, c, 3pg), at Nelson
Auckland 38 (5t, 5c, pg) v Wellington 17 (2t, 2c, pg), at Auckland

Final: Auckland 40 aet (6t, 5c) v Canterbury 33 aet (2t, pt, 2c, 4pg), at Auckland

CHAMPIONSHIP

Semi-finals: Waikato 48 (6t, 6c, 2pg) v Northland 26 (4t, 3c), at Hamilton
Otago 20 (2t, 2c, 2pg) v Hawke's Bay 19 (3t, 2c), at Dunedin

Final: Waikato 36 (5t, 4c, pg) v Otago 13 (t, c, 2pg), at Hamilton

ALMANACK NEW ZEALAND MITRE 10 CUP XV

George Bridge
Canterbury

Melani Nanai   Quinn Tupaea   Sevu Reece
Auckland   *Waikato*   *Waikato*

T.J. Faiane
Auckland

Fletcher Smith
Waikato

Brad Weber
Hawke's Bay

Akira Ioane
Auckland

Dillon Hunt   Pari Pari Parkinson   Luke Romano   Dalton Papali'i
North Harbour   *Tasman*   *Canterbury*   *Auckland*

Tyrel Lomax   Andrew Makalio   Wyatt Crockett
Tasman   *Tasman*   *Tasman*

Reserves: Samisoni Taukei'aho (*Waikato*), Reuben O'Neill (*Taranaki*), Marcel Renata (*Auckland*), James Blackwell (*Wellington*), Gareth Evans (*Hawke's Bay*), Bryn Hall (*North Harbour*), Josh Ioane (*Otago*), Will Jordan (*Tasman*).

RECORDS

BY THE TEAMS

BEST PERFORMANCES 2018

RECORD 1976–2018

First Division 1976–2005, Air New Zealand Cup 2006–2009, ITM Cup 2010–2015, Mitre 10 Cup 2016-

In a Season

Most points	450	Waikato	521	Otago, 1998
Most tries	66	Waikato	74	Wellington, 2017
Most conversions	54	Waikato	57	Canterbury, 2017
Most penalty goals	17	Otago	45	Otago, 2012
Most dropped goals	0		12	Bay of Plenty, 1985

In a Match

Highest Score	71	Waikato v Northland, 6 Oct	97	Auckland v King Country, 1993
Biggest winning margin	48	Auckland v Southland (56–8)	94	Auckland v King Country, 1993 (97–3)
Most tries	11	Waikato v Northland, 6 Oct	15	Auckland v King Country, 1993
Most conversions	8	Auckland v Southland	12	Canterbury v Southland, 2012
Most penalty goals	4	Canterbury v Auckland, f	9	Taranaki v Bay of Plenty, 2011
Most dropped goals	0		4	Bay of Plenty v Waikato, 1985

BY THE PLAYERS

BEST PERFORMANCES 2018

RECORD 1976–2018
First Division 1976–2005, Air New Zealand Cup 2006–2009, ITM Cup 2010–2015, Mitre 10 Cup 2016-

In a Season

Most points	130	F.H. Smith (*Waikato*)	196	T.E. Brown (*Otago*), 1998
Most tries	14	S.L. Reece (*Waikato*)	15	T.J. Wright (*Auckland*), 1984
				B.J. Laney (*Otago*), 1998

In a Match

Most points	25	J.R. Ioane (*Otago*) v Bay of Plenty	37	B.A. Blair (*Canterbury*) v Counties Manukau, 1999
Most tries	4	T. Li (*North Harbour*) v Taranaki	5	T.J. Wright (*Auckland*) v Manawatu, 1984
		S.L. Reece (*Waikato*) v Northland, sf		W.R. Gordon (*Waikato*) v Southland, 1990
				C.J. Spencer (*Auckland*) v Otago, 1996
				M.P. Robinson (*Taranaki*) v Southland, 1997
				J. Maddock (*Canterbury*) v North Harbour, 2002
				S.W. Sivivatu (*Waikato*) v Auckland, 2004
				T. Li (*North Harbour*) v Taranaki, 2017
Most conversions	7	F.H. Smith (*Waikato*) v Bay of Plenty	12	T.J. Taylor (*Canterbury*) v Southland, 2012
		B.D. Cameron (*Canterbury*) v Hawke's Bay		
		F.H. Smith (*Waikato*) v Northland, 6 Oct		
Most penalty goals	4	B.D. Cameron (*Canterbury*) v Auckland, f	9	B.J. Barrett (*Taranaki*) v Bay of Plenty, 2011
Most dropped goals	0		4	R.J. Preston (*Bay of Plenty*) v Waikato, 1985

Leading point-scorers in the Mitre 10 Cup:

F.H. Smith	*Waikato*	130
B.D. Cameron	*Canterbury*	121
M.J. Hunt	*Tasman*	116
J.R. Ioane	*Otago*	116
H.R.J. Plummer	*Auckland*	113
B.E.C. Gatland	*North Harbour*	109
J.M. Debreczeni	*Northland*	100

Leading Try scorers in the Mitre 10 Cup:

S.L. Reece	*Waikato*	14
T. Li	*North Harbour*	10
W.T. Jordan	*Tasman*	9
S.T.M. Rayasi	*Auckland*	9
S.F. Taukei'aho	*Waikato*	9

MITRE 10 HEARTLAND CHAMPIONSHIP

Before the 13th edition of the Heartland Championship began, there were three provinces that had not won either the Meads Cup or Lochore Cup. Two of those three — Thames Valley and Horowhenua Kapiti — were winners for the first time, with Thames Valley becoming Heartland Champion and Meads Cup winner, and Horowhenua Kapiti winning the Lochore Cup. This now leaves just West Coast as the only province not to have won either Cup.

Not only did Thames Valley win one of the trophies for the first time, they and King Country both made the top four for the first time to contest the Meads Cup. All 12 unions have now done so.

The 448 tries scored and 309 conversions kicked were the most ever, surpassing the 2016 records of 437 tries and 283 conversions. For the first time ever there were no dropped goals scored.

ROUND ROBIN SUMMARY

	P	W	D	L	B^4	B^8	Pts	T	C	PG	DG	Total	T	C	PG	DG	Total
									FOR					AGAINST			
Wanganui	8	8	0	0	7	0	39	47[1]	35	8	0	331	16[1]	11	3	0	113
South Canterbury	8	6	0	2	7	1	32	53	35	2	0	341	21	11	8	0	151
King Country	8	6	0	2	6	1	31	43	29	10	0	303	33	21	8	0	231
Thames Valley	8	5	0	3	7	1	28	40[1]	21	10	0	274	30[1]	21	13	0	233
Horowhenua Kapiti	8	4	0	4	6	2	24	32	24	15	0	253	36	22	9	0	251
Wairarapa Bush	8	4	0	4	4	1	21	29[1]	19	9	0	212	28	17	7	0	195
North Otago	8	4	0	4	2	2	20	29	22	8	0	213	30	19	7	0	209
Mid Canterbury	8	3	0	5	5	2	19	33[1]	23	4	0	225	34	21	7	0	233
West Coast *	8	4	0	4	5	1	16	35[1]	21	3	0	228	34	25	7	0	241
Buller	8	2	0	6	5	3	16	31	22	8	0	223	41	30	8	0	289
Poverty Bay	8	2	0	6	6	2	16	27	17	8	0	193	44[2]	30	6	0	302
East Coast	8	0	0	8	1	1	2	15[1]	8	2	0	99	67[2]	48	4	0	447
TOTALS								414	276	87	0	2895	414	276	87	0	2895

B^4 bonus point for scoring four or more tries in a match.
[1] includes one penalty try (7 points)
* deducted six points for fielding an ineligible player

B^8 bonus point for a loss by seven points or less.
[2] includes two penalty tries (14 points)

West Coast, Buller and Poverty Bay all finished on 16 points. The first tiebreak rule used when three or more teams finish on the same number of points is ranking by points differential which was West Coast (-13), Buller (-66) and Poverty Bay (-109).

PLAYOFF SUMMARY

The top four teams played off for the Meads Cup, and the teams finishing fifth to eighth played off for the Lochore Cup. In the semi-finals, the top qualifier was home to the fourth-placed qualifier and the second-placed qualifier was home to the third-place qualifier. In the final, the highest qualifier of the two participants played at home..

MEADS CUP (1st–4th)

Semi-finals: Thames Valley 17 (2t, 2c, pg) v Wanganui 7 (t, c), at Wanganui
South Canterbury 58 (7t, 7c, 3pg) v King Country 21 (3t, 3c), at Timaru

Final: Thames Valley 17 (2t, 2c, pg) v South Canterbury 12 (2t, c), at Timaru

LOCHORE CUP (5th–8th)

Semi-finals: Wairarapa Bush 30 (3t, 3c, 3pg) v North Otago 21 (3t, 3c), at Masterton
Horowhenua Kapiti 34 (4t, 4c, 2pg) v Mid Canterbury 24 (3t, 3c, pg), at Levin

Final: Horowhenua Kapiti 26 (2t, 2c, 4pg) v Wairarapa Bush 23 (2t, 2c, 3pg), at Levin

HEARTLAND CHAMPIONSHIP RECORDS

BY THE TEAMS

	BEST PERFORMANCE 2018		RECORD 2006–2018	
In a Season				
Most points	411	South Canterbury	440	Wanganui, 2016
Most tries	62	South Canterbury	63	Wanganui, 2008
Most conversions	43	South Canterbury	45	Wanganui, 2008
Most penalty goals	21	Horowhenua Kapiti	30	Wairarapa Bush, 2012
Most dropped goals	0		2	on ten occasions (*eight teams*)
In a Match				
Most points	100	South Centerbury v Ngati Porou East Coast	116	North Otago v East Coast, 2010
Biggest winning margin	93	South Centerbury v Ngati Porou East Coast (*100-7*)	113	North Otago v East Coast, 2010 (*116–3*)
Most tries	16	South Centerbury v Ngati Porou East Coast	17	North Otago v East Coast, 2010
Most conversions	10	South Centerbury v Ngati Porou East Coast	14	North Otago v East Coast, 2010
Most penalty goals	5	Horowhenua Kapiti v Thames Valley	7	Thames Valley v Mid Canterbury, 2009
				Thames Valley v East Coast, 2011
				Poverty Bay v Buller, 2013
Most dropped goals	0		1	54 occasions

BY THE PLAYERS

	BEST PERFORMANCE 2018	RECORD 2006–2018
In a Season		
Most points	118 J.S. So'oialo (*Horowhenua Kapiti*)	147 J.J. Lash (*Buller*), 2017
Most tries	9 T.B. Matoramusha (*Mid Canterbury*) A.M. Thrupp (*King Country*) K.V. Leatigaga (*South Canterbury*)	14 P. Fetuai (*Wanganui*), 2006
In a Match		
Most points	28 W.A. Wright (*South Canterbury*) v King Country	35 S.C. Leighton (*Poverty Bay*) v Thames Valley, 2007
Most tries	5 S. Malatai (*Wairarapa Bush*) v Buller	5 L.M. Herden (*North Otago*) v East Coast, 2010
Most conversions	8 G.M. Walters (*Wairarapa Bush*) v Buller E.H. Reihana (*King Country*) v Poverty Bay	9 R.F. Aloe (*Horowhenua Kapiti*) v East Coast, 2008 B. Patston (*North Otago*) v East Coast, 2010
Most penalty goals	5 J.S. So'oialo (*Horowhenua Kapiti*) v Thames Valley	7 D.P. Harrison (*Thames Valley*) v Mid Canterbury, 2009; J.R. Reynolds (*Thames Valley*) v East Coast, 2011 S.P. Parkes (*Poverty Bay*) v Buller, 2013
Most dropped goals	0	1 on 54 occasions (*38 players*)

Leading Points-scorers in the Championship:

J.S. So'oialo	*Horowhenua Kapiti*	118
C.D. Clare	*Wanganui*	117
W.A. Wright	*South Canterbury*	104
E.H. Reihana	*King Country*	99
R. Broughton	*Thames Valley*	91

Leading Try scorers in the Championship:

T.B. Matoramusha	*Mid Canterbury*	9
A.M. Thrupp	*King Country*	9
K.V. Leatigaga	*South Canterbury*	9
D.J. Fransen	*Mid Canterbury*	7
S.T. Sauqaqa	*South Canterbury*	7
W.A. Wright	*South Canterbury*	7
S. Malatai	*Wairarapa Bush*	7

AUCKLAND

2018 Status: Mitre 10 Cup Premiership
Founded 1883. Original member 1892
President: B.M. (Bruce) Gemmell
Chairman: S.M. (Stuart) Mather
Chief executive officer: J.M. (Jarrod) Bear
Coach: Alama Ieremia
Assistant coaches: Sir G.W. (Graham) Henry, Tai Lavea, F.I. (Filo) Tiatia
Main ground: Eden Park, Auckland
Capacity: 47,000
Colours: Blue and white

RECORDS

Most appearances	196	Snow White, 1949–63
Most points	2746	Grant Fox, 1982–93
Most tries	112	Terry Wright, 1984–93
Most points in a season	322	Grant Fox, 1990
Most tries in a season	19	Terry Wright, 1984
Most conversions in a season	77	Grant Fox, 1990
Most penalty goals in a season	48	Grant Fox, 1989, 1990
Most dropped goals in a season	8	Grant Fox, 1990
Most points in a match	43	Adrian Cashmore v Mid Canterbury, 1995
Most tries in a match	8	John Kirwan v North Otago, 1993
Most conversions in a match	12	Grant Fox v Marlborough, 1984
		Brett Craies v Horowhenua, 1986
		Grant Fox v Nelson Bays, 1991
		Lachie Munro v North Otago, 2008
Most penalty goals in a match	7	Grant Fox v Canterbury, 1990
		Grant Fox v Waikato, 1992
Highest team score	139	v North Otago, 1993
Record victory (points ahead)	134	139–5 v North Otago, 1993
Highest score conceded	59	v Waikato, 2004
Record defeat (points behind)	48	11–59 v Waikato, 2004

New coaching team, new squad, new attitude.

There was a fresh feel to Auckland rugby's work in 2018, but the final outcome of a Premiership crown — its 17th provincial title in all, and first since 2007 — must have exceeded even the most ardent fan's expectations. There was some doubt as to whether the coaching staff of Alama Ieremia, Filo Tiatia, Tai Lavea, Sir Graham Henry and Mike Casey had the players from which to launch Auckland's resurgence. Those fears were eased with a consistent selection policy, especially in the backline, and some astute signings who came good.

Despite not seeing any of Ofa Tu'ungafasi, again on All Blacks duty, only 56 minutes of Patrick Tuipulotu, in a cameo hat-trick display, and designated captain Blake Gibson for just the first four games before injury, the coaches pulled the right strings for most of the time. A whole raft of players had moved on, or were moved on. Dan Bowden had retired, there was a pre-season hooking crisis, and Vince Aso and Scott Scrafton missed the entire campaign with injury. Loose forwards Sione Havili (Tasman) and Samuel Slade (Manawatu) were loaned out. In all, 27 of the 45 players used in 2017 did not appear in 2018.

Auckland eased into its work, solid but unspectacular victories over Counties Manukau — for the Dan Bryant Memorial Trophy — and Northland, leading into three convincing defeats of Waikato — for the Stan Thomas Memorial Trophy — Tasman and Canterbury. The latter two wins saw the competition sit up and take notice, such was Auckland's dominance. A flat patch followed, escaping from New Plymouth with the points and then a surprise loss on Eden Park to Otago, a tight result in the capital, before a rousing finish to the season, dispatching Southland and North Harbour — for the Battle of the Bridge — and then comfortably accounting for Wellington in the semi-final. Auckland Rugby and Eden Park Trust threw the gates open for the final against Canterbury, which saw more than 20,000 create a tremendous atmosphere. What followed was a 100-minute epic, Auckland showing resilience and impact off the bench to close it out 40–33 in extra time, the second victory in six weeks over the defending champs.

Auckland's pre-eminence throughout the season was built on an organised defence, set-piece accuracy, physicality at the breakdown and an ability to strike when needed. Jordan Trainor scored five tries from fullback but looked a far different, more confident, player from the uncertain figure of 2017. Melani Nanai also scored five tries and set up several others with his elusive running, while on the other wing Salesi Rayasi, unused in 2017, ran in nine tries and played his way into a Hurricanes contract with his searing pace and finishing ability. He kept Caleb Clarke on ice, the 19-year-old yet to make a telling impact at provincial level. Tumua Manu, occasionally used as a wing last season, was so effective in midfield he scored seven tries, combined nicely with captain TJ Faiane, and won a Chiefs contract. Faiane himself is fit to rank as the country's most improved player, having his best Auckland campaign to date, scoring six tries and showing his strong technique in the collisions. His heads-up play in the final to set up Manu was a key moment in Auckland's comeback.

First-five Harry Plummer built on the promise of 2018, appearing in all 12 games. His kicking off the tee was not always on song, but he landed several decisive goals in the latter part of the season and racked up 113 points. Halfback Jonathan Ruru acted like a fourth loose forward and mostly took the right option. Leon Fukofuka was consigned to a support role, but he did score the winning try in the final. Akira Ioane was consistently good, powering off the scrum base, scoring seven tries, and especially dominant in the playoffs. His omission from the All Blacks was strange.

So well did Dalton Papali'i play in his nine games that he was selected for the All Blacks. He made a competition-high 169 tackles, missing just six, but also showed versatility and some softer touches. Canadian international Evan Olmstead was probably the best signing. He made his presence felt at the breakdown and in the lineouts and was most unlucky to miss a Super Rugby deal. Before he was injured, lock Jack Whetton was in good form and his reward was a Highlanders contract. Michael Fatialofa returned later from injury and did his job. Former Manu Samoa international Fa'atiga Lemalu toiled away. Marcel Renata and Sam Prattley used their experience to good effect in the front row, while former Brumbies hooker Robbie Abel wore the No. 2 jersey with aplomb. He scored a brace from lineout drives against Waikato. Taleni Seu played well in the final two games after a long injury layoff, while Mike Sosene, Waimana Riedlinger-Kapa, Adrian Choat, Ezekiel Lindenmuth and Hoskins Sotutu all showed promise.

Jacob Umaga was an interesting newcomer from England. The son of former Manu Samoa fullback Mike Umaga, he mostly played off the bench at either first five or fullback, though his best outing was ironically in the defeat to Otago.

Higher honours went to:
New Zealand:	R. Ioane, D. Papali'i, P. Tuipulotu, O. Tu'ungafasi
New Zealand Maori:	R. Abel, A. Ioane, M. Renata, J. Ruru
New Zealand Under 20:	J. Akau'ola-Laula, C. Clarke, R. Cobb, H. Plummer, W. Riedlinger-Kapa, H. Sotutu, T. Tele'a
New Zealand Sevens:	C. Clarke, R. Khan, J. Ravouvou, S. Rayasi

AUCKLAND REPRESENTATIVES 2018

	Club	Games for Union	Points for Union
Robert Abel	College Rifles	10	15
Jarred Adams	Suburbs	9	0
Adrian Choat	Waitemata	3	5
Caleb Clarke	Suburbs	10	10
Lyndon Dunshea	University	2	0
Tinoai "TJ" Faiane	Pakuranga	28	35
Michael Fatialofa	Ponsonby	24	5
Marco Fepulea'i	Ponsonby	11	5
Leon Fukofuka	Marist	27	5
Blake Gibson	Ponsonby	25	15
Akira Ioane	Ponsonby	39	55
Daniel Kirkpatrick	University	2	6
Taniela Koroi	Marist	2	0
Jamie Lane	Ponsonby	5	0
Fa'atiga Lemalu	Papatoetoe	11	10
Desma Liaina	Eden	3	5
Ezekiel Lindenmuth	Suburbs	5	0
Tumua Manu	College Rifles	16	35
Melani Nanai	Manukau Rovers	35	60
Evan Olmstead	Suburbs	12	0
Dalton Papali'i	Pakuranga	13	5
Harry Plummer	Grammar TEC	15	117
Sam Prattley	Pakuranga	53	5
Joseva Ravouvou	College Rifles	10	20
Salese Rayasi	Marist	11	45
Marcel Renata	University	32	10
Waimana Riedlinger-Kapa	Ponsonby	3	0
Jonathan Ruru	University	12	15
Leif Schwenke	Suburbs	1	0
Taleni Seu	Grammar TEC	23	25
Michael Sosene-Feagai	Mt Wellington	12	15
Hoskins Sotutu	Marist	10	0
Taniela Tele'a	Marist	4	0
Jordan Trainor	Ponsonby	19	37
Patrick Tuipulotu	Ponsonby	22	40
Jacob Umaga	Eden	9	2
Jack Whetton	Grammar TEC	27	10

INDIVIDUAL SCORING

	Tries	Con	PG	DG	Points
Plummer	1	42	8	–	113
Rayasi	9	–	–	–	45
Manu	7	–	–	–	35
Ioane	6	–	–	–	30
Faiane	6	–	–	–	30
Nanai	5	–	–	–	25
Trainor	5	–	–	–	25
Abel	3	–	–	–	15
Tuipulotu	3				15
Ruru	3	–	–	–	15
Sosene-Feagai	3	–	–	–	15
Femalu	2	–	–	–	10
Clarke	2	–	–	–	10
Kirkpatrick	–	3	–	–	6
Gibson	1	–	–	–	5
Papali'i	1	–	–	–	5
Liaina	1	–	–	–	5
Choat	1	–	–	–	5
Fepulea'i	1	–	–	–	5
Fukofuka	1	–	–	–	5
Umaga	–	1	–	–	2
Totals	**61**	**46**	**8**	**0**	**421**
Opposition scored	35*	23	12	0	259

* includes one penalty try (7 points)

AUCKLAND 2018

Player	Counties Manukau	Northland	Waikato	Tasman	Canterbury	Taranaki	Otago	Wellington	Southland	North Harbour	Wellington	Canterbury	TOTALS
J.V. Trainor	15	15	15	15	15	15	–	s	15	15	15	15	11
J.I.F. Umaga	s	s	s	s	s	–	15	15	–	s	s	–	9
M.H. Nanai	14	14	14	14	14	14	–	14	14	14	14	14	11
S.T.M. Rayasi	11	11	11	11	–	11	11	11	11	11	11	11	11
C.D. Clarke	–	s	s	–	–	–	14	–	s	s	s	s	7
J. Ravouvou	–	–	–	–	11	–	s	–	–	–	–	–	2
T.P. Manu	13	13	13	13	13	13	13	13	13	13	13	13	12
T. Faiane	12	12	12	12	12	12	–	12	12	12	12	12	11
T.R. Tele'a	–	–	–	–	s	s	s	12	–	–	–	–	4
H.R.J. Plummer	10	10	10	10	10	10	10	10	10	10	10	10	12
D.J.P. Kirkpatrick	s	–	–	–	–	–	–	–	s	–	–	–	2
L.P.C. Fukofuka	9	9	9	s	s	s	–	9	–	–	–	s	8
J.L. Ruru	s	s	s	9	9	9	9	s	9	9	9	9	12
D. Lianina	–	–	–	–	–	–	–	–	s	s	s	–	3
A.L. Ioane	8	8	8	8	8	8	8	8	s	8	8	8	12
B.T. Gibson (capt)	7	7	7	7	–	–	–	–	–	–	–	–	4
D.R. Papali'i	6	6	6	s	7	7	7	7	–	6	–	–	9
E.D. Olmstead	s	s	s	6	6	6	4	6	s	5	6	6	12
H. Sotutu	s	s	s	–	s	s	6	–	8	s	s	s	10
W. Riedlinger-Kapa	–	–	–	–	–	–	s	–	6	6	–	–	3
A.J. Choat	–	–	–	–	–	–	–	–	7	–	7	7	3
J.C. Whetton	5	5	5	5	5	5	5	–	–	–	–	–	7
J.H. Lane	4	–	–	–	s	–	–	s	–	–	–	–	3
F. Lemalu	–	4	4	s	4	4	s	4	4	4	4	4	11
P.T. Tuipulotu	–	–	–	4	–	–	–	–	–	–	–	–	1
L.J. Dunshea	–	–	–	–	–	s	–	–	–	–	–	–	1
M.J. Fatialofa	–	–	–	–	–	–	4	5	s	5	5	5	5
T.J.A. Seu	–	–	–	–	–	–	–	–	–	–	s	s	2
M.L. Fepulea'i	3	–	s	s	s	–	s	s	3	s	s	s	10
J.J. Adams	1	s	s	–	–	s	–	–	s	s	s	s	9
S.M.J. Prattley	s	1	1	1	1	–	1	1	–	1	1	1	10
T.T. Koroi	s	s	–	–	–	–	–	–	–	–	–	–	2
M.T. Renata	–	3	3	3	3	3	3	s	3	3	3	3	11
E. Lindenmuth	–	–	–	–	s	1	s	s	1	–	–	–	5
M.A. Sosene-Feagai	2	s	s	s	s	s	2	s	2	s	s	s	12
L. Schwenke	s	–	–	–	–	–	–	–	–	–	–	–	1
R.J. Abel	–	2	2	2	2	2	s	2	–	2	2	2	10

S.M.J. Prattley captained v Otago; T. Faiane captained the other seven matches B.T. Gibson did not appear in.

AUCKLAND TEAM RECORD, 2018

Played 12　　Won 11　　Lost 1　　Points for 421　　Points against 259

Date	Opponent	Location	Score	Tries	Con	PG	DG	Referee
August 18	Counties Manukau (P)	Auckland	23–19	Rayasi, Gibson, Nanai	Plummer	Plummer (2)		G.W. Jackson
August 26	Northland (P/C)	Whangarei	28–12	Nanai (2), Plummer, Rayasi	Plummer (4)			R.P. Kelly
August 30	Waikato (P/C)	Auckland	35–17	Abel (2), Trainor (2), Rayasi	Plummer, Umaga	Plummer (2)		J.D. Munro
September 7	Tasman (P)	Auckland	36–10	Tuipulotu (3), Nanai, Ioane	Plummer (4)	Plummer		N.E.R. Hogan
September 16	Canterbury (P)	Christchurch	34–29	Faiane (3), Ruru, Manu	Plummer (3)	Plummer		B.D. O'Keeffe
September 22	Taranaki (P)	New Plymouth	31–30	Rayasi (2), Ioane, Manu, Ruru	Plummer (3)			G.W. Jackson
September 28	Otago (P/C)	Auckland	26–31	Manu (2), Papali'i, Ioane	Plummer (3)			M.I. Fraser
October 7	Wellington (P)	Wellington	29–24	Manu, Faiane, Rayasi, Trainor	Plummer (3)	Plummer		N.P. Briant
October 10	Southland (P/C)	Invercargill	56–8	Sosene-Feagai (2), Rayasi, Lemalu, Manu, Clarke, Laiina, Choat	Plummer (5), Kirkpatrick (3)			J.J. Doleman
October 14	North Harbour (P)	Auckland	45–29	Faiane (2), Rayasi (2), Ruru, Abel, Trainor	Plummer (5)			C.J. Stone
October 20	Wellington (P semi-final)	Auckland	38–17	Ioane (2), Nanai, Lemalu, Fepulea'i	Plummer (5)	Plummer		B.E. Pickerill
October 27	Canterbury (P final)	Auckland	40–33 aet	Manu, Ioane, Trainor, Clarke, Sosene-Feagai, Fukofuka	Plummer (5)			G.W. Jackson

aet *after extra time*

BAY OF PLENTY

2018 Status: Mitre 10 Cup Championship
Founded 1911. Affiliated 1911
President: P.J. (Phil) Barnett
Chairman: P.L. (Paul) Owen
Chief executive officer: M.W. (Mike) Rogers
Coach: C.R. (Clayton) McMillan
Assistant coaches: R.P. (Rodney) Gibbs, D.W. (David) Hill, D.T. (Damian) Karauna
Main ground: Rotorua International Stadium (since 2016)
Capacity: 20,000
Colours: Blue and gold.

RECORDS

Most appearances	161	Greg Rowlands, 1969–82
Most points	1008	Greg Rowlands, 1969–82
Most tries	62	Graeme Moore, 1967–80
Most points in a season	245	Andrew Miller, 1996
Most tries in a season	14	Damon Kaui, 1995
Most conversions in a season	53	Andrew Miller, 1996
Most penalty goals in a season	48	Eion Crossan, 1991
Most dropped goals in a season	13	Ron Preston, 1985
Most points in a match	36	Adrian Cashmore v Thames Valley, 1993
Most tries in a match	5	Ian Backhouse v North Otago, 1965
		Damon Kaui v Thames Valley, 1995
Most conversions in a match	9	Eion Crossan v Poverty Bay, 1991
Most penalty goals in a match	6	Ron Preston v Poverty Bay, 1982
		Eion Crossan v North Harbour, 1990
		Eion Crossan v Fiji President's XV, 1991
		Eion Crossan v Western Samoa, 1991
		Erin Cossey v Hawke's Bay, 1994
		Andrew Miller v Counties, 1995
		Andrew Miller v King Country, 1996
		Glen Jackson v Northland, 2001
		Glen Jackson v Otago, 2004
		Mike Delany v Waikato, 2009
Highest team score	88	v East Coast, 1972
Record victory (points ahead)	79	88–9 v East Coast, 1972
		82–3 v Thames Valley, 1995
Highest score conceded	93	v New Zealand XV, 1993
Record defeat (points behind)	88	5–93 v New Zealand XV, 1993

Bay of Plenty started their season with a solid win over Taranaki. This was followed with a victory over Counties Manukau, but in hindsight this game was a sign of things to come. For the first 40 minutes Bay of Plenty dined on 90 per cent possession and territory and went into halftime with just ten points in the bank. They eventually won by a small margin, but the signs were there that scoring tries and securing bonus points may be on the difficult side.

Six consecutive defeats then followed which included a one-point loss in the final minute to Hawke's Bay, being soundly beaten by Ranfurly Shield holders Waikato in the worst effort of the season, and a conversion attempt from in front hitting the post and bouncing away for a two-point loss to Manawatu instead of a draw.

The final defeat in the run was to Otago when the Bay finally found some attacking ability and for the first time were able to score more than three tries in a game. But in their exuberance to mount attack after attack they gave away two intercept tries and also one from spilled possession, all 90 metres from their own tryline. Hard to win a game when 21 points are gifted to the opposition. The last two games against Southland and Northland were won, albeit by narrow margins, for an overall season of four games won and six lost which was rather deflating after the success of 2017.

Chase Tiatia was again in good form at fullback, his experience in guiding the new players out wide being of immense value. Kaleb Trask had a promising first season at this level and will benefit greatly from it. He ended the year with three games at first five-eighth.

Of the wings Fa'asiu Fuatai played every game and scored two tries to highlight the inability of the midfielders to create opportunities or distribute the ball. Bailey Simonsson impressed but also lacked the opportunities as the ball seldom came his way. Mathew Garland was also a useful wing, but injury ended his season.

After a broken jaw curtailed his 2017 season, Liam Steel played every game this year, but struggled with creating chances for his wingers, often being caught in possession, taking the wrong options or his hands letting him down. Terrence Hepetema was solid but not as dominant as the previous year. Mike Delany was again the director of proceedings at first five-eighth and performed well until a shoulder injury against North Harbour ended his season, and he later announced his retirement. Jason Robertson also succumbed to injury when breaking a leg against Manawatu.

Richard Judd was at the top of his game at halfback and Luke Campbell, as always, was more than able backup, starting the last three games when Judd picked up a niggling injury.

Number eight Hoani Matenga's experience was a great asset in his return to the Bay. On the flanks Mitch Karpik was impressive, especially trying to catch runaway wingers against Otago. Hugh Blake was useful until injury ended his season and Tyler Ardron, who took over the captain's role during the season, was a tireless leader on attack and defence. Tanerau Latimer returned to the team after an absence of six years overseas, his experience proving invaluable. However, injury curtailed his season and was another to announce his retirement at season's end.

Aaron Carroll, Kane Le'aupepe and Baden Wardlaw were the most used locks. All three gave a good account of themselves at this level and can be well pleased with their efforts. Zane Kapeli and Nick Ross were called into the team when injuries arose, with Kapeli making the most of his chances after a very late call-up before the Taranaki game.

Props Ross Geldenhuys, Jeff Thwaites, James Lay and Solomona Sakalia were the workhorses of the front row and provided a very stable platform for the scrum. Sakalia's season ended early when he snapped his Achilles tendon against Manawatu. Hooker and captain Liam Polwart was injured late in the opening game against Taranaki which ended his season. Angus McDonald, on the back of a good club season, made the most of his chances and Tom Crozier was brought in on loan to become the starting hooker. Valentine Meachen made a late start due to injury but managed three appearances off the bench at the end of the season.

New arrivals in 2018 were Trael Joass (Tasman), Ross Geldenhuys (Natal Sharks), Tom Crozier (on loan from Canterbury and Manawatu rep 2017) with Fa'asiu Fuatai, Tanerau Latimer and Hoani Matenga all back from overseas, while from the club ranks came a number of players with previous first-class experience in Reece Macdonald (loaned to King Country 2017), Aaron Carroll (loaned to Thames Valley 2017) Kane Le'aupepe (Wellington 2016) Nick Ross (Waikato 2014), Zane Kapeli (Waikato 2015), Valentine Meachen (Wellington 2016) and Jason Robertson (Waikato 2016).

A feature was the introduction during the year of Kaleb Trask, Cole Forbes, Emoni Narawa and Lalomilo Lalomilo from the successful national champion Under 19 team, although Trask was in the original Steamers' squad.

Of last year's team Aidan Ross and Lalakai Foketi were unavailable due to injury, James O'Reilly and Henry Stowers had returned to Wellington, Jesse Parete had transferred back to Taranaki, Te Aihe Toma was loaned to Counties Manukau and Troy Callander, Tom Franklin, Monty Ioane and Jordan Lay had all taken contracts overseas while Joe Webber had committed to the NZ Sevens programme.

Higher honours went to:
New Zealand: S. Cane, N. Harris
New Zealand Maori: M. Karpik, H. Matanga
New Zealand Under 20: T. Mafileo, K. Trask
New Zealand Sevens: S. Curry, T. Joass (from August), N. McGarvey-Black, L. Masirewa, B. Simonsson, T. Stanaway, R. Ware, J. Webber

BAY OF PLENTY REPRESENTATIVES 2018

	Club	Games for Union	Points for Union		Club	Games for Union	Points for Union
Tyler Ardron	Papamoa	15	10	Tanerau Latimer	Rangiuru	84	27
Hugh Blake	Te Puke Sports	24	20	James Lay	Whakarewarewa	20	10
Luke Campbell	Te Puke Sports	26	38	Kane Leaupepe	Te Puke Sports	8	15
Aaron Carroll	Mt Maunganui	9	15	Reece Macdonald	Te Puna	1	2
Tom Crozier	Sumner [1]	8	10	Hoani Matenga	Rangiuru	9	0
Josh Davey	Mt Maunganui	3	0	Angus McDonald	Te Puna	6	0
Mike Delany	Mt Maunganui	77	640	Valentine Meachen	Greerton Marist	3	0
Cole Forbes	Te Puke Sports	1	0	Emoni Narawa	Tauranga Sports	1	5
Fa'asiu Fuatai	Rangataua	10	10	Liam Polwart	Greerton Marist	15	5
Mathew Garland	Whakarewarewa	8	0	Jason Robertson	Te Puke Sports	5	7
Ross Geldenhuys	[2]	10	0	Nick Ross	Mt Maunganui	2	0
Terrence Hepetema	Te Puna	28	55	Solomona Sakalia	Mt Maunganui	40	10
Trael Joass	Mt Maunganui	7	0	Bailey Simonsson	Greerton Marist	6	15
Richard Judd	Mt Maunganui	17	20	Liam Steel	Mt Maunganui	14	5
Zane Kapeli	Te Puna	6	0	Isaac Te Aute	Rangiuru	20	5
Mitchell Karpik	Rangataua	16	5	Jeff Thwaites	Te Puna	31	5
Joe Key	Greerton Marist	1	0	Chase Tiatia	Rangataua	35	50
Aileone "AJ" Lafaele-Mua	Tauranga Sports	5	0	Kaleb Trask	Tauranga Sports	7	28
Lalomilo Lalomilo	Te Puke Sports	1	0	Baden Wardlaw	Rotoiti	8	0

[1] *Canterbury RU* [2] *arrived from overseas*

INDIVIDUAL SCORING

	Tries	Con	PG	DG	Points
Delany	2	10	9	–	57
Trask	1	10	1	–	28
Tiatia	4	–	–	–	20
Leaupepe	3	–	–	–	15
Carroll	3	–	–	–	15
Judd	3	–	–	–	15
Simonsson	3	–	–	–	15
Lay	2	–	–	–	10
Crozier	2	–	–	–	10
Fuatai	2	–	–	–	10
Robertson	–	2	1	–	7
Campbell	1	1	–	–	7
Penalty try	1	–	–	–	7
Polwart	1	–	–	–	5
Ardron	1	–	–	–	5
Hepetema	1	–	–	–	5
Blake	1	–	–	–	5
Thwaites	1	–	–	–	5
Steel	1	–	–	–	5
Narawa	1	–	–	–	5
Macdonald	–	1	–	–	2
Totals	**34**	**24**	**11**	**0**	**253**
Opposition scored	40*	33	8	0	292

* includes one penalty try (7 points)

BAY OF PLENTY 2018

	Taranaki	Counties Manukau	Canterbury	Hawke's Bay	North Harbour	Waikato	Manawatu	Otago	Southland	Northland	TOTALS
C.J. Tiatia	15	15	11	15	15	–	s	15	15	15	9
K.R. Trask	s	–	15	–	–	15	15	10	10	10	7
F. Fuatai	14	14	14	14	14	s	11	11	11	11	10
M.D. Garland	11	11	–	11	–	11	12	–	–	–	5
B.G. Simonsson	–	–	s	–	s	14	14	14	14	–	6
E.R. Narawa	–	–	–	–	–	–	–	–	–	14	1
L.T. Steel	13	13	s	13	11	13	13	13	13	13	10
T.R. Joass	s	s	13	s	13	–	–	–	s	s	7
L. Lalomilo	–	–	–	–	–	–	–	s	–	–	1
T.R.T. Hepetema	12	12	12	12	12	12	–	12	12	12	9
M.P. Delany	10	10	10	10	10	–	–	–	–	–	5
J.R. Robertson	–	s	–	s	s	10	10	–	–	–	5
R.S. Macdonald	–	–	–	–	–	–	–	s	–	–	1
C.D. Forbes	–	–	–	–	–	–	–	–	–	s	1
R.P. Judd	9	9	9	9	–	9	9	s	–	–	7
L.A. Campbell	s	s	s	s	9	s	s	9	9	9	10
I.N. Te Aute	–	–	–	–	s	–	–	–	s	s	3
H.M. Matenga	8	8	8	8	8	–	8	8	8	8	9
A. Lafaele Mua	s	–	s	–	–	s	s	–	–	–	4
M.R. Karpik	7	7	7	7	7	s	/	/	/	7	10
H.P. Blake	6	–	–	s	s	7	–	–	–	–	4
Z.R. Kapeli	s	s	–	–	–	6	s	–	–	s	6
T.J. Ardron	–	6	4	–	6	8	6	6	6	6	8
T.D. Latimer	–	s	6	6	s	–	–	–	s	–	5
A.P. Carroll	5	5	s	s	5	s	s	s	s	s	9
K.T.V. Leaupepe	4	4	–	4	–	5	5	5	5	4	8
B.M. Wardlaw	–	–	5	5	–	s	4	4	4	5	7
N.J. Ross	–	–	–	–	4	4	–	–	–	–	2
J.R. Thwaites	3	3	s	s	s	s	s	s	s	3	10
J.M. Lay	1	1	s	s	s	s	s	1	1	1	10
S.L. Sakalia	s	s	1	1	1	1	1	–	–	–	7
R. Geldenhuys	s	s	3	3	3	3	3	3	3	s	10
J.A.L. Davey	–	–	–	–	–	–	–	s	s	s	3
L.J. Polwart (capt)	2	–	–	–	–	–	–	–	–	–	1
A.D. McDonald	s	2	s	–	s	s	–	s	–	–	6
J.T.T. Key	–	s	–	–	–	–	–	–	–	–	1
T.D. Crozier	–	–	2	2	2	2	2	2	2	2	8
A.V.J. Meachen	–	–	–	–	–	–	s	–	s	s	3

M.P. Delany captained in matches 2–5, T.D. Latimer co-captaining with Delany v Canterbury and Hawke's Bay. T.J. Ardron captained the final five matches.

BAY OF PLENTY TEAM RECORD, 2018

Played 10　Won 4　Lost 6　Points for 253　Points against 292

Date	Opponent	Location	Score	Tries	Con	PG	DG	Referee
August 18	Taranaki (P/C)	Rotorua	30–10	Polwart, Leaupepe, Carroll	Delany (3)	Delany (3)		B.E. Pickerill
August 23	Counties Manukau (P/C)	Pukekohe	22–17	Tiatia (2), Judd	Delany (2)	Delany		A.W.B. Mabey
September 1	Canterbury (P/C)	Tauranga	19–31	Tiatia, Ardron, Hepetema	Delany (2)			M.C.J. Winter
September 8	Hawke's Bay (C)	Napier	28–29	Judd (2), Delany	Delany (2)	Delany (3)		R.P. Kelly
September 16	North Harbour (P/C)	Albany	20–32	Delany, Lay	Delany, Robertson	Delany (2)		N.J. Webster
September 21	Waikato (C)	Rotorua	21–54	Blake, Simonsson, Leaupepe	Trask (2), Robertson			A.W.B. Mabey
September 27	Manawatu (C)	Rotorua	15–17	Carroll, Campbell	Trask	Robertson		M.G. Lash
October 3	Otago (C)	Dunedin	34–45	Simonsson, Trask, Penalty try, Crozier, Carroll	Trask, Macdonald	Trask		J.R. Nutbrown
October 7	Southland (C)	Invercargill	26–22	Simonsson, Crozier, Fuatai, Leaupepe	Trask (2), Campbell			T.M.T. Cottrell
October 13	Northland (C)	Tauranga	38–35	Lay, Thwaites, Steel, Narawa, Fuatai, Tiatia	Trask (4)			T.M.T. Cottrell

BULLER

2018 Status: Heartland
Founded 1894. **Affiliated** 1894
Chairman: H.W. (Hugh) McMillan
Chief executive officer: B.A. (Brian) Ahern (to July)
Rugby Manager: A.C. (Andrew) Duncan (from July)
Coach: C.M. (Craig) Scanlon
Assistant coaches: P.J. (Phil) Beveridge,
                      N.J. (Nathan) Thompson
Main ground: Victoria Square, Westport
Capacity: 5000
Colours: Cardinal and blue

RECORDS

Highest attendance	5000	*West Coast-Buller v South Africa, 1956*
Most appearances	174	*L.G. Brownlee, 1999-2018*
Most points	575	*D.J. Baird, 1981–91*
Most tries	44	*T.J. Stuart, 1984–99*
Most points in a season	147	*J.J. Lash, 2017*
Most tries in a season	11	*I. Ravudra, 2014*
Most conversions in a season	32	*J.J. Lash, 2016*
Most penalty goals in a season	27	*D.J. Baird, 1985*
Most dropped goals in a season	7	*D.J. Baird, 1984*
Most points in a match	25	*J.J. Lash, v Mid Canterbury, 2017*
Most tries in a match	4	*J. Easton v Wellington Colts, 1935*
		T.J. Stuart v West Coast, 1992
		M. Taylor v East Coast, 2007
		I. Ravudra v Wairarapa Bush, 2014
		S.T. Sauqaqa v Thames Valley, 2015
Most conversions in a match	7	*J.J. Lash v Wairarapa Bush, 2014*
		J.J. Lash v East Coast, 2017
Most penalty goals in a match	6	*D.J. Baird v East Coast, 1987*
		C.J. Hart v East Coast, 1999
		S.N. Jack, v Wairarapa Bush, 2002
		A.P. Stephens v Horowhenua Kapiti, 2010
Highest team score	67	*v East Coast, 2014*
Record victory (points ahead)	61	*67–6 v East Coast, 2014*
Highest score conceded	81	*v Wanganui, 1994*
Record defeat (points behind)	73	*0–73 v Horowhenua Kapiti, 1999*

In a disappointing season, Buller lost their first six matches to be in 11th place on the points table and out of contention for a playoff place in either Heartland Cup with still two games to play. Victories came in the final two matches against Mid Canterbury and Poverty Bay, which showed what might have been but in the end was no more than consolation.

The forward pack produced a very good lineout and scrum that provided plenty of ball for the backline. The front row of Logan Mundy, Anthony Ellis and Jack Best were workhorses and as good as any other front row in the Heartland Championship. Anthony Ellis has the ability to fill all three front-row positions and Logan Mundy played his 100th match for the union against

Wairarapa Bush. Assistant coach Phil Beveridge, who retired at the end of last season, made an appearance at prop in the final match of the season due to injuries in the front row.

Robbie Bonisch and Caleb Aperahama were an excellent pair at lock, dominant in the lineout and providing plenty of good go-forward in the tight. Number eight Jeff Lepa turned in some fine performances as did flanker Sam Godwin against Thames Valley.

Luke Brownlee announced his retirement prior to the Mid Canterbury match. It was his 174th first-class match for the province and the record appearance holder's last act in the Buller jersey was to successfully convert a try with the final kick of the game. He has given outstanding service to his union since he made his debut in 1999.

The two imports, Mike Wells and Robbie Malneek, were the pick of the backline. Malneek had the versatility to appear at fullback and first five-eighth, but when paired with Wells in the midfield for the second half of the season the backline functioned much better immediately. Wells also proved himself a reliable goalkicker.

James Lash was not as influential as previously due to a knee injury against King Country that caused him to miss matches, and when he did return he did not resume goalkicking duties straight away. Halfback and captain Andrew Stephens reached his 100th match for the province against Wanganui and gave yet another season of faithful service behind the pack. Wing Joel Hands looked a good prospect, scoring an excellent solo try debuting as a substitute against West Coast.

Buller won the Seddon Shield from Nelson Bays 26–24 at Murchison on 4 August but lost it to Marlborough 21–22 at the same venue seven days later. Neither match is ranked as first-class. The union celebrated its 125th jubilee during 2018.

Higher honours went to:
New Zealand Heartland: J.J. Lash, A.P. Stephens

BULLER REPRESENTATIVES 2018

	Club	Games for Union	Points for Union		Club	Games for Union	Points for Union
Caleb Aperahama	Canterbury University [1]	7	15	Jeff Lepa	White Star	17	5
Jack Best	Westport	8	5	Robbie Malneek	Central [2]	7	25
Phil Beveridge	White Star	155	56	Sam Marris	White Star	65	35
Robbie Bonisch	White Star	17	5	Ropati Matangi	White Star	8	0
Luke Brownlee	White Star	174	17	Logan Mundy	White Star	104	10
Brad Collins	White Star	4	0	Kahu Parata	Westport	14	10
Sean Eggers	Ngakawau-Karamea	3	0	Iliesa Ravudra	White Star	43	140
Anthony Ellis	Ngakawau-Karamea	31	15	Petaia Saukuru	Westport	20	5
Maifea Feso	White Star	8	5	Willis Scott	Nelson [2]	2	0
Peter Foote	Westport	2	0	Andrew Stephens	Ngakawau-Karamea	102	261
Sam Godwin	Canterbury University [1]	7	0	Anthony Tailua	White Star	27	78
Joel Hands	Westport	4	10	Zach Walsh	Westport	8	0
Corey Jenkins	Westport	7	0	Michael Wells	[3]	8	56
James Lash	Ngakawau-Karamea	36	448				

[1] Canterbury RU   [2] Tasman RU   [3] arrived from overseas

INDIVIDUAL SCORING

	Tries	Con	PG	DG	Points
Wells	4	12	4	–	56
Lash	1	9	4	–	35
Ravudra	5	–	–	–	25
Malneek	5	–	–	–	25
Tailua	4	–	–	–	20
Aperahama	3	–	–	–	15
Hands	2	–	–	–	10
Best	1	–	–	–	5
Feso	1	–	–	–	5
Ellis	1	–	–	–	5

	Tries	Con	PG	DG	Points
Marris	1	–	–	–	5
Parata	1	–	–	–	5
Saukuru	1	–	–	–	5
Bonisch	1	–	–	–	5
Brownlee	–	1	–	–	2
Totals	**31**	**22**	**8**	**0**	**223**
Opposition scored	41	30	8	0	289

BULLER 2018

	North Otago	King Country	Thames Valley	Wairarapa Bush	West Coast	Wanganui	Mid Canterbury	Poverty Bay	TOTALS
R.T. Malneek	15	15	10	10	13	13	13	–	7
A. Tailua	14	14	15	15	15	15	15	15	8
I. Ravudra	11	11	11	11	11	11	11	11	8
S.A. Marris	s	–	14	14	–	–	s	s	5
P.T. Saukuru	–	–	s	s	s	–	–	–	3
B.R. Collins	–	–	s	s	–	s	–	s	4
J.G. Hands	–	–	–	–	s	14	14	14	4
M.O. Wells	13	13	13	13	12	12	12	13	8
M.T. Feso	12	12	12	12	14	s	s	12	8
J.J. Lash	10	10	–	–	10	10	10	10	6
A.P. Stephens (capt)	9	9	9	9	9	9	9	9	8
C.W. Jenkins	–	–	s	s	–	s	s	s	5
P.J. Lepa	8	8	8	8	8	8	8	8	8
L.G. Brownlee	7	7	7	7	7	7	7	–	7
S.R. Godwin	6	6	6	–	6	6	6	6	7
K.G. Parata	s	s	s	s	s	s	s	7	8
W.T. Scott	5	–	–	6	–	–	–	–	2
R. Bonisch	4	4	4	4	4	4	4	4	8
Z.L. Walsh	s	s	s	s	s	s	s	s	8
C.A. Aperahama	–	5	5	5	5	5	5	5	7
J.W. Best	3	3	3	3	3	s	3	3	8
L.M. Mundy	1	1	1	1	1	1	1	1	8
S.H.R. Eggers	s	s	–	–	–	s	–	–	3
P.G. Foote	–	–	s	–	–	–	–	s	2
P.J. Beveridge	–	–	–	–	–	–	–	s	1
A.W. Ellis	2	2	2	2	2	2	2	2	8
R. Matangi	s	s	s	s	s	3	s	s	8

BULLER TEAM RECORD, 2018

Played 8 Won 2 Lost 6 Points for 223 Points against 289

Date	Opponent	Location	Score	Tries	Con	PG	DG	Referee
August 25	North Otago (H)	Oamaru	24–30	Malneek (2), Ravudra, Best	Lash (2)			H.G. Reed
September 1	King Country (H)	Westport	28–30	Feso, Lash, Wells	Wells (2)	Wells (3)		T.N. Griffiths
September 8	Thames Valley (H)	Westport	22–43	Ellis, Aperahama, Tailua	Wells (2)	Wells		H.G. Reed
September 15	Wairarapa Bush (H)	Masterton	29–61	Marris, Parata, Aperahama, Ravudra, Saukuru	Wells (2)			T. Kawahara *Japan*
September 22	West Coast (H)	Westport	28–34	Tailua, Hands, Malneek, Ravudra	Wells (4)			J.D. Munro
September 29	Wanganui (H)	Wanganui	14–45	Tailua, Malneek	Wells (2)			M.C.J. Winter
October 6	Mid Canterbury (H)	Westport	37–19	Wells (2), Tailua, Malneek	Lash (3), Brownlee	Lash (3)		R.M. Mahoney
October 13	Poverty Bay (H)	Gisborne	41–27	Ravudra (2), Wells, Aperahama, Bonisch, Hands	Lash (4)	Lash		R.M. Mahoney

CANTERBURY

2018 Status: Mitre 10 Cup Premiership
Founded 1879. Affiliated 1894
President: V.E.T. (Vance) Stewart
Chairman: P.A. (Peter) Winchester
Chief executive officer: Nathan Godfrey (to August),
T.P. (Tony) Smail (from October)
Coach: J.S. (Joe) Maddock
Assistant coaches: Mark Brown, N.K. (Nathan) Mauger,
R.D. (Reuben) Thorne
Main ground: Christchurch Stadium
Capacity: 20,000
Colours: Red and black

RECORDS

Most appearances	220	*Fergi McCormick, 1958–75*
Most points	1625	*Robbie Deans, 1979–90*
Most tries	94	*Paula Bale, 1989–96*
Most points in a season	279	*Robbie Deans, 1989*
Most tries in a season	24	*Paula Bale, 1989*
Most conversions in a season	52	*Greg Coffey, 1991*
		Ben Blair, 2001
Most penalty goals in a season	50	*Robbie Deans, 1989*
Most dropped goals in a season	10	*Andrew Mehrtens, 1994*
Most points in a match	44	*Jon Preston v West Coast, 1992*
Most tries in a match	7	*Bruce McPhail v Combined Services, 1959*
Most conversions in a match	20	*Jon Preston v West Coast, 1992*
Most penalty goals in a match	7	*Robbie Deans v Counties, 1984*
		Andrew Mehrtens v Fiji, 2003
		Cameron McIntyre v Wellington, 2003
Highest team score	128	*v West Coast, 1992*
Record victory (points ahead)	128	*128–0 v West Coast, 1992*
Highest score conceded	60	*v Wellington, 2017*
Record defeat (points behind)	46	*14–60 v Wellington, 2017*

For just the second time since 2007 Canterbury did not win the National Championship, going down in the final to Auckland in extra time. While this constitutes a near miss in a season of nine wins and three losses, the victories had to be achieved in different fashion in 2018.

The backline was not as potent as it was in 2017, scoring less than half the tries they achieved in last year's Mitre 10 Cup — 28 versus 58. Having to replace the trio of Richie Mo'unga, Tim Bateman and Rob Thompson in the 10, 12 and 13 combination was a hard act and the 2018 version inevitably did not have the same creativity and fluidity to it.

George Bridge had an excellent season at fullback, being safe under the high ball and an exciting counter-attacker. Halfback Mitchell Drummond had a somewhat slow start but his form in the second half of the season was very assured. Braydon Ennor was the best performing of the four midfielders used, transitioning very well from wing to centre.

Caleb Makene and Josh McKay both proved useful wings when given an opportunity. In his second season Brett Cameron at first five-eighth scored 121 points with some excellent goalkicking, and he had very good all-round matches against Manawatu and Taranaki.

Canterbury's forwards remained strong with plenty of experience in vital positions. Not required by the All Blacks during the French tests and Rugby Championship, Luke Romano had an outstanding season at lock. A strong ball runner, heavy tackler and lineout winner, he must surely have been unlucky not to have made the main 32-man squad for the All Blacks end of year tour. Instead he was one of the 19 specifically chosen for the test against Japan only, and then, unfortunately had to withdraw injured.3

His locking partner Mitchell Dunshea had his best season yet, with particularly prominent displays against Manawatu and North Harbour.

Number eight and co-captain Whetu Douglas broke a thumb in the round-robin match against Auckland which ruled him out of the rest of the campaign. He was a big loss to the side with his experience and energy. Due to his All Blacks' commitments, last year's captain Luke Whitelock appeared just three times.

After a solitary debut appearance off the bench last year, Tom Christie showed up well at openside flanker in his first full season. It was a bit of a surprise that he did not start in either of the playoff matches. However, this underlined the depth Canterbury had in the loose forwards with Tom Sanders, Reed Prinsep and Billy Harmon all featuring when they appeared.

Loosehead prop Alex Hodgman performed well in anchoring a strong front row, keeping out the challenge of the returning Daniel Lienert-Brown, while Australian Sef Fa'agase was a fit mobile tighthead prop. At the age of 37 veteran prop Chris King was one of only two forwards to appear in all 12 games.

With the absence of the injured Ben Funnell, Nathan Vella stepped well as the first-choice hooker while newcomer Brodie McAlister looked promising.

There were a number of absent players from last year's squad. Gone were Tim Bateman (Japan), Dominic Bird (France), Jed Brown (Tasman), Wyatt Crockett (Tasman), Chris Gawler (Taranaki), Dylan Nel (Otago), Jack Straker (Northland), Jack Stratton (Waikato), Rob Thompson (Manawatu), Matt Todd (Japan) and Poasa Waqanibau (Fiji), while front rowers Ben Funnell, Oliver Jager and Siate Tokolahi all missed the season through injury.

Gains in from overseas were Sam Beard (South Canterbury/Bay of Plenty), Phil Burleigh (Bay of Plenty/Chiefs/Highlanders, one test for Scotland), Whetu Douglas (Waikato/Crusaders), Chris King (Canterbury 2002–04, Crusaders/Highlanders) and Sef Fa'agase (Queensland) plus Greg Pleasants-Tate from Auckland and Hugh Renton from Hawke's Bay.

Higher honours went to:
New Zealand: G. Bridge, B. Cameron, R. Crotty, M. Drummond, O. Franks, J. Moody, R. Mo'unga, C. Taylor, M. Todd, L. Whitelock, S. Whitelock
New Zealand Maori: W. Harmon, R. Prinsep
New Zealand Under 20: T. Christie, N. Punivai, W. Tucker
New Zealand Sevens: S. Dickson, A. Nicole

CANTERBURY REPRESENTATIVES 2018

	Club	Games for Union	Points for Union		Club	Games for Union	Points for Union
Harrison Allan	Sydenham	4	0	Chris King	Christchurch	32	10
Sam Beard	Burnside	12	5	Daniel Lienert-Brown	Chch HSOB	29	15
George Bridge	Chch HSOB	29	85	Caleb Makene	Lincoln University	14	25
Phil Burleigh	New Brighton	10	5	Brodie McAlister	Sydenham	7	5
Brett Cameron	Lincoln University	23	201	Josh McKay	Lincoln University	22	56
Tom Christie	Christchurch	12	5	Joe Moody	Lincoln	32	15
Connor Collins	Lincoln University	7	0	Ben Morris	Lincoln University	2	0
Hamish Dalzell	Lincoln University	20	5	Greg Pleasants-Tate	Prebbleton	5	20
Whetu Douglas	Canterbury University	6	0	Reed Prinsep	Chch HSOB	46	30
Mitchell Drummond	Chch HSOB	49	74	Ngane Punivai	Lincoln University	13	5
Mitchell Dunshea	Lincoln University	35	25	Hugh Renton	Christchurch	4	0
Ere Enari	Lincoln University	20	0	Luke Romano	Hurunui	40	25
Braydon Ennor	Canterbury University	19	80	Tom Sanders	Lincoln University	44	45
Sef Fa'agase	Darfield	11	5	Nic Souchon	Lincoln University	2	0
Connor Garden-Bachop	Lincoln University	3	10	Samu Tawake	Sumner	1	0
Billy Harmon	New Brighton	25	20	William Tucker	Christchurch	1	0
James Hawkey	Nelson Marist [1]	2	0	Nathan Vella	New Brighton	32	35
Alex Hodgman	Linwood	55	10	Filimoni Waqainabete	Sumner	4	0
				Luke Whitelock	Canterbury University	66	45

[1] Tasman RU

INDIVIDUAL SCORING

	Tries	Con	PG	DG	Points		Tries	Con	PG	DG	Points
Cameron	1	37	14	–	121	Fa'agase	1	–	–	–	5
Ennor	6	–	–	–	30	King	1	–	–	–	5
Drummond	5	1	–	–	27	McAlister	1	–	–	–	5
Bridge	5	–	–	–	25	Burleigh	1	–	–	–	5
Penalty try	3	–	–	–	21	Hodgman	1	–	–	–	5
Pleasants-Tate	4	–	–	–	20	Christie	1	–	–	–	5
Prinsep	4	–	–	–	20	Harmon	1	–	–	–	5
Makene	3	–	–	–	15	Beard	1	–	–	–	5
McKay	3	–	–	–	15	Punivai	1	–	–	–	5
Dunshea	2	–	–	–	10	Sanders	1	–	–	–	5
Garden-Bachop	2	–	–	–	10						
Lienert-Brown	1	–	–	–	5	**Totals**	**51**	**38**	**14**	**0**	**379**
Romano	1	–	–	–	5						
Vella	1	–	–	–	5	Opposition scored	35	27	13	0	268

CANTERBURY 2018

	Tasman	Wellington	Bay of Plenty	Manawatu	North Harbour	Auckland	Otago	Hawke's Bay	Taranaki	Counties Manukau	Tasman	Auckland	TOTALS
G.C. Bridge	–	15	15	15	15	15	15	15	15	15	15	15	11
J.A. McKay	15	14	14	14	14	14	14	14	–	–	14	14	10
C.L. Makene	14	11	11	11	11	11	11	–	–	s	11	11	10
F.T.V. Waqainabete	s	–	s	s	s	–	–	–	–	–	–	–	4
C. Garden-Bachop	–	–	–	–	–	–	–	s	14	14	–	–	3
B.M. Ennor	11	13	–	–	–	13	13	13	13	13	13	13	9
N.G.J. Punivai	s	s	13	13	13	s	s	11	11	11	s	s	12
S.T. Beard	13	12	12	s	12	s	s	s	12	12	s	s	12
P.D. Burleigh	12	–	–	12	s	12	12	12	s	10	12	12	10
J.N.M. Hawkey	–	–	s	–	–	–	–	–	s	–	–	–	2
B.D. Cameron	10	10	10	10	10	10	10	10	10	s	10	10	12
M.D. Drummond (co-capt)	9	9	9	s	9	9	9	9	9	9	9	9	12
C.D. Collins	s	–	s	9	s	–	s	s	s	–	–	–	7
E.C.S. Enari	–	–	–	–	–	–	–	–	–	s	s	s	3
W.H. Douglas (co-capt)	8	8	s	8	8	8	–	–	–	–	–	–	6
L.C. Whitelock	–	–	8	–	–	–	–	–	–	–	8	8	3
T.M. Christie	7	7	–	s	7	7	s	7	7	7	s	s	11
T.B. Sanders	6	s	7	7	–	s	6	–	–	6	s	s	9
R.J. Prinsep	s	6	6	6	6	6	8	8	–	8	6	6	11
H.T. Renton	–	–	–	–	s	–	–	s	8	s	–	–	4
W.K. Harmon	–	–	–	–	–	–	7	6	6	–	7	7	5
M.T.W. Dunshea	5	5	s	5	5	s	5	5	5	s	5	5	12
L. Romano	4	4	4	s	–	4	4	4	4	4	4	4	11
H.A. Dalzell	s	s	5	4	4	5	s	–	s	5	–	–	9
B.J. Morris	–	–	–	–	s	–	–	–	–	–	–	–	1
W.A. Tucker	–	–	–	–	–	–	–	s	–	–	–	–	1
C.C. King	3	s	s	3	s	s	3	s	s	s	s	s	12
A.T.O.A. Hodgman	1	1	s	–	1	1	s	1	1	–	s	1	10
D.P. Lienert-Brown	s	s	1	1	s	s	1	–	–	–	–	–	8
S.F. Fa'agase	s	3	3	s	3	3	–	3	3	3	3	3	11
H.M. Allan	–	–	–	s	–	–	–	s	–	1	–	s	4
S.O.F. Tawake	–	–	–	–	–	–	s	–	–	–	–	–	1
J.P.T. Moody	–	–	–	–	–	–	–	–	–	s	1	–	2
N.B. Vella	2	2	s	s	2	–	–	s	2	2	2	2	10
G.W. Pleasants-Tate	s	s	2	2	–	2	–	–	–	–	–	–	5
B.L. McAlister	–	–	–	–	s	s	2	2	–	s	s	s	7
N.P. Souchon	–	–	–	–	–	–	s	–	s	–	–	–	2

CANTERBURY TEAM RECORD, 2018

Played 12 Won 9 Lost 3 Points for 379 Points against 268

Date	Opponent	Location	Score	Tries	Con	PG	DG	Referee
August 17	Tasman (P)	Blenheim	17–25	Pleasants-Tate (2)	Cameron (2)	Cameron		R.P. Kelly
August 25	Wellington (P)	Christchurch	27–20	Ennor, Prinsep, Drummond, Makene	Cameron (2)	Cameron		J.J. Doleman
September 1	Bay of Plenty (P/C)	Tauranga	31–19	McKay (2), Lienert-Brown, Penalty try	Cameron (3)	Cameron		M.C.J. Winter
September 6	Manawatu (P/C)	Christchurch	34–23	Prinsep, Pleasants-Tate, Makene, Cameron, Romano	Cameron (3)	Cameron		C.J. Stone
September 12	North Harbour (P)	Albany	31–21	Vella, Bridge, Prinsep, Dunshea	Cameron (4)	Cameron		A.W.B. Mabey
September 16	Auckland (P)	Christchurch	29–34	Pleasants-Tate, Fa'agase, King, McAlister	Cameron (3)	Cameron		B.D. O'Keeffe
September 22	Otago (P/C)	Dunedin	47–25	Bridge, Burleigh, Dunshea, McKay, Makene, Ennor, Prinsep	Cameron (6)			N.P. Briant
September 30	Hawke's Bay (P/C)	Christchurch	49–24	Ennor (2), Hodgman, Drummond, Bridge, Christie, Garden-Bachop	Cameron (7)			J.J. Doleman
October 6	Taranaki (P)	Christchurch	41–7	Drummond, Garden-Bachop, Harmon, Beard, Punivai, Ennor	Cameron (4)	Cameron		J.J. Doleman
October 13	Counties Manukau (P)	Pukekohe	19–14	Bridge, Ennor, Penalty try	Drummond			A.W.B. Mabey
October 19	Tasman (P semi-final)	Nelson	21–16	Drummond (2)	Cameron	Cameron (3)		M.I. Fraser
October 27	Auckland (P final)	Auckland	33–40 aet	Penalty try, Bridge, Sanders	Cameron (2)	Cameron (4)		G.W. Jackson

aet *after extra time*

COUNTIES MANUKAU

2018 Status: Mitre 10 Cup Premiership
Founded 1926 as South Auckland and affiliated to Auckland.
Granted full union status as South Auckland Counties in 1955.
Name changed to Counties 1956, to Counties Manukau 1996.
President: K.D. (Kere) Maihi
Chairman: C.W. (Craig) Carter
Chief executive officer: B.A. (Barton) Hoggard
Coach: D.B. (Darryl) Suasua
Assistant coaches: G.W. (Grant) Henson, Semo Sititi
Main ground: Navigation Homes Stadium, Pukekohe
Capacity: 18,000
Colours: Red, white and black

RECORDS

Most appearances	201	Alan Dawson, 1976–89
Most points	698	Danny Love, 1993–96
Most tries	59	Alan Dawson, 1976–89
Most points in a season	208	Danny Love, 1995
Most tries in a season	22	Luke Erenavula, 1993
Most conversions in a season	52	Danny Love, 1993
Most penalty goals in a season	47	Stu Hollier, 1989
Most dropped goals in a season	4	Bob Lendrum, 1976
		Joe Harvey, 1983
Most points in a match	37	Jim Graham v East Coast, 1972
Most tries in a match	5	K.Koiatu v King Country, 2004
Most conversions in a match	14	Jim Graham v East Coast, 1972
Most penalty goals in a match	6	Stu Hollier v France, 1989
		Stu Hollier v Thames Valley, 1989
		Danny Love v Manawatu, 1994
		James Semple v Manawatu, 2011
		Baden Kerr v Auckland 2012
Highest team score	108	v Horowhenua, 1994
Record victory (points ahead)	103	103–0 v Poverty Bay, 1993
Highest score conceded	100	v Auckland, 2004
Record defeat (points behind)	85	15–100 v Auckland, 2004

Counties Manukau supporters will not look back with fondness on the Steelers' 2018 season.

Their two wins, plus nine bonus points, were enough to keep them clear of Taranaki and relegation. Too often there were glimpses of the Steelers' true potential, then a loose pass or ill-discipline would prove costly.

However, on closer analysis, they were competitive in every match, barring the 53–12 defeat to Wellington. Seven of the eight losses were by 10 points or less. The disappointing statistic will be the five straight home defeats, while they lost two of their crossover games, to Bay of Plenty and Northland.

Mitigating factors were a crippling injury toll and the loss of several key players, such as Baden Kerr, Pauliasi Manu and Augustine Pulu to Japan, and Tim Nanai-Williams to France, while Jimmy Tupou was also out for the season. There were a clutch of retirements, while All Blacks prop Nepo Laulala only returned for the last 34 minutes of the season, to ensure he was available for the All Blacks' northern tour.

Chiefs halfback Jonathan Taumateine was injured for the entire campaign. Kieran Read did make his first appearance in Steelers' colours, but that was in a non-first-class pre-season encounter. The odds are now long on the All Blacks' captain ever playing an official match for the province where he was schooled.

It all started so well for the Steelers, however, using their physicality and set-piece grunt to heap early pressure on Auckland at Eden Park. But that game was dropped, as were the next two, and it required a gritty effort to edge Hawke's Bay in Napier. The Stags were convincingly defeated, but the tame manner in which the Jonah Lomu Memorial Trophy was again lost was disappointing.

The second stanza of the Tasman game saw the Steelers play some of their best rugby, and they almost forced a draw after trailing 21–0.

Lu Laulala was mercurial at fullback, with exquisite moments of skill interspersed with unforced errors. The wings were dangerous, Tevita Nabura scoring four tries and hitting hard on defence, while Toni Pulu, back after missing 2017 with injury, again showed his searing pace. His try against Taranaki, beating six defenders, was a prime example. He was one of three who reached 50 games for the province.

Orbyn Leger moved around the backline, and built on his promising 2018 Blues debut, winning his Steelers' blazer, but never really stamping his authority. Cardiff Vaega returned from Hawke's Bay and stepped up his output. Nigel Ah Wong scored two tries and set up more either at wing or centre.

Etene Nanai-Seturo's long-awaited debut was delayed by a hamstring injury, but he showed his class, and footwork, on occasion, mostly at centre or fullback.

Tongan international No. 10 Latiume Fosita, transferred from Auckland, looked good on occasion with his passing and kicking games, but failed to exert consistent control. Te Aihe Toma and Liam Daniela were a pair of sparky halfbacks, if not in the Pulu class.

The loss of designated captain Sam Henwood to concussion in just the third match was a blow. To that point he had been the best Steelers' player with his all-round game and two tries. His replacement as skipper, Matiaha Martin, hacked away in the tight. Lock Sikeli Nabou raised his 50-game milestone but operated mainly off the bench.

Kalolo Tuiloma could never regain full fitness from a niggly calf. Coree Te Whata-Colley was solid in the scrums, but heavily penalised. Loosehead Sean Bagshaw also brought up 50 games for the union.

Hooker Joe Royal was full value, playing every game and scoring four tries. His play around the field was effective, and he threw well into the lineout, though this source became unreliable for the Steelers late in the season or when he was off the field.

Jarrod Firth returned to Steelers' colours after several seasons in France, but was used sparsely as a sub, including being loaned to Taranaki.

There were good moments from loose forwards Matt Vaai and Dan Hyatt, but that was symptomatic of the Steelers' 2018 woes: inconsistency and errors amid flashes of brilliance.

Higher honours went to:
New Zealand: N. Laulala, K. Read, SB. Williams
New Zealand Under 20: S. Asomua
New Zealand Sevens: S. Molia, E. Nanai-Seturo, A. Rokolisoa

COUNTIES MANUKAU REPRESENTATIVES 2018

	Club	Games for Union	Points for Union		Club	Games for Union	Points for Union
Nigel Ah Wong	Manurewa	19	35	Sione Molia	Karaka	14	30
Suetena Asomua	Waiuku	1	0	Sikeli Nabou	Ardmore Marist	53	30
Sean Bagshaw	Onewhero	50	0	Tevita Nabura	Waiuku	18	25
Liam Daniela	Bombay	11	5	Etene Nanai-Seturo	Bombay	6	0
Caleb Fa'alili	Manurewa	1	0	Toni Pulu	Bombay	51	65
Jarrod Firth	Papakura	30	0	Viliame Rarasea	Ardmore Marist	43	15
Latiume Fosita	Ardmore Marist	8	31	Savelio Ropati	Ardmore Marist	8	0
Sam Furniss	Patumahoe	10	0	Joseph Royal	Patumahoe	20	30
Kalione Hala	Karaka	4	0	Mark Royal	Patumahoe	3	0
Sam Henwood	Pukekohe	25	30	Howard Sililoto	Manurewa	8	5
Daniel Hyatt	Waiuku	22	25	Gafatasi Sua	Manurewa	40	10
Luteru Laulala	Ardmore Marist	30	74	Viliami Taulani	Manurewa	10	0
Nepo Laulala	Ardmore Marist	1	0	Coree Te Whata-Colley	Bombay	20	0
Daymon Leasuasu	Ardmore Marist	5	0	Te Aihe Toma	Manurewa	10	5
Orbyn Leger	Karaka	20	10	Kalolo Tuiloma	Bombay	25	35
Fotu Lokotui	Ardmore Marist	18	30	Matthew Vaai	Manurewa	18	0
Matiaha Martin	Bombay	28	5	Cardiff Vaega	Karaka	29	25
Michael McKee	Waiuku	4	0				

INDIVIDUAL SCORING

	Tries	Con	PG	DG	Points		Tries	Con	PG	DG	Points
Fosita	–	14	1	–	31	Ah Wong	2	–	–	–	10
L. Laulala	1	7	2	–	25	Vaega	2	–	–	–	10
J. Royal	4	–	–	–	20	Penalty try	1	–	–	–	7
Molia	4	–	–	–	20	Sililoto	1	–	–	–	5
Nabura	4	–	–	–	20	Martin	1	–	–	–	5
Pulu	3	–	–	–	15	Toma	1	–	–	–	5
Lokotui	3	–	–	–	15						
Tuiloma	2	–	–	–	10	**Totals**	**33**	**21**	**3**	**0**	**218**
Henwood	2	–	–	–	10						
Hyatt	2	–	–	–	10	Opposition scored	39*	23	10	0	275

* includes two penalty tries (14 points)

COUNTIES MANUKAU 2018	Auckland	Bay of Plenty	Taranaki	Hawke's Bay	Southland	Wellington	Tasman	Northland	North Harbour	Canterbury	TOTALS
K.H.K. Hala	15	–	s	–	–	–	–	–	–	–	2
L.E. Laulala	–	15	15	15	15	15	s	10	s	10	9
E. Nanai-Seturo	–	–	–	–	s	s	15	15	15	15	6
S.L.J. Molia	14	14	–	–	–	–	s	13	–	s	5
T. Nabura	11	11	11	11	11	11	11	11	11	11	10
T.N. Pulu	–	–	14	14	–	14	14	14	14	14	7
N.F. Ah Wong	13	13	13	–	14	s	13	s	13	13	9
S.C. Furniss	s	s	s	13	13	–	–	–	–	–	5
O.N.T. Leger	12	12	12	s	s	13	12	12	s	s	10
C.K. Vaega	s	s	–	12	12	12	–	s	12	12	8
L. Fosita	10	10	10	10	10	10	10	–	10	–	8
T.A.T.M.L.A. Toma	9	9	9	9	9	9	9	s	9	s	10
L.T. Daniela	–	–	s	s	s	s	s	9	s	9	8
S.T. Henwood (capt)	8	8	7	–	–	–	–	–	–	–	3
S. Ropati	–	–	8	s	s	–	–	–	–	7	4
D.T. Hyatt	–	–	–	8	8	8	8	8	8	–	6
F.S. Lokotui	7	7	–	–	7	7	7	7	7	s	8
S. Nabou	s	–	–	s	s	s	s	6	6	6	8
M. Vaai	s	6	6	6	6	6	6	s	s	8	10
V.T.H. Laulani	–	s	s	–	–	–	–	–	–	–	2
C. Fa'alili	–	–	–	7	–	–	–	–	–	–	1
M.J.F. McKee	6	s	s	s	–	–	–	–	–	–	4
M. Martin	5	5	5	5	5	5	5	5	5	5	10
V.L. Rarasea	4	4	4	4	4	4	4	s	s	s	10
D. Leasuasu	–	–	–	–	–	s	s	4	4	4	5
K.E. Tuiloma	3	–	3	3	3	3	–	–	–	–	5
H.J.F. Sililoto	1	s	s	–	–	s	1	1	s	s	8
M.J.T.K.T.R. Royal	s	–	–	s	s	–	–	–	–	–	3
C.J.W. Te Whata-Colley	s	3	s	s	s	s	3	3	3	3	10
S. Bagshaw	–	1	1	1	1	1	s	s	1	1	9
J.V. Firth	–	s	–	–	–	–	s	s	–	–	3
S. Asomua	–	–	–	–	–	–	–	–	s	–	1
N.E. Laulala	–	–	–	–	–	–	–	–	–	s	1
J.W. Royal	2	2	2	2	2	2	2	2	2	s	10
G.W. Sua	s	s	s	s	s	s	s	s	s	2	10

M. Martin captained in the last seven matches.

COUNTIES MANUKAU TEAM RECORD, 2018

Played 10 Won 2 Lost 8 Points for 218 Points against 275

Date	Opponent	Location	Score	Tries	Con	PG	DG	Referee
August 18	Auckland (P)	Auckland	19–23	Tuiloma, Henwood, Sililoto	Fosita (2)			G.W. Jackson
August 23	Bay of Plenty (P/C)	Pukekohe	17–22	J. Royal, Molia, Henwood	Fosita			A.W.B. Mabey
August 29	Taranaki (P)	Pukekohe	19–26	Tuiloma, Nabura, Pulu	Fosita, Laulala			N.P. Briant
September 2	Hawke's Bay (P/C)	Napier	29–25	Nabura, Hyatt, J. Royal, Martin	Fosita (3)	Fosita		M.I. Fraser
September 8	Southland (P/C)	Invercargill	43–26	Lokotui, L. Laulala, Toma, Ah Wong, J. Royal, Vaega	Fosita (4), Laulala	Laulala		J.J. Doleman
September 15	Wellington (P)	Pukekohe	12–53	Hyatt, Pulu	Fosita			R.P. Kelly
September 23	Tasman (P)	Nelson	19–21	Molia, J. Royal, Nabura	Laulala (2)			T.N. Griffiths
September 30	Northland (P/C)	Pukekohe	20–24	Molia, Lokotui, Pulu	Laulala	Laulala		B.D. O'Keeffe
October 6	North Harbour (P)	Albany	26–36	Vaega, Nabura, Lokotui, Penalty try	Fosita (2)			J.D. Munro
October 13	Canterbury (P)	Pukekohe	14–19	Ah Wong, Molia	Laulala (2)			A.W.B. Mabey

NGATI POROU EAST COAST

2018 Status: Heartland
Founded 1921 as East Coast and affiliated 1921.
Name changed to Ngati Porou East Coast 2017
President: B.N. (Bailey) Mackey
Chairman: C.W. (Campbell) Dewes
Chief executive officer: Cushla Tangaere-Manuel
Co-coaches: W.L. (Wayne) Ensor and T.D. (Troy) Para
Main ground: Whakarua Park, Ruatoria
Capacity: 3000
Colours: Sky blue

RECORDS

Highest attendance	4000	v Poverty Bay (Div 3 final), 1999
Most appearances	115	E.M. Waitoa, 1979–2006
Most points	406	E.J. Manuel, 1985–98
Most tries	24	J.R. Kururangi, 1979–96
Most points in a season	145	M.R. Flutey, 2000
Most tries in a season	9	S. Vorenasu, 2011
Most conversions in a season	20	M.R. Flutey, 2001
		J.R. Semple, 2012
Most penalty goals in a season	30	M.R. Flutey, 2000
Most dropped goals in a season	3	M.R. Flutey, 2000
Most points in a match	22	V.P. Taingahue v Buller, 1999
Most tries in a match	3	W. Peachy v Bush, 1954
		T.M. Reedy v Horowhenua, 1958
		J.R. Kururangi v West Coast, 1992
		J. Higgins v Poverty Bay, 1993
		M. Vere v Buller, 1999
		T.W. Delamere v Horowhenua Kapiti, 2000
		H.F. Haerewa v Poverty Bay, 2012
		S.P. Destounis, v Poverty Bay, 2016
Most conversions in a match	8	V.P. Taingahue v Buller, 1999
Most penalty goals in a match	7	M.R. Flutey v Nelson Bays, 2001
Highest team score	74	v Buller, 1999
Record victory (points ahead)	69	72–3 v West Coast, 1992
Highest score conceded	116	v North Otago, 2010
Record defeat (points behind)	113	3–116 v North Otago, 2010

Ngati Porou East Coast once again had another winless season in the Heartland Championship. While the match against South Canterbury had an unfortunate outcome, there were good spells during the other matches. The closest the union came to breaking their duck was the derby match against Poverty Bay when an unconverted Sam Parkes try levelled the score at 19–19 with five minutes left, but the conceding of an intercept try in the final minute resulted in another defeat.

The team suffered with the inability to put the same team out consistently, as every week there would be key players unavailable and not just with injury. Of the 40 players used, only nine had played ten or more matches for the province before the season started. And in such a wide geographical area training could only be held once a week. They could ill afford to lose players of the calibre of Patrick Allen (Poverty Bay) and the Palmer brothers (overseas) from last year's team as they did. To offset this to some extent, the union did the gain the services of experienced players lock Adaam Ross and prop Hakarangi Tichborne, both previously having represented Mid Canterbury and Manawatu.

The best of the forwards was the captain and lock Hone Haerewa who gave several splendid efforts. Also showing up well were debutants Jack Richardson at flanker and hooker Wyntah Riki. Hakarangi Tichborne and Adaam Ross showed the benefit of their experience, with Tichborne unfortunately having his season end early with injury.

Halfback Sam Parkes gave his utmost in every game. He would surely make the Heartland team if he appeared for another province. The midfield combination of the experienced campaigners Tau Moeke and Verdon Bartlett worked well on both sides of the ball until Moeke became unavailable, while pacy fullback Morrison Siliko also had good moments.

No player was called upon for higher honours.

NGATI POROU EAST COAST REPRESENTATIVES 2018

	Club	Games for Union	Points for Union		Club	Games for Union	Points for Union
Patrick Allen	Ruatoria City	9	0	Jayden Milner	Ruatoria City	27	11
Tim Barbarich	Ruatoria City	22	0	Tau "TK" Moeke	Hikurangi	38	55
Verdon Bartlett	Tihirau Victory Club	69	36	Ahomatua Morice	Hikurangi	1	0
Pera Bishop	Ruatoria City	40	5	Reg Namana	Uawa	4	0
Claude "CJ" Fox	Ruatoria City	4	0	Tanetoa Parata	Hikurangi	25	5
Lorne Goldsmith-Boyce	Ruatoria City	5	0	Sam Parkes	Uawa	36	53
Benny Haerewa	Tihirau Victory Club	8	0	Vern Parkes	Uawa	1	0
Hone Haerewa	Tokararangi	31	22	Anaru Potae	Te Teko [5]	5	0
Ngarangi Haerewa	Tihirau Victory Club	8	23	Teina Potae	Tokararangi	8	0
Faafoi Ioapo	Northern United [2]	1	0	Trent Proffit	Hikurangi	6	5
Fabian Kahaki	Hikurangi	14	0	Jack Richardson	Ruatoria City	8	5
Mangu Kemp	Uawa	3	0	Wyntah Riki	Uawa	8	0
Rikki Kernohan	Uawa	10	0	Adaam Ross	Kamo [6]	9	0
Teina Kirikiri	Uawa	1	0	Jesse Rye	Uawa	2	0
Daniel Knubley	Uawa	13	0	BJ Sidney	Uawa	8	12
Scott Lasenby	Uawa	11	0	Morrison Siliko	Ponsonby [7]	6	5
Epeli Lotawa	United Matamata Sports [3]	9	20	Hoani Te Moana	Tihirau Victory Club	12	0
David Manuel	Hikurangi	9	0	Hakarangi Tichborne	Linton Army [8]	4	10
Perrin Manuel [1]	Tech OB [4]	25	16	Slade Tiopira	Waiapu	5	8
Buchanan Maxwell	Ruatoria City	7	5	Raniera Whakataka	Uawa	1	0

[1] Player of Origin [2] Wellington RU [3] Waikato RU [4] Hawke's Bay RU

[5] Bay of Plenty RU [6] Northland RU [7] Auckland RU [8] Manawatu RU

INDIVIDUAL SCORING

	Tries	Con	PG	DG	Points
N. Haerewa	1	6	2	–	23
S. Parkes	2	3	2	–	22
Lotawa	3	–	–	–	15
Tichborne	2	–	–	–	10
Penalty try	1	–	–	–	7
Moeke	1	–	–	–	5
P. Manuel	1	–	–	–	5
Richardson	1	–	–	–	5
Milner	1	–	–	–	5

	Tries	Con	PG	DG	Points
Maxwell	1	–	–	–	5
H. Haerewa	1	–	–	–	5
Siliko	1	–	–	–	5
Proffit	1	–	–	–	5
Totals	**17**	**9**	**4**	**0**	**117**
Opposition scored	76*	53	5	0	505

* includes 2 penalty tries (14 points).

NGATI POROU EAST COAST 2018

	Poverty Bay	King Country	Horowhenua Kapiti	Wairarapa Bush	South Canterbury	Poverty Bay	Mid Canterbury	Wanganui	West Coast	TOTALS
M. Siliko	–	15	15	15	–	15	15	–	15	6
J.P. Milner	15	11	s	14	15	11	11	15	11	9
F. Kahaki	14	s	s	s	–	s	s	11	s	8
T.M.T. Potae	11	12	s	11	11	12	12	12	–	8
A. Morice	s	–	–	–	–	–	–	–	–	1
B. Haerewa	–	14	11	s	s	10	10	–	–	6
B.J. Sidney	–	–	14	–	–	–	–	s	13	3
E. Lotawa	–	–	–	–	14	14	14	14	14	5
D. Manuel	–	–	–	–	–	–	s	s	s	3
V.R.M. Bartlett	13	13	13	13	12	13	13	13	12	9
V. Parkes	–	–	–	–	13	–	–	–	–	1
T.K. Moeke	12	–	12	12	–	–	–	–	–	3
M.P. Kemp	–	s	–	s	s	–	–	–	–	3
S.T.W. Tiopira	s	–	–	–	–	–	–	–	–	1
J. Rye	–	–	–	–	–	–	–	s	s	2
N. Haerewa	10	10	10	10	10	s	–	10	10	8
C.J. Fox	s	s	–	–	s	–	–	s	–	4
S.P. Parkes	9	9	9	9	9	9	9	9	9	9
B. Maxwell	–	8	8	8	8	8	8	8	–	7
T.C. Proffit	7	–	–	s	–	–	–	–	s	3
P. Allen	6	–	–	–	–	–	–	–	–	1
R.M. Kernohan	4	6	6	6	–	6	–	6	6	7
J. Richardson	–	7	7	7	7	7	7	7	7	8
S.T. Parata	–	–	–	s	–	–	–	–	–	1
H.J. Te Moana	–	–	–	–	6	s	4	s	8	5
L. Goldsmith-Boyce	–	s	–	–	s	–	s	s	–	4
A.T. Ross	5	5	5	5	5	5	5	5	5	9
H. Haerewa (capt)	s	4	4	–	–	4	6	4	4	7
S.T. Lasenby	s	s	s	4	4	s	s	–	s	8
R. Namana	–	–	–	–	s	–	s	–	–	2
P.J. Manuel	8	3	3	3	–	3	3	3	3	8
H.T.K. Tichborne	1	1	1	1	–	–	–	–	–	4
A. Potae	3	–	–	–	–	–	–	–	–	1
T.J. Barbarich	s	s	s	s	s	s	s	–	s	8
F. Ioapo	–	–	–	–	1	–	–	–	–	1
R. Whakataka	2	–	–	–	–	–	–	–	–	1
T. Kirikiri	s	–	–	–	–	–	–	–	–	1
W. Riki	–	2	2	2	2	2	2	2	2	8
P.P. Bishop	–	s	s	s	3	1	1	s	1	8
D.W. Knubley	–	–	–	–	s	–	s	1	s	4

P. Allen captained v Poverty Bay (1st); P.J. Manuel v Wairarapa Bush; V.R.M. Bartlett v South Canterbury.

NGATI POROU EAST COAST TEAM RECORD, 2018

Played 9 Won 0 Lost 9 Points for 117 Points against 505

Date	Opponent	Location	Score	Tries	Con	PG	DG	Referee
June 2	Poverty Bay	Tolaga Bay	18–58	Moeke, P. Manuel	S. Parkes	S. Parkes (2)		D.J. MacPherson
August 25	King Country (H)	Te Kuiti	17–75	Tichborne (2), Richardson,	N. Haerewa			G.W. Jackson
September 1	Horowhenua Kapiti (H)	Ruatoria	8–46	N. Haerewa		N. Haerewa		N.E.R. Hogan
September 8	Wairarapa Bush (H)	Ruatoria	5–26	Milner				M.I. Fraser
September 15	South Canterbury (H)	Timaru	7–100	S. Parkes	N. Haerewa			T.M.T. Cottrell
September 22	Poverty Bay (H)	Ruatoria	19–26	Penalty try, Maxwell, S. Parkes	S. Parkes			M.G. Lash
September 29	Mid Canterbury (H)	Ashburton	7–56	Lotawa	S. Parkes			H.G. Reed
October 6	Wanganui (H)	Tolaga Bay	10–56	H. Haerewa	N. Haerewa	N. Haerewa		R.P. Kelly
October 13	West Coast (H)	Greymouth	26–62	Lotawa (2), Sililoko, Proffit	N. Haerewa (3)			M.G. Lash

HAWKE'S BAY

2018 Status: Mitre 10 Cup Championship
Founded 1884. Original member 1892
President: P.G. (Paul) Daniel
Chairman: B.J. (Brendon) Mahony
Chief executive officer: M.J. (Mike) Bishop (to Feb),
J.L. (Jay) Campbell (from Feb)
Coach: M.D. (Mark) Ozich
Assistant coach: J.D. (Josh) Syms
Main ground: McLean Park, Napier
Capacity: 16,500
Colours: Black and white

RECORDS

Most appearances	158	N.W. Thimbleby, 1959–71
Most points	998	J.B. Cunningham, 1990–98
Most tries	73	B.A. Grenside, 1919–31
Most points in a season	237	J.B. Cunningham, 1994
Most tries in a season	18	B.A. Grenside, 1926
		P.J. Cooke, 1986
Most conversions in a season	47	J.B. Cunningham, 1995
Most penalty goals in a season	37	M.W. Berquist, 2009
Most dropped goals in a season	7	B.D.M. Furlong, 1968
		M.K. Sisam, 1979
Most points in a match	36	M.K. Sisam v East Coast, 1979
Most tries in a match	6	R.P. Hunter v East Coast, 1979
Most conversions in a match	13	J.B. Cunningham v Cook Islands, 1995
Most penalty goals in a match	7	J.B. Cunningham v Manawatu, 1993
		J.B. Cunningham v King Country, 1994
		R.G.E. Lewis v North Harbour, 2001
Highest team score	99	v Cook Islands, 1995
		v Mid Canterbury, 2003
Record victory (points ahead)	99	99–0 v Cook Islands, 1995
Highest score conceded	86	v Waikato, 1999
Record defeat (points behind)	86	0–86 v Waikato, 1999

The 2018 season was a much improved one for Hawke's Bay, making the championship semifinals where they lost to a last-minute penalty goal by Otago in Dunedin. With a young side and 17 debutants among the 32 players used, the Magpies finished with a five wins–six loss record. Only against Tasman in the rain did Hawke's Bay really struggle. The emphasis was on attack and the 46 tries was the most Hawke's Bay has ever scored in a Mitre 10 Cup season since the restructuring of the domestic competitions in 2006.

The Magpies' gave debuts to six of last year's national champion Hastings Boys High School first XV now in their first year out of school. Four of them ended up playing in more than half the matches, with loose forward Devan Flanders earning a three-year contract with the Hurricanes, Kianu Kereru-Symes ending up as the first-choice hooker when captain Ash Dixon suffered injury against Counties Manukau, Lincoln McClutchie finished the season as first-choice first five-eighth when Tiaan Falcon was injured in the Ranfurly Shield challenge against Waikato, and halfback Folau Fakatava received a full contract from the Highlanders. They are all players with bright futures. Along with Danny Toala and Josiah Tavita-Metcalfe, Hawke's Bay ought to feel the benefit of this bold move in the not too distant future.

The forward pack had a lot more experience to it than last year and was therefore more competitive. Consistency of selection contributed a lot to this as well with nothing like the disruption due to injuries as occurred last year. A strong point was the rolling maul from the lineout which produced a number of tries.

Loose forward Gareth Evans continued the notable form he had displayed in Super Rugby for the Hurricanes with his best season for Hawke's Bay. For the first time he was injury free, and his nine appearances in 2018 equalled the nine matches he had accumulated over the previous four injury-plagued seasons.

Evans, along with Siosiua 'Josh' Kaifa and Marino Mikaele-Tu'u, were a hard-working loose forward trio, Mikaele-Tu'u having a standout match against Northland. Lock/blindside flanker Geoff Cridge was another to show his worth in an injury-free season after past seasons containing a lot of recovery time on the sideline.

The locks Michael Allardice and Tom Parsons combined well at set-piece time and in general play, with Parsons another to have his best season in the black and white jersey. Props Mark Braidwood and Ben May, also both free of injury in contrast to last year, produced good games, and were well backed up by Joe Apikotoa and Pouri Rakete-Stones.

In the backline, JJ Taulagi was always a threat to the opposition with his running from fullback and showed himself to be a good goalkicker. At times he did look casual but not to any detriment. Jonah Lowe and Mason Emerson were two quick wings who used their pace to usually finish any chances that came their way.

Utility back Stacey Ili played mostly at centre and had a good left boot on him, while Pasqualle Dunn was the preferred second five-eighth. Halfback Brad Weber would have to have been a contender for best halfback in the Mitre 10 Cup, such was his form and influence, and looked after the young backline outside him. He must have gone very close to All Blacks' selection for the end-of-year tour.

Of last year's squad, Hugh Renton (Canterbury), TJ Vaega (returned to Auckland), Cardiff Vaega (returned to Counties Manukau), Richard Buckman (Japan), Ihaia West (France), Chris Eaton (Spain), Tony Lamborn (Southland), Nick Palmer (returned to Australia) and Jarvy Aoake (Waikato) had all moved on while Tim Farrell and Sam McNicol were injured and Jorian Tangaere had an enforced injury retirement. Not required by the All Blacks, Israel Dagg was playing in Japan.

New players arriving in with previous first-class experience were Joe Apikotoa (Wellington), Siosiua 'Josh' Kaifa (Auckland), Sam Ulufonua (Auckland), JJ Taulagi (Sunwolves and Samoa), and Stacey Ili (Auckland) from overseas while Tom Parsons returned from Manawatu.

Higher honours went to:
New Zealand:	G. Evans, B. Retallick
New Zealand Maori:	A. Dixon, J. Lowe, B. May, B. Weber
New Zealand Under 20:	D. Flanders, W. Tremain

HAWKE'S BAY REPRESENTATIVES 2018

	Club	Games for Union	Points for Union
Michael Allardice	Pirates	51	20
Joe Apikotoa	Taradale	11	5
Mark Braidwood	Tech OB	27	15
Michael Buckley	Napier OB Marist	8	10
Geoff Cridge	Hastings RS	27	10
Ash Dixon	Tech OB	85	45
Pasqualle Dunn	Central HB RS	15	20
Mason Emerson	Hastings RS	33	40
Gareth Evans	Havelock North	18	15
Folau Fakatava	Hastings RS	8	10
Tiaan Falcon	Clive	24	48
Devan Flanders	Havelock North	9	0
Solomone Funaki	MAC	1	0
Stacy Ili	Napier OB Marist	10	10
Siosiua "Josh" Kaifa	Clive	11	15
Kianu Kereru-Symes	Tamatea	8	10
Jason Long	Hastings RS	36	20
Jonah Lowe	Clive	35	77
Ben May	Central HB RS	18	5
Lincoln McClutchie	Tamatea	6	0
Marino Mikaele-Tu'u	Hastings RS	21	25
Tom Parsons	Central HB RS	26	10
Ben Power	Havelock North	8	10
Pouri Rakete-Stones	Pirates	18	0
JJ Taulagi	Clive	11	67
Josiah Tavita-Metcalfe	Hastings RS	1	0
Danny Toala	Hastings RS	4	0
Sasa Tofilau	Clive	8	10
William Tremain	Napier OB Marist	4	0
Shae Tucker	Napier OB Marist	1	0
Sam Ulufonua	Havelock North	5	0
Brad Weber	Napier OB Marist	27	49

INDIVIDUAL SCORING

	Tries	Con	PG	DG	Points
Taulagi	4	19	3	–	67
Falcon	–	11	4	–	34
Weber	6	2	–	–	34
Lowe	5	–	–	–	25
Kaifa	3	–	–	–	15
Dunn	3	–	–	–	15
Braidwood	2	–	–	–	10
Dixon	2	–	–	–	10
Emerson	2	–	–	–	10
Fakatava	2	–	–	–	10
Parsons	2	–	–	–	10
Tofilau	2	–	–	–	10
Kereru-Symes	2	–	–	–	10
Ili	2	–	–	–	10
Mikaele-Tu'u	2	–	–	–	10
Power	2	–	–	–	10
Buckley	2	–	–	–	10
May	1	–	–	–	5
Apikotoa	1	–	–	–	5
Evans	1	–	–	–	5
Totals	**46**	**32**	**7**	**0**	**315**
Opposition scored	44	38	15	0	341

HAWKE'S BAY 2018

	Southland	Otago	Counties Manukau	Bay of Plenty	Waikato	North Harbour	Northland	Canterbury	Manawatu	Tasman	Otago	TOTALS
J-J Taulagi	15	15	15	15	15	15	15	15	15	15	15	11
J.H. Lowe	14	14	14	14	14	14	14	14	14	14	14	11
M.R. Emerson	11	11	11	11	11	11	11	s	11	s	11	11
M.F. Buckley	s	s	–	–	s	s	–	11	s	11	s	8
S.I.A. Ili	13	13	13	13	13	13	13	–	13	10	13	10
S.P. Tucker	–	–	–	–	–	–	–	13	–	–	–	1
S.T.M. Tofilau	12	s	s	12	s	s	–	12	–	13	–	8
P.M. Dunn	s	12	12	s	12	12	12	–	12	–	12	9
D.S. Toala	–	–	–	–	–	–	–	s	s	12	s	4
T.J. Falcon	10	10	10	10	10	–	–	–	–	–	–	5
L.F. McClutchie	–	–	–	–	–	10	10	10	10	s	10	6
B.M. Weber	9	9	9	9	9	9	9	–	9	9	9	10
F.M.N. Fakatava	s	s	s	–	s	s	–	9	s	s	–	8
G.O. Evans	8	8	8	8	8	8	7	–	7	–	7	9
S.A. Kaifa	7	7	7	7	s	7	s	7	s	7	s	11
M.E.R. Mikaele-Tu'u	6	6	6	6	6	6	8	–	8	8	8	10
D.J. Flanders	s	s	s	–	–	s	s	8	s	6	s	9
W.A. Tremain	–	s	s	s	7	–	–	–	–	–	–	4
A.S. Funaki	–	–	–	–	–	–	–	s	–	–	–	1
M.G. Allardice	5	5	–	5	5	5	5	s	5	5	5	10
T.I. Parsons	4	4	4	4	4	4	4	4	4	s	4	11
S.F.M.H. Ulufonua	s	–	5	–	–	–	s	5	–	4	–	5
G.O. Cridge	–	–	s	s	s	s	6	6	6	s	6	9
S.J.L. Apikotoa	3	s	s	s	3	s	s	3	s	3	s	11
M. Braidwood	1	1	1	1	s	1	1	s	1	s	1	11
P.G. Rakete-Stones	s	s	s	–	s	s	–	s	s	s	–	8
B. May	s	3	3	3	1	3	3	–	3	–	3	9
J.B. Long	–	–	–	–	s	–	s	1	s	1	s	6
J. Tavita-Metcalfe	–	–	–	–	–	–	–	–	–	s	–	1
A.L. Dixon (capt)	2	2	2	–	–	–	–	–	–	–	–	3
B.R.D. Power	s	s	s	2	–	s	s	2	–	–	s	8
K.R. Kereru-Symes	–	–	–	s	2	2	2	s	2	2	2	8

T.I. Parsons captained v Canterbury; B.M. Weber and G.O. Evans co-captained the other games A.L.Dixon did not appear in.

HAWKE'S BAY TEAM RECORD, 2018

Played 11   Won 5   Lost 6   Points for 315   Points against 341

Date	Opponent	Location	Score	Tries	Con	PG	DG	Referee
August 19	Southland (C)	Invercargill	31–10	Dixon (2), Braidwood, Kaifa	Falcon (4)	Falcon		J.R. Nutbrown
August 24	Otago (C)	Dunedin	31–25	Kaifa, Taulagi, May, Emerson, Weber	Falcon (3)			S. Kubo *Japan*
September 2	Counties Manukau (P/C)	Napier	25–29	Lowe (2), Kaifa, Fakatava	Falcon	Falcon		M.I. Fraser
September 8	Bay of Plenty (C)	Napier	29–28	Weber (2), Lowe, Apikotoa	Falcon (3)	Falcon		R.P. Kelly
September 13	Waikato (C) (RS)	Hamilton	22–42	Weber, Parsons, Tofilau	Taulagi (2)	Falcon		N.P. Briant
September 22	North Harbour (P/C)	Napier	34–51	Kereru-Symes, Lowe, Taulagi, Weber	Taulagi (4)	Taulagi (2)		M.C.J. Winter
September 26	Northland (C)	Napier	55–41	Ili (2), Power (2), Dunn (2), Evans, Mikaele-Tu'u, Taulagi	Taulagi (3), Weber (2)			N.E.R. Hogan
September 30	Canterbury (P/C)	Christchurch	24–49	Tofilau, Buckley, Fakatava	Taulagi (3)	Taulagi		J.J. Doleman
October 5	Manawatu (C)	Napier	45–17	Dunn, Kereru-Symes, Parsons, Braidwood, Taulagi, Lowe, Buckley	Taulagi (5)			B.D. O'Keeffe
October 11	Tasman (P/C)	Nelson	0–29					M.I. Fraser
October 20	Otago (C semi-final)	Dunedin	19–20	Mikaele-Tu'u, Weber, Emerson	Taulagi (2)			B.D. O'Keeffe

RS *Ranfurly Shield*

HOROWHENUA KAPITI

2018 Status: Heartland
Founded 1893. Affiliated 1893 as Horowhenua.
Name change to Horowhenua Kapiti 1997
President: G.B. (Gerald) De Castro
Chairman: J.R. (John) Mowbray
Chief executive officer: C.J. (Corey) Kennett
Coach: C.R.K. (Chris) Wilton
Assistant coach: M.P. (Mark) Rutene
Main ground: Levin Park Domain
Capacity: 12,000
Colours: Red, white and blue

RECORDS

Highest attendance	6500	*Hurricanes v Crusaders pre-season, 2014*
Most appearances	153	*P.M. Hirini, 1986–2000*
Most points	440	*C.W. Laursen, 1984–89*
Most tries	69	*D.C. Laursen, 1980–92*
		P.M. Hirini, 1986–2000
Most points in a season	136	*C.J. Spencer, 1993*
Most tries in a season	13	*D.C. Laursen, 1987*
		C.J. Kennett, 1993
Most conversions in a season	26	*C.J. Spencer, 1993*
		R.F. Aloe, 2008
Most penalty goals in a season	29	*C.W. Laursen, 1987*
Most dropped goals in a season	5	*M. Liddicoat, 1979*
Most points in a match	29	*J.P.M. Hamilton v West Coast, 2010*
		B.C. Laursen v Poverty Bay, 2015
Most tries in a match	5	*D.C. Laursen v West Coast, 1991*
Most conversions in a match	9	*D.P. Nepia v Buller, 1999*
	9	*R.F. Aloe v East Coast, 2008*
Most penalty goals in a match	6	*J. Proctor v Wanganui, 2009*
		J.S. So'oialo v Buller 2017
Highest team score	73	*v Buller, 1999*
		v East Coast, 2008
Record victory (points ahead)	73	*73–0 v Buller, 1999*
Highest score conceded	108	*v Counties, 1994*
Record defeat (points behind)	96	*12–108 v Counties, 1994*

Horowhenua Kapiti had a record of six wins and four losses in 2018. Three of those defeats came at the hands of teams who ultimately finished in the top four as the union finished fifth to enter the Lochore Cup playoffs. A 34–24 win over Mid Canterbury in the semi-final reversed the defeat suffered in the round robin, while the tense 26–23 win over Wairarapa Bush in the final secured the Lochore Cup, enabling Horowhenua Kapiti to celebrate their 125th jubilee with silverware.

With the majority of last year's forward pack available, the directness of going forward over the advantage line continued as a successful tactic. The big experienced lock and captain Ryan Shelford again gave invaluable service and was well supported by fellow lock Tainui Woodmass, props Robin Praat and Scott Cameron and number eight Tyson Maki. New hooker Dean Ropata had a successful debut season. The leading performer in the forwards, though, was flanker Aaron Lahmert who was effective at the breakdown and carried well.

Changes were made to the backline after the loss to South Canterbury. At halfback Leon Ellison was preferred to Tainui Brown, and first five-eighth Ethan Reti and fullback James So'oialo swapped places. So'oialo was much more effective after this and finished top points-scorer in the Heartland competition with 118 points through some excellent goalkicking. Timoci Seruwalu and Kalim Kelemete were both hard to stop in midfield and along with wing Willie Paia'aua scored 15 tries between them. At least one of the three scored a try in nine of the ten games. On the other wing, Himiona Henare had a promising debut season.

Horowhenua Kapiti CEO Corey Kennett, who represented the union in 55 games as a flanker 1991–1995, made an unscheduled reappearance in 2018. For the match against Ngati Porou East Coast he travelled to Ruatoria with the team as a normal part of his role. On the day of the game lock Tainui Woodmass pulled out with sickness, and with no reinforcement being able to get to Ruatoria in time for the game, Kennett agreed to take a spot on the subs bench but only take the field in the event of an injury. With six substitutes on the field, lock Joel Winterburn suffered an injury and on Corey went for the last five minutes at the age of 47. He had played regularly for the Levin College Old Boys reserve team in 2018 that won the reserve grade championship.

Higher honours went to:
New Zealand Heartland: S.A. Cameron, A.D. Lahmert, W.E. Paia'aua

HOROWHENUA KAPITI REPRESENTATIVES 2018

	Club	Games for Union	Points for Union		Club	Games for Union	Points for Union
Anthony Ackerman	Levin College OB	3	0	Robin Praat [1]	Massey University [3]	38	0
Tainui Brown	Levin College OB	21	10	Ethan Reti	Waikanae	9	16
Scott Cameron	Waikanae	47	48	Dean Ropata	Toa	9	0
Leon Ellison	Toa	8	14	Edward Seiuli	Toa	1	0
Michael "TJ" Fermanis	Toa	7	10	Timoci Seruwalu	Ngamatapouri [4]	10	30
Anthony Fox	Waikanae	49	35	Ryan Shelford	Paraparaumu	88	27
Himiona Henare	Levin College OB	9	10	James So'oialo	Tawa [2]	20	251
Kalim Kelemete	Tawa [2]	19	25	Kane Tamou	Foxton	13	5
Corey Kennett	Levin College OB	56	154	Dylan Taylor	Paraparaumu	12	5
Aaron Lahmert	Waikanae	45	37	Tiwana Thompson-Paringatai	Waikanae	15	0
Stewart MacGregor	Athletic	6	10	Cyprus Warren	Toa	1	0
Chase Makamaka	Toa	4	0	Joel Winterburn	Rahui	18	10
Tyson Maki	Levin College OB	32	27	Tainui Woodmass	Shannon	21	0
David McErlean	Foxton	38	30	Tom Zimmerman	Foxton	11	0
Willie Paia'aua	Levin College OB	25	67				

[1] Player of Origin   [2] Wellington RU   [3] Manawatu RU   [4] Wanganui RU

INDIVIDUAL SCORING

	Tries	Con	PG	DG	Points
So'oialo	3	23	19	–	118
Paia'aua	6	–	–	–	30
Seruwalu	6	–	–	–	30
Lahmert	4	–	–	–	20
Reti	–	5	2	–	16
Kelemete	3	–	–	–	15
Ellison	2	2	–	–	14
Henare	2	–	–	–	10
Fermanis	2	–	–	–	10
MacGregor	2	–	–	–	10
Cameron	2	–	–	–	10

	Tries	Con	PG	DG	Points
Tamou	1	–	–	–	5
Taylor	1	–	–	–	5
Winterburn	1	–	–	–	5
Maki	1	–	–	–	5
Shelford	1	–	–	–	5
McErlean	1	–	–	–	5
Totals	**38**	**30**	**21**	**0**	**313**
Opposition scored	41	27	13	0	298

HOROWHENUA KAPITI 2018

	Mid Canterbury	Ngati Porou East Coast	South Canterbury	North Otago	Wairarapa Bush	King Country	Thames Valley	Wanganui	Mid Canterbury	Wairarapa Bush	TOTALS
E.T. Reti	–	10	10	15	15	15	15	15	s	s	9
C. Warren	–	–	–	–	–	–	–	s	–	–	1
H.T.W.K. Henare	15	14	14	–	14	14	14	14	15	15	9
W.E. Paia'aua	14	11	11	11	11	11	11	–	–	11	8
D.C. Taylor	11	s	s	14	–	s	–	–	–	–	5
E. Seiuli	–	–	–	–	–	–	–	11	–	–	1
T.S. Seruwalu	13	13	13	12	12	12	12	12	13	13	10
K.J.P. Kelemete	12	12	12	13	13	13	13	13	14	14	10
S.D. MacGregor	–	s	s	–	–	–	s	s	11	–	5
J.S. So'oialo	10	15	15	10	10	10	10	10	10	10	10
D.T. Brown	9	s	9	s	s	–	s	s	9	9	9
K.E.M. Tamou	s	9	–	–	–	–	–	–	s	s	4
L.P. Ellison	–	–	s	9	9	9	9	9	12	12	8
M. Fermanis	8	8	–	s	s	s	–	7	s	–	7
T.J. Maki	–	–	s	8	8	8	8	8	8	8	8
A.D. Lahmert	7	7	7	7	7	7	6	–	7	7	9
J. Winterburn	6	5	6	6	6	6	–	6	6	6	9
T.L. Zimmerman	s	6	8	–	–	–	s	s	–	–	5
A.B. Ackerman	–	s	s	–	–	–	–	–	–	–	2
C.J. Kennett	–	s	–	–	–	–	–	–	–	–	1
A.J. Fox	–	–	–	–	s	s	7	–	s	s	5
F.T. Woodmass	5	–	5	5	5	5	5	5	5	5	9
R.T. Shelford (capt)	4	4	4	4	4	4	4	4	4	4	10
S.A. Cameron	3	3	3	3	3	3	3	3	3	3	10
R.A. Praat	1	1	s	1	1	1	–	1	1	1	9
C.M. Makamaka	s	s	1	–	–	–	1	–	–	–	4
T.S. Tiwana-Paringatai	–	–	s	s	s	s	s	s	s	s	8
D.J. McErlean	2	s	–	s	s	s	s	s	s	s	9
D. Ropata	–	2	2	2	2	2	2	2	2	2	9

HOROWHENUA KAPITI TEAM RECORD, 2018

Played 10 Won 6 Lost 4 Points for 313 Points against 298

Date	Opponent	Location	Score	Tries	Con	PG	DG	Referee
August 25	Mid Canterbury (H)	Foxton	24–30	So'oialo, Henare, Fermanis, Paia'aua	So'oialo (2)			M.C.J. Winter
September 1	Ngati Porou East Coast (H)	Ruatoria	46–8	Seruwalu (2), Paia'aua (2), Tamou, MacGregor	Reti (5)	Reti (2)		N.E.R. Hogan
September 9	South Canterbury (H)	Wellington	29–52	So'oialo, Ellison, Paia'aua, Lahmert	So'oialo (2), Ellison	So'oialo		T.N. Griffiths
September 15	North Otago (H)	Oamaru	27–24	Taylor, Kelemete, Seruwalu	So'oialo (3)	So'oialo (2)		J.J. Doleman
September 22	Wairarapa Bush (H) (BSC)	Levin	37–21	Seruwalu (2), Kelemete, Winterburn	So'oialo (4)	So'oialo (3)		H.G. Reed
September 29	King Country (H)	Paraparaumu	36–30	Lahmert (2), Cameron, Paia'aua, Fermanis	So'oialo (4)	So'oialo		R.P. Kelly
October 6	Thames Valley (H)	Te Aroha	27–29	Paia'aua, So'oialo	So'oialo	So'oialo (5)		A.W.B. Mabey
October 13	Wanganui (H) (BSC)	Wanganui	27–57	Seruwalu, MacGregor, Henare, Cameron	So'oialo (2)	So'oialo		T.N. Griffiths
October 20	Mid Canterbury (LC semi-final)	Levin	34–24	Maki, Ellison, Kelemete, Shelford	So'oialo (3), Ellison	So'oialo (2)		C.J. Stone
October 28	Wairarapa Bush (LC final)	Levin	26–23	Lahmert, McErlean	So'oialo (2)	So'oialo (4)		R.P. Kelly

BSC *Bruce Steel Cup*

KING COUNTRY

2018 Status: Heartland
Founded 1922. Affiliated 1922
President: L.M. (Max) Lamb
Chairman: I.C. (Ivan) Haines
General Manager: S.M. (Susan) Youngman
Coach: C.W. (Craig) Jeffries
Assistant coach: C.J. (Charles) Hubbard
Main grounds: Owen Delany Park, Taupo; Rugby Park, Te Kuiti
Capacity: 15,000
Colours: Gold and maroon

RECORDS

Highest attendance	12,000	King Country v South Africa, 1994 (Taupo)
Most appearances	147	P.L. Mitchell, 1988–2001
Most points	917	H.C. Coffin, 1984–95
Most tries	46	M.R. Kidd, 1974–84
Most points in a season	230	H.C. Coffin, 1992
Most tries in a season	11	D.M. Flavell, 1981
		S.J. Bradley, 1992
Most conversions in a season	40	H.C. Coffin, 1992
Most penalty goals in a season	45	H.C. Coffin, 1992
Most dropped goals in a season	8	I.N. Ingham, 1966
Most points in a match	33	H.C. Coffin v Poverty Bay, 1992
Most tries in a match	4	C.A. Crossman v Auckland XV, 1936
		J. Haitana & H. Dixon v Thames Valley, 1938
		T. Katene v Golden Bay-Motueka, 1955
		J.A.W. McIlroy v Horowhenua, 1965
		D.W. Koni v Taranaki, 1969
		D.M. Flavell v East Coast, 1979
		N.A. Harrison v East Coast, 1981
		N.A. Harrison v Horowhenua, 1984
		J.W. Wells v East Coast, 1992
Most conversions in a match	10	H.C. Coffin v Poverty Bay, 1992
Most penalty goals in a match	7	L.W.T. Peina v Wanganui, 2000
Highest team score	99	v East Coast, 1992
Record victory (points ahead)	99	99–0 v East Coast, 1992
Highest score conceded	97	v Auckland, 1993
Record defeat (points behind)	94	3–97 v Auckland, 1993

Making a massive improvement on 2017's solitary win, King Country had their best-ever season in the Heartland Championship, finishing third in the round robin to earn a place in the Meads Cup playoffs for the very first time. The Rams won their first four games, and although well beaten by South Canterbury in the semi-final in a disappointing finish, a good platform has seemingly been set for next year.

Carl Carmichael, who captained the side, was a powerful scrummager and tireless leader. He received good support in the forward effort in particular from hard-working flanker Oliver Kay and loan player Chulainn Mabett-Sowerby who was hard to stop at number eight. Having appeared mainly at number eight previously, Rob Sherson made a successful conversion to lock, appearing in every game, and was again good value. Tighthead prop Manawa Veitayaki, son of Joeli who repped for the union 1991–1996, was ever-present in his debut season. Another in his first season, Liam Rowlands started as reserve hooker but played so well he ended up as first choice by season end.

The star of the backline was centre Alex Thrupp whose nine tries made him equal top try-scorer in the Heartland Championship. And with the return of Joe Perawiti at second five-eighth, these two formed a very good partnership in midfield, with Perawiti a forceful runner and strong defender. Dean Church maintained his pace and is still an elusive wing. Evaan Reihana, son of All Black Bruce Reihana, was a very composed first five-eighth and accurate goalkicker in his debut season at first-class level, kicking a last-minute penalty goal to win the match against Buller. Halfback Zayn Tipping made a welcome return after missing all of last year with injury but was not quite the player of two seasons ago. Newcomer Tana Tuhakaraina ended the season prominently at fullback.

Of last year's team, Aarin Dunster and Josh Dais had both retired, and surprisingly, Anthony Wise was not required. For the first time since 2005, King Country hosted a match at Taumarunui after an upgrade was made to the facilities there.

Higher honours went to:
New Zealand Heartland: C.W. Carmichael, D.R. Church, A.M. Thrupp

KING COUNTRY REPRESENTATIVES 2018

	Club	Games for Union	Points for Union		Club	Games for Union	Points for Union
Pihana Astle-Harris	Piopio	6	0	Stormy McCarthy	Piopio	17	12
Declan Barnett	Te Puke Sports [2]	2	20	Joe Perawiti [1]	Otorohanga Sports [3]	27	35
Baven Brown	Waitete	11	20	Evaan Reihana	Te Awamutu Sports [3]	9	99
Carl Carmichael	Taumarunui RS	28	10	Cameron Robinson	Taupo Sports	4	0
Dean Church	Waitomo	73	213	Liam Rowlands	Taupo Sports	9	15
Doug Clapcott	Piopio	9	5	Rob Sherson	Taumarunui RS	64	66
Shilo Cullen	Taupo Sports	9	5	Peter Smith	Kio Kio United	7	0
Joseva Curuki	Taumarunui Districts	4	0	Alex Thrupp	Waitomo	24	72
Kaleb Foote	Piopio	2	5	Zayn Tipping	Taupo Sports	46	194
Phillip Green	Taupo Sports	3	0	Sam Trangmar	Waitomo	2	0
Charlie Henare	Taupo Sports	11	0	Tana Tuhakaraina	Te Puna [2]	6	10
Michael Horrocks	Taumarunui RS	13	0	Manawa Veitayaki	Taupo Sports	9	0
Tim Hounsell	Taupo Sports	6	5	Ratu Vosaki	Taupo Sports	10	10
Oliver Kay	Waitomo	25	10	Sisa Vosaki	Taupo Sports	11	0
Chulainn Mabbett-Sowerby	Te Puke Sports [2]	9	20	Sean Wanden	Waitomo	33	32

[1] *Player of Origin*   [2] *Bay of Plenty RU*   [3] *Waikato RU*

INDIVIDUAL SCORING

	Tries	Con	PG	DG	Points
Reihana	1	32	10	–	99
Thrupp	9	–	–	–	45
Church	6	–	–	–	30
Barnett	4	–	–	–	20
Mabbett-Sowerby	4	–	–	–	20
Brown	3	–	–	–	15
Rowlands	3	–	–	–	15
Wanden	2	–	–	–	10
R.Vosaki	2	–	–	–	10
Sherson	2	–	–	–	10
Perawiti	2	–	–	–	10
Tuhakaraina	2	–	–	–	10
Cullen	1	–	–	–	5
Tipping	1	–	–	–	5
Hounsell	1	–	–	–	5
Clapcott	1	–	–	–	5
Carmichael	1	–	–	–	5
Foote	1	–	–	–	5
Totals	**46**	**32**	**10**	**0**	**324**
Opposition scored	40	28	11	0	289

KING COUNTRY 2018

	Ngati Porou East Coast	Buller	North Otago	Thames Valley	Wanganui	Horowhenua Kapiti	Poverty Bay	Mid Canterbury	South Canterbury	TOTALS
D.G. Barnett	15	–	–	–	–	–	–	–	15	2
S.T.M.E. McCarthy	s	15	15	s	–	–	–	–	–	5
T. Tuhakaraina	–	–	14	15	15	15	15	15	–	6
D.R. Church	14	14	–	–	–	14	11	11	11	6
S.A. Cullen	11	11	11	11	11	s	s	s	s	9
R.S. Vosaki	s	s	s	14	s	–	s	–	s	7
C.J. Robinson	–	–	s	–	–	–	–	–	–	1
B.L. Brown	–	–	–	–	14	11	14	14	14	5
A.M. Thrupp	13	13	13	13	13	13	13	13	13	9
J.E. Perawiti	12	12	12	12	12	12	12	12	12	9
E.H. Reihana	10	10	10	10	10	10	10	10	10	9
Z.J. Tipping	9	9	9	9	9	9	9	9	9	9
T. Hounsell	s	s	s	s	–	–	s	s	–	6
C. Mabbett-Sowerby	8	8	8	8	8	8	8	8	8	9
O.W. Kay	7	7	6	6	7	7	7	7	7	9
S. Vosaki	6	6	s	–	6	6	6	–	s	7
P. Smith	s	s	7	7	–	s	s	–	s	7
S.H. Trangmar	–	–	–	s	s	–	–	–	–	2
K. Foote	–	–	–	–	–	–	–	6	6	2
R.L. Sherson	5	5	5	5	5	5	5	5	5	9
P.J. Green	4	4	–	–	–	–	s	–	–	3
D.J. Clapcott	s	s	4	s	s	4	4	4	4	9
M.L.M.L. Horrocks	–	–	s	4	4	s	–	–	s	6
M. Veitayaki	3	3	s	3	3	s	3	3	3	9
C.W. Carmichael (capt)	1	1	1	1	1	1	1	1	1	9
J.K. Curuki	s	s	3	–	–	–	–	–	–	3
P.P. Astle-Harris	–	s	–	s	s	3	–	s	s	6
C.K. Henare	–	–	–	–	–	–	s	s	s	3
S.P.B. Wanden	2	2	2	s	2	2	s	–	–	7
L. Rowlands	s	s	s	2	s	s	2	2	2	9

KING COUNTRY TEAM RECORD, 2018

Played 9　Won 6　Lost 3　Points for 324　Points against 289

Date	Opponent	Location	Score	Tries	Con	PG	DG	Referee
August 25	Ngati Porou East Coast (H)	Te Kuiti	75–17	Church (3), Barnett (3), Wanden, Cullen, Thrupp, Reihana, R. Vosaki	Reihana (7)	Reihana (2)		G.W. Jackson
September 1	Buller (H)	Westport	30–28	Church (3), Mabbett-Sowerby	Reihana (2)	Reihana (2)		T.N. Griffiths
September 8	North Otago (H)	Taumarunui	22–18	Thrupp, Sherson, Tipping	Reihana (2)	Reihana		D.J. MacPherson
September 15	Thames Valley (H)	Te Aroha	37–29	Perawiti, R. Vosaki, Mabbett-Sowerby, Tuhakaraina, Hounsell	Reihana (3)	Reihana (2)		R.M. Mahoney
September 22	Wanganui (H)	Te Kuiti	19–36	Brown, Wanden, Clapcott	Reihana (2)			N.J. Webster
September 29	Horowhenua Kapiti (H)	Paraparaumu	30–36	Thrupp, Mabbett-Sowerby, Perawiti, Rowlands	Reihana (2)	Reihana (2)		R.P. Kelly
October 6	Poverty Bay (H)	Taupo	59–38	Thrupp (3), Brown (2), Rowlands (2), Carmichael	Reihana (8)	Reihana		H.G. Reed
October 13	Mid Canterbury (H)	Ashburton	31–29	Thrupp (2), Mabbett-Sowerby, Sherson, Tuhakaraina	Reihana (3)			N.J. Webster
October 20	South Canterbury (MC semi-final)	Timaru	21–58	Barnett, Foote, Thrupp	Reihana (3)			N.J. Webster

MANAWATU

2018 Status: Mitre 10 Cup Championship
Founded 1886. Original member 1892
President: B.S. (Bruce) Hemara
Chairman: T.J. (Tim) Myers
Chief executive officer: S.M. (Shannon) Paku
Coach: J.M. (Jeremy) Cotter
Assistant coach: A.J. (Aaron) Good
Main ground: Central Energy Trust Arena, Palmerston North
Capacity: 17,000
Colours: Green and white

MANAWATU RUGBY

RECORDS

Highest attendance	24,996	Manawatu-Horowhenua v British Isles, 1959
Most appearances	145	G.A. Knight, 1975–86
Most points	641	J.J. Holland, 1991–96
Most tries	66	K.W. Granger, 1971–84
Most points in a season	182	J.M. Smith, 1991
Most tries in a season	14	P.L. Alston, 1991
Most conversions in a season	38	D.L. Rollerson, 1981
		J.M. Smith, 1991
Most penalty goals in a season	27	M.C. Finlay, 1984
		A. McMaster, 1987
Most dropped goals in a season	9	J.P.J. Carroll, 1978
Most points in a match	35	J.M. Smith v Horowhenua, 1992
Most tries in a match	5	J.P. Butt v Wanganui, 1944
		N.J. Mears v Horowhenua, 1958
		G.P.D. Henare v Horowhenua, 1987
Most conversions in a match	11	J.M. Smith v Poverty Bay, 1991
Most penalty goals in a match	6	M.R. Love v Waikato, 1983
		M.C. Finlay v Wanganui, 1984
		A. McMaster v Waikato, 1987
		J.J. Holland v Counties, 1994
		I. Thompson v Northland, 2009
Highest team score	94	v Poverty Bay, 1991
Record victory (points ahead)	87	94–7 v Poverty Bay, 1991
Highest score conceded	109	v British & Irish Lions, 2005
Record defeat (points behind)	103	6–109 v British & Irish Lions, 2005

There was considerable confidence in the squad chosen for the 2018 campaign and the first-round win over Waikato strengthened that confidence. However, two heavy losses followed, to Taranaki and Otago, and failure to gain a win in any of the following four games, shattered all hopes of gaining a semi-final berth. There were good efforts against Canterbury and Tasman but, overall, it was a disappointing season. Conceding an average of 35 points per game indicates a leaky defence. The wins over Bay of Plenty and Southland, late in the campaign, merely restored some respectability, both opponents sharing the lower end of the championship ladder with Manawatu. The forwards rarely gained dominance and this affected the backline which contained numerous talented performers but seldom exhibited efficient, error free play. Some fine tries were scored but there were only a few moments when fans rose from their seats.

Tom Parsons returned to Hawke's Bay and with Jackson Hemopo receiving a well-deserved call-up to the All Blacks Manawatu lacked power behind the front row. Experienced props Fraser Armstrong and Michael Ala'alatoa were joined in the front row by Sam Stewart who had arrived early in the year from Southland. Nick Crosswell, nearing a century of games for the Turbos, was moved to lock. Liam Hallam-Eames was suspended for four games after an incident against Waikato. Brad Tucker, from Waikato, and Tom Hughes, returning from Canterbury after Hallam-Eames was suspended, were the other locks used. Heiden Bedwell-Curtis, the 2017 captain, departed for Japan and Antonio Kiri Kiri took over the leadership. He was supported in the loose by Brice Henderson and the improving Liam Mitchell. Sam Slade was brought in from Auckland and Adrian Wyrill from Taranaki.

There was little between the two halfbacks Kayne Hammington and Jamie Booth, both being very efficient. First-five Jade Te Rure was injured in the third game leaving Sam Malcolm, called home from Sydney, to take command until Otere Black returned from injury. Malcolm later moved to fullback and proved to be perhaps the most consistent among the backs. Rob Thompson's return from Canterbury was a popular signing and he didn't disappoint. His experience and skill shone through, particularly in the earlier games. The experienced Lifeimi Mafi returned from Ireland but the 36-year-old was not the explosive player that was seen in the Manawatu jersey during 2002-03. The usually reliable Hamish Northcott was the only midfielder to appear in every game. Hastings-born Junior Laloifi had made a name for himself across the Tasman where he appeared for Australia Sevens teams and the Queensland Reds. He gained the label 'the prince of pace' and he exhibited his blistering speed during the early games when he scored in each of the first three games. Television commentators were excited by the 23-year-old fullback but, as the team struggled through the remainder of the season, less was seen of him.

Nehe Milner-Skudder, Jackson Hemopo and Ngani Laumape were released from the All Blacks squad on occasions, Laumape giving a grand display against Southland. The Turbos sadly lacked the explosive power that each of this trio is known for.

Higher honours went to:
New Zealand: J. Hemopo, N. Laumape, N. Milner-Skudder, A.L. Smith
Maori All Blacks: O. Black, J. Hemopo, R. Thompson
New Zealand Sevens: K.T. Baker

MANAWATU REPRESENTATIVES 2018

	Club	Games for Union	Points for Union		Club	Games for Union	Points for Union
Michael Ala'alatoa	Feilding OB Oroua	36	20	Nehe Milner-Skudder	University	41	35
Fraser Armstrong	OB Marist	36	5	Liam Mitchell	Te Kawau	14	5
Sione Asi	Kia Toa	10	0	Hamish Northcott	University	53	25
Otere Black	College OB	45	369	Sean Paranihi	Feilding OB Oroua	16	0
Jamie Booth	University	42	35	Faalelei Sione	Canberra Vikings[2]	9	10
Tim Cadwallader	College OB	29	10	Sam Slade	Ponsonby[3]	8	0
Nick Crosswell	Feilding	93	20	Sam Stewart	Te Kawau	10	0
Liam Hallam-Eames	OB Marist	15	0	Gene Syminton	College OB	2	0
Kayne Hammington	Feilding	40	15	Michael Tagicakibau	Kia Toa	4	5
Jackson Hemopo	Kia Toa	22	20	Jade Te Rure	Kia Toa	34	189
Brice Henderson	College OB	21	5	Rob Thompson	University	9	15
Tom Hughes	Sydenham[1]	8	0	James Tofa	College OB	7	5
Jackson Iose	Kia Toa	1	0	Brad Tucker	OB Marist	9	5
Antonio Kiri Kiri	OB Marist	62	55	Te Rangatira Waitokia	University	10	0
Junior Laloifi	Feilding OB Oroua	9	25	Sam Wasley	Feilding	1	0
Ngani Laumape	Kia Toa	14	50	Ben Werthmuller	OB Marist	1	0
Lifeimi Mafi	Kia Toa	25	35	Adrian Wyrill	Tukapa[4]	4	5
Sam Malcolm	University	20	47				

[1] Canterbury RU [2] Australia [3] Auckland RU [4] Taranaki RU

INDIVIDUAL SCORING

	Tries	Con	PG	DG	Points		Tries	Con	PG	DG	Points
Malcolm	2	8	3	–	35	Henderson	1	–	–	–	5
Black	–	11	2	–	28	Mafi	1	–	–	–	5
Laloifi	5	–	–	–	25	Mitchell	1	–	–	–	5
Thompson	3	–	–	–	15	Tagicakibau	1	–	–	–	5
Ala'alatoa	2	–	–	–	10	Tofa	1	–	–	–	5
Kiri Kiri	2	–	–	–	10	Tucker	1	–	–	–	5
Laumape	2	–	–	–	10	Wyrill	1	–	–	–	5
Sione	2	–	–	–	10						
Te Rure	–	3	1	–	9	**Totals**	**28**	**22**	**6**	**0**	**202**
Booth	1	–	–	–	5	Opposition scored	53	34	8	0	357
Crosswell	1	–	–	–	5						
Hemopo	1	–	–	–	5						

MANAWATU 2018	Waikato	Taranaki	Otago	Canterbury	Northland	Tasman	Wellington	Bay of Plenty	Hawke's Bay	Southland	TOTALS
J. Laloifi	15	15	15	15	15	15	–	11	11	11	9
Te R.W. Waitokia	14	14	–	14	–	14	15	–	14	–	6
N.R. Milner-Skudder	11	11	14	–	–	–	–	–	–	14	4
J. Tofa	–	s	11	s	14	12	11	s	–	–	7
M.L. Tagicakibau	–	–	–	11	11	11	–	14	–	–	4
R. Thompson	12	13	13	13	13	–	14	13	13	13	9
L.O. Mafi	13	–	s	12	12	s	13	–	–	–	6
B.B. Werthmuller	–	–	–	–	–	–	s	–	–	–	1
H.C. Northcott	s	12	12	s	s	13	12	12	s	s	10
K.H. Laumape	–	–	–	–	–	–	–	–	12	12	2
J. Te Rure	10	s	10	–	–	–	–	–	s	s	5
S.B. Malcolm	s	10	s	10	10	10	s	15	15	15	10
O.W. Black	–	–	–	–	s	s	10	10	10	10	6
K.W. Hammington	9	9	s	s	9	s	9	s	s	9	10
J.P. Booth	s	s	9	9	s	9	s	9	9	s	10
B.W. Henderson	8	8	8	8	8	–	s	8	8	s	9
S.D. Wasley	s	–	–	–	–	–	–	–	–	–	1
J.O. Iose	–	s	–	–	–	–	–	–	–	–	1
A.I. Kiri Kiri (Capt)	7	7	7	7	7	7	–	7	7	7	9
A.E. Wyrill	–	–	–	–	s	s	7	–	s	–	4
L.F. Mitchell	6	6	6	6	6	–	6	6	6	4	9
S.V. Slade	–	s	s	s	s	6	s	–	s	8	8
J.N. Hemopo	–	–	–	–	–	s	–	–	–	6	2
N.J. Crosswell	5	5	4	4	4	–	5	s	–	5	8
L.J. Hallam-Eames	4	–	–	–	–	5	4	4	4	s	6
B.C. Tucker	s	4	s	5	5	8	8	s	5	–	9
T.W. Hughes	–	–	5	s	–	4	–	5	–	–	4
S.F. Asi	3	s	s	s	s	–	–	–	–	–	7
M.S. Ala'alatoa	–	3	3	3	3	3	s	3	3	3	9
F.P. Armstrong	1	1	1	–	1	1	s	1	1	1	9
S.B. Paranihi	s	–	–	1	–	–	3	s	s	s	6
F. Sione	s	s	s	s	s	s	1	s	s	–	9
T.J. Cadwallader	2	2	2	2	2	–	–	–	s	–	6
S.W. Stewart	s	s	s	s	s	2	2	2	2	2	10
G.W. Syminton	–	–	–	–	–	–	s	–	–	s	2

Crosswell was captain against Wellington

MANAWATU TEAM RECORD, 2018

Played 10　Won 3　Lost 7　Points for 202　Points against 357

Date	Opponent	Location	Score	Tries	Con	PG	DG	Referee
August 18	Waikato (C)	Palmerston North	24–19	Laloifi (2), Sione, Thompson	Te Rure, Malcolm			M.I. Fraser
August 24	Taranaki (C/P, RS)	New Plymouth	21–41	Laloifi, Crosswell, Thompson	Malcolm (2), Te Rure			M.I. Fraser
September 1	Otago (C)	Palmerston North	17–50	Thompson, Laloifi, Sione	Te Rure			P.M. Williams
September 6	Canterbury (C/P)	Christchurch	23–34	Mitchell, Mafi	Malcolm (2)	Malcolm (3)		C.J. Stone
September 14	Northland (C)	Whangarei	19–49	Tofa, Laloifi, Wyrill	Malcolm, Black			M.C.J. Winter
September 19	Tasman (C/P)	Palmerston North	19–29	Malcolm, Ala'alatoa, Tagicakibau	Malcolm, Black			B.D. O'Keeffe
September 23	Wellington (C/P)	Palmerston North	7–49	Henderson	Malcolm			C.J. Stone
September 27	Bay of Plenty (C)	Rotorua	17–15	Booth, Malcolm	Black (2)	Black		M.G. Lash
October 5	Hawke's Bay (C)	Napier	17–45	Tucker, Ala'alatoa	Black (2)	Black		B.D. O'Keeffe
October 14	Southland (C)	Palmerston North	38–26	Kiri Kiri (2), Laumape (2), Hemopo	Black (5)	Te Rure		P.M. Williams

MID CANTERBURY

2018 Status: Heartland
Founded 1904 as Ashburton with affiliation to South Canterbury, 1905–1926 affiliated to Canterbury. Granted full union status in 1927 as Ashburton County; 1952 name changed to Mid Canterbury.
President: J.C. (Jock) Ross
Chairman: G.P. (Gerard) Rushton
Chief executive officer: I.J. (Ian) Patterson
Coach: Sean Carter
Assistant coaches: Dale Palmer, J.J. (Jason) Rickard
Main ground: Ashburton Showgrounds
Capacity: 10,000
Colours: Forest green and gold

RECORDS

Highest attendance	8656	Mid Canterbury v British Isles, 1983
Most appearances	158	J.C. Ross, 1970–87
Most points	598	A.H.A. Smith, 1955–68
Most tries	47	G.R. Bryant, 1968–77
Most points in a season	200	S.R. Middleton, 1994
Most tries in a season	13	M.L. Sau, 2017
Most conversions in a season	34	S.R. Middleton, 1994
		J.R. Percival, 2017
Most penalty goals in a season	44	S.R. Middleton, 1994
Most dropped goals in a season	12	M.B. Roulston, 1982
Most points in a match	22	M.C. Williams v East Coast, 2014
Most tries in a match	5	G.R. Bryant v Nelson Bays, 1977
Most conversions in a match	8	S.R. Middleton v West Coast, 1998
Most penalty goals in a match	6	S.R. Middleton v Horowhenua Kapiti, 1998
		D.J. Maw v West Coast, 2007
		M.C. Williams v Wanganui, 2014
Highest team score	90	v West Coast, 1998
Record victory (points ahead)	77	90–13 v West Coast, 1998
Highest score conceded	99	v Hawke's Bay, 2003
Record defeat (points behind)	91	8–99 v Hawke's Bay, 2003

Mid Canterbury was fortunate to finish eighth in the round robin and make the Lochore Cup semi-finals with a record of three wins and five defeats. If West Coast had not been deducted six competition points the day before the final round, Mid Canterbury would have finished ninth and missed the playoffs.

The back division contained two speedsters on the wings in former Zimbabwe Under 20 rep Brian Matoramusha and origin player Dan Fransen, scoring a combined 16 tries with Matoramusha's nine being equal top in the Heartland Championship. In his second season Tom Hanham-Carter showed some deft touches at centre, but second five-eighth Andrew Letham had another injury-plagued year. Jarred Percival started at first five-eighth but was shifted back to fullback for the second half of the season to make way for newcomer Nathan McCloy. Halfback Will MacKenzie was a capable performer who cleared the ball efficiently.

The forward pack was not one of the biggest in the competition but was a mobile one. Lock

Eric Duff was not quite as good as he was last year, but his lineout play was still of a high standard. Angus Lindsay was shifted to flanker and carried on with his good work from last season. Flanker Seta Koroitamana was a standout throughout the season with his pace and strong ball-carrying. Loosehead prop Tom Heywood, just 21, was a real workhorse throughout the season and unfortunately missed the semi-final through injury. Hooker and captain Jackson Donlan played every game.

Prominent players from last year's squad who were absent included Maleli Sau, Nete Caucau (both back in Fiji), and Willie McGoon (Hawke's Bay).

Higher honours went to:
New Zealand Heartland: S.S. Koroitamana

MID CANTERBURY REPRESENTATIVES 2018

	Club	Games for Union	Points for Union		Club	Games for Union	Points for Union
Osea Baisagale	Methven	2	0	Jesse Houston	Lincoln University [2]	1	0
Matt Bentley	Rakaia	10	0	Seta Koroitamana	Rakaia	49	133
Tyler Blackburn	Methven	25	5	Atolofi Lapa	Hampstead	1	0
Tom Blyth	Rakaia	8	0	Andrew Letham	Rakaia	34	123
Logan Bonnington	Southern	39	21	Angus Lindsay	Celtic	23	30
Sam Cottam	Christchurch [2]	7	0	Will MacKenzie	Southern	66	0
Jackson Donlan	Rakaia	47	16	Isireli Masiwini	Celtic	13	15
Eric Duff	Southern	49	31	Brian Matoramusha	Celtic	8	47
Aron Einarsson	Christchurch HSOB [2]	8	5	Nathan McCloy	Celtic	9	34
Penisimani Fakatoka	Rakaia	5	0	Angus McKenzie	Southern	5	0
Dan Fransen [1]	Sydenham [2]	15	40	Shepherd Mhembere	Celtic	3	0
Hugh Griffiths	Methven	5	0	Timoci Nabakeke	Rakaia	21	28
Matt Groom	Methven	24	5	Jarred Percival	Christchurch HSOB [2]	28	259
Tom Hanham-Carter	Rakaia	16	15	Leauma Tu Uga	Celtic	3	5
Tom Heywood	Rakaia	15	5	Adam Williamson	Southern	17	0

[1] *Player of Origin*   [2] *Canterbury RU*

INDIVIDUAL SCORING

	Tries	Con	PG	DG	Points		Tries	Con	PG	DG	Points
Matoramusha	9	1	–	–	47	Heywood	1	–	–	–	5
Fransen	7	–	–	–	35	Hanham-Carter	1	–	–	–	5
McCloy	–	14	2	–	34	Einarsson	1	–	–	–	5
Letham	–	9	1	–	21	Bonnington	1	–	–	–	5
Koroitamana	4	–	–	–	20	Tu Uga	1	–	–	–	5
Masiwini	3	–	–	–	15	Groom	1	–	–	–	5
Percival	1	2	2	–	15						
Nabakeke	2	–	–	–	10	**Totals**	36	26	5	0	249
Lindsay	2	–	–	–	10						
Penalty try	1	–	–	–	7	*Opposition scored*	38	25	9	0	267
Duff	1	–	–	–	5						

MID CANTERBURY 2018	Horowhenua Kapiti	North Otago	West Coast	Wanganui	South Canterbury	Ngati Porou East Coast	Buller	King Country	Horowhenua Kapiti	TOTALS
T.N. Nabakeke	15	14	s	14	15	11	15	s	s	9
D.J. Fransen	14	15	15	15	14	14	14	14	14	9
T.B. Matoramusha	11	s	11	11	11	–	s	11	11	8
H.R. Griffiths	–	11	14	–	–	s	11	–	s	5
O.B. Baisagale	–	–	–	–	–	s	s	–	–	2
T.K. Hanham-Carter	13	13	13	13	13	s	13	13	13	9
I. Masiwini	12	–	–	s	s	13	s	12	12	7
A.J. Letham	s	12	12	12	12	–	–	–	–	5
J.R. Percival	10	10	10	10	10	15	–	15	15	8
N.J. McCloy	s	s	s	s	s	10	10	10	10	9
A.W. MacKenzie	9	s	9	9	9	9	9	s	9	9
T.A.C. Blackburn	s	9	s	s	s	12	12	9	–	8
A.D. Einarsson	8	8	–	8	8	8	8	s	8	8
S.S. Koroitamana	7	7	8	7	7	–	7	8	6	8
A.J. Lindsay	6	6	6	6	6	7	6	7	7	9
J.D.W. Houston	–	–	7	–	–	–	–	–	–	1
S.C. Mhembere	–	–	s	–	s	–	–	–	s	3
A. Lapa	–	–	–	–	s	–	–	–	–	1
E.J. Duff	5	5	5	5	5	5	5	5	5	9
M.J. Bentley	4	4	s	–	–	s	s	s	–	6
T.E.L. Blyth	s	s	4	4	4	6	s	6	–	8
L.P. Bonnington	–	–	–	s	–	4	4	4	4	5
S.W. Cottam	3	3	–	–	3	–	–	–	–	3
T.J. Heywood	1	1	1	1	1	1	1	1	–	8
M.R. Groom	–	–	3	3	s	3	3	3	3	7
A.C.J. Williamson	–	–	s	–	–	–	–	s	s	3
P. Fakatoka	–	–	–	s	–	s	s	–	s	4
L. Tu Uga	–	–	–	–	–	s	–	s	1	3
J.L. Donlan (capt)	2	2	2	2	2	2	2	2	2	9
A.A.J. McKenzie	–	s	s	–	s	s	s	–	–	5

MID CANTERBURY TEAM RECORD, 2018

Played 9　Won 3　Lost 6　Points for 249　Points against 267

Date	Opponent	Location	Score	Tries	Con	PG	DG	Referee
August 25	Horowhenua Kapiti (H)	Foxton	30–24	Matoramusha, Masiwini, Nabakeke, Duff	Percival (2)	Percival (2)		M.C.J. Winter
September 1	North Otago (H)	Ashburton	33–34	Fransen (2), Nabakeke, Koroitamana, Heywood	Letham (4)			J.R. Nutbrown
September 8	West Coast (H)	Ashburton	36–29	Koroitamana (2), Percival, Matoramusha, Fransen	Letham (4)	Letham		J.D. Munro
September 15	Wanganui (H)	Wanganui	12–30	Hanham-Carter, Matoramusha	Letham			C.J. Stone
September 22	South Canterbury (H) (HS)	Timaru	10–41	Fransen (2)				J.J. Doleman
September 29	Ngati Porou East Coast (H)	Ashburton	56–7	Masiwini (2), Einnarson, Penalty try, Bonnington, Fransen, Tu Uga, Lindsay	McCloy (7)			H.G. Reed
October 6	Buller (H)	Westport	19–37	Groom, Lindsay, Matoramusha	McCloy (2)			R.M. Mahoney
October 13	King Country (H)	Ashburton	29–31	Matoramusha (3), Fransen	McCloy (3)	McCloy		N.J. Webster
October 20	Horowhenua Kapiti (LC semi-final)	Levin	24–34	Matoramusha (2), Koroitamana	McCloy (2), Matoramusha	McCloy		C.J. Stone

HS *Hanan Shield*

NORTH HARBOUR

2018 Status: Mitre 10 Cup Premiership
Founded 1985. Affiliated 1985
President: John McKittrick
Chairman: S.R. (Shaun) Nixon
General Manager: D.B. (David) Gibson
Coach: T.J. (Tom) Coventry
Assistant coaches: D.K. (Daniel) Halangahu, Noel McNamara
Main ground: North Harbour Stadium, Albany
Capacity: 25,000
Colours: White, black and cardinal

RECORDS

Most appearances	145	Ron Williams, 1985–94
		Walter Little, 1987–2000
Most points	1052	Warren Burton, 1990–96
Most tries	63	Richard Kapa, 1985–93
Most points in a season	258	Warren Burton, 1995
Most tries in a season	16	Glenn Davis, 1999
Most conversions in a season	53	Warren Burton, 1991
Most penalty goals in a season	47	Warren Burton, 1995
Most dropped goals in a season	3	Jamie Cameron, 1991
Most points in a match	34	Frano Botica v Queensland Country, 1985
Most tries in a match	5	Glenn Davis v Poverty Bay-East Coast, 1999
		Tevita Li v Taranaki, 2017
Most conversions in a match	10	Frano Botica v Taranaki, 1989
		Jamie Cameron v Marlborough, 1990
		Warren Burton v Wanganui, 1991
Most penalty goals in a match	6	Warren Burton v Counties, 1990
		Warren Burton v Wellington, 1990
		Warren Burton v Otago, 1994
		Warren Burton v Hawke's Bay, 1996
Highest team score	99	v Horowhenua Kapiti, 2008
Record victory (points ahead)	93	99–6 v Horowhenua Kapiti, 2008
Highest score conceded	71	v Auckland, 1995
Record defeat (points behind)	55	10–65 v Canterbury 2002

North Harbour played some good rugby in the Premiership but will be disappointed to have fallen short of a semi-finals berth after such a fine 2017.

Harbour started well enough with seven debutants, winning its first two games, if narrowly. But then followed a run of three straight defeats, which put semi-final aspirations under the blowtorch. Four victories on the bounce brought the side storming back into contention, but Auckland administered a reality check, to regain the Battle of the Bridge silverware, on the final day of the regular season.

Harbour was solid enough in most areas but was off the pace against the four Premiership semi-finalists, and tended to drop the ball in promising situations. A core group of 15 players played in almost all the games, signifying a settled selection policy.

Missing from 2017 were Jarrad Hoeata (Taranaki), Brandon Nansen (France), Chris Smylie (retired), Shaun Treeby (Japan), Josh Tyrell (UK), Matt Vaega (Japan) and Ben Volavola (France).

Incoming were James Dargaville (Australia), Dillon Hunt (Otago), Harrison Levien (Waikato), Loketi Manu (Auckland), Nic Mayhew (Australia), Ben Nee-Nee (Auckland), Jacob Pierce (Auckland) and Sione Teu (Otago).

Shaun Stevenson was again outstanding at fullback, scoring four tries and setting up several more. His combination with wings Matt Duffie and Tevita Li, often on the counter-attack, was especially effective.

Duffie scored five tries, finishing some in fine style, but his work under the high ball was not flawless, and his overall play fell short of his 2017 standards, when he made the All Blacks.

Li, who brought up 50 games for the union, was often unstoppable with his pace and strength, following on from his 11 tries in 2017. He crossed for 10, including a quartet against Taranaki.

James Dargaville, signed from the Brumbies, was solid enough at centre, but loan player Loketi Manu only made three appearances. Daniel Hilton-Jones showed promise when given space to move. Harrison Groundwater was solid if not spectacular at second five.

Bryn Gatland passed 100 points again and often did some very good and influential things, but his general play was not as slick as it was in 2016–17.

Bryn Hall backed up another big Crusaders campaign with consistently sound rugby, while his understudy Lewis Gjaltema added impact late in games.

Number eights Murphy Taramai and Hapakuki Moala-Liava'a often worked well in tandem, Taramai bringing his high work rate from the start and Moala-Liava'a, a powerful ball carrier, offering impact later in games.

Flanker Dillon Hunt was Harbour's best player, strong over the ball, and scoring four tries. His was a good signing, having returned home to his native province. Glenn Preston bounced back from a season-ending Blues injury to put in some good shifts on the blindside.

Gerard Cowley-Tuioti was as industrious as ever at lock, while Ben Nee-Nee won 32 lineouts and impressed around the field. Jacob Pierce became Harbour rep No. 423 with his early debut. He started just one game, but that was enough to be signed by the Blues.

In the front row, Nic Mayhew was injured early, while Chris Eves mostly wore the No17 jersey. Mike Tamoaieta was not the scrummaging force he was in 2017. Karl Tu'inukuafe was not seen due to his meteoric rise into the All Blacks. Sione Mafileo shouldered most of the tighthead workload, while Luatangi Li, brother of Tevita, acquitted himself well either starting or off the bench.

James Parsons led the team well again and maintained a high standard of play. His sweet reverse pass to set up Duffie against Canterbury was a season highlight, while his two tries from lineout drives and a conversion against Hawke's Bay capped a memorable 100th game for this stalwart of the union.

Coaches Tom Coventry and Daniel Halangahu are now moving on to the Blues, so a new staff will need to continue the good work of the last four or five seasons.

Higher honours went to:
New Zealand: D. Hunt, K. Tu'inukuafe
New Zealand Maori: C. Eves, B. Hall, S. Stevenson

NORTH HARBOUR REPRESENTATIVES 2018

	Club	Games for Union	Points for Union
Gerard Cowley-Tuioti	Massey	46	15
James Dargaville	Northcote	6	0
Danny Drake	Northcote	4	0
Matt Duffie	Takapuna	29	75
Chris Eves	Massey	23	15
Bryn Gatland	Takapuna	31	328
Lewis Gjaltema	East Coast Bays	12	0
Harrison Groundwater	East Coast Bays	17	20
Bryn Hall	Northcote	68	69
Daniel Hilton-Jones	North Shore	23	15
Dillon Hunt	Marist	8	20
Tevita Li	Massey	55	180
Luatangi Li	East Coast Bays	8	5
Sione Mafileo	North Shore	43	10
Loketi Manu	College Rifles [1]	4	0
Nic Mayhew	Northcote	31	10
Hapakuki Moala-Liava'a	Massey	30	0
Ben Nee-Nee	Northcote	9	0
James Parsons	Takapuna	103	97
Jacob Pierce	North Shore	8	0
Glenn Preston	Marist	33	5
Nick Smith	Northcote	1	0
Shaun Stevenson	Marist	21	55
Mike Tamoaieta	Glenfield	18	0
Murphy Taramai	Northcote	31	10
Mark Telea	Massey	16	5
Sione Teu	North Shore	5	5
Luteru Tolai	Northcote	6	0
Palatoni "Toni" Tu'ungafasi	Northcote	3	5

[1] Auckland RU

INDIVIDUAL SCORING

	Tries	Con	PG	DG	Points
Gatland	2	27	15	–	109
T. Li	10	–	–	–	50
Duffie	5	–	–	–	25
Hunt	4	–	–	–	20
Stevenson	4	–	–	–	20
Parsons	3	1	–	–	17
Groundwater	3	–	–	–	15
Penalty try	2	–	–	–	14
Hilton-Jones	2	–	–	–	10
Hall	1	1	–	–	7
Taramai	1	–	–	–	5
Cowley-Tuioti	1	–	–	–	5
Teu	1	–	–	–	5
Telea	1	–	–	–	5
L. Li	1	–	–	–	5
Tu'ungafasi	1	–	–	–	5
Totals	**42**	**29**	**15**	**0**	**317**
Opposition scored	40*	31	11	0	297

* includes one penalty try (7 points)

NORTH HARBOUR 2018

	Northland	Waikato	Tasman	Wellington	Canterbury	Bay of Plenty	Hawke's Bay	Taranaki	Counties Manukau	Auckland	TOTALS
S.T. Stevenson	15	15	15	15	15	15	15	15	15	15	10
M.D. Duffie	14	14	14	14	14	14	14	14	–	–	8
T. Li	11	11	11	11	11	11	11	11	11	11	10
M.E. Telea	s	s	s	s	–	–	s	s	14	14	8
J.M. Dargaville	13	13	–	13	13	13	13	–	–	–	6
L.O.H. Manu	–	s	13	–	–	–	–	s	–	s	4
D.P. Hilton-Jones	–	–	s	s	–	s	s	13	13	13	7
H.H. Groundwater	12	12	12	12	12	12	12	12	12	12	10
B.E.C. Gatland	10	10	10	10	10	10	10	10	10	10	10
N.W. Smith	–	–	–	–	–	–	–	–	s	–	1
B.D. Hall	9	9	9	9	9	9	9	9	9	9	10
L.M. Gjaltema	–	s	s	s	s	s	s	s	s	s	9
M.V.U. Taramai	8	6	–	7	7	s	s	8	8	8	9
H. Moala-Liava'a	–	8	8	s	8	8	8	s	s	s	9
D. Hunt	7	7	7	–	–	7	7	7	7	7	8
G.L. Preston	6	s	6	6	6	–	–	6	6	6	8
S.F.F. Teu	–	–	s	8	s	6	6	–	–	–	5
B.P. Nee-Nee	5	5	5	s	5	5	–	5	5	5	9
G.E. Cowley-Tuioti	4	4	4	4	4	4	4	4	4	4	10
J.W.L. Pierce	s	s	s	5	s	s	s	s	–	–	8
D.J. Drake	–	–	–	–	–	s	5	–	s	s	4
S.T. Mafileo	3	3	3	3	3	s	s	3	3	3	10
N.J. Mayhew	1	1	–	–	–	–	–	–	–	–	2
M. Tamoaieta	s	s	s	s	s	3	3	–	–	–	7
C.I. Eves	s	s	1	1	1	s	s	s	s	s	10
L. Li	–	–	s	s	s	1	1	1	1	1	8
J.P. Tu'ungafasi	–	–	–	–	–	–	–	s	s	s	3
J.W. Parsons (capt)	2	2	2	2	2	2	2	2	2	2	10
L.H.V. Tolai	–	s	–	–	s	s	s	s	s	–	6

NORTH HARBOUR TEAM RECORD, 2018

Played 10   Won 6   Lost 4   Points for 317   Points against 297

Date	Opponent	Location	Score	Tries	Con	PG	DG	Referee
August 16	Northland (P/C)	Albany	21–20	Hunt, T. Li	Hall	Gatland (3)		N.P. Briant
August 25	Waikato (P/C)	Hamilton	29–28	T. Li (2), Penalty try, Taramai	Gatland (2)	Gatland		C.J. Stone
September 1	Tasman (P)	Albany	20–32	Cowley-Tuioti, Duffie	Gatland (2)	Gatland (2)		G.W. Jackson
September 9	Wellington (P)	Wellington	23–35	T. Li, Duffie	Gatland (2)	Gatland (3)		M.G. Lash
September 12	Canterbury (P)	Albany	21–31	Duffie, Stevenson, Teu	Gatland (3)			A.W.B. Mabey
September 16	Bay of Plenty (P/C)	Albany	32–20	Parsons, Hall, T. Li, Gatland	Gatland (3)	Gatland (2)		N.J. Webster
September 22	Hawke's Bay (P/C)	Napier	51–34	Parsons (2), Duffie, Stevenson, T. Li, Gatland, Groundwater	Gatland (4), Parsons	Gatland (2)		M.C.J. Winter
September 29	Taranaki (P)	New Plymouth	55–26	T. Li (4), Hunt (2), Hilton-Jones, Duffie, Telea	Gatland (5)			T.N. Griffiths
October 6	Counties Manukau (P)	Albany	36–26	Groundwater, Penalty try, Hilton-Jones, Stevenson, Hunt	Gatland (3)	Gatland		J.D. Munro
October 14	Auckland (P)	Auckland	29–45	L. Li, Stevenson, Groundwater, Tu'ungafasi	Gatland (3)	Gatland		C.J. Stone

NORTH OTAGO

2018 Status: Heartland
Founded 1904. with affiliation to Otago.
Granted full union status 1927.
President: D.J.L. (David) Douglas
Chairman: W.L. (Warren) Prescott
Chief executive officer: C.S. (Colin) Jackson
Coach: N.G. (Nigel) Walsh
Assistant coach: J.A. (Jason) Forrest
Main ground: Centennial Park, Oamaru
Capacity: 7000
Colours: Gold

RECORDS

Highest attendance	6500	North Otago v Marlborough (Div 3 final), 1997
Most appearances	123	M.J. Mavor, 1995–2009
Most points	429	P.M. Ford, 1964–74
Most tries	39	V.T. Fifita, 2000–04
Most points in a season	159	S.M. Porter, 2002
Most tries in a season	15	V.T. Fifita, 2002
Most conversions in a season	42	M. Adair, 2005
Most penalty goals in a season	30	C.J.W. Finch, 1997
		S.M. Porter, 2000
Most dropped goals in a season	4	M.E. Kenworthy, 1986
Most points in a match	28	C.J.W. Finch v Poverty Bay, 1998
		S.M. Porter v Poverty Bay, 2000
Most tries in a match	5	L.M. Herden v East Coast, 2010
Most conversions in a match	9	B. Patston v East Coast, 2010
Most penalty goals in a match	7	C.J.W. Finch v South Canterbury, 1998
Highest team score	116	v East Coast, 2010
Record victory (points ahead)	113	116–3 v East Coast, 2010
Highest score conceded	139	v Auckland, 1993
Record defeat (points behind)	134	5–139 v Auckland, 1993

Despite starting the season with two wins, North Otago lost four of the next five and required a win in their last round robin game, against Wairarapa Bush at Masterton, to confirm a Lochore Cup semi-final. This was duly done with a very good performance, but to underline their inconsistency seven days later the Old Golds lost to the same team at the same venue to end their season.

In a very good forward pack, flanker Filipo Veamatahau was the standout playing with energy and skill, and number eight Mika Mafi always gave his best at all times. It was a shame Mafi did not play in the semi-final due to injury. Hard-working lock Josh Clark was a forceful presence in the tight. Two promising players who appeared were debutant Anthony Amato at lock and second season flanker Junior Fakatoufifita.

The front row of Ralph Darling, Meli Kolinisau and captain and hooker Sam Sturgess was a formidable one and a significant part of one of the best scrums in the Heartland Championship. Darling played his 100th match for the union in the semi-final defeat.

Inoke Naufahu was a good halfback but outside him the first-five eighth position was a problem one with three players tried. Josh Buchan was more effective at fullback than at first five-eighth but remained a reliable goalkicker. In the midfield Taina Tamou started off in fine form but seemed to fade. The standout in the backline was wing Simon Lilicama, being a strong runner who always looked dangerous with ball in hand.

Prominent players missing from last year were Robbie Smith (unavailable), Lemi Masoe (South Canterbury), Dan Lewis and Tom MacDonald (both returned to England).

Higher honours went to:
New Zealand Heartland: R.K. Darling, M. Kolinisau.

NORTH OTAGO REPRESENTATIVES 2018

	Club	Games for Union	Points for Union		Club	Games for Union	Points for Union
Anthony Amato	Oamaru OB	3	5	Mikaele Mafi	Excelsior	15	20
Braden Barnes	Kurow	4	0	Kieran McClea	Otago University [3]	2	0
Josh Buchan [1]	Pirates Old Boys [2]	18	160	Kayne Middleton	Excelsior	6	0
Tyler Burgess	Kurow	7	5	Antonio Misiloi	Excelsior	1	0
Josh Clark	Green Island [3]	31	5	Inoke Naufahu	Oamaru OB	20	35
Ralph Darling	Oamaru OB	100	68	Hamaua Samasoni	Harbour [3]	6	15
Matthew Duff	Excelsior	50	11	Pita Sinamoni	Kaikorai [3]	3	5
Junior Fakatoufifita	Athletic Marist	17	30	Hamish Slater	Excelsior	2	0
Kelepi Funaki	Oamaru OB	7	0	Glen Sturgess	Valley	7	5
Thomas Furnival	Kurow	1	0	Sam Sturgess	Valley	23	20
Jake Greenslade	Valley	14	5	Taina Tamou	Athletic Marist	9	5
Kafaongo Katoa	Athletic Marist	2	0	Paul Tupai	Southern [3]	8	5
Francis Kelly	Excelsior	9	5	Filipo Veamatahau	Oamaru OB	34	17
Melikisua Kolinisau	Valley	34	0	Matthew Vocea	Valley	31	71
Simon Lilicama	Athletic Marist	20	62	Jared Whitburn	Athletic Marist	28	11

[1] Player of Origin   [2] Southland RU   [3] Otago RU

INDIVIDUAL SCORING

	Tries	Con	PG	DG	Points		Tries	Con	PG	DG	Points
Buchan	3	25	8	–	89	G. Sturgess	1	–	–	–	5
Lilicama	4	–	–	–	20	S. Sturgess	1	–	–	–	5
Naufahu	4	–	–	–	20	Kelly	1	–	–	–	5
Fakatoufifita	4	–	–	–	20	Tupai	1	–	–	–	5
Samasoni	3	–	–	–	15	Vocea	1	–	–	–	5
Darling	2	–	–	–	10	Greenslade	1	–	–	–	5
Mafi	2	–	–	–	10						
Sinamoni	1	–	–	–	5	**Totals**	**32**	**25**	**8**	**0**	**234**
Amato	1	–	–	–	5						
Tamou	1	–	–	–	5	Opposition scored	33	22	10	0	239
Burgess	1	–	–	–	5						

NORTH OTAGO 2018

	Buller	Mid Canterbury	King Country	Horowhenua Kapiti	Thames Valley	West Coast	South Canterbury	Wairarapa Bush	Wairarapa Bush	TOTALS
H. Slater	15	15	–	–	–	–	–	–	–	2
S. Lilicama	14	14	14	15	15	14	14	14	14	9
F.F. Kelly	11	11	15	11	11	11	11	13	13	9
M. Vocea	–	s	11	s	s	s	s	11	11	8
A.P. Misiloi	–	–	–	–	14	–	–	–	–	1
P.E. Tupai	13	13	13	13	13	12	12	10	–	8
H. Samasoni	–	–	s	14	–	13	13	s	s	6
T. Tamou	12	12	12	12	12	s	s	12	12	9
J.S. Buchan	10	10	10	10	10	15	15	15	15	9
T.P. Burgess	–	s	s	s	s	10	10	–	10	7
K. Middleton	–	–	–	–	–	–	–	–	s	1
I.L. Naufahu	9	9	9	s	s	9	9	9	9	9
G.D. Sturgess	s	s	s	–	–	s	s	s	s	7
K.A. McClea	–	–	–	9	9	–	–	–	–	2
M.T.T. Mafi	8	8	8	8	8	8	8	8	–	8
F. Veamatahau	7	6	6	7	7	7	–	5	5	8
J. Fakatoufifita	6	s	7	s	s	s	7	6	6	9
M.R.V. Duff	s	7	s	6	6	s	s	7	7	9
P.P. Sinamoni	5	5	5	–	–	–	–	–	–	3
J.P. Whitburn	4	–	–	5	–	4	4	–	–	4
A. Amato	s	–	4	4	–	–	–	–	–	3
J.A. Clark	–	4	–	–	5	5	5	4	4	6
B.J. Barnes	–	–	s	s	4	–	s	–	–	4
K.K. Funaki	3	s	–	s	s	s	s	3	–	7
R.K. Darling	1	1	1	1	1	1	1	1	1	9
T.G. Furnival	s	–	–	–	–	–	–	–	–	1
M. Kolinisau	–	3	3	3	3	3	3	s	3	8
S.W. Sturgess (capt)	2	2	2	2	2	2	2	2	2	9
J.S. Greenslade	s	–	s	s	s	6	6	–	8	7
K.T. Katoa	–	–	–	–	s	–	–	s	–	2

NORTH OTAGO TEAM RECORD, 2018

Played 9 Won 4 Lost 5 Points for 234 Points against 239

Date	Opponent	Location	Score	Tries	Con	PG	DG	Referee
August 25	Buller (H)	Oamaru	30–24	Darling, Lilicama, Sinamoni	Buchan (3)	Buchan (3)		H.G. Reed
September 1	Mid Canterbury (H)	Ashburton	34–33	Buchan, Darling, Naufahu, Fakatouifita, Lilicama	Buchan (3)	Buchan		J.R. Nutbrown
September 8	King Country (H)	Taumarunui	18–22	Fakatouifita, Amato, Samasoni		Buchan		D.J. MacPherson
September 15	Horowhenua Kapiti (H)	Oamaru	24–27	Lilicama, Samasoni, Buchan	Buchan (3)	Buchan		J.J. Doleman
September 22	Thames Valley (H)	Te Aroha	21–43	Lilicama, Tamou, Naufahu	Buchan (3)			T. Kawahara *Japan*
September 29	West Coast (H)	Oamaru	40–19	Mafi, Buchan, Naufahu, Burgess, G. Sturgess, S. Sturgess	Buchan (5)			A.W.B. Mabey
October 6	South Canterbury (H) (HS)	Oamaru	22–41	Mafi, Naufahu, Kelly	Buchan (2)	Buchan		M.C.J. Winter
October 13	Wairarapa Bush (H)	Masterton	24–0	Tupai, Fakatouifita, Samasoni	Buchan (3)	Buchan		H.G. Reed
October 20	Wairarapa Bush (LC semi-final)	Masterton	21–30	Fakatouifita, Vocea, Greenslade	Buchan (3)			H.G. Reed

HS *Hanan Shield*

NORTHLAND

2018 Status: Mitre 10 Cup Championship
Founded 1920 as North Auckland. Affiliated 1920.
Name changed to Northland 1994
President: S.L. (Sharon) Morgan
Chairman: A.C. (Ajit) Balasingham
Chief executive officer: A.K. (Alister) McGinn
Coach: D.J.C. (Derren) Witcombe
Assistant coach: G.N. (George) Konia
Main ground: Okara Park, Whangarei
Capacity: 24,000
Colours: Cambridge blue

RECORDS

Most appearances	165	Joe Morgan, 1967–81
Most points	1656	Warren Johnston, 1986–97
Most tries	71	Norman Berryman, 1991–2003
Most points in a season	283	David Holwell, 1997
Most tries in a season	21	Norman Berryman, 1994
Most conversions in a season	85	David Holwell, 1997
Most penalty goals in a season	34	Warren Johnston, 1989
Most dropped goals in a season	10	Eddie Dunn, 1979
Most points in a match	38	David Holwell v Thames Valley, 1997
Most tries in a match	7	Norman Berryman v Wairarapa Bush, 1994
Most conversions in a match	14	David Holwell v Thames Valley, 1997
Most penalty goals in a match	6	Chippie Semenoff v Thames Valley, 1978
		Warren Johnston v Wairarapa Bush, 1993
		Warren Johnston v France, 1994
		Warren Johnston v Wairarapa Bush, 1995
		Ash Moeke v North Harbour, 2012
		Dan Hawkins v North Harbour, 2014
		Peter Breen v Otago, 2017
Highest team score	113	v Thames Valley, 1997
Record victory (points ahead)	99	113–14 v Thames Valley, 1997
Highest score conceded	84	v Otago, 1998
Record defeat (points behind)	74	10–84 v Otago, 1998

Although they once again reached the Championship semi-finals, Northland will feel frustrated with their season. They scored some outstanding tries but could also be very inconsistent, particularly the defence in the second half of the season. The Taniwha had good leads against Hawke's Bay, and Waikato in the semi final, but lost both games when conceding a lot of points very quickly. The only time Northland were not in the contest was the big loss to Waikato in the round-robin match.

After surprisingly being asked to start on the wing, his return to centre once again made Rene Ranger the dominant personality in the team with his experience and expertise. His defence was impeccable and was always aware of opportunities and his support with ball in hand.

At fullback Matt Wright was a mixture and appeared down on pace, but he finished the season with a good match in the semi-final and did kick the late winning penalty goal to defeat Taranaki. Jordan Hyland showed determination on wing but was under-used. With Jone Macilai absent through injury, newcomer Scott Gregory filled the void and, with some appearances at second five-eighth, was a very good find for the Taniwha.

Blake Hohaia was steady at second five-eighth but did not feature much on attack, while import Jack Debreczeni was a good acquisition at first five-eighth. He reached 100 points for the season with some magnificent goalkicking, at one stage being successful with 21 consecutive attempts at goal. Northland had two excellent halfbacks in Sam Nock and Jono Kitto, with Nock the preferred starter, but Kitto seemed more of a threat to the opposition with his running.

As with halfback, Northland had two very skilful hookers in captain Matt Moulds and Jordan Olsen, with Olsen also assuming the captaincy when Moulds did not start. The very experienced loosehead prop Ross Wright missed the majority of matches with injury, while tighthead prop Ropate Rinakama used his strength and experience to advantage in the tight while appearing in every match.

The trio of Murray Douglas, Josh Goodhue and Tom Robinson covered the lock and blindside flanker positions well, all contributing to a very good scrum and lineout, plus strong defence and ball carrying. When all three were rested for the Bay of Plenty match the lineout noticeably struggled.

Loose forwards Matt Matich and Kara Pryor both had high work rates, working well in tandem, but were affected with injury by season's end. In the last two matches Matich played just 16 minutes off the bench before reinjuring himself, while Pryor did not appear at all.

Northland had a high turnover in players with a number of the 2017 team playing elsewhere in 2018 — Solomon Alaimalo (Tasman), Dan Hawkins (Japan), Peter Breen (Australia), Dan Pryor (Japan), Jack Ram (England), Michael Faleafa (France), Tim Bond (Waikato), Josh Larsen (Otago), Phil Kite (France), Howard Sililoto (Counties Manukau), Chris Apoua (Southland) — while Jone Macilai and Namatahi Wa'a did not feature due to injury.

Arrivals in were Jack Straker (Canterbury), former NZ Under 20/Bay of Plenty rep Jono Kitto (returned from England), Wiseguy Faiane (Auckland), Isileli Tu'ungafasi (Auckland), Kane Jacobson (North Harbour), Jack Debreczeni (Melbourne Rebels) and Regan Verney (Wellington), although Verney did not take the field due to injury.

Higher honours went to:
New Zealand: Jack Goodhue
New Zealand Maori: S. Nock, R. Wright
New Zealand Under 20: S. Gregory
New Zealand Sevens: S. Gregory

NORTHLAND REPRESENTATIVES 2018

	Club	Games for Union	Points for Union		Club	Games for Union	Points for Union
Lucas Albornoz	Waipu	2	0	Matt Moulds	Otamatea	54	15
Paddy Jo Atkins	Wellsford	6	0	Sam Nock	Kerikeri	37	32
Noah Cooper	Kerikeri	4	5	Jordan Olsen	Mid Northern	38	10
Jack Debreczeni	Eastern	11	100	Kara Pryor	Hora Hora	46	20
Murray Douglas	Awanui	18	10	Rene Ranger	Wellsford	86	145
Wiseguy Faiane	Old Boys Marist	2	4	Ropate Rinakama	Waipu	21	5
Josh Goodhue	Kamo	31	20	Renata Roberts-Te Nana	Old Boys Marist	4	5
Scott Gregory	Hikurangi	10	10	Tom Robinson	Kerikeri	12	10
Blake Hohaia	Kamo	15	15	Aorangi Stokes	Old Boys Marist	8	15
Jordan Hyland	Wellsford	40	50	Jack Straker	Kamo	10	0
Kane Jacobson	Kamo	5	0	Mac Sykes	Kamo	10	0
Jono Kitto	Hikurangi	10	15	Myles Thoroughgood	Kamo	7	0
Taniela Manu	Old Boys Marist	11	0	Isileli Tu'ungafasi	Mid Northern	11	0
Matt Matich	Western Sharks	28	30	Tamati Tua	Hikurangi	23	15
Jaycob Matiu	Hora Hora	26	5	Boyd Wiggins	Old Boys Marist	1	0
Campbell Matthews	Hikurangi	2	0	Matt Wright	Wellsford	49	96
Temo Mayanavanua	Waipu	6	0	Ross Wright	Wellsford	87	25
Sam McNamara	Waipu	6	0				

INDIVIDUAL SCORING

	Tries	Con	PG	DG	Points		Tries	Con	PG	DG	Points
Debreczeni	2	30	10	–	100	Olsen	1	–	–	–	5
M. Wright	3	1	2	–	23	Pryor	1	–	–	–	5
Hyland	4	–	–	–	20	Matiu	1	–	–	–	5
Kitto	3	–	–	–	15	Goodhue	1	–	–	–	5
Ranger	3	–	–	–	15	Roberts-Te Nana	1	–	–	–	5
Tua	3	–	–	–	15	Rinakama	1	–	–	–	5
Nock	3	–	–	–	15	Cooper	1	–	–	–	5
Robinson	2	–	–	–	10	Faiane	–	2	–	–	4
Hohaia	2	–	–	–	10						
Matich	2	–	–	–	10	**Totals**	**40**	**33**	**12**	**0**	**302**
Gregory	2	–	–	–	10						
Douglas	2	–	–	–	10	Opposition scored	50*	36	10	0	354
Stokes	2	–	–	–	10						

* includes one penalty try (7 points)

NORTHLAND 2018

	North Harbour	Auckland	Taranaki	Otago	Manawatu	Southland	Hawke's Bay	Counties Manukau	Waikato	Bay of Plenty	Waikato	TOTALS
M.K. Wright	15	15	15	15	15	15	15	15	–	15	15	10
J.S.C. Hyland	14	14	14	14	14	14	14	14	14	14	14	11
S.J. Gregory	S	S	S	S	11	12	11	12	–	11	11	10
N. Cooper	–	–	–	–	S	11	–	–	S	S	–	4
R.C. Roberts-Te Nana	–	–	–	–	–	S	S	11	11	–	–	4
T.R. Tua	13	13	11	11	–	–	–	–	S	13	12	7
R.M.N. Ranger	11	11	13	13	13	13	13	13	13	–	13	10
B.M. Hohaia	12	12	12	12	12	–	12	S	12	12	S	10
J.M. Debreczeni	10	10	10	10	10	10	10	10	10	10	10	11
M.B. Thoroughgood	–	S	–	S	S	S	S	S	15	–	–	7
W.S. Faiane	–	–	–	–	–	–	–	–	–	S	S	2
S.J. Nock	9	9	9	9	S	9	9	–	S	9	9	10
J.M. Kitto	S	S	S	S	9	S	S	9	9	–	S	10
M.A. Sykes	–	–	–	–	–	–	S	–	S	–	–	2
J. Matiu	8	S	–	–	S	6	6	8	S	8	8	9
M.E.S. Matich	S	8	8	8	8	8	8	–	8	–	S	9
K.A. Pryor	7	7	–	S	6	7	7	7	7	–	–	8
K.P. Jacobson	S	S	7	7	7	–	–	–	–	–	–	5
A.T.H. Stokes	–	–	–	–	–	–	–	S	S	7	7	4
T.T. Manu	–	–	–	–	–	–	–	–	–	6	–	1
M.I. Douglas	6	6	5	–	S	5	5	5	5	–	–	8
J.K. Goodhue	5	5	4	5	4	–	4	4	4	–	5	9
T.N. Robinson	4	4	6	6	5	–	–	–	6	–	6	7
T.S. Mayanavanua	–	–	S	4	–	4	S	S	–	5	–	6
S.J. McNamara	–	–	–	S	–	S	S	6	–	4	S	6
L. Albornoz	–	–	–	–	–	–	–	–	S	S	4	2
J.J. Straker	3	S	S	S	S	S	S	1	–	1	S	10
R.G. Wright	1	1	1	1	–	–	–	–	–	–	1	5
I. Tu'ungafasi	S	S	S	S	1	1	1	S	1	S	S	11
R.R. Rinakama	S	3	3	3	3	3	3	S	3	3	3	11
P-J. Atkins	–	–	–	–	S	S	S	3	S	S	–	6
B.L. Wiggins	–	–	–	–	–	–	–	–	S	–	–	1
M.G. Moulds (capt)	2	2	–	–	S	S	S	2	2	2	2	9
J.D. Olsen	S	S	2	2	2	2	2	S	S	S	S	11
C.I.I. Matthews	–	–	–	S	–	S	–	–	–	–	–	2

J.D. Olsen captained the team in the five matches M.G. Moulds did not start in or play.

NORTHLAND TEAM RECORD, 2018

Played 11 | Won 4 | Lost 7 | Points for 302 | Points against 354

Date	Opponent	Location	Score	Tries	Con	PG	DG	Referee
August 16	North Harbour (P/C)	Albany	20–21	Robinson, Kitto	Debreczeni (2)	Debreczeni (2)		N.P. Briant
August 26	Auckland (P/C)	Whangarei	12–28	Hohaia, Ranger	Debreczeni			R.P. Kelly
September 2	Taranaki (P/C)	Whangarei	18–17	Robinson, Tua	M. Wright	M. Wright (2)		M.G. Lash
September 7	Otago (C)	Dunedin	23–27	Tua, Debreczeni	Debreczeni (2)	Debreczeni (3)		N.J. Webster
September 14	Manawatu (C)	Whangarei	49–19	Matich, Olsen, Hyland, Debreczeni, Gregory, Pryor, Hohaia	Debreczeni (4)	Debreczeni (2)		M.C.J. Winter
September 20	Southland (C)	Whangarei	26–10	Douglas (2), Matich, Nock	Debreczeni (3)	Debreczeni		B.E. Pickerill
September 26	Hawke's Bay (C)	Napier	41–55	M. Wright (2), Matiu, Hyland, Ranger	Debreczeni (5)	Debreczeni (2)		N.E.R. Hogan
September 30	Counties Manukau (P/C)	Pukekohe	24–20	Kitto, Goodhue, Hyland	Debreczeni (3)	Debreczeni		B.D. O'Keeffe
October 6	Waikato (C)	Whangarei	28–71	Ranger, Roberts-Te Nana, Nock, Stokes	Debreczeni (4)			B.E. Pickerill
October 13	Bay of Plenty (C)	Tauranga	35–38	Stokes, Rinakama, Cooper, Tua, Hyland	Debreczeni (3), Faiane (2)			T.M.T. Cottrell
October 20	Waikato (C semi-final)	Hamilton	26–48	Nock, Gregory, M. Wright, Kitto	Debreczeni (3)			P.M. Williams

OTAGO

2018 Status: Mitre 10 Cup Championship
Founded 1881. Affiliated 1895
President: D.G. (Des) Smith
Chairman: K.T. (Keith) Cooper
General Manager: R.P. (Richard) Kinley
Coach: Ben Herring
Assistant coaches: T.J.S. (Tom) Donnelly, Ryan Martin
Main ground: Forsyth Barr Stadium
Capacity: 28,000
Colours: Dark blue

RECORDS

Most appearances	170	Richard Knight, 1981–92
Most points	1520	Greg Cooper, 1984–96
Most tries	73	Paul Cooke, 1990–96
Most points in a season	279	Greg Cooper, 1991
Most tries in a season	16	John Timu, 1988
		John Timu, 1990
		Paul Cooke, 1995
		Brendon Laney, 1998
Most conversions in a season	50	Greg Cooper, 1998
Most penalty goals in a season	54	Greg Cooper, 1989
Most dropped goals in a season	9	Lee Smith, 1986
Most points in a match	39	Paul Turner v East Coast, 1986
Most tries in a match	5	George Owles v South Canterbury, 1920
		Bill Meates v South Canterbury, 1948
		Bruce Hunter v Marlborough, 1969
		Graham Sims v West Coast, 1972
Most conversions in a match	14	Paul Turner v East Coast, 1986
Most penalty goals in a match	7	Greg Cooper v NZ Combined Services, 1989
		Greg Cooper v Canterbury, 1991
		Blair Feeney v Wellington, 2002
Highest team score	91	v East Coast, 1986
Record victory (points ahead)	85	88–3 v North Otago, 1983
Highest score conceded	68	v Wellington, 2007
Record defeat (points behind)	61	7–68 v Wellington, 2007

Otago's season ended in disappointment with defeat to Waikato in the Championship final, thus missing promotion to the Premiership, just two weeks after the satisfaction of having deprived Waikato of the Ranfurly Shield.

The season started off poorly when losing their opening two matches, then the 50–17 win over Manawatu in the third match turned the season around. All remaining round-robin matches against Championship teams were won, including the Ranfurly Shield from top of the table Waikato, and in what must rank as their best performance of the year Otago was the only side to defeat Premiership winners Auckland.

Having missed all last year with injury, Michael Collins was a safe fullback and passed 50 games for the union. He also took over the captaincy in the second half of the season. NZ Sevens rep Vilimoni Koroi played some useful games at both fullback and wing, always looking to attack. Jona Nareki maintained his reputation as a dangerous wing that he earned in his debut season last year while on the other wing Mitchell Scott was an improved performer. They scored six and five tries respectively.

After a below par performance in the opening match against Wellington, Matthew Faddes and Petelesio Tomkinson ended the season as one of the best midfield combinations in the Mitre 10 Cup with their ability to break the line, excellent distribution and aggressive defence.

In his second season at first five-eighth Josh Ioane built well on last year. He was more authoritative in his tactical appreciation, including running more, and his goalkicking was up several notches. His penalty goal, with the last kick of the game, won the semi-final against Hawke's Bay.

After a solitary debut appearance last year, Kurt Hammer became first-choice halfback when Josh Renton was injured in the second match. With some good displays he retained his starting position when Renton returned.

Dylan Nel had an excellent season at number eight. Exhibiting a very high work rate, he did everything required whether it was tackling, ball carrying and strength over the ball at the tackle.

Another second-season rep to come to the fore was loose forward Slade McDowall. With James Lentjes a late starter due to injury, McDowall got the chance to show his worth.

Sione Misiloi was one of only two forwards to appear in all 12 matches, having the versatility to play at number eight, blindside flanker and lock. Lock Josh Dickson was among the best lineout jumpers in the country, winning the most lineout ball in the entire competition.

Loosehead prop Aki Seiuli was in very good form with his scrummaging and running game and it was a blow that a knee injury against Northland in the fourth match ended his season. First Tom Hill and then Jonah Aoina filled his position. At tighthead prop the experienced Hisa Sasagi scrummed well in a good Otago scrum.

Captain and hooker Sam Anderson-Heather did not appear in the second half of the season due to injury and Liam Coltman was able to make three appearances for Otago in between his All Blacks' commitments.

Missing from last year's team were Fletcher Smith (Waikato), Tei Walden (Taranaki), Jonathan Ruru (Auckland), Sione Teu and Dillon Hunt (both North Harbour) with Adam Knight, Blair Tweed, Josh Furno, Craig Millar and Leroy van Dam all overseas.

Those that arrived in were Josh Larsen (Northland), Tom Hill (Tasman), Finn Hart-Strawbridge and Dylan Nel (both Canterbury), while 2018 debutants Sione Misiloi had represented North Otago on loan in 2016 and Angus Williams had represented NZ Universities 2016 and 2017.

Higher honours went to:
New Zealand: L. Coltman, B. Smith
New Zealand Maori: J. Ioane
New Zealand Under 20: R. Jackson, V. Koroi
New Zealand Sevens: T. Haugh, V. Koroi, J. Nareki

OTAGO REPRESENTATIVES 2018

	Club	Games for Union	Points for Union
Sam Anderson-Heather	Dunedin	62	45
Jonah Aoina	Kaikorai	11	15
George Bower	Harbour	8	0
Donald Brighouse	Dunedin	49	10
Michael Collins	Taieri	51	60
Liam Coltman	Alhambra Union	67	15
Naulia Dawai	Harbour	37	75
Josh Dickson	University	43	15
Sam Dickson	University	2	0
Matthew Faddes	University	49	90
Kurt Hammer	Taieri	12	5
Finn Hart-Strawbridge	Green Island	2	9
Taylor Haugh	University	4	0
Tom Hill	Taieri	11	0
Josh Ioane	Southern	21	158
Ricky Jackson	University	4	0
Joketani Koroi	Harbour	13	10
Vilimoni Koroi	Alhambra Union	21	35
Josh Larsen	Taieri	5	0
James Lentjes	Taieri	36	40
Melani Matavao	Harbour	7	5
Slade McDowall	Kaikorai	17	5
Sione Misiloi	Harbour	12	0
Jona Nareki	Alhambra Union	19	75
Dylan Nel	Sumner [1]	10	10
Sekonaia Pole	Harbour	37	5
Josh Renton	Kaikorai	44	10
Tom Rowe	Zingari Richmond	16	0
Yoshihisa "Hisa" Sasagi	Southern	45	0
Mitchell Scott	Taieri	27	50
Aki Seiuli	Taieri	61	25
Josh Timu	University	4	0
Hame Toma	Dunedin	2	0
Petelesio "Sio" Tomkinson	Harbour	38	49
Matt Whaanga	Taieri	10	5
Angus Williams	University	1	0

[1] Canterbury RU

INDIVIDUAL SCORING

	Tries	Con	PG	DG	Points
Ioane	4	30	12	–	116
Faddes	7	–	–	–	35
Nareki	6	–	–	–	30
Scott	5	–	–	–	25
Tomkinson	2	4	2	–	24
V. Koroi	4	–	–	–	20
Dauwai	2	–	–	–	10
Nel	2	–	–	–	10
Collins	2	–	–	–	10
J. Koroi	2	–	–	–	10
Hart-Strawbridge	–	–	3	–	9
Hammer	1	–	–	–	5
Whaanga	1	–	–	–	5
Brighouse	1	–	–	–	5
Matavao	1	–	–	–	5
Aoina	1	–	–	–	5
McDowall	1	–	–	–	5
J. Dickson	1	–	–	–	5
Lentjes	1	–	–	–	5
Totals	**44**	**34**	**17**	**0**	**339**
Opposition scored	51*	38	8	0	357

* includes one penalty try (7 points)

OTAGO 2018

	Wellington	Hawke's Bay	Manawatu	Northland	Southland	Canterbury	Auckland	Bay of Plenty	Tasman	Waikato	Hawke's Bay	Waikato	TOTALS
V.T. Koroi	15	15	14	s	s	s	14	15	15	s	11	11	12
M.W.V. Collins	–	–	15	15	15	15	15	–	–	15	15	15	8
J.C. Timu	14	14	–	–	–	–	–	–	–	–	–	–	2
J.M. Nareki	11	11	11	11	11	11	11	11	s	11	–	–	10
T.C. Haugh	s	s	–	–	–	–	–	–	s	–	s	–	4
M.J. Scott	–	–	s	14	14	14	s	14	14	14	14	14	10
M.A. Faddes	13	13	s	s	13	13	13	13	11	13	13	13	12
P.F. Tomkinson	12	12	13	13	12	12	s	12	13	12	12	12	12
M.A. Whaanga	s	s	12	12	s	s	12	s	12	–	–	s	10
F.C. Hart-Strawbridge	10	–	–	–	–	–	–	–	10	–	–	–	2
J.R. Ioane	–	10	10	10	10	10	10	–	10	10	10	10	10
J.D. Renton	9	9	–	–	–	–	–	–	s	s	s	s	6
K.M. Hammer	s	s	9	9	9	9	s	9	–	9	9	9	11
M. Matavao	–	–	s	s	s	s	9	s	9	–	–	–	7
D.M. Nel	8	–	8	8	8	8	s	8	–	8	8	8	10
S.R. McDowall	7	7	s	s	s	7	7	–	7	7	7	s	11
J.R. Koroi	6	s	s	s	6	–	6	6	s	6	6	6	11
S.R. Dickson	s	s	–	–	–	–	–	–	–	–	–	–	2
S.F. Misiloi	s	8	6	6	4	s	8	s	8	4	4	4	12
R.N.T. Dauwai	–	6	7	7	7	6	–	7	6	s	s	s	10
H.M. Toma	–	–	–	–	s	–	–	–	–	–	–	–	1
J.A.R. Lentjes	–	–	–	–	–	–	s	s	s	s	s	7	5
J.M. Dickson	5	5	5	5	5	5	5	5	–	5	5	5	11
T.B. Rowe	4	4	4	4	s	4	4	4	–	s	–	–	10
J.S. Larsen	–	–	–	–	–	–	s	s	5	s	–	s	5
Y. Sasagi	3	3	3	s	s	–	3	3	–	3	3	3	10
A. Seiuli	1	1	1	1	–	–	–	–	–	–	–	–	4
T.R. Hill	s	s	s	s	1	1	–	1	1	s	s	s	11
D.I.M. Brighouse	s	s	s	3	3	–	s	s	3	–	–	–	8
J.T. Aoina	–	–	–	–	s	s	1	s	s	1	1	1	8
G.G. Bower	–	–	–	–	–	3	s	–	s	s	s	s	6
A.L. Williams	–	–	–	–	s	–	–	–	–	–	–	–	1
S.G. Anderson-Heather (capt)	2	2	–	–	2	2	s	–	–	–	–	–	5
S.J. Pole	s	s	2	2	s	s	2	2	s	2	2	s	12
L.J. Coltman	–	–	s	–	–	–	–	–	–	–	s	2	3
R.D. Jackson	–	–	–	s	–	–	–	s	2	–	–	–	3

M.J. Scott captained v BOP and Tasman; M.W.V. Collins captained the remaining six matches S.G. Anderson-Heather did not play or start in.

OTAGO TEAM RECORD, 2018

Played 12　Won 7　Lost 5　Points for 339　Points against 357

Date	Opponent	Location	Score	Tries	Con	PG	DG	Referee
August 19	Wellington (P/C)	Wellington	16–34	Hammer	Tomkinson	Hart-Strawbridge (3)		P.M. Williams
August 24	Hawke's Bay (C)	Dunedin	25–31	Ioane, Dauwai, V. Koroi	Ioane (2)	Ioane (2)		S. Kubo *Japan*
September 1	Manawatu (C)	Palmerston North	50–17	Nel, Dawai, Collins, Whaanga, Brighouse, Nareki, Matavao	Ioane (6)	Ioane		P.M. Williams
September 7	Northland (C)	Dunedin	27–23	Nel, Nareki, J. Koroi	Ioane (3)	Ioane (2)		N.J. Webster
September 15	Southland (C)	Invercargill	43–24	Scott (3), Nareki (2), Faddes, Aoina	Ioane (4)			J.D. Munro
September 22	Canterbury (P/C)	Dunedin	25–47	Collins, Ioane, Nareki	Ioane (2)	Tomkinson (2)		N.P. Briant
September 28	Auckland (P/C)	Auckland	31–26	Faddes (3), V. Koroi, Nareki	Ioane (3)			M.I. Fraser
October 3	Bay of Plenty (C)	Dunedin	45–34	Ioane (2), Faddes (2), V. Koroi (2),	Ioane (6)	Ioane		J.R. Nutbrown
October 7	Tasman (P/C)	Dunedin	21–47	Faddes, Tomkinson, McDowall	Tomkinson (3)			P.M. Williams
October 13	Waikato (C) (RS)	Hamilton	23–19	Scott, J. Dickson, J. Koroi	Ioane	Ioane (2)		B.E. Pickerill
October 20	Hawke's Bay (C semi-final)	Dunedin	20–19	Scott, Tomkinson	Ioane (2)	Ioane (2)		B.D. O'Keeffe
October 26	Waikato (C final)	Hamilton	13–36	Lentjes	Ioane	Ioane (2)		B.D. O'Keeffe

RS *Ranfurly Shield*

POVERTY BAY

2018 Status: Heartland
Founded 1890. Affiliated 1893
President: R.W. (Richard) Glover
Chairman: G.B. (George) Brown
Chief executive officer: M.L. (Marty) Davis (to February); J.I. (Josh) Willoughby (from June)
Coach: K.M.F. (Mana) Otai
Assistant coach: D.E. (Dwayne) Russell
Main ground: Rugby Park, Gisborne
Capacity: 18,000
Colour: Scarlet

RECORDS

Highest attendance	15,000	*Poverty Bay-East Coast v British Isles, 1971*
Most appearances	150	*S.T. Ngatu, 2003–2018*
Most points	791	*S.C. Leighton, 2004–12*
Most tries	35	*P.S.R. Ransley, 1961–74*
Most points in a season	144	*S.C. Leighton, 2007*
Most tries in a season	11	*J. Moeke, 1997;*
		J. Stewart, 2010
		J. Stewart, 2011
Most conversions in a season	30	*S.C. Leighton, 2007*
Most penalty goals in a season	27	*D.M. Boyle, 1999*
Most dropped goals in a season	3	*G.B. Ross, 1976; J. Whittle, 1979*
Most points in a match	35	*S.C. Leighton v Thames Valley, 2007*
Most tries in a match	4	*J.L. Penny v Olympians Club, 1953*
		K.A. Twigley v East Coast, 1966
		I.A. Kirkpatrick v East Coast, 1971
		K.D. Ferris v East Coast, 1983
		A.B. Hansen v North Otago, 1987
Most conversions in a match	9	*R.P. Owen v East Coast, 1983*
Most penalty goals in a match	7	*S.P. Parkes v Buller, 2013*
Highest team score	75	*v East Coast, 1980*
Record victory (points ahead)	75	*75–0 v East Coast, 1980*
Highest score conceded	121	*v Waikato, 1998*
Record defeat (points behind)	121	*0–121 v Waikato, 1998*

Poverty Bay finished 11th in the Heartland Championship with a record of two wins and six losses. A win in the final match against Buller would have given Poverty Bay a Lochore Cup playoff place but was lost 27–41. The match against eventual champions Thames Valley was somehow lost 34–37. Ahead 34–27, and with 14 men, Poverty Bay conceded a converted try and a penalty goal all in the last two minutes, while a missed penalty kick in the final minute against West Coast resulted in a one-point defeat.

These near misses were balanced by the scoring of last-minute tries to win the Wairarapa Bush and East Coast fixtures, which showed the side played with determination for the full 80 minutes in each game throughout the season. The team scored some brilliant tries, but it was defence that usually let them down. Only against Wanganui was the side outclassed.

After last year's promising debut, Andrew Tauatevalu continued to impress with some standout performances, appearing at wing, first five-eighth and fullback. In the back three he was more able to show the pace he possesses. Te Peehi Fairlie ran with determination on the wing and was top try-scorer with seven. At halfback Mario Counsell and Willie Grogan again shared the duties and were a contrasting pair, while Tom Iosefo was the best of the first-five eighths used and Mapa Tuipulotu was prominent in midfield.

Newcomer Callum McDonald, from Australia but Rotorua born, had an exceptional season in the forward pack, the lively openside flanker was fearless on defence, always in support, and hard to stop on attack. Origin player Micaiah Torrance-Read had a consistently high work rate at lock and was the main lineout winner. It was unfortunate a red card and subsequent suspension ended his season prematurely. Andrew Petelo was an excellent prop at tighthead, being at the forefront of all the front-row work. Number eight Jesse Kapene and lock Sam McDell both had good debut seasons, starting on the reserves bench and being first choice in their positions by the end of the season. Captain and hooker Tamanui Hill played every game.

Star players of last year's team James Grogan (Taranaki) and Siosiua Moala (overseas) were absent and Ethine Reeves was unavailable for half the season due to work commitments. Record appearance holder Sione Ngatu played his 150th first-class match for the province in the Queen's Birthday fixture against East Coast and then announced his retirement. Poverty Bay had the loan services of 2008 Auckland rep Mapa Tuipulotu, Samoan sevens rep Tom Iosefo, experienced wing Willie McGoon and former Tasman prop Andrew Petelo.

Higher honours went to:
New Zealand Heartland: C. McDonald

POVERTY BAY REPRESENTATIVES 2018

	Club	Games for Union	Points for Union		Club	Games for Union	Points for Union
Semisi Akana	Ngatapa	19	10	Willie McGoon	Havelock North [2]	3	0
Juston Allen	Gisborne OB Marist	17	15	Sione Ngatu	Ngatapa	150	81
Hamuera Baker	Waikohu	2	0	Toru Noanoa	Waikohu	14	5
Campbell Chrisp	Ngatapa	48	5	Andrew Petelo	Poneke [3]	9	20
Jacob Cook	Gisborne OB Marist	27	6	Matthew Raleigh	Ngatapa	6	5
Mario Counsell	Waikohu	47	15	Ethine Reeves	Waikohu	46	114
Stefan Destounis	Gisborne HSOB	1	0	Cameron Rowden	Ngatapa	5	10
Te Peehi Fairlie	YMP	14	40	Oka Sanerivi	Ngatapa	7	0
Jesse Fleming	Waikohu	12	5	Shayde Skudder	YMP	15	0
William Grogan	Gisborne OB Marist	28	5	Kelvin Smith	Waikohu	39	70
Tamanui Hill	Gisborne HSOB	30	35	Tawhao Stewart	Waikohu	9	5
Sandy Hohipa-Campbell	Waikohu	7	0	Willis Tamatea	YMP	39	5
Kenneth Houkamau	Waikohu	30	11	Andrew Tauatevalu	Gisborne HSOB	17	118
Tom Iosefo	MAC [2]	4	20	Kurt Taylor	Wairoa Athletic [2]	1	0
Jesse Kapene	Wairoa Athletic [2]	10	5	Rikki Terekia	Gisborne OB Marist	1	0
Anthony Karauria	Ngatapa	16	5	Micaiah Torrance-Read [1]	Spotswood United [4]	13	0
Siaosi "George" Lelenoa	Hamilton Marist	1	0	Jody Tuhaka	Gisborne HSOB	20	5
Korey Love	Gisborne HSOB	7	5	Mapa Tuipulotu	Fraser Tech [5]	6	0
Sam McDell	Ngatapa	10	0	Fawn White	YMP	15	0
Callum McDonald	Gisborne OB Marist	9	5				

[1] Player of Origin [2] Hawke's Bay RU [3] Wellington RU [4] Taranaki RU [5] Waikato RU

INDIVIDUAL SCORING

	Tries	Con	PG	DG	Points		Tries	Con	PG	DG	Points
Tauatevalu	6	13	3	–	65	Raleigh	1	–	–	–	5
Fairlie	7	–	–	–	35	Counsell	1	–	–	–	5
Smith	3	4	2	–	29	McDonald	1	–	–	–	5
Reeves	1	5	4	–	27	Grogan	1	–	–	–	5
Petelo	4	–	–	–	20	Noanoa	1	–	–	–	5
Iosefo	4	–	–	–	20						
Hill	3	–	–	–	15	**Totals**	**36**	**22**	**9**	**0**	**251**
Rowden	2	–	–	–	10						
Kapene	1	–	–	–	5	Opposition scored	58*	40	8	0	398

* includes two penalty tries (14 points)

POVERTY BAY 2018

	Ngati Porou East Coast	Taranaki	Wairarapa Bush	South Canterbury	Wanganui	West Coast	Ngati Porou East Coast	Thames Valley	King Country	Buller	TOTALS
E.S. Reeves	15	15	15	15	–	–	–	–	–	s	5
C. Rowden	s	s	–	–	–	s	14	–	–	–	4
A.H. Tauatevalu	14	11	14	10	10	15	15	15	15	15	10
T.P.H.H. Fairlie	13	14	11	14	11	14	11	11	14	14	10
O.P.A.W.R. Sanerivi	11	–	–	s	–	s	s	s	s	s	7
K.D. Love	–	–	s	11	s	–	–	–	11	11	5
M. Raleigh	–	–	s	s	15	s	–	s	–	s	6
W.B. McGoon	–	–	–	–	14	11	–	–	13	–	3
J. Fleming	12	13	13	13	–	–	–	–	–	13	5
T. Stewart	s	s	–	–	–	–	–	–	–	–	2
A.T. Karauria	–	12	–	–	12	12	13	13	12	–	6
M.A. Tuipulotu	–	–	12	12	13	13	12	12	–	–	6
K.M. Smith	10	10	10	–	–	10	10	–	s	12	7
T. Iosefo	–	–	–	–	–	–	14	10	10	10	4
M.B. Counsell	9	s	9	9	s	s	s	9	9	9	10
H. Baker	s	9	–	–	–	–	–	–	–	–	2
W.D. Grogan	–	–	s	s	9	9	9	s	s	s	8
J. Kapene	8	s	s	6	6	6	8	8	8	8	10
K.R. Houkamau	–	8	8	8	8	8	–	–	s	s	7
S. Destounis	7	–	–	–	–	–	–	–	–	–	1
W.T. Tamatea	6	6	–	s	s	–	s	–	–	–	5
K. Taylor	s	–	–	–	–	–	–	–	–	–	1
C. McDonald	–	7	7	7	7	7	7	7	7	7	9
F.D. White	–	–	6	–	s	s	6	6	6	6	7
J.M. Allen	5	–	–	–	–	–	–	–	–	–	1
J.E. Cook	4	5	5	5	5	s	–	–	4	4	9
S. McDell	s	s	s	s	s	5	5	5	5	5	10
M. Torrance-Read	–	4	4	4	4	4	4	4	–	–	7
S.T. Ngatu	3	–	–	–	–	–	–	–	–	–	1
J.K. Tuhaka	1	–	–	–	–	–	–	–	–	–	1
S.T.T.P. Hohipa-Campbell	s	–	–	–	–	–	–	–	–	–	1
S.K. Lelenoa	–	3	–	–	–	–	–	–	–	–	1
C.P.L. Chrisp	–	1	1	1	1	s	s	s	s	s	9
S.M. Akana	–	s	–	–	–	–	s	s	s	s	5
A.A. Petelo	–	s	3	3	3	3	3	3	3	3	9
T.M. Noanoa	–	–	s	s	s	1	1	1	1	1	8
T.G. Hill (capt)	2	2	2	2	2	2	2	2	2	2	10
R. Terekia	s	–	–	–	–	–	–	–	–	–	1
S. Skudder	–	s	s	s	s	–	s	s	s	–	7

POVERTY BAY TEAM RECORD, 2018

Played 10 Won 3 Lost 7 Points for 251 Points against 398

Date	Opponent	Location	Score	Tries	Con	PG	DG	Referee
June 2	Ngati Porou East Coast	Tolaga Bay	58–18	Tauatevalu (3), Smith (2), Reeves, Fairlie, Rowden, Kapene	Reeves (3), Tauatevalu, Smith	Reeves		D.J. MacPherson
July 28	Taranaki (RS)	Tikorangi	0–78					J.D. Munro
August 25	Wairarapa Bush (H)	Gisborne	27–22	Fairlie (2), Smith, Petelo	Reeves (2)	Reeves		N.P. Briant
September 1	South Canterbury (H)	Timaru	11–40	Raleigh		Reeves (2)		N.J. Webster
September 8	Wanganui (H)	Gisborne	0–53					T.M.T. Cottrell
September 15	West Coast (H)	Greymouth	30–31	Tauatevalu (2), Petelo, Fairlie	Smith (2)	Smith, Tauatevalu		M.G. Lash
September 22	Ngati Porou East Coast (H)	Ruatoria	26–19	Tauatevalu, Hill, Rowden, Counsell	Tauatelavu (2), Smith			M.G. Lash
September 29	Thames Valley (H)	Gisborne	34–37	Iosefo (2), Hill, McDonald	Tauatevalu (4)	Tauatevalu (2)		J.D. Munro
October 6	King Country (H)	Taupo	38–59	Fairlie (2), Iosefo (2), Hill, Grogan	Tauatevalu (4)			H.G. Reed
October 13	Buller (H)	Gisborne	27–41	Petelo (2), Fairlie, Noanoa	Tauatevalu (2)	Smith		R.M. Mahoney

RS *Ranfurly Shield*

SOUTH CANTERBURY

2018 Status: Heartland
Founded 1888. Original member 1892
President: M.G. (Murray) Roberts
Chairman: R.T. (Ray) Teahen
Chief Executive Officer: C.W. (Craig) Calder
Coach: B.A. (Barry) Matthews
Assistant coach: G.W. (Grant) McFarlane
Main ground: Alpine Energy Stadium, Timaru
Capacity: 17,000
Colours: Emerald green and black

RECORDS

Highest attendance	17,000	*South Canterbury v France, 1961*
Most appearances	152	*S.J. Todd, 1986–2001*
Most points	1048	*B.J. Fairbrother, 1981–92*
Most tries	60	*S.J. Todd 1986–2001*
Most points in a season	175	*B.J. Fairbrother, 1991*
Most tries in a season	13	*J.S. Ellery, 1960*
		C.J. Dorgan, 1992
		B.J. Laney, 1992
Most conversions in a season	31	*B.J. Fairbrother, 1989*
Most penalty goals in a season	31	*B.J. Fairbrother, 1990*
Most dropped goals in a season	8	*B.J. Fairbrother, 1987*
		B.J. Fairbrother, 1991
Most points in a match	32	*G.I. Dempster v Wairarapa Bush, 1996*
Most tries in a match	4	*G.V. Gerard v Southland, 1926*
		E.W. Ryan v Ashburton County, 1935
		E.W. Ryan v Wellington XV, 1937
		J.M. Cole v North Otago, 1958
		E.C. Smith v Nelson, 1961
		B.J. Matthews v North Otago, 1992
		D.J. Hunter v Poverty Bay, 1993
		I.G. Howden v Marlborough, 1996
		S. Kiole v West Coast, 2002
		E. Tau v Poverty Bay, 2015
Most conversions in a match	8	*B.J. Fairbrother v West Coast, 1989*
		B.J. Fairbrother v North Otago, 1991
		B.J. Fairbrother v North Otago, 1992
		C.S. Gard v North Otago, 1993
		B.J. Laney v North Otago, 1994
		G.I. Dempster v Wairarapa Bush, 1996
Most penalty goals in a match	7	*B.J. Fairbrother v East Coast, 1990*
Highest team score	100	*v Ngati Porou East Coast, 2018*
Record victory (points ahead)	93	*100–7 v Ngati Porou East Coast, 2018*
Highest score conceded	103	*v Canterbury, 2001*
Record defeat (points behind)	103	*0–103 v Canterbury, 2001*

The Meads Cup continued to elude South Canterbury, suffering defeat in a home final to Thames Valley 12-17, whom they had defeated two weeks earlier. On the day, leading 12-3 at halftime, the team just could not score in the second half while conceding two converted tries. The union and its supporters must be wondering what they have to do to be Heartland Champion, because the team certainly had the individual and collective talent in both the forward and back divisions to achieve it. Their 62 tries in the championship was just one short of the record.

The forward pack could lay claim to being the best in the Heartland Championship, having the size required to physically dominate, and it provided plenty of ball for the backline. The only two changes the coach Barry Matthews had to make in the forwards during the season were both due to injury when lock Solomone Lavaka suffered a broken arm and at hooker where Pita Anae Ah Sue returned in time for the playoffs. Their replacements former captain Kieran Coll and Marac Beckham ably substituted. Otherwise, the props Matthew Fetu and Garrett Casey, lock Veikoso Poloniati and the loose forward trio of Timote Tuipolotu, Nick Strachan and Loni Toumohuni assured their starts through consistent performance. The loose forwards, in particular, stood out in every game with their support, carrying and defensive work.

Against North Otago Matthew Fetu became the 13th player to play 100 games for the province.

Nineteen-year-old debutant Rico Syme grew in confidence at fullback when he came in halfway through the campaign and the two wings Kalavini Leatigaga and Setefano Sauqaqa were big fast men who were always dangerous with ball in hand, scoring nine and seven tries respectively. Leatigaga's total made him equal top try-scorer in the competition.

Centre Shayne Anderson produced plenty of strong running and was a very reliable defender. Having spent most of the season performing well at second five-eighth, Miles Medlicott was moved into the ten jersey for the playoffs, while Willie Wright again turned in some fine games at halfback.

Higher honours went to:
New Zealand Heartland: V.J. Poloniati, W.A. Wright

SOUTH CANTERBURY REPRESENTATIVES 2018

	Club	Games for Union	Points for Union		Club	Games for Union	Points for Union
Pita Anae Ah Sue	Timaru Old Boys	5	0	Brad "BJ" Oliver	Geraldine	15	0
Shayne Anderson	Marist Albion [2]	14	15	Kalolo Otutaha	Christchurch [2]	5	5
Marac Beckham	Geraldine	17	25	Veikoso Poloniati	MacKenzie	10	5
Garret Casey	Celtic	13	20	Zac Saunders	Celtic	9	20
Kieran Coll	Christchurch [2]	33	58	Setefano Sauqaqa	MacKenzie	14	35
Theo Davidson	Waimate	32	35	Henry Scott [1]	Christchurch [2]	5	10
Daniel Dorgan [1]	Christchurch [2]	6	27	Matthew Stewart	Celtic	4	0
Matthew Etheredge	Christchurch [2]	8	6	Nick Strachan	Celtic	80	72
Sione Fa'aoso	Waimate	4	5	Rico Syme	Christchurch [2]	6	20
Tokoma'ata Fakatava	Waimate	9	0	Kadin Te Nana	Geraldine	2	0
Matthew Fetu	Celtic	103	35	Loni Toumohunui	Waimate	20	40
Andrew Gooden	Geraldine	10	0	Jared Trevathan	MacKenzie	54	146
Ben Hewitson	Pleasant Point	56	5	Timote Tuipolotu	Waimate	10	5
Solomone Lavaka	Temuka	6	10	Brad Tunnicliffe	Timaru Old Boys	4	15
Kalavini Leatigaga	Temuka	24	116	Dominic Visesio	Celtic	6	0
Lemi Masoe	Oamaru Old Boys [3]	1	0	Willie Wright	Celtic	37	234
Miles Medlicott	Waimate	51	33				

[1] *Player of Origin*   [2] *Canterbury RU*   [3] *North Otago RU*

INDIVIDUAL SCORING

	Tries	Con	PG	DG	Points		Tries	Con	PG	DG	Points
Wright	7	27	5	–	104	Lavaka	2	–	–	–	10
Leatigaga	9	–	–	–	45	Scott	2	–	–	–	10
Sauqaqa	7	–	–	–	35	Coll	1	–	–	–	5
Dorgan	1	11	–	–	27	Otutaha	1	–	–	–	5
Casey	4	–	–	–	20	Tuipolotu	1	–	–	–	5
Saunders	4	–	–	–	20	Poloniati	1	–	–	–	5
Strachan	4	–	–	–	20	Medlicott	1	–	–	–	5
Toumohunui	4	–	–	–	20	Fa'aoso	1	–	–	–	5
Syme	4	–	–	–	20						
Anderson	3	–	–	–	15	**Totals**	62	43	5	0	411
Tunnicliffe	3	–	–	–	15						
Davidson	–	5	–	–	10	Opposition scored	26	16	9	0	189
Beckham	2	–	–	–	10						

SOUTH CANTERBURY 2018

	Wanganui	Poverty Bay	Horowhenua Kapiti	Ngati Porou East Coast	Mid Canterbury	Wairarapa Bush	North Otago	Thames Valley	King Country	Thames Valley	TOTALS
B.D. Tunnicliffe	15	15	–	s	14	–	–	–	–	–	4
R.J. Syme	–	–	–	–	15	15	15	15	15	15	6
S.T. Sauqaqa	14	14	14	14	–	14	14	14	14	14	9
K.V. Leatigaga	11	11	11	11	11	11	11	11	11	11	10
S.F. Fa'aoso	–	–	–	–	s	–	–	s	s	s	4
S.W. Anderson	13	12	13	–	13	13	13	13	13	13	9
H.J. Scott	s	13	s	15	–	–	s	–	–	–	5
M.W. Medlicott	12	s	12	13	12	12	10	12	10	10	10
Z.C.C. Saunders	s	s	15	12	s	–	12	s	12	12	9
L. Masoe	–	–	–	s	–	–	–	–	–	–	1
J.D. Trevathan	10	–	s	–	–	–	s	–	s	s	5
D.A. Dorgan	–	10	10	10	10	10	–	10	–	–	6
W.A. Wright	9	–	9	9	9	9	9	9	9	9	9
T.R. Davidson	s	9	s	s	s	–	–	s	–	–	6
K. Te Nana	–	s	–	–	–	–	–	–	s	–	2
L. Toumohuni	s	8	8	8	8	8	8	8	8	8	10
N.J.C. Strachan (capt)	8	7	7	7	7	–	7	7	7	7	9
M.N. Etheredge	7	–	–	–	–	–	–	–	–	–	1
A.S. Gooden	6	6	6	s	s	7	s	s	s	s	10
T.S. Tuipolotu	s	s	s	6	6	6	6	6	6	6	10
B.J. Oliver	–	s	s	s	s	–	–	–	s	s	7
V.J. Poloniati	5	5	5	5	5	5	5	5	5	5	10
S.P. Lavaka	4	4	4	4	4	4	–	–	–	–	6
K.P. Coll	–	–	–	s	–	–	4	4	4	4	5
M.J. Stewart	–	–	–	–	s	–	s	–	–	–	2
K.M.H.L.P. Otutaha	3	1	3	–	1	3	–	–	–	–	5
M. Fetu	1	s	1	1	2	1	1	1	1	1	10
G.J. Casey	s	3	s	3	3	s	3	3	3	3	10
B.C. Hewitson	–	–	–	–	–	–	–	s	s	–	2
P.A. Ah Sue	2	–	–	–	–	s	s	–	2	2	5
M.E.L. Beckham	s	s	2	2	2	–	2	2	2	s	8
T.M.H.K. Fakatava	–	2	s	–	–	–	–	–	–	–	2
D. Visesio	–	–	–	s	s	–	s	s	s	s	6

W.A. Wright captained v Wairarapa Bush.

SOUTH CANTERBURY TEAM RECORD, 2018

Played 10　Won 7　Lost 3　Points for 411　Points against 189

Date	Opponent	Location	Score	Tries	Con	PG	DG	Referee
August 25	Wanganui (H)	Wanganui	10–21	Casey	Davidson	Wright		N.E.R. Hogan
September 1	Poverty Bay (H)	Timaru	40–11	Anderson (2), Sauqaqa, Leatigaga, Saunders, Strachan	Dorgan (5)			N.J. Webster
September 9	Horowhenua Kapiti (H)	Wellington	52–29	Wright (2), Toumohuni, Saunders, Dorgan, Sauqaqa, Beckham, Lavaka	Dorgan (6)			T.N. Griffiths
September 15	Ngati Porou East Coast (H)	Timaru	100–7	Tunnicliffe (3), Strachan (3), Sauqaqa (2), Scott (2), Wright, Saunders, Toumohunui, Leatigaga, Lavalea, Coll	Wright (6), Davidson (4)			T.M.T. Cottrell
September 22	Mid Canterbury (H) (HS)	Timaru	41–10	Wright (2), Syme (2), Casey, Leatigaga, Otutaha	Wright (3)			J.J. Doleman
September 29	Wairarapa Bush (H)	Masterton	24–27	Syme, Beckham, Leatigaga, Sauqaqa	Wright (2)			B.E. Pickerill
October 6	North Otago (H) (HS)	Oamaru	41–22	Leatigaga (2), Tuipolotu, Toumohuni, Anderson, Wright	Wright (4)	Wright		M.C.J. Winter
October 13	Thames Valley (H)	Timaru	33–24	Poloniati, Saunders, Medlicott, Syme, Sauqaqa	Wright (4)			M.C.J. Winter
October 20	King Country (MC semi-final)	Timaru	58–21	Leatigaga (2), Casey (2), Sauqaqa, Wright, Fa'aoso	Wright (7)	Wright (3)		N.J. Webster
October 27	Thames Valley (MC final)	Timaru	12–17	Toumohuni, Leatigaga	Wright			J.R. Nutbrown

HS *Hanan Shield*

SOUTHLAND

2018 Status: Mitre 10 Cup Championship
Founded 1887. Affiliated 1894
President: K.I. (Kim) McDowall
Chairman: B.J. (Bernie) McKone
General Manager: A.I. (Andrew) Moreton (to Feb),
   Brian Hopley (from March)
Coach: D.N. (Dave) Hewett
Assistant coaches: J.M. (Jason) Kawau, D.J. (Dale) McLeod
Main ground: Rugby Park Stadium, Invercargill
Capacity: 20,200
Colours: Maroon

RECORDS

Most appearances	139	Jason Rutledge, 2000–2016
Most points	976	Simon Culhane, 1988–98
Most tries	46	Bruce Pascoe, 1983–89
Most points in a season	194	Simon Culhane, 1994
Most tries in a season	13	Simon Forrest, 1992
Most conversions in a season	38	Simon Culhane, 1997
Most penalty goals in a season	41	Eion Crossan, 1989
Most dropped goals in a season	10	Brian McKechnie, 1977
Most points in a match	37	Simon Culhane v Manawatu, 1994
Most tries in a match	5	Simon Forrest v Poverty Bay, 1992
Most conversions in a match	11	Simon Culhane v Malborough, 1997
Most penalty goals in a match	8	Simon Culhane v Manawatu, 1994
Highest team score	92	v Marlborough, 1997
Record victory (points ahead)	74	79–5 v Poverty Bay, 1992
Highest score conceded	95	v Waikato, 1998
Record defeat (points behind)	88	7–95 v Waikato, 1998

Southland experienced another winless season in 2018 and have now lost their last 21 matches in the Mitre 10 Cup. There were slight improvements in the points for and points conceded columns but the closest the Stags came to breaking their duck was against Bay of Plenty when leading 22–19 until conceding a converted try with six minutes left. Injury caused disruption to continuity with a number of first-choice players having to miss matches during the season.

A factor also not helping was the new coach Dave Hewett having to rebuild with just 13 players reappearing from the 31 used last year. Absent were Ryan Tongia (Hawke's Bay), Liam Howley (Otago), Tim Boys (retired), Tupou Sopoaga (Wellington), Mike McKee (Counties Manukau), Tepasu Thomas (Canterbury), while overseas were Neria Fomai, James Schrader, Elliot Dixon and Guy Millar. Ruled out because of injury were Greg Dyer and captain designate Brayden Mitchell while Scott Eade was unavailable.

Arrivals in were Jackson Ormond (Taranaki), Tony Lamborn (Hawke's Bay), Chris Apoua (Northland), Nicolas Costa (Auckland), Broc Hooper (NZ Universities), Jesse MacDonald (Hawke's Bay/Tasman), and from overseas were Andrew Ready (Queensland Reds) and returning former Stags James Wilson and Tayler Adams from England and Australia respectively.

The team's most valuable player was the experienced James Wilson. Whether at first five-eighth or in the midfield, he was consistently to the fore with his individual effort and organisation of the less experienced backline around him.

Jackson Ormond, with more than 50 games for Taranaki behind him, was a disappointment. Matthew Johnson was not as influential as last year having not played any rugby at all in the first six months of the year. He was the only Stags player fully contracted to a New Zealand Super Rugby team for 2018 but did not play a single game for the Blues having undergone open heart surgery in January.

The two halfbacks, Jay Renton and Nic Costa, appeared in every game, with Costa gaining the starting role in the final two matches.

The best of the forwards was unquestionably Manaaki Selby-Rickit. The 2-m 112-kg lock made a big advance on last year's debut season, always in the thick of things with his strong carrying, presence in the lineout and work in the tight.

Others who made a favourable impression in the forward effort were loose forwards Tony Lamborn and Phil Halder, while tighthead prop Morgan Mitchell was a consistent performer. Lock Ben Fotheringham showed up well in the Ranfurly Shield challenge and flanker Wade McRae and hooker Flynn Thomas had their seasons end early with injury.

Two debutants who could develop well for Southland are second five-eighth Ray Nu'u and 125-kg 20-year-old number eight Viliami 'Lio' Tosi, a former NZ Schools rugby league rep.

Higher honours went to:
New Zealand Under 20:   J. Renton, F. Thomas

SOUTHLAND REPRESENTATIVES 2018

	Club	Games for Union	Points for Union		Club	Games for Union	Points for Union
Tayler Adams	Star	28	18	Ray Nu'u	Wyndham	7	0
Chris Apoua	Midlands	9	0	Jackson Ormond	Woodlands	6	0
Jack Capil	Star	4	0	Lewis Ormond	Woodlands	19	30
Nick Costa	Woodlands	10	5	Andrew Ready	[2]	8	0
Ethan De Groot	Blues	6	0	Jay Renton	Blues	17	0
Ben Fotheringham	Marist	11	0	Manaaki Selby-Rickit	Star	15	20
Bill Fukofuka	Blues	47	30	Shaun Stodart	Marist	20	0
Phil Halder	Marist	27	0	Ray Tatafu	Blues	10	0
Broc Hooper	Pirates Old Boys	10	2	Isaac Te Tamaki	E.N. Barbarians	9	15
Brenton Howden	E.N. Barbarians	5	0	Flynn Thomas	Marist	16	5
Matthew Johnson	Marist	20	10	Viliami Tosi	Marist	2	0
Tony Lamborn	Edendale	9	5	Presley Tufuga	Woodlands	1	0
Jesse MacDonald	Central [1]	6	0	Tauaosi Tuimavave	Woodlands	18	22
Wade McRae	Pirates Old Boys	9	0	Rory van Vugt	E.N. Barbarians	5	5
Morgan Mitchell	Star	39	20	Joseph Walsh	Woodlands	24	5
Aleki Morris-Lome	Woodlands	18	10	James Wilson	Blues	75	307
Reuben Northover	Marist	12	0				

[1] Tasman RU   [2] Arrived from overseas

INDIVIDUAL SCORING

	Tries	Con	PG	DG	Points
Wilson	1	15	6	–	53
Mitchell	4	–	–	–	20
L. Ormond	4	–	–	–	20
Te Temaki	3	–	–	–	15
Selby-Rickit	3	–	–	–	15
Fukofuka	2	–	–	–	10
Lamborn	1	–	–	–	5
Thomas	1	–	–	–	5
van Vugt	1	–	–	–	5

	Tries	Con	PG	DG	Points
Costa	1	–	–	–	5
Tuimavave	1	–	–	–	5
Walsh	1	–	–	–	5
Adams	–	–	1	–	3
Hooper	–	1	–	–	2
Totals	**23**	**16**	**7**	**0**	**168**
Opposition scored	59	49	3	0	402

SOUTHLAND 2018

	Hawke's Bay	Tasman	Wellington	Counties Manukau	Otago	Northland	Waikato	Bay of Plenty	Auckland	Manawatu	TOTALS
T. Tuimavave	15	15	–	–	–	–	15	15	–	–	4
I.R. Te Tamaki	14	14	14	14	14	14	14	14	–	14	9
J.T. Ormond	11	–	11	11	s	11	–	–	14	–	6
L.H. Ormond	s	11	s	15	15	s	11	11	15	15	10
R.F. van Vugt	–	s	–	11	15	–	–	11	11	–	5
A.M. Morris-Lome	13	13	13	s	–	–	–	13	s	–	6
M. Johnson	12	12	12	13	13	13	s	s	12	13	10
R.I. Nu'u	–	–	s	12	–	s	12	12	s	12	7
J.W.R. Wilson (co-capt)	10	10	10	10	12	12	13	13	–	10	9
B.K. Hooper	s	s	15	s	s	10	10	10	s	s	10
T.J.K. Adams	–	–	–	–	10	–	s	–	10	–	3
J.L. Renton	9	9	9	9	s	9	9	9	s	s	10
N. Costa	s	s	s	s	9	s	s	s	9	9	10
T.A. Lamborn	8	8	8	–	6	7	6	8	7	8	9
B.S. Fukofuka	s	–	s	8	8	8	8	s	8	s	9
P.W. Halder	7	7	7	7	7	–	7	7	–	7	8
W.G. McRae	6	6	6	6	–	–	–	–	–	–	4
B.A. Howden	–	s	–	s	–	s	s	–	4	–	5
J.W. Capil	–	–	–	s	s	6	–	–	–	–	3
P. Tufuga	–	–	–	–	–	–	–	s	–	–	1
P.V. Tosi	–	–	–	–	–	–	–	–	s	s	2
M.W.H. Selby-Rickit	5	5	5	–	5	5	5	5	5	5	9
B.J. Fotheringham	4	4	s	4	4	4	4	4	s	4	10
R.K. Tatafu	s	s	4	5	s	s	s	6	6	6	10
M.D. Mitchell	3	3	–	3	3	3	3	3	–	3	8
J.S. Walsh	1	s	s	–	–	–	–	–	s	s	5
S.D.G. Stodart	s	1	1	–	1	1	1	s	1	–	8
C. Apoua	s	s	s	1	s	s	s	–	3	s	9
R.A. Northover	–	–	3	s	–	–	–	s	s	–	4
E.L. De Groot	–	–	–	s	s	s	1	–	1	–	6
F.C. Thomas (co-capt)	2	2	2	s	2	2	–	–	–	–	6
A.J. Ready	s	s	s	2	–	–	s	s	s	s	8
J.L.R.J. MacDonald	–	–	–	–	s	s	2	2	s	2	6

T.A. Lamborn captained v Auckland.

SOUTHLAND TEAM RECORD, 2018

Played 10　Won 0　Lost 10　Points for 168　Points against 402

Date	Opponent	Location	Score	Tries	Con	PG	DG	Referee
August 19	Hawke's Bay (C)	Invercargill	10–31	Te Tamaki	Wilson	Wilson		J.R. Nutbrown
August 26	Tasman (P/C)	Blenheim	24–45	Lamborn, Thomas, Selby-Rickit, Van Vugt	Wilson (2)			J.R. Nutbrown
August 31	Wellington (P/C)	Wellington	7–52	Fukofuka	Wilson			S. Kubo *Japan*
September 8	Counties Manukau (P/C)	Invercargill	26–43	Fukofuka, Mitchell, L. Ormond, Costa	Wilson (3)			J.J. Doleman
September 15	Otago (C)	Invercargill	24–43	Mitchell, Selby-Rickit, Te Tamaki	Wilson (3)	Wilson		J.D. Munro
September 20	Northland (C)	Whangarei	10–26	Selby-Rickit	Hooper	Wilson		B.E. Pickerill
September 29	Waikato (C) (RS)	Hamilton	11–42	Tuimavave		Wilson (2)		J.R. Nutbrown
October 7	Bay of Plenty (C)	Invercargill	22–26	L. Ormond, Mitchell, Te Tamaki	Wilson (2)	Wilson		T.M.T. Cottrell
October 10	Auckland (P/C)	Invercargill	8–56	Walsh		Adams		J.J. Doleman
October 14	Manawatu (C)	Palmerston North	26–38	L. Ormond (2), Mitchell, Wilson	Wilson (3)			P.M. Williams

RS *Ranfurly Shield*

TARANAKI

2018 Status: Mitre 10 Cup Premiership
Founded 1889. Original member 1892
President: Robyn Houghton
Chairman: Lindsay Thomson
Chief executive officer: Jeremy Parkinson
Coach: Willie Rickards
Assistant coach: Paul Tito, Leo Crowley
Main ground: Yarrow Stadium, New Plymouth
Capacity: 12,000
Colours: Amber and black

RECORDS

Most appearances	222	Ian Eliason, 1964–81
Most points	1723	Kieran Crowley, 1980–94
Most tries	64	Kieran Crowley, 1980–94
Most points in a season	233	Jamie Cameron, 1995
Most tries in a season	13	Charlie McAlister, 1985
Most conversions in a season	49	Kieran Crowley, 1983
Most penalty goals in a season	39	Jamie Cameron, 1995
Most dropped goals in a season	11	Ross Brown, 1964
Most points in a match	34	Jamie Cameron v Nelson Bays, 1995
Most tries in a match	5	George Loveridge v Wanganui, 1913
		Dave Vesty v Thames Valley, 1971
		Mark Robinson v Southland, 1997
Most conversions in a match	13	Kieran Crowley v East Coast, 1983
Most penalty goals in a match	9	Beauden Barrett v Bay of Plenty, 2011
Highest team score	104	v Nelson Bays, 1995
Record victory (points ahead)	97	97–0 v East Coast, 1983
Highest score conceded	80	v Otago, 1996
Record defeat (points behind)	60	16–76 v North Harbour, 1989

Although holding the Ranfurly Shield, Taranaki Rugby was on the back foot before the first bead of sweat had been raised on the pre-season run. Taranaki Rugby could be without a home. Engineering reports on the two stands had declared them earthquake risks. It didn't seem to matter for the first Ranfurly Shield game as it was played on a field new to first-class rugby at Tikorangi — home of the Clifton Club. New field but some old-fashioned mud. Hawera hosted its fourth Ranfurly Shield match (first in 98 years), when a spirited Wanganui team exposed some frailties in the holder's team.

Once some compromises had been made, including seating only at the ends of the ground and changes effected including new changing sheds, Yarrow Stadium was open for business. The result confirmed that most people prefer to watch rugby from the side, not the ends, of the field — but there was no alternative.

For the third consecutive time Waikato comprehensively ended Taranaki's Ranfurly Shield tenure in what was Taranaki's 100th Shield match. Taranaki was to finish the season with seven consecutive losses including two near misses, the most galling of which was to the champion Auckland side where a successful last-minute conversion could have reversed the result. After winning the round robin last year, no one would have challenged the relegation this year, but it came in a year when Taranaki had nine, almost 10 All Blacks on their books. Sadly, seeing the

All Blacks in provincial colours is a rarity these days. Likewise, imported players being tagged to a club they may never visit. A seemingly never-ending run of injuries was the main factor in a record 44 players being used during the season.

Beaudein Waaka began the year with one successful goal kick to his name from five years earlier. He was a reliable fullback and equal top try scorer who could not have got closer to 100 points. Prior to leaving for overseas, Seta Tamanivalu played in every minute of nine premiership games for just three tries. His nephew, Manasa Mataele, played in eight games for four tries. There was much interest in Waisake Naholo's younger brother Kiniviliame, but he was not sighted beyond the first two Ranfurly Shield games. Tei Walden, recently of Otago, was a steadying influence in midfield. Injury restricted the availability of the much-talented Stephen Perofeta to just four starts. Brayton Northcott-Hill made a promising start to his career. Brendon Leonard, former Waikato and All Blacks halfback, returned from overseas and found a home here. Half of a Ranfurly Shield match and 74 minutes of a Mitre 10 match was all we saw of All Black Te Toiroa Tahuriorangi. It was a welcome home to New Zealand and England Sevens representative Warwick Lahmert. Halfback Logan Crowley maintained an industrious family tradition.

Captain Mitch Crosswell was the only player to start every match. Toa Halafihi was his high-energy self for the first half of the season. Just when his name was being mentioned more widely as one to keep an eye on, we sadly saw just half a season from Lachlan Boshier. Young Tom Florence was drawing attention to himself for the right reasons. A red card in the penultimate match prevented a returning Jarrad Hoeata starting in every Mitre 10 match. Reuben O'Neil played in every game covering both sides of the scrum, and went very close to becoming an All Black. The future did not look bright for Angus Ta'avao at the beginning of the calendar year, but opportunity was presented and with a run of good form he became an All Black in the Rugby Championship. Jesse Parete brought a lot of energy home from Bay of Plenty. Chris Gawler, returning home from Lincoln University, looks to become a valuable investment. Following a great Super Rugby campaign Ricky Riccitelli had a quiet season for Taranaki. Adrian Wyrill played for both Taranaki and Manawatu, likewise Jarrod Firth for Taranaki and Counties Manukau in the Mitre 10 competition in 2018.

Higher honours went to:

New Zealand:	B. Barrett, J. Barrett, S. Barrett, W. Naholo, A. Ta'avao-Matau, T. Tahuriorangi
New Zealand Under 20:	T. Florence, C. Matoe
Maori All Blacks:	T. Walden, R. Ware

TARANAKI REPRESENTATIVES 2018

	Club	Games for Union	Points for Union		Club	Games for Union	Points for Union
Liam Blyde	Clifton	1	0	Stephen Perofeta	Clifton	25	54
Kaylum Boshier	NPOB	1	5	Jayson Potroz	Tukapa	3	15
Lachlan Boshier	NPOB	31	35	Leighton Price	Tukapa	27	5
Mitchell Crosswell (capt)	Tukapa	51	25	Jared Proffit	Spotswood	26	5
Logan Crowley	Coastal	14	0	Ricky Riccitelli	Tukapa	18	15
Jarrod Firth	†	2	0	Xavier Roe	Okaiawa	4	0
Tom Florence	NPOB	10	5	Asaeli Sorovaki	Spotswood	7	0
Chris Gawler	Coastal	11	0	Pita-Gus Sowakula	Spotswood	15	15
Toa Halafihi	Spotswood	42	60	Kyle Stewart	Stratford	5	0
Jarrad Hoeata	Southern	79	20	Angus Ta'avao-Matau	Tukapa	34	5
Jack Jordan	Stratford	1	0	Te Toiroa Tahuriorangi	NPOB	33	20
Warwick Lahmert	Spotswood	6	5	Seta Tamanivalu	Spotswood	61	130
Brendon Leonard	Patea	4	0	Kane Thompson	Stratford	13	5
Avon Lewis	Inglewood	8	15	Tupou Va'ai	NPOB	3	0
Donald Maka	Stratford	18	5	Latu Vaeno	Spotswood	26	35
Manasa Mataele	Spotswood	21	35	Beaudein Waaka	Clifton	30	111
Ciarahn Matoe	Coastal	11	32	Sean Wainui	NPOB	35	50
Scott Mellow	Tukapa	7	0	Daniel Waite	NPOB	7	24
Kiniviliame Naholo	Clifton	2	15	Shaan Waite	NPOB	1	0
Brayton Northcott-Hill	NPOB	10	17	Regan Ware	Bell Block	8	10
Reuben O'Neil	NPOB	30	5	Teihorangi Walden	Spotswood	10	5
Jesse Parete	Southern	9	5	Adrian Wyrill	Tukapa	18	15

† Counties Manukau

INDIVIDUAL SCORING

	Tries	Con	PG	DG	Points		Tries	Con	PG	DG	Points
Waaka	4	23	11	–	99	L. Boshier	1	–	–	–	5
D. Waite	2	7	–	–	24	Crosswell	1	–	–	–	5
Mataele	4	–	–	–	20	Florence	1	–	–	–	5
Vaeno	4	–	–	–	20	Halafihi	1	–	–	–	5
Northcott-Hill	3	1	–	–	17	Lahmert	1	–	–	–	5
K. Naholo	3	–	–	–	15	Maka	1	–	–	–	5
Potroz	3	–	–	–	15	Parete	1	–	–	–	5
Tamanivalu	3	–	–	–	15	Thompson	1	–	–	–	5
Matoe	2	1	–	–	12	Walden	1	–	–	–	5
Lewis	2	–	–	–	10						
Ware	2	–	–	–	10	**Totals**	**43**	**32**	**11**	**0**	**314**
Penalty try	1	–	–	–	7						
K. Boshier	1	–	–	–	5	Opposition scored	50	34	9	0	345

TARANAKI 2018

Player	Poverty Bay	Wanganui	Bay of Plenty	Manawatu	Counties Manukau	Northland	Waikato	Tasman	Auckland	North Harbour	Canterbury	Wellington	TOTALS
J.P. Potroz	15	15	–	–	–	–	–	–	–	–	s	–	3
B.R.T. Waaka	–	10	15	15	15	15	15	15	15	15	11	15	11
R.E. Ware	–	–	–	s	s	14	14	–	14	14	14	14	8
A.P. Lewis	14	14	s	–	–	–	–	s	–	–	–	–	4
L.M. Vaeno	13	–	s	14	14	13	s	14	–	–	s	s	9
K.N. Naholo	11	11	–	–	–	–	–	–	–	–	–	–	2
L.G. Blyde	s	–	–	–	–	–	–	–	–	–	–	–	1
M.M.B.T. Mataele	–	–	–	11	11	11	11	11	11	11	–	11	8
S. Tamanivalu	–	–	14	13	13	–	13	13	13	13	13	13	9
S.T. Wainui	–	–	11	–	–	–	–	–	–	–	–	–	1
B.K. Northcott-Hill	12	13	–	s	–	s	s	s	s	s	15	s	10
T.T. Walden	–	–	13	12	12	12	12	12	12	12	12	12	10
D.S. Waite	10	–	12	10	10	10	10	–	–	–	–	–	6
S. Perofeta	–	12	10	–	–	–	–	–	10	10	–	–	4
C.R. Matoe	s	s	–	–	s	–	–	10	s	s	10	10	8
L.E. Crowley	9	9	9	9	s	9	s	s	s	–	–	s	10
S.A. Waite	s	–	–	–	–	–	–	–	–	–	–	–	1
B.G. Leonard	–	–	–	s	–	–	–	9	9	9	–	–	4
T.T.H. Tahuriorangi	–	s	–	–	9	–	–	–	–	–	–	–	2
W.H. Lahmert	–	s	s	–	–	–	–	–	–	–	9	9	4
X.O'C. Roe	–	–	–	–	s	9	–	–	–	s	s	–	4
S.T. Halafihi	8	8	8	8	s	s	8	8	–	–	–	–	8
T.H.T. Florence	7	7	–	–	–	s	–	s	7	7	7	7	8
A.E. Wyrill	–	s	s	–	–	–	–	–	–	–	–	s	3
L.S. Boshier	–	–	7	7	7	7	7	–	–	–	–	–	5
M.C. Crosswell (capt)	6	6	6	6	6	6	6	7	8	8	6	6	12
K.L. Boshier	s	–	–	–	–	–	–	–	–	–	–	–	1
P.G.N. Sowakula	–	–	–	s	8	8	s	6	6	6	–	–	7
K.G. Thompson	5	4	–	s	s	–	s	s	–	–	–	4	7
J.W.Z. Parete	–	–	5	5	5	5	5	–	–	s	8	8	8
L.T. Price	–	s	s	–	–	s	–	5	5	5	5	5	8
J.C. Jordan	4	–	–	–	–	–	–	–	–	–	–	–	1
J.M.R.A. Hoeata	s	5	4	4	4	4	4	4	4	4	4	–	11
T.P.O. Va'ai	–	–	–	–	–	–	–	–	s	s	s	–	3
A.S. Sorovaki	3	s	–	–	–	–	–	–	–	–	–	–	2
R.G. O'Neil	s	3	1	1	1	3	3	3	3	3	3	3	12
A.W.F. Ta'avao-Matau	–	–	3	3	3	–	–	–	–	–	–	–	3
J.P. Proffit	1	s	s	–	s	1	1	1	s	s	s	1	11
C.M. Gawler	s	1	s	s	–	s	s	s	1	1	1	s	11
K.L. Stewart	–	–	–	s	–	–	–	–	s	s	s	s	5
J.V. Firth	–	–	–	–	–	s	s	–	–	–	–	–	2
D.S.K.M. Maka	2	2	s	s	s	2	–	–	s	s	s	s	10
S.B. Mellow	s	s	–	–	–	s	s	–	–	–	s	s	7
J.R. Riccitelli	–	–	2	2	2	–	2	2	2	2	2	2	9

TARANAKI TEAM RECORD 2018

Played 12 Won 4 Lost 8 Points for 314 Points against 345

Date	Opponent	Location	Score	Tries	Con	PG	DG	Referee
July 28	Poverty Bay (RS)	Tikorangi	78–0	Vaeno (3), K. Naholo (2), Potroz (2), Northcott-Hill (2), D. Waite, Maka, K. Boshier	D. Waite (7), Northcott-Hill, Matoe			J. Munro
August 4	Wanganui (RS)	Hawera	33–10	Lewis (2), K. Naholo, penalty try, Northcott-Hill	Waaka (3)			M. Lash
August 18	Bay of Plenty (P/C)	Rotorua	10–30	Tamanivalu	Waaka	Waaka		B. Pickerill
August 24	Manawatu (RS) (P/C)	New Plymouth	41–21	Mataele, Waaka, Walden, Halafihi, D. Waite	Waaka (5)	Waaka (2)		M. Fraser
August 29	Counties Manukau (P)	Pukekohe	26–19	Waaka (2), L. Boshier	Waaka	Waaka (3)		B. Pickerill
September 2	Northland (P/C)	Whangarei	17–18	Vaeno, Mataele	Waaka (2)	Waaka		M. Lash
September 9	Waikato (RS) (P/C)	New Plymouth	19–23	Ware, Mataele, Tamanivalu	Waaka (2)			B. O'Keeffe
September 14	Tasman (P)	Nelson	17–53	Matoe, Thompson	Waaka (2)	Waaka		J. Nutbrown
September 22	Auckland (P)	New Plymouth	30–31	Tamanivalu, Florence, Crosswell, Matoe	Waaka (2)	Waaka (2)		G. Jackson
September 29	North Harbour (P)	New Plymouth	26–55	Ware, Mataele, Waaka, Parete	Waaka (3)			T. Griffiths
October 6	Canterbury (P)	Christchurch	7–41	Potroz	Waaka			J. Doleman
October 12	Wellington (P)	New Plymouth	10–34	Lahmert	Waaka	Waaka		B. O'Keeffe

TASMAN

2018 Status: Mitre 10 Cup Premiership
Founded and **affiliated 2005** (December)
President: R.S. (Ramon) Sutherland
Chairman: W.A. (Wayne) Young
Chief executive officer: A.J.F. (Tony) Lewis
Coach: L.R. (Leon) MacDonald
Assistant coaches: S.A. (Shane) Christie, Clarke Dermody, A.D. (Andrew) Goodman
Main ground: Trafalgar Park, Nelson
Capacity: 18,000
Colours: Navy blue and red

RECORDS

Most appearances	104	Robbie Malneek, 2006–2017
Most points	628	Marty Banks, 2013–2016
Most tries	25	Robbie Malneek
Most points in a season	173	Marty Banks, 2014
Most tries in a season	10	Peter Playford, 2006
Most conversions in a season	37	Marty Banks, 2014
Most penalty goals in a season	33	Marty Banks, 2016
Most dropped goals in a season	1	by five players
Most points in a match	28	Marty Banks v Northland, 2013
Most tries in a match	4	Peter Playford v Canada A, 2006
		Peter Playford v Northland, 2006
Most conversions in a match	7	Aaron Kimura v Northland, 2006
		Marty Banks v Manawatu, 2013
Most penalty goals in a match	8	Tom Marshall v Bay of Plenty, 2010
Most dropped goals in a match	1	by five players
Highest team score	64	v Waikato, 2013
Record victory (points ahead)	56	56-0 v Southland, 2016
Highest score conceded	52	v Counties Manukau, 2017
Record defeat (points behind)	42	7–49 v Auckland, 2007

After finishing the round robin in second place, with their best ever record of nine wins and just one defeat, Tasman's season ended with a disappointing home defeat to Canterbury in the Premiership semi-final. Leading 13–6 at halftime, the Mako could not maintain their ascendancy in the second half, going down 16–21, with two yellow cards not helping the cause. Since winning the Championship in 2013, Tasman have made the Premiership semi-finals in all five succeeding years, a feat only Canterbury has been able to match in the same period.

Tasman owed much of its success to its strong forward pack, in particular the performance of the tight five, whose scrummaging, mauling and lineout regularly set the tone for the side's performance.

Wyatt Crockett, Andrew Makalio and Tyrel Lomax formed one of the best front rows in the country. The retired All Black Crockett was an outstanding scrummager at loosehead, and it was noticeable that when he was subbed off in the semi-final that Tasman's effort there was reduced. His experience was also invaluable to the young players around him. Andrew Makalio was a forceful tackler, a hard man to stop with ball in hand, and solid performer in his set-piece roles.

With a season of Super Rugby behind him, 22-year-old tighthead prop Tyrel Lomax built on last year's debut season to show considerable improvement, particularly with his mobility, to win All Blacks' selection for the test against Japan. All three appeared in every match.

The two young locks 2.04-m Pari Pari Parkinson and 1.99-m Quinten Strange turned 22 years old during the Mitre 10 Cup. With veteran Alex Ainley battling injury all year and appearing in only the final two matches, the two youngsters probably got more game time than originally planned. Both blossomed with some very fine performances at the heart of the set pieces.

Ethan Blackadder was a tireless worker at blindside flanker, where his attack and defence work was consistently of a high standard, and the only Mako to play every minute of the season. Specialist openside flanker Jed Brown was a valuable acquisition, also doing a lot of the unfashionable work required at the tackle and breakdown.

Number eight Vernon Fredericks had his season end with injury in the opening match. Loan player Taina Fox-Matamua was the best of the replacements used.

At halfback Finlay Christie was in excellent form with his crisp passing, sniping running around the edges and quick decision making. Mitchell Hunt was one of the best first five-eighths in the Mitre 10 Cup. He directed the team well with a good balance between kicking, running and moving the ball on. Hunt also passed 100 points for the season with reliable goal-kicking.

Captain David Havili and Levi Aumua were a very effective midfield partnership with contrasting styles. The 118-kg centre Aumua was always difficult to contain with his strong direct running while Havili showed good line-breaking ability and distribution.

At fullback, 20-year-old Will Jordan was top try scorer with nine tries. His sensational running skills, allied with pace, were all on display again. He possesses a good clearing kick, but his tackling was inconsistent.

New arrival Solomon Alaimalo was the best of the wings. He did not reach the excellent form he displayed for the Chiefs in Super Rugby, but was always dangerous, particularly from broken play.

Of last year's team elsewhere were Robbie Malneek (on loan to Buller), Viliami Lolohea (Auckland), Trael Joass (Bay of Plenty), Jordan Taufua (injured but was intending to play in Japan), Tom Hill (Otago), Andrew Petelo (Wellington), Ti'i Paulo (retired) with James Lowe, Peter Samu, and Siosiua Halanukonuka all overseas. Before the season started, Shane Christie announced a premature retirement due to the ongoing effects of concussion, with Billy Guyton doing the same during the Mitre 10 Cup. Kane Hames played no rugby at all in 2018 due to concussion.

New players into the province with previous first-class experience were Jed Brown and Wyatt Crockett (both Canterbury), Solomon Alaimalo (Northland), and Ray Niuia (North Harbour).

Higher honours went to:
New Zealand:	S. Frizell, T. Lomax, T. Perry, L. Squire
New Zealand Maori:	T. Lomax, PP Parkinson
New Zealand Under 20:	Leicester Fainga'anuku, J. Spowart
New Zealand Sevens:	Lotima Fainga'anuku, T. Joass (to July), A. Knewstubb (to May), T. Ng Shiu

TASMAN REPRESENTATIVES 2018

	Club	Games for Union	Points for Union
Alex Ainley	Wanderers	92	45
John Akau'ola-Laula	Pakuranga United [1]	5	5
Solomon Alaimalo	Stoke	9	20
Tomas Aoake	Stoke	5	0
Levi Aumua	Renwick	18	25
Ethan Blackadder	Nelson	31	25
Jed Brown	Stoke	8	0
Finlay Christie	Stoke	31	15
Te Ahirau Cirikidaveta	Stoke	3	5
Ryan Coxon	Wanderers	10	0
Wyatt Crockett	Nelson	11	5
Michael Curry	Moutere	7	0
Leicester Fainga'anuku	Nelson	2	0
Lotima "Tima" Fainga'anuku	Nelson	26	25
Ben Finau	Moutere	3	0
Taina Fox-Matamua	Ponsonby [1]	5	0
Vernon Fredericks	Moutere	56	20
Shannon Frizell	Marist	24	30
Jack Grooby	Stoke	9	5
David Havili	Nelson	42	87
William Havili	Nelson	1	0
Sione Havili-Talitui	College Rifles [1]	5	5
Mitchell Hunt	Stoke	34	240
Will Jordan	Nelson	21	70
Tyrel Lomax	Stoke	19	5
Andrew Makalio	Marist	32	35
Isiah Miller	Nelson	1	0
Alex Nankivell	Stoke	35	30
Ray Niuia	Waitohi	10	0
Jacob Norris	Marist	2	5
Tim O'Malley	Waitohi	19	50
Pari Pari Parkinson	Stoke	21	5
Rupena Parkinson	Stoke	2	0
Tim Perry	Nelson	62	25
Blair Prinsep	Stoke	13	0
Isaac Salmon	Nelson	10	0
Jamie Spowart	Marist	3	5
Braden Stewart	Central	7	0
Quinten Strange	Nelson	26	20

[1] Auckland RU

INDIVIDUAL SCORING

	Tries	Con	PG	DG	Points
Hunt	4	27	14	–	116
Jordan	9	–	–	–	45
Alaimalo	4	–	–	–	20
Makalio	4	–	–	–	20
O'Malley	1	7	–	–	19
D. Havili	3	–	–	–	15
Aumua	2	–	–	–	10
Strange	2	–	–	–	10
Blackadder	2	–	–	–	10
Lotima Fainga'anuku	2	–	–	–	10
Christie	2	–	–	–	10
Havili-Talitui	1	–	–	–	5
Frizell	1	–	–	–	5
Lomax	1	–	–	–	5
Spowart	1	–	–	–	5
Cirikidaveta	1	–	–	–	5
Crockett	1	–	–	–	5
Norris	1	–	–	–	5
Akau'ola-Laula	1	–	–	–	5
P. Parkinson	1	–	–	–	5
Grooby	1	–	–	–	5
Totals	**45**	**34**	**14**	**0**	**335**
Opposition scored	29	22	9	0	216

TASMAN 2018

	Canterbury	Southland	North Harbour	Auckland	Taranaki	Manawatu	Counties Manukau	Wellington	Otago	Hawke's Bay	Canterbury	TOTALS
W.T. Jordan	15	15	15	15	15	s	15	15	15	15	15	11
J.W. Spowart	14	–	–	–	–	14	11	–	–	–	–	3
S. Alaimalo	11	11	11	11	11	11	–	11	–	13	11	9
Lot. T. Fainga'anuku	–	14	14	14	14	–	14	14	11	11	14	9
W.L. Havili	–	–	–	–	–	–	s	–	–	–	–	1
T. Aoake	–	–	–	–	–	–	–	–	14	14	s	3
Lei. O.K. Fainga'anuku	–	–	–	–	–	–	–	–	s	s	–	2
L. Aumua	13	13	13	s	13	13	13	13	13	–	13	10
R.W. Parkinson	–	–	–	–	–	–	–	–	–	s	–	1
D.K. Havili (capt)	12	12	12	12	12	15	12	12	12	–	12	10
A.P. Nankivell	s	s	s	13	s	12	s	s	–	–	–	8
M.J. Hunt	10	s	10	10	10	s	10	10	10	10	10	11
T.P. O'Malley	–	10	–	s	s	10	–	s	s	12	s	8
J.B.T. Grooby	9	9	–	s	s	s	s	s	9	s	–	9
B.I. Finau	s	s	–	–	–	–	–	–	–	–	–	2
F.T. Christie	–	–	9	9	9	9	9	9	s	9	9	9
V.J. Fredericks	8	–	–	–	–	–	–	–	–	–	–	1
I.W.P. Miller	–	8	–	–	–	–	–	–	–	–	–	1
S.M. Frizell	–	–	8	–	–	–	–	–	–	–	–	1
T.A. Cirikidaveta	–	–	–	s	–	–	8	–	–	–	–	2
T.J. Fox-Matamua	–	–	–	–	8	8	s	8	8	–	–	5
B.J. Stewart	–	–	–	–	–	–	–	–	s	s	s	3
J.C. Brown	7	7	7	7	7	–	7	–	–	7	7	8
E.J. Blackadder	6	6	6	8	6	6	6	6	6	6	6	11
S.T. Havili-Talitui	s	s	–	6	s	7	–	–	–	–	–	5
J.K. Norris	–	–	–	–	–	–	–	7	7	–	–	2
P-P.M. Parkinson	5	5	5	5	5	s	5	5	5	5	5	11
Q.J. Strange	4	4	4	4	4	5	4	4	4	–	4	10
M. Curry	s	s	s	s	s	4	–	–	–	8	8	7
J.S. Akau'ola-Laula	–	–	–	–	–	s	s	s	s	s	–	5
A.N. Ainley	–	–	–	–	–	–	–	–	–	4	s	2
T.S. Lomax	3	3	3	3	3	s	3	3	3	3	3	11
W.W.V. Crockett	1	s	s	1	1	1	1	1	1	1	1	11
B.E. Prinsep	s	s	–	–	s	3	–	s	s	–	s	7
R.C. Coxon	–	1	–	s	s	s	s	s	s	s	–	8
T.G. Perry	–	–	1	–	–	–	–	–	–	–	s	2
I.A. Salmon	–	–	s	s	–	–	s	–	–	s	–	4
A. Makalio	2	2	2	s	2	2	s	2	2	2	2	11
R. Niuia	s	s	–	2	s	s	2	s	s	s	s	10

W.W.V. Crockett captained v Hawke's Bay.

TASMAN TEAM RECORD, 2018

Played 11 Won 9 Lost 2 Points for 335 Points against 216

Date	Opponent	Location	Score	Tries	Con	PG	DG	Referee
August 17	Canterbury (P)	Blenheim	25–17	Aumua, Strange, Alaimalo	Hunt (2)	Hunt (2)		R.P.Kelly
August 26	Southland (P/C)	Blenheim	45–24	Jordan (2), Makalio, Alaimalo, Strange, Blackadder, Havili-Talitui	O'Malley (4), Hunt			J.R. Nutbrown
September 1	North Harbour (P)	Albany	32–20	Lotima Fainga'anuku, Jordan, Frizell, Christie	Hunt (3)	Hunt (2)		G.W. Jackson
September 7	Auckland (P)	Auckland	10–36	Blackadder	Hunt	Hunt		N.E.R. Hogan
September 14	Taranaki (P)	Nelson	53–17	Makalio (2), Lomax, D. Havili, Hunt, Jordan, Alaimalo	Hunt (5), O'Malley	Hunt (2)		J.R. Nutbrown
September 19	Manawatu (P/C)	Palmerston North	29–19	Spowart, Aumua, Jordan, Hunt	O'Malley (2), Hunt	Hunt		B.D. O'Keeffe
September 23	Counties Manukau (P)	Nelson	21–19	Cirikidaveta, Crockett, Jordan	Hunt (3)			T.N. Griffiths
September 29	Wellington (P)	Wellington	28–22	Christie, Alaimalo, Norris, Akau'ola-Laula	Hunt	Hunt (2)		N.P. Briant
October 7	Otago (P/C)	Dunedin	47–21	Jordan (3), Hunt, Makalio, D. Havili, Lotima Fainga'anuku	Hunt (6)			P.M. Williams
October 11	Hawke's Bay (P/C)	Nelson	29–0	P-P. Parkinson, O'Malley, Hunt, Grooby	Hunt (3)	Hunt		M.I. Fraser
October 19	Canterbury (P semi-final)	Nelson	16–21	D. Havili	Hunt	Hunt (3)		M.I. Fraser

THAMES VALLEY

2018 Status: Heartland
Founded and affiliated 1922
President: K.J. (Kelly) Plummer
Chairman: G.W. (Graham) Hallett
Chief executive officer: Edmond Leahy
Coach: M.W. (Matthew) Bartleet
Assistant coaches: D.P. (David) Harrison, J.R. (Joe) Murray
Main ground: Paeroa Domain
Capacity: 3000
Colours: Gold and red

RECORDS

Highest attendance	7000	*Thames Valley v Auckland (Ranfurly Shield), 1989*
Most appearances	144	*B.C. Duggan, 1970–84*
Most points	665	*D.P. Harrison, 2004–15*
Most tries	42	*I.F. Campbell, 1981–94*
Most points in a season	127	*J.R. Reynolds, 2011*
Most tries in a season	14	*I.F. Campbell, 1988*
Most conversions in a season	30	*D.B. McCallum, 1995*
Most penalty goals in a season	25	*J.R. Reynolds, 2011*
Most dropped goals in a season	4	*T.E. Shaw, 1962*
		R.W. Kemp, 1968
Most points in a match	27	*D.B. McCallum v East Coast, 1995*
		M. Griffin v King Country, 2003
Most tries in a match	4	*I.F. Campbell v North Otago, 1990*
		G.A. Ellis v North Otago, 1994
		G.W. McLiver v Marlborough, 1995
Most conversions in a match	8	*G.A. Ellis v West Coast, 1994*
		M.A. Handley v North Otago, 1994
Most penalty goals in a match	7	*D.P. Harrison v Mid Canterbury, 2009*
	7	*J.R. Reynolds v East Coast, 2011*
Highest team score	86	*v North Otago, 1994*
Record victory (points ahead)	79	*86–7 v North Otago, 1994*
Highest score conceded	113	*v Northland, 1997*
Record defeat (points behind)	99	*14–113 v Northland, 1997*

After finishing the 2017 season in ninth place, Thames Valley made a dramatic improvement in 2018 which resulted in their winning the Mitre 10 Heartland Championship and becoming holders of the Meads Cup. Sixteen players with previous representative experience formed a valuable foundation for the coaches to build on, and the Swamp Foxes were further strengthened by the addition of several worthy newcomers in key positions. Head coach Matthew Bartleet, together with his two assistants, David Harrison and Joe Murray, quickly settled on a preferred starting line-up and the team played open and attractive rugby to score a Thames Valley record of 44 tries in the Heartland competition.

Throughout the season the forward pack steadily improved and developed into a very effective combination which was more than a match for its opponents in the finals. Team spirit intensified as the season progressed as did the players' self-belief in their ability to be successful. The manner in which they stepped up their defence in the final matches against Wanganui and South Canterbury is a tribute to their attitude and commitment. To win five games away from home, including a semi-final and a final, is an amazing achievement for a team which had never previously progressed beyond a semi-final in the Lochore Cup and one which had never featured in the Meads Cup playoff series.

Out wide Harry Lafituanai, Sam McCahon and Kieran Lee formed a potent attacking trio and they were well supported by two promising newcomers in Ethan Seymour and Matthew Abraham. Jesse Dodunski, returning after a year's absence, was a capable fullback, but his season was curtailed by injury. Shaun Hill again demonstrated his strength in the midfield and it was unfortunate that an injury prevented him from playing in the final and taking his place in the New Zealand Heartland XV. Halfback Ben Bonnar was back to his best form with Matt Fisher, returning to the side after a year's break, being a worthy substitute. At first five-eighth Reece Boughton played a key role in the team's success. He scored 86 points with his boot and proved to be an astute tactical kicker.

Alex Bradley, Brett Ranga and former New Zealand Secondary Schools' representative Christian Kelleher were a dynamic loose forward trio and they scored a total of ten tries. For the second year in a row Brett Ranga was named Player of the Year. Newcomer Cameron Dromgool joined Connor McVerry as a lock and although they were the shortest pairing in the competition they demonstrated much courage and skilful play. Glen McIntyre, who had last appeared in 2016, was a dedicated and powerful hooker. The regular prop forwards, Te Huia Kutia and Sitiveni Tupou, made huge strides this season with the latter becoming something of a cult figure. When he was available the Chilean prop Sergio de la Fuente provided good cover, with the highlight of his season being the try he scored in the final against South Canterbury. The surprise of the year was former outside back, and veteran of 65 games for Thames Valley, Lance Easton's transformation into a prop forward. Easton appeared in every game and after a shaky start he proved his worth with some strong scrummaging in the final matches.

After an outstanding season with Thames Valley, Alex Bradley was named as captain of the New Zealand Heartland team, an honour richly deserved and well merited as were the selections of Ranga, McIntyre, McCahon and Hill (unavailable).

Higher honours went to:
New Zealand Heartland: A.J. Bradley, S.M. McCahon, G.F. McIntyre, B.D. Ranga

THAMES VALLEY REPRESENTATIVES 2018

	Club	Games for Union	Points for Union		Club	Games for Union	Points for Union
Matiu Abraham	Thames	7	15	Harry Lafituanai	Melville [2]	18	35
Ben Bonnar	Waihou	27	23	Kieran Lee	Melville [2]	10	30
Alex Bradley	Waihou	18	30	Keegan Lewis	Waihou	6	0
Reece Boughton	Thames	10	91	Logan Matai-Povey	Tairua	3	0
Sergio De La Fuente	Thames	6	5	Sam McCahon	Waihou	18	30
Jesse Dodunski	Waihi Athletic	5	5	Glen McIntyre	Waihou	18	10
Cameron Dromgool	Te Aroha COB	10	5	Connor McVerry [1]	Fraser Tech [2]	27	0
Lance Easton	Tairua	75	97	Shin Ouchi	Waihou	5	0
Nathan Emery	Te Aroha COB	3	0	Brett Ranga	Waihi Athletic	42	40
Matthew Fisher	Hauraki North	18	0	Matthew Rolston	Waihi Athletic	21	0
Matthew Hart	Waihi Athletic	16	5	Ethan Seymour	Waihi Athletic	9	15
Shaun Hill	Hauraki North	15	20	Sitiveni Topou	Thames	15	10
Christian Kelleher	Hamilton Marist [2]	10	15	Ben Vincent	Thames	3	0
Te Huia Kutia	Tairua	8	0				

[1] Player of Origin   [2] Waikato RU

INDIVIDUAL SCORING

	Tries	Con	PG	DG	Points		Tries	Con	PG	DG	Points
Boughton	1	25	12	–	91	Topou	2	–	–	–	10
McCahon	6	–	–	–	30	Penalty try	1	–	–	–	7
Lee	6	–	–	–	30	Dodunski	1	–	–	–	5
Lafituanai	4	–	–	–	20	Bonnar	1	–	–	–	5
Ranga	4	–	–	–	20	Dromgool	1	–	–	–	5
Kelleher	3	–	–	–	15	De La Fuente	1	–	–	–	5
Abraham	3	–	–	–	15						
Seymour	3	–	–	–	15	**Totals**	**44**	**25**	**12**	**0**	**308**
Bradley	3	–	–	–	15						
Hill	2	–	–	–	10	Opposition scored	33*	23	13	0	252
McIntyre	2	–	–	–	10						

* includes one penalty try (7 points)

THAMES VALLEY 2018

	West Coast	Wairarapa Bush	Buller	King Country	North Otago	Poverty Bay	Horowhenua Kapiti	South Canterbury	Wanganui	South Canterbury	TOTALS
J.T. Dodunski	15	15	15	15	–	–	–	–	–	–	4
H.K. Lafituanai	14	14	14	14	15	15	15	15	15	13	10
K.F. Lee	11	11	11	11	11	11	11	11	11	11	10
E.L. Seymour	s	–	s	s	14	14	14	14	14	15	9
N. Emery	–	–	–	s	s	–	–	s	–	–	3
S.M. McCahon	13	13	13	13	13	13	13	13	13	12	10
S.M.G. Hill (capt)	12	12	–	12	12	–	12	12	12	–	7
M.J.K. Abraham	s	s	12	–	s	12	–	–	s	14	7
R. Boughton	10	10	10	10	10	10	10	10	10	10	10
B.T. Bonnar	9	9	9	9	9	9	s	9	9	9	10
M.A. Fisher	s	s	s	s	s	s	9	s	–	s	9
A.J. Bradley	8	8	8	8	8	8	8	8	8	8	10
C.T. Kelleher	7	7	7	7	7	7	7	7	7	7	10
B. Vincent	6	–	s	6	–	–	–	–	–	–	3
M.J. Hart	s	s	s	s	s	s	s	s	–	–	8
B.D. Ranga	–	6	6	–	6	6	6	6	6	6	8
C.E. McVerry	5	5	5	5	5	5	–	–	5	5	8
C.M. Dromgool	4	4	4	4	4	4	4	4	4	4	10
M.J. Rolston	s	–	s	s	s	s	5	s	–	–	7
K.S. Lewis	–	s	–	–	–	–	–	5	–	s	3
S.V. Topou	3	3	3	3	3	3	3	3	3	3	10
T.H.A. Kutia	1	1	–	–	1	1	1	1	1	1	8
L.C. Easton	s	s	1	1	s	s	s	s	s	s	10
S. De La Fuente	–	s	–	s	–	s	s	s	–	s	6
G.F. McIntyre	2	2	2	2	2	2	2	2	2	2	10
L.T. Matai-Povey	s	–	s	–	–	–	–	–	–	–	2
S. Ouchi	–	s	s	s	s	–	–	s	–	–	5

B.D. Ranga captained in the three matches S.M.G. Hill did not play in.

THAMES VALLEY TEAM RECORD, 2018

Played 10   Won 7   Lost 3   Points for 308   Points against 252

Date	Opponent	Location	Score	Tries	Con	PG	DG	Referee
August 25	West Coast (H)	Te Aroha	25–27	Hill, McCahon, Lee	Boughton (2)	Boughton (2)		D.J. MacPherson
September 1	Wairarapa Bush (H)	Masterton	44–32	McCahon (2), Dodunski, Kelleher, Lee, Bonnar	Boughton (4)	Boughton (2)		T.M.T. Cottrell
September 8	Buller (H)	Westport	43–22	Seymour (2), Abraham, Lafituanai, Dromgool, Ranga, Boughton	Boughton (4)			H.G. Reed
September 15	King Country (H)	Te Aroha	29–37	McCahon, Lee, McIntyre, Seymour	Boughton (3)	Boughton		R.M. Mahoney
September 22	North Otago (H)	Te Aroha	43–21	Lee (2), McCahon, Abraham, Lafituanai, Kelleher	Boughton (2)	Boughton (3)		T. Kawahara *Japan*
September 29	Poverty Bay (H)	Gisborne	37–34	Bradley, Topou, Penalty try, Abraham, Lafituanai	Boughton (2)	Boughton (2)		J.D. Munro
October 6	Horowhenua Kapiti (H)	Te Aroha	29–27	Bradley (2), Ranga, McCahon, Hill	Boughton (2)			A.W.B. Mabey
October 13	South Canterbury (H)	Timaru	24–33	Ranga, Kelleher, Lee, Lafituanai	Boughton (2)			M.C.J. Winter
October 20	Wanganui (MC semi-final)	Wanganui	17–7	Topou, McIntyre	Boughton (2)	Boughton		R.P. Kelly
October 27	South Canterbury (MC final)	Timaru	17–12	Ranga, De La Fuente	Boughton (2)	Boughton		J.R. Nutbrown

WAIKATO

2018 Status: Mitre 10 Cup Championship
Founded 1909 as South Auckland.
Affiliated 1909. Name changed to Waikato 1921
President: Duane Monkley
Chairman: Colin Groves
Chief executive officer: Blair Foote
Coach: Jono Gibbes
Assistant coaches: Nathan White, Roger Randle
Main ground: FMG Stadium, Hamilton
Capacity: 27,000
Colours: Red, yellow and black

RECORDS

Most appearances	148	Ian Foster, 1985–98
Most points	1604	Matthew Cooper, 1990–99
Most tries	70	Bruce Smith, 1979–84
Most points in a season	269	Brett Craies, 1989
Most tries in a season	17	Bruce Smith, 1981
Most conversions in a season	69	Brett Craies, 1989
Most penalty goals in a season	57	Matthew Cooper, 1993
Most dropped goals in a season	10	John Boe, 1981
Most points in a match	35	Bruce Reihana v North Otago, 2000
Most tries in a match	5	Gary Major v East Coast, 1981
		Bruce Smith v Nadi, 1982
		Bruce Smith v South Australia, 1983
		Ian Wilson v South Canterbury, 1984
		Rob Gordon v Southland, 1990
		Roger Randle v Poverty Bay, 1998
		Sitiveni Sivivatu v Auckland, 2004
Most conversions in a match	12	Matthew Cooper v Wairarapa Bush, 1990
		Glen Jackson v West Coast, 2000
Most penalty goals in a match	7	Andrew Strawbridge v Wellington, 1985
		Trent Renata v Bay of Plenty, 2013
Highest team score	121	v Poverty Bay, 1998
Record victory (points ahead)	121	121–0 v Poverty Bay, 1998
Highest score conceded	96	v Harlequins Invitation XV, 1995
Record defeat (points behind)	71	25–96 v Harlequins Invitation XV, 1995

Winning promotion to the Premiership would have been a prime objective of Waikato in 2018. However, losing their first three games almost caused a review, but six consecutive wins starting with a big win over Wellington and a third consecutive convincing victory in the Ranfurly Shield challenge against Taranaki created the momentum for a successful season. A short Ranfurly Shield tenure ended to Otago, who had also relieved Waikato of the Shield five years earlier. Scoring the most tries (66) and the most points (452) sits nicely alongside Mitre 10 Championship winner.

Nine players appeared in all 12 games and a further six players in 11 games is a sign of sound selection. Arriving from Otago with a modest but useful goal-kicking record, first five-eighth Fletcher Smith hit the ground running, converting 54 of 65 tries at an 83 per cent success rate, making him the leading points scorer in the competition. That 83 per cent is by far the best record for a Waikato player.

Sevu Reece was the leading try scorer in the competition but will have learned that off-field behaviour is also among selection criteria. Matt Lansdown, whose career had begun in Northland, performed well enough at fullback to gain selection for the Maori All Blacks. Veteran Dwayne Sweeney captained the side and gave an interesting demonstration of 'leading from the front'. He scored the first try for Waikato in each of his three Ranfurly Shield games. Captain of the 2017 New Zealand Secondary Schools team Quinn Tupaea was a most impressive centre, playing in every game. Jack Stratton, who had earlier played for Canterbury and the Crusaders, welcomed the greater opportunity of Waikato and did not disappoint. The O'Donnell brothers returned from Taranaki.

Samisoni Taukei'aho appeared in all twelve games and was the leading forward try scorer in the competition, touching down nine times. Joshua Iosefo-Scott started every match at tighthead prop. It was no surprise to see him selected for a Super Rugby team — the Highlanders where he will be joined by fellow Waikato prop Ayden Johnstone. It was disappointing not to see Atu Moli on the field beyond the first round of Super Rugby, but welcomed home was the six times-capped Wallaby Toby Smith. Tim Bond, who had played for Northland last year, was a first-choice lock, who was to captain Waikato against Northland. James Tucker, who had promised much in recent years, had a great season. It will be worth keeping an eye on New Zealand Under 20 lock Laghlan McWhannell. Mitch Jacobson contributed to what may become a Jacobson legacy of Waikato Rugby. Jordan Manihera was a high-energy number eight.

Higher honours went to:
New Zealand: A. Lienert-Brown, D. McKenzie
New Zealand Under 20: L. McWhannell, O. Norris, X Roe, B. Sullivan, Q. Tupaea
Maori All Blacks: M. Lansdown
New Zealand Sevens: J. Bunce, D. Collier, T. Mikkelson, I. Te Tamaki

WAIKATO REPRESENTATIVES 2018

	Club	Games for Union	Points for Union		Club	Games for Union	Points for Union
Jono Armstrong	Hautapu	24	0	Laghlan McWhannell	Hautapu	13	5
Tim Bond	University	11	0	Jordan Manihera	HOB	30	55
Jahrome Brown	Melville	2	0	Michael Mayhew	Hautapu	7	5
Jordan Bunce	Fraser Tech	2	0	Declan O'Donnell	Melville	34	50
Adam Burn	HOB	55	20	Kylem O'Donnell	Melville	14	5
Sam Caird	Hautapu	10	0	Pepesano Patafilo	[2]	3	5
Tyler Campbell	University	25	25	Sevu Reece	HOB	33	134
Mosese Dawai	[1]	5	5	Fletcher Smith	University	12	130
Sosaia Fale	HOB	10	0	Toby Smith	HOB	57	45
Haereiti Hetet	Otorohanga	5	0	Jack Stratton	University	11	5
Joshua Iosefa-Scott	Melville	20	5	Bailyn Sullivan	Marist	16	25
Murray Iti	Otorohanga	23	20	Dwayne Sweeney (capt)	Morrinsville Sports	93	132
Mitch Jacobson	Hautapu	37	10	Raniera Takarangi	HOB	7	15
Ayden Johnstone	Hautapu	21	0	Samisoni Taukei'aho	Fraser Tech	23	60
Sefo Kautai	Marist	21	5	James Tucker	Marist	34	25
Matthew Lansdown	Fraser Tech	22	47	Quinn Tupaea	HOB	12	35
Sekope Lopeti-Moli	Hautapu	17	10				

[1] Counties Manukau   [2] Wellington RU

INDIVIDUAL SCORING

	Tries	Con	PG	DG	Points
F. Smith	2	54	4	–	130
Reece	14	–	–	–	70
Taukei'aho	9	–	–	–	45
Tupaea	7	–	–	–	35
Campbell	3	–	–	–	15
Manihera	3	–	–	–	15
Sullivan	3	–	–	–	15
Sweeney	3	–	–	–	15
Takarangi	3	–	–	–	15
Tucker	3	–	–	–	15
D. O'Donnell	2	–	–	–	10
Iti	2	–	–	–	10
Lansdown	2	–	–	–	10
Penalty try	1	–	–	–	7
Burn	1	–	–	–	5
Dawai	1	–	–	–	5
Iosefa-Scott	1	–	–	–	5
Jacobson	1	–	–	–	5
Lopeti-Moli	1	–	–	–	5
K. O'Donnell	1	–	–	–	5
Patafilo	1	–	–	–	5
T. Smith	1	–	–	–	5
Stratton	1	–	–	–	5
Totals	**66**	**54**	**4**	**0**	**452**
Opposition scored	40	25	10	0	282

WAIKATO 2018

	Manawatu	North Harbour	Auckland	Wellington	Taranaki	Hawke's Bay	Bay of Plenty	Southland	Northland	Otago	Northland	Otago	TOTALS
M.R.T. Lansdown	10	10	s	15	15	15	15	s	15	15	15	15	12
F.J. Bunce	–	–	–	–	–	–	s	15	–	–	–	–	2
D.P.T.K. O'Donnell	14	14	–	–	–	–	–	–	–	s	s	s	5
T.A.J. Campbell	s	s	15	14	14	s	14	14	14	11	14	14	12
M.R. Dawai	–	–	14	s	–	s	s	–	s	–	–	–	5
S.L. Reece	11	11	11	11	11	11	11	11	11	–	11	11	11
Q.P.C. Tupaea	13	13	s	13	13	13	13	13	12	13	13	13	12
B.W.M. Sullivan	s	s	13	–	s	14	–	–	13	14	s	s	9
D.W.H. Sweeney (capt)	12	12	12	12	12	12	12	12	–	12	12	12	11
P. Patafilo	–	–	–	s	–	–	–	s	s	–	–	–	3
F.H. Smith	15	15	10	10	10	10	10	10	10	10	10	10	12
K.F.T. O'Donnell	9	s	s	9	–	–	–	–	–	–	s	s	6
J.B. Stratton	s	9	9	–	9	9	9	9	9	9	9	9	11
R. Takarangi	–	–	–	s	s	s	s	s	s	s	–	–	7
M.E. Iti	8	–	–	–	–	s	8	8	–	–	s	s	6
J.M. Manihera	6	8	8	8	8	8	–	–	8	8	8	8	10
M.L. Jacobson	7	7	–	7	7	7	7	7	s	7	7	7	11
J.D. Armstrong	–	s	s	–	–	–	s	s	7	s	–	–	6
J.D.R. Brown	–	–	7	–	–	–	–	–	–	–	–	–	1
A.N. Burn	s	6	6	s	6	6	6	6	s	s	6	6	12
J.F. Tucker	5	5	s	6	5	s	5	5	6	6	5	5	12
L.E. McWhannell	–	s	4	5	s	5	4	s	5	5	s	4	11
T.O. Bond	4	4	5	4	4	4	–	4	4	4	4	s	11
S.W. Caird	s	–	–	s	–	–	s	–	–	–	–	–	3
J.Z.A. Iosefa-Scott	3	3	3	3	3	3	3	3	3	3	3	3	12
S.S.V. Kautai	s	–	–	–	–	–	–	–	–	–	–	–	1
H.B.G. Hetet	s	s	–	–	s	s	s	–	–	–	–	–	5
C.A. Johnstone	1	1	s	s	1	1	1	1	1	s	1	1	12
T.J. Smith	–	–	1	1	–	–	–	s	s	1	s	s	7
S.I.K. Fale	–	s	s	s	s	s	s	s	s	–	s	s	10
S.F. Taukei'aho	2	2	s	2	2	2	2	s	2	2	2	2	12
M.S. Mayhew	s	s	2	–	–	–	–	s	–	–	–	–	4
S. Lopeti-Moli	–	–	–	s	s	s	s	2	–	s	s	s	8

WAIKATO TEAM RECORD 2018

Played 12 Won 8 Lost 4 Points for 452 Points against 282

Date	Opponent	Location	Score	Tries	Con	PG	DG	Referee
August 18	Manawatu (C)	Palmerston North	19–24	Reece, Taukei'aho, D. O'Donnell	F.Smith (2)			M. Fraser
August 25	North Harbour (C)	Hamilton	28–29	Manihera, D. O'Donnell, Tupaea, Campbell	F. Smith (4)			C. Stone
August 30	Auckland (P/C)	Auckland	17–35	Dawai, Taukei'aho, K. O'Donnell	F. Smith			J. Munro
September 5	Wellington (P/C)	Hamilton	43–31	Reece (3), Manihera, Takarangi, Taukei'aho	F. Smith (5)	F. Smith		B. Pickerill
September 9	Taranaki (RS) (P/C)	New Plymouth	33–19	Sweeney, Burn, Tucker, Taukei'aho, Tupaea	F. Smith (4)			B. O'Keeffe
September 13	Hawke's Bay (RS) (C)	Hamilton	42–22	Sweeney, Reece, Manihera, Iti, F. Smith, Takarangi	F. Smith (6)			N. Briant
September 21	Bay of Plenty (C)	Rotorua	54–21	Taukei'aho (2), Tupaea (2), Tucker, Jacobson, Lopeti-Moli, Lansdown	F. Smith (7)			A.Mabey
September 29	Southland (RS) (C)	Hamilton	42–11	Taukei'aho (2), Sweeney, Reece, Iti, T. Smith	F. Smith (6)			J. Nutbrown
October 6	Northland (C)	Whangarei	71–28	Sullivan (2), Tupaea (2), Reece (2), F. Smith, Tucker, Takarangi, penalty try, Patafilo	F. Smith (7)			B. Pickerill
October 13	Otago (RS) (C)	Hamilton	19–23	Iosefa-Scott, Campbell, Sullivan	F. Smith (2)			B. Pickerill
October 19	Northland (semi-final)	Hamilton	48–26	Reece (4), Taukei'aho, Stratton	F. Smith (6)	F. Smith (2)		P. Williams
October 26	Otago (Final)	Hamilton	36–13	Reece (2), Tupaea, Lansdown, Campbell	F. Smith (4)	F. Smith		B. O'Keeffe

Photo by Bruce Jarvis Photographic Services Ltd

ALL BLACKS 2018 STEINLAGER SERIES V FRANCE

BACK ROW: G. Enoka (*Manager — Leadership*), J. Toomaga-Allen, J. Barrett, V. Fifita, S. Barrett, L. Squire, O. Tu'ungafasi, M. Cron (*Asst Coach*). ***FOURTH ROW***: K. Simperingham (*S&C Coach*), J. Iversen (*Logistics Manager*), C. Taylor, T. Perry, S. Frizell, R. Ioane, J. Goodhue, N. Harris, S. McLeod (*Asst Coach*), N. Gill (*Head S&C Coach*). ***THIRD ROW***: G. Duncan (*Muscle Therapist*), J. Hamilton (*Analyst*), A. Page (*Doctor*), D. McKenzie, L. Coltman, L. Whitelock, A. Savea, N. Milner-Skudder, A. Ioane, J. Locke (*Media Manager*), D. Shand (*Manager — Business & Operations*). ***SECOND ROW***: I. Foster (*Asst Coach*), B. Thiel (*Team Services Manager*), R. Mo'unga, N. Laumape, J. Taufua, J. Moody, A. Lienert-Brown, W. Naholo, R. Crotty, H. Chapman (*Asst Analyst*), P. Gallagher (*Physio*). ***FRONT ROW***: T.J. Perenara, O. Franks, B. Barrett, B. Smith, S. Whitelock (*Captain*), S. Hansen (*Head Coach*), S. Cane, B. Retallick, S. Williams, A. Smith. ***INSETS***: G. Fox (*Selector*), K. Darry (*Nutritionist*), L. Romano, Te T. Tahuriorangi, T. Franklin, R. Riccitelli, M. Todd, J. Hemopo, K. Tu'inukuafe.

ALL BLACKS — 2018 INVESTEC RUGBY CHAMPIONSHIP AND HOLDERS OF THE BLEDISLOE CUP

BACK ROW: G. Enoka (*Manager — Leadership*), S. Williams, J. Hemopo, J. Barrett, S. Barrett, L. Squire, O. Tu'ungafasi, M. Cron (*Asst Coach*). **FOURTH ROW**: A. Page (*Doctor*), D. Shand (*Manager — Business & Operations*), J. Iversen (*Logistics Manager*), C. Taylor, T. Perry, S. Frizell, R. Ioane, J. Goodhue, N. Harris, S. McLeod, N. Gill (*Head S&C Coach*). **THIRD ROW**: J. Hamilton (*Analyst*), G. Duncan (*Muscle Therapist*), R. Mo'unga, Te T. Tahuriorangi, D. McKenzie, L. Coltman, L. Whitelock, A. Savea, N. Milner-Skudder, K. Darry (*Nutritionist*), J. Locke (*Media Manager*). **SECOND ROW**: I. Foster (*Asst Coach*), B. Thiel (*Team Services Manager*), N. Laumape, T.J. Perenara, K. Tu'inukuafe, J. Moody, A. Lienert-Brown, W. Naholo, R. Crotty, H. Chapman (*Asst Analyst*), P. Gallagher (*Physio*). **FRONT ROW**: D. Coles, O. Franks, B. Barrett, B. Smith, K. Read (*Captain*), S. Hansen (*Head Coach*), S. Whitelock, B. Retallick, S. Cane, A. Smith. **INSETS**: K. Simperingham (*S&C Coach*), V. Fifita, G. Fox (*Selector*), A. Ta'avao-Matau, J. Toomaga-Allen, R. Riccitelli.

ALL BLACKS — 2018 VISTA NORTHERN TOUR, JAPAN TEST

BACK ROW: A. Page (*Doctor*), G. Enoka (*Manager — Leadership*), D. Papalii, J. Barrett, G. Evans, M. Cron (*Asst Coach*), S. McLeod (*Asst Coach*).
FOURTH ROW: J. Hamilton (*Analyst*), G. Duncan (*Muscle Therapist*), M. Proctor, D. Havili, D. Hunt, J. Iversen (*Logistics Manager*), N. Gill (*S&C Coach*), J. Roche (*Physio*). *THIRD ROW*: K. Simperingham (*Asst S&C Coach*), B. Cameron, B. Hall, G. Bridge, J. Hemopo, T. Perry, T. Lomax, K. Darry (*Nutritionist*), D. Shand (*Manager — Business & Operations*), J. Locke (*Media Manager*). *SECOND ROW*: I. Foster (*Asst Head Coach*), B. Thiel (*Team Services Manager*), Te T. Tahuriorangi, M. Drummond, A. Aumua, L. Coltman, A. Ta'avao-Matau, R. O'Neill, H. Chapman (*Asst Analyst*), P. Gallagher (*Physio*).
FRONT ROW: N. Laumape, W. Naholo, P. Tuipulotu, R. Mo'unga, L. Whitelock (*Captain*), S. Hansen (*Head Coach*), D. Coles, O. Tu'ungafasi, N. Milner-Skudder, V. Fifita. *INSET*: G. Fox (*Selector*).

Photo by Jarvis Photographic Services Ltd

ALL BLACKS — 2018 VISTA NORTHERN TOUR

BACK ROW: G. Enoka (*Manager — Leadership*), P. Tuipulotu, V. Fifita, J. Barrett, K. Barrett, R. Ioane, L. Squire, M. Cron (*Asst Coach*). **FOURTH ROW**: A. Page (*Doctor*), G. Duncan (*Muscle Therapist*), J. Iversen (*Logistics Manager*), D. Papalii, A. Savea, N. Laulala, M. Todd, N. Harris, S. McLeod (*Asst Coach*), N. Gill (*S&C Coach*). **THIRD ROW**: J. Hamilton (*Analyst*), B. Thiel (*Team Services Manager*), R. Mo'unga, D. McKenzie, J. Goodhue, O. Tu'ungafasi, C. Taylor, K. Darry (*Nutritionist*), D. Shand (*Manager — Business & Operations*), J. Locke (*Media Manager*). **SECOND ROW**: I. Foster (*Asst Head Coach*), K. Simperingham (*Asst S&C Coach*), Te T. Tahuriorangi, T.J. Perenara, K. Tu'inukuafe, J. Moody, A. Lienert-Brown, W. Naholo, R. Crotty, H. Chapman (*Asst Analyst*), P. Gallagher (*Physio*). **FRONT ROW**: D. Coles, O. Franks, B. Barrett, B. Smith, K. Read (*Captain*), S. Hansen (*Head Coach*), S. Whitelock, B. Retallick, S. Williams, A. Smith. **INSETS**: G. Fox (*Selector*), A. Ta'avao-Matau.

Photo by Bruce Jarvis Photographic Services Ltd

BLACK FERNS 2018 INTERNATIONAL SERIES V AUSTRALIA

BACK ROW: J. Tout (S&C Coach), J. Ngan-Woo, L. Perese, A. Nelson, C. Smith, J. Patea-Fereti, C. Alley, J. Haggart (Asst Coach), S. Smith (Doctor), W. Clarke (Asst Coach). **THIRD ROW**: A. Hodge (Analyst), M. Tagoai, C. Tofa, A. Itunu, A. Saili, M. Parkes, C. McMenamin, K. Demant, P. Love, L. Cournane (Manager). **SECOND ROW**: G. Milne (Physio), T. Te Tamaki (Physio), T. Fitzpatrick, S. Waaka, K. Cottrell, K. Sue, L. Elder, Te K. Ngata-Aerengamate, R. Demant, H. Porter (Campaign Manager), M. Keys (Media Manager). **FRONT ROW**: E. Blackwell, L. Itunu, K. Cocksedge, G. Moore (Head Coach), F. Fa'amausili (Captain), S. Winiata, R. Wickliffe, A. Savage.

Photo by Bruce Jarvis Photographic Services Ltd

BLACK FERNS 2018 NORTHERN TOUR

BACK ROW: J. Haggart (*Asst Coach*), J. Ngan-Woo, L. Perese, A. Nelson, C. Smith, J. Patea-Fereti, C. Alley, S. Smith (*Doctor*), W. Clarke (*Asst Coach*). **THIRD ROW**: A. Hodge (*Analyst*), M. Tagoai, C. Tofa, A. Itunu, M. Parkes, C. McMenamin, K. Demant, P. Love, K. Moata'ane, J. Tout (*S&C Coach*). **SECOND ROW**: L. Cournane (*Manager*), T. Te Tamaki (*Physio*), A. Leti-I'iga, N. Moors, S. Waaka, L. Anderson, K. Sue, L. Elder, Te K. Ngata-Aerengamate, R. Demant, M. Keys (*Media Manager*). **FRONT ROW**: E. Blackwell, L. Itunu, K. Cocksedge, G. Moore (*Head Coach*), F. Fa'amausili (*Captain*), S. Winiata, R. Wickliffe, A. Savage.

MĀORI ALL BLACKS 2018 TOUR TO THE USA, BRAZIL & CHILE

BACK ROW: R. Randle (*Asst Coach*), B. Harmon, S. Stevenson, I. Walker-Leawere, P.P. Parkinson, H. Matenga, R. Prinsep, R. Thompson, M. Lansdown. *THIRD ROW*: M. Sexton (*Campaign Manager*), R. Durie (*Doctor*), R. Abel, I. Salmon, R. Wright, S. Thomas (*S&C Coach*), J. Ross (*Analyst*), J. Maddock (*Asst Coach*). *SECOND ROW*: A. Letts (*Asst Physio*), A. Draper (*Physio*), R. Ware, M. Karpik, J. Ruru, J. Lowe, T. Walden, J. Ioane, S. Nock, T. Ward (*Manager*). *FRONT ROW*: M. Renata, A. Ioane, C. Eves, L. Crawford (*Kaumatua*) A. Dixon (*Captain*), C. McMillan (*Head Coach*), B. May, B. Weber, O. Black. *INSETS*: J. Trainor, T. Lomax, B. Hall, J. Hemopo, M. Proctor.

Photo by Bruce Jarvis Photographic Services Ltd

ALL BLACKS SEVENS

Commonwealth Games Gold Medallists, Gold Coast, 2018

BACK ROW: M. Harvey (*S&C Coach*), T. Cama (*Asst Coach*), E. Nanai Seturo, A. Knewstubb, T. Joass, A. Rokolisoa, V. Koroi, T. Martin (*Analyst*), D. Banks (*Physio*). ***FRONT ROW:*** C. Laidlaw (*Head Coach*), S. Molia, S. Dickson, S. Curry (*Co-captain*), T. Mikkelson (*Co-captain*), K. Baker, D. Collier, R. Ware, R. Everiss (*Manager*). ***INSETS:*** C. Clarke, N. McGarvey, J. Webber.

Photo by Sean Willis

BLACK FERNS SEVENS – DUBAI SEVENS, 2018

BACK ROW: A. Bunting (*Head Coach*), C. Sweeney (*Asst Coach*) K. Niederer (*Physio*), T. Te Tamaki, M. Blyde, R. Pouri-Lane, T. Nathan-Wong, T. Kidwell (*Manager*), S. Ross (*Asst Coach*), B. Anderson (*S&C Coach*). ***FRONT ROW:*** K. Whata-Simpkins, S. Waaka, K. Brazier, A. Saili, S. Goss (*Captain*), R. Tui, S. Baker, T. Fitzpatrick, G. Broughton. ***ABSENT:*** N. Armstrong (*Physio*).

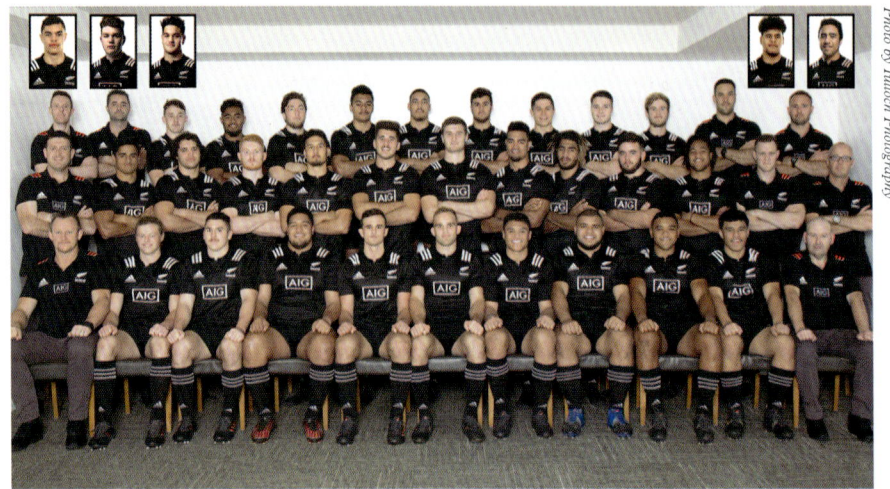

NEW ZEALAND UNDER 20
World Rugby Under 20 Championship, France, 2018

BACK ROW: J. Bishop (*Doctor*), K. Houltham (*Physio*), J. Renton, V. Koroi, F. Thomas, T. Tele'a, B. Proctor, J. Spowart, W. Tremain, K. Trask, X. Roe, D. Hill (*Asst Coach*), S. Pinford (*S&C Coach*). **SECOND ROW:** D. Hewett (*Set Piece Coach*), B. Sullivan, D. Flanders, T. Florence, W. Riedlinger-Kapa, L. McWhannell, W. Tucker, J. Akau'ola-Laula, H. Sotutu, R. Cobb, L. Fainga'anuku, W. Rickards (*Asst Coach*). **FRONT ROW:** C. Philpott (*Head Coach*), S. Gregory, R. Jackson, K. Uluilakepa, H. Plummer, T. Christie (*Captain*), C. Clarke, S. Asi, T. Mafileo, X. Numia, M. Vercoe (*Manager*). **INSETS:** N. Punivai, O. Norris, Q. Tupaea, S. Asomua, S. Matenga

NEW ZEALAND HEARTLAND XV

BACK ROW: S. Koroitamana, S. Holani, T. Tauwhare, G. McIntyre, P. Nabainivalu, A. Thrupp, A. Lahmert, W. Paia'aua. **SECOND ROW:** M. Rutene (*Asst Coach*), P. Masoe (*Physio*), S. Cameron, M. Kolinisau, C. McDonald, J. Goodger, V. Poloniati, C. Hart, B. Ranga, C. Scanlon (*Coach*), P. McHugh (*Doctor*), G. Hodder (*Manager*). **FRONT ROW:** C. Carmichael, D. Church, W. Wright, A. Stephens, R. Darling (*Vice-captain*), A. Bradley (*Captain*), C. Clare (*Vice-captain*), J. Lash, S. McCahon, C. Crowley.

Photo by Farrelly Photos

BLUES

BACK ROW: J. Pierce, S. Scrafton, J. Goodhue, L. Dunshea, J. Tupou, B. Nee-Nee, G. Cowley-Tuioti, M. Martin, B. Afeaki (*Scrum Coach*). ***FIFTH ROW***: S. Jackson (*Asst Coach*), M. Collins, M. Duffie, G. Preston, B. Gibson, M. Taramai, O. Leger, R. Ioane, A. Hodgman, A. Draper (*Physio*). ***FOURTH ROW***: C. Clarke, K. Pryor, M. Moulds, T. Tua, D. Papalii, M. Johnson, J. Hyland, O. Black, S. Williams. ***THIRD ROW***: D. Ellis (*Asst Coach*), M. Tamoaieta, L. Apisai, P. Manu, S. Havili, J. Ruru, J. Trainor, I. Salmon, R. Wright, T. Manu, TJ. Faiane, J. Yarnton (*Asst Analyst*). ***SECOND ROW***: Dr A. Storey (*Sports Science Manager*), T. Webber (*Analyst*), J. McGarvey (*Doctor*), S. Nock, S. Mafileo, S. Peročeta, T. Hepetema, D. Kirkpatrick, B. Gatland, J. Smethurst (*Physio*), J. Price (*S&C Coach*), J. Ryan (*Asst S&C Coach*). ***FRONT ROW***: R. Fry (*Manager*), M. Nanai, A. Ioane, J. Kaino, A. Pulu (*Captain*), T. Umaga (*Head Coach*), J. Parsons, O. Tu'ungafasi, P. Tuipulotu, G. Moala, A. Rogers (*Asst Coach*). ***ABSENT***: A. Kiri Kiri.

Photo by Richard Spranger Photography

CHIEFS

BACK ROW: A. Sharples *(Nutrition Intern)*, L. Elisara *(PDM)*, L. Laulala, T. Falcon, J. Fa'auli, Te T. Tahuriorangi, J. Taumateine, T. Banfield *(Asst S&C Coach)*, A. Moore *(S&C Intern)*. ***FOURTH ROW***: M. Robert *(Analyst)*, B. Smith *(Sports Scientist)*, M. Karpik, S. Taukei'aho, S. McNicol, K. Tu'inukuafe, R. Verney, M. McKenzie, L. Polwart, B. Sullivan, A. Ross, N. Laulala, D. Baker *(Nutritionist)*, C. Bradey *(GPS)*. ***THIRD ROW***: D. Galbraith *(Sports Psychologist)*, K. Rottier *(Head Physio)*, C. Argus *(Head S&C Coach)*, S. Stevenson, L. Jacobson, B. Wardlaw, F. Hoeata, S. Wainui, S. Kautai, A. Moli, J. Thwaites, A. Nankivell, B. Mills *(Senior S&C Coach)*, T. Te Tamaki *(Physio)*. ***SECOND ROW***: N. Hall *(Manager)*, Z. Khouri *(Doctor)*, R. Hall *(Head Analyst)*, L. Boshier, J. Parete, M. Brown, A. Ta'avao-Matau, M. Allardice, S. Alaimalo, T. Ardron, S. Prattley, P. Sowakula, D. Fisher *(Chair)*, M.Collins *(CEO)*, T. Cawood *(Chair)*. ***FRONT ROW***: C. Cooper *(Head Coach)*, T. Matson *(Asst Coach)*, T. Pulu, T. Seu, N. Harris, A. Lienert-Brown, L. Messam, C. Ngatai *(Co-captain)*, S. Cane *(Co-captain)*, B. Retallick, D. McKenzie, B. Weber, T. Nanai-Williams, D. Bird, N. Barnes *(Asst Coach)*, A. Strawbridge *(Asst Coach)*.

Photo by Mark Tantrum Photography

HURRICANES

BACK ROW: W. Goosen, M. Renata, N. Vella, V. Aso, A. Fidow, J. O'Reilly, J. Garden-Bachop, N. Laumape, I. West, J. Booth, B. Colclough *(Analyst Intern)*. ***THIRD ROW***: F. Christie, N. Milner-Skudder, F. Armstrong, V. Fifita, G. Evans, J. Blackwell, R. Prinsep, M. Douglas, T. Smith, B. Lam, P. Minehan *(Baggageman/Masseur)*. ***SECOND ROW***: D. Gray *(Head S&C Coach)*, J. Dickie *(S&C Coach)*, D. Wildash *(Asst S&C Coach)*, D. Larsen *(R&D Manager)*, S. Henwood, I. Walker-Leawere, B. Thomson, M. Fatialofa, S. Lousi, J. Bar;ett, R. Riccitelli, J. Lowe, C. Shaw *(Head Physio)* L. Santos *(Asst Physio)* R. Runciman *(Analyst)* S. Tafua *(Analyst)* J. Ross *(Head Analyst)* N. Hogg *(Mental Skills)*. ***FRONT ROW***: A. Perrot-David *(PDM)* T. Ward *(Manager)* D. Cron *(Scrum Coach)* M. Proctor, J. Savea, B. Barrett, D. Coles, B. Shields *(Captain)* C. Boyd *(Head Coach)* T.J. Perenara, B. May, J. Toomaga-Allen, C. Eves, A. Savea, R. Watt *(Coach)*, J. Holland *(Coach)*. ***ABSENT***: T. Dorfing *(Doctor)* J. Plumtree *(Asst Coach)*.

CRUSADERS

Winners of the 2018 Investec Super Rugby Championship

BACK ROW: M. Ala'alatoa, S. Tamanivalu, H. Bedwell-Curtis, E. Blackadder, M. Dunshea, S. Barrett, Q. Strange, O. Jager, W. Douglas, J. Moody, P. Samu, T. Sanders. **FOURTH ROW**: P. Bowden (*Analyst*), S. Thomas (*Head S&C Coach*), B. Ennor, G. Bridge, T. Fainga'anuku, J. Goodhue, W. Jordan, D. Havili, T. Perry, J. Taufua, J. Stratton, N. Tucker (*Physio*), A. Goodman (*Support Coach*). **THIRD ROW**: J. Roche (*Head Physio*), J. Gardner (*Head Analyst*), S. Anderson-Heather, A. Makalio, H. Allan, M. Mataele, B. Hall, B. Harmon, C. Taylor, D. Brighouse, G. Duder (*S&C*), M. Swan (*Doctor*). **SECOND ROW**: B. Mooar (*Coach*), R. O'Gara (*Coach*), J. Ryan (*Coach*), M. Hunt, M. Delany, R. Mo'unga, J. Macilai, S. Siataga, M. Drummond, E. Enari, B. Cameron, J. Miles (*Logistics*), S. Fletcher (*Manager*). **FRONT ROW**: I. Dagg, L. Romano, O. Franks, K. Read, R. Crotty (*Vice-captain*), S. Whitelock (*Captain*), M. Todd (*Vice-captain*), W. Crockett, C. King, B. Funnell, T. Bateman.

Photo by Ken Baker Photography

Photo by McRobie Studios, Dunedin

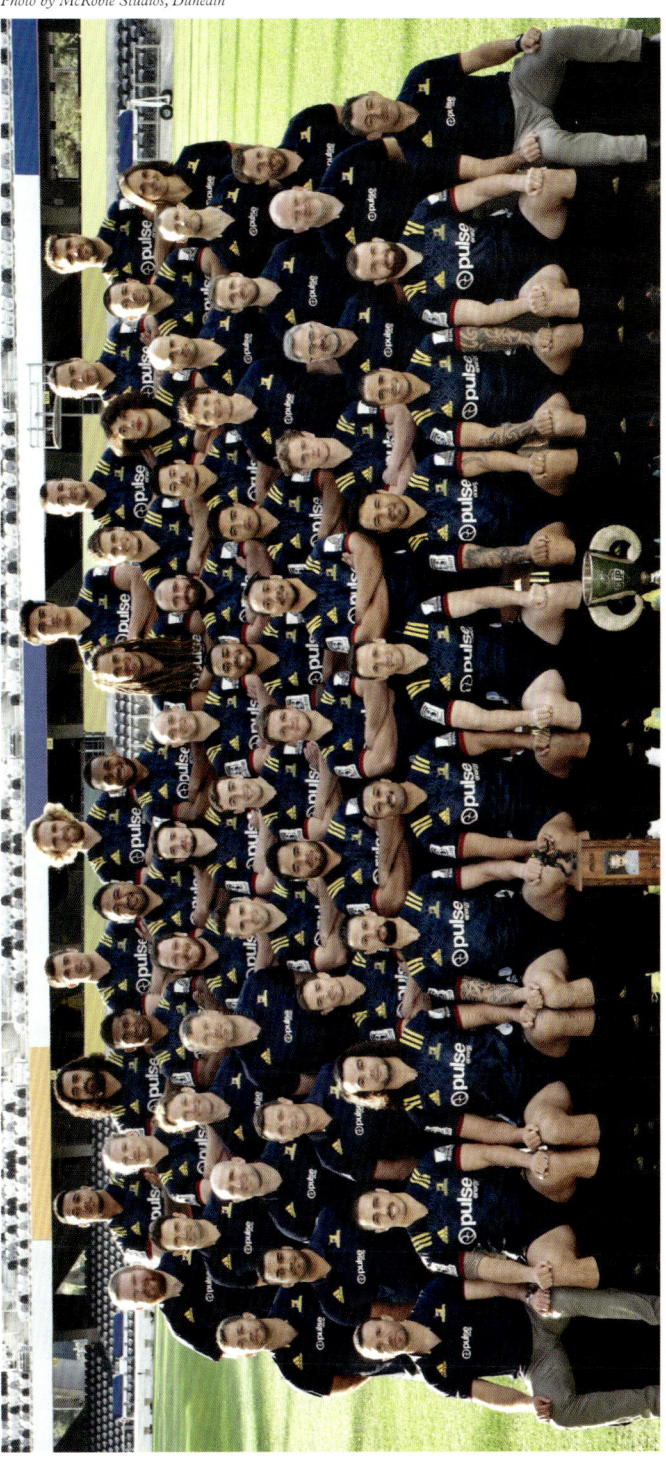

HIGHLANDERS

BACK ROW: S. Frizell, J. Hemopo, L. Squire, J. Dickson, P.P. Parkinson, A. Ainley, T. Lomax, L. Whitelock. **FIFTH ROW**: H. Hyndman (*Baggage Master*), J. Lentjes, W. Naholo, K. Tuiloma, T. Nabura, D Fryor, D. Hunt, T. Umaga-Jensen, R. Thompson, F. Simpson (*Dietician*) **FOURTH ROW**: A. Letts (*Physio*), M. Ranby (*PDM*), G. Millar, R. Buckman, M. Faddes, G. Pleasants-Tate, P. Tomkinson, I. Blake (*Asst S&C Coach*), J. Montgomery (*Asst Physio*). **THIRD ROW**: C. Brown (*Skills Coach*), C. Dermody (*Scrum Coach*), G. Delaney (*Asst Coach*), F. Smith, J. McKay, T. Li, J. Ioane, A. Beardmore (*S&C Coach*), A. Watts (*Analyst*), H. Chapman (*Asst Analyst*). **SECOND ROW**: A. Singh (*Doctor*), R. Clark (*CEO*), K. Hammington, S. Tokolahi, T. Walden, A. Seiuli, J. Renton, G. O'Brien (*General Manager, Rugby*), P. McLaughlan (*Team Manager*). **FRONT ROW**: A. Mauger (*Head Coach*), D. Lienert-Brown, T. Franklin, E. Dixon, L. Sopoaga, B. Smith (*Co-captain*), A. Dixon (*Co-captain*), A. Smith, L. Coltman, M. Hammett (*Asst Coach*). **ABSENT**: M. Mikaele-Tu'u.

NORTHLAND

BACK ROW: K. Kinoshita (*Asst Analyst*), M. Carpinter (*Analyst*), M. Sykes, J. Kitto, A. Stokes, I. Tu'ungafasi, M. Thoroughgood, W. Faiane, C. Lewis (*PDM*), F. Deformes (*Asst Scrum Coach*), B. Parkes (*Asst S&C Coach*). **SECOND ROW:** H. Slobbe (*Head S&C Coach*), J. Smethurst (*Physio*), A. Balasingham (*Chairman*), A. McGinn (*CEO*), P. Atkins, L. Albornoz, S. McNamara, T. Blundell, N. Cooper, J. Debreczeni, T. Mayanavanua, J. Straker, K. Jacobson, R. Roberts-Te Nana, S. Gregory, G. Konia (*Asst Coach*), D. Witcombe (*Head Coach*), B. Te Haara (*Manager*), G. Subritzky (*Asst Manager*). **FRONT ROW:** T. Tua, R. Rinakama, J. Matiu, J. Goodhue, K. Pryor, M. Wright, J. Olsen, M. Moulds (*Captain*), R. Ranger, M. Douglas, J. Hyland, M. Matich, J. Macilai, B. Hohaia, T. Robinson. **ABSENT:** R. Wright, S Nock, J. Goodhue, R. Verney, B. Wiggins, L. Clark, C. Matthews, T. Manu.

NORTH HARBOUR

BACK ROW: D. Hunt, D. Hilton-Jones, S. Stevenson, B. Nee-Nee, J. Pierce, D. Drake, J. Fiebig, S. Teu, H. Moala-Liava'a, R. Hilton-Jones (*Director of Rugby*). **THIRD ROW:** S. Nixon (*Chairman*), P. White (*Manager*), N. Smith, H. Groundwater, J. Dargaville, C. Winstanley (*Doctor*), M. Telea, T. Tu'ungafasi, C. Eves, J. McKittrick (*President*), D. Gibson (*General Manager*). **SECOND ROW:** D. Halangahu (*Asst Coach*), D. Allnutt (*Gear Manager*), A. King (*S&C Coach*), S. Dunbar, L. Manu, L. Li, L. Tolai, J. Bergin, L. Gjaltema, A. Beeton (*Analyst*), M. Wenham (*Physio*), N. McNamara (*Asst Coach*). **FRONT ROW:** T. Coventry (*Coach*), M. Taramai, G. Preston, S. Mafileo, T. Li, J. Parsons (*Co-captain*), B. Hall, G. Cowley-Tuioti, B. Gatland, N. Mayhew, C. Kelly (*Asst manager*). **ABSENT:** M. Duffie (*Co-captain*), M. Tamoaieta, K. Tu'inukuafe, I. Stewart (*Doctor*), B. Afeaki (*Scrum Coach*).

NORTH HARBOUR HIBISCUS

BACK ROW: K. Williams, S. Lomu, P. Tapsell, S. Fisher, O. Ward-Duin, JJ. Taylor, F. Makasini. **THIRD ROW:** E. Harbour (*Trainer*), J. Newman, T-N. Tuterangiwhiu, C. Tofa, C. McMeekin, K. Christiansen, T. Nanjan, A. Robertshaw, B. Mitchinson (*Manager*). **SECOND ROW:** B. Lamont (*Asst Manager*), D. McGrory (*Asst coach*), M. Whitehead, K. Hilton, N-D. Ngarongo-Porima, K. Macdonald, M. Collins (*Head Coach*), J. Bartlett (*Physio*). **FRONT ROW:** S. McIlroy, B-J. Jones, H. Muir, S. Tupe (*Vice-captain*), R. Wood (*Captain*), J. Vizirgianakis, I. Timani, C. Cox, R-L. Wharawhara. **ABSENT:** W. Walker (*Asst Coach*), G. Vegar, C. Wikaira, L. Crossman, F. Fatanitavake, J. Palmer, B. Ellison, H. Tarau-Peehikuru.

AUCKLAND STORM

BACK ROW: A-P. Nelson, E. Blackwell, K. Demant. **THIRD ROW:** O. Tafoulua, M. Vaiouga, R. Demant, A. Itunu. **SECOND ROW:** W. Sotutu (*Asst Coach*), M. Suzuki, M. Fujimoto, L. Sikoloni, K. Cribb (*Trainer*). **FRONT ROW:** A. Warbrooke, J. Fa'amausili (*Coach*), C. McMenamin (*Captain*), A. Po'oi, A. Wright (*Manager*), J-R. Reu. **ABSENT:** J. Aiono, F. Fa'amausili, J. Fanene, M. Fineaso-Levi, L. Fuikefu, S. Gautusa, M. Hufanga, L. Itunu, H. Leiataua, L. Mafi, V. Moimoi, N. Moors, C. Nanai, M. Nena, G. Milne (*Physio*), L. Sa'u, C. Smith, H. Watene.

AUCKLAND
Winners of the Mitre 10 Cup Premiership

BACK ROW: L. Dunshea, S. Rayasi, T. Seu, J. Lane, W. Riedlinger-Kapa, E. Olmstead, M. Fatialofa. **FOURTH ROW:** J. Moore (*PDM*), C. Clarke, T. Tele'a, H. Plummer, J. Ravouvou, F. Lemalu, H. Sotutu, A. Choat, C. Stuart (*Doctor*). **THIRD ROW:** H. McCrae (*Massage Therapist*), W. Hiramatsu (*S&C Intern*), J. Bear (*CEO*), M. Sosene-Feagai, J. Ruru, R. Abel, J. Trainor, E. Lindenmuth, M. Fepulea'i, J. Yarnton (*Analyst*), K. Ogura (*Analyst Intern*). **SECOND ROW:** K. Cribb (*S&C Intern*), S. Mather (*Chairman*), Sir G. Henry (*Asst Coach*), L. Schwencke, J. Umaga, T. Manu, J. Adams, D. Kirkpatrick, D. Liaina, M. Plummer (*Physio*), P. Downes (*S&C Coach*), N. Burton (*S&C Intern*), J. Giles (*Asst S&C*). **FRONT ROW:** M. Casey (*Asst Coach*), L. Fukofuka, T. Lavea (*Asst Coach*), M. Nanai, A. Ioane, TJ. Faiane (*Co-captain*), A. Ieremia (*Head Coach*), B. Gibson (*Co-Captain*), S. Prattley, M. Renata, F. Tiatia (*Asst Coach*), J. Whetton, M. Taylor (*Manager*). **ABSENT:** T. Koroi, D. Papalii, P. Tuipulotu (*Co-captain*), B. Ward (*Asst Manager*).

COUNTIES POWER HEAT

BACK ROW: W. Flesher, S. To'a, J. Absher, S. Brown, G. Gago. **SECOND ROW:** C. Aitken (*Analyst*), H. Pomare, G. Lidgard, A. Mamea, L. Kanatea-Ofa (*Manager*), J. Clark (*Coach*). **FRONT ROW:** O. Tierney, F. Piliu, L. Lima, A. Marino-Tauhinu (*Captain*), L. Steed, E. Kitson, J. Auva'a. **ABSENT:** A. Watene, K. Wira-Kohu, K. Veainu, L. Veainu, S. Thompson, H. Te Iringa, A. Te Iringa, L. Tauhalaliku, V. Subritzky-Nafatali, A. Savage, L. Perese, Te K. Ngata-Aerengamate, V. Meki, A. Matau, Z. Leaupepe, T. Leaf, J. Lavea, M. Eli. A. Brider, N. Bhana, G. Aiono, J. Maka (*Asst Coach*), S. Penney (*Technical Advisor*), J. Levi (*Asst Coach*), P. Shaw (*Trainer*), H. Lemon (*Physio*).

COUNTIES MANUKAU STEELERS

BACK ROW: S. Fifita, Te A. Toma, S. Nginingini, J. Taumateine, L. Laulala, E. Nanai-Seturo, L. Daniela, M. Royal, F. Lokotui, K. Hala. **THIRD ROW:** J. Souchon (*Head analyst*), T. Ralph (*Physio*), H. Sililoto, L. Fosita, S. Molia, K. Tuiloma, S. Asomua, S. Furniss, O. Leger, J. Royal, R. Huet (*Senior Analyst*), P. Shaw (*Asst Trainer*), B. Tarapa (*Masseur*). **SECOND ROW:** S. Kim (*Doctor*), J. Knox (*Sports Sciences Manager*), M. Leilua (*Manager*), C. Te Whata-Colley, N. Ah Wong, T. Nabura, D. Leasuasu, M. Vaai, V. Taulani, S. Ropati, N. Laulala, C.Carter (*Chairman*), K. Maihi (*President*), B. Hoggard (*CEO*). **FRONT ROW:** G. Henson (*Asst Coach*), G. Su'a, J. Firth, V. Rarasea, S. Nabou, M. Martin (*Captain*), D. Suasua (*Coach*), S. Henwood (*Captain*), T. Pulu, S. Bagshaw, D. Hyatt, C. Vaega, S. Sititi (*Asst Coach*). **ABSENT:** K. Read, S. Williams, C. Fa'alili, M. McKee.

THAMES VALLEY
Winners of the Meads Cup

BACK ROW: J. van Doorn (*Physio*), T. Erceg, K. Lewis, M. Rolston, H. Lafituanai, A. Bradley, D. Harrison (*Asst Coach*). **THIRD ROW:** J. Murray (*Asst Coach*), M. Fisher, S. De La Fuente, C. Dromgool, C. McVerry, E. Seymour, S. Ouchi, B. Vincent. **SECOND ROW:** C. Wisnewski (*Chef*), L. McIver (*Manager*), A. Rackham (*Physio*), L. Easton, Te H. Kutia, N. Emery, M. Bartleet (*Head Coach*), M. Holmes (*Trainer*), C. Bishop (*Asst Manager*). **FRONT ROW:** G. Hallett (*Chairman*), K. Lee, R. Boughton, S. Topou, B. Ranga (*Co-captain*), S. Hill (*Co-captain*), M. Abraham, S. McCahon, B. Bonnar, K. Plummer (*President*). **IN FRONT:** S. Tupou (*Ball Boy*). **ABSENT:** L. Matai-Povey, J. Dodunski, G. McIntyre, M. Hill, M. Hart, E. Leahy (*CEO*), C. Kelleher, C. Berridge.

WAIKATO
Winners of the Mitre 10 Cup Championship

BACK ROW: K. Abbott (*Nutritionist*), L. Vasu (*Asst Trainer*), J. Iosefa-Scott, T. Bond, S. Caird, L. McWhannell, J. Manihera, S. Lopeti-Moli, J. Christy (*Analyst*) T. Te Tamaki (*Head Physio*). **FOURTH ROW:** Z. Khouri (*Doctor*), A. Johnstone, J. Stratton, M. Dawai, A. Moli, J. Brown, S. Kautai, B. Sullivan, E. Pene (*Asst Physio*), R. Stephenson (*PDM*). **THIRD ROW:** M. Crawfod (*Manager*), J. Bunce, M. Lansdown, J. Armstrong, Q. Tupaea, M. Iti, M. Mayhew, S. Taukei'aho, B. Foote (*CEO*). **SECOND ROW:** T. Hurst (*Head Trainer*), S. Reece, P. Patafilo, F. Smith, T. Campbell, H. Hetet, S. Fale, K. O'Donnell, N. Longopoa, N. White (*Asst Coach*). **FRONT ROW:** R. Randle (*Asst Coach*), D. O'Donnell, M. Jacobson, T. Smith, D. Sweeney (*Co-captain*), L. Jacobson (*Co-captain*), A. Burn, J. Tucker, J. Gibbes (*Head Coach*). **ABSENT:** A. Lienert-Brown, D. McKenzie, R. Takarangi, P. Kennedy (*Doctor*).

WAIKATO FPC

BACK ROW: A. Gaby-Sutherland, T. Natua, D. Fermanis, R. Parone, G. Houpapa-Barrett, E-L Heta. **THIRD ROW:** A. Josephs (*Trainer*), K. Simon, V. Edmonds, N. Hamilton, M. Riki-Te Kanawa, T. Reid, L. Mitchell, A. Tangen-Wainohu, M-S Rabukatoka (*Trainer*). **SECOND ROW:** R. Smiler (*Manager*), A. Marsters, L. Kloppers, T. Kalounivale, K. Faneva, E. Faiaoga, D. Treadaway, N. Kewish (*Manager*). **FRONT ROW:** J. Semple (*Coach*), K. Paul, A. Bayler, R. Hayes, S. Talawadua (*Co-captain*), C. Alley (*Co-captain*), C. Wihone, A. Yama, W. Maxwell (*Coach*). **ABSENT:** K. Turvey (*Physio*), L. Ngalu-Lavemai, N. Delamere, D. Paenga, A. Whitiora.

BAY OF PLENTY STEAMERS

BACK ROW: T. Stebbing (*Asst S&C Trainer*), R. Macdonald, T. Joass, A. Mua, E. Narawa, T. Mafileo, S. Siataga, V. Meachen, A. McDonald, C. McNeil (*Asst S&C Trainer*). **THIRD ROW:** P. Barnett (*President*), P. Cameron (*Physio*), M. Roberts (*Analyst*), J. Lay, K. Trask, L. Steel, T. Crozier, C. McMillan (*Head Coach*), C. Forbes, J. Davey, F. Fuatai, L. Lalomilo, B. Mayo (*Head S&C Trainer*), B. Drabble (*Statistician*). **SECOND ROW:** H. Ngawhika (*Operations Manager*), I. Te Aute, T. McHugh, B. Simonsson, Z. Kapeli, N. Ross, B. Wardlaw, K. Le'aupepe, H. Matenga, A. Carroll, M. Garland, R. Geldenhuys, J. Robertson, W. Brill (*Campaign Manager*). **FRONT ROW:** R. Gibbs (*Asst Coach*), L. Campbell, R. Judd, M. Karpik, M. Delany (*Vice-captain*), L. Polwart (*Vice-captain*), T. Ardron (*Captain*), T. Latimer, J. Thwaites, H. Blake, T. Hepetema, C. Tiatia, D. Hill (*Asst Coach*). **INSETS:** S. Cane, N. Harris, A. Ross, D. Karauna, S. Sakalia, L. Foketi, J. Key.

BAY OF PLENTY VOLCANIX

BACK ROW: F. Gutschlag (*Physio*), S. Tapsell, L. Florence, O. Williams, O. Richardson, A. Mulu, R. Luka, P. Playle, L. Hardy (*Masseuse*), A. Thompson (*Manager*). **SECOND ROW:** R. Innis (*Analyst*), Z. Winslade (*Asst Coach*), E. Magee, B. Jacob, C. Perrott, A. Aldridge, M. Wardlaw, K. Henwood, T. Lemon, R. Holmes, M. Lewis (*Asst coach*), C. Wilson (*Physio*). **FRONT ROW:** S. King (*S & C Trainer*), A. Mohi, R. Wickliffe, L. Elder, K. Reynolds, C. Yule (*Captain*), T-R. Raharuhi, K. Hudson, Z. Wilson, B. Webby (*Head Coach*), T. Wilson (*S & C Trainer*). **ABSENT:** J. Tuilaepa, B. Meyer, J. Benioni, B. Walker, K. Heyblom, T. Fitzgerald, M. McLean-Kora, C. Corbett, Te R. Mohi, H. Tapiata.

NGATI POROU EAST COAST

BACK ROW: W. Riki, D. Manuel, M. Siliko, N. Haerewa. **THIRD ROW:** J. Rye, B.J. Sidney, T. Barbarich, H. Te Moana, D. Knubley, T. Proffit, J. Richardson. **SECOND ROW:** L. Goldsmith (*Manager*), W. Ensor (*Coach*), S. Lasenby, E. Lotawa, A. Ross, R. Kernohan, W. Haerewa (*Trainer*), T. Para (*Asst Coach*), C. Tangaere-Manuel (*CEO*). **FRONT ROW:** F. Kahaki, S. Parkes, V. Bartlett, H. Haerewa, P. Manuel, P. Bishop, J. Milner. **ABSENT:** Te T. Maxwell, H. Tichborne, T.K. Moeke, B. Haerewa, T. Potae, R. Namana.

POVERTY BAY

BACK ROW: O. Sanerivi, A. Karauria, F. White, J. Kapene, W. Grogan, K. Love. **THIRD ROW:** C. McDonald, M. Tu'ipulotu, S. Akana, S. McDell, J. Cook, A. Petelo, T. Iosefo. **SECOND ROW:** G. MacDonald (*Physio*), S. Smith (*Manager*), M. Otai (*Head Coach*), J. Willoughby (*CEO*), G. Brown (*Chairman*), D. Russell (*Assst Coach*), M. Nikora (*S&C Coach*). **FRONT ROW:** C. Chrisp, C. Rowden, M. Counsell, K. Houkamau, T. Hill (*Captain*), J. Fleming, K. Smith, T. Noanoa, M. Raleigh. **ABSENT:** S. Skudder, M. Torrance, W. Tamatea, M. Brown, T. Stewart, Te P. Fairlie, A. Tau'atevalu, W. McGoon, E. Reeves, S. Wong (*Doctor*), P. McHugh (*Doctor*).

KING COUNTRY RAMS

BACK ROW: P. Astle-Harris, T. Tuhakaraina, C. Mabbett-Sowerby, D. Clapcott, P. Green, K. Foote, M. Horrocks, A. Thrupp. *THIRD ROW:* C. Hancock (*Physio*), J. Curuki, P. Smith, M. Veitayaki, C. Henare, S. Cullen, R. Vosaki, C. Hubbard (*Asst Coach*), N. Clarke (*Manager*). *SECOND ROW:* G. Meads (*Tech Advisor*), C. Bell (*Trainer*), L. Rowlands, B. Brown, S.Trangmar, D. Barnett, E. Reihana, T. Hounsell, S. Luoni (*Tech Advisor*), C. Jeffries (*Head Coach*). *FRONT ROW:* O. Kay, Z. Tipping, J. Perawiti (*Vice-captain*), C. Carmichael (*Captain*), R. Sherson, D. Church, S. Wanden. *ABSENT:* S. Vosaki, S. McCarthy.

TARANAKI BULLS

BACK ROW: N. Coombes (*Asst Physio*), S. Mellow, S. Perofeta, M. Mataele, L. Vaeno, K. Stewart, C. Matoe, D. Maka, T. Stuck (*Skills Coach*). *FOURTH ROW:* P. Riley (*Doctor*), D. Neilson (*Analyst*), S. Ritchie (*Asst S&C Coach*), K. Naholo, A. Wyrill, J. Proffit, C. Gawler, B. Northcott-Hill, L. Crowley (*Asst Coach*), R. Houghton (*President*), J. Parkinson (*CEO*), D. Spicer (*Manager*). *THIRD ROW:* J. Hooper (*Scrum Coach*), T. Florence, P-G Sowakula, J. Parete, T. Va'ai, K. Thompson, L. Price, F. Hoeata, L. Thomson (*Chairman*). *SECOND ROW:* A. Larkin (*Physio*), L. Holland (*PDM*), L. Crowley, B. Waaka, B. Leonard, R. Ware, D. Waite, W. Lahmert, X. Roe, R. Riccitelli, M. Radich (*Nutritionist*), A. Hay (*S&C Coach*). *FRONT ROW:* P. Tito (*Asst Coach*), L. Boshier, R. O'Neill, T. Walden (*Co-captain*), A. Ta'avao (*Captain*), M. Crosswell (*Co-captain*), J. Hoeata, S. Tamanivalu, T. Halafihi, W. Rickards (*Head Coach*). *ABSENT:* P. Marsh (*Asst Analyst*), R. Vaughan (*Sport Psychologist*), B. Barrett, J. Barrett, S. Barrett, W. Naholo, Te T. Tahuriorangi, S. Wainui, M. Brown, M. Graham, M. McKenzie, A. Lewis, A. Sorovaki, J. Firth, J. Potroz, B. Slater, J. Jordan, S. Waite, K. Boshier, L. Blyde.

TARANAKI WHIO
BACK ROW: N. Jones, B. Munro-Smith, M. Dallinger, N. Haupapa. ***THIRD ROW:*** N. Milby (*Physio*), T. Moeahu, F. Edmonds, L. Appert, U. Atonio, A. Fakavamoeanga, L. Barnard, M. Stone (*Coach*). ***SECOND ROW:*** B. Peterson (*Trainer*), S. Brown, E. Johns, C. Poletti, V. McCullough, B. Poingdestre, J. Aitken-Fowler, D. Davies (*Manager*), B. Siffleet (*Coach*). ***FRONT ROW:*** K. Batchelor, A. Blackburn-Kingi, B. Sim, J. Smith (*Captain*), N. Pera, C. Austin. ***ABSENT:*** M. Allen, K. Henry, H. Dando, K. Parkinson, K. Walsh-Tito. ***INSET:*** P. Matheson (*Manager/Player*).

WANGANUI
BACK ROW: G. Hakaraia, K. Latu, S. Scott, E. Robinson, P. Nabainivalu, T. Gilbert, S. Dibben, H. Symes, T. Rogers-Holden, A. Middleton, K. Dabenaise. ***SECOND ROW:*** C. Back (*Manager*), H. Fitzgerald (*Physio*), T. Symes, D. Whale, B. Hudson, P-T. Hay-Horton, C. Jackson, H. Williams, S. Madams, J. Hodges, M. Tafili, K. Kuruyabaki, D. Robinson (*Asst Manager*). ***FRONT ROW:*** K. Stembridge (*Physio*), C. Crowley, J. Fifita, V. Tofa, J. Hughes, J. Caskey (*Head Coach*), C. Hart (*Vice-captain*), R. Tutauha (*Captain*), P. Rowe (*Technical Advisor*), J. Yarrall, L. Horrocks, W. Cottrell, M. McGrath (*Selector*). ***INSETS:*** C. Clare, D. Gallien.

HAWKE'S BAY MAGPIES

BACK ROW: T. Gittings (*Manager*), I. Taylor (*Doctor*), J. Tavita-Metcalfe, H. Brighouse, J. Kaifa, D. Flanders, S. Ulufonua. J. Apikotoa, T. Farrell, S. Funaki, J.J. Taulagi, P. O'Shaughnessy (*Analyst*), B. Jenkinson (*Asst Manager*). **SECOND ROW:** K. Bibby (*S&C Intern*), M. Nicol (*Physio*), J. Syms (*Asst Coach*), L. McClutchie, S. Ili, B. Power, W. Tremain, S. Tofilau, M. Buckley, D. Toala, K. Kereru-Symes, F. Fakatava, M. Ozich (*Coach*), L. Stephenson (*S&C Coach*), F. Dionese (*Asst S&C Coach*). **FRONT ROW:** M. Emerson, P. Dunn, J. Lowe, M. Mikaele-Tu'u, G. Cridge, T. Parsons, B. Weber (*Vice-captain*), G. Evans (*Vice-captain*), M. Allardice, B. May, J. Long, M. Braidwood, T. Falcon, P. Rakete-Stones. **ABSENT:** A. Dixon (*Captain*), B. Retallick, F. Selesele, S. Tucker, J. Devery.

MANAWATU CYCLONES

BACK ROW: A. Knight, A. Kuruyabaki, J. Fagan-Pease, S. Hemingway, A. Rivers, L. Sae. **THIRD ROW:** J. Nuku, M. Live, R. Rakatau, S. Wilkins, N. Chase, K. Takitimu-Cook, M. Leota. **SECOND ROW:** R-L Rawleigh, K. Belcher (*Physio*), M. Canterbury (*Asst Manager*), S. Lewis (*Asst Coach*), F. Feaunati (*Head Coach*), A. Ballie (*Analyst*), K. Murphy (*Trainer*), M. Gaffney. **FRONT ROW:** K. Tipene, C. Dallinger, S. Porima, N. Dickins (*Co-captain*), S. Winiata (*Co-captain*), K. Sue, R. Finau, S. Olsen, L. Brown. **ABSENT:** L. Balsillie, V. Greig, M. Polson, S. McKenzie, S. Tipene, C. Windle, W. Stent (*Manager*).

MANAWATU TURBOS

BACK ROW: B. Werthmuller, S. Slade, L. Mitchell, L. Hallam-Eames, T. Hughes, B. Tucker, S. Wasley, B. Iose, J. Hemopo, N. Milner-Skudder. ***THIRD ROW:*** I. Tuputala (*Analyst*), Te R. Waitokia, M. Tagicakibau, S. Asi, J. Iose, S. Stewart, F. Sione, B. Henderson, R. Thompson, S. Pinfold (*Trainer*). ***SECOND ROW:*** K. Hughes (*Physio*), V. Wilson (*Manager*), J. Laloifi, N. Laumape, G. Syminton, S. Paranihi, L. Mafi, J. Tofa, A. Good (*Asst Coach*), J. Cotter (*Coach*). ***FRONT ROW:*** K. Hammington, J. Te Rure, T. Cadwallader, F. Armstrong, N. Crosswell, A. Kiri Kiri (*Captain*), M. Ala'alatoa, H. Northcott, O. Black, J. Booth, S. Malcolm. ***ABSENT:*** A. Wyrill, S. Lombard (*Doctor*).

WAIRARAPA BUSH

BACK ROW: N. Hohepa, M. Ale, T. Isaac, T. Potoru, J. Pakoti. ***FOURTH ROW:*** E. Rayaqayaqa, T. Flutey, P. Gluck, F. Yeats, R. Knell, M. Henderson, M. Lealeva'a. ***THIRD ROW:*** D. Tafatu (*Trainer*), D. Castorina (*Physio*), D. Pickering, S. Gammie, A. Smith, S. Law, D. van Deventer (*Asst Coach*), W. Reiri (*Strapper*). ***SECOND ROW:*** T. Nathan (*Chairman*), S. O'Gorman (*Manager*), J. Harwood (*Head Coach*), S. Malatai, M. Tufuga, J. Mapusua, B. Weatherstone (*President*), B. Hansen (*Masseuse*), O. Browne (*Asst Physio*). ***SEATED:*** I. Katia, C. Hayton. T. Haira, L. McFadzean, J. Goodger (*Captain*), K. Tufuga (*Vice-captain*), N. Olson, G. Walters, R. Anderson. ***ABSENT:*** C. Baker, L. Buchanan, S. Shaw, P. Weepu (*Asst Coach*).

HOROWHENUA KAPITI
Winners of the Lochore Cup

BACK ROW: T. Barnsley (*Physio*), T. Brown, T. Paringatai, S. MacGregor, K. Kelemete, J. So'oialo, E. Seiuli, K. Tamou, J. White (*Analyst*). **SECOND ROW:** M. Rutene (*Asst Coach*), C. Wilton (*Coach*), H. Henare, T. Zimmerman, J. Winterburn, T. Woodmass, D. Ropata, T.J. Fermanis, E. Reti. L. Ellison, N. Picchi (*Manager*), N. Taylor (*Asst Manager*). **FRONT ROW:** J. Mowbray (*Chairman*), D. McErlean, S. Cameron, A. Lahmert, A. Fox, R. Shelford (*Captain*), R. Praat, T. Maki, W. Paia'aua, C. Kennett (*CEO*). **ABSENT:** T. Seruwalu, C. Makamaka, C. Warren, D. Taylor, A. Ackerman, M. Wineera, T. Luke, D. Jackson (*Strapper*).

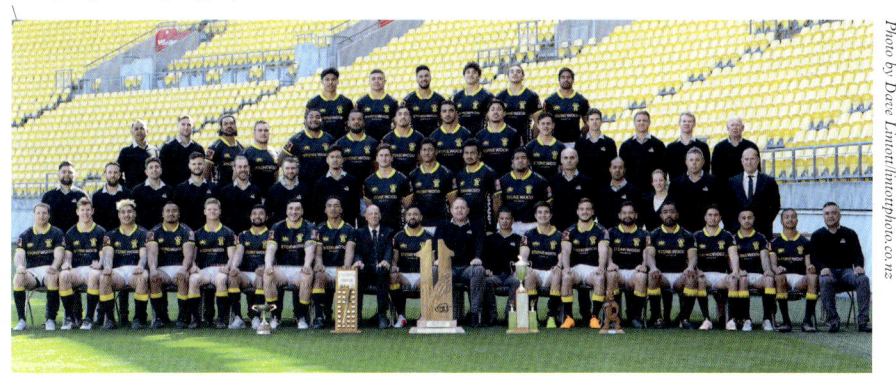

WELLINGTON LIONS

BACK ROW: X. Numia, D. Kirifi, P. Turia, T. Umaga-Jensen, P. Umaga-Jensen, T. Renata. **THIRD ROW:** A. Narayan (*Doctor*), C. Jane (*Asst Coach*), L. Filipo, J. Hintz, T. Tuimauga, M. Kafatolu, B. Proctor, T. Ben-Nicholas, B. Lam, C. Price, B. Treanor (*Physio*), B. Sigmund (*PDM*), M. Ganley (*Physio*), A. Muir (*Scrum Coach*). **SECOND ROW:** K. Shigeeda (*S&C Intern*), J. Dickie (*Head S&C*), J. Marshall (*S&C*), M Higgins (*S&C*), V. Serangeli (*Head Analyst*), J. Ross (*Analyst*), S. Taufua (*Analyst*), W. Mangos, S. Lousi, I. Walker-Leawere, K. Uluilakepa, G. Stanbridge (*Kit Manager*), L. Santos (*Head Physio*), N. Hogg (*Mental Skills*), G. Halford (*Scrum Coach*), M. Evans (*CEO*). **FRONT ROW:** T. Waldrom, J. Blackwell, A. Fidow, A. Aumua, J. O'Reilly, G. Foe, J. Toomaga-Allen, G. Taufale, B. Gardner (*President*), M. Proctor (*Captain*), C. Gibbes (*Head Coach*), A. Bell (*Asst Coach*), J. Garden-Bachop, W. Goosen, L. Apisai, T. Fahamokioa, S. Rangihuna, K. Hauiti-Parapara, M. Tuitama, M. Poutoa (*Manager*). **ABSENT:** A. Barendregt, D. Coles, V. Fifita, T.J. Perenara, A. Savea, T.J. Va'a.

WELLINGTON PRIDE
Winners of the Farah Palmer Cup Championship

BACK ROW: A. Jones (*Skills Coach*), R. Uluinayau, M-L Sa'u, I. Laupolo, J. Ngan-Woo, J. Taumoli, A. Rasch, D. Faleafaga, M. Parkes, T. Bentley, M. Poutoa (*Asst Coach*), M. Symes (*S&C Trainer*). **SECOND ROW:** B. Joyes (*Physio*), B. Mockett (*Analyst*), K. Mei, G. Williamson, R. Stirling, A. Uila, B. Tauaneai, E. Taito, A. Print, M. Tagoai, P. Matthews (*Physio*), M. Conley (*Manager*). **FRONT ROW:** R. Bond (*Head Coach*), A. Te Iwimate, S. Whareaorere, F. Makisi, B. Robertson, J. Patea-Fereti (*Captain*), A. Leti-Iiga, T. Tumaii, N. Foaese, S. Mose-Samou, B. Reidy (*Asst Coach*). **ABSENT:** A-M. Afuie, C. Clarke, M. Heslop, S. Levave, S. Toala-Ryder, T. Paulo.

TASMAN MAKO

BACK ROW: R. Niuia, T. Fainga'anuku, W. Jordan, J. Grooby, B. Prinsep, I. Salmon, T. Aoake, R. Parkinson, J. Spowart, W. Havili, F. Christie, J. Brown, T. O'Malley, L. Fainga'anuku, J. Taufua. **SECOND ROW:** A. Goodman (*Asst Coach*), M. Vercoe (*Manager*), K. Harrington (*Physio*), L. Aumua, T. Lomax, Te A. Cirikidaveta, I. Miller, Q. Strange, P.P. Parkinson, J. Akau'ola-Laula, S. Frizell, S. Alaimalo, T. Fox-Matamua, J. Norris, R. Coxon, R. Marsden (*Physio*), J. Holden (*S&C Coach*), B. Thornalley (*Asst Manager*), N. Price (*Analyst*). **FRONT ROW:** L. MacDonald (*Head Coach*), V. Fredericks, B. Guyton, T. Perry, A. Ainley, M. Hunt (*Vice-captain*), D. Havili (*Captain*), W. Crockett (*Vice-captain*) E. Blackadder, A. Nankivell, A. Makalio, S. Christie (*Asst Coach*) C. Dermody (*Asst Coach*).

BULLER

BACK ROW: P. Foote, B. Collins, I. Ravudra, J. Best, R. Matangi, A. Tailua, A. Ellis, K. Parata, S. Marris, M. Feso, C. Jenkins, A. Duncan (*Manager BRU*). **SECOND ROW:** S. Carey (*Physio*), R. Malneek, M. Wells, R. Bonisch, S. Godwin, C. Aperahama, J. Lepa, W. Scott, Z. Walsh, J. Hands, S. Jar (*ICIR*). **FRONT ROW:** P. Beveridge (*Asst Coach*), P. Bonisch (*Manager*), H. McMillan (*Chairman*), J. Lash, L. Brownlee, A. Stephens (*Captain*), L. Mundy, C. Scanlon (*Coach*), N. Thompson (*Asst Coach*), C. Adams (*Analyst*). **ABSENT:** S. Eggers, P. Saukuru.

WEST COAST

BACK ROW: D. Davies, S. McClure, S. Soper, P. Te Rakau, R. Stanton, J. Tomlinson, S. Holani, K. Curtis. **SECOND ROW:** L. McNeish (*Manager*), K. Koch (*Physio*), S. Cuttance (*Coach*), J. van Vliet, J. MacRae, T. Tu'ulua, D. Foord, A. Tukana, B. Tauwhare, O. Varley, M. Connors (*Asst Manager*), K. Parker (*Asst Coach*), B. Pearson (*Trainer*). **FRONT ROW:** J. Pitman-Joass, J. Ferguson, T. Reekie (*Vice-captain*), T. Tauwhare (*Captain*), M. Mudu, D. Wood, O. Dimmick. **ABSENT:** D. Delany. **INSETS:** N. Smith, J. Manning, S. Shepherd (*Physio*).

CANTERBURY

BACK ROW: H. Renton, B. Morris, W.Tucker, H. Dalzell, M. Dunshea, O. Jager, N. Punivai. **FOURTH ROW:** C. Garden-Bachop, H. Allan, T. Christie, B. Harmon, F. Waqainabete, B. Ennor, G. Bridge, S. Fa'agase, C. King, S. Tawake, P. Bowden (*Analyst*). **THIRD ROW:** G. Duder (*S&C Coach*), M. Swan (*Doctor*), G. Pleasants-Tate, J. Hawkey, B. McAlister, C. Beard, P. Burleigh, J. McKay, S. Hunter (*Asst Logistics*), N. Tucker (*Physio*). **SECOND ROW:** M. Brown (*Asst Coach*), T. Williamson (*Manager*), A. Tiplady (*Doctor*), B. Cameron, E. Enari, C. Makene, N. Souchon, C. Collins, M. Bowden (*PDM*), J. Miles (*Logistics*), R. Thorne (*Asst Coach*). **FRONT ROW:** J. Maddock (*Head Coach*), D. Lienert-Brown, N. Vella, R. Prinsep, M. Drummond (*Captain*), W. Douglas (*Captain*), L. Romano, A. Hodgman, T. Sanders, N. Mauger (*Asst Coach*). **ABSENT:** L. Whitelock, S. Whitelock, C. Taylor, R. Mo'unga, O. Franks, R. Crotty, J. Moody, S. Tokolahi.

CANTERBURY FPC
Winners of the Farah Palmer Cup Premiership

BACK ROW: K. Tavendale, O. McGoverne, N. Poletti, C. Bremner, M. Rossiter, G. Ponsonby, C. Siataga. **THIRD ROW:** S. Dobson (*Analyst*), S. Curtis, L. Cunningham, C. Greenslade, P. Love, L. McIntyre, L. Jenkins, T. Curtis, M. Vanner (*Trainer*). **SECOND ROW:** A. Busbridgel (*Analyst*), M. Williams (*Physio*), C. Thompson, F. Burkin, G. O'Rourke, B. Davidson, T. Gapper, D. Hiini, N. Wong (*Manager*), J. Jowsey (*Asst Coach*). **FRONT ROW:** K. Kite (*Head Coach*), M. Puckett, A. Bremner, L. Anderson, S. Te Ohaere-Fox, K. Cocksedge, J. Hansen, G. Brooker, M. Ruscoe (*Asst Coach*). **INSETS:** A. Sisifa, G. Steinmetz, E. Uren, A. Tiplady (*Doctor*).

MID CANTERBURY

BACK ROW: B. Matoramusha, P. Sofai, S. Mhembere, A. Lindsay, A. Einarsson, T. Heywood, A. McKenzie, N. McCloy, D. Palmer (*Asst Coach*). **MIDDLE ROW:** J. Tranter (*Analyst*), S. Carter (*Head Coach*), I. Masiwini, L. Tu Uga, S. Cottam, M. Bentley, T. Hanham-Carter, A. Letham, J. Percival, S. Koroitamana, J. Rickard (*Asst Coach*), T. Harrison (*Manager*). **FRONT ROW:** J. Ross (*President*), G. Clarke (*Trainer*), D. Fransen, M. Groom, E. Duff, J. Donlan (*Captain*), T. Blackburn, P. Fakatoka, O. Baisagale, H. Griffiths, J. Hodgins (*Physio*), G. Rushton (*Chairman*). **ABSENT:** W. Mackenzie, A. Williamson, J. Houston, L. Bonnington, T. Nabakeke, T. Blyth.

SOUTH CANTERBURY

BACK ROW: Z. Saunders, K. Leatigaga, B. Hewitson, B.J. Oliver, T. Davidson. **SECOND ROW:** G. Miller (*Trainer*), G. Thompson (*Physio*), M. Beckham, A. Gooden, T. Tuipolotu, G. Casey, K. Te Nana, J. Simpson (*Technical Advisor*). **FRONT ROW:** C. Coll (*Manager*), M. Fetu, L. Toumohunui, G. McFarlane (*Asst Coach*), N. Strachan (*Captain*), B. Matthews (*Coach*), W. Wright (*Vice-captain*), M. Medlicott, M. Roberts (*President*). **ABSENT:** K. Coll, S. Anderson, R. Syme, S. Sauqaqa, V. Poloniati, H. Scott, D. Dorgan, J. Trevathan, B. Tunnicliffe, P. Ah Sue.

OTAGO
2018 Ranfurly Shield Holders

BACK ROW: N. Dawai, D. Nel, J. Koroi, T. Rowe, J. Dickson, J. Larsen, M. Whaanga, S. Misiloi, J. Lentjes, T. Hill. **FOURTH ROW:** T. Grant (*Team Support*), J. Bishop (*Doctor*), S. McDowall, J. Aoina, G. Bower, P. Tomkinson, R. Jackson, S. Dickson, A. Wilson (*Physio*). **THIRD ROW:** A. Staples (*Analyst*), A. Hunter (*Manager*), T. Haugh, S. Pole, J. Timu. J. Ioane, M. Scott, A. Williams, K. Bloxham (*Trainer*), K. Jury (*Skills Coach*). **SECOND ROW:** R. Kinley (*General Manager*), D. Smith (*President*), J. Nareki, V. Koroi, F. Strawbridge, K. Hammer, M. Matavao, K. Cooper (*Chairman*), R. Martin (*Asst Coach*). **FRONT ROW:** T. Donnelly (*Asst Coach*), J. Renton, H. Sasagi, M. Collins, S. Anderson-Heather (*Captain*), A. Seiuli, L. Coltman, D. Brighouse, M. Faddes, B. Herring (*Head Coach*). **ABSENT:** H. Toma.

SOUTHLAND STAGS

BACK ROW: A. Mackintosh (*Physio*), B. Hopley (*General Manager*). **FOURTH ROW:** R. Smith (*Manager*), C. Stewart (*Doctor*), R. Nu'u, A. Ready, G. Dyer, J. Renton, I. Te Tamaki, N. Costa, B. Hooper, A. Curry (*Asst S&C Coach*), J. Franklin (*Chairman*). **THIRD ROW:** S. Curry (*S&C Coach*), W. McRae, T. Lamborn, R. van Vugt, J. Ormond, V. Tosi, J. MacDonald, A. Morris-Lome, C. Apoua, R. Bennett (*Analyst*). **SECOND ROW:** D. MacLeod (*Defence Coach*), M. Johnson, B. Fotheringham, E. de Groot, L. Ormond, M. Selby-Rickit, J. Capil, B. Howden, R. Northover, R. Tatafu, R. Fahey (*Asst Manager*), K. McDonald (*Physio*). **FRONT ROW:** D. Hewett (*Head Coach*), S. Stodart, J. Walsh, B. Fukofuka, T. Adams, F. Thomas (*Co-captain*), J. Wilson (*Co-captain*), B. Mitchell, M. Mitchell, P. Halder, T. Tuimavave, J. Kawau (*Asst Coach*). **ABSENT:** P. Tufuga, J. McKenzie (*PDM*), A. Hall (*Nutritionist*).

WAIRARAPA BUSH

2018 Status: Heartland
Founded: Wairarapa 1886 and original member 1892.
Bush 1890 and affiliated 1893. Amalgamated 1971.
President: B.A. (Brian) Weatherstone
Chairman: T.H.G. (Tim) Nathan
Chief executive officer: A.R. (Tony) Hargood
Coach: J.R. (Joe) Harwood
Assistant coaches: Deon van Deventer, P.A.T. (Piri) Weepu
Main ground: Memorial Park, Masterton
Capacity: 10,000
Colours: Green

RECORDS

Highest attendance	12,000	*Wairarapa Bush v British Isles, 1971 and 1983*
Most appearances	132	*G.K. McGlashan, 1971–83*
Most points	561	*P. Harding-Rimene, 1999–2008*
Most tries	43	*M.T. Foster, 1984–92*
Most points in a season	166	*G.M. Walters, 2012*
Most tries in a season	14	*S.F. Simanu, 2005*
Most conversions in a season	28	*M.F.C. Benton, 1987*
Most penalty goals in a season	34	*G.M. Walters, 2012*
Most dropped goals in a season	7	*K.W. Carter, 1985*
Most points in a match	26	*M.J. Berry v South Canterbury, 1995*
Most tries in a match	5	*S. Malatai v Buller, 2018*
Most conversions in a match	11	*M.F.C. Benton v Horowhenua, 1987*
Most penalty goals in a match	6	*J.T. Te Huia v Buller, 2010*
		G.M. Walters v South Canterbury, 2012
Highest team score	82	*v Horowhenua, 1987*
Record victory (points ahead)	73	*82–9 v Horowhenua, 1987*
Highest score conceded	96	*v Canterbury, 2006*
Record defeat (points behind)	86	*10–96 v Canterbury, 2006*

The 2018 season was a much improved one for Wairarapa Bush, winning half their ten matches and being narrowly beaten in the Lochore Cup final after finishing sixth in the round robin. The best performance was the surprise win over eventual runners-up South Canterbury while the loss to North Otago in the last round was a poor effort. Just seven days later that poor effort against North Otago was successfully reversed in the Lochore Cup semi-final with a gutsy win.

The forward pack suffered in size to some of the packs they faced, and the scrum certainly struggled, but the pack was a mobile one. Number eight Kirk Tufuga was a strong runner and prop Sam Gammie made a successful conversion from lock to loosehead prop with numerous tackles, carries in the tight and six tries. James Goodger was superb in the lineout and led by example in his general play, having taken over the captaincy when original captain Cyrus Baker missed the whole campaign due to injury sustained in a pre-season match.

At first five-eighth Glen Walters was the kingpin in the backline with his tactical control and excellent goalkicking. He was unavailable for the first match against North Otago and made a big difference when he was back for the return encounter in the following week's semi-final. He then missed the Lochore Cup final, having taken up an overseas contract. Outside him Michael Lealava'a was a very composed second five-eighth, having excellent games in the good wins over

Buller, West Coast and semi-final.

Fast wing Soli Malatai had a standout game against Buller when he scored five tries on his 21st birthday to set a new record for Wairarapa Bush. He scored an excellent try in the Lochore Cup final too. In an odd selection the experienced Inia Katia was asked to play much of the season at fullback after being Wairarapa Bush club player of the year in his usual position at halfback for the champion club Gladstone. The intention was for him to then move into his preferred halfback position during the second half. He did not let the team down but none of the other halfbacks used was superior.

Higher honours went to:
New Zealand Heartland: J.W.P.R. Goodger

WAIRARAPA BUSH REPRESENTATIVES 2018

	Club	Games for Union	Points for Union		Club	Games for Union	Points for Union
Marcus Ale	Greytown	5	0	Soli Malatai	Marist	17	50
Robert Anderson	Eketahuna	29	31	Jeremiah Mapusua	Marist	8	0
Lance Buchanan	Greytown	4	0	Lachlan McFadzean	Carterton	44	0
Tristan Flutey	Martinborough	6	5	Nick Olson	Greytown	84	120
Sam Gammie	Eketahuna	23	42	Elijah-James Pakoti	Martinborough	18	5
Paddy Gluck	Marist	3	0	Daryl Pickering	Carterton	12	5
James Goodger	Marist	50	59	Thomas Potoru	Gladstone	3	0
Tipene Haira	Martinborough	30	33	Tim Priest	Martinborough	30	223
Cameron Hayton	Gladstone	52	81	Epeli Rayaqayaqa	Gladstone	15	40
Matthew Henderson	Greytown	7	10	Sam Shaw	Eketahuna	2	0
Nick Hohepa	Greytown	26	5	Andrew Smith	Gladstone	17	12
Tavita Isaac	Greytown	17	5	Kirk Tufuga [1]	Massey University [4]	10	0
Inia Katia	Gladstone	73	60	Max Tufuga	Massey University [4]	9	0
Ryan Knell	Gladstone	9	0	Glen Walters	Hutt OB Marist [3]	39	386
Sean Law	Northcote Birkenhead [2]	2	0	Finn Yeats	Greytown	4	5
Michael Lealava'a	Wainuiomata [3]	10	20				

[1] Player of Origin [2] North Harbour RU [3] Wellington RU [4] Manawatu RU

INDIVIDUAL SCORING

	Tries	Con	PG	DG	Points		Tries	Con	PG	DG	Points
Walters	2	22	12	–	90	Hohepa	1	–	–	–	5
Malatai	7	–	–	–	35	Goodger	1	–	–	–	5
Gammie	6	–	–	–	30	Katia	1	–	–	–	5
Lealava'a	4	–	–	–	20	Anderson	1	–	–	–	5
Rayaqayaqa	3	–	–	–	15	Yeats	1	–	–	–	5
Haira	–	2	3	–	13	Pickering	1	–	–	–	5
Olson	2	–	–	–	10						
Henderson	2	–	–	–	10	**Totals**	**34**	**24**	**15**	**0**	**265**
Penalty try	1	–	–	–	7						
Flutey	1	–	–	–	5	Opposition scored	33	22	11	0	242

WAIRARAPA BUSH 2018

	Poverty Bay	Thames Valley	Ngati Porou East Coast	Buller	Horowhenua Kapiti	South Canterbury	West Coast	North Otago	North Otago	Horowhenua Kapiti	TOTALS
I.S.T. Katia	15	15	9	15	15	15	15	15	15	15	10
T.C. Priest	–	–	–	–	–	–	–	–	–	s	1
T.R. Flutey	14	14	14	–	14	14	–	–	–	s	6
T. Potoru	11	s	–	s	–	–	–	–	–	–	3
N.K. Olson	s	11	s	14	–	s	–	–	–	–	5
S. Malatai	–	–	11	11	11	11	11	11	11	11	8
F. Yeats	–	–	–	–	–	–	s	14	14	14	4
C.M. Hayton	–	–	–	–	–	–	s	s	s	–	3
M.F. Henderson	13	s	13	13	s	13	14	–	–	–	7
R.J. Anderson	–	–	s	s	s	12	13	13	13	13	8
S. Law	–	–	–	–	13	–	–	s	–	–	2
M.S. Lealava'a	12	13	12	12	12	s	12	12	12	12	10
G.M. Walters	10	10	10	10	10	10	10	–	10	–	8
T.T. Haira	s	12	15	s	s	s	s	10	–	10	9
P.S. Gluck	9	9	–	–	–	–	s	–	–	–	3
D.J. Pickering	–	–	s	9	9	9	9	9	9	9	8
K.M.S. Tufuga	8	8	8	8	8	8	8	8	8	8	10
M.A. Ale	7	7	s	s	s	–	–	–	–	–	5
S. Shaw	6	–	–	–	–	–	–	–	–	s	2
T.A. Isaac	s	6	6	6	6	6	6	6	6	6	10
E. Rayaqayaqa	s	s	s	s	s	7	7	7	s	–	9
R.N. Knell	–	s	7	7	7	s	s	s	7	7	9
L.J.M. McFadzean	5	s	5	5	5	5	5	5	s	s	10
J.W.P.R. Goodger (capt)	4	4	4	4	4	4	4	4	4	4	10
A.D. Smith	s	5	–	–	–	s	s	s	5	5	7
E-J. Pakoti	3	–	s	s	3	2	2	2	2	2	9
M.H.P.V. Tufuga	1	3	3	3	–	3	3	3	3	3	9
J.M. Mapusua	s	s	–	–	s	s	s	s	s	s	8
S.G. Gammie	–	1	1	1	1	1	1	1	1	1	9
N.J. Hohepa	2	2	2	2	2	s	s	s	s	s	10
L. Buchanan	s	s	s	s	–	–	–	–	–	–	4

WAIRARAPA BUSH TEAM RECORD, 2018

			Played 10	Won 5	Lost 5	Points for 265		Points against 242
Date	Opponent	Location	Score	Tries	Con	PG	DG	Referee
August 25	Poverty Bay (H)	Gisborne	22–27	Flutey, Hohepa, Walters	Walters (2)	Walters		N.P.Briant
September 1	Thames Valley (H)	Masterton	32–44	Olson, Rayaqayaqa, Penalty try, Goodger	Walters (2)	Walters (2)		T.M.T. Cottrell
September 8	Ngati Porou East Coast (H)	Ruatoria	26–5	Gammie (2), Henderson, Lealava'a	Walters (3)			M.I. Fraser
September 15	Buller (H)	Masterton	61–29	Malatai (5), Katia, Lealava'a, Olson, Walters	Walters (8)			T. Kawahara *Japan*
September 22	Horowhenua Kapiti (H) (BSC)	Levin	21–37	Gammie (2)	Walters	Walters (3)		H.G. Reed
September 29	South Canterbury (H)	Masterton	27–24	Rayaqayaqa (2), Malatai, Gammie	Walters (2)	Walters		B.E. Pickerill
October 6	West Coast (H)	Greymouth	23–5	Henderson, Anderson, Yeats	Walters	Walters (2)		N.J. Webster
October 13	North Otago (H)	Masterton	0–24					H.G. Reed
October 20	North Otago (LC semi-final)	Masterton	30–21	Lealava'a (2), Pickering	Walters (3)	Walters (3)		H.G. Reed
October 28	Horowhenua Kapiti (LC final)	Levin	23–26	Malatai, Gammie	Haira (2)	Haira (3)		R.P. Kelly

BSC *Bruce Steel Cup*

WANGANUI

2018 Status: Heartland
Founded 1888. Original member 1892
President: D.R. (David) Hoskin
Chairman: J.M. (Jeff) Phillips
Chief executive officer: B.S. (Bridget) Belsham
Coach: J.M. (Jason) Caskey
Assistant coaches: J.P. (Jason) Hamlin
Main ground: Cooks Gardens
Capacity: 15,000
Colours: Royal blue, black and white

RECORDS

Highest attendance	6500	*Wanganui v Scotland, 1996*
Most appearances	146	*T.T.T. Olney, 1973–90*
Most points	980	*R.B. Barrell, 1963–77*
Most tries	48	*J.D. Hainsworth, 1984–95*
Most points in a season	184	*G.R.J. Lennox, 1994*
Most tries in a season	14	*H.S. Gordon, 1988*
	14	*P. Fetuia, 2006*
Most conversions in a season	44	*M.K. Davis, 2008*
Most penalty goals in a season	39	*R.B. Barrell, 1975*
Most dropped goals in a season	6	*L.T. Head, 1952*
Most points in a match	32	*K.H. Chase v East Coast, 1989*
Most tries in a match	6	*D.F. Philipson v Taranaki, 1919*
Most conversions in a match	10	*L.K. Harding v West Coast, 1993*
		G.R.J. Lennox v Buller, 1994
Most penalty goals in a match	6	*R.B. Barrell v Manawatu, 1971*
		R.B. Barrell v Taranaki, 1975
		M.K. Davis v East Coast, 2011
Highest team score	81	*v West Coast, 1993*
		v Buller, 1994
Record victory (points ahead)	77	*80–3 v King Country, 2017*
Highest score conceded	88	*v Taranaki, 2000*
Record defeat (points behind)	84	*0–84 v Taranaki, 1995*

A surprise 7–17 defeat to Thames Valley in their home semi-final of the Meads Cup brought Wanganui's season to an abrupt end. It was the shock result of the 2018 Heartland Championship.

Until then Wanganui had won all eight championship matches, including a deserved 21–10 win over expected closest challenger South Canterbury. The defensive qualities of the team were a feature of their play, remarkably conceding only one bonus point in the entire round robin. And although beaten by Taranaki in their Ranfurly Shield challenge, they had produced a very creditable performance where the second half score was 5–5.

From first game to last, the two standouts in the backline again were halfback Lindsay Horrocks and utility Craig Clare. As well as serving the backline well, Horrocks had an accurate kicking game and was a good defender around the ruck. He was surely unlucky not to have made the New Zealand Heartland team. Whether at fullback or first five-eighth Clare was in sublime form and an excellent goalkicker.

Injury in the Ranfurly Shield challenge meant Cameron Crowley made a slow start to the

Championship, and he retired at the conclusion of the two matches played by the New Zealand Heartland team. On the other wing, 19-year-old Harry Symes had a very promising debut season, exhibiting really good pace until dislocating his shoulder against King Country.

Another newcomer who held his spot was fullback Tyler Rogers-Holden. It was his emergence that prompted the coach Jason Caskey to shift Craig Clare into first five-eighth in place of Dane Whale. Former Buller rep Penijamini Nabainivalu arrived from Wellington and with Kaveni Dabenaise formed a good partnership in midfield with their pace and ability to breach the opposition line.

Hooker and captain Roman Tutauha made a delayed entry due to a broken arm suffered in the club final and blindside flanker Campbell Hart captained the team in Tutauha's absence. With the extra responsibility, Hart played some outstanding games and his New Zealand Heartland selection was well deserved. The locking pair of 2.02m Welshman Henri Williams and Sam Madams were both hard working and a tower of strength in the lineouts.

Last year's number eight Bryn Hudson had an injury-plagued season and Michael Tafili was brought in on loan from Counties Manukau. He made a big impression, providing strong ball-carrying ability and aggressive defence. His having to leave the field injured after 50 minutes of the semi-final was a blow. With two good openside flankers in Angus Middleton and Jamie Hughes, the coach had the luxury of rotating them.

The depth in the front row was well utilised with the experienced Viki Tofa and Kamipeli Latu, second season Gabriel Hakaraia and debutant Wiremu Cottrell all getting good game time with no noticeable loss of effect. Hooker Jack Yarrall had played one game in 2016 and with Tutauha's injury showed himself an able replacement for his captain.

Higher honours went to:
New Zealand Heartland: C.D. Clare, C.J. Crowley, C.J. Hart, P.B. Nabainivalu

WANGANUI REPRESENTATIVES 2018

	Club	Games for Union	Points for Union		Club	Games for Union	Points for Union
Jackson Campbell	Ruapehu	1	0	Kameli Kuruyabaki	Taihape	17	28
Craig Clare	Ruapehu	26	260	Kamipeli Latu	Border	33	15
Wiremu Cottrell	Taihape	8	0	Sam Madams	Marist	50	15
Cameron Crowley	Marist	51	140	Angus Middleton	Border	20	25
Kaveni Dabenaise	Border	19	40	Penijamini Nabainivalu	Marist	9	5
Simon Dibben	Marist	54	97	Ethan Robinson	Kaierau	9	5
Joshua Fifiita	Ruapehu	4	0	Tyler Rogers-Holden	Border	8	25
Dylan Gallien	Taihape	5	5	Shandon Scott	Kaierau	6	7
Tremaine Gilbert	Taihape	46	52	Harry Symes	Border	6	10
Gabriel Hakaraia	Ruapehu	16	10	Tom Symes	Border	2	5
Campbell Hart	Ruapehu	24	16	Michael Tafili	Manurewa [1]	5	10
Peter-Travis Hay-Horton	Taihape	3	0	Viki Tofa	Marist	45	30
Jack Hodges	Border	1	5	Roman Tutauha	Ruapehu	62	26
Lindsay Horrocks	Border	61	62	Dane Whale	Taihape	35	76
Bryn Hudson	Ngamatapouri	37	46	Henri Williams	Fraser Tech [2]	10	0
Jamie Hughes	Ruapehu	29	28	Jack Yarrall	Marist	11	5

[1] *Counties Manukau RU*   [2] *Waikato RU*

INDIVIDUAL SCORING

	Tries	Con	PG	DG	Points
Clare	5	34	8	–	117
Rogers-Holden	5	–	–	–	25
Dabenaise	4	–	–	–	20
Tofa	4	–	–	–	20
Whale	3	1	–	–	17
Middleton	3	–	–	–	15
Horrocks	3	–	–	–	15
Dibben	2	–	–	–	10
H. Symes	2	–	–	–	10
Kuruyabaki	2	–	–	–	10
Tafili	2	–	–	–	10
Hart	2	–	–	–	10
Scott	1	1	–	–	7
Penalty try	1	–	–	–	7
Gilbert	1	–	–	–	5

	Tries	Con	PG	DG	Points
Hakaraia	1	–	–	–	5
Latu	1	–	–	–	5
Gallien	1	–	–	–	5
Nabainavalu	1	–	–	–	5
Crowley	1	–	–	–	5
Madams	1	–	–	–	5
Hodges	1	–	–	–	5
T. Symes	1	–	–	–	5
Yarrall	1	–	–	–	5
Robinson	1	–	–	–	5
Totals	**50**	**36**	**8**	**0**	**348**
Opposition scored	23*	16	4	0	163

* includes two penalty tries (14 points)

WANGANUI 2018

	Taranaki	South Canterbury	West Coast	Poverty Bay	Mid Canterbury	King Country	Buller	Ngati Porou East Coast	Horowhenua Kapiti	Thames Valley	TOTALS
S.P. Scott	15	s	–	s	s	–	s	s	–	–	6
C.D. Clare	–	15	15	15	15	15	10	10	10	10	9
T.T.H. Rogers-Holden	–	–	s	11	s	s	15	15	15	15	8
H.I.A. Symes	14	14	14	14	14	14	–	–	–	–	6
C.J. Crowley	11	–	–	–	11	11	11	11	–	11	6
S.K. Dibben	s	11	11	–	–	–	14	–	14	14	6
T.O.H. Symes	–	–	–	–	–	–	s	14	–	–	2
K.N. Kuruyabaki	13	s	–	s	–	s	13	12	13	s	8
E.T. Robinson	s	–	s	s	s	s	–	s	s	–	7
K. Dabenaise	–	13	13	13	13	13	–	13	11	13	8
P.B. Nabainivalu	12	12	12	12	12	12	12	–	12	12	9
D.J. Whale	10	10	10	10	10	10	s	–	s	–	8
L.D. Horrocks	9	9	9	9	9	9	9	s	9	9	10
J.T. Fifita	s	s	s				–	9	–	–	4
T.J. Gilbert	8	8	–	8	s	s	s	6	s	s	9
M.T. Tafili	–	–	–	s	8	8	8	–	–	8	5
B.D. Hudson	–	–	–	–	–	–	–	8	8	–	2
J.N. Hughes	7	7	7	s	7	s	7	–	s	7	9
C.J. Hart	6	6	–	6	6	6	6	s	6	6	9
A.H. Middleton	s	s	8	7	s	7	s	7	7	s	10
J.L. Campbell	–	–	6	–	–	–	–	–	–	–	1
H.O. Williams	5	5	5	5	5	5	5	s	5	5	10
S.A. Madams	4	4	s	4	4	4	4	4	4	4	10
P-T.H. Hay-Horton	s	s	4	–	–	–	–	–	–	–	3
J.I. Hodges	–	–	–	–	–	–	5	–	–	–	1
V.M. Tofa	3	–	3	s	–	3	s	3	3	–	7
K.T. Latu	1	1	1	–	s	1	1	–	1	1	8
W.H. Cottrell	s	s	–	1	1	s	–	1	s	s	8
G.T.E. Hakaraia	s	3	s	3	3	–	3	s	s	3	9
J.S. Yarrall	2	s	s	2	2	2	2	s	s	s	10
D.R. Gallien	s	2	2	s	–	s	–	–	–	–	5
R.B.K. Tutauha (capt)	–	–	–	–	–	–	s	2	2	2	4

D.J. Whale captained v Taranaki, West Coast; C.J. Hart captained v South Canterbury, Poverty Bay, Mid Canterbury, King Country, Buller.

WANGANUI TEAM RECORD, 2018

Played 10 Won 8 Lost 2 Points for 348 Points against 163

Date	Opponent	Location	Score	Tries	Con	PG	DG	Referee
August 4	Taranaki (RS)	Hawera	10–33	Gilbert, Dibben				M.G. Lash
August 25	South Canterbury (H)	Wanganui	21–10	Hakaraia, Dibben	Clare	Clare (3)		N.E.R. Hogan
September 1	West Coast (H)	Greymouth	33–21	Whale (2), Clare, Latu, Middleton	Clare (4)			B.E. Pickerill
September 8	Poverty Bay (H)	Gisborne	53–0	Rogers-Holden (2), Dabenaise, H. Symes, Whale, Clare, Kuruyabaki, Scott	Clare (4), Scott	Clare		T.M.T. Cottrell
September 15	Mid Canterbury (H)	Wanganui	30–12	Clare, Tafili, Dabenaise, Gallien	Clare (2)	Clare (2)		C.J. Stone
September 22	King Country (H)	Te Kuiti	36–19	Tofa, Tafili, Horrocks, Dabenaise, H. Symes	Clare (4)	Clare		N.J. Webster
September 29	Buller (H)	Wanganui	45–14	Horrocks, Clare, Nabainavalu, Crowley, Tofa, Madams	Clare (6)	Clare		M.C.J. Winter
October 6	Ngati Porou East Coast (H)	Tolaga Bay	56–10	Rogers-Holden, Hodges, Tofa, T. Symes, Penalty try, Hart, Middleton, Yarrall	Clare (7)			R.P. Kelly
October 13	Horowhenua Kapiti (H) (BSC)	Wanganui	57–27	Rogers-Holden (2), Middleton, Tofa, Hart, Horrocks, Dabenaise, Kuruyabaki, Robinson	Clare (5), Whale			T.N. Griffiths
October 20	Thames Valley (MC semi-final)	Wanganui	7–17	Clare	Clare			R.P. Kelly

BSC *Bruce Steel Cup*
RS *Ranfurly Shield*

WELLINGTON

2018 Status: Mitre 10 Cup Premiership
Founded 1879. Original member 1892
President: B.F. (Brendan) Gard'ner
Chairman: I.G. (Iain) Potter
Chief Executive Officer: S.P. (Steve) Rogers (to Aug),
M.G. (Matt) Evans (interim)
Coach: C.J. (Chris) Gibbes
Assistant coaches: A.H.R. (Andre) Bell, C.S. (Cory) Jane,
K.P. (Kurt) McQuilkin
Main ground: Westpac Stadium, Wellington
Capacity: 34,500
Colours: Black

RECORDS

Most appearances	173	*Graham Williams, 1964–76*
Most points	909	*Allan Hewson, 1977–86*
Most tries	105	*Bernie Fraser, 1975–86*
Most points in a season	199	*John Gallagher, 1987*
Most tries in a season	24	*Bernie Fraser, 1981*
Most conversions in a season	47	*Jackson Garden-Bachop, 2017*
Most penalty goals in a season	38	*Jon Preston, 1994*
Most dropped goals in a season	7	*John Dougan, 1971*
Most points in a match	34	*David Holwell v Bay of Plenty, 2002*
Most tries in a match	7	*Nigel Geany v Wanganui, 1991*
Most conversions in a match	14	*Peter O'Shaughnessy, v Horowhenua, 1988*
		Simon Mannix v Rosario, 1995
Most penalty goals in a match	7	*Jackson Garden-Bachop v North Harbour, 2016*
Highest team score	118	*v Rosario, 1995*
Record victory (points ahead)	101	*118–17 v Rosario, 1995*
Highest score conceded	82	*v Otago, 1998*
Record defeat (points behind)	72	*10–82 v Otago, 1998*

With a record of six wins and five losses in their first season back in the Premiership, Wellington comfortably made the top four to enter the semi-finals. There they were beaten by eventual winners Auckland 17–38.

Of their defeats, all matches played against the other top four teams were lost (three by less than seven points), the other being to eventual Championship winners Waikato when Wellington made changes to their team. The victories were all dominant affairs, with the lowest score achieved in winning them being 34.

Wellington had very few changes from last year's squad. Gone were Julian Savea and Brad Shields (both overseas), Daniel Kirkpatrick (Auckland), and Joe Apikotoa (Hawke's Bay) while Alex Fidow was absent injured. Having missed all of last year with concussion concerns, prop Reg Goodes announced his retirement from rugby in February. Gains were the return from overseas of Thomas Waldrom (who last represented the union in 2008, and who had won four caps for England since), and Joel Hintz (Canterbury).

Starting the season on the wing Wes Goosen was then shifted to fullback, which proved to be an inspired move from coach Chris Gibbes. From the back Goosen produced a number of brilliant attacking performances and was also a first-rate defender.

On the wings Malo Tuitama was a very determined runner and had his best return with six tries. Ben Lam also scored six tries, including a hat-trick against Southland. Overall, though, he did not quite attain the standard he exhibited for the Hurricanes in Super Rugby.

Free from injury, captain and centre Matt Proctor reproduced the form he showed in 2016 and was rewarded with test selection against Japan. He also passed 50 games for Wellington. The coach alternated between 19-year-old Billy Proctor and 21-year-old Thomas Umaga-Jensen at second five-eighth. They received four starts each in the round robin with Proctor claiming the position for the semi-final. Both look to have good futures.

Jackson Garden-Bachop was again good value at first five-eighth with an all-round game. He was another to pass 50 games for the union. Sheridan Rangihuna started the season as first-choice halfback but in the second half of the season lost his place in the side with Kemara Hauiti-Parapara promoted to starting halfback and Carlos Price coming off the bench.

Wellington was well off for loose forwards. Thomas Waldrom only appeared in half the games and announced his retirement at the end of the season. After the loss to Waikato the highly promising Teariki Ben-Nicholas became the preferred number eight and stepped up well on last year's debut season.

Du Plessis Kirifi had a season interrupted by injury and in his absence Mateaki Kafatolu showed himself to be a capable openside flanker. After missing All Blacks selection for the Rugby Championship, blindside flanker Vaea Fifita was recalled to national duty after an outstanding match against Counties Manukau.

With Sam Lousi making a late entry due to knee surgery, Isaia Walker-Leawere and James Blackwell gave a good account of themselves at lock, particularly Blackwell who was one of the form locks of the Mitre 10 Cup. He was powerful on defence, made numerous carries and was a strong scrummager.

Wellington also had an abundance of front-row talent. After opening with Tolu Fahamokioa and Joel Hintz as props, the coach finally settled on 2018 New Zealand under 20 rep Xavier Numia and a fully fit Jeffrey To'omaga-Allen. Talented hooker Asafo Aumua made a slow start after not having played since a fractured wrist in April, but he built nicely and at season end his trademark charges were on display along with lineout throwing accuracy and strong defensive work around the field.

Dane Coles played his first games for Wellington since 2013 when coming off the bench twice in his rehabilitation from the serious knee injury against France last November.

Higher honours went to:
New Zealand: D. Coles, V. Fifita, T. Perenara, M. Proctor, A. Savea
New Zealand Maori: M. Proctor, I. Walker-Leawere
New Zealand Under 20: X. Numia, C. Price, B. Proctor, K. Uluilakepa
New Zealand Sevens: D. Schrijvers

WELLINGTON REPRESENTATIVES 2018

	Club	Games for Union	Points for Union
Asafo Aumua	Avalon	31	85
Alexander Barendregt	OB University	1	0
Teariki Ben-Nicholas	OB University	16	10
James Blackwell	Petone	30	20
Dane Coles	Poneke	69	90
Otutolu "Tolu" Fahamokioa	Tawa	34	30
Vaea Fifita	Wellington	36	65
Losi Filipo	Petone	8	10
Greg Foe	Poneke	26	10
Jackson Garden-Bachop	Northern United	52	400
Wes Goosen	OB University	40	90
Kemara Hauiti-Parapara	Tawa	22	10
Joel Hintz	OB University	11	0
Mateaki Kafatolu	Petone	16	10
Du Plessis Kirifi	Northern United	15	10
Ben Lam	Tawa	20	60
Sam Lousi	Marist St Pat's	22	15
Will Mangos	OB University	17	5
Xavier Numia	Oriental Rongotai	7	5
James O'Reilly	Hutt OB Marist	26	15
Sitiveni Paongo	Tawa	14	20
Thomas "TJ" Perenara	Northern United	16	15
Carlos Price	Petone	8	0
Billy Proctor	Marist St Pat's	13	5
Matt Proctor	Oriental Rongotai	52	60
Sheridan Rangihuna	Hutt OB Marist	32	10
Trent Renata	Oriental Rongotai	15	32
Ardie Savea	Oriental Rongotai	34	80
Galu Taufale	Poneke	25	25
Jeffery To'omaga-Allen	Marist St Pat's	41	30
Tietie Tuimauga	Johnsonville	2	0
Malo Tuitama	Oriental Rongotai	27	65
Pakai Turia	Poneke	10	2
Kaliopasi Uluilakepa	Petone	2	5
Peter Umaga-Jensen	Wainuiomata	11	10
Thomas Umaga-Jensen	Wainuiomata	17	50
Tennessee "TJ" Va'a	Wainuiomata	4	2
Thomas Waldrom	Avalon	84	110
Isaia Walker-Leawere	Poneke	22	25

INDIVIDUAL SCORING

	Tries	Con	PG	DG	Points
Garden Bachop	1	28	10	–	91
Tuitama	6	–	–	–	30
Lam	6	–	–	–	30
T. Umaga-Jensen	5	–	–	–	25
Goosen	4	–	–	–	20
Aumua	4	–	–	–	20
O'Reilly	3	–	–	–	15
Walker-Leawere	3	–	–	–	15
Fifita	3	–	–	–	15
Renata	1	3	–	–	11
Blackwell	2	–	–	–	10
M. Proctor	2	–	–	–	10
Taufale	2	–	–	–	10
Ben-Nicholas	2	–	–	–	10
Kirifi	1	–	–	–	5
Fahamokioa	1	–	–	–	5
Uluilakepa	1	–	–	–	5
Filipo	1	–	–	–	5
Hauiti-Parapara	1	–	–	–	5
B. Proctor	1	–	–	–	5
Waldrom	1	–	–	–	5
Kafatolu	1	–	–	–	5
P. Umaga-Jensen	1	–	–	–	5
Numia	1	–	–	–	5
Paongo	1	–	–	–	5
Va'a	–	1	–	–	2
Turia	–	1	–	–	2
Totals	**55**	**33**	**10**	**0**	**371**
Opposition scored	31	23	13	0	240

WELLINGTON 2018

	Otago	Canterbury	Southland	Waikato	North Harbour	Counties Manukau	Manawatu	Tasman	Auckland	Taranaki	Auckland	TOTALS
T.W.K. Renata	15	15	–	15	s	–	s	–	s	s	s	8
W.T. Goosen	11	11	15	–	15	15	15	13	15	15	15	10
M. Tuitama	14	s	11	14	11	11	–	11	14	11	11	10
M.B. Lam	–	14	14	–	14	14	11	15	11	14	14	9
L.F. Filipo	–	–	–	11	–	–	14	14	–	–	s	4
M.P. Proctor (capt)	–	13	13	13	13	13	13	–	13	13	13	9
B.D. Proctor	13	s	s	s	12	12	–	12	s	12	12	10
P.I.J. Umaga-Jensen	12	–	–	12	–	–	s	–	–	–	–	3
T.N.M. Umaga-Jensen	s	12	12	–	s	s	12	s	12	s	–	9
J.K. Garden-Bachop	10	10	10	s	10	10	10	10	10	10	10	11
T.V. Va'a	–	–	s	–	–	–	–	–	–	–	–	1
P. Turia	–	–	–	10	–	s	–	–	–	–	–	2
S.M. Rangihuna	9	9	–	–	s	s	s	–	–	–	–	5
K.H. Hauiti-Parapara	s	s	–	9	9	9	9	9	9	9	9	10
T.T.R. Perenara	–	–	9	–	–	–	–	–	–	–	–	1
C.T. Price	–	–	s	9	–	–	–	s	s	s	s	6
T.R. Waldrom	8	8	–	8	–	–	8	–	s	–	–	5
T.G. Ben-Nicholas	s	–	8	6	8	8	–	8	8	8	8	9
D.P.A. Kirifi	7	7	–	–	7	–	–	7	–	–	s	5
V.T.L. Fifita	6	6	6	–	6	6	–	–	6	–	–	6
G.F. Foe	s	–	s	7	–	s	s	–	–	–	–	5
M. Kafatolu	–	s	–	s	s	7	7	s	7	7	7	9
A.S. Savea	–	–	7	–	–	–	–	–	–	–	–	1
G.F. Taufale	–	–	s	–	s	6	6	6	s	s	–	8
I.E.T. Walker-Leawere	5	5	–	5	5	5	5	5	5	5	5	10
J. Blackwell	4	4	4	–	4	4	4	4	4	4	6	10
W.K. Mangos	s	s	5	4	5	–	s	s	–	–	–	7
S.T. Lousi	–	–	–	–	–	–	–	–	s	s	4	3
J.N. Hintz	3	s	3	3	3	s	s	s	s	s	s	11
O.A. Fahamokioa	1	1	1	1	s	s	1	s	s	1	s	11
K. Uluilakepa	s	–	s	–	–	–	–	–	–	–	–	2
A.J. Barendregt	s	–	–	–	–	–	–	–	–	–	–	1
J.L. To'omaga-Allen	–	3	–	–	–	3	3	3	3	3	3	7
X.S. Numia	–	–	s	s	1	1	s	1	1	–	–	7
T. Tuimauga	–	–	–	s	s	–	–	–	–	–	–	2
S.F. Paongo	–	–	–	–	–	–	–	–	–	s	1	2
J.P. O'Reilly	2	2	s	s	s	s	s	s	s	–	–	9
A. Aumua	s	s	2	2	2	2	2	2	2	2	2	11
D.S. Coles	–	–	–	–	–	–	–	–	–	s	s	2

T.R. Waldrom captained v Otago; G.F. Taufale captained v Tasman.

WELLINGTON TEAM RECORD, 2018

Played 11　　Won 6　　Lost 5　　Points for 371　　Points against 240

Date	Opponent	Location	Score	Tries	Con	PG	DG	Referee
August 19	Otago (P/C)	Wellington	34–16	Goosen (2), Tuitama (2)	Garden-Bachop (4)	Garden-Bachop (2)		P.M. Williams
August 25	Canterbury (P)	Christchurch	20–27	T. Umaga-Jensen, O'Reilly, Kirifi	Garden-Bachop	Garden-Bachop		J.J. Doleman
August 31	Southland (P/C)	Wellington	52–7	Lam (3), T. Umaga-Jensen, Aumua, Fahamokioa, Blackwell, Ulilakepa	Garden-Bachop (5), Va'a			S. Kubo *Japan*
September 5	Waikato (P/C)	Hamilton	31–43	Renata, Walker-Leawere, M. Proctor, Tuitama, Filipo	Garden-Bachop (2), Turia			B.E. Pickerill
September 9	North Harbour (P)	Wellington	35–23	Aumua, Hauiti-Parapara, Tuitama, Goosen, Garden-Bachop	Garden-Bachop (2)	Garden-Bachop (2)		M.G. Lash
September 15	Counties Manukau (P)	Pukekohe	53–12	Fifita (2), O'Reilly (2), Walker-Leawere, Tuitama, B. Proctor, Aumua	Garden-Bachop (5)	Garden-Bachop		R.P. Kelly
September 23	Manawatu (P/C)	Palmerston North	49–7	Lam (2), Waldrom, Kafatolu, T. Umaga-Jensen, Blackwell, Aumua, Walker-Leawere, P. Umaga-Jensen	Renata (2)			C.J. Stone
September 29	Tasman (P)	Wellington	22–28	Numia, Taufale, T. Umaga-Jensen	Garden-Bachop (2)	Garden-Bachop		N.P. Briant
October 4	Auckland (P)	Wellington	24–29	Taufale, T. Umaga-Jensen, Lam	Garden-Bachop (3)	Garden-Bachop		N.P. Briant
October 12	Taranaki (P)	New Plymouth	34–10	Fifita, Ben-Nicholas, M. Proctor, Tuitama, Paongo	Garden-Bachop (2), Renata	Garden-Bachop		B.D. O'Keeffe
October 20	Auckland (P semi-final)	Auckland	17–38	Goosen, Ben-Nicholas	Garden-Bachop (2)	Garden-Bachop		B.E. Pickerill

WEST COAST

2018 Status: Heartland
Founded 1890. Affiliated 1893
President: G.N. (Gavin) Davy
Chairman: M.J. (Mike) Meehan
Chief executive officer: Mike Connors
Coach: S.J. (Sean) Cuttance
Assistant coach: K.G. (Kyle) Parker, B.G. (Bruce) Pearson
Main ground: John Sturgeon Park, Greymouth
Capacity: 8000
Colours: Red and white

RECORDS

Highest attendance	5500	West Coast v British Isles, 1983
Most appearances	100	M.T. Mudu, 2004–2018
Most points	712	M.A. Foster, 1992–2000
Most tries	27	K.J.J. Beams, 1965–78
Most points in a season	176	M.A. Foster, 1999
Most tries in a season	9	P.A. Teen, 1975
Most conversions in a season	20	M.A. Foster, 1999
Most penalty goals in a season	38	M.A. Foster, 1999
Most dropped goals in a season	9	A.P. O'Regan, 1987
Most points in a match	24	M.A. Foster v Horowhenua Kapiti, 1999
Most tries in a match	4	K. McNee v Buller, 1964
		F.P. O'Donnell v Buller, 1970
		P.A. Teen v Nelson Bays, 1975
		R.J. Stanton v Ngati Porou East Coast, 2018
Most conversions in a match	6	L.T. Martyn v Golden Bay-Motueka, 1933
Most penalty goals in a match	6	P.W. Hutchison v East Coast, 1991
		C.N. Simpson v South Canterbury, 2007
Highest team score	62	v Ngati Porou East Coast, 2018
Record victory (points ahead)	42	45–3 v Golden Bay-Motueka, 1933
Highest score conceded	128	v Canterbury, 1992
Record defeat (points behind)	128	0–128 v Canterbury, 1992

West Coast's season was unfortunately defined by the stripping of six competition points the day before the final round for having fielded an ineligible player in the first four games. Despite winning the final match, the team finished ninth and out of the playoffs. If the six points had not been lost, West Coast would have finished sixth and hosted Wairarapa Bush in a Lochore Cup semi-final.

At times there was a lack of cohesiveness between the forward and back divisions. Sometimes the forward pack would play well and the backline would look out of sorts, or vice versa. Despite this, the side recorded four wins in their eight matches and came close to beating Heartland heavyweight Wanganui, only the conceding of a converted try with three minutes left pushed the score out to 21–33.

In the backline Sean McClure had a solid season at centre, but the standout was his midfield partner former Tasman rep Sione Holani who created a fine impression with his strong running and determined tackling. On the wing Regan Stanton scored four tries against East Coast to equal the union's record. In his debut season Oliver Dimmick started promisingly at halfback, but Jarrod Ferguson regained the jersey towards the end of the season.

Maleli Mudu became the first player to reach 100 games for West Coast in the final fixture against East Coast. His three tries during the season took his tally to 25, just two short of the record.

Functioning well at the set pieces, the personnel of the forward pack was a settled one, with the only change having to be made, apart from injury, being Daniel Foord replacing Tyler Morgan-Kearns at prop at the halfway point of the season. The loose forward unit of Amenatave Tukana, Steven Soper and Brad Tauwhare was an experienced one, while the import locks Josh Manning and Tumama Tu'ulua battled away well in the tight, including providing plenty of ball from the lineout. Captain and hooker Troy Tauwhare stood out as a tireless worker and prop Daniel Davies progressed well in his second season.

Having last appeared in 2015, 33-year-old lock Brad Houston had the misfortune to suffer a heart attack on the field in the opening match against Thames Valley and was taken to hospital. Thankfully he recovered, but it would seem to be an unfortunate end to his playing career.

West Coast's home ground of Rugby Park was permanently renamed John Sturgeon Park on 6 October in recognition of the enormous contribution John Sturgeon has made to West Coast and New Zealand rugby.

Higher honours went to:
New Zealand Heartland: S.F. Holani, T.K. Tauwhare

WEST COAST REPRESENTATIVES 2018

	Club	Games for Union	Points for Union		Club	Games for Union	Points for Union
Andrew Connors [1]	[2]	35	50	Jesse Pitman-Joass	Grey Valley	7	0
Nick Cumming [1]	Sumner [3]	25	149	Tom Reekie	Marist	17	85
Kevin Curtis	Blaketown	25	11	Nathan Smith [1]	Shirley [3]	18	4
Daniel Davies	South Westland	17	5	Steven Soper	Grey Valley	16	30
Oliver Dimmick	Wests	8	11	Regan Stanton	Blaketown	38	87
Jarrod Ferguson	Kiwi	21	15	Brad Tauwhare	Kiwi	40	45
Daniel Foord	Kiwi	15	5	Troy Tauwhare	Kiwi	64	49
Sione Holani	Grey Valley	5	5	Peter Te Rakau	Kiwi	21	25
Brad Houston	Blaketown	65	65	Joshua Tomlinson	Wests	9	0
Vincent Lucas	Wests	2	0	Tumama Tu'ulua	Auckland Uni [4]	7	5
Jesse MacRae	South Westland	25	0	Amenatave Tukana	Belfast [3]	24	36
Joshua Manning	Christchurch Marist [3]	31	10	Jaysn Van Vliet	Kiwi	6	0
Sean McClure	Kiwi	50	79	Oliver Varley	Marist	3	0
Tyler Morgan-Kearns	Grey Valley	4	0	Duncan Wood	Blaketown	6	5
Maleli Mudu	Marist	100	146				

[1] Player of Origin   [2] Returned from overseas[3] Canterbury RU   [4] Auckland RU

INDIVIDUAL SCORING

	Tries	Con	PG	DG	Points
Reekie	2	18	3	–	55
Stanton	6	–	–	–	30
Tukana	4	–	–	–	20
McClure	4	–	–	–	20
Mudu	3	–	–	–	15
Te Rakau	3	–	–	–	15
Soper	3	–	–	–	15
Dimmick	1	3	–	–	11
B. Tauwhare	2	–	–	–	10
Penalty try	1	–	–	–	7

	Tries	Con	PG	DG	Points
Tu'ulua	1	–	–	–	5
Wood	1	–	–	–	5
Cumming	1	–	–	–	5
Holani	1	–	–	–	5
T. Tauwhare	1	–	–	–	5
Curtis	1	–	–	–	5
Totals	**35**	**21**	**3**	**0**	**228**
Opposition scored	34	25	7	0	241

WEST COAST 2018

	Thames Valley	Wanganui	Mid Canterbury	Poverty Bay	Buller	North Otago	Wairarapa Bush	Ngati Porou East Coast	TOTALS
P.E. Te Rakau	15	15	15	11	11	15	11	s	8
N.K. Cumming	–	–	s	15	–	–	–	–	2
J.J. Pitman-Joass	–	–	–	–	15	–	15	15	3
D.R.W. Wood	14	14	14	14	–	14	s	–	6
M.T. Mudu	11	11	11	s	s	11	s	11	8
V.J. Lucas	–	–	–	s	–	s	–	–	2
R.J. Stanton	13	13	13	–	14	12	14	14	7
S.R. McClure	–	12	12	13	13	13	13	13	7
N.L. Smith	12	s	–	–	–	s	10	–	4
A.D. Connors	s	–	–	–	–	–	–	–	1
S.F. Holani	–	s	–	12	12	–	12	12	5
T.J. Reekie	10	10	10	10	10	10	–	10	7
O.H. Dimmick	9	s	9	9	9	9	s	s	8
J.C. Ferguson	–	9	s	s	s	s	9	9	7
A.V. Tukana	8	8	8	8	8	8	8	8	8
S.G. Soper	7	7	7	7	7	–	–	7	6
B.G. Tauwhare	6	6	6	–	6	6	6	6	7
K.J. Curtis	s	s	s	s	s	7	7	s	8
J.P. Tomlinson	–	–	s	6	s	s	s	s	6
T.M.L. Tu'ulua	5	4	4	4	–	4	4	4	7
B.G. Houston	4	–	–	–	–	–	–	–	1
J.J. Manning	s	5	5	5	5	5	5	s	8
J.P. Van Vliet	–	–	s	s	4	s	s	5	6
D.J. Davies	3	3	3	3	3	3	3	3	8
T.J. Kearns	1	1	1	1	–	–	–	–	4
J.S. MacRae	s	s	s	s	s	s	s	s	8
D.M. Foord	–	–	s	s	1	1	1	1	6
O.J. Varley	–	–	–	–	–	s	s	s	3
T.K. Tauwhare (capt)	2	2	2	2	2	2	2	2	8

WEST COAST TEAM RECORD, 2018

Played 8　Won 4　Lost 4　Points for 228　Points against 241

Date	Opponent	Location	Score	Tries	Con	PG	DG	Referee
August 25	Thames Valley (H)	Te Aroha	27–25	Mudu, Te Rakau, Stanton, Tukana	Reekie (2)	Reekie		D.J. MacPherson
September 1	Wanganui (H)	Greymouth	21–33	Reekie, Penalty try, B. Tauwhare	Reekie, Dimmick			B.E. Pickerill
September 8	Mid Canterbury (H)	Ashburton	29–36	Tukana, Tu'ulua, Wood, McClure	Reekie (3)	Reekie		J.D. Munro
September 15	Poverty Bay (H)	Greymouth	31–30	Soper (2), Dimmick, McClure, Cumming	Reekie (3)			M.G. Lash
September 22	Buller (H)	Westport	34–28	Te Rakau (2), Holani, Stanton, Tukana	Reekie (3)	Reekie		J.D. Munro
September 29	North Otago (H)	Oamaru	19–40	Tukana, T. Tauwhare, Mudu	Reekie (2)			A.W.B. Mabey
October 6	Wairarapa Bush (H)	Greymouth	5–23	Curtis				N.J. Webster
October 13	Ngati Porou East Coast (H)	Greymouth	62–26	Stanton (4), McClure (2), B. Tauwhare, Soper, Reekie, Mudu	Reekie (4), Dimmick (2)			M.G. Lash

RANFURLY SHIELD 2018

The Ranfurly Shield changed hands twice in 2018.

Taranaki had comfortable victories against their Heartland opponents, although the second half scoring was 5–5 in the defence against Wanganui.

Waikato avoided the shortest reign in Ranfurly Shield history when they withstood the challenge from Hawke's Bay just four days after lifting the Shield from Taranaki.

A similar scoring pattern occurred in both matches the Shield changed hands, wherein the challenger made a fast start and then withstood a comeback to hold on and claim the trophy. Waikato led 33–5 at halftime against Taranaki and were scoreless in the second half in winning 33–19, while Otago led 17-0 after 19 minutes to win 23–19.

Results

Taranaki

686	July 28	v Poverty Bay	Tikorangi	won	78–0
687	August 4	v Wanganui	Hawera	won	33–10
688	August 24	v Manawatu	New Plymouth	won	41–21
689	September 9	v Waikato	New Plymouth	lost	19–33

Waikato

690	September 13	v Hawke's Bay	Hamilton	won	42–22
691	September 29	v Southland	Hamilton	won	42–11
692	October 13	v Otago	Hamilton	lost	19–23

First and most recent Ranfurly Shield match	Played	Won	Lost	Drawn as holder	Drawn as challenger	Points for	Points against
Auckland (1904–2015)	203	158	39	5	1	5849	2220
Bay of Plenty (1920–2015)	24	2	23	–	–	328	655
Buller (1907–2001)	12	–	11	–	1	36	328
Bush (1927–1968)	7	–	7	–	–	41	285
Canterbury (1920–2017)	195	148	40	6	1	5676	2501
Counties Manukau (1958–2017)	33	7	24	–	2	566	872
East Coast (1953–2013)	7	–	7	–	–	22	430
Golden Bay-Motueka (1958)	1	–	1	–	–	8	56
Hawke's Bay (1905–2018)	96	61[1]	31	3	1	2038	1474
Horowhenua Kapiti (1914–2015)	10	–	10	–	–	92	563
King Country (1922–2016)	20	–	20	–	–	120	664
Manawatu (1914–2018)	38	14	23	–	1	511	728
Manawhenua (1927–1929)	6	3	3	–	–	84	110
Marlborough (1908–2005)	20	7	13	–	–	245	539
Mid Canterbury (1933–2017)	15	–	15	–	–	111	620
Nelson (1924–1959)	2	–	2	–	–	17	66
Nelson Bays (1973–2005)	6	–	6	–	–	46	334
North Harbour (1986–2016)	20	4	16	–	–	462	608
North Otago (1938–2011)	13	–	13	–	–	78	738
Northland (1935–2015)	48	17	30	1	–	715	1053
Otago (1904–2018)	83	37	43	1	2	1193	1147
Poverty Bay (1911–2018)	17	–	17	–	–	78	790
South Auckland (1911)	1	–	1	–	–	5	21
South Canterbury (1920–2006)	26	3	23	–	–	263	821
Southland (1906–2018)	73	30	40	–	3	1072	1398
Taranaki (1906–2018)	100	49	45	3	3	1631	1618
Tasman (2008–2012)	2	–	2	–	–	60	75
Thames Valley (1951–2016)	15	–	15	–	–	76	665
Waikato (1932–2018)	108	67	37	3	1	3138	1668
Wairarapa (1905–1969)	30	12	17	–	1	431	504
Wairarapa Bush (1973–2015)	9	–	9	–	–	67	491
Wanganui (1907–2018)	31	–	30	–	1	239	985
Wellington (1904–2014)	98	50	42	1	5	1545	1343
West Coast (1932–2000)	15	–	15	–	–	107	588

[1] includes one game where shield did not change hands because of a residential breach.

HIGHEST WINNING MARGIN BY A SHIELD HOLDER
134 points   Auckland 139   North Otago 5 at Oamaru 1993

HIGHEST WINNING MARGIN BY A CHALLENGER
45 points   Waikato 52   North Harbour 7 at Albany 2007

INDIVIDUAL PERFORMANCES

Most matches	57	G.J. Fox, Auckland
Most points	932	G.J. Fox, Auckland
Most tries	53	T.J. Wright, Auckland
Most conversions	233	G.J. Fox, Auckland
Most penalty goals	142	G.J. Fox, Auckland
Most dropped goals	14	R.H. Brown, Taranaki; D. Trevathan, Otago
Most goals from a mark	3	J.H. Dufty, Auckland
Most points in a match	40	J.J. Kirwan, Auckland v North Otago, 1993
Most tries in a match	8	J.J. Kirwan, Auckland v North Otago, 1993
Most conversions in a match	12	B.M. Craies, Auckland v Horowhenua, 1986; G.J. Fox, Auckland v Nelson Bays, 1991; G.W. Jackson, Waikato v West Coast, 2000; L.H. Munro, Auckland v North Otago, 2008
Most penalty goals in a match	7	R.M. Deans, Canterbury v Counties, 1984 C.J. McIntyre, Canterbury v Wellington, 2003
Most dropped goals in a match	3	R.H. Brown, Taranaki v Wanganui, 1964; R.H. Brown, Taranaki v North Auckland, 1964; G.P. Coffey, Canterbury v Auckland, 1990; A.P. Mehrtens, Canterbury v Southland, 1995

SUCCESSFUL CHALLENGES

Auckland	15	Otago	6	Marlborough	1
Canterbury	15	Hawke's Bay	5	Manawatu	1
Waikato	11	Northland	4	Bay of Plenty	1
Wellington	10	Wairarapa	3	North Harbour	1
Southland	7	South Canterbury	2	Counties Manukau	1
Taranaki	6	Manawhenua	1		

Auckland were also the first holders, presented the Shield by the NZRFU in 1902 for having the best record that year.

TENURES

Longest tenure	Challenges resisted		Shortest tenure		Days
Auckland	1985–93	61	Hawke's Bay	2013	6
Auckland	1960–63	25	Wellington	1963	7
Canterbury	1982–85	25	Waikato	2007	7
Hawke's Bay	1922–27	24	Otago	2013	9
Auckland	1905–13	23	Auckland	1972	10
Canterbury	1953–56	23	North Auckland	1960	11
Canterbury	2000–03	23	Wairarapa	1950	14
Hawke's Bay	1966–69	21	South Canterbury	1950	14
Waikato	1997–00	21	Auckland	1952	14

North Auckland resisted one challenge;
the other unions were defeated by the first challenger.

HAPPENINGS

The 25th Annual National Deaf Rugby Championship was held over the Easter weekend at Linfield Park, Christchurch, and won by Southern Zone. Results:

>**Southern Zone 36** (Phillip King 2, Ashley Bensley 2, Murray Spears, Henry Tangiwai-Scott tries; Herbie Agnew 3 conversions) defeated **Central Zone 0**.
>
>**Southern Zone 24** (Brett Harborne 2, Ashley Bensley, Darren Popata tries; Agnew 2 conversions) defeated **Northern Zone 12** (James Copeland, Wiremu Ellis tries; Copeland conversion).
>
>**Central Zone 31** (Matt Hollis 2, Darryl Alexander, Theo Waterhouse, Henry Schuster tries; Alexander 3 conversions) defeated **Northern Zone 29** (Kupa Parker 2, Tama Albert, Tutu Timiiti tries; James Copeland 3 conversions and penalty goal).
>
>There were no fixtures for the national team as a proposed visit by Argentina Deaf was postponed until 2019.

• • •

The Sharks scored 100 points in the two Super games played in New Zealand, defeating Blues 63—40 at Albany before losing to the Hurricanes 38—37 at Napier. The Sharks points came from 10 tries, 10 conversions and 10 penalty goals.

• • •

On 31 March Robert du Preez of the Sharks scored 38 points (1t, 6c, 7p) in their Super Rugby match against the Blues on Eden Park. This is the most points scored by any player in a first-class match on Eden Park.

• • •

On 28 April both the Reds at Brisbane and the Highlanders at Pretoria had three Smiths in their match day 23. In both matches two of the Smiths scored tries: Jean-Pierre Smith and George Smith for the Reds v Lions and Aaron Smith and Fletcher Smith for the Highlanders v Bulls.

• • •

All Blacks were among families of a number of top performing athletes at the Commonwealth Games. Bob O'Dea (1953/54) was grandfather of Ben and Sam O'Dea, bronze medallists in Beach Volleyball. Hud Rickit (1981) is the father of Te Paea Selby Rickit, fourth placed in netball. Reagan King (2002) is the brother of Joelle King, double gold medallist and bronze for squash. Kawhena Woodman (1984), father of Portia Woodman, gold medallist in Sevens. Sonny Bill Williams (2010—18), brother of Niall Williams, gold medallist in Sevens.

• • •

When the Chiefs defeated the Highlanders 45—22 in Suva, the Chiefs led 42—0 at halftime. Thus 64 points and all 10 tries were scored at the one end of the field.

• • •

The 36 points scored by former Otago and Highlanders player Hayden Parker for the Sunwolves against the Reds is the fourth highest score by a player in Super Rugby.

• • •

• • •

Brothers Samuel and Luke Whitelock became the first pair of brothers to captain the All Blacks. Samuel captained for four tests: the first three against France and the second test against Argentina in Buenos Aires. Luke captained for the test against Japan. All five tests were won.

• • •

Brothers Beauden and Jordie Barrett became the 13th and 14th players to score four tries for the All Blacks in a test match. Beauden was the first All Black to score four tries against Australia and first All Black to score four tries on Eden Park. Jordie was the first All Black to score four tries against Italy and the first All Black to score four tries in Rome.

• • •

Working overtime. Not so long ago the game of rugby stopped for halftime at 40 minutes and full-time at 80 minutes. If that had still been the case, Jordie Barrett would only have scored two tries against Italy because his second try was scored at 41 minutes 56 seconds in the first half and his fourth try was scored at 82 minutes 16 seconds in the second half.

• • •

Some may have thought Beauden Barrett performed below his high standard of recent years; however, he continues to set records. He was the top points-scorer in international rugby 2018 and just the second player and first All Black to be top points-scorer in consecutive years since professionalism. He kicked the most conversions in test match rugby for the third consecutive year. He is the only first five-eighth to score four tries in a test match. He has now scored a record 25 tries as the most in history by a first five-eighth. Barrett has scored 23 tries in the last three years. Current World Rugby Player of the Year Johnny Sexton hasn't scored any tries in the last three years. He scored six tries against Australia this year which gives him 10 against Australia in his career. His 30 points scored on Eden Park was the most by any player in a test match against Australia. Barrett's teams continue to average better than five tries per test.

• • •

Much has been made of New Zealand spreading their rugby knowledge through playing, captaining and coaching overseas. The reverse is also true. Tyler Ardron (31 caps for Canada) captained Bay of Plenty, and Tony Lamborn (18 caps for USA) captained Southland in the Mitre 10 competition 2018.

• • •

Mrs Christine Wilson, who died in Christchurch on 26 May 2018, had a unique position in All Blacks rugby history, as both the sister of two All Blacks and the mother of two All Blacks. Her younger brothers, Stephen and Graeme Bachop, were All Blacks. In Stephen's case in 1992—94 when he played 18 games and five tests and Graeme's in 1987—95 (54 games and 31 tests). Stephen also played international rugby for Samoa and Graeme for Japan. The two brothers were on opposite sides at the 1999 World Cup in Wales. Mrs Wilson's sons, Aaron and Nathan Mauger, were also All Blacks, with Aaron playing 46 games and 45 tests 2001—07 and Nathan two games in 2001.

• • •

Jon Elrick, a prolific scorer in a 15-season career with Takapuna in North Harbour's premier club competition, probably set a national record during the 2018 season. The former Harbour and Northland representative five-eighths, having missed a number of games, scored what was for him a moderate tally of 84 points in 2018. But that was enough for him to claim what is believed to be a record for club rugby in a Mitre 10 Cup provincial union. Elrick now has an overall aggregate in club rugby of 2363 points, placing him ahead of the 2332 points Colin Williamson compiled in a lengthy club career in Christchurch in the 1980s—90s. Whether Elrick adds to his tally might be in doubt as he is now in his mid-30s.

• • •

In previous editions we have reported on the progress of Kelly Graham's playing record for the Otane Sports club first team in Hawke's Bay, having made his debut in 1992. In the last edition we mentioned that the final match of the 2017 season was his 450th consecutive match from that 1992 debut. In 2018, his 27th season, in which he turned 44 years old, he played the first five matches and decided to stand aside temporarily to allow other members of the squad match play, with the club having good playing numbers this year. This brought his phenomenal streak to end at 455 consecutive matches. During the season he played in 15 of the first team's 19 matches. But, as well as his playing record on the field, his off-field work for the club has been just as impressive. He is currently club president, chairman, captain, and treasurer, and been in all four roles for several years, and was rewarded with life membership more than 10 years ago. A truly remarkable contribution to the Otane Sports club by Kelly Graham.

• • •

For the first time, players appeared in first-class rugby who were born in the 2000s.
Born on 24 March 2000, at Stoke-on-Trent, England, Thomas Furnival played for North Otago in their opening Heartland match against Buller on 25 August. It was his only match of the year for North Otago. Born on 27 January 2000, at Eua Island, Tonga, Tupou Vaai debuted for Taranaki against Auckland on 22 September and made two further appearances.

• • •

For the second consecutive year Southland were winless in the Mitre 10 Cup, having now suffered 21 consecutive defeats in the competition. In the top tier of the National Championship (Division One, ANZ Cup, ITM Cup, M10 Cup), the following runs of 15 or more consecutive defeats have been recorded:

30	Northland 2003—04—05—06
21	Southland 2016—17—18
19	Southland 1990, 1995, 1997
19	Northland 2014—15—16
18	Northland 1992, 1998—99
15	Hawke's Bay 1992—93, 2006

• • •

North Harbour hooker James Parsons had a memorable match when North Harbour visited Hawke's Bay at McLean Park, Napier on 22 September.
It was his 100th match for North Harbour. He scored two tries. He kicked his first goal in first-class rugby when he kicked the conversion to Harrison Groundwater's 79th-minute try. He was unwittingly involved in North Harbour then playing out the remainder of the game with 16 men. While he was preparing the conversion attempt, North Harbour sent on reserve hooker Luteru Tolai as his replacement. After Parsons had kicked the conversion, he ran back to his side of halfway for the restart, unaware that Tolai was on the field and that he (Parsons) ought to have retired to the bench. Somehow the sideline officials had not ensured Parsons' coming-off.

• • •

Terry Smith, who died in Sydney aged 81 on 30 August, was an experienced journalist who made many visits to New Zealand on Wallabies tours and with the New South Wales state side, especially in the 1980s and 90s. Smith, who was on the staff of several Sydney-based newspapers in a career spanning more than 50 years, also covered cricket, golf and boxing.

• • •

Talent emerging in the teenage national squads during the year included several who are closely related to well-known players, past and present. The NZ Under 20 squad had Caleb Clarke (son of Eroni), Hoskins Sotutu (son of Waisake) and Billy Proctor (brother of Matt). The NZ Schools team had Niko Jones (son of Sir Michael). The Barbarians Schools team had Caleb Cavubati (son of Bill), Stewart Cruden (brother of Aaron), Hamdahn Tuipulotu (brother of Patrick), Robert Rush (son of Eric) and Noah Perelini (son of Apollo). The NZ Maori Under 18 team had Ruben Love (son of Matene).

• • •

Six players played their 100th game for a provincial union in 2018. In chronological order they were: Logan Mundy (Buller), James Parsons (North Harbour), Andrew Stephens (Buller), Matthew Fetu (South Canterbury), Maleli Mudu (West Coast) and Ralph Darling (North Otago). Since the advent of the Mitre 10 Cup and Heartland Championship competitions in 2006, a total of 43 players have reached the milestone of 100 games for a provincial union. Only eight of those 43 played their first 100 games from 2006 or after, the other 35 players starting their provincial careers before 2006 and reaching their 100th game in 2006 or after. Or put another way, in the 13 seasons of the Mitre 10 Cup and Heartland Championship, just eight players have played their first 100 games for a union.
The eight in chronological order are:

Josh Bekhuis	Southland (first 2006, 100th 2014)
Rob Foreman	Manawatu (first 2006, 100th 2014)
Robbie Malneek	Tasman (first 2006, 100th 2015)
Culum Retallick	Bay of Plenty (first 2007, 100th 2016)
Cole Baldwin	Wanganui (first 2006, 100th 2017)
James Parsons	North Harbour (first 2007, 100th 2018)
Andrew Stephens	Buller (first 2007, 100th 2018)
Ralph Darling	North Otago (first 2007, 100th 2018)

At the current rates noted above, a Mitre 10 Cup player will have to play at least nine seasons to reach 100 games, while a Heartland Championship player will have to play at least 12 seasons to reach 100 games.

• • •

Black Ferns Sevens captain Sarah Goss was on the road towards success as a fast and clean competitive shearer until rugby intervened. Shearing was in the family and Sarah started when aged seven and by the time she was 12 she could shear 200 in a day. Her best day shearing lambs is 311 in eight hours.
Competing at the prestigious annual Golden Shears competition at Masterton in 2007 the 14-year-old was runner-up in the novice class and later second place in the junior grade and, in 2012, third in the intermediate grade. She won the junior title at the 2010 Royal Easter Show at Auckland. At the 2012 NZ shearing championships, at Te Kuiti, she was runner-up in the

invitation class. In 2013 Goss, aged 20, won the invitation charity event at the Golden Shears and returned there the following year to defend her title. But she had no time to prepare.

During February 2014, Sarah Goss was in America with the Black Ferns Sevens team playing at tournaments at Atlanta and Sao Paulo. After a long flight from Buenos Aires she landed at Auckland airport at 1 am then, after a few hours break, another flight saw her land at Palmerston North at 9 am. Then a drive home to Kimbolton, collect her shearing gear, and drive down to Masterton where she took the stand in the evening, shearing five sheep in 9 min 33.918 sec to finish in fifth place. She was the first woman to compete in three Golden Shears finals.

Sarah's competitive nature comes from her parents. Father Alan was Golden Shears intermediate champion in 1985 while mother Ronnie won the 2008 open wool handling class. At the 2014 world shearing and wool handling championships, held in Ireland, Ronnie finished second.

• • •

The 2018 ASB Rugby Awards were held at Sky City Convention Centre, Auckland, on 13 December. The winners are recorded elsewhere in this publication, but we record here the finalists for some of the awards (winner in bold).

- Sky Television Fans Try of the Year: Kelly Brazier (Black Ferns Sevens), **Chris Hala'ufia** (St Peter's College), Richie Mo'unga (Crusaders).
- Charles Monro Rugby Volunteer of the Year: **Irene Eruera-Taiapa** (Horowhenua Kapiti), Steve Webling (Taranaki), Kim Wheeler (King Country).
- New Zealand Rugby Referee of the Year: **Glen Jackson**, Richard Kelly, Rebecca Mahoney.
- New Zealand Rugby Age Grade Player of the Year: Sam Darry (Canterbury), **Tom Christie** (Canterbury), Risaleaana Pori-Lane (Tasman), Kaleb Trask (Bay of Plenty).
- Mitre 10 Heartland Championship Player of the Year: Craig Clare (Wanganui), **Brett Ranga** (Thames Valley), Willie Wright (South Canterbury).
- Richard Crawshaw Memorial All Blacks Sevens Player of the Year: **Scott Curry**, Vilimoni Koroi, Regan Ware.
- Black Ferns Sevens Player of the Year: **Michaela Blyde**, Kelly Brazier, Sarah Goss.
- Duane Monkley Medal: TJ Faiane (Auckland), **Luke Romano** (Canterbury), Fletcher Smith (Waikato).
- Fiao'o Faamausili Medal: **Kendra Cocksedge** (Canterbury), Krysten Cottrell (Hawke's Bay), Jackie Patea-Fereti (Wellington).
- Investec Super Rugby Player of the Year: Solomon Alaimalo (Chiefs), **Richie Mo'unga** (Crusaders), Matt Todd (Crusaders).
- Tom French Memorial Maori Player of the Year: Sarah Goss, Rieko Ioane, **Codie Taylor.**
- ASB National Coach of the Year: **Alama Ieremia** (Auckland), Kieran Kite (Canterbury Women), Scott Robertson (Crusaders).
- ASB New Zealand Coach of the Year: Allan Bunting (Black Ferns Sevens), Steve Hansen (All Blacks), **Clark Laidlaw** (All Blacks Sevens).
- New Zealand Rugby Women's Player of the Year: **Kendra Cocksedge**, Aroha Savage, Selica Winiata.
- Kelvin R Tremain Memorial Player of the Year: **Kendra Cocksedge**, Richie Mo'unga, Brodie Retallick, Codie Taylor.
- adidas National Team of the Year: Auckland, **Crusaders**, Thames Valley.
- adidas New Zealand Team of the Year: All Blacks, All Blacks Sevens, **Black Ferns Sevens**.

2018 SEASON'S STATISTICS

LEADING SCORERS IN ALL FIRST-CLASS MATCHES IN NEW ZEALAND AND FOR NEW ZEALAND TEAMS OVERSEAS

(Record: 519, G.J. Fox, 1989 in 32 games, 2 Tries, 122 Con, 88 PG, 1 DG)

	Teams	M	Tries	Con	PG	DG	Total
B.J. Barrett	Hurricanes/New Zealand	27	14	61	18	2	252
D.S. McKenzie	Chiefs/New Zealand	26	13	49	23	–	232
H.R.J. Plummer	NZ Under 20/Auckland	20	7	70	16	–	223
R. Mo'unga	Crusaders/New Zealand	21	5	57	21	–	202
M.J. Hunt	Crusaders/Tasman	31	7	56	15	–	190
L.Z. Sopoaga	Highlanders	18	4	41	21	–	171
B.E.C. Gatland	Blues/North Harbour	21	4	36	22	–	158
F.H. Smith	Highlanders/Waikato	18	4	56	6	–	150
J.R. Ioane	Highlanders/Otago/NZ Maori	22	5	35	12	–	131
C.D. Clare	Wanganui/NZ Heartland	11	7	34	8	–	127
B.D. Cameron	Crusaders/Canterbury/New Zealand	14	1	37	14	–	121
J.S. So'oialo	Horowhenua Kapiti	10	3	23	19	–	118
M.B. Lam	Hurricanes/Wellington	27	22	–	–	–	110
G.C. Bridge	Crusaders/Canterbury/New Zealand	30	22	–	–	–	110
W.A. Wright	South Canterbury/NZ Heartland	11	8	27	5	–	109
R.E. Ioane	Blues/New Zealand	26	21	–	–	–	105
J.M. Debreczeni	Northland/UK Barbarians	12	2	30	10	–	100

LEADING TRY-SCORERS

(Record: 36, J.J. Kirwan, 1987 in 32 games)

Tries	Games		Teams
22	27	M.B. Lam	Hurricanes/Wellington
22	30	G.C. Bridge	Crusaders/Canterbury/New Zealand
21	26	R.E. Ioane	Blues/New Zealand
16	24	K.H. Laumape	Hurricanes/New Zealand/Manawatu
14	24	T. Li	Highlanders/North Harbour
14	31	A.L. Ioane	Blues/Auckland/NZ Maori
14	11	S.L. Reece	Waikato
14	24	W.R. Naholo	Highlanders/New Zealand
14	27	B.J. Barrett	Hurricanes/New Zealand
13	26	D.S. McKenzie	Chiefs/New Zealand
12	21	M.M.B.T. Mataele	Crusaders/Taranaki
12	26	S. Alaimalo	Chiefs/Tasman
10	19	S.F. Taukei'aho	Chiefs/Waikato
10	16	T.P. Manu	Blues/Auckland
10	23	J.M. Barrett	Hurricanes/New Zealand

THREE (or more) TRIES IN A MATCH
(Record: 8, T.R. Heeps, New Zealand v Northern NSW, 1962;
J.J. Kirwan, Auckland v North Otago, 1993)

5	S. Malatai	Wairarapa Bush v Buller
4	M.B. Lam	Hurricanes v Rebels
4	K.H. Laumape	Hurricanes v Blues, 7 July
4	B.J. Barrett	New Zealand v Australia, 25 August
4	T. Li	North Harbour v Taranaki
4	R.J. Stanton	West Coast v Ngati Porou East Coast
4	S.L. Reece	Waikato v Northland, 20 October
4	J.M. Barrett	New Zealand v Italy
3	S.M. Frizell	Highlanders v Blues, 20 April
3	M.B. Lam	Hurricanes v Lions
3	J.W. Spowart	New Zealand Under 20 v Japan Under 20
3	A.H. Tauatevalu	Poverty Bay v Ngati Porou East Coast, 2 June
3	R.E. Ioane	New Zealand v France, 23 June
3	R. Hodge	Rebels v Highlanders
3	G.C. Bridge	Crusaders v Blues, 14 July
3	L.M. Vaeno	Taranaki v Poverty Bay
3	D.R. Church	King Country v Ngati Porou East Coast
3	D.G. Barnett	King Country v Ngati Porou East Coast
3	M.B. Lam	Wellington v Southland
3	D.R. Church	King Country v Buller
3	S.L. Reece	Waikato v Wellington
3	P.T. Tuipulotu	Auckland v Tasman
3	B.D. Tunnicliffe	South Canterbury v Ngati Porou East Coast
3	N.J.C. Strachan	South Canterbury v Ngati Porou East Coast
3	M.J. Scott	Otago v Southland
3	T. Faiane	Auckland v Canterbury, 16 September
3	M.A. Faddes	Otago v Auckland
3	A.M. Thrupp	King Country v Poverty Bay
3	W.T. Jordan	Tasman v Otago
3	T.B. Matoramusha	Mid Canterbury v King Country
3	A.J. Bradley	NZ Heartland v Vanua XV
3	K.H. Laumape	New Zealand v Japan
3	M.R. Karpik	NZ Maori v Chile
3	D.S. McKenzie	New Zealand v Italy

21 (or more) POINTS IN A MATCH
(Record: 45, S.D. Culhane, New Zealand v Japan, 1995, 1 try, 20 conversions)

38	R. Du Preez	Sharks v Blues, 1t, 6c, 7pg
30	B.J. Barrett	New Zealand v Australia, 25 August, 4t, 5c
29	R. Hodge	Rebels v Highlanders, 3t, 4c, 2pg
28	W.A. Wright	South Canterbury v King Country, 1t, 7c, 3pg
26	D.S. McKenzie	Chiefs v Sunwolves, 2t, 8c
25	R. Mo'unga	Crusaders v Highlanders, 6 July, 1t, 4c, 4pg
25	E.H. Reihana	King Country v Ngati Porou East Coast, 1t, 7c, 2pg

25	S. Malatai	Wairarapa Bush v Buller, 5t
25	J.R. Ioane	Otago v Bay of Plenty, 2t, 6c, 1pg
24	D.S. McKenzie	New Zealand v France, 23 June, 2t, 7c
22	M.J. Hunt	Crusaders v French Barbarians, 2t, 6c
22	J.S. So'oialo	Horowhenua Kapiti v Thames Valley, 1t, 1c, 5pg
22	R. Mo'unga	New Zealand v Japan, 1t, 7c, 1pg
21	H.R.J. Plummer	New Zealand Under 20 v Tonga Under 20, 1t, 8c
21	B.R.T. Waaka	Taranaki v Manawatu, 1t, 5c, 2pg
21	B.R.T. Waaka	Taranaki v Counties Manukau, 2t, 1c, 3pg
21	M.J. Hunt	Tasman v Taranaki, 1t, 5c, 2pg
21	G.M. Walters	Wairarapa Bush v Buller, 1t, 8c

SIX (or more) CONVERSIONS IN A MATCH
(Record: 20, J.P. Preston, Canterbury v West Coast, 1992;
S.D. Culhane, New Zealand v Japan, 1995)

8	D.S. McKenzie	Chiefs v Sunwolves
8	H.R.J. Plummer	New Zealand Under 20 v Tonga Under 20
8	G.M. Walters	Wairarapa Bush v Buller
8	E.H. Reihana	King Country v Poverty Bay
7	D.S. McKenzie	New Zealand v France, 23 June
7	D.S. Waite	Taranaki v Poverty Bay
7	E.H. Reihana	King Country v Ngati Porou East Coast
7	F.H. Smith	Waikato v Bay of Plenty
7	N.J. McCloy	Mid Canterbury v Ngati Porou East Coast
7	B.D. Cameron	Canterbury v Hawke's Bay
7	C.D. Clare	Wanganui v Ngati Porou East Coast
7	F.H. Smith	Waikato v Northland, 6 October
7	W.A. Wright	South Canterbury v King Country
7	R. Mo'unga	New Zealand v Japan
7	O.W. Black	NZ Maori v Chile
6	R. Du Preez	Sharks v Blues
6	K.R. Trask	New Zealand Under 20 v Japan Under 20
6	D.S. McKenzie	Chiefs v Highlanders, 30 June
6	J.M. Barrett	Hurricanes v Blues, 7 July
6	J.R. Ioane	Otago v Manawatu
6	D.A. Dorgan	South Canterbury v Horowhenua Kapiti
6	F.H. Smith	Waikato v Hawke's Bay
6	W.A. Wright	South Canterbury v Ngati Porou East Coast
6	B.D. Cameron	Canterbury v Otago
6	C.D. Clare	Wanganui v Buller
6	F.H. Smith	Waikato v Southland
6	J.R. Ioane	Otago v Bay of Plenty
6	M.J. Hunt	Tasman v Otago
6	F.H. Smith	Waikato v Northland, 20 October
6	J.J. Lash	NZ Heartland v Vanua XV

SIX (or more) PENALTY GOALS IN A MATCH
*(Record: 9, A.P. Mehrtens, New Zealand v Australia, at Auckland, 1999;
A.P. Mehrtens, New Zealand v France, at Paris, 2000;
B.J. Barrett, Taranaki v Bay of Plenty, 2011)*

7	R. Du Preez	Sharks v Blues

TWO (or more) DROPPED GOALS IN A MATCH
(Record: 5, M.K. Sisam, Hawke's Bay v East Coast, 1979)

No player drop kicked more than one goal in a match in 2018

SCORED IN ALL FOUR WAYS
No player scored all four ways in a match in 2018

CURRENT PLAYER STATISTICS

CAREER RECORDS OF PLAYERS APPEARING IN FIRST-CLASS RUGBY IN NEW ZEALAND, 2018

100 GAMES OF FIRST-CLASS RUGBY

W.W.V. Crockett	366	P. Manu	165	S. Tamanivalu	122		
L.J. Messam	327	L.J. Coltman	164	M.D. Drummond	122		
K.J. Read	313	B.C.F. Funnell	162	M.P. Proctor	122		
J. Kaino	295	J.M.R.A. Hoeata	162	D.S. McKenzie	121		
O.T. Franks	271	P.J. Beveridge	157	A.R. Lienert-Brown	116		
B.R. Smith	266	S.T. Ngatu	156	A.P. Stephens	115		
C.C. King	265	D.W.H. Sweeney	153	S.B. Williams	115		
S.L. Whitelock	264	C.J. Ngatai	161	G.O. Evans	114		
R.J. Crotty	259	J.L. To'omaga-Allen	152	M. Fetu	114		
A.L. Smith	257	A.W. Pulu	151	T.G. Perry	114		
D.S. Coles	244	A.S. Savea	150	S.J. Tupou	114		
I.J.A. Dagg	233	T.S.G. Franklin	149	R.K. Darling	113		
B. May	223	S.J. Taufua	149	N.E. Laulala	113		
B.J. Barrett	220	B.D. Hall	148	T.J. Smith	111		
T.D. Latimer	220	C.I. Eves	147	S.K. Barrett	110		
M.B. Todd	218	A.O.H.M. Tu'ungafasi	146	B.N. Thomson	109		
S.J. Savea	212	A.W.F. Ta'avao-Matau	145	R. Mo'unga	109		
A.L. Dixon	200	R.T. Malneek	144	L.M. Mundy	108		
J.W. Parsons	200	S.M.J. Prattley	142	D.K. Havili	107		
T.T.R. Perenara	193	A.N. Ainley	140	L.I.J. Squire	107		
S.J. Cane	192	J.P.T. Moody	140	A.L. Ioane	105		
B.A. Retallick	189	C.J.D. Taylor	139	D.J. Pryor	105		
L. Romano	187	I.T. West	139	C.D. Clare	104		
L.C. Whitelock	179	W.R. Naholo	137	M.R. McKenzie	104		
E.C. Dixon	176	B.M. Weber	135	L. Masoe	104		
B.D.F. Shields	176	D.J. Bird	134	P.T. Tuipulotu	103		
L.G. Brownlee	174	R.J. Buckman	133	R. Thompson	103		
T.R. Waldron	174	G. Moala	133	M.T. Mudu	102		
R.M.N. Ranger	172	M.P. Delany	132	N.P. Harris	101		
T.E.S. Bateman	171	T. Li	124	A.Seiuli	100		
L.Z. Sopoga	171						

500 POINTS IN FIRST-CLASS RUGBY

B.J. Barrett	1934	D.S. McKenzie	910	M.R. McKenzie	570
L.Z. Sopoaga	1544	M.P. Delaney	824	O.W. Black	508
I.T. West	1121	S.J. Savea	605	I.J.A. Dagg	500
R. Mo'unga	915	J.J. Lash	573		

50 TRIES IN FIRST-CLASS RUGBY

S.J. Savea	121	B.J. Barrett	72	G. Moala	55
W.R. Naholo	86	T. Li	65	C.J. Ngatai	51
B.R. Smith	82	T.T.R. Perenara	65	S. Tamanivalu	50
I.J.A. Dagg	77	K.J. Read	62	A.L. Smith	50
L.J. Messam	76	R.E. Ioane	58	R.S. Crotty	50

FIRST-CLASS STATISTICS
to January 1, 2019

250 GAMES OF FIRST-CLASS RUGBY

K.F. Mealamu	2000-15	384	C.J. Spencer	1992-2005	273
W.W.V. Crockett	2005-18	366	J.A. Collins	1994-2010	273
C.E. Meads	1955-74	361	O.T. Franks	2007-18	271
S.B.T. Fitzpatrick	1983-97	346	M.J.A. Cooper	1985-99	270
R.H. McCaw	2000-15	334	D.E. Holwell	1995-2010	270
T.D. Woodcock	2000-15	331	J.M. Muliaina	1999-2014	270
M.A. Nonu	2002-15	330	B.G. Williams	1968-84	269
J.F. Umaga	1994-2011	329	K.R. Tremain	1957-72	268
A.M. Haden	1971-86	327	J.J. Kirwan	1983-94	267
L.J. Messam	2003-18	327	A.M. Ellis	2004-16	266
Q.J. Cowan	2000-16	326	L.R. MacDonald	1994-2009	266
R.W. Loe	1980-97	321	B.R. Smith	2007-18	266
G.W. Whetton	1979-95	313	C.G. Smith	2003-15	265
K.J. Read	2005-18	313	C.C. King	2002-18	265
Z.V. Brooke	1985-97	311	S.L. Whitelock	2008-18	264
A.K. Hore	1999-2016	311	G.L. Slater	1991-2005	262
W.F. McCormick	1958-78	310	R.D. Thorne	1996-2	262
C.S. Ralph	1996-2008	306	H.T.P. Elliot	2005-17	261
G.J. Fox	1982-95	303	K.J. Crowley	1980-94	260
A.D. Oliver	1993-2007	298	T.J. Blackadder	1990-2001	260
N.J. Hewitt	1988-2001	296	C.H. Hoeft	1993-2005	260
J. Kaino	2003-18	295	I.A. Eliason	1964-82	259
S.C. McDowall	1982-98	294	E. Clarke	1990-2005	259
R.M. Brooke	1987-2001	289	R.S. Crotty	2008-18	259
C.R. Flynn	2001-17	289	S.J. Bachop	1986-99	257
D.W. Carter	2002-15	287	C.S. Jane	2003-17	257
I.D. Jones	1988-2000	287	A.L. Smith	2008-18	257
I.A. Kirkpatrick	1966-79	285	G.A. Knight	1972-86	254
J.W. Marshall	1992-2005	284	G.M. Somerville	1997-2008	254
P.A.T. Weepu	2003-17	284	I.J. Clarke	1951-63	253
W.K. Little	1988-2000	283	S.M. Going	1962-78	251
A.P. Mehrtens	1993-2005	282	C.R. Jack	1998-11	250
A.J. Wyllie	1964-80	279	B.J. Robertson	1971-84	250
A.M. Stone	1980-94	275			

1000 POINTS IN FIRST-CLASS RUGBY

	Career	Games	Tries	Con	PG	DG/Mark	Points
G.J. Fox	1982–95	303	29	901	683	47	4112
D.W. Carter	2002–2015	287	78	649	646	19	3683
A.P. Mehrtens	1993–2005	282	40	556	572	54	3190
M.J.A. Cooper	1985–99	270	79	475	420	2	2577
K.J. Crowley	1980–94	260	86	375	376	9	2261
G.J.L Cooper	1984–96	188	60	385	388	14	2221
D.E. Holwell	1995–2010	270	39	451	366	2	2201
W.B. Johnston	1986–2001	220	29	421	396	5	2179
R.M. Deans	1979–90	187	45	390	370	1	2073
W.F. McCormick	1958–78	310	57	457	314	9	2065
T.E. Brown	1995–2011	211	29	345	373	14	1996
B.J. Barrett	2010-18	220	72	382	267	3	1934
A.R. Cashmore	1992–2005	185	64	351	290	2	1898
C.J. Spencer	1992–2005	273	101	329	222	11	1860
D.B. Clarke	1951–64	226	22	365	318	28/3	1851
S.R. Donald	2001–17	241	68	337	273	2	1839
S.D. Culhane	1988–99	155	20	292	312	19	1671
J.B. Cunningham	1990–98	136	52	316	226	1	1569
B.A. Blair	1999–2006	148	59	302	221	–	1562
L.Z. Sopoaga	2010-18	171	26	299	267	5	1544
A.W. Cruden	2008–17	201	33	245	267	2	1462
G.W. Jackson	1996–2004	175	41	267	215	8	1408
D.W. Hill	1997–2006	177	30	279	230	1	1401
A.R. Hewson	1973–88	154	19	247	229	17	1308
J.P. Preston	1987–98	171	21	242	231	–	1281
M. Williment	1958–68	121	17	296	188	16	1255
F.M. Botica	1985–2001	149	37	262	171	7	1213
L.W. Mains	1967–76	142	13	213	227	13	1193
E.J. Crossan	1987–96	91	29	189	220	–	1157
G.D. Rowlands	1969–82	179	41	198	186	15	1151
C.L. McAlister	2002–11	151	19	205	207	1	1129
I.T. West	2012–18	139	26	224	179	2	1121
J.W. Wilson	1992–2002	233	151	76	68	4	1123
W.J. Burton	1990–96	93	10	215	204	5	1099
J.A. Gallagher	1984–90	139	67	196	144	1	1095
J.A. Gopperth	2002–09	125	27	228	167	2	1094
B.J.W. Fairbrother	1981–92	118	20	132	183	61	1076
R.B. Barrell	1963–79	147	20	125	225	10	1030
D.P. Lilley	1993–2003	162	41	139	176	6	1029
G.W. Anscombe	2010–14	83	27	163	182	1	1010

100 TRIES IN FIRST-CLASS RUGBY

	Games	Tries		Games	Tries
J.J. Kirwan	267	199	I.A. Kirkpatrick	285	114
T.J. Wright	217	177	N.R. Berryman	188	114
D.C. Howlett	240	173	J. Vidiri	154	112
B.G. Fraser	201	171	E. Clarke	259	111
C.M. Cullen	233	164	C.I. Green	159	111
Z.V. Brooke	311	161	J.T. Rokocoko	214	111
J.F. Umaga	329	156	H.E. Gear	228	111
J.W. Wilson	233	151	G.B. Batty	142	109
R.A. Jarden	134	145	B.R. Ford	196	109
R.Q. Randle	188	141	J.K.R. Timu	182	108
B.G. Williams	269	137	R.L. Gear	197	108
K.R. Tremain	268	136	T.W. Mitchell	155	106
P.J. Cooke	192	134	S.S. Wilson	202	106
C.S. Ralph	306	133	E.J. Rush	196	104
J.T. Lomu	203	126	B.W. Smith	146	102
S.W. Sivivatu	191	125	R.M. Smith	152	102
M. Clamp	141	123	A.R. Sutherland	208	102
S.J. Savea	545	121	P. Bale	129	101
A.E. Cooke	131	119	C.J. Spencer	273	101
M.A. Nonu	330	117			

MOST DROPPED GOALS IN FIRST-CLASS RUGBY

B.J.W. Fairbrother	61	M.A. Herewini	47	P. Martin	34
A.P. Mehrtens	54	R.J. Preston	39	B.J. McKechnie	33
M.B. Roulston	49	J.W. Boe	37	E.J. Dunn	32
G.J. Fox	47	R.H. Brown	35	D. Trevathan	31

MOST POINTS IN A FIRST-CLASS MATCH

	Match	Tries	Con	PG	DG	Total
S.D. Culhane	New Zealand v Japan, 1995	1	20	–	–	45
J.P. Preston	Canterbury v West Coast, 1992	1	20	–	–	44
R.M. Deans	New Zealand v South Australia, 1984	3	14	1	–	43
A.R. Cashmore	Auckland v Mid Canterbury, 1995	5	9	–	–	43
J.F. Karam	New Zealand v South Australia, 1974	2	15	1	–	41
J.J. Kirwan	Auckland v North Otago, 1993	8	–	–	–	40
P.W. Turner	Otago v East Coast, 1986	2	14	1	–	39
J.W. Wilson	New Zealand Colts v Thames Valley, 1993	4	5	3	–	39
D.J. Kellett	Western Samoa v Marlborough, 1993	3	12	–	–	39
R.A. Jarden	New Zealand v Central West (Aust), 1951	6	10	–	–	38
D.E. Holwell	Northland v Thames Valley, 1997	2	14	–	–	38
B.A. Blair	New Zealand v Ireland A, 2001	3	4	5	–	38
R.J. du Preez	Sharks v Blues 2018	1	6	7	–	38
J.L. Graham	Counties v East Coast, 1972	–	14	3	–	37
S.D. Culhane	Southland v Manawatu, 1994	1	1	8	2	37
J.B. Cunningham	Central Vikings v South Canterbury, 1997	3	11	–	–	37
B.A. Blair	Canterbury v Counties Manukau, 1999	3	11	–	–	37

REFEREES
by Chris Jansen

2018 NEW ZEALAND RUGBY NATIONAL REFEREES SQUAD

	Union	Squad Debut	Tests	SR	P	HC	FPC	Sevens	Nat[1]	Prov[2]	RS[3]	Total
N.P. Briant	Bay of Plenty	2009	8	50	55	11	2	29	15	–	10	170
T.M.T. Cottrell	Hawke's Bay	2017	–	–	2	8	2	1	–	1	–	14
J.J. Doleman	Auckland	2014	–	–	13	18	2	21	2	–	1	56
M.I. Fraser	Wellington	2007	6	48	58	17	2	5	17	1	8	154
T.N. Griffiths	Manawatu	2016	–	–	2	14	1	–	–	–	–	17
N.E.R. Hogan	Wellington	2017	–	–	2	8	4	2	–	–	–	16
G.W. Jackson	Bay of Plenty	2010	30	77	53	8	–	–	7	1	6	176
R.P. Kelly	Taranaki	2009	–	–	43	15	1	53	4	3	2	119
M.G. Lash	Tasman	2013	–	–	23	10	–	2	7	–	2	42
A.W.B. Mabey	Auckland	2014	–	–	19	16	1	–	2	–	1	38
D.J. Macpherson	Poverty Bay	2018	–	–	–	2	1	1	–	1	–	5
J.D. Munro	Canterbury	2011	–	–	5	12	2	2	1	–	1	22
J.R. Nutbrown	Canterbury	2014	–	13	20	6	1	–	9	–	2	49
Dr. B.D. O'Keeffe	Wellington	2012	13	36	41	6	1	1	1	7	6	106
B.E. Pickerill	North Harbour	2012	4	18	37	8	1	3	10	–	3	81
H.G. Reed	Hawke's Bay	2016	–	–	–	15	1	–	1	–	–	17
C.J. Stone	Taranaki	2012	–	–	15	20	2	2	–	1	–	40
N.J. Webster	North Otago	2016	–	–	2	16	–	–	–	–	–	18
M.C.J. Winter	Waikato	2015	–	–	5	19	1	5	1	–	–	31
P.M. Williams	Taranaki	2014	8	19	26	7	–	3	6	2	2	71

SR   Super Rugby
P   Mitre 10 Cup (total includes former ITM Cup fixtures)
HC   Heartland Championship
FPC   Farah Palmer Cup
[1]NZR appointment — international tour, Ranfurly Shield (non-Mitre 10 Cup), national trial, and women's international.
[2]interprovincial (non-Mitre 10 Cup, non-Heartland Championship, non-Ranfurly Shield)
[3]Ranfurly Shield — also included within N1 or Nat (if a non-Mitre 10 Cup match)

REFEREE APPOINTMENTS 2018

Jamie Bell (Bay of Plenty)

January	13/14		National Sevens	Rotorua
December	15/16		National Sevens	Tauranga

Nick Briant

March	3	SR	Jaguares v Hurricanes	Buenos Aires
	17	SR	Highlanders v Crusaders	Dunedin
	31	SR	Blues v Sharks	Auckland
May	19	SR	Lions v Brumbies	Johannesburg
	26	SR	Stormers v Lions	Cape Town
June	2	SR	Blues v Rebels	Auckland
	16		Japan v Italy	Tokyo
	30	SR	Brumbies v Hurricanes	Canberra
August	16	P	North Harbour v Northland	Albany
	25	HC	Poverty Bay v Wairarapa Bush	Gisborne
	29	P	Counties Manukau v Taranaki	Pukekohe
September	8	FPC	Bay of Plenty v Waikato	Matata
	13	P/RS	Waikato v Hawke's Bay	Hamilton
	22	P	Otago v Canterbury	Dunedin
	29	P	Wellington v Tasman	Wellington

Referees

October	4	P	Wellington v Auckland	Wellington

Stu Catley (Hawke's Bay)

December	15/16		National Sevens	Tauranga

Tipene Cottrell

September	1	HC	Wairarapa Bush v Thames Valley	Masterton
	8	HC	Poverty Bay v Wanganui	Gisborne
	15	HC	South Canterbury v East Coast	Timaru
	29	FPC	Taranaki v Otago	New Plymouth
October	7	P	Southland v Bay of Plenty	Invercargill
	13	P	Bay of Plenty v Northland	Tauranga
December	15/16		National Sevens	Tauranga

James Doleman

January	13/14		National Sevens	Rotorua
	26–28		Australia World Rugby Sevens	Sydney
February	3/4		New Zealand World Rugby Sevens	Hamilton
March	2 – 4		USA World Rugby Sevens	Las Vegas
	10/11		Canada World Rugby Sevens	Vancouver
April	6–8		Hong Kong World Rugby Sevens	Hong Kong
	28–29		Singapore World Rugby Sevens	Singapore
June	2/3		England World Rugby Sevens	London
	9/10		France World Rugby Sevens	Paris
	15		Crusaders v French Barbarians	Christchurch
August	25	P	Canterbury v Wellington	Christchurch
September	1	FPC	Otago v North Harbour	Dunedin
	8	P	Southland v Counties Manukau	Invercargill
	15	HC	North Otago v Horowhenua Kapiti	Oamaru
	22	HC	South Canterbury v Mid Canterbury	Timaru
	30	P	Canterbury v Hawke's Bay	Christchurch
October	6	P	Canterbury v Taranaki	Christchurch
	10	P	Southland v Auckland	Invercargill
	13	FPC s-f	Otago v Hawke's Bay	Dunedin
November	30/1		Dubai World Rugby Sevens	Dubai
December	8–9		South Africa World Rugby Sevens	Cape Town

Mike Fraser

March	10	SR	Jaguares v Waratahs	Buenos Aires
	24	SR	Hurricanes v Highlanders	Wellington
April	20	SR	Waratahs v Lions	Sydney
May	4	SR	Chiefs v Jaguares	Rotorua
	12	SR	Stormers v Chiefs	Cape Town
	19	SR	Sharks v Chiefs	Durban
June	9	PNC	Fiji v Samoa	Suva
	22		Highlanders v French Barbarians	Dunedin
	30	RWCQ	Samoa v Germany	Apia
July	14	SR	Chiefs v Hurricanes	Hamilton
	21	SR q-f	Crusaders v Sharks	Christchurch
August	18	P	Manawatu v Waikato	Palmerston North
	24	P/RS	Taranaki v Manawatu	New Plymouth
September	2	P	Hawke's Bay v Counties Manukau	Napier
	8	HC	East Coast v Wairarapa Bush	Ruatoria
	15	FPC	Manawatu v Bay of Plenty	Palmerston North
	28	P	Auckland v Otago	Auckland

October	6	FPC	Wellington v Taranaki	Porirua
	11	P	Tasman v Hawke's Bay	Nelson
	19	P s-f	Tasman v Canterbury	Nelson

Tim Griffiths

September	1	HC	Buller v King Country	Westport
	8	HC	Horowhenua Kapiti v South Canterbury	Levin
	15	FPC	Wellington v Otago	Porirua
	23	P	Tasman v Counties Manukau	Nelson
	29	P	Taranaki v North Harbour	New Plymouth
October	13	HC	Wanganui v Horowhenua Kapiti	Wanganui

Nick Hogan

January	13/14		National Sevens	Rotorua
August	25	HC	Wanganui v South Canterbury	Wanganui
September	1	HC	East Coast v Horowhenua Kapiti	Ruatoria
	7	P	Auckland v Tasman	Auckland
	15	FPC	Taranaki v Hawke's Bay	New Plymouth
	23	FPC	Tasman v Wellington	Nelson
	26	P	Hawke's Bay v Northland	Napier
October	6	FPC	North Harbour v Waikato	Albany
December	15/16		National Sevens	Tauranga

Glen Jackson

February	16	SR	Lions v Sharks	Johannesburg
	24	6N	Ireland v Wales	Dublin
March	9	SR	Highlanders vs Stormers	Dunedin
	17	SR	Brumbies v Sharks	Canberra
	30	SR	Chiefs v Highlanders	Hamilton
April	21	SR	Sharks v Stormers	Durban
	28	SR	Bulls v Highlanders	Pretoria
May	5	SR	Stormers v Bulls	Cape Town
	19	SR	Blues v Crusaders	Auckland
	26	SR	Chiefs v Waratahs	Hamilton
June	23		South Africa v England	Cape Town
July	14	SR	Highlanders v Rebels	Dunedin
	21	SR q-f	Hurricanes v Chiefs	Wellington
August	18	P	Auckland v Counties Manukau	Auckland
	25	HC	King Country v East Coast	Te Kuiti
September	1	P	North Harbour v Tasman	Albany
	8	RC	Australia v South Africa	Brisbane
	22	P	Taranaki v Auckland	New Plymouth
October	27	P f	Auckland v Canterbury	Auckland
November	10		Italy v Georgia	Florence
	17		France v Argentina	Lille

Richard Kelly

January	13/14		National Sevens	Rotorua
	26–28		Australia World Rugby Sevens	Sydney
February	3/4		New Zealand World Rugby Sevens	Hamilton
March	2–4		USA World Rugby Sevens	Las Vegas
	10/11		Canada World Rugby Sevens	Vancouver
April	6–8		Hong Kong World Rugby Sevens	Hong Kong
	13–15		Commonwealth Games Rugby Sevens	Gold Coast

July	20–22		Rugby World Cup Sevens	San Francisco
August	17	P	Tasman v Canterbury	Blenheim
	26	P	Northland v Auckland	Whangarei
September	8	P	Hawke's Bay v Bay of Plenty	Napier
	15	P	Counties Manukau v Wellington	Pukekohe
	22	FPC	Waikato v Auckland	Hamilton
	29	HC	Horowhenua Kapiti v King Country	Paraparaumu
	6	HC	East Coast v Wanganui	Ruatoria
October	13	HC	South Canterbury v Thames Valley	Timaru
	20	MC s-f	Wanganui v Thames Valley	Wanganui
	28	LC f	Horowhenua Kapiti v Wairarapa Bush	Levin

Mike Lash

August	4	RS	Taranaki v Wanganui	Hawera
September	2	P	Northland v Taranaki	Whangarei
	9	P	Wellington v North Harbour	Wellington
	15	HC	West Coast v Poverty Bay	Greymouth
	22	HC	East Coast v Poverty Bay	Ruatoria
	27	P	Bay of Plenty v Manawatu	Rotorua
October	10	P	Southland v Auckland	Invercargill
	13	HC	West Coast v East Coast	Greymouth

Angus Mabey

August	23	P	Counties Manukau v Bay of Plenty	Pukekohe
September	12	P	North Harbour v Canterbury	Albany
	16	FPC	North Harbour v Tasman	Albany
	21	P	Bay of Plenty v Waikato	Rotorua
	29	HC	North Otago v West Coast	Oamaru
October	6	HC	Thames Valley v Horowhenua Kapiti	Paeroa
	13	P	Counties Manukau v Canterbury	Pukekohe

Damian Macpherson

January	13/14		National Sevens	Rotorua
August	25	HC	Thames Valley v West Coast	Paeroa
September	8	HC	King Country v North Otago	Taumarunui

James Munro

July	28	RS	Taranaki v Poverty Bay	Clifton
August	30	P	Auckland v Waikato	Auckland
September	8	HC	Mid Canterbury v West Coast	Ashburton
	15	P	Southland v Otago	Invercargill
	22	HC	Buller v West Coast	Westport
	29	HC	Poverty Bay v Thames Valley	Gisborne
October	6	P	North Harbour v Counties Manukau	Albany
	13	FPC	Canterbury v Manawatu	Christchurch

Jamie Nutbrown

February	23	SR	Highlanders v Blues	Dunedin
March	10	SR	Reds v Bulls	Brisbane
	24	SR	Jaguares v Lions	Buenos Aires
April	13	SR	Hurricanes v Chiefs	Wellington
June	3	JWC	Australia U20 v Japan U20	Narbonne
	7	JWC	Ireland U20 v Georgia U20	Narbonne
	17	JWC	Argentina U20 v Australia U20	Beziers

August	19	P	Southland v Hawke's Bay		Invercargill
	26	P	Tasman v Southland		Blenheim
September	1	HC	Mid Canterbury v North Otago		Ashburton
	8	FPC	Otago v Hawke's Bay		Dunedin
	14	P	Tasman v Taranaki		Nelson
	29	P/RS	Waikato v Southland		Hamilton
October	3	P	Otago v Bay of Plenty		Dunedin
	27	MC f	South Canterbury v Thames Valley		Timaru

Ben O'Keeffe

February	24	SR	Crusaders v Chiefs	Christchurch
March	2	SR	Blues v Chiefs	Auckland
	17	6N	Wales v France	Cardiff
April	7	SR	Brumbies v Reds	Canberra
	14	SR	Highlanders v Brumbies	Dunedin
	21	SR	Bulls v Rebels	Pretoria
	27	SR	Stormers v Rebels	Cape Town
May	12	SR	Crusaders v Waratahs	Christchurch
	18	SR	Hurricanes v Reds	Wellington
June	1	SR	Highlanders v Hurricanes	Dunedin
	9		South Africa v England	Johannesburg
	30	SR	Sunwolves v Bulls	Singapore
July	7	SR	Hurricanes v Blues	Wellington
	14	SR	Reds v Sunwolves	Brisbane
August	18	RC	South Africa v Argentina	Durban
September	1	FPC	Tasman v Taranaki	Nelson
	9	P/RS	Taranaki v Waikato	New Plymouth
	16	P	Canterbury v Auckland	Christchurch
	19	P	Manawatu v Tasman	Palmerston North
	30	P	Counties Manukau v Northland	Pukekohe
October	5	P	Hawke's Bay v Manawatu	Napier
	12	P	Taranaki v Wellington	New Plymouth
	20	P s-f	Otago v Hawke's Bay	Dunedin
	26	P f	Waikato v Otago	Hamilton
	3	Pro14	Edinburgh v Scarlets	Edinburgh
November	10		Wales v Australia	Cardiff
	24		Ireland v USA	Dublin

Chris Paul (South Canterbury)

September	30	FPC	Canterbury v Counties Manukau	Christchurch

Brendon Pickerill

February	23	SR	Rebels v Reds	Melbourne
March	10	SR	Hurricanes v Crusaders	Wellington
	18	SR	Waratahs v Rebels	Sydney
April	21	SR	Crusaders v Sunwolves	Christchurch
May	19	SR	Waratahs v Highlanders	Sydney
June	9	PNC	Tonga v Georgia	Suva
	16	PNC	Tonga v Samoa	Suva
	30	RWCQ	Cook Islands v Hong Kong	Rarotonga
July	6	SR	Crusaders v Highlanders	Christchurch
August	18	P	Bay of Plenty v Taranaki	Rotorua
September	1	HC	West Coast v Wanganui	Greymouth

	5	P	Waikato v Wellington	Hamilton
	20	P	Northland v Southland	Whangarei
	22	FPC	Otago v Counties Manukau	Dunedin
October	6	P	Northland v Waikato	Whangarei
	13	P/RS	Waikato v Otago	Hamilton
	20	P s-f	Auckland v Wellington	Auckland
	26		Japan v World XV	Osaka

Hugh Reed

August	25	HC	North Otago v Buller	Oamaru
September	8	HC	Buller v Thames Valley	Westport
	15	FPC	Counties Manukau v Auckland	Pukekohe
	22	HC	Horowhenua Kapiti v Wairarapa Bush	Levin
	29	HC	Mid Canterbury v East Coast	Ashburton
October	6	HC	King Country v Poverty Bay	Taupo
	13	HC	Wairarapa Bush v North Otago	Masterton
	20	LC s-f	Wairarapa Bush v North Otago	Masterton

Cameron Stone

August	25	P	Waikato v North Harbour	Hamilton
September	6	P	Canterbury v Manawatu	Christchurch
	8	FPC	Taranaki v North Harbour	New Plymouth
	15	HC	Wanganui v Mid Canterbury	Wanganui
	23	P	Manawatu v Wellington	Palmerston North
October	6	FPC	Manawatu v Hawke's Bay	Palmerston North
	14	P	Auckland v North Harbour	Auckland
	20	LC s-f	Horowhenua Kapiti v Mid Canterbury	Levin

Daniel Waenga (Bay of Plenty)

September	21	FPC	Bay of Plenty v Taranaki	Rotorua
December	15/16		National Sevens	Tauranga

Nick Webster

September	1	HC	South Canterbury v Poverty Bay	Timaru
	7	P	Otago v Northland	Dunedin
	16	P	North Harbour v Bay of Plenty	Albany
	22	HC	King Country v Wanganui	Te Kuiti
October	6	HC	West Coast v Wairarapa Bush	Greymouth
	13	HC	Mid Canterbury v King Country	Ashburton
	20	MC s-f	South Canterbury v King Country	Timaru
November	1		NZ Heartland XV v Vanua XV	Taupo

Michael Winter

January	13/14		National Sevens	Rotorua
August	25	HC	Horowhenua Kapiti v Mid Canterbury	Foxton
September	1	P	Bay of Plenty v Canterbury	Tauranga
	14	P	Northland v Manawatu	Whangarei
	22	P	Hawke's Bay v North Harbour	Napier
	29	HC	Wanganui v Buller	Wanganui
October	6	HC	North Otago v South Canterbury	Oamaru
December	15/16		National Sevens	Tauranga

Paul Williams

February	10	PRO 14	Edinburgh v Leinster	Edinburgh
	24	SR	Sunwolves v Brumbies	Tokyo

Month	Date	Comp	Match	Venue
March	17	SR	Jaguares v Reds	Buenos Aires
	31	SR	Brumbies v Waratahs	Canberra
April	7	SR	Chiefs v Blues	Hamilton
	28	SR	Blues v Jaguares	Auckland
May	11	SR	Blues v Hurricanes	Auckland
	25	SR	Jaguares v Sharks	Buenos Aires
June	16		Australia v Ireland	Melbourne
	30	SR	Highlanders v Chiefs	Suva
July	6	SR	Reds v Rebels	Brisbane
August	19	P	Wellington v Otago	Wellington
September	1	P	Manawatu v Otago	Palmerston North
	29	HC	Wairarapa Bush v South Canterbury	Masterton
October	7	P	Otago v Tasman	Dunedin
	14	P	Manawatu v Southland	Palmerston North
	20	P s-f	Waikato v Northland	Hamilton
November	4		NZ Heartland XV v NZ Marist XV	Taupo
	17		England v Japan	London
	24		Scotland v Argentina	Edinburgh

RWCQ   Rugby World Cup Qualifier
JWC   Junior World Championship
RC   Rugby Championship
6N   Six Nations
PNC   Pacific Nations Cup
PRO14 PRO 14 League in UK
SR   Super Rugby
P   Mitre 10 Cup
HC   Heartland Championship
MC   Meads Cup
LC   Lochore Cup
FPC   Farah Palmer Cup

Two overseas referees controlled two Mitre 10 Cup & two Heartland Championship fixtures:

Shuhei Kubo (Japan) Aug 24, Otago v Hawke's Bay; Aug 31, Wellington v Southland.
Teru Kajiwara (Japan) Sep 15, Wairarapa Bush v Buller; Sep 22, Thames Valley v North Otago.
Paul Williams replaced Jaco Peyper (illness) during the Super Rugby fixture Blues v Hurricanes in Auckland May 11.

INTERNATIONAL ASSISTANT REFEREES AND TELEVISION MATCH OFFICIALS

Nick Briant
June	9		Japan v Italy		Oita
	23		Japan v Georgia		Aichi

Mike Fraser
June	16		Fiji v Georgia		Suva

Glen Jackson
June	9		South Africa v England		Johannesburg
	16		South Africa v England		Bloemfontein
September	15	RC	Australia v Argentina		Gold Coast
November	24		England v Australia		London

Richard Kelly
	30	RWCQ	Samoa v Germany		Apia

Angus Mabey
June	30	RWCQ	Cook Islands v Hong Kong		Rarotonga

Shane McDermott
	23		Japan v Georgia	(TMO)	Aichi

Glenn Newman
February	4	6N	Italy v England	(TMO)	Rome
	10	6N	England v Wales	(TMO)	London
September	8	RC	Australia vs South Africa	(TMO)	Brisbane
	15	RC	Australia v Argentina	(TMO)	Gold Coast

Ben O'Keeffe
March	10	6N	Ireland v Scotland		Dublin
June	16		South Africa v England		Bloemfontein
	23		South Africa v England		Cape Town
August	25	RC	Argentina v South Africa		Mendoza
November	17		Scotland v South Africa		Edinburgh

Aaron Paterson
June	16	PNC	Tonga v Samoa	(TMO)	Suva
	16	PNC	Fiji v Georgia	(TMO)	Suva
	30	RWCQ	Samoa v Germany	(TMO)	Apia

Brendon Pickerill
June	23		Fiji v Tonga		Suva
November	3		England v South Africa		London
	10		Wales v Australia		Cardiff

Ben Skeen
March	10	6N	France v England	(TMO)	Paris
	17	6N	England v Ireland	(TMO)	London
June	9		Australia v Ireland	(TMO)	Brisbane
	16		Australia v Ireland	(TMO)	Melbourne
	23		Australia v Ireland	(TMO)	Sydney

November	10		Scotland v Fiji	Edinburgh
	17		Scotland v South Africa	Edinburgh

Cameron Stone

June	9	PNC	Tonga v Georgia	Suva
	16	PNC	Tonga v Romania	Suva
	23		Australia v Ireland	Sydney
	30	RWCQ	Samoa v Germany	Apia

Paul Williams

February	3	6N	France v Ireland	Paris
	11	6N	Scotland v France	Edinburgh
June	9		Australia v Ireland	Brisbane
	23		Australia v Ireland	Sydney
September	8	RC	Australia vs South Africa	Brisbane
	15	RC	Australia v Argentina	Gold Coast

Michael Winter

June	30	RWCQ	Cook Islands v Hong Kong	Rarotonga

(TMO) Television Match Official
JWC Junior World Championship
PNC Pacific Nations Cup
RC   Rugby Championship
6N   Six Nations

2018 INTERNATIONAL REFEREES

N.P. Briant — 2014 Fiji v Cook Islands (RWCQ), Romania v Canada; 2016 Georgia v Tonga, Tonga v USA; 2017 Tonga v Wales, Fiji v Tonga (RWCQ), Japan v Australia; 2018 Japan v Italy.

M.I. Fraser — 2013 Georgia v USA, Wales v Tonga; 2014 Canada v Scotland, Tonga v USA; 2018 Fiji v Samoa, Samoa v Germany (RWCQ).

G.W. Jackson — 2012 England v Fiji, Georgia v Japan; 2013 Italy v Australia, France v Tonga; 2014 Argentina v Ireland, South Africa v Scotland, Australia v Argentina, France v Fiji, Ireland v Australia; 2015 France v Scotland, Wales v Ireland, Argentina v South Africa, Ireland v Canada (RWC), Australia v Fiji (RWC), Tonga v Namibia (RWC), USA v Japan (RWC); 2016 Italy v England, Scotland v France, South Africa v Ireland, South Africa v Argentina, France v Australia; 2017 Italy v Ireland, South Africa v France, Australia v South Africa, Wales v Australia; 2018 Ireland v Wales, South Africa v England, Australia v South Africa, Italy v Georgia, France v Argentina.

Dr B.D. O'Keeffe — 2016 Samoa v Georgia, Japan v Scotland, Scotland v Argentina; 2017 Italy v France, South Africa v France, South Africa v Australia, Ireland v South Africa, England v Australia; 2018 Wales v France, South Africa v England, South Africa v Argentina, Wales v Australia, Ireland v USA.

B.E. Pickerill — 2017 Germany v USA; 2018 Tonga v Georgia, Tonga v Samoa, Cook Islands v Hong Kong (RWCQ).

P.M. Williams — 2016 Romania v USA; 2017 Italy v Scotland, Fiji v Italy, Samoa vs Fiji (RWCQ), Ireland v Fiji; 2018 Australia v Ireland, England v Japan, Scotland v Argentina.

INTERNATIONAL REFEREES
to 1 January, 2019

Bishop, D.J. (Southland) 1986–95	26
Bray, L.E. (Wellington) 2001–08	9
Briant, N.P. (Bay of Plenty) 2014–18	8
Brown, K.W. (Southland) 2008–11	8
Campbell, A. (Auckland) 1908	2
Dainty, C.J. (Wellington) 1982–86	2
Deaker, K.M. (Hawke's Bay) 2001–08	23
Doocey, T.F. (Canterbury) 1976–83	3
Downes, A.D. (Otago) 1913	1
Duffy, B.W. (Taranaki) 1977	1
Duncan, J. (Otago) 1908	1
Evans, F.T. (Canterbury) 1904	1
Farquahar, A.B. (Auckland) 1961–64	6
Fleury, A.L. (Otago) 1959	1
Fong, A.S. (West Coast) 1946–50	2
Forsyth, R.A. (Taranaki) 1958	1
Francis, R.C. (Wairarapa Bush) 1984–86	10
Fraser, M.I. (Wellington) 2013–18	6
Fright, W.A. (Canterbury) 1956	2
Frood, J. (Otago) 1952	1
Garrard, W.G. (Canterbury) 1899	1
Gillies, C.R. (Waikato) 1958–59	4
Griffiths, A.A. (Waikato) 1952	1
Harrison, G.L. (Wellington) 1979–83	4
Hawke, C.J. (South Canterbury) 1990–2001	24
Hill, E.D. (Auckland) 1949	1
Hollander, S. (Canterbury) 1930–31	4
Honiss, P.G. (Canterbury & Waikato) 1997–2008	46
Jackson, G.W. (Bay of Plenty) 2012–18	30
King, J.S. (Wellington) 1937	2
Lawrence, B.J. (Bay of Plenty) 2005–11	25
Lawrence, K.H. (Bay of Plenty) 1985–91	13
Macassey, L.E. (Otago) 1937	1
McAuley, C.J. (Otago) 1962	1
McDavitt, P.A. (Wellington) 1972–77	5
McKenzie, E. (Wairarapa) 1921	1
McKenzie, H.J. (Wairarapa) 1936	1
McLachlan, L.L. (Otago) 1989–94	7
McMullen, R.F. (Auckland) 1973	1
Matheson, A.M. (Taranaki) 1946	1
Millar, D.H. (Otago) 1965–78	8
Moffit, J. (Wellington) 1936	1
Munro, V.G. (Canterbury) 2009–10	2
Murphy, J.P. (North Auckland) 1959–69	13
Neilson, A.E. (Wellington) 1921	2
Nicholson, G.W. (Auckland) 1913	1
O'Brien, P.D. (Southland) 1994–2005	37
O'Keeffe, Dr B.D. (Wellington) 2016–18	13
Parkinson, F.G.M. (Manawatu) 1955–56	3
Pickerill, B.E. (North Harbour) 2017–18	4
Pollock, C.J. (Hawke's Bay) 2005–15	22
Pring, J.P.G. (Auckland) 1966–72	8
Robson, C.F. (Waikato) 1963	1
Simpson, J.L. (Wellington) 1913	1
Skeen, B.D. (Auckland) 2008–09	2
Sullivan, G. (Taranaki) 1950	1
Sutherland, F.E. (Auckland) 1930	1
Taylor, A.R. (Canterbury) 1965–72	3
Thompson, M.W. (Auckland) 1983	2
Tindill, E.W.T. (Wellington) 1950–55	3
Wahlstrom, G.K. (Auckland) 1994–97	6
Walsh, L. (Canterbury) 1949	1
Walsh, S. (Wellington) 1994–97	5
Walsh, S.R. (North Harbour) 1998–2008	33
White, J.M (Auckland) 2013	2
Williams, J. (Otago) 1905	1
Williams, P.M. (Taranaki) 2016–18	8
Williamson G.L. (Wellington) 2010–13	2
Wise, G.J. (Hawke's Bay) 2004	1
Wolstenholme, B. (Poverty Bay) 1955	1

100 AND MORE FIRST-CLASS MATCHES
to 1 January, 2019

P.D. O'Brien	1988–2005	230	G.K. Wahlstrom	1985–2002	132
P.G. Honiss	1992–2008	227	R.P. Kelly	2009–2018	119
S.R. Walsh	1994–2008	214	G.L. Williamson	2003–2014	117
B.J. Lawrence	1997–2012	204	Dr. J.M. White	2000–2013	116
C.J. Pollock	2000–2016	204	D.J. Bishop	1976–1995	114
C.J. Hawke	1983–2001	183	G.J. Wise	1996–2007	114
K.M. Deaker	1996–2008	181	K.W. Brown	1999–2012	112
G.W. Jackson	2010–2018	176	Dr. B.D. O'Keeffe	2012–2018	105
N.P. Briant	2009–2018	170	S. Walsh	1980–2000	103
M.I. Fraser	2007–2018	154	K.H. Lawrence	1971–1992	100
L.E. Bray	1991–2008	144			

MOST INTERNATIONAL APPOINTMENTS BY REFEREES

N. Owens	Wales	2003–2018	86	D.A. Pearson	England	2003–2012	28
W. Barnes	England	2006–2018	82	W.J. Erickson	Australia	1994–2002	27
J.I. Kaplan	South Africa	1996–2013	70	S.M. Lawrence	South Africa	2000–2011	27
C.P. Joubert	South Africa	2003–2016	69	A.J. Watson	South Africa	1996–2004	27
A.C.P. Rolland	Ireland	2001–2014	67	D.J. Bishop	New Zealand	1986–1995	26
R. Poite	France	2006–2018	61	B. Gabbei	Germany	1993–2006	26
S.R. Walsh	New Zealand/			S.M. Young	Australia	1994–2006	26
	Australia	1998–2014	60	K.V.J. Fitzgerald	Australia	1985–1991	25
C.R. White	England	1998–2009	51	M. Jonker	South Africa	2005–2014	25
J. Garces	France	2010–2018	48	B.J. Lawrence	New Zealand	2005–2011	25
S.J. Dickinson	Australia	1997–2011	47	C. Norling	Wales	1978–1991	25
P.G. Honiss	New Zealand	1997–2008	46	J.P. Doyle	England	2009–2017	24
G.J. Clancy	Ireland	2006–2016	45	C.J. Hawke	New Zealand	1990–2001	24
J.D. Peyper	South Africa	2011–2018	45	K.M. Deaker	New Zealand	2001–2008	23
D.A. Lewis	Ireland	1998–2010	45	K.D. Kelleher	Ireland	1959–1971	23
W.D. Bevan	Wales	1985–2000	44	D.G. Walters	Wales	1959–1966	23
J.M. Fleming	Scotland	1985–2001	41	J. Dume	France	1993–2003	22
A.J. Spreadbury	England	1990–2008	41	M. Joseph	Wales	1966–1977	22
P. Gauzere	France	2010–2018	39	C.J. Pollock	New Zealand	2005–2015	22
E.F. Morrison	England	1991–2001	38	R.C. Williams	Ireland	1957–1964	21
P.D. O'Brien	New Zealand	1994–2005	37	F.A. Howard	England	1984–1992	20
J. Jutge	France	1996–2007	35	A.R. Gardner	Australia	2011–2018	19
A.J. Cole	Australia	1997–2005	31	A.M. Hosie	Scotland	1973–1984	19
G.W. Jackson	New Zealand	2012–2018	30	S.J. Lander	England	1999–2003	19
J.D. Lacey	Ireland	2010–2018	30	L.W. Pearce	England	2013–2018	19
P.L. Marshall	Australia	1993–2003	30	N.C. Whitehouse	Wales	1998–2006	19
D.T.M. McHugh	Ireland	1994–2004	29				

SEVENS RUGBY
NEW ZEALAND SEVENS SQUADS 2018

The All Blacks Sevens undertook the heaviest schedule of tournaments since 2002 with 13 events. Without doubt the highlights were the winning of the gold medals at the Commonwealth Games and at the Rugby World Cup Sevens. Winning the double was surprising considering the team had not appeared in the final of the other tournaments. Not since the opening rounds of the HSBC World Series, in December 2017, when runners-up at Dubai and Cup winners at Cape Town, had the team taken part in a final. The team finished a distant third in the series. However, the 2018/19 series commenced in December with a gutsy win in Dubai, entering the final with only nine fit players and defeating USA 21–5 in the Cup final. It was an inexperienced squad that took part at Hong Kong one week before the Commonwealth Games tournament, Rokolisoa being the only player to play at both events. Injuries to several experienced members hampered selections but this allowed some promising newcomers to emerge. Scott Gregory and Taylor Haugh made their debuts at the Oceania tournament in Fiji.

The National Sevens tournament was held twice during 2018. The first, in January, was won by Waikato and the second, in December, won by Tasman. The union chose to bring the tournament forward to allow more time to prepare for the international events commencing in the new year.

INDIVIDUAL SCORING

	Tries	Con	Points		Tries	Con	Points
Knewstubb	17	62	209	Rayasi	7	–	35
Ravouvou	30	–	150	Nareki	5	3	31
Baker	16	32	144	Joass	6	–	30
Koroi	12	31	122	Gregory	5	–	25
Ware	24	–	120	Haugh	1	8	21
Curry	22	3	116	Khan	–	10	20
Molia	21	–	105	Bunce	3	–	15
McGarvey-Black	13	13	91	Stanaway	2	–	10
Collier	17	–	85	Te Tamaki	2	–	10
Nanai-Seturo	14	–	70	Webber	–	3	6
Dickson	12	1	62	Clarke	1	–	5
Masirewa	11	–	55	Simonsson	1	–	5
Mikkelson	11	–	55				
Rokolisoa	6	12	54	**TOTALS**	278	178	1746
Ng Shiu	10	–	50				
Nicole	9	–	45	*Opposition scored 887 points*			

Final points for 2017/18 World Rugby Sevens Series: South Africa 182, Fiji 180, New Zealand 150, Australia 123, England 122, USA 117, Argentina 105, Kenya104, Canada 76, Samoa 59, Spain 56, Scotland 55, France 53, Wales 49, Ireland 27, Russia 26, Papua New Guinea 6, Uganda 4, Japan 3, Uruguay 2, South Korea 1. The series was held over ten tournaments between December 2017 and June 2018.

Previous winners: New Zealand 2000, 2001, 2002, 2003, 2004, 2005, 2007, 2008, 2011, 2012, 2013, 2014; Fiji 2006, 2015, 2016; South Africa 2009, 2017; Samoa 2010.

World Rugby Sevens Series Cup championship titles (1999 to 1 January 2019): New Zealand 52, Fiji 37, South Africa 26, England 19, Samoa 10, Australia 7, Argentina 2, Scotland 2, United States 2, France 1, Kenya 1, Canada 1.

Player	Province	Australia	New Zealand	USA	Canada	Hong Kong	C'wealth Games	Singapore	England	France	RWC	Fiji	Dubai	South Africa	TOTALS
Kurt Baker	Manawatu	*	s	–	*	–	*	*	*	*	*	–	–	–	8
Jordan Bunce	Waikato	–	–	–	–	*	–	–	–	–	–	*	–	–	2
Caleb Clarke	Auckland	s	*	–	–	–	–	–	–	–	–	–	–	–	2
Dylan Collier	Waikato	–	–	*	*	–	*	*	*	*	*	*	*	*	10
Scott Curry	Bay of Plenty	*	*	*	*	–	*	–	*	*	*	–	*	–	9
Sam Dickson	Canterbury	*	*	*	*	–	*	–	*	*	–	*	*	–	9
Tima Fainga'anuku	Tasman	–	–	–	–	–	s	–	–	–	–	–	–	–	1
Scott Gregory	Northland	–	–	–	–	–	–	–	–	–	–	*	*	*	3
Taylor Haugh	Otago	–	–	–	–	–	–	–	–	–	–	*	–	s	2
Trael Joass	Tasman/BOP	–	–	*	*	–	*	*	–	–	–	*	–	*	7
Rocky Khan	Auckland	–	–	–	–	*	–	–	–	–	–	–	–	–	1
Andrew Knewstubb	Tasman/Horo Kapi	*	–	*	*	–	*	–	*	–	–	*	*	*	9
Vilimoni Koroi	Otago	*	*	*	–	–	*	–	–	–	–	–	s	*	6
Ngarohi McGarvey-Black	Bay of Plenty	–	–	*	*	–	–	*	–	–	–	*	*	*	6
Luke Masirewa	Bay of Plenty	*	*	–	*	*	–	–	–	–	–	*	*	*	7
Tim Mikkelson	Waikato	*	*	*	–	–	*	*	*	*	*	–	–	–	8
Sione Molia	Counties Manukau	*	*	*	–	*	*	*	*	*	*	–	*	*	10
Etene Nanai-Seturo	Counties Manukau	*	*	*	*	–	*	*	*	–	–	–	–	*	8
Jona Nareki	Otago	–	–	–	–	*	–	s	*	*	*	*	–	*	6
Tone Ng Shiu	Tasman	–	–	–	–	*	–	*	*	*	–	*	*	*	7
Amanaki Nicole	Canterbury	–	–	–	–	*	–	–	–	–	–	*	*	*	4
Joe Ravouvou	Auckland	*	*	*	*	–	*	–	*	*	*	*	–	–	9
Salesi Rayasi	Auckland	–	–	–	–	*	–	–	*	*	*	–	–	–	4
Akuila Rokolisoa	Counties Manukau	–	–	–	–	*	*	*	*	s	*	–	–	–	7
Daniel Schrijvers	Wellington	–	–	–	*	–	–	–	–	–	–	–	–	–	1
Bailey Simonsson	Bay of Plenty	–	–	–	–	*	–	–	–	*	–	–	–	–	2
Teddy Stanaway	Bay of Plenty	*	*	–	–	–	–	–	*	–	–	–	–	–	3
Isaac Te Tamaki	Waikato	–	–	–	–	*	–	–	–	–	–	–	–	–	1
Regan Ware	Bay of Plenty	*	*	*	*	–	–	–	*	*	*	–	*	–	9
Joe Webber	Bay of Plenty	–	*	s	*	–	–	–	–	–	–	–	–	–	3

Captaincy was shared during the year: Curry and Mikkelson (Australia, New Zealand, USA, Commonwealth Games, RWC); Curry (Canada); Khan and Ng Shiu (Hong Kong); Mikkelson and Molia (Singapore); Baker and Molia (England and France); Dickson and Collier (Fiji); Curry and Molia (Dubai); Molia and Collier (South Africa).

Coach: Clark Laidlaw
Manager: Ross Everiss *(Bay of Plenty)*
Assistant coach: Tomasi Cama *(Manawatu)*
Physiotherapist: Damian Banks *(Bay of Plenty)*

At Hong Kong:
Coach: Roger Randle *(Waikato)*
Manager: Grant Wilson *(Auckland)*
Physiotherapist: Ema Pene *(Waikato)*

NEW ZEALAND AT AUSTRALIA SEVENS
Allianz Stadium, Sydney   January 26–28, 2018

Date	Opponent	Result	Tries	Conversions
Jan 26	Russia	won 61–0	Ravouvou (2), Dickson (2), Ware, Curry, Knewstubb, Molia, Nanai-Seturo	Knewstubb (5), Koroi (3)
Jan 27	Samoa	won 31–0	Dickson (2), Ravouvou, Baker, Nanai-Seturo	Knewstubb (2), Koroi
Jan 27	Fiji	lost 17–19	Knewstubb, Ware, Masirewa	Knewstubb
Jan 28	Australia (Cup q-f)	lost 12–24	Koroi (2)	Knewstubb
Jan 28	England (semi-final for 5th)	won 10–5	Ravouvou, Masirewa	
Jan 28	Fiji (final for 3rd)	won 31–7	Ware, Molia, Koroi, Clarke, Mikkelson	Koroi (3)

Australia defeated South Africa 29–0 in the Cup final.

NEW ZEALAND AT NEW ZEALAND SEVENS
Waikato Stadium, Hamilton   February 3/4, 2018

Date	Opponent	Result	Tries	Conversions
Feb 3	France	won 52–7	Curry (2), Ravouvou, Mikkelson, Molia, Ware, Nanai-Seturo, Masirewa	Koroi (5), Webber
Feb 3	Scotland	won 24–5	Mikkelson, Curry, Koroi, Dickson	Koroi (2)
Feb 3	Argentina	won 17–12	Stanaway, Koroi, Ravouvou	Webber
Feb 4	England (Cup q-f)	won 19–12	Mikkelson, Koroi, Curry	Koroi (2)
Feb 4	Fiji (Cup semi-final)	lost 12–14	Dickson, Koroi	Koroi
Feb 4	Australia (final for 3th)	lost 7–8	Curry	Webber

Fiji defeated South Africa 24–17 in the Cup final

NEW ZEALAND AT USA SEVENS
Sam Boyd Stadium, Las Vegas   March 2–4, 2018

Date	Opponent	Result	Tries	Conversions
Mar 2	Uruguay	won 28–7	Ware (2), Mikkelson, Ravouvou	Koroi (3), Knewstubb
Mar 2	Argentina	lost 19–26	Molia, Ravouvou, Nanai-Seturo	Koroi, Curry
Mar 3	Scotland	won 26–17	Ware (2), Molia, Dickson	Knewstubb (3)
Mar 3	Fiji (Cup q-f)	lost 10–14	Koroi, Molia	
Mar 4	England (semi-final for 5th)	won 19–14	McGarvey-Black (2), Collier	Knewstubb (2)
Mar 4	Australia (final for 5th)	won 17–12	Koroi, Dickson, Molia	Knewstubb

USA defeated Argentina 28–0 in the Cup final

NEW ZEALAND AT CANADA SEVENS
BC Place Stadium, Vancouver   March 10/11, 2018

Date	Opponent	Result	Tries	Conversions
Mar 10	Scotland	won 31–26	Ware (2), Curry (2), Joass	Knewstubb (3)
Mar 10	Russia	won 31–5	Ravouvou (3), Dickson, Masirewa	McGarvey-Black (3)
Mar 10	South Africa	won 33–14	Collier (2), Curry, McGarvey-Black, Masirewa	McGarvey-Black (4)
Mar 11	USA (Cup q-f)	lost 0–17		
Mar 11	England (semi-final for 5th)	lost 17–21	Curry (2), Ravouvou	McGarvey-Black
Fiji defeated Kenya 31–12 in the Cup final				

NEW ZEALAND AT HONG KONG SEVENS
Hong Kong Stadium, Hong Kong   April 6–8, 2018

Date	Opponent	Result	Tries	Conversions
Apr 6	Russia	won 36–5	Ravouvou (2), Nicole, Rokolisoa, Ng Shiu, Te Tamaki	Rokolisoa (2), Khan
Apr 7	Samoa	won 19–12	Ravouvou, Te Tamaki, Masirewa	Khan (2)
Apr 7	Fiji	lost 7–50	Nicole	Rokolisoa
Apr 8	USA (Cup q-f)	won 35–7	Rokolisoa (2), Ravouvou, Masirewa, Rayasi	Khan (5)
Apr 8	Kenya (Cup semi-final)	lost 12–21	Nicole, Nareki	Khan
Apr 8	South Africa (for 3rd)	lost 7–29	Ng Shiu	Khan
Fiji defeated Kenya 24–12 in the Cup final				

NEW ZEALAND AT XXI COMMONWEALTH GAMES
Robina Stadium, Gold Coast, Australia   April 14/15, 2018

Date	Opponent	Result	Tries	Conversions
Apr 14	Zambia	won 54–0	Baker, Mikkelson, Ware, Molia, Knewstubb, Koroi, Nanai-Seturo, Rokolisoa	Knewstubb (2), Rokolisoa (2), Baker (2), Koroi
Apr 14	Kenya	won 40–7	Nanai-Seturo (2), Curry, Ware, Molia, Knewstubb	Knewstubb (2), Koroi (2), Baker
Apr 14	Canada	won 33–7	Ware (2), Baker, Curry, Koroi	Knewstubb (3), Baker
Apr 15	England (semi-final)	won 17–12	Ware (2), Nanai-Seturo	Koroi
Apr 15	Fiji (final)	won 14–0	Nanai-Seturo, Ware	Koroi (2)
England defeated South Africa 21–14 in the playoff for the bronze medal				

NEW ZEALAND AT SINGAPORE SEVENS
National Stadium, Singapore   April 28/29, 2018

Date	Opponent	Result	Tries	Conversions
Apr 28	Wales	won 32–7	Ravouvou, Collier, Baker, Joass, Nanai-Seturo, Ng Shiu	Knewstubb
Apr 28	Australia	lost 12–19	Joass, Collier	Baker
Apr 28	Scotland	won 22–12	Ravouvou (2), Collier, Baker	McGarvey-Black
Apr 29	Fiji (Cup q-f)	lost 19–24	Baker (2), Ravouvou	Baker (2)
Apr 29	Kenya (semi-final for 5th)	won 17–7	Baker, Collier, Joass	Baker
Apr 29	Samoa (for 5th)	won 36–17	Nareki, Molia, Ng Shiu, Baker, Stanaway, Nanai-Seturo	Baker (2), Rokolisoa

Fiji defeated Australia 28–22 in the Cup final

NEW ZEALAND AT ENGLAND SEVENS
Twickenham, London   June 2/3, 2018

Date	Opponent	Result	Tries	Conversions
June 2	Scotland	won 24–12	Baker, Molia, Nanai-Seturo, Rayasi	Baker (2)
June 2	Argentina	won 36–5	Curry, Mikkelson, Baker, Rayasi, Nareki, Nanai-Seturo	Baker (2), Nareki
June 2	Fiji	lost 7–27	Dickson	Baker
June 3	South Africa (Cup q-f)	lost 5–14	Collier	
June 3	Australia (semi-final for 5th)	won 38–7	Ware (2), Curry, Mikkelson, Baker, Ng Shiu	Baker (2), Rokolisoa, Nareki
June 3	USA (for 5th)	won 26–5	Ware, Rayasi, Rokolisoa, Mikkelson	Baker (2), Rokolisoa

Fiji defeated South Africa 21–17 in the Cup final

NEW ZEALAND AT FRANCE SEVENS
Stade Jean Bouin, Paris   June 9/10, 2018

Date	Opponent	Result	Tries	Conversions
June 9	Kenya	won 24–5	Collier (2), Baker, Mikkelson	Baker (2)
June 9	Samoa	won 22–17	Molia (2), Baker, Ware	Baker
June 9	Fiji	lost 17–26	Curry (2), Rayasi	Curry
June 10	USA (Cup q-f)	won 33–7	Ware (2), Rayasi (2), Curry	Baker (4)
June 10	South Africa (Cup semi-final)	lost 12–24	Nareki, Ravouvou	Nareki
June 10	Canada (for 3rd)	won 38–5	Nareki, Molia, Collier, Ravouvou, Simonsson, Dickson	Rokolisoa (4)

South Africa defeated England 24–14 in the Cup final.

NEW ZEALAND AT RUGBY WORLD CUP SEVENS
AT&T Park, San Francisco, USA　　　　　　　　　　　　　　　　　　July 20–22, 2018

Date	Opponent	Result	Tries	Conversions
July 20	Russia	won 29–5	Ravouvou (2), Baker, Knewstubb, Mikkelson	Baker, Knewstubb
July 21	France (q-f)	won 12–7	Baker, Ravouvou	Baker
July 22	Fiji (Cup semi-final)	won 22–17	Ravouvou (2), Collier, Ware	Baker
July 22	England (Cup final)	won 33–12	Molia (2), Ravouvou, Rokolisoa, Joass	Baker (3), Curry

South Africa defeated Fiji 24–19 for the bronze medal

NEW ZEALAND AT OCEANIA SEVENS
ANZ Stadium, Suva, Fiji　　　　　　　　　　　　　　　　　　　　　November 9/10, 2018

Date	Opponent	Result	Tries	Conversions
Nov 9	Nauru	won 62–0	Knewstubb (2), McGarvey-Black (2), Ng Shiu, Bunce, Gregory, Masirewa, Joass, Nicole	Knewstubb (4), Haugh (2)
Nov 9	New Caledonia	won 47–0	McGarvey-Black (2), Ravouvou, Knewstubb, Nicole, Ng Shiu, Bunce	Haugh (6)
Nov 10	Papua New Guinea (Cup q-f)	won 47–0	McGarvey-Black (2), Collier, Gregory, Ravouvou, Knewstubb, Bunce	Knewstubb (3), McGarvey-Black (2), Dickson
Nov 10	Australia (Cup semi-final)	won 14–5	McGarvey-Black (2)	Knewstubb, McGarvey-Black
Nov 10	Fiji (Cup final)	lost 12–17	Knewstubb, Collier	Knewstubb

NEW ZEALAND AT DUBAI SEVENS
The Sevens, Dubai　　　　　　　　　　　　　　　　　　　　November 30/December 1, 2018

Date	Opponent	Result	Tries	Conversions
Nov 30	Wales	won 28–7	Curry (2), Knewstubb, Gregory	Knewstubb (4)
Nov 30	Spain	won 28–17	Curry (2), Collier, Knewstubb	Knewstubb (4)
Nov 30	USA	won 24–7	Dickson, Knewstubb, Collier, Masirewa	Knewstubb (2)
Dec 1	Scotland (Cup q-f)	won 21–7	McGarvey-Black, Knewstubb, Nicole	Knewstubb (3)
Dec 1	England (Cup semi-final)	won 7–5	Ng Shiu	Knewstubb
Dec 1	USA (Cup final)	won 21–5	Ng Shiu, Collier, McGarvey-Black	Knewstubb (2), Koroi

NEW ZEALAND AT SOUTH AFRICA SEVENS
Cape Town Stadium, Cape Town   December 8/9, 2018

Date	Opponent	Result	Tries	Conversions
Dec 8	Zimbabwe	won 35–0	Gregory (2), Masirewa (2), Knewstubb	Knewstubb (2), Koroi (2), McGarvey-Black
Dec 8	Samoa	lost 17–21	Molia (2), Ng Shiu	Knewstubb
Dec 8	South Africa	won 26–21	Molia (2), Knewstubb, Koroi	Knewstubb (2), Koroi
Dec 9	Australia (Cup q-f)	won 26–17	Nicole (3), Nanai-Seturo	Knewstubb (3)
Dec 9	USA (Cup semi-final)	lost 12–31	Knewstubb, Haugh	Knewstubb
Dec 9	South Africa (for 3rd)	lost 5–10	Molia	

Fiji defeated USA 29–15 in the Cup final

PLAYING RECORD OF NEW ZEALAND SEVENS TEAMS

	Tournaments			Games				Points	
	Attended	Won	Runner-up	Played	Won	Draw	Lost	For	Against
1973	1	–	–	3	2	–	1	58	50
1983	1	–	–	5	4	–	1	114	4
1984	1	–	1	5	4	–	1	74	40
1985	1	–	–	4	3	–	1	88	18
1986	3	3	–	16	15	–	1	414	72
1987	2	1	1	11	10	–	1	284	66
1988	2	1	1	11	10	–	1	274	37
1989	2	2	–	11	11	–	–	316	71
1990	1	–	1	5	4	–	1	134	44
1991	1	–	1	5	4	–	1	150	18
1992	1	–	1	5	4	–	1	130	34
1993	3	–	–	17	12	–	5	420	175
1994	2	1	–	10	9	–	1	361	89
1995	5	2	1	22	19	–	3	681	182
1996	5	3	2	29	27	–	2	1263	236
1997	4	1	1	21	18	–	3	670	287
1998	11	6	2	59	54	–	5	2134	473
1999	10	7	2	54	49	1	4	1574	426
2000	10	6	3	59	55	–	4	2048	354
2001	10	7	1	60	56	–	4	2042	330
2002	13	8	2	75	68	1	6	2377	565
2003	7	1	3	40	34	–	6	1285	411
2004	8	3	2	46	39	–	7	1396	395
2005	8	3	1	48	41	–	7	1509	441
2006	9	2	1	48	36	2	10	1380	551
2007	8	4	–	44	40	–	4	1391	355
2008	8	4	2	47	43	–	4	1350	367
2009	9	2	2	49	37	–	12	1262	514
2010	9	2	2	51	43	1	7	1531	541
2011	9	4	1	50	43	–	7	1479	519
2012	9	3	4	54	46	–	8	1375	556
2013	10	3	4	60	52	–	8	1651	584
2014	10	4	3	60	50	–	10	1645	511
2015	8	1	3	47	33	1	13	1039	692
2016	11	3	1	64	45	3	16	1357	860
2017	11	1	2	64	48	–	16	1396	802
2018	13	3	1	73	52	–	21	1746	887
TOTALS	**236**	**91**	**52**	**1332**	**1120**	**9**	**203**	**38398**	**12557**

SEVENS RECORDS
to January 1, 2019

BY NEW ZEALAND TEAMS

Most successive wins	47	2007–08
Most successive tournament wins	7	2007–08
Most successive appearances in finals	12	1986–92

Tournament records
Most points	463	Portugal, 1996
Most tries	69	Portugal, 1996
Most conversions	59	Portugal, 1996

Match records
Highest team score	94	v Moldova, Portugal, 1996
Record victory (*points ahead*)	94	94–0, v Moldova, 1996
Highest score conceded	61	v Fiji, Japan, 1996
Record defeat (*points behind*)	56	5–61, v Fiji, Japan, 1996
Most tries	14	v Moldova, Portugal, 1996
Most conversions	12	v Moldova, Portugal, 1996
		v Hungary, Portugal, 1996

BY THE PLAYERS

Career records
Attended most tournaments	94	DJ Forbes
Most points	2122	T. Cama
Most tries	216	T.J. Mikkelson

Tournament records
Most points	136	C.M. Cullen, Hong Kong, 1996
Most tries	20	B.R.M. Fleming, Portugal, 1996
Most conversions	28	D.A. Smith, Portugal, 1996

Match records
Most points	37	C.M. Cullen, v Sri Lanka, Hong Kong, 1996
Most tries	7	C.M. Cullen, v Sri Lanka, Hong Kong, 1996
Most conversions	9	T.J. Wright, v Korea, Sydney, 1989
		M. Ashford, v Sri Lanka, Dubai, 2001

NEW ZEALAND SEVENS REPRESENTATIVES, 1973–2018

	Tournaments
Ahki, P.J. (*North Harbour*) 2013–14–16	7
Ai'i, O. (*Auckland*) 1999–00–01–02–04–05	25
Alley, G. (*North Harbour*) 1992–93	2
Andrews, L.S. (*Otago*) 1999	2
Anesi, S.R. (*Waikato*) 2004–06	7
Arnold, T.C. (*Bay of Plenty*) 2009–10–11–12	19
Ashford, M.R. (*Auckland*) 2001–05	10
Atiga, B.A.C. (*Auckland*) 2007	1
Austin, H.S.E. (*Taranaki*) 1999	1
Auva'a, O.J. (*Auckland*) 2006–09	5
Bachop, G.T.M. (*Canterbury*) 1990–91–92–94	5
Baker, K.T. (*Manawatu*) 2008–09–17–18 (*Taranaki*) 2010–12–13–14–16	37
Bale, P. (*Canterbury*) 1990–92–93	3
Barrett, B.J. (*Taranaki*) 2010	2
Batty, G.B. (*Wellington*) 1973	1
Baxter, C.N.O. (*Bay of Plenty*) 2003–06–07	9
Berryman, N.R. (*Northland*) 1997	1
Blackadder, T.J. (*Canterbury*) 1993	2
Blackie, J.M. (*Otago*) 2002–03–04–05–06	12
Blowers, A.F. (*Auckland*) 1995	3
Blythe, T.G. (*Waikato*) 1999 (*Bay of Plenty*) 2001	3
Booth, J.P. (*Manawatu*) 2017	2
Botica, F.M. (*North Harbour*) 1985–86–87–88	8
Bourke, C.R. (*Hawke's Bay*) 2004	3
Brooke, Z.V. (*Auckland*) 1986–87–88–89–90	10
Brooke-Cowden, M. (*Auckland*) 1986–87	5
Bruning, K.T. (*Waikato*) 1994 (*Nelson Bays*) 1995	3
Bryant, R.J. (*Taranaki*) 1997	1
Bunce, F.E. (*North Harbour*) 1993	2
Bunce; J.F. (*Manawatu*) 2015 (*Waikato*) 2018	4
Bunting, A.M. (*Bay of Plenty*) 2002–03	6
Cama, T. (*Manawatu*) 2005–07–08–09–10–11–12–13–14	63
Camburn, M. (*North Harbour*) 2005	3
Cashmore, A.R. (*Auckland*) 1995	4
Christie, S.A. (*Tasman*) 2011	2
Clamp, M. (*Wellington*) 1984–85–86	4
Clarke, C.D. (*Auckland*) 2018	2
Clarke, E. (*Auckland*) 1993	1
Clutterbuck, M.J. (*Bay of Plenty*) 2014	1
Cocker, E. (*Otago*) 2005–06–07 (*Auckland*) 2008–09	28
Collier, D.J. (*Waikato*) 2015–16–17–18	33
Colling, G.L. (*Otago*) 1973	1
Collins, N.I. (*Bay of Plenty*) 2001–02	6
Crowley, A.E. (*Taranaki*) 1987–88–89–91	6
Cullen, C.M. (*Manawatu*) 1995–96 (*Wellington*) 1998–00	7
Curry, S.B. (*Manawatu*) 2010–12–13 (*Bay of Plenty*) 2011–14–15–16–17–18	50
Curtis, A.A.D. (*Wellington*) 2013–14–15 (*Manawatu*) 2017	19
Dagg, I.J.A. (*Hawke's Bay*) 2007–08	6
Daniel, B.W. (*Bay of Plenty*) 1997	3
Dauwai, A. (*Thames Valley*) 2006	2
Dawson, A.J. (*Counties*) 1983–85	2
De Goldi, C.D. (*Bay of Plenty*) 1998–99–00 (*Auckland*) 2001–02–03–04	41
Dickson, S.N. (*Canterbury*) 2012–13–14–15–16–17–18	47
Donald, A.J. (*Wanganui*) 1983	1
Duggan, R.J.L. (*Waikato*) 1997	1
Ellis, M.C.G. (*Otago*) 1993	1
Ellison, T.E. (*Wellington*) 2005–06	5
Ensor A.C. (*Otago*) 2014	1
Erenavula, L. (*Counties*) 1994	2
Evans, N.J. (*North Harbour*) 2002	8
Faddes, M.A. (*Otago*) 2013	3
Fainga'anuku, L.T. (*Tasman*) 2018	1
Farani, D. (*Wellington*) 1997	1
Flavell, T.V. (*North Harbour*) 1998	2

	Tournaments
Fleming, B.R.M.	
(*Bay of Plenty*) 1995	
(*Canterbury*) 1996–97–98	
(*Wellington*) 1998–99–00–01–02	
(*Otago*) 2003–04	35
Foote, B.M. (*Waikato*) 1997	
(*North Harbour*) 1998	3
Forbes, D.J. (*Auckland*) 2006–07	
(*Counties Manukau*) 2008–09–10–	
11–12–13–14–15–16–17	94
Forster, S.T. (*Otago*) 1993	2
Fry, R.J. (*Auckland*) 1983–84	2
Fuatai, F. (*Otago*) 2017	2
Gallagher, J.A. (*Wellington*) 1989–90	3
Gear, R.L. (*Auckland*) 1998–99–01	9
Gear, H.E. (*North Harbour*) 2003	
(*Wellington*) 2010–12	4
Going, S.J.	
(*Northland*) 1999–00–01–02–03	29
Goodhue, E.J. (*Northland*) 2015	2
Granger, K.W. (*Manawatu*) 1983	1
Grant, P.W. (*Otago*) 2008–09–10	15
Green, C.I. (*Canterbury*) 1986	2
Gregory, S.J. (*Northland*) 2018	3
Grice, R.J.L. (*Waikato*) 2011	3
Guildford, Z.R. (*Hawke's Bay*) 2010	1
Haami, B.D. (*Taranaki*) 2000	2
Halai, F. (*Waikato*) 2010–11–12	15
Hales, D.A. (*Canterbury*) 1973	1
Hamilton, L.G. (*North Harbour*) 2009	1
Hamilton, A.R.	
(*Hawke's Bay*) 1994–95–96	5
Haugh, T.C. (*Otago*) 2018	2
Heem, B.I. (*Auckland*) 2010–11–12	
(*Tasman*) 2013–14	22
Hoeata, J.M.R.A. (*Taranaki*) 2006	2
Holmes, B. (*North Auckland*) 1973	1
Hona, J. (*Bay of Plenty*) 2005	4
Houston, J.D.W. (*Canterbury*) 2017	1
Howarth, S.P. (*Auckland*) 1991	1
Hudson, C. (*Canterbury*) 1999–00	6
Hunt, N. (*Wellington*) 2005–06–07–08	
(*Bay of Plenty*) 2009	28
Ieremia, A. (*Wellington*) 1997	1
Ioane, A. (*Counties Manukau*) 1997	2

	Tournaments
Ioane, A.L. (*Auckland*) 2014–16	11
Ioane, R.E. (*Auckland*) 2015–16	11
Ioasa, T.S.J.	
(*Hawke's Bay*) 2001–04–05–06–07–08	
(*Wellington*) 2002–03	48
Iopu, I.P. (*Auckland*) 2012	
(*Taranaki*) 2016–17	9
Izatt, C.S. (*Manawatu*) 1999	2
Jackman, M.B. (*HB/Cant*) 2012–13	
–14	10
Jane, C.S. (*Wellington*) 2006	5
Joass, T.J. (*Tasman*) 2017	
(*Tas/BOP*) 2018	14
John, O.W. (*Counties Manukau*) 1996	2
Jones, M.T.	
(*Bay of Plenty*) 1993–94–95–96–97	11
Kaino, J. (*Auckland*) 2005	2
Kaka, G.G. (*Hawke's Bay*)	
2013–14–15–16	33
Kamana, T.J.K.J. (*Waikato*) 2007	2
Karauna, D.T. (*Waikato*) 1996–97–	
98–00–01–02–03	35
Kepu, S.K.M. (*Auckland*) 2001	1
Keresoma, M.M. (*Auckland*) 2012–13	3
Khan, R.N. (*Auckland*) 2013–16–17–18	12
King, P.S.V.	
(*Bay of Plenty*) 2006–07–08–09–10	
(*North Harbour*) 2011–12	33
Kinikinilau, R.U.	
(*Wellington*) 2002–03–04–05–06	
(*Waikato*) 2007	13
Kiri Kiri, A.I. (*Manawatu*) 2015–16	4
Kirk, D.E. (*Otago*) 1984	
(*Auckland*) 1985–86	5
Kirwan, J.J. (*Auckland*)	
1984–85–86–88	5
Knewstubb, A.S. (*Tasman*) 2017	
(*Tas/Horo Kap*) 2018	18
Koloto, E.T. (*Manawatu*) 1987	2
Konia, G.N. (*Hawke's Bay*) 1997	1
Koonwaiyou, A. (*Auckland*) 2002	1
Koroi, V.T. (*Otago*) 2017–18	14
Lahmert, W.H. (*Taranaki*) 2012–13	5
Lam, M.B. (*Auckland*) 2012–13–	
14–16	15
Lam, P.R.	
(*Auckland*) 1989–90–91–92–93	7

Tournaments

Latimer, T.D.	
(Bay of Plenty) 2004–05–06	15
Lawrence, Z.W.	
(North Harbour) 2005–06–07	
(Bay of Plenty) 2008–09–10	35
Lee, F.A. *(Counties Manukau)* 2010	4
Leo'o, J.J. *(Canterbury)* 2000–01	8
Lewis, A.J. *(Otago)* 1984	1
Lindsay, A.C. *(Canterbury)* 1983–84	2
Llewellyn, R.A.M. *(Canterbury)* 2012	1
Lomu, J.T. *(Counties Manukau)* 1994–95–96–98–99	
(Wellington) 2000–01	13
Lynn, K.G. *(Southland)* 2008	2
McMaster, A. *(Manawatu)* 1987	2
McPhee, J.B. *(North Harbour)* 2010	2
McQuoid, G.A. *(Bay of Plenty)* 2004	3
MacDonald, L.T.J.	
(Bay of Plenty) 2005–09	3
McGarvey-Black, N.M.	
(Bay of Plenty) 2018	6
McKenzie, M.R. *(Southland)* 2014	2
Mafi, L.O. *(Manawatu)* 2003	
(Taranaki) 2004–05	8
Maher, J.T. *(Counties Manukau)* 2006	2
Maidens, T.K. *(Hawke's Bay)* 1995	1
Malo, J.R. *(Waikato)* 2012	1
Marshall, J.R. *(Tasman)* 2011	2
Martin, E.M. *(Waikato)* 1996	1
Martin, R.E. *(Bay of Plenty)* 2001–02	11
Martine, H.R.I.	
(King Country) 2000	1
Masirewa, L.R. *(Waikato)* 2012–13	
(Bay of Plenty) 2018	12
Masirewa, W.	
(Counties Manukau) 1996–97–98	10
Masoe, M.C. *(Taranaki)* 2001–02–04	22
Messam, L.J. *(Bay of Plenty)* 2002	
(Waikato) 2003–04–05–06–10–16	26
Mikkelson, T.J. *(Waikato)* 2007–08–09–10–11–12–13–14–15–16–17–18	84
Miller, A.J. *(Bay of Plenty)* 1997	1
Mills, J.G. *(Auckland)* 1984	1
Milne, B.W.T. *(Southland)* 2002	2
Molia, S.L.J.	
(Counties Manukau) 2016–17–18	29
Monaghan, A.C.	
(Northland) 1998–00	18

Tournaments

Muliaina, J.M.	
(Auckland) 1999–00–01–02	11
Munro, L.H. *(Auckland)* 2006	4
Murray, C.D. *(Counties)* 1994	1
Naholo, W.R. *(Taranaki)* 2012–13–14	8
Nanai-Seturo, E.W.P.S.	
(Counties Manukau) 2018	8
Nanai-Williams, T.T.	
(Counties Manukau) 2008–09	7
Naoupu, G.E. *(Canterbury)* 2005	3
Nareki, J.M. *(Otago)* 2018	6
Nepia, D.S.M.	
(Bay of Plenty) 2000–01	5
Newby, C.A. *(Bay of Plenty)* 1999	
(North Harbour) 1999–00–01–02	13
Ng Shiu, I.J.S. *(Tasman)* 2017–18	15
Ngaluafe, N.S.J. *(Southland)* 2016	1
Nicole, A.P. *(Canterbury)* 2018	4
Nonoa, S.I. *(Waikato)* 1998	1
Nonu, M.A. *(Wellington)* 2004	2
Nowell, B.C. *(Canterbury)* 2008	2
O'Donnell, D.P.T. *(Waikato)* 2010–11–14–15	12
O'Donnell, K.F.T. *(Taranaki)* 2011–12	5
Ormsby, K.M.T.	
(Counties Manukau) 2000	1
Ormond, J.T. *(Taranaki)* 2010–11	3
Ormond, L.H. *(Taranaki)* 2015–16–17	12
Osborne, G.M.	
(Nth Harbour) 1992–93–94–96–97	6
Paramore, J. *(Counties)* 1993	2
Parkinson, D.T. *(Auckland)* 1998–99	
(Otago) 2001	
(North Harbour) 2003	15
Parkinson, M.T.	
(North Harbour) 1999–2003–04	
(Bay of Plenty) 2005	14
Peacocke, G.M.	
(North Harbour) 1996–97	3
Pearson, M.B. *(Wellington)* 2015	1
Pedersen, H.L. *(Otago)* 2005	2
Pelenise, A.	
(Canterbury) 2005–06–07	13
Phillips, C.M.	
(North Auckland) 1986	3
Philpott, S. *(Canterbury)* 1988	2

Tournaments

Pierce, M.S.L.
(*North Harbour*) 1989–91–92–93–95 6
Piutau, S.T. (*Auckland*) 2011–12 8
Popoali'i, B. (*Wellington*) 2009
(*Otago*) 2011 8
Puletua, J.R. (*Auckland*) 2009 1
Pulu, A.W.
(*Counties Manukau*) 2015–16 7
Putt, K.B. (*Waikato*) 1987–89 2

Qio, J. (*NZ Fijians*)[1] 1999 1

Raikabula, L.
(*Wellington*) 2006–11–12–13–14–15
(*Hawke's Bay*) 2007
(*Manawatu*) 2008–09–10 70
Raikuna, D.A. (*Counties Manukau*) 2011
(*North Harbour*) 2013–14 12
Raki, L.E. (*Counties Manukau*) 1985–87 3
Ralph, C.S.
(*Bay of Plenty*) 1996–97–98
(*Canterbury*) 2000 7
Ranby, R.M. (*Waikato*) 2005 2
Randle, R.Q.
(*Hawke's Bay*) 1995–96–97–98
(*Waikato*) 2000–01–02 10
Ranger, R.M.N.
(*Northland*) 2006–07–08 8
Ravouvou, J. (*Auckland*) 2017–18 14
Rayasi, P. (*Wellington*) 1993 1
Rayasi, S.T.M. (*Auckland*) 2018 4
Reid, H.B. (*Otago*) 2001
(*North Harbour*) 2002–03–04
(*Bay of Plenty*) 2005–06 28
Reid, H.R. (*Bay of Plenty*) 1983 1
Reihana, B.T. (*Waikato*) 1998–02 2
Rich, G.J.W. (*Auckland*) 1983–84–85 3
Rickards, W.T.C.
(*Southland*) 2006–07–08–09 8
Robertson, G.A. (*Waikato*) 2011 3
Rokocoko, J.T. (*Auckland*) 2002–05 8
Rokolisoa, A.T.
(*Counties Manukau*) 2018 7
Ropiha, B.J. (*Hawke's Bay*) 2016 1
Ruddell, N.K. (*North Auckland*) 1986 1
Ruru, J.L. (*Otago*) 2016 2
Rush, E.J. (*Auckland*) 1988–89–90–91
(*North Harbour*) 1992–93–94–95–
96–97–98–99–00–01–02–03–04 62

Tournaments

Samuels, T.D.G. (*Hawke's Bay*) 2017 1
Savea, A.S. (*Wellington*) 2012–16 8
Savea, S.J. (*Wellington*) 2008–09 7
Savou, T.H. (*Manawatu*) 1998 1
Schmidt-Uili, P.T. (*Manawatu*) 1998 2
Schrijvers, D.J. (*Wellington*) 2018 1
Schuster, N.J.
(*Wellington*) 1986–88–89–90 6
Scown, A.I. (*Taranaki*) 1973 1
Scrimgeour, O.J.
(*Bay of Plenty*) 1995–96
(*Waikato*) 1995–96–97–98–99 22
Senio, K. (*Auckland*) 2001 2
Seymour, D.J.
(*Canterbury*) 1988–89–90–91–
92–93–99–00–02
(*Hawke's Bay*) 1994–95–96
(*Wellington*) 1997–98–99 35
Shelford, W.T.
(*North Harbour*) 1985–86–87 5
Simonsson, B.G. (*Bay of Plenty*) 2017–18 3
Skudder, G.R. (*Waikato*) 1973 1
Smith, B.R. (*Otago*) 2010 1
Smith, B.W. (*Waikato*) 1983 1
Smith, David (*Auckland*) 2008 1
Smith, D.A. (*Canterbury*) 1996 3
Smith, W.R. (*Canterbury*)
1984–85–86 4
Smylie, C.B. (*North Harbour*) 2002 2
Soakai, A. (*Otago*) 2006–07 9
So'oialo, R. (*Wellington*) 2000–01–02 6
Souness, B.J. (*Taranaki*) 2009–10–11 17
Spooner-Neera, T.A. (*Hawke's Bay*)
2013 4
Stanaway, T.Z.B.P. (*Bay of Plenty*)
2015–16–17–18 9
Stanley, J.T. (*Auckland*) 1983 1
Steinmetz, P.C. (*Wellington*) 1999 3
Stevens, I.N. (*Wellington*) 1973 1
Stowers, S.L. (*Auckland*) 2004
(*Counties Manukau*) 2009–10–12–
13–14–15–16–17 42
Sutherland, A.R.
(*Marlborough*) 1973 1
Sweeney, D.W.H. (*Waikato*) 2006 6

Tagaloa, T.D.L. (*Wellington*) 1991 1
Tairea, F.T. (*Auckland*) 2009 1

Tournaments

Tamani, G.B. (*Japan*)[1] 1997	1
Tanivula, I. (*Auckland*) 2002	2
Taramai, M.V.U. (*Wellington*) 2014–15	4
Taufahema, T. (*Auckland*) 1998	5
Tauiwi, J.J.	
(*Bay of Plenty*) 1994–95–96–97	14
Te Aute, I.N. (*Bay of Plenty*) 2016	1
Te Nana, K.S.	
(*Wellington*) 1996–97–98–99	
(*North Harbour*) 1999–00–01–02–03	42
Te Tamaki, I.R. (*Waikato*) 2015–16–17–18	15
Thomas, J.T. (*Waikato*) 1998	1
Thomson, A.J. (*Otago*) 2007	4
Thomson, N.J. (*Canterbury*) 2006–07	6
Thorpe, A.J. (*Canterbury*) 1984	1
Tiatia, J.A.	
(*Canterbury*) 2000–01–02–03–04	21
Tietjens, G.F. (*Waikato*) 1983	1
Tilsley, G. (*Wellington*) 2011	
(*Manawatu*) 2014	6
Timu, J.K.R. (*Otago*) 1993	2
Tipoki, T.R. (*Auckland*) 1997–98	
(*North Harbour*) 1998–99–02	10
Toeava, I. (*Auckland*) 2005	3
Tokula, S. (*Waikato*) 2009–10	12
Tololima-Auva'a, O.J. see **Auva'a, O.J.**	
(*Auckland*) 2006	
Tuatagaloa, B. (*Wellington*) 2012	
(*Canterbury*) 2013	9
Tuhakaraina, M.	
(*Bay of Plenty*) 1999–00	2
Tui'avii, D. (*Wellington*) 1993	1
Tuilevu, A. (*Waikato*) 1997–98	5
Tuitavake, A.S.	
(*North Harbour*) 2002–03–04	20
Tuitavake, N.H.	
(*North Harbour*) 2008–09–10	12
Tulou, A. (*Wellington*) 2008	1
Tuoro, C.K.	
(*Counties Manukau*) 2008–09	10
Tupuola, T. (*Wellington*) 2010	2
Umaga-Marshall, T.P.	
(*Wellington*) 2006–09	4
Vaka, S.T.	
(*Counties Manukau*) 2014–15	4

Tournaments

Valence, A.	
(*Auckland*) 1998–99–00–01–02–05–06	
(*Hawke's Bay*) 2003–04	67
van Lieshout, J.J.A.	
(*Counties Manukau*) 2016	2
Verran, J.A. (*Canterbury*) 2012	1
Vidiri, J.	
(*Counties Manukau*) 1995–96–98	
(*Auckland*) 2000	6
Visinia, L. (*Auckland*) 2012	2
Vito, V.V.J. (*Wellington*) 2007–08–09	8
Waaka, B.R.T. (*Taranaki*) 2015–16–17	14
Waldrom, S.L. (*Wellington*) 2002	
(*Taranaki*) 2007–10	5
Walker, N.A.	
(*Bay of Plenty*) 2002–03–04	15
Waqaseduadua, V.M.	
(*North Harbour*) 2005–09	4
Ware, R.E. (*Waikato*) 2015–16	
(*Bay of Plenty*) 2017–18	27
Webb, G.A. (*Otago*) 2003	1
Webber, T.J. (*Waikato*) 2011–12–13–14–15–16–17–18	34
Whitelock, A.J. (*Canterbury*) 2014	2
Williams, S.	
(*Counties Manukau*) 2016	7
Williams-Spiers, G.D.	
(*Auckland*) 2012	1
Wilson, B.A. (*North Harbour*) 2005	1
Wilson, J.C. (*Bay of Plenty*) 1999–00	
(*Auckland*) 2001–02	
(*Wellington*) 2003–04–05	32
Wilson, J.H. (*Bay of Plenty*) 2012	3
Wolfe, T.W.N. (*Taranaki*) 1993	1
Woods, P.G.A. (*Bay of Plenty*) 1993	
(*Nth Harbour*) 1994–95–96–97–98	15
Wotherspoon, K.J.	
(*Hawke's Bay*) 1996	1
Wright, T.J.	
(*Auckland*) 1986–87–88–89–90–91–92	11
Wulf, R.N.	
(*North Harbour*) 2004–05–06	7
Wyllie, A.J. (*Canterbury*) 1973	1
Yates, S.P. (*Canterbury*) 2007–08	12

[1]Tournament reserve players called upon when injuries prevented New Zealand from having fit reserves for the final.

NEW ZEALAND INTERNATIONAL SEVENS
FMG Waikato Stadium, Hamilton February 3–4, 2018

POOL PLAY

A   Fiji 28, Wales 0; Australia 21, Spain 5; Fiji 24, Spain 12;
Australia 26, Wales 7; Wales 29, Spain 21; Fiji 26, Australia 15.

B   England 47, Russia 0; South Africa 36, Papua New Guinea 5;
England 27, Papua New Guinea 0; South Africa 38, Russia 0;
Papua New Guinea 33, Russia 7; South Africa 28, England 7.

C   New Zealand 52, France 7; Argentina 19, Scotland 14; New Zealand 24, Scotland 5;
France 28, Argentina 14; Scotland 26, France 14; New Zealand 17, Argentina 12.

D   Kenya 19, Samoa 14; USA 28, Canada 14; Kenya 19, Canada 14;
Samoa 14, USA 10; Samoa 22, Canada 14; USA 19, Kenya 19.

CUP CHAMPIONSHIP

Quarter-finals   Fiji 12, Samoa 10; New Zealand 19, England 12;
Australia 33, Kenya 12; South Africa 22, Scotland 0.
Semi-finals   Fiji 14, New Zealand 12; South Africa 24, Australia 5.
Final   Fiji 24, South Africa 17.
Play off for 3rd   Australia 8, New Zealand 7.
5th place semi-final   Samoa 22, England 17; Kenya 33, Scotland 19.
5th place play-off   Samoa 19, Kenya 15.

CHALLENGE TROPHY

Quarter-finals   Canada 19 Wales 14; Argentina 21 Russia 12;
USA 29 Spain 12; Papua New Guinea 35 France 0.
Semi-finals   Argentina 14 Canada 12; USA 42 Papua New Guinea 12.
Final   USA 24 Argentina 5.

13th place semi-final Wales 33 Russia 7; France 19 Spain 14.
13th place play-off   France 19 Wales 17.

Tournament referees: James Doleman (*New Zealand*), Craig Evans (*Wales*), Sam Grove-White (*Scotland*), Richard Kelly (*New Zealand*), Damon Murphy (*Australia*), Rasta Rasivhenge (*South Africa*), Rasta Rasivhenge (*South Africa*), Matt Rodden (*Hong Kong*), Tevita Rokovereni (*Fiji*), Jordan Way (*Australia*).

New Zealand International Sevens Tournaments

	Cup final	Plate winner	Bowl winner	Shield winner
2000	Fiji 24, New Zealand 14	Canada	France	
2001	Australia 19, Fiji 17	Samoa	South Africa	Japan
2002	South Africa 17, Samoa 14	Argentina	France	Cook Is
2003	New Zealand 38, England 26	Samoa	Canada	Tonga
2004	New Zealand 33, Fiji 15	Tonga	Argentina	USA
2005	New Zealand 31, Argentina 7	Australia	Kenya	Niue
2006	Fiji 27, South Africa 22	England	Scotland	Tonga
2007	Samoa 17, Fiji 14	England	Argentina	Portugal
2008	New Zealand 22, Samoa 7	South Africa	England	USA
2009	England 19, New Zealand 17	South Africa	Cook Is	Scotland
2010	Fiji 19, Samoa 14	Australia	Wales	USA
2011	New Zealand 29, England 14	Fiji	Kenya	USA
2012	New Zealand 24, Fiji 7	South Africa	Kenya	Scotland
2013	England 24, Kenya 19	Australia	Canada	Wales
2014	New Zealand 21, South Africa 0	Australia	Kenya	USA
2015	New Zealand 27, England 21	Fiji	France	Canada
2016	New Zealand 24, South Africa 21	Australia	Samoa	France

	Cup final	Challenge Trophy winner
2017	South Africa 26, Fiji 5	Kenya
2018	Fiji 24, South Africa 17	USA

NATIONAL SEVENS

Rotorua International Stadium   January 13/14, 2018

POOL PLAY

A   Counties Manukau 45, Wanganui 12; Taranaki 12, Waikato 12;
       Waikato 19, Counties Manukau 12; Taranaki 42, Wanganui 5;
       Taranaki 19, Counties Manukau 12; Waikato 45, Wanganui 5.
B   Bay of Plenty 43, Mid Canterbury 0; Auckland 19, Canterbury 0;
       Bay of Plenty 19, Canterbury 10; Auckland 39, Mid Canterbury 10;
       Bay of Plenty 24, Auckland 14; Canterbury 22, Mid Canterbury 12.
C   Wellington 24, Southland 5; Tasman 24, Northland 5;
       Wellington 26, Northland 5; Tasman 24, Southland 7;
       Tasman 22, Wellington 7; Northland 19, Southland 17.
D   Otago 26, Manawatu 19; North Harbour 19, Hawke's Bay 12;
       North Harbour 40, Otago 7; Manawatu 32, Hawke's Bay 5;
       Hawke's Bay 20, Otago 14; North Harbour 33, Manawatu 5.

CUP CHAMPIONSHIP

Quarter-finals   Waikato 35, Auckland 0; Wellington 15, North Harbour 12;
                   Tasman 24, Manawatu 12; Taranaki 24, Bay of Plenty 17.
Semi-finals   Waikato 22, Wellington 5; Tasman 17, Taranaki 12.
Final   Waikato 21, Tasman 17.

PLATE CHAMPIONSHIP

Semi-finals   Auckland 19, North Harbour 14; Bay of Plenty 26, Manawatu 7.
Final   Bay of Plenty 31, Auckland 12

BOWL CHAMPIONSHIP

Quarter-finals   Counties Manukau 38, Mid Canterbury 7; Hawke's Bay 31, Southland 0;
                   Otago 24, Northland 0; Canterbury 29, Wanganui 10.
Semi-finals   Counties Manukau 40, Hawke's Bay 5; Canterbury 22, Otago 12.
Final   Counties Manukau 26, Canterbury 5.

SHIELD CHAMPIONSHIP

Semi-finals   Southland 32, Mid Canterbury 24; Northland 38, Wanganui 12.
Final   Northland 31, Southland 19.

Tournament referees: Jamie Bell, James Doleman, Nick Hogan, Richard Kelly, Damian Macpherson, Michael Winter.

NATIONAL SEVENS

Tauranga Domain   December 15/16, 2018

POOL PLAY

A   Counties Manukau 24, Wairarapa Bush 0; North Harbour 26, Manawatu 12;
    Counties Manukau 22, North Harbour 7; Manawatu 22, Wairarapa Bush 14;
    Counties Manukau 24, Manawatu 7; North Harbour 50, Wairarapa Bush 0.
B   Waikato 27, Southland 14; Auckland 24, Otago 14;
    Waikato 38, Otago 21; Southland 26, Auckland 5;
    Waikato 19, Auckland 0; Southland 17, Otago 7.
C   Wellington 26, South Canterbury 0; Tasman 40, Northland 7;
    Wellington 38, Northland 0; Tasman 26, South Canterbury 7;
    Tasman 24, Wellington 10; Northland 19, South Canterbury 0.
D   Canterbury 17, Hawke's Bay 12; Taranaki 10, Bay of Plenty 0;
    Canterbury 24, Bay of Plenty 7; Hawke's Bay 38, Taranaki 12;
    Taranaki 24, Canterbury 5; Hawke's Bay 21, Bay of Plenty 17.

CUP CHAMPIONSHIP

Quarter-finals   Counties Manukau 19, Southland 10; Wellington 33, Hawke's Bay 0;
                   Tasman 24, Taranaki 19; North Harbour 24, Waikato 0.
Semi-finals   Counties Manukau 12, Wellington 10; Tasman 33, North Harbour 7.
Final   Tasman 12, Counties Manukau 7.

PLATE CHAMPIONSHIP

Semi-finals   Hawke's Bay 19, Southland 7; Taranaki 22, Waikato 21.
Final   Taranaki 19, Hawke's Bay 5.

BOWL CHAMPIONSHIP

Quarter-finals   Otago 29, Manawatu 5; Canterbury 21, South Canterbury 14;
                   Bay of Plenty 41, Northland 0; Auckland 26, Wairarapa Bush 12.
Semi-finals   Otago 12, Canterbury 7; Auckland 24, Bay of Plenty 21.
Final   Auckland 22, Otago 14.

SHIELD CHAMPIONSHIP

Semi-finals   Manawatu 21, South Canterbury 19; Northland 35, Wairarapa Bush 12.
Final   Manawatu 14, Northland 7.

Tournament referees: Jamie Bell, Stu Catley, Tipene Cottrell, Nick Hogan, Daniel Waenga, Michael Winter.

Joe Tauiwi Memorial Trophy *(Player of the Tournament)*
2001 Rua Tipoki (*North Harbour*), 2002 Tafai Ioasa (*Wellington*), 2004 Rudi Wulf (*North Harbour*), 2005 Amasio Valence (*Auckland*), 2006 Gary Saifoloi (*Auckland*), 2007 Tomasi Cama (*Manawatu*), 2008 David Raikuna (*Counties Manukau*), 2009 Luke Hamilton (*North Harbour*), 2010 Ben Souness (*Taranaki*), 2011 Malakai Fekitoa (*Auckland*, *2012* Buxton Popoaili'i (*Otago*), 2013 David Raikuna (*North Harbour*), 2014 George Tilsley (*Manawatu*), 2015 Luke Masirewa (*Waikato*), 2016 Augustine Pulu (*Counties Manukau*) , 2017 Andrew Knewstubb (*Tasman*), 2018 (*January*) Jordan Bunce (*Waikato*); (*December*) James Lash (*Tasman*).

NATIONAL SEVENS
TOURNAMENT TROPHY WINNERS

	Venue	Cup	Plate	Bowl	Shield
1975	Auckland	Marlborough			
1976	Christchurch	Marlborough			
1977	Blenheim	Manawatu			
1978	Hamilton	Manawatu			
1979	Palmerston Nth	Manawatu			
1980	Palmerston Nth	Auckland			
1981	Palmerston Nth	Taranaki			
1982	Feilding	Taranaki			
1983	Feilding	Auckland			
1984	Feilding	Auckland			
1985	Feilding	Counties			
1986	Feilding	Nth Harbour			
1987	Christchurch	Nth Harbour	Canterbury	Horowhenua	
1988	Pukekohe	Auckland	Manawatu	Wai Bush	
1989	Palmerston Nth	Auckland	Taranaki	Wanganui	Hawke's Bay
1990	Palmerston Nth	Canterbury	Bay of Plenty	Wanganui	Manawatu B
1991	Palmerston Nth	Auckland	Counties	Canterbury	East Coast
1992	Palmerston Nth	Nth Harbour	Counties	Auckland	Manawatu B
1993	Palmerston Nth	Canterbury	Nth Harbour	Taranaki	King Country
1994	Palmerston Nth	Counties	Nth Harbour	Canterbury	Manawatu B
1995	Palmerston Nth	Counties	Wellington	King Country	Manawatu B
1996	(Mar) Palm Nth	Waikato	C'nties M'kau	Wai Bush	Poverty Bay
1996	(Nov) Palm Nth	Waikato	Wellington	Wai Bush	Wanganui
1997	Rotorua	Waikato	Auckland	Otago	Wai Bush
1998	Rotorua	Waikato	Canterbury	Wai Bush	Otago
1999	Palmerston Nth	Nth Harbour	Canterbury	King Country	Nelson Bays
2000	Palmerston Nth	Nth Harbour	Wanganui	Nelson Bays	Southland
2001	Palmerston Nth	Nth Harbour	C'nties M'kau	Manawatu	West Coast
2002	Palmerston Nth	Wellington	Waikato	Marlborough	West Coast
2004	Queenstown	Nth Harbour	Auckland	Canterbury	Manawatu
2005	Queenstown	Auckland	Wellington	Otago	Manawatu
2006	Queenstown	Auckland	Bay of Plenty	Southland	Cantabrians
2007	Queenstown	Auckland	C'nties M'kau	Wellington	Northland

	Venue	Cup	Plate	Bowl	Shield
2008	Queenstown	Auckland	Manawatu	Wellington	Tasman
2009	Queenstown	Nth Harbour	Wellington	Otago	Southland
2010	Queenstown	Waikato	Nth Harbour	Horo' Kapiti	Tasman
2011	Queenstown	Auckland	Nth Harbour	Manawatu	Canterbury
2012	Queenstown	Auckland	Taranaki	Tasman	Bay of Plenty
2013	Queenstown	Taranaki	Auckland	Hawke's Bay	C'nties M'kau
2014	Rotorua	Wellington	Manawatu	Nth Harbour	Waikato
2015	Rotorua	Waikato	Taranaki	NthHarbour	Canterbury
2016	Rotorua	C'nties M'kau	Auckland	Northland	Wanganui
2017	Rotorua	C'nties M'kau	Auckland	Bay of Plenty	Otago
2018					
(Jan)	Rotorua	Waikato	Bay of Plenty	C'nties M'kau	Northland
(Dec)	Tauranga	Tasman	Taranaki	Auckland	Manawatu

CLUB FINALS
Results of the 2018 senior club finals.

Auckland — Gallaher Shield:
28 July: Ponsonby 35 v University 23
In the second half Ponsonby went from 17–18 down to 32–18 in front and eventually claim their 49th title.

Bay of Plenty – Baywide Premier Trophy:
28 July: Te Puke Sports 27 v Te Puna 13
Halftime 11–10. Te Puna's first final.

Buller – Senior Shield:
7 July: Westport 52 v White Star 24
Repeat finalists from 2017. Westport led 14–12 at halftime and raced ahead to 52–12 for their first title since 2003. Mitieli Kaloudigibeci scored four of their eight tries.

Buller–West Coast – Ngakawau Jubilee Trophy
2 June: Kiwi 48 v Westport 31
At 22–19 ahead in the second half, Kiwi gained two penalty tries from five metre scrums to pull clear. Last combined competition was 2010.

Canterbury

**Ellesmere–Mid Canterbury–North Canterbury combined –
Luisetti Combined Country Cup:**
16 June: Waihora 36 v Rakaia 24
In the final ten minutes Waihora kicked a penalty goal and then scored a converted try.

Metropolitan – Hawkins Trophy:
29 July: Lincoln University 26 v New Brighton 7
Halftime 20–0. Fourth consecutive title for Lincoln University. New Brighton scored in the final minute.

Ellesmere sub union – Coleman Shield:
11 August: Waihora 20 v Darfield 10
Halftime 0–3. Darfield beaten in third consecutive final.

North Canterbury sub union – Hunnibel Memorial Trophy:
11 August: Glenmark–Cheviot 23 v Saracens 10
Halftime 20–5.

Counties Manukau – McNamara Cup:
21 July: Ardmore Marist 52 aet v Patumahoe 26 aet
21–21 at halftime and 26–26 after 80 minutes, Ardmore Marist scored four tries in extra time.

Ngati Porou East Coast – Rangiora Keelan Memorial Shield:
28 July: Uawa 25 v Tokararangi 21
Halftime 22–7, and there was no scoring in the last 19 minutes. Uawa's first title since 2009. Whiti Timutimu, a Hawke's Bay women's rep 2001–2002, refereed.

Hawke's Bay – Maddison Trophy Cup (new):

28 July: Clive 37 v Napier OB Marist 7
Repeat finalists from last year. Halftime 13–7. Napier OB Marist had won both previous encounters in 2018 by more than 70 points.

Horowhenua Kapiti – Ramsbotham Cup:

28 July: Toa 41 v Rahui 32
Toa's first title since 2005. Rahui led twice in the second half. Five sets of brothers were in the Toa match day 22.

King Country – Meads Shield:

28 July: Taupo Sports 17 v Piopio 10
Halftime 7–3. Three tries to one. Piopio's first final since 1989.

Manawatu – Hankins Shield:

28 July: Feilding OB–Oroua 24 v Feilding 22
First title for the combined club. A penalty goal with four minutes left put Feilding OB–Oroua back in front. The match ended with Feilding in possession 10 metres out from the FOB–Oroua posts then conceding a penalty.

Mid Canterbury – Watters Cup:

4 August: Celtic 28 v Southern 24
Down 21–24, Celtic turned down three kickable penalties in the final 10 minutes in favour of a scrum then two tap kicks, scoring the winning try from the second tap kick for their first title since 2006. For combined competition with Ellesmere and North Canterbury sub-unions see **Canterbury**.

Northland

Northland Premiership – Joe Morgan Memorial Trophy:
21 July: Kamo 35 v Waiapu 10
Halftime 11–10.

Bay of Islands sub union – Championship Shield:
7 July: Moerewa–United Kawakawa 24 v Kaikohe 18
Repeat finalists from last year. A converted try with two minutes left put the defending champions back in front. Only four teams participated. Moerewa–United Kawakawa subsequently lost a promotion-relegation match into the Northland Premiership.

Mangonui sub union – Bell Shield:
28 July: Eastern United 31 v Kaitaia 10
Halftime 16–0. Eastern United successfully defended their title.

North Harbour – A.S.B. Cup:

21 July: Northcote 25 v East Coast Bays 20
Northcote came from 11–20 down in the second half to win. It was East Coast Bays first final since 1994.

North Otago – Citizen's Shield:

21 July: Valley 28 v Kurow 22
The match ended with Kurow in possession five metres from the Valley posts and then conceding a penalty.

Otago

Metropolitan – Speight's Championship Shield:
4 August: Harbour 30 aet v University 30 aet
30–30 after 80 minutes. University scored an 80th minute converted try to force extra time. Harbour missed a drop goal attempt in final minute of extra time. Harbour's first ever title, University's 50th title.

Central Region – Super Liquor Trophy:
28 July: Upper Clutha 27 v Cromwell 8
Halftime 10–8. No scoring in last 24 minutes of match. First title for Upper Clutha since 1979.

Southern Region – Speight's Cup:
28 July: Clutha 43 v Crescent 25
Repeat finalists from last year. Halftime 24–8, with Robin Fesilafai scoring a second half hat trick in Clutha's fourth title in a row.

Central Region–Southern Region: Countrywide Shield
4 August: Clutha 31 v Upper Clutha 28
Halftime 10–15. A last minute try to Daniel Miller enabled Clutha to win the Countrywide Shield for the fourth consecutive time.

Poverty Bay – Lee Brothers Shield:

21 July: Waikohu 40 v YMP 26
Halftime 13–6. Waikohu led 40–9 during the second half for their first ever title.

Southland – Galbraith Shield:

21 July: Marist 38 v Pirates Old Boys 13
Marist successfully defended the title, first time in their history they have won two titles in a row.

South Canterbury – Hamersley Cup:

28 July: Celtic 25 v Waimate 22
Celtic made it ten consecutive titles after leading 16–5 at halftime. Waimate scored four tries to two.

Taranaki – McMasters Shield:

15 July: New Plymouth OB 29 v Coastal 9
Three converted tries in the last 15 minutes saw Old Boys go from 8–9 to 29–9, the last of them coming in the final minute.

Tasman – Tasman Trophy:

21 July: Nelson 16 Nelson Marist 6
A scoreless second half in the rain, Nelson celebrated their 150th jubilee this year.

Marlborough sub union – Champion of Champions Trophy:
4 June: Waitohi 20 v Renwick 19
Waitohi scored their only try with 12 minutes left to lead 20–19. There was no further scoring.

Nelson Bays sub union – Strange Memorial Cup + Centennial Cup:
4 June: Stoke 19 v Marist 10
Stoke scored three tries to one, for their first title since 2010.

Thames Valley – McClinchy Cup:
28 July: Waihi Athletic 26 v Thames RS 17
Waihi Athletic led 13–10 at halftime and a penalty goal right on fulltime made it 26–17 for their first ever title.

Waikato – Breweries Shield:
28 July: Hamilton OB 42 v Hautapu 27
Hamilton OB led 42–15 after 71 minutes to successfully defend the title.

Wanganui – President's Rosebowl:
21 July: Ruapehu 41 v Pirates 17
Shaquille Wara scored three of Ruapehu's seven tries as they successfully defended their title.

Wairarapa Bush – Tui Cup:
28 July: Gladstone 32 v Carterton 10
Gladstone led 32–3 with three minutes left, to claim back to back titles for the first time.

Wellington – Jubilee Cup:
4 August: Old Boys University 37 v Northern United 31
Halftime 25–3. Old Boys University withstood a second half comeback for their second consecutive title. Northern United had won both previous encounters during the year.

West Coast – Taylorville Wallsend Trophy:
21 July: Kiwi 17 v Blaketown 5
Played in the rain, a third consecutive title for Kiwi who also completed a perfect season 16 wins from 16 games. Halftime, 5–0. Same finalists as last year.

For combined competition with Buller see **Buller–West Coast.**

Most consecutive championships:
14 Star (Southland) 1890–1903
10 Athletic (North Otago) 1906–1915; Celtic (South Canterbury) 2009–2018
8 Star (Southland) 1919–1926; Westport (Buller) 1963–1970; Invercargill (Southland) 1987–1994; Ponsonby (Auckland) 2004–2011

Most consecutive Sub Union championships:
13 Mahia (Wairoa) 1981–1993
11 Dannevirke O.B. (Dannevirke) 1946–1955, (Central HB–Dannevirke) 1956

JOCK HOBBS MEMORIAL NATIONAL UNDER 19 TOURNAMENT

The fifth edition of this tournament was played from 9–15 September at Owen Delany Park, Taupo. On the final day four of the eight matches were shown live on Sky TV. The matches are not of first-class status.

Each squad was made up of 25 players who were registered to play club rugby in their Provincial Union and who were under 19 as at 1 January 2018.

The seedings for the National Tournament, based on placings in prior tournaments held within each Super Rugby franchise (Crusaders and Highlanders combined), were:

Premiership (top eight) — Graham Mourie Cup
Auckland (*Blues 2*), Bay of Plenty (*Chiefs 1*), Canterbury (*Southern 1*), Hawke's Bay (*Hurricanes 2*), North Harbour (*Blues 1*), Taranaki (*Chiefs 2*), Tasman (*Southern 2*), Wellington (*Hurricanes 1*).

Championship (bottom eight) – Michael Jones Trophy
Auckland Development (*Blues 4*), Counties Manukau (*Chiefs 4*), Heartland, Manawatu (*Hurricanes 3*), Northland (*Blues 3*), Otago (*Southern 3*), Southland (*Southern 4*), Waikato (*Chiefs 3*).

2018 RESULTS
PREMIERSHIP — GRAHAM MOURIE CUP (1ST–8TH)
Day One: September 9
Bay of Plenty 90 – Hawke's Bay 0; North Harbour 28 – Tasman 25; Canterbury 37 – Auckland 8; Wellington 62 – Taranaki 8
Day Two: September 12
Semi-finals: Bay of Plenty 68 – North Harbour 12; Canterbury 39 – Wellington 22
Ranking: Tasman 35 – Hawke's Bay 33; Auckland 41 – Taranaki 20
Day Three: September 15
1st/2nd Final: Bay of Plenty 35 – Canterbury 30
3rd/4th North Harbour 21 – Wellington 10; *5th/6th* Auckland 35 – Tasman 31; *7th/8th* Hawke's Bay 40 – Taranaki 13

CHAMPIONSHIP — MICHAEL JONES TROPHY (9TH–16TH)
Day One: September 9
Otago 29 – Auckland Development 22; Counties Manukau 27 – Manawatu 22; Waikato 67 – Heartland 5; Southland 29 – Northland 22
Day Two: September 12
Semi-finals: Otago 27 – Counties Manukau 25; Waikato 59 – Southland 0
Ranking: Auckland Development 40 – Manawatu 17; Northland 38 – Heartland 35
Day Three: September 15
9th/10th Final: Waikato 30 – Otago 5
11th/12th Counties Manukau 29 – Southland 24;
13th/14th Auckland Development 59 – Northland 14; *15th/16th* Manawatu 21 – Heartland 12

D.J. GRAHAM AWARD (PLAYER OF THE TOURNAMENT)
2014	Mitchell Karpik	(*Auckland A*)
2015	Charlie Gamble	(*Canterbury*)
2016	Luke Jacobson	(*Waikato*)
2017	Sione Talitui	(*Auckland*)
2018	Kaleb Trask	(*Bay of Plenty*)

Top Try-scorer

2014	(4)	Setariki Koroitamana (*Heartland*)
2015	(5)	Jonathan Taumateine (*Counties Manukau*)
2016	(5)	Salimoni Tukania (*Counties Manukau*)
2017	(4)	Ajay Mua (*Bay of Plenty*), Jaya More (*Southland*)
2018	(5)	Jack McConnell (*Waikato*), Siave Seti (*Waikato*), Bartje Wierenga (*Bay of Plenty*)

Top Points-scorer

2014	(46)	Jaye Thompson (*Southland*)
2015	(69)	Jonathan Taumateine (*Counties Manukau*)
2016	(51)	Mathew Lansdown (*Waikato*)
2017	(60)	Harry Plummer (*Auckland*)
2018	(54)	Kaleb Trask (*Bay of Plenty*)

FINISHING POSITIONS

	2014	2015	2016	2017	2018
Auckland	3	7	2	1	5
Auckland Development	13	16	7	16	13
Bay of Plenty	8	13	10	5	1
Canterbury	2	1	4	4	2
Counties Manukau	16	9	9	9	11
Hawke's Bay	12	12	12	11	7
Heartland	11	15	15	12	16
Manawatu	10	8	6	8	15
North Harbour	7	6	13	3	3
Northland	15	14	14	15	14
Otago	5	4	5	13	10
Southland	9	11	16	10	12
Taranaki	6	3	8	14	8
Tasman	14	10	11	6	6
Waikato	4	2	1	2	9
Wellington	1	5	3	7	4

2018 SQUADS (APPEARANCES IN BRACKETS):

Auckland: *Captain:* Lemeki Namoa *Coach:* James Hantz
Caleb Clarke (3); Robert Cobb (3); McCarthy Cocker-Filikitonga (3); John Cooper (3); Lesinali Faleafa (3); Cameron Finefeuiaki (3); Noah Foster (3); Jack Gray (3); Carter Hackett (2); Frazer Harrison (3); Felix Kalapu (3); Isileli Manu (3); Junior Matautia (3); Paul Mohi (3); Lemeki Namoa (3); Albert Ngata (1)); Fatongia Paea (3); Otunuku Pauta (3); Obey Samate (0); Oliver Shepherd (3); Theodore Steffany (3); Thomas Strachan (3); Nua Tapuai Soti (2); Te Ariki Te Puni (3); Tamatoa Tepaea (2).

Auckland Development: *Captain:* Michaile Van Wyk *Coach:* Greg Aldous
Griffin Bayley (3); Sam Beere (3); Jack Casey-Pickering (0); Jackson Clarke (3); Joseph Elisara (1); Simon Fauoo (3); Samuela Fihaki (3); Levi Filiga (2); Hugo Garcia Rafael (3); Rosia Ioane (3); Josefa Kolinisau (3); John Latu (3); Tyberg Mauafua (2); Pita Niubalavu (1); Mordecai Pulu (3); Danny Silivelio (3); Viliami Sipa (3); Champagnat Solomon-Mua (3); Ben Sterritt (3); Vai'ese Su'a (3); Kainaliu Teaupa (3); Lisivani Tuifua (3); Toa Tupuna (3); Michaile Van Wyk (3); Josh Wheeler (3).

Bay of Plenty: *Captain:* Kaipo Brown *Coach:* Mike Rogers
Angus Baker (2); Kaipo Brown (3); Leroy Carter (3); Mafi Fafita (3); Taniela Filimone (1); Cole Forbes (3); Kohan Herbert (3); Lalomilo Lalomilo (3); Gordie Lloyd (3); Miracle Lolofie (3); Iosefa Maloney (3); Coby Milne (2); Emoni Narawa (3); Semisi Paea (3); Jonas Pomare (3); Dennon Robinson (2); Peter Seeling (3); Tevita Sole (3); Jayjay Suemai (3); Apitone Toia (3); Kaleb Trask (3); Etonia Waqa (2); Bartje Wieringa (2); Dylan Williams (3); Keita Yamamoto (2).

Canterbury: *Captain:* Cullen Grace *Coach:* Grant Keenan
Josh Bokser (3); Finlay Brewis (3); Fergus Burke (3); Luke Donaldson (3); Thomas Edwards (3); Nick Frost (3); Connor Garden-Bachop (3); Mitchell Gibson (3); Sam Gilbert (3); Connor Gordon (3); Cullen Grace (3); Alex Harford (2); Finlay Joyce (0); Perry Karati (3); Coel Kerr (3); Shilo Klein (3); Matthew Letoga (3); Reon Lowery (3); Dallas McLeod (3); Connor McManus (3); Burns Mills (3); Fletcher Morgan (1); Fletcher Newell (3); Rico Syme (2); Boris Van Bruchem (3).

Counties Manukau: *Captain:* Zuriel Togiatama (2),
Chay Mackwood (1) *Coach:* Glen Rowe
Callum Bean (3); Lachlan Douglas (3); Glynne Evans (2); Lionel Evans (3); Charlie Fakaonga (2); Abraham Falani (3); Joshua Gray (3); Nathan Green (3); James King (2); Ronan Lawrence (2); Chay Mackwood (3); Jermaine Malaga (1); Heremaia Murray (2); Aue Parima (1); Jesse Pascoe (3); Faalae Peni (3); Tala Potifara (3); Salesitangi Savelio (3); Zachary Smith (3); Jireh Tiumalu (3); Karapani Togafau Aperila (2); Zuriel Togiatama (2); Rodney Tongatea (3); Reuben Unga (3); Malkome Vaka (2); George Wynn (3).

Hawke's Bay: *Captain:* Lincoln McClutchie *Coach:* Blair Cross
Flynn Allen (3); Josh Combs (3); Kyle Cornelissen (3); Billie Croswell (1); Jacob Devery (3); Tyrone Dodd-Edwards (3); Folau Fakatava (1); Lolani Faleiva (2); Devan Flanders (2); Rangatira Fox (3); Nathan Giles (3); Nick Hutton (2); Luke Johnson (2); Thomas Kirikiri (2); Clerk Kopelani (3); Lincoln McClutchie (3); Nikau McGregor (3); Lee Moleli (3); Trei Nepe-Apatu (3); Cameron Pratt (3); Daniel Saifiti (2); Jon Scales (3); Dan Sharplin (2); Jacob Stephenson (3); Danny Toala (3); Jasper Wylie (3).

Heartland: *Captain:* Kafaongo Katoa *Coach:* Aleni Feagaiga
Bryan Arnold Wairarapa Bush (3); Issac Bracewell Wairarapa Bush (2); Austin Brear Thames Valley (3); Joseph Gordon Wairarapa Bush (3); Zac Gregory Thames Valley (2); Joel Hands Buller (3); Kafaongo Katoe North Otago (3); Te Huia Kutia Thames Valley (3); Ioelu Leo Leo Mid Canterbury (3); Max Linklater West Coast (2); Jake Lochore King Country (1); Jeremiah Mapusua Wairarapa Bush (3); Matt Masoe Wairarapa Bush (3); Caleb McNoe South Canterbury (3); Jason Myers Wanganui (3); Connor Paki Horowhenua Kapiti (3); Sean Pape Horowhenua Kapiti (3); Moses Pearce Horowhenua Kapiti (3); Xavier Pereka Horowhenua Kapiti (3); Hamish Prattley South Canterbury (2); Baxter Richards Thames Valley (2); Niao Savage Ngati Porou East Coast (2); Winiata Tarawa Poverty Bay (2); Desmond Tyrell Wanganui (3); Bray Ward Thames Valley (3).

Manawatu: Co Captains – David Parker, Jamie Tinetti *Coach:* Shane Ratima
Rawiri Chambers (2); Griffin Culver (3); Zane Dallinger (3); Jayden Falcon (3); Matt Finsden (1); Jack Fleury (3); Michael Halatuituia (3); Jack Harris (3); Hugh Hawkey (3); Jacob Hewetson Talamaivao (3); Michael Ioane (3); Pawhare Kershaw (3); Awatere Kiwara (3); Josh McIntyre (3); Tiari Mumby (3); David Parker (3); Jackson Scully (3); Greg Shaw (3); Sam Stewart (3); Jack Sturmey (3); Trevahn Ta'ufo'ou (3); Kolo Tavake (2); Jamie Tinetti (3); Te Tahinga Whaanga Davies (3); Tobias Wickham-Manuel (3).

North Harbour: *Captain:* Jack Heighton *Coach:* Steven Bates
Thomas Barham (3); Jordyn Evans (3); Kalin-Lee Felise (3); Jack Heighton (3); Cameron Hey (2); Maxwell Hicks (3); Samuel Johnson (3); Matthew Jerlina (3); Isileli Kioa (3); Connor Leather (3); Abel Magalogo (2); Spencer McDowall (3); Tamerau McGahan (2); Brad McNaughten (3); David Meki (3); Heremoni Nepo-Tuivaiti (3); Patrick Pati (2); Mosese Pepa (3); James Roots (3); Filipo Sefulu (3); Preston Smith-Owen (1); Joshua Tanner (3); Tuna Tautalafau (3); Nadi Tulia (3); Ezra Vai (2).

Northland: *Captain:* Sadius Cook-Savage (2),
Keanu Cook-Savage (1) *Coach:* Mark Kapa
Tamati Abel (3); Puru Aboagye (3); Thomas Anderson (3); Ilai Arona (3); Gil Cann-Vaana (3); Jaydon Connolly (2); Keanu Cook-Savage (3); Sadius Cook-Savage (2); Tyler Foster (3); Nikau Graham (3); William Grant (3); Miles Halvorson (3); Matthew Harrison (3); Mason Hohaia (3); Nasinu Kuli (3); Jayden Leaupepe (3); Ngatai Manukau-Togiavalu (3); Jake McClure (2); Ben Monaghan (2); Javahn Repia (3); Royce Sanderson (3); Rhys Shadbolt (3); Ethan Sherwood (1); Jackson Sparksman-Brott (3); Mikaere Wiki (3).

Otago: *Captain:* Josh Hill *Coach:* Seilala Mapusua
TJ Ane (3); Henry Bell (3); Harrison Boyle (3); Adam Brash (2); Ross Burton (1); Sam Dickson (3); Kody Edwards (3); Levi Emery (3); Jake Fowler (3); Josh Hill (3); Sean Jansen (3); Llewellyn Johnson (1); Kane Johnston (3); Sam Jones (3); Moala Katoa (3); Delaney McKenzie (3); Gus McPherson (3); Layne Opetaia (3); Abraham Pole (3); Brady Robertson (3); Mamea Taimalie (3); JJ Tonks (1); Graham Urquhart (3); Sepa Vaka (3); Robbie Wong-Tai (1).

Southland: *Captain:* Curtis Williams *Coach:* Daryl Thompson
Josh Bolger (3); Jacob Carmichael (3); Zak Dunnage (2); Henry Earland (3); Kalani Elder (3); Jayden Henderson (3); Campbell Hosie (1); Shane Johnston (2); Rikirangi Kawe-Gage (3); Jake Lawlor (2); Josh Mason (3); Devon McLeod (3); Jack Nally (2); Ben Paulin (3); Ben Pope (2); Albert Qoro (3); Taniora Raniera (3); Dominic Ririnui-Sipa (3); Conor Rodden (2); Kaleb Talamahina (3); Taine Te Whata (3); James Wairau (1); Nathan Wairau (0); Sy Waiti (3); Curtis Williams (3).

Taranaki: *Captain:* Michael Loft *Coach:* Rhys Connell
Austin Brown (3); Toby Burkett (3); Luke Dravitzki (3); Tevita Fa'ukafa (3); Parris Faapulou (3); Melakhi Falaniko (3); Daniel Guthrie (1); Jack Hartley (3); Zach Henderson (3); Josh Iwikau (3); Michael Loft (3); Kane Perrett (3); Chad Petersen (3); Mason Porteous (3); Isaac Ratumaitavuki-Kneepkens (1); Maika Rova (3); Hanley Setu (2); Josh Setu (3); Jackson Sinclair (3); Tobias Stark (3); Liam Thomson (1); Brent Tucker (3); Tupou Vaa'i (3); Jahmarl Weir (1); Connor White (3).

Tasman: *Captain:* Sam Moli *Coach:* Dan Perrin
Eden Beech (3); Caleb Coventry (3); Tom Eelman (3); Leicester Faingaanuku (1); Max Fraine (2); Josh Grant (3); Quinn Harrison-Jones (3); Caleb Havili (3); Vailua Kaloni (3); Luis Lemperle (2); Josh McPherson (3); Neo Milligan-Richard (0); Sam Moli (3); Max Nalder (3); Luke Nicolson (3); Karl Ratcliffe (2); Taine Robinson (3); Nigel Satherley (3); Joe Sharland (3); Humphrey Sheild (3); Matt Stevenson (1); Kershawl Sykes Martin (3); Joe Taylor (3); Kyle Te Tai (1); Sosefo Vaka (2); Peter Vakaloa (1).

Waikato: *Captain:* Sam Cooper *Coach:* Daniel Teka
Charles Alaimalo (3); Sam Cooper (3); Rhys Dickinson (2); George Dyer (2); Samipeni Finau (3); Kaea Hongara (3); Logan Karl (3); TJ Kihi (2); Brian Lima (3); Joseph Mason (3); Jack McConnell (3); Jamie McInnes (0); Calum McNab (3); Keaton Neels (3); Oliver Norris (3); R Kelly Paekau (3); Stanley Paese (3); Jonty Powers (3); Siave Seti (3); Quade Tapsell (3); Wesley Tapueluleu (3); James Thompson (3); Malakai Uasi (3); Joshua Vuta (3); Raiki Willison (2).

Wellington: *Captain:* Naitoa Ah Kuoi (2), Taine Plumtree (1) *Coach:* Dion Waller
Naitoa Ah Kuoi (2); Nicholas Apikotoa (3); Caleb Delaney (3); Xavier English (3); Misilifi Faimalo (3); Tisileli Finau (1); Tanara Haenga (3); Callum Harkin (2); Kienan Higgins (3); George Jacobs (3); Shamus Langton (3); Mellenniumma Leota (1); Laurence-Jarel Lim (3); Tominiko Maiava (1); Ricky Manulaiatea (3); Desmond Matofai (3); Faafetai Neli (3); Raniera Petersen (2); Taine Plumtree (3); Albert Polu (3); Kyle Preston (3); Todd Svenson (3); DJ Taoipu (3); Tane Te Aho (3); Reuben Va'a (2); Jack Wright (3).

SECONDARY SCHOOLS RUGBY

Following a three-day development camp at the Massey University Sport & Rugby Institute in Palmerston North the NZ Schools squad was chosen to visit Australia and the Barbarians Schools squad chosen to play two games in Wellington.

The Schools team won all three games in Brisbane and played at three different venues — Tonga at Sunnybank RFC, Barbarians at Tennyson Field and Australia at Ballymore Stadium. Blair Murray was awarded the Bronze Boot. Funaki, Punivai, Reihana and Williams were also members of the 2017 squad.

NEW ZEALAND SCHOOLS, 2018

	School	Date of birth	Height	Weight
Iona Apineru	St Patrick's College, Silverstream	12/8/00	1.92	113
Louie Chapman	Christchurch BHS	1/5/00	1.74	69
Sam Darry	Christ's College	18/7/00	2.03	97
Chay Fihaki	Sacred Heart College	3/1/01	1.93	94
Taufa Funaki	Sacred Heart College	29/7/00	1.76	91
Matt Graham-Williams	St Kentigern College	16/8/00	1.90	126
Niko Jones	St Peter's College, Auckland	22/7/00	1.85	99
Jacob Kneepkens	Francis Douglas Memorial College	3/8/01	1.89	85
Joshua Lord	Hamilton BHS	17/1/01	2.06	98
Josiah Marakau	Feilding High School	30/3/00	1.82	91
Thomas Martin	Hamilton BHS	13/9/00	1.94	103
Saula Mau	Auckland Grammar	29/4/00	1.95	144
Blair Murray	New Plymouth BHS	9/10/01	1.73	71
Simon Parker	St Peter's School, Cambridge	6/5/00	1.98	107
George Prain	Rangiora HS	30/8/00	1.82	95
Isaiah Punivai (captain)	St Kentigern College	1/12/00	1.89	98
Rivez Reihana	St Kentigern College	25/5/00	1.88	93
Anton Segner	Nelson College	24/7/01	1.93	105
Zarn Sullivan	King's College	10/7/00	1.92	93
Tiaan Tauakipulu	St Kentigern College	3/5/01	1.87	111
Patrick Thacker	Christ's College	2/8/00	1.79	109
Tyrone Thompson	Napier BHS	28/5/00	1.89	106
Soane Vikena	Mt Albert Grammar	7/1/01	1.85	101
Ethan Webster-Nonu	Scots College	10/4/01	1.77	89
Tamati Williams	St Kentigern College	10/8/00	1.97	133
Gideon Wrampling	St Paul's Collegiate	26/7/01	1.88	98

Coaches: Brad Mooar (*Crusaders*), Sam Moore (*assistant, New Plymouth BHS*)
Manager: Nick Reid (*Awatapu College*)
Strength & conditioning coach: Ewan Brumwell (*Otago*)
Physiotherapist: Richie Marsden (*Tasman*)
Video analyst: Doug Neilson (*Taranaki*)

INDIVIDUAL SCORING

	Tries	Con	PG	DG	Points
Reihana	1	9	–	–	23
Murray	4	–	–	–	20
Wrampling	4	–	–	–	20
Williams	2	–	–	–	10
Sullivan	–	5	–	–	10
Chapman	1	–	–	–	5
Darry	1	–	–	–	5
Jones	1	–	–	–	5
Kneepkens	1	–	–	–	5
Maraku	1	–	–	–	5
Mau	1	–	–	–	5
Segner	1	–	–	–	5
Tauakipulu	1	–	–	–	5
Thompson	1	–	–	–	5
Vikena	1	–	–	–	5
Totals	21	14	0	0	133
Opposition scored	6	5	1	0	43

NEW ZEALAND SCHOOLS, 2018

	Tonga Schools	Australia Schools Barbarians	Australia Schools	TOTALS
Murray	15	15	15	3
Webster-Nonu	14	–	–	1
Maraku	11	s	s	3
Kneepkens	–	11	11	2
Punivai	13	13	13	3
Wrampling	12	14	14	3
Fihaki	s	12	12	3
Reihana	10	s	10	3
Sullivan	s	10	s	3
Funaki	9	s	9	3
Chapman	s	9	s	3
Jones	8	8	8	3
Segner	7	s	7	3
Prain	s	7	–	2
Apineru	6	–	6	2
Parker	s	6	s	3
Lord	5	s	s	3
Darry	–	5	5	2
Martin	4	4	4	3
Mau	3	s	3	3
Thacker	–	3	s	2
Williams	1	s	1	3
Graham-Williams	s	1	s	3
Vikena	2	–	2	2
Thompson	s	2	s	3
Tauakipulu	s	s	–	2

NEW ZEALAND SCHOOLS, 2018

PLAYED 3 WON 3 POINTS FOR 133 POINTS AGAINST 43

Date	Opponent	Location	Score	Tries	Con	PG	DG	Referee
September 27	Tonga Schools	Brisbane	54–0	Wrampling (2), Williams, Vikena, Segner, Jones, Maraku, Murray	Reihana (5), Sullivan (2)			Aaron Pook
October 1	Australia Schools Barbarians	Brisbane	55–31	Wrampling (2), Murray (2), Thompson, Darry, Chapman, Kneepkens, Tauakipulu	Sullivan (3), Reihana (2)			Brodie Ingram
October 6	Australia Schools	Brisbane	24–12	Mau, Williams, Reihana, Murray	Reihana (2)			Damon Murphy

NEW ZEALAND BARBARIANS SCHOOLS

Results:
September 27 v **NZ Maori Under 18**, at Porirua Park, Wellington. Lost 20–21. Uelese, Perelini, Cavubati tries; Evans conversion and penalty goal.

October 1 v **Fiji Schools**, at Porirua Park, Wellington. Lost 10–15. Ngakuru, Cavubati triess.

Backs: James Arscott (*Otago BHS*), Caleb Cavubati (*Scots C*), Stewart Cruden (*Palmerston North BHS*), Corey Evans (*captain – Auckland Grammar*), Lukas Halls (*King's C*), Tahu Kaa (*Christchurch BHS*), Peniasi Lasaqa (*St Kentigern C*), Samuel Smith (*Wairarapa C*), Roderick Solo (*Scots C*), Ropati So'oalo (*Aotea C*), Kristian Standen (*New Plymouth BHS*).

Forwards: Arthur Allen (*Christ's C*), Zachary Gallagher (*Christ's C*), Joshua Gimblett (*Napier BHS*), Benet Kumeroa (*Auckland Grammar*), Mahonri Ngakuru (*St Kentigern C*), Jacob Payne (*Southland BHS*), Noah Perelini (*King's C*), Robert Rush (*St Kentigern C*), Poukohe Sorenson (*Rotorua BHS*), Hamdahn Tuipulotu (*St Peter's C*), Ovaleni 'Junior' Uelese (*Scots C*), Keelan Whitman (*St Patrick's C, Wellington*).

Coach: Cory Brown (*Highlanders*)
Assistant coach: Mark Hooper (*Kelston BHS*)
Manager: Cam Kilgour
Trainer: Joel Marshall

NATIONAL UNDER 18 MAORI TEAM

A squad of Maori under-18 players was assembled for two fixtures.

September 27 v **New Zealand Barbarians Schools**, at Porirua Park, Wellington. Won 21–20. Love, Parkinson, Dale tries; Cook-Savage 2, Gordon conversions.

October 5 v **Fiji Schools**, at Porirua Park, Wellington. Won 20–15. Rueben, Hemi tries; Cook-Savage 2 conversions, 2 penalty goals.

Squad: Nikora Broughton (*Hato Paora C*), Te Paea Cook-Savage (*St Paul's Collegiate*), Taylor Dale (*Otago BHS*), Tiaki Fabish (*Napier BHS*), Bailey Gordon (*Western Heights HS*), Jack Gray (*Grammar TEC RFC, Auckland*), Chris Hemi (*St Patrick's C, Silverstream*), Damarus Hokianga (*Hastings BHS*), Ruben Love (*Palmerston North BHS*), Niko Manaena (*Southland BHS*), Thomas Murray-Edwards (*New Plymouth BHS*), Leo Ngatai-Tafau (*St Peter's C, Auckland*), Oliver Parkinson (*Auckland GS*), Terrell Peita (*Mt Albert Grammar*), Raniera Petersen (*Upper Hutt Rams RFC*), Billy Priestley (*Gisborne BHS*), Cortez-Lee Ratima (*Hamilton BHS*), Te Rama Reuben (*Rotorua BHS*), Zach Ririnui (*Rotorua BHS*), Daniel Rona (*New Plymouth BHS*), Kynan Stowers-Smith (*St Bede's C*), Leo Thompson (*Napier BHS*), Jordan Thompson-Dunn (*Hastings BHS*), Jayden Walker (*Napier BHS*), Samuel Walton-Sexton (*Karamu HS*).

Coaches: Kahu Carey, Rua Wanoa
Assistant coaches: Stacey Grant, Anthony Rehutai, Ngatai Walker, Jeremy Wara
Manager: Mark Seymour

NEW ZEALAND BARBARIANS AREA SCHOOLS

Selected from the smaller country high schools, this squad assembled at the Massey University Sport and Rugby Institute, Palmerston North, September 11–15. On the final day a game was played against Manawatu Under-16 at the Institute. Manawatu won 31–17. For the Area Schools, McKinnel, Senior, Tuapawa tries; Beck conversion.

Results:
Squad: Caleb Beck (*Hurunui AS, Canterbury*), Kyhia Bovill (*Onewhero AS, Counties Manukau*), Jarod Bryant (*Rai Valley AS, Tasman*), Oscar Canseco-Munoz (*Tolaga Bay AS, East Coast*), Connor Guest (*Captain, Tauraroa AS, Northland*), Danny Henderson (*Tauraroa AS, Northland*), Liam Henderson (*Tauraroa AS, Northland*), Murray McFarlane (*Taihape AS, Wanganui*), Tiaan McKinnel (*Roxburgh AS, Otago*), Trinity McQueen (*Mercury Bay AS, Thames Valley*), John Henry Martin (*Panguru AS, Northland*), William Martin (*Te Waha o Rerekohu, East Coast*), Makoroa Mataira (*Raglan AS, Waikato*), Clay Morgan (*Tapawera AS, Tasman*), Keagan Mulholand (*Maniototo AS, Otago*), Tyrese Payne (*Taihape AS, Wanganui*), Bohan Rogers (*Cheviot AS, Canterbury*), Dough Smith (*Maniototo AS, Otago*), Hori Te Tai (*Panguru AS, Northland*), Teihana Senior (*Te Wharekura o te Kaokaoroa o Patetere, Waikato*), Mark James Tuapawa (*Tolaga Bay AS, East Coast*), Jacob Walden (*Onewhero AS, Counties Manukau*).

Bovill, Bryant, Danny and Liam Henderson and Guest were also members of the 2017 squad.

Coach: Justin Marsh (*Tongariro AS*)
Assistant coaches: Steve Beck (*Hurunui College*), Hone Manuel (*Te Whare Kura O Manaia*), Ratu Mataira (*Raglan AS*).
Manager: Michael Smith (*Mercury Bay AS*)

SCHOOLS RUGBY REVIEW
by Adam Julian

St Peter's College (Auckland) produced a stirring run of victories to capture their third National Top Four title, and first since 2000, in Palmerston North. Finishing fourth in the round robin of the 1A competition, St Peter's won their next five knockout games by a combined margin of eight points to capture the Barbarians Cup. St Peter's won the title without offering a bundle of scholarships, unlike their Auckland semi-final opponents St Kentigern College who had their 21-game local win streak snapped at the worst possible time.

While First XV rugby grapples with the demands of professionalism, it has struggled to maintain equality of competition and opportunity which is why St Peter's win was so warmly embraced. A total of 53 players were selected for the New Zealand Secondary Schools development camp this year — 21 being from six private schools, St Kentigern College, King's College, St Peter's School (Cambridge), St Paul's Collegiate, Scots College and Christ's College. According to the Ministry of Education, less than five percent of all students in New Zealand attend private schools yet nearly half of the contenders for the final New Zealand team in 2018 were from private schools.

The New Zealand Secondary Schools extended their unbeaten run to 16 games (the record is 22), but the Barbarians Schools suffered losses, both games by narrow margins, to a raw and talented Fijian outfit and a New Zealand Maori Under-18 selection. The Maori concept has grown in stature in the three years it has existed and should remain on the itinerary for some time.

NATIONAL TOP FOUR
St Peter's College stunned Napier BHS in the final 31–28 with captain Niko Jones (son of Sir Michael Jones) prominent during the second half.

Results:
Semi-finals: Napier BHS 31, Christchurch BHS 12; St Peter's College 8, Hamilton BHS 7.
3 v 4: Hamilton BHS 43, Christchurch BHS 25
Final: St Peter's College 31, Napier BHS 28

GIRLS TOP FOUR
Hamilton Girls' High School were crowned national champions for a third time trouncing Manukura in the final. Hamilton won all 16 games this season and scored 962 points in reversing their loss in the final a year earlier. Manukura, a small Maori school in Palmerston North, have only had a First XV for four years. Hamilton holds both the National Sevens and First XV crowns.

Results:
Semi-finals: Hamilton GHS 62, Aorere College 5; Manukura 41, Southland GHS 29.
3 v 4: Aorere College 39, Southland GHS 24.
Final: Hamilton Girls' High School 42, Manukura 5

NATIONAL CO-ED TOP FOUR
St Peter's Cambridge became the first team since St Kentigern College in 2011 to successfully defend the National co-ed title.

Results:
Semi-finals: St Peter's Cambridge 55, Mount Albert Grammar 18;
Rangiora HS 15, Feilding HS 12.
3 v 4: Mount Albert Grammar School 16, Feilding High School 10
Final: St Peter's Cambridge 33, Rangiora High School 26

MOASCAR CUP

It was a busy year for the Moascar Cup with four different holders — the most since five schools shared the prize in 1972. Nelson College started the season as holders and defeated St Andrew's College 37–12, Shirley Boys' High School 27–3 and St Thomas of Canterbury College 25–11, but came unstuck against UC Cup Champions, Christchurch BHS 12–22 ending a tenure of 14 defences.

Christchurch BHS was able to foil the challenges of Lincoln HS 45–7, Rangiora HS 54–22, Christ's College 18–18 and Otago BHS 29–26, but surrendered the cup in their National Top Four semi-final against Napier BHS who relinquished the prize two days later in the National Top Four final against St Peter's College.

HIGHLIGHTS

- There were two 18–18 draws in major finals. Christchurch Boys' High School rallied from an 8–18 deficit to claim the UC Championship for the 11th time against Christ's College on a superior try count (3–2), while Takapuna Grammar School were unlucky not to claim outright honours in the North Harbour decider against Westlake Boys' High School.
- St Patrick's College, Silverstream, successfully defended their Premier 1 Wellington title defeating St Patrick's College, Wellington 29–22 in the final. Silverstream have won 22 games in a row in the Premier 1 competition.
- Otago Boys' High School returned to the secondary school grade for the first time since 2014 and beat John McGlashan College 24–17 in the final.
- St Paul's Collegiate, Hamilton reclaimed the Central North Island title beating Feilding High School 24–17 in the final. St Paul's have won the Central North Island crown four times in the past five seasons. Feilding have been a top four side every year since the Taine Randell Cup started in 2012.
- Rangiora High School beat Christchurch Boys' High School for the first time 35–33 to end Christchurch's 21-game unbeaten local streak.
- Hamilton Boys' High School won the Super 8 final with a last play penalty 23–22 against Napier Boys' High School. It was the 21st season of Super 8.

WOMENS RUGBY
THE ALMANACK NEW ZEALAND XV

Selica Winiata
Manawatu

Renee Wickliffe　　　　　　Stacey Waaka　　　　　　Portia Woodman
Bay of Plenty　　　　　　　*Waikato*　　　　　　　*Counties Manukau*

Kelly Brazier
Bay of Plenty

Ruahei Demant
Auckland

Kendra Cocksedge
Canterbury

Aroha Savage
Counties Manukau

Lesley Elder　　　Charmaine Smith　　　Eloise Blackwell　　　Sarah Goss
Bay of Plenty　　　*Auckland*　　　　　　*Auckland*　　　　　　*Manawatu*

Aldora Itunu　　　Fiao'o Faamausili (capt)　　　Phillipa Love
Auckland　　　　　*Auckland*　　　　　　　　　*Canterbury*

Reserves –

Te Kura Ngata-Aerengamate (*Counties Manukau*), Leilani Perese (*Counties Manukau*), Aleisha Nelson (*Auckland*), Jackie Patea-Fereti (*Wellington*), Charmaine McMenamin (*Auckland*), Kristina Sue (*Manawatu*), Chelsea Alley (*Waikato*), Michaela Blyde (*Bay of Plenty*).

COMMENTS

We introduce a Women's XV to record the outstanding players during the year. With the limited number of provincial games and Black Ferns fixtures we include in our considerations the performances of the Black Ferns Sevens squad. Stacey Waaka had a full year with both the Black Ferns and Black Ferns Sevens. Waaka, along with Woodman, Brazier, Goss and Blyde, were powerful players in the Black Ferns Sevens squad that won gold at the Commonwealth Games and again at the Rugby World Cup Sevens. Michaela Blyde scored 57 tries and was again World Rugby's Sevens Player of the Year. Portia Woodman scored 58 tries. Of the 232 tries scored by the Black Ferns Sevens team during their eight tournaments, perhaps the most memorable was Kelly Brazier's long run in extra time of the final at the Commonwealth Games. In the drama-filled final with the scores level at fulltime and both teams exhausted, extra time was required to determine a winner, Brazier made the break and ran into history, eventually collapsing across the tryline to claim the gold medal. Her 80-metre run was no different to a track athlete surging to the finish line.

In addition to the sevens players mentioned, we were also impressed with Niall Williams who can no longer be in the shadow of her All Black brother. Williams did a lot of damage with her powerful runs. Theresa Fitzpatrick, Gayle Broughton, Tyla Nathan-Wong, Ruby Tui and Tenika Willison were grand contributors towards the sevens' success. The outstanding form of Sarah Goss was another of the year's highlights, an inspiring captain who led from the front.

When we thought Fiao'o Faamausili had retired, the veteran Black Ferns captain bounced back, marking her return with three tries in the Sydney test. The Laurie O'Reilly Cup was retained after two wins over Australia, and USA were trounced at Chicago, but the Black Ferns met their match in France where they drew the series against the Six Nations champions.

The champion Canterbury team have several players close to Black Ferns honours, fullback Olivia McGoverne being among them. Krysten Cottrell stood out in the Hawke's Bay side, as did Chelsea Alley for Waikato and Jackie Patea-Fereti for Wellington. Ayesha Leti-I'iga's form for Wellington was rewarded with Black Ferns honours. Younger players to impress were Risi Pouri-Lane and Marcelle Parkes.

PLAYERS OF THE YEAR

Kendra Margaret Cocksedge (*Canterbury*) produced another outstanding season for both Canterbury and the Black Ferns and extended many of her own try-scoring and goal-kicking records. Her 10 tries and 116 points bettered her 2016 records for Canterbury and she has now scored 800 points for her union. Her 27 points against Auckland included four tries and, two weeks later, scored another 27 points in the Farah Palmer Cup final against Counties Manukau with two tries, a penalty, and converted all seven tries scored by Canterbury.

An astute director of the backline, this halfback is like a terrier, superbly fit, ever alert for attacking opportunities, and often darts through gaps, catching the opposition off-guard. She has been a key playmaker in the successes of Canterbury and the Black Ferns. In December Cocksedge became the first female recipient of the Kelvin Tremain Memorial trophy, NZR's award for player of the year.

Born at New Plymouth on 1 July 1988, Cocksedge grew up near Okato and is related to the Barrett family. She attended Okato Primary School and New Plymouth GHS (2002–06) and represented Taranaki Schools 2002–06 and Hurricanes Schools 2003–06. She played cricket for Taranaki 2002–06, CD 2004–07 and was in the New Zealand A squad 2007–08.

Offered a cricket scholarship at Lincoln University, Cocksedge moved to Canterbury in 2007, but it was to be rugby that gradually commanded her sporting interests. She quickly established the halfback position in the Canterbury team during 2007 and in October the 19-year-old made her Black Ferns debut, coming off the bench against Australia at Wanganui. Cocksedge has been a permanent member of Black Ferns squads since her debut and for many years shared the halfback position with the experienced Emma Jensen and it wasn't until 2015 that she became a regular in the number nine shirt. In the three tests against England in 2012 she started at first five-eighth.

Cocksedge has now played 47 tests and scored a record 282 points. She has played 123 first-class games and is the first woman to surpass 1000 points.

Sarah Leigh Goss (*Manawatu*) led the most successful national team of the 2018 season. The 2017 NZR Women's Player of the Year captained the Black Ferns Sevens team to win the gold medal at both the Commonwealth Games in Australia and the World Cup Sevens at San Francisco. Since losing in January to Australia in the final of the World Series tournament in Sydney the team has been undefeated in all seven tournaments, winning all 39 games. An inspiring leader, Goss is a strong carrier with the ball, possesses speed, and is effective at the breakdowns and solid on defence.

Born at Feilding on 9 December 1992, Goss attended Utuwai and Kimbolton primary schools before becoming keen on rugby during her years at Feilding High School 2006–10. A member of the Manawatu Secondary Schools' Girls team 2007–10, she captained the 2010 team to win the Hurricanes regional competition without conceding a point. Joining Feilding Old Boys Oroua club she represented Manawatu 2011–13, commencing at centre in the first year then moving to five-eighth and eventually to flanker in 2013. Goss became a sevens specialist but appeared for the Black Ferns in 2016 with two tests against Australia and the following year a full season of eight tests including the successful Rugby World Cup campaign.

A successful career as a shearer (see Happenings) was put on hold once sevens became the priority. Since 2012 Goss has attended a Black Ferns Sevens record of 39 tournaments, scored 80 tries and captained the team since 2015. She has been in the Manawatu sevens squad that won national titles in 2013, 2014, 2016 and 2018.

Sarah Goss is one of an increasing number of talented and skilful players producing attractive and entertaining rugby which has encouraged tremendous growth in women's rugby.

SEASON IN REVIEW
By Melodie Robinson

The 2018 rugby season for our women's athletes didn't start well when the Black Ferns Sevens kicked off their year at the Dubai Sevens. The sevens team, looking powerful in pool play, got tipped up in the quarter-finals by the United States 14–12 — thanks to the States using their physicality to stunt the Kiwi attack. The next tournament for the Black Ferns was late January in Sydney, and despite an improved performance in making the final, they were overwhelmed by the home team favourites by a resounding 31–0, putting Australia in the box seat for the world series title with just three tournaments for the Kiwis to catch up.

But in the New Zealand rugby vernacular a loss is a learning experience; so it was back to the drawing board for coach Allan Bunting as the World Series took a break and the New Zealand side started to focus on winning a Commonwealth Games title in April. In the meantime, the XVs team had some good news with the historic announcement that 30 women would receive salaries, including maternity incentives, to encourage women to stay in the game. A further 20 would train with the squad and receive payments if called upon.

Back into the action and at the Commonwealth Games, the Black Ferns had some big wins in pool play, the closest being a 24–7 win over Canada, and they won their semi-final against England 26–5 with Portia Woodman wowing the crowds in a typical manner. It seemed everyone knew it would be Australia and New Zealand in the final, but no one predicted the way this game would play out and who would be the commanding figure. At 12–all, Australia had possession, but one of their inexperienced athletes kicked the ball to touch, meaning the game went to extra time. In scorching heat, after around 19 minutes of play, it was the most experienced Black Fern on the pitch, Kelly Brazier, who ran 80 metres to score the winning try, winding herself when she touched down, and stunning the Aussies in the audience to silence. Meanwhile back in New Zealand rugby fans were jumping off the couches in glee. With a gold medal to avenge the silver at the Olympics, the Black Ferns' sevens season was back on track.

The only incident to mar the final was the headline on stuff.co.nz referring to star wing Michaela Blyde's exploits as 'the girlfriend of Aiden Ross wins gold medal'. Suffice to say the online abuse meant the company changed it quick smart.

The team went on to win the next three World Sevens Series events in Japan, Canada and Paris, but unfortunately their poor start at Dubai meant they had an eight-point deficit which they couldn't make up and Australia won the overall title, despite only winning two tournaments.

On to the Sevens Rugby World Cup in San Francisco and the Black Fern Sevens cruised through to the semi-finals again. And once again it was their nemesis the United States waiting for them. And it was tight — the Black Ferns winning 26–21 in the end — and on to France in the final. In typical French fashion they surrendered to the enemy and it was a rather disappointing final in that the Kiwis won 29–0. Another trophy in the cabinet and a very successful year for Sarah Goss and her team.

In August the spotlight was to shine on the XVs side, the Black Ferns up against Australia in a two-test series. Significantly it was a double header with the All Blacks and Wallabies, on both sides of the Tasman. Linking with such a big brand as the All Blacks proved a positive for the women as they pulled in a record crowd of 28,842 in Sydney, with the Black Ferns winning 31–11. Fiao'o Faamausili, despite signalling her impending retirement in 2017, was outstanding, dabbing down a hat-trick. In Auckland the crowd was arguably disappointing, the Kiwi fans not willing to sit at Eden Park for longer than one test match. But the match itself wasn't a let-down with the home team winning 45–17, the performance from the pack just outstanding again. The other disappointment, however, was that only one name from the sevens made herself available — centre Stacey Waaka. The rest took a break after an intense eight months.

The Farah Palmer Cup kicked off at the beginning of September, 12 teams this year, with more live games on television. The competition mimics the men's with it divided into the premiership and championship. However, there was some criticism during the season of the big gap between the top sides and the bottom along with blowout scores. What the critics don't take into account is that women's rugby is still growing, just under 28,000 were playing at last count, a number which keeps growing year on year — the main growth is in small blacks — girls aged 5 to 12. All a long way off boosting the numbers of the Farah Palmer Cup. The story line was again around the incredibly fit and entertaining Canterbury team who defended their title 52–29 over Counties, and Wellington who gained promotion to the premiership with their 57–5 win over Otago. Of interest is that Auckland only won one round robin game despite having numerous Black Ferns in their squad, many of whom earned selection in the Black Ferns team.

After the provincial competition finished, the Black Ferns were back on board, their next test match was in Chicago; it was the first game in which the United States had hosted New Zealand on their home soil. The Black Ferns test was the appetiser to the Maori All Blacks versus the Eagles and Italy against Ireland. Interestingly, the speed of pass and accuracy of the Black Ferns was arguably quicker than either match following. The defence was strong too, with the Americans unable to even score a try, making the result 67–6 — probably the best Black Ferns performance so far.

It was a quick turnaround for the Ferns' strongest challenge all year, two tests back to back against France, the side that coach Glenn Moore has signalled is the team to beat. Amazingly, this was also the first time France had hosted New Zealand for a test match. In Toulon, the score was nil-all at halftime and so the Ferns reverted to the strength of their pack to set up a try to lock Eloise Blackwell, which was converted by Kendra Cocksedge. Another came out wide for wing Renee Wickliffe, and while they won 14–0, suddenly the Black Ferns didn't look quite as invincible next to the athleticism and youth of the French team. Their set piece — particularly the scrum — went backwards, which gave little chance for the backs to attack.

The second test match was not the result the Kiwis would want to finish the season with. They kicked poorly in open play, often straight into the arms of the French back three. Their scrum was under pressure again, and they were outplayed in most facets of the game. An injury to fleet flanker Lesley Elder meant the French had three mobile, big, fast flankers who outplayed their opposition. Despite the Black Ferns' disadvantages, however, the test was great to watch with stunning tries to both sides, the home team beating New Zealand for the first time in an official test 30–27, and with French vice-president Serge Simon saying that 1.8 million tuned into the broadcast. And later in November Jessy Tremouliere became the first French player, male or female, to win World Rugby's player of the year award. For the Kiwis Michaela Blyde won World Sevens player of the year at the glamorous night in Monaco, the second year in a row the winger picked up the award.

The Black Ferns Sevens team finished off their year being awarded the prestigious Lonsdale Cup by the New Zealand Olympic Committee. They are the first rugby team to receive the award, which was first awarded in 1961. They join illustrious names such as Sir Murray Halberg, Dame Valerie Adams, Lisa Carrington, Sir John Walker and Sir Peter Snell which demonstrates the impact this team has had on the sporting landscape.

For the XVs team the news that New Zealand won the hosting rights for the Women's Rugby World Cup 2021 is a much-needed boost for the longer version of the game. The New Zealand Rugby Union is already one of the best operationally for hosting rugby events when it comes to efficiency, but this is an incredible opportunity to change from a traditional rugby event to an entertainment event. Taking the ASB tennis model to the dedicated stadiums would be ideal, where it's not just about the sport, it's about the food, music and kids' entertainment with pop-up venues and technology integrated to make a unique experience for fans. They'll need something original to try to lure fans up to Northland, that's for sure.

Finally, what a wonderful night for women's rugby at the 2018 ASB Rugby Awards, with Kendra

Cocksedge becoming the first female recipient of the Kelvin R Tremain Memorial Player of the Year award. Kendra also won the Women's Player of the Year and took out the Fiao'o Fa'amausili Medal. It was a truly history-making evening, with Michaela Blyde winning Black Ferns Sevens Player of the Year and the Black Ferns Sevens winning adidas New Zealand Team of the Year.

NEW ZEALAND BLACK FERNS

NEW ZEALAND, 2018

	Union	Date of Birth	Height	Weight	Tests at 1/1/18
C.H. (Chelsea) Alley	Waikato	7/11/92	1.78	81	15
L.E. (Lucy) Anderson	Canterbury	18/5/91	1.76	92	0
E.S. (Eloise) Blackwell	Auckland	28/12/90	1.82	89	32
K.M. (Kendra) Cocksedge	Canterbury	1/7/88	1.57	61	42
K.J. (Krysten) Cottrell	Hawke's Bay	17/2/92	1.62	65	0
D.R. (Ruahei) Demant	Auckland	21/4/95	1.69	81	0
K.W. (Kiritapu) Demant	Auckland	8/10/96	1.73	65	2
L.T. (Lesley) Elder (nee Ketu)	Bay of Plenty	10/1/87	1.66	62	9
F.M. (Fiao'o) Faamausili (capt)	Auckland	30/9/80	1.63	75	52
T.M. (Theresa) Fitzpatrick	Auckland	25/2/95	1.68	75	7
A.T. (Aldora) Itunu	Auckland	28/6/91	1.78	110	15
L.F. (Linda) Itunu	Auckland	21/11/84	1.73	83	34
A.A. (Ayesha) Leti-I'iga	Wellington	3/1/99	1.66	79	0
P.E.A. (Phillipa) Love	Canterbury	8/4/90	1.73	90	2
C.J. (Charmaine) McMenamin	Auckland	13/5/90	1.73	84	14
D.B. (Nathalia) Moors	Auckland	7/12/95	1.63	71	0
A.P. (Aleisha) Nelson	Auckland	2/3/90	1.82	104	26
J.M.F. (Joanah) Ngan-Woo	Wellington	15/12/95	1.82	88	0
T.R. (Te Kura) Ngata-Aerengamate	Counties Manukau	21/10/91	1.64	96	19
M.J. (Marcelle) Parkes	Wellington	9/9/97	1.77	78	0
J.S. (Jackie) Patea-Fereti	Wellington	30/9/86	1.78	83	12
L.L.R. (Leilani) Perese	Counties Manukau	1/1/93	1.79	125	0
A.F. (Alena) Saili	Southland	13/12/98	1.73	79	0
A. (Aroha) Savage	Counties Manukau	10/3/90	1.78	85	28
C.B. (Charmaine) Smith	Auckland	15/11/90	1.83	77	16
K.J. (Kristina) Sue	Manawatu	13/3/87	1.60	63	10
M.F. (Monica) Tagoal	Wellington	17/10/98	1.67	75	0
L.C.S. (Cristo) Tofa	North Harbour	11/12/87	1.69	105	0
S.J.A.K. (Stacey) Waaka	Waikato	3/11/95	1.70	72	11
R.W.M. (Renee) Wickliffe	Bay of Plenty	30/5/87	1.64	63	30
S.C. (Selica) Winiata	Manawatu	14/11/86	1.55	58	31

Kilisitina Moata'ane (*Otago*) was an original selection to tour USA and France but withdrew with injury and replaced by Lucy Anderson. Chelsea Alley returned home after USA test and replaced by Kiritapu Demant. Tourists Anderson, Ngan-Woo, Kiritapu Demant and Tofa were not selected in any of the three playing squads. .

Coach: Glenn Moore
Assistant coach: Wesley Clarke, John Haggart
Manager: Lauren Cournane
Campaign manager: Hannah Porter
Physiotherapist: Georgia Milne (August only), Teresa Te Tamaki
Doctor: Dr Steve Smith
Strength & conditioning coach: Jamie Tout
Analyst: Arran Hodge

NEW ZEALAND IN AUSTRALIA, NEW ZEALAND AND FRANCE, 2018

BLACK FERNS 2018

	Australia	Australia	USA	France	France	TOTALS
Winiata	15	15	15	15	15	5
Wickliffe	14*	14	14*	14	14	5
Saili	11	11	–	–	–	2
Leti-I'iga	–	–	11	11*	11	3
Tagoai	–	–	s	s	s	3
Waaka	13	13	13	13	13*	5
Fitzpatrick	12	12*	–	–	–	2
Alley	s	s	12*	–	–	3
R. Demant	10*	10*	10	12	12	5
Cottrell	s	s	s	10	10*	5
Moors	–	–	–	–	s	1
Cocksedge	9*	9*	9*	9*	9*	5
Sue	s	s	s	s	s	5
Savage	8	8	8	8	6	5
Elder	7	7*	7*	7*	–	4
Parkes	–	–	–	s	s	2
McMenamin	6*	6	6*	6*	7*	5
L. Itunu	s	s	s	s	8*	5
Smith	5*	5	5*	5*	5	5
Patea-Fereti	s	s	s	s	s	5
Blackwell	4	4*	4	4	4	5
A. Itunu	3*	3*	3*	3*	3*	5
Perese	s	s	s	s	s	5
Love	1*	1*	1*	1*	1*	5
Tofa	s	s	–	–	–	2
Nelson	–	–	s	s	s	3
Faamausili	2*	2*	2	2*	2	5
Ngata-Aerengamate	s	s	s	s	–	4

INDIVIDUAL SCORING

	Tries	Con	PG	DG	Points
Cocksedge	3	18	2	–	57
Faamausili	5	–	–	–	25
Blackwell	4	–	–	–	20
Wickliffe	4	–	–	–	20
A. Itunu	3	–	–	–	15
Winiata	3	–	–	–	15
Waaka	2	–	–	–	10
Alley	1	–	–	–	5
Fitzpatrick	1	–	–	–	5
Leti-I'iga	1	–	–	–	5
Love	1	–	–	–	5
R. Demant	–	1	–	–	2
Totals	**28**	**19**	**2**	**–**	**184**
Opposition scored	8	3	6	–	64

NEW ZEALAND IN AUSTRALIA, NEW ZEALAND, USA AND FRANCE 2018

Played 5 Won 4 Lost 1 Points for 184 Points against 64

Date	Opponent	Location	Score	Tries	Con	PG	DG	Referee
August 18	Australia	Sydney	31–11	Faamausili (3), A. Itunu, Cocksedge	Cocksedge (3)			Tim Baker, Hong Kong
August 25	Australia	Auckland	45–17	Love, A. Itunu, Blackwell, Cocksedge, Fitzpatrick, Wickliffe, Winiata	Cocksedge (5)			Ian Tempest, England
November 3	USA	Chicago	67–6	Wickliffe (2), Blackwell (2), A. Itunu, Alley, Faamausili, Winiata, Cocksedge, Waaka, Leti-I'iga	Cocksedge (5), R. Demant			Aimee Barrett-Theron, South Africa
November 9	France	Toulon	14–0	Blackwell, Wickliffe	Cocksedge (2)			Sara Cox, England
November 17	France	Grenoble	27–30	Waaka, Faamausili, Winiata	Cocksedge (3)	Cocksedge (2)		Joy Neville, Ireland

Test venues: ANZ Stadium, Sydney; Eden Park, Auckland; Soldier Field, Chicago; Stade Felix Mayol, Toulon; Stade des Alpes, Grenoble.

NEW ZEALAND WOMEN'S REPRESENTATIVES, 1989–2018

	Internationals Games	Points
Aiatu, Muteremoana S. 1981– (Wellington) 2011	1	–
Alley, Chelsea H. 1992– (Waikato) 2013–14–17–18 (North Harbour) 2015–16	18	20
Andrew, Shannon R. 1972– (Auckland) 1996	2	–
Aniseko, Fa'anati 1989– (Auckland) 2007	2	5
Apiata, Jacquileen W. 1966– (Canterbury) 1989–90–91– 92–93–94–95	5	–
Atkins, Leanne T. 1976– (Northland) 1994	–	–
Baker, Lise (Wellington) 1990	–	–
Baker, Miriama 1962– (Auckland) 1989–91	–	–
Baker, Shakira J. 1992– (Wellington) 2011 (Manawatu) 2012–14	13	40
Ballinger, Shona 1970– (Wellington) 1990–91	–	–
Barclay, F.J. *see* King, F.J.		
Berry, Zoey P. 1987– (Canterbury) 2012	1	–
Blackledge, V.E. *see* Grant, V.E.		
Blackwell, Eloise S. 1990– (Auckland) 2011–12–13–14–15–16–17–18	37	35
Blyde, Cherrie (Taranaki) 1992	–	–
Borthwick, Nicole M. 1980– (Auckland) 2005	2	7
Bosman (nee Ngatai), Melodie, 2010. *see* Ngatai, M.M.		
Brazier, Kelly A. 1989– (Otago) 2009–10–12–13–14–16 (Canterbury) 2011 (Bay of Plenty) 2017	37	190
Brett, Lesley 1968– (Canterbury) 1990–91	3	12
Broughton, Florence (Wellington) 1990	–	–
Canterbury, Marina R. 1984– (Hawke's Bay) 2005	5	10
Chase, Debbie P.M. 1966– (Canterbury) 1990–91–93	3	12
Chittock, Barbara J. 1985– (Canterbury) 2009	–	–

	Internationals Games	Points
Coady, Olivia R. 1990– (Canterbury) 2008–09	4	5
Cobley, Rhonda J. 1971– (Canterbury) 1992–94	–	–
Cocksedge, Kendra M. 1988– (Canterbury) 2007–08–09–10–11– 12–13–14–15–16–17–18	47	282
Codling, Monalisa M. 1977– (Otago) 1998 (Auckland) 1999–02–03–04–05– 06–07–08–10	30	25
Cootes, Vanessa 1969– (Waikato) 1995–96–97–98–00– 01–02	16	215
Cottrell, Krysten J. 1992– (Hawke's Bay) 2018	5	–
Crossman, Lydia J. 1986– (Hawke's Bay) 2011 (Auckland) 2012	5	–
Cunningham, Vicky (Auckland) 1997	1	–
Davie, Mary (Canterbury) 1992–93	–	–
Dawson, Susan 1971– (Northland) 1999–00–02	4	5
de Jong, Catherine L. 1984– (Otago) 2005	1	–
Demant, D. Ruahei 1995– (Auckland) 2018	5	2
Demant, Kiritapu W. 1996– (Auckland) 2015	2	–
Edwards (nee Shelford), Exia T. 1975– (Bay of Plenty) 1998–99–00– 01–02–03–04–05–06	27	90
Edwards, Maree 1975– (Otago) 1998–00 (Canterbury) 2003	4	5
Edwards, Tangaloa (Auckland) 1989	–	–
Elder (nee Ketu), Lesley T. 1987– (Waikato) 2015–17 (Bay of Plenty) 2018	13	5
Ellis, Judith M. 1966– (Canterbury) 1993–94–95	1	–
Engebretsen, Lauren J. 1983– (Waikato) 2004	3	–
Epiha, Eva A. 1974– (Auckland) 1994	–	–
Everitt, Rawinia P. 1986– (Auckland) 2011–12 (Counties Manukau) 2013–14–16–17	21	25

	Internationals Games	Points
Ewe, Donna 1964– (Auckland) 1990–91	3	–
Fa'amausili, Fiao'o 1980– (Auckland) 2002–03–05–06–07– 08–09–10–11–12–13–14–15–16– 17–18	57	85
Fa'aope, Lili (Canterbury) 1989–90	–	–
Farr, Amy M. 1982– (Wellington) 2007	1	0
Fereti (nee Patea), **Jackie S.** see **Patea, J.S.**		
Fitzgibbon, Maree 1966– (Canterbury) 1989–90–91	3	–
Fitzpatrick, Theresa M. 1995- (Auckland) 2017–18	9	15
Ford, Amanda 1970– (Canterbury) 1989–90–91	1	4
Ford, Deborah 1965– (Canterbury) 1989–90–91	–	–
Frost, Seuga 1966– (Canterbury) 1990–91	–	–
Garden, Susan 1961–2008 (Canterbury) 1989–90–91 (Otago) 1992	–	–
Gavet, Sandra 1961– (Auckland) 1990–92	–	–
Goss, Sarah L. 1992– (Manawatu) 2016–17	10	5
Grant (*nee* Blackledge), Victoria E. 1982– (Auckland) 2006–07–08–09–10–11 (Waikato) 2013	17	30
Gray, Isabel 1974– (Wellington) 1999–02–05	5	5
Gubb (nee Halapua), **Charlene P.T.** see **Halapua, C.P.T.**		
Halapua, Charlene P.T. 1988– (Auckland) 2015–16–17	9	5
Harrison, Sarah (Wellington) 1999	2	–
Hayes, Carol (Southland) 1989–91–92–93	–	–
Heenan, Janet M. 1969– (Northland) 1996–98	5	–
Heighway, Victoria L 1980– (Auckland) 2000–01–02–03–04– 05–06–07–08–09–10	32	10
Hiemer, Riki (Wellington) 1997	2	–
Hina, Trisha R. 1977– (Auckland) 2010	4	–
Hireme, A. Honey 1981– (Waikato) 2014–15–16–17	18	75
Hirovanaa, Monique J. 1966– (Auckland) 1994–95–96–97– 98–99–00–01–02	24	65
Hohepa, Carla G. 1985– (Otago) 2007–08–09–10 (Waikato) 2016–17	19	80
Hull, R.M. see **Mahoney, R.M.**		
Hopkins, Anna 1970– (Wellington) 1991	–	–
Huxford, Sarah (Wellington) 1993	–	–
Inwood, Nicola A. 1970– (Canterbury) 1989–90–91	3	–
Itunu, Aldora T. 1991– (Auckland) 2015–16–17–18	20	30
Itunu, Linda F. 1984– (Auckland) 2003–04–06–07–08– 09–10–14–15–17–18	39	10
Jensen, Emma M. 1977– (Waikato) 2002–03–04 (Auckland) 2005–06–07–08–09– 10–11–12–13–14–15	49	53
John, Chris (Canterbury) 1990	–	–
Johnson, Fiona C. 1970– (Wellington) 1990	–	–
Kahura, Dianne M.T. 1969– (Auckland) 1998–99–00–02	12	95
Kay, Rhonda 1976– (Waikato) 2000	1	–
Ketu, Lesley T. see **Elder, L.T.**		
King (*nee* Barclay), Fiona J. 1972– (Otago) 1996–97–98–99–00– 01–02	18	5
Kingi, Mere A. 1974– (Auckland) 2003–04	5	10
Kiwi, Kellie H. 1972– (Bay of Plenty) 1996–97–98	8	15
Knight, Neroli 1974– (Wellington) 1990–91–99–00–01	4	–
Konui, Toni R.H. 1966– (Auckland) 1998	3	–
Kupa, Mel (Hawke's Bay) 1997	2	–
Lavea, Justine 1984– (Auckland) 2004–05–07–09–10– 11–12–13–14 14 (Counties Manukau) 2015	34	30
Lavea, Vaniya N.H. 1981– (Auckland) 2003–04–07	5	–
Leiataua, Onjeurlina F. 1995– (Auckland) 2013	1	–
Lemon, Tracey M. 1970–2012 (Auckland) 1991–94–95	2	–
Lene, Stacey O. 1980– (Canterbury) 2003–04–05	7	35
Leti-I'iga, Ayesha A. 1999– (Wellington) 2018	3	5
Levave, Sanita D. 1988– (Wellington) 2014	5	–

New Zealand Women's Representatives, 1989–2018

Name	Internationals Games	Points
Lili'i, Adrienne P. 1970– (Auckland) 1999–02–03–04 (Waikato) 2000	12	5
Littleworth, Helen M. 1966– (Canterbury) 1989–90–91–92–93–94 (Otago) 1995–96	8	20
Liua'ana, Rebecca 1970– (Wellington) 1999–00–01–02	10	10
Lotui'iga, L. Brigitta 1968– (Auckland) 1998	5	–
Love, Phillipa E.A. 1990– (Otago) 2014 (Canterbury) 2017–18	7	5
McKay, K. Ruth 1986– (Manawatu) 2007–08–09–10–12–13–14	25	–
McKenzie, Margaret J. 1970– (Otago) 2000–05	5	5
McMenamin, Charmaine J. 1990– (Auckland) 2013–16–17–18	19	5
Mahon, Helen L. 1968– (Canterbury) 1989 (Wellington) 1991 (Waikato) 1992	3	12
Mahoney (*nee* Hull), Rebecca M. 1983– (Manawatu) 2004–08 (Hawke's Bay) 2006 (Wellington) 2009–10–11	16	25
Makata, Rachel J. 1974– (Auckland) 2006	2	5
Maliukaetau, F. Diane L. 1986– (Auckland) 2005–06	6	5
Mallard, Beth L. 1981– (Otago) 2006–07–08–09	8	–
Manuel, Huriana R. 1986– (Auckland) 2005–06–07–08–09–10–14	25	70
Marsh, A. *see* **Rule, A.**		
Martin, Rochelle L. 1973– (Wellington) 1994–95 (Auckland) 1996–97–98–99–00–02–04–05–06	32	70
Matapo, P.E.A. 'Kelani' 1983– (Auckland) 2011	1	–
Mata'u, Aotearoa K. 1997– (Counties Manukau) 2016–17	8	5
Mihinui, M.T. Eliza 1960– (Auckland) 1994	–	–
Moore, Aroha 1978– (Auckland) 2004	3	–
Moors, D.B. 'Natahlia' 1995– (Auckland) 2018	1	–
Mortimer, Stephanie A. 1981– (Canterbury) 2003–04–05–06	11	50
Mulipola, Tala 1981– (Auckland) 2000–01–03	7	5
Murphy, Amanda J. 1985– (Canterbury) 2009–11	2	–
Myers, H.J. *see* **Porter, H.J.**		
Natua Toka I. 1991– (Waikato) 2015–16–17	16	25
Nelson, Aleisha P. 1990– (Auckland) 2012–14–15–16–17–18	29	10
Nemaia, Ana (Auckland) 1989	–	–
Nesbit, Joanne (Canterbury) 1989	–	–
Ngata-Aerengamate, Te Kura R. 1991– (Counties Manukau) 2014–15–16–17–18	23	5
Ngatai, Melodie M. 1976– (Auckland) 2004 (Waikato) 2005 (Hawke's Bay) 2006–11 (Canterbury) 2010–13	17	–
Nielsen, Jacinta 1972– (Otago) 1997–98–00	7	–
O'Leary, Pauline (Wanganui) 1993	–	–
O'Reilly, Lauren M. 1967– (Canterbury) 1992–93–94	1	–
Paasi, Poinisitia 1970– (Wellington) 2001–07	4	–
Paitai, Elsie 1963– (Auckland) 1990–91	–	–
Palmer, Farah R. 1972– (Otago) 1996–98–99–00 (Waikato) 1997 (Manawatu) 2001–02–03–04–05–06	35	25
Papalii, Christine 1962– (Auckland) 1989–90–92	–	–
Parkes, Marcelle J. 1997– (Wellington) 2018	2	–
Patea Fereti, Jackie S. 1986– (Wellington) 2012–13–14–16–18	17	–
Paul, Geraldine 1965– (Bay of Plenty) 1989–91–97 (Taranaki) 1994	4	10
Paul, Tamaku 1979– (Bay of Plenty) 2001	1	–
Penetito, Karina E. *see* **Stowers, K.E.**		
Perese, Leilani L.R. 1993– (Counties Manukau) 2018	5	–
Piho, Mata 1972– (Otago) 1998–00	3	–
Porter (*nee* Myers), Hannah J. 1979– (Otago) 2000–02 (Auckland) 2003–04–05–06–08	22	169
Reader, Heidi C. 1971– (Otago) 1993 (Waikato) 1994–96 (Bay of Plenty) 1995	3	38

	Internationals Games	Points
Rees, Vivian L. 1971– (Wellington) 1993–94–95	2	2
Rere (Ratu), Ericka 1963– (Wellington) 1990–91–92 (Bay of Plenty) 1993	3	–
Reynolds, Julie 1966– (Canterbury) 1993–94	–	–
Richards, Anna M. 1964– (Auckland) 1990–91–92–93–94– 96–97–98–99–00–01–02–03–04– 05–06–07–08–10	49	89
Richards, Fiona C. 1970– (Canterbury) 1993–94–95–96 (Auckland) 1997–98–99	14	–
Richardson, Claire 1984– (Otago) 2003–04–05–06–07–12 (Auckland) 2013–14	23	54
Rikihana-Broughton, Julie (Wellington) 1990	–	–
Robertson, Casey J. 1981– (Canterbury) 2002–03–04–05–06– 09–10–11–12–13–14	38	10
Robinson, Melodie C. 1973– (Wellington) 1996–97–98–99 (Auckland) 2001–02	18	20
Robinson, Vita J. 1982– (Auckland) 2007–09–10–11–13	14	–
Rodd, Christine A. 1959– (Canterbury) 1990–91	2	–
Ross, L. Christine 1964– (Mid C'bury) 1989–92–96 (Canterbury) 1990–91	5	52
Rowat, Claire L. 1983– (Wellington) 2009	–	–
Rule (*nee* Marsh), Amiria 1983– (Canterbury) 2000–01–02–03–5– 06–09–11–13–14	34	75
Ruscoe, Melissa J. 1976– (Canterbury) 2004–05–06–07– 08–10	22	32
Rush, Annaleah M. 1976– (Otago) 1996–97–98–99 (Auckland) 2000–01–02	20	156
Rush, Erin 1970– (Wellington) 2003	2	–
Saili, Alena F. 1998– (Southland) 2018	2	–
Savage, Aroha 1990– (Auckland) 2010–11–12 (Counties Manukau) 2013–14–16– 17–18	33	20
Sheck, Regina 1969– (Auckland) 1994–96–97–98 (Waikato) 1999–00–01–02–03–04	25	25
Shelford, Exia T. *see* **Edwards, E.T.**		
Shortland, Suzanne 1974– (Auckland) 1997–98–99–00–01–02	18	20
Simpson-Brown, Lenadeen H. 1964– (Canterbury) 1994 (Waikato) 1995–96–97	8	15

	Internationals Games	Points
Sio, Nina 1963– (Auckland) 1989–91–92 (Waikato) 1994	4	–
Sione, Joan L. 1986– (Auckland) 2005–10	6	5
Sisifa, Angelene A.F. 1989– (Otago) 2015–16	7	–
Smith, Charmaine B. 1990– (North Harbour) 2015–16–17 (Auckland) 2018	21	15
Smith, Kimberly M. 1985– (Canterbury) 2005–06–07–08–09	11	–
Solomon, Pikihuia P. 1983– (Otago) 2005	2	10
Stowers, Karina E. (*nee* **Penetito**) 1986– (Auckland) 2005–09–10–11–12–13	18	–
Su'a, S.M.A. 'Nara' 1969– (Auckland) 1996	2	5
Suasua-White, D. *see* **White, D.M.**		
Subritzky-Nafatali, Victoria S. 1991– (Otago) 2012–14 (Counties Manukau) 2015–16–17	19	34
Sue, Kristina J. 1987– (Manawatu) 2016–17–18	15	–
Sutorius, Aimee E. 1979– Wellington) 2007–08–09	3	–
Tagoai, Monica F. 1998– (Wellington) 2018	3	–
Tahu, Bella M. 1970– (Auckland) 1996	3	–
Talawadua, Sosoli J. 1989– (Waikato) 2016–17	8	5
Tamihana, Florence (Wellington) 1995	1	–
Taufateau, Doris J.T. 1987– (Auckland) 2008–10–11	5	–
Taylor, Karen 1968– (Bay of Plenty) 1996	2	5
Teddy, Waimania L. 1979– (Auckland) 2005–06–07	6	–
Te Tamaki, Teresa K. 1981– (Auckland) 2007–08–11 (Waikato) 2012–15	10	–
Tekeu, No'o (–) 1990	–	–
Te Ohaere-Fox, Stephanie A. 1985– (Canterbury) 2008–09–10–12– 13–14 (Wasps) 2011	24	–
Thomas, Emma H. 1958– (Bay of Plenty) 1996–97–98	9	–
Tiplady, Anika M. 1980– (Manawatu) 2007 (Canterbury) 2009	2	–
Tiplady-Hurring, Halie A. 1986– (Canterbury) 2008–10–14 (Otago) 2012	13	15

	Internationals Games	Points
Tiriamai, Kimi 1964– (Auckland) 1990–91	2	–
Tofa, L. Cristo. S. 1987– (North Harbour) 2018	2	–
Tubic, Hazel S. 1990– (Auckland) 2011–12 (Counties Manukau) 2016–17	11	12
Va'aga, Helen 1977– (Auckland) 2002–03–05–06	10	10
Vaeteru, Teina (–) 1990	–	–
Vaughan, Janna M. 1988– (Manawatu) 2015–16	6	10
Waaka, Cheryl M. 1970– (Auckland) 1997–98–00–01–02– 03–04 (Northland) 1999	20	35
Waaka, Stacey J.A.K. 1995– (Waikato) 2015–17–18	16	30
Wall, Louisa H. 1972– (Waikato) 1994 (Auckland) 1995–96–97–98–99	15	95
Waters, Tracey J.R. 1973– (Canterbury) 1995–96–98	10	5
Wharton, Julie (Auckland) 1990	–	–
Whata-Simpkins, Katarina R. 1990– (Wellington) 2011	1	0
White, Davida M. 1967– (Auckland) 1993–94–95–96– 98–00	13	0
Wickliffe, Renee W.M. 1987– (Auckland) 2009–10–11 (Counties Manukau) 2013–14–15– 16–17 (Bay of Plenty) 2018	35	85
Wihongi, Kamila T. 1982– (Otago) 2005	1	–
Williams, Amy L. 1986– (Hawke's Bay) 2005–06	6	–
Williams, Tasha H. 1973– (Manawatu) 1994	1	10
Willoughby, Shannon M. 1982– (Otago) 2005–06	8	–
Wilson, Tammi 1973– (Auckland) 1998–99–00–01–02	16	196
Wilton, Kathleen A. 1984– (Otago) 2007–11–12–13–14	18	–
Winiata, Selica C. 1986– (Manawatu) 2008–12–13–14–15– 16–17–18	36	190
Wong, Natasha A. 1967– (Canterbury) 1990–91–92–93–94	3	–
Wood, Rebecca J. 1987- (North Harbour) 2017	7	–
Woodman, Portia L. 1991– (Auckland) 2013 (Counties Manukau) 2016–17	16	110
Woodman, Sharnita K. 1986– (Counties Manukau) 2016	2	–
Yates, Sandy 1979– (Counties Manukau) 2001	1	–

BLACK FERNS RECORDS

NEW ZEALAND INTERNATIONAL CAPTAINS

Fiao'o Fa'amausili	2012–18	35
Farah Palmer	1997–2006	30
Melissa Ruscoe	2007–10	8
Lenadeen Simpson-Brown	1994–96	6
Helen Littleworth	1991	3
Victoria Grant	2010–11	3
Rochelle Martin	2005–06	2
Victoria Heighway	2009	2
Davida White	1998	1
Anna Richards	2005	1
Casey Robertson	2011	1
Amiria Rule	2014	1

MOST APPEARANCES IN INTERNATIONALS

F.M. Faamausili	2002-18	57	K.A. Brazier	2009-17	37
A.M. Richards	1991-10	49	E.S. Blackwell	2011-18	37
E.M. Jensen	2002-15	49	S.C. Winiata	2008-18	36
K.M. Cocksedge	2007-18	47	F.R. Palmer	1996-06	35
C.J. Robertson	2002-14	38	R.W.M. Wickliffe	2009-18	35
L.F. Itunu	2003-18	38			

MOST SUCCESSIVE INTERNATIONALS

E.M. Jensen	2003–15	44

MOST POINTS IN INTERNATIONALS

	Tries	Con	PG	DG	Total		Tries	Con	PG	DG	Total
K.M. Cocksedge	16	74	18	-	282	K.A. Brazier	11	45	15	-	190
V. Cootes	43	-	-	-	215	S.C. Winiata	38	-	-	-	190
T. Wilson	21	29	11	-	196	A.M. Rush	14	34	6	-	156
H.J. Porter	5	42	20	-	169						

MOST POINTS IN AN INTERNATIONAL

V. Cootes	v France, 1996	45	(9 tries)
P.L. Woodman	v Hong Kong, 2017	40	(8 tries)
T. Wilson	v USA, 1999	36	(6 tries, 3 conversions)
L.C. Ross	v France, 1996	34	(2 tries, 12 conversions)
K.M. Cocksedge	v Hong Kong, 2017	31	(1 try, 13 conversions)
T. Wilson	v Germany, 1998	30	(4 tries, 5 conversions)

MOST TRIES IN AN INTERNATIONAL

V. Cootes	v France, 1996	9	V. Cootes	v USA, 1998	5
P.L. Woodman	v Hong Kong, 2017	8	V. Cootes	v Germany, 2002	5
T. Wilson	v USA, 1999	6	S.C. Winiata	v Samoa, 2014	5
V. Cootes	v USA, 1996	5			

MOST PENALTY GOALS IN AN INTERNATIONAL

| K.A. Brazier | v England, 2013 | 4 | K.M. Cocksedge | v England, 2015 | 4 |

MOST CONVERSIONS IN AN INTERNATIONAL

| K.M. Cocksedge | v Hong Kong, 2017 | 13 | L.C. Ross | v Canada, 1996 | 9 |
| L.C. Ross | v France, 1996 | 12 | H.C. Reader | v USA, 1996 | 8 |

INTERNATIONAL MATCH RECORD

Year	v	Opponent	Venue	Result		
1991	v	Canada[1]	Glamorgan	won	24	8
	v	Wales[1]	Llanharen	won	24	6
	v	USA[1] (semi-final)	Cardiff	lost	0	7
1994	v	Australia	Sydney	won	37	0
1995	v	Australia	Auckland	won	64	0
1996	v	Australia	Sydney	won	28	5
	v	Canada	St Albert	won	88	3
	v	USA	Edmonton	won	86	8
	v	France	Edmonton	won	109	0
1997	v	England	Burnham	won	67	0
	v	Australia	Dunedin	won	40	0
1998	v	Germany[1]	Amsterdam	won	134	6
	v	Scotland[1]	Amsterdam	won	76	0
	v	Spain[1] (quarter-final)	Amsterdam	won	46	3
	v	England[1] (semi-final)	Amsterdam	won	44	11
	v	USA[1] (final)	Amsterdam	won	44	12
	v	Australia	Sydney	won	27	3
1999	v	Canada	Palmerston North	won	73	0
	v	USA	Palmerston North	won	65	5
2000	v	Canada	Winnipeg	won	41	0
	v	USA	Winnipeg	won	45	0
	v	England	Winnipeg	won	32	13
2001	v	England	Rotorua	won	15	10
	v	England	Albany	lost	17	22
2002	v	Germany[1]	Barcelona	won	117	0
	v	Australia[1]	Barcelona	won	36	3
	v	France[1] (semi-final)	Barcelona	won	30	0

	v	England[1] (final)	Barcelona	won	19	9
2003	v	World XV	Auckland	won	37	0
	v	World XV	Whangarei	won	38	19
2004	v	Canada	Vancouver	won	32	5
	v	USA	Calgary	won	35	0
	v	England	Edmonton	won	38	0
2005	v	Scotland	Ottawa	won	30	9
	v	Canada	Ottawa	won	43	3
	v	Canada	Ottawa	won	32	5
	v	England	Auckland	won	33	8
	v	England	Hamilton	won	24	15
2006	v	Canada[1]	Edmonton	won	66	7
	v	Samoa[1]	Edmonton	won	50	0
	v	Scotland[1]	Edmonton	won	21	0
	v	France[1] (semi-final)	Edmonton	won	40	10
	v	England[1] (final)	Edmonton	won	25	17
2007	v	Australia	Wanganui	won	21	11
	v	Australia	Wellington	won	29	12
2008	v	Australia	Canberra	won	37	3
	v	Australia	Canberra	won	22	16
2009	v	England	London	won	16	3
	v	England	London	lost	3	10
2010	v	South Africa[1]	London	won	55	3
	v	Australia[1]	London	won	32	5
	v	Wales[1]	London	won	41	8
	v	France[1] (semi-final)	London	won	45	7
	v	England[1] (final)	London	won	13	10
2011	v	England	London	lost	0	10
	v	England	London	lost	7	21
	v	England	London	draw	8	8
2012	v	England	Esher	lost	13	16
	v	England	Aldershot	lost	8	17
	v	England	London	lost	23	32
2013	v	England	Auckland	won	29	10
	v	England	Hamilton	won	14	9
	v	England	Pukekohe	won	29	8
2014	v	Australia	Rotorua	won	38	3
	v	Samoa	Auckland	won	90	12
	v	Canada	Tauranga	won	16	8
	v	Canada	Whakatane	won	33	21
	v	Kazakhstan[1]	Marcoussis	won	79	5
	v	Ireland[1]	Marcoussis	lost	14	17
	v	USA[1]	Marcoussis	won	34	3
	v	Wales[1]	Paris	won	63	7
	v	USA[1]	Paris	won	55	5
2015	v	Canada	Calgary	won	40	22
	v	England	Red Deer	won	26	7
	v	USA	Edmonton	won	49	14

2016	v Australia	Auckland	won	67	3
	v Australia	Albany	won	29	3
	v England	London	won	25	20
	v Canada	Dublin	won	20	10
	v Ireland	Dublin	won	38	8
2017	v Canada	Wellington	won	28	16
	v Australia	Christchurch	won	44	17
	v England	Rotorua	lost	21	29
	v Wales[1]	Dublin	won	44	12
	v Hong Kong[1]	Dublin	won	121	0
	v Canada[1]	Dublin	won	48	5
	v USA[1] (semi-final)	Belfast	won	45	12
	v England[1] (final)	Belfast	won	41	32
2018	v Australia	Sydney	won	31	11
	v Australia	Auckland	won	45	17
	v USA	Chicago	won	67	6
	v France	Toulon	won	14	0
	v France	Grenoble	lost	27	30

[1]World Cup

SUMMARY OF INTERNATIONALS

Played: 93 Points for: 3709
Won: 81 Points against: 812
Lost: 11
Drawn: 1

RESULTS FROM 2018 FIRST-CLASS SEASON IN NEW ZEALAND
AND TEAMS OF NEW ZEALANDERS OVERSEAS

Key:	P	Farah Palmer Cup Premiership
	C	Farah Palmer Cup Championship
	P/C	Crossover match between teams from the FPC Premiership and Championship divisions
	sf	semi-final
	f	final
	rel. p-o	relegation playoff
	ST	J.J. Stewart Trophy
	*	not first-class

January							
Sat/Sun	13/14 *		National Sevens				Rotorua
Fri-Sun	26-28 *		Australia WR Sevens				Sydney
April							
Fri-Sun	13-15 *		Commonwealth Games Sevens				Gold Coast
Sat/Sun	21/22 *		Japan WR Sevens				Kitakyushu
May							
Sat/Sun	12/13 *		Canada WR Sevens				Victoria
June							
Fri-Sun	8-10 *		France WR Sevens				Paris
Fri/Sat	20/21 *		Rugby World Cup Sevens				San Francisco
August							
Sat	18		New Zealand	31	Australia	11	Sydney
Sat	25		New Zealand	45	Australia	17	Auckland
September							
Sat	1	P	Manawatu	44	Auckland	17	Pakuranga
		P	Canterbury	55	Bay of Plenty	5	Tauranga
		P	Waikato	33	Counties Manukau	27	Taupiri
		C	Hawke's Bay	25	Wellington	22	Napier
		C	Otago	27	North Harbour	13	Dunedin
		C	Tasman	65	Taranaki	12	Motueka
Fri	7	P/C	Auckland	86	Tasman	0	Auckland
Sat	8	P	Waikato	44	Bay of Plenty	7	Tauranga
		P	Counties Manukau	31	Manawatu	22	Papakura
		P/C	Wellington	43	Canterbury	38	Porirua
		C	Otago	31	Hawke's Bay	12	Dunedin
		C	North Harbour	59	Taranaki	0	Inglewood
Sat	15	P, ST	Canterbury	28	Waikato	10	Christchurch

Results From 2018 First-Class Season In New Zealand

Day	Date	Type	Team 1	Score	Team 2	Score	Venue
		P	Counties Manukau	31	Auckland	12	Pukekohe
		P	Manawatu	22	Bay of Plenty	10	Palmerston North
		C	Hawke's Bay	55	Taranaki	10	Inglewood
		C	Wellington	38	Otago	10	Porirua
Sun	16	C	North Harbour	51	Tasman	14	Albany
Fri	21	P/C	Bay of Plenty	73	Taranaki	0	Rotorua
Sat	22	P	Waikato	45	Auckland	14	Taupiri
		P/C	Counties Manukau	39	Otago	8	Dunedin
		C	Hawke's Bay	52	North Harbour	10	Napier
Sun	23	P	Canterbury	48	Manawatu	12	Palmerston North
		C	Wellington	88	Tasman	3	Nelson
Fri	28	P	Bay of Plenty	34	Auckland	29	Auckland
Sat	29	P	Waikato	31	Manawatu	8	Hamilton
		C	Wellington	50	North Harbour	10	Mairangi Bay
		C	Otago	65	Taranaki	0	New Plymouth
Sun	30	P, ST	Canterbury	39	Counties Manukau	22	Christchurch
		C	Hawke's Bay	47	Tasman	12	Napier
October							
Sat	6	P, ST	Canterbury	37	Auckland	12	Christchurch
		P	Counties Manukau	26	Bay of Plenty	22	Pukekohe
		P/C	Manawatu	22	Hawke's Bay	10	Palmerston North
		P/C	Waikato	44	North Harbour	7	Albany
		C	Otago	48	Tasman	7	Blenheim
		C	Wellington	118	Taranaki	0	Porirua
Sat	13	P sf	Canterbury	31	Manawatu	12	Christchurch
		P sf	Counties Manukau	24	Waikato	14	Hamilton
		C sf	Wellington	33	North Harbour	7	Porirua
		C sf	Otago	34	Hawke's Bay	10	Dunedin
		rel. p-o	Bay of Plenty	25	Auckland	22	Tauranga
Sat	20	P f	Canterbury	52	Counties Manukau	29	Christchurch
		C f	Wellington	57	Otago	5	Porirua
Sat/Sun	20/21 *		USA WR Sevens				Glendale
November							
Sat	3		New Zealand	67	USA	6	Chicago
Fri	9		New Zealand	14	France	0	Toulon
Fri/Sat	9/10		Oceania Sevens				Suva
Sat	17		France	30	New Zealand	27	Grenoble
	29/30 *		Dubai WR Sevens				Dubai
December							
Sat/Sun	15/16 *		National Sevens				Tauranga

WOMEN'S CLUB FINALS

Results of the 2018 senior club finals. Counties Manukau and North Harbour clubs participated in the Auckland competition.

Union	Winner		Runner-up	
Auckland	College Rifles	22	Marist	18
Bay of Plenty	Rangataua	22	Rangiuru	21
Canterbury	Christchurch[1]	59	Cant. University	17
Hawke's Bay	Clive[1]	48	Taradale	28
Manawatu	Feilding OB Oroua	34	Kia Toa	29
Otago	University	20	Pirates	10
Taranaki	Coastal	10	Clifton	5
Tasman	Moutere[1]	22	Waimea OB	14
Waikato	Melville	34	Hamilton OB	0
Wellington	Northern United	20	Oriental Rongotai	15

[1] also won in 2017

FARAH PALMER CUP

The number of teams increased to twelve with the return of Taranaki. Teams were ranked based on the 2017 results with the top six teams playing in the premiership division and the remaining six in the championship division. Similar to the men's competition, crossover games were played with each team playing one team from the other division.

Final standings after round robin:

	P	W	D	L	B⁴	B⁷	Pts	T	C	PG	DG	Total	T	C	PG	DG	Total
										FOR					AGAINST		
PREMIERSHIP DIVISION																	
Canterbury	6	5	–	1	6	1	27	40	18	3	–	245	17	8	1	–	104
Waikato	6	5	–	1	5	–	25	31	20	4	–	207	14	6	3	–	91
Counties Manukau	6	4	–	2	6	1	23	29	14	1	–	176	22	10	2	–	136
Manawatu	6	3	–	3	4	–	16	22	7	2	–	130	22	14	3	–	147
Bay of Plenty	6	2	–	4	2	1	11	23	12	4	–	151	28	15	2	–	176
Auckland	6	1	–	5	2	1	7	28	15	–	–	170	28	18	5	–	191
CHAMPIONSHIP DIVISION																	
Wellington	6	5	–	1	5	1	26	55	39	2	–	359	12	7	4	–	86
Otago	6	4	–	2	4	–	20	31	14	2	–	189	16	10	3	–	109
Hawke's Bay	6	4	–	2	3	–	19	30	15	7	–	201	18	7	1	–	107
North Harbour	6	2	–	4	2	–	10	23	13	3	–	150	30	14	3	–	187
Tasman	6	1	–	5	1	–	5	16	9	1	–	101	54	28	2	–	332
Taranaki	6	–	–	6	–	–	0	4	1	–	–	22	71	40	–	–	435
TOTALS								332	177	29	0	2101	332	177	29	0	2101

B⁴ *bonus points for four or more tries in a match.*   B⁷ *bonus points for loss by seven or fewer points.*

PREMIERSHIP

Semi-finals: Canterbury 31, Manawatu 12, at Christchurch
Canterbury 52, Counties Manukau 29, at Christchurch

Final: Canterbury 13, Counties Manukau 7, at Pukekohe

CHAMPIONSHIP

Semi-final: Wellington 33, North Harbour 7, at Porirua
Otago 34, Hawke's Bay 10, at Dunedin

Final: Wellington 57, Otago 5, at Porirua

LEADING POINTS-SCORERS

Amanda Rasch	Wellington	118
Kendra Cocksedge	Canterbury	116

LEADING TRY-SCORERS

Ayesha Leti-I'iga	Wellington	11
Kendra Cocksedge	Canterbury	10

CAREER CHAMPIONSHIP RECORDS

Points
800	Kendra Cocksedge (Canterbury)
538	Emma Jensen (Waik/Auck/HB)
426	Selica Winiata (Manawatu)

Tries
65	Selica Winiata (Manawatu)
53	Kendra Cocksedge (Canterbury)
46	Fiao'o Fa'amausili (Auckland)

Games
113	Emma Jensen (Waik/Auck/HB)
106	Fiao'o Fa'amausili (Auckland)
106	Justine Lavea (Auckland/Counties Manukau)

GRAND FINAL RESULTS

	Winner		Runner-up		Venue
1999	Auckland	22	Wellington	0	Wellington
2000	Auckland	22	Otago	12	Auckland
2001	Auckland	28	Wellington	3	Auckland
2002	Auckland	53	Wellington	3	Auckland
2003	Auckland	35	Wellington	0	Auckland
2004	Auckland	29	Canterbury	10	Auckland
2005	Auckland	36	Canterbury	3	Auckland
2006	Wellington	11	Auckland	10	Auckland
2007	Auckland	32	Otago	27	Auckland
2008	Auckland	13	Canterbury	12	Auckland
2009	Auckland	24	Canterbury	20	Christchurch
2011	Auckland	34	Wellington	8	Hamilton
2012	Auckland	38	Canterbury	12	Christchurch
2013	Auckland	20	Canterbury	10	Wellington
2014	Auckland	28	Waikato	14	New Plymouth
2015	Auckland	39	Wellington	9	Napier
2016	Counties Manukau	41	Auckland	22	Pukekohe
2017	Canterbury	13	Counties Manukau	7	Pukekohe
2018	Canterbury	52	Counties Manukau	29	Christchurch

CHAMPIONSHIP RECORDS

BY THE TEAMS

	BEST PERFORMANCE 2018		RECORD
Season Totals			
Most points	449 by Wellington	449	by Wellington, 2018
Most tries	69 by Wellington	69	by Wellington, 2018
Most conversions	49 by Wellington	49	by Wellington, 2018
Most penalty goals	7 by Hawke's Bay	14	by Otago, 2013
Most dropped goals	0	2	by Manawatu, 2002; Auckland, 2012
Match Records			
Most points	118 by Wellington v Taranaki	118	by Wellington v Taranaki, 2018
Most tries	18 by Wellington v Taranaki	18	by Auckland v North Harbour, 1999; by Wellington v Taranaki, 2018
Most conversions	14 by Wellington v Taranaki	14	by Wellington v Taranaki, 2018
Most penalty goals	2 on seven occasions	6	by Auckland v Wellington, 2001
Most dropped goals	0	1	on seven occasions
Biggest winning margin	118 by Wellington v Taranaki (118–0)	118	by Wellington v Taranaki (118–0), 2018

BY THE PLAYERS

	BEST PERFORMANCE 2018		RECORD
Season Totals			
Most points	118 Amanda Rasch (Wellington)	118	Amanda Rasch (Wellington), 2018
Most tries	11 Ayesha Leti-I'iga (Wellington)	16	Mele Hufanga (Auckland 2015
Most conversions	46 Amanda Rasch (Wellington)	46	Amanda Rasch (Wellington), 2018
Most penalty goals	5 Krysten Cottrell (Hawke's Bay)	12	Chelsea Alley (Waikato) 2013
Most dropped goals	0	2	Rebecca Hull (Manawatu), 2002; Bella Milo (Auckland) 2012
Match Totals			
Most points	43 Amanda Rasch (Wellington) v Taranaki	45	Kelly Brazier (Otago) v Hawke's Bay, 2012
Most tries	4 Kendra Cocksedge (Canterbury) v Auckland	8	Annaleah Rush (Otago) v Hanan Shield Dist), 1999
Most conversions	14 Amanda Rasch (Wellington) v Taranaki	14	Amanda Rasch (Wellington) v Taranaki, 2018
Most penalty goals	2 by five players on six occasions	6	Annaleah Rush (Auckland) v Wellington, 2001
Most dropped goals	0	1	by six players on nine occasions

AUCKLAND STORM

2018 Status: Premiership
NPC participation: 1999–
Coach: John Fa'amausili
Assistant coaches: Waisake Sotutu
Home grounds: Eden Park; Bell Park, Pakuranga

RECORDS

Most appearances	106	*Fiao'o Fa'amausili, 1999–2018*
Most points	452	*Emma Jensen, 2004–17*
Most tries	46	*Fiao'o Fa'amausili, 1999–2017*
Most points in a season	101	*Tammi Wilson, 1999*
Most tries in a season	16	*Mele Hufanga 2015*
Most conversions in a season	27	*Bella Milo, 2012*
Most penalty goals in a season	9	*Emma Jensen, 2014*
Most dropped goals in a season	2	*Bella Milo, 2012*
Most points in a match	31	*Tammi Wilson v North Harbour, 1999*
Most tries in a match	4	*Louisa Wall v North Harbour, 1999;*
		v Northland, 1999;
		Victoria Grant v Otago, 2008;
		Jade Le Pesq v Manawatu, 2012
		Mele Hufanga v Wellington, 2014;
		v Hawke's Bay, 2014;
		v Canterbury 2015;
		Natahlia Moors v Bay of Plenty 2015
Most conversions in a match	13	*Tammi Wilson v North Harbour, 1999*
Most penalty goals in a match	6	*Annaleah Rush v Wellington, 2001*
Highest team score	116	*v North Harbour, 1999*
Record victory (points ahead)	116	*116–0 v North Harbour, 1999*
Highest score conceded	43	*34–43 v Waikato, 2017*
Record defeat (points behind)	231	*14–45 v Waikato, 2018*

The slump in form that had affected Auckland and the Blues in recent seasons has also affected the Storm yet no one anticipated the Storm losing six of its seven games. The only bright performance was against relatively new participants Tasman. Finishing at the foot of the Premiership ladder, Storm's final game was a playoff against Bay of Plenty in the relegation fixture. This too was lost and, for the first time, the country's most populated union drops out of the premier grade for 2019.

The Storm had the services of more Black Ferns than any other union, including the arrival of Charmaine Smith from North Harbour, yet were well beaten by Counties Manukau, Waikato and Canterbury. Several Black Ferns who had taken part in the August series against Australia were rested for the opening game, against Manawatu. The shock 44–17 loss firmly placed the Storm back onto its heels. It was a poor season but it is expected the team will romp through its Championship games in 2019 and make a quick return to the Premiership division.

Kiritapu Demant joined the Black Ferns in France but was not required for either test.

Higher honours went to:
New Zealand: E. Blackwell, R. Demant, F. Fa'amausili, T.M. Fitzpatrick, A. Itunu, L. Itunu, C. McMenamin, N. Moors, A. Nelson, C. Smith
New Zealand Sevens: T.M. Fitzpatrick, T.B. Nathan-Wong, N.L.V. Williams

AUCKLAND REPRESENTATIVES 2018

	Club	Games for Union	Points for Union
Jacqui Aiono	Marist	6	10
Eloise Blackwell	Eden	50	50
Kiritapu Demant	College Rifles	29	86
Ruahei Demant	College Rifles	29	122
Fiao'o Fa'amausili	Marist	106	230
Joanna Fanene	Marist	12	30
Alaimoana Fineaso-Levi	Marist	11	15
Leilani Fuikefu	Marist	2	0
Maiko Fujimoto	Ponsonby	5	0
Savah Gautusa	College Rifles	5	0
Mele Hufanga	Marist	46	195
Aldora Itunu	Ponsonby	37	70
Linda Itunu	Ponsonby	52	45
Hasting Leiataua	Marist	18	30
Charmaine McMenamin	Ponsonby	46	50
Lose Mafi	Marist	15	10
Vainga Moimoi	College Rifles	4	0
Natahlia Moors	Ponsonby	12	60
Corina Nanai	College Rifles	8	5
Aleisha Nelson	Ponsonby	61	60
Margarette Nena	Eden	3	0
Alakoka Po'oi	College Rifles	2	0
Jennifer-Rose Reu	Marist	7	0
Lauren Sa'u	Marist	4	5
Luti Sikoloni	Marist	5	5
Charmaine Smith	College Rifles	5	10
Misaki Suzuki	Marist	7	0
Olalini Tafoulua	Marist	5	0
Margaret Vaiouga (nee Saena)	Marist	9	10
Aeron Warbrooke	Ponsonby	23	5
Hinemoa Watene	College Rifles	5	10

INDIVIDUAL SCORING

	Tries	Con	PG	DG	Points
R. Demant	6	16	–	–	62
Fanene	3	–	–	–	15
Hufanga	3	–	–	–	15
Moors	3	–	–	–	15
Aiono	2	–	–	–	10
Leiataua	2	–	–	–	10
Smith	2	–	–	–	10
Vaiouga	2	–	–	–	10
K. Demant	1	–	–	–	5
Fa'amausili	1	–	–	–	5
Fineaso-Levi	1	–	–	–	5
A. Itunu	1	–	–	–	5
McMenamin	1	–	–	–	5
Nanai	1	–	–	–	5
Sa'u	1	–	–	–	5
Sikoloni	1	–	–	–	5
Warbrooke	1	–	–	–	5
Totals	**32**	**16**	**0**	**0**	**192**
Opposition scored	32	19	6	0	216

AUCKLAND 2018	Manawatu	Tasman	Counties Manukau	Waikato	Bay of Plenty	Canterbury	Bay of Plenty	TOTALS
K.W. Demant	–	–	–	15	15	15	15	**4**
D.B. Moors	15	14	14	–	–	14	–	**4**
H. Leiataua	–	15	15	14	11	s	s	**6**
L. Fuikefu	14	s	–	–	–	–	–	**2**
H.H. Watene	11	–	–	–	–	–	–	**1**
L. Mafi	s	–	–	s	s	11	11	**5**
C. Nanai	–	11	11	11	14	–	14	**5**
L.T. Sa'u	13	13	–	13	13	–	–	**4**
S.S. Gautusa	12	–	13	s	s	s	–	**5**
D.R. Demant	s	12	12	10	10	13	13	**7**
M.M. Hufanga	–	–	s	12	12	12	12	**5**
M.T. Nena	10	10	10	–	–	–	–	**3**
A.K. Warbrooke	9	9	9	s	s	9	9	**7**
J-R. Reu	s	s	s	9	9	10	10	**7**
C.J. McMenamin (capt)	8	8	8	–	–	–	8	**4**
J. Fanene	–	s	s	8	8	8	6	**6**
M. Suzuki	7	7	7	7	7	7	7	**7**
A. Po'oi	6	–	–	–	–	s	–	**2**
L.F. Itunu	s	6	6	–	–	s	s	**5**
A. Fineaso-Levi	5	–	–	6	6	6	5	**5**
C.B. Smith	–	5	5	5	5	5	–	**5**
O.M. Tafoulua	4	–	–	s	s	4	s	**5**
E.S. Blackwell	–	4	4	4	4	–	4	**5**
J.F. Aiono	3	s	–	s	s	–	–	**4**
A.P. Nelson	s	3	3	3	3	3	3	**7**
M. Vaiouga	1	1	1	s	s	s	–	**6**
L. Sikoloni	s	s	s	–	–	s	s	**5**
A.T. Itunu	–	s	s	1	1	1	1	**6**
M. Fujimoto	2	s	–	s	2	–	s	**5**
V.L. Moimoi	s	–	–	–	s	s	2	**4**
F.M. Fa'amausili	–	2	2	2	–	2	–	**4**

Blackwell (v Waikato and Bay of Plenty) and R. Demant (v Canterbury) captained the team during McMenamin's absence.

AUCKLAND TEAM RECORD, 2018

Played 7　Won 1　Lost 6　Points for 192　Points against 216

Date	Opponent	Location	Score	Tries	Con	PG	DG	Referee
September 1	Manawatu (P)	Pakuranga	17–44	Aiono (2), R. Demant	R. Demant			L.A. Jenner
September 7	Tasman (P/C)	Auckland	86–0	R. Demant (3), Vaiouga (2), Smith (2), Moors (2), Sa'u, McMenamin, Warbrooke, Sikoloni, Leiataua	R. Demant (8)			L.A. Jenner
September 15	Counties Manukau (P)	Pukekohe	12–31	Moors, R. Demant	R. Demant			H.G. Reed
September 22	Waikato (P)	Taupiri	14–45	Hufanga (2)	R. Demant (2)			R.P. Kelly
September 28	Bay of Plenty (P)	Auckland	29–34	Leiataua, Nanai, Hufanga, Fanene, Fineaso-Levi	R. Demant (2)			R.M. Mahoney
October 6	Canterbury (P, ST)	Christchurch	12–37	Faamausili, A. Itunu	R. Demant			B.J. Andrew
October 13	Bay of Plenty (relegation play-off)	Tauranga	22–25	Fanene (2), K. Demant, R. Demant	R. Demant			M.C.J. Winter

ST *Stewart Trophy*

BAY OF PLENTY VOLCANIX

2018 Status: Premiership
NPC participation: 1999–2005, 2014–
Coach: Brendon Webby
Assistant coaches: Zane Winslade, Mike Lewis
Home Grounds: Tauranga Domain; Matata RFC;
Rotorua International Stadium

RECORDS

Most appearances	35	Lisa Mansell, 1999–2015
Most points	90	Tamaku Paul, 1999–2002
Most tries	18	Tamaku Paul, 1999–2002
Most points in a season	55	Tamaku Paul, 1999
Most tries in a season	11	Tamaku Paul, 1999
Most conversions in a season	12	Puawai Hohepa, 2004
Most penalty goals in a season	4	Renee Wickliffe, 2018
Most dropped goals in a season	1	Puawai Hohepa, 2000
Most points in a match	20	Tamaku Paul v Counties Manukau, 1999
Most tries in a match	4	Tamaku Paul v Counties Manukau, 1999
Most conversions in a match	5	Exia Shelford v Counties Manukau, 2003
Most penalty goals in a match	2	Heidi Reader v Northland, 1999; Puawai Hohepa v Waikato, 2000 Kymbillie Raynes v North Harbour, 2016 Renee Wickliffe v Auckland 2018
Highest team score	73	v Taranaki 2018
Record victory (points ahead)	73	73–0 v Taranaki 2018
Highest score conceded	101	v Auckland, 2015
Record defeat (points behind)	101	0–101 v Auckland, 2015

Having won the Championship division in 2017 the Volcanix was promoted to the stronger Premiership division and after two hefty losses, to Canterbury and Waikato, proved to be strong competitors during the rest of the season. The highlights were defeating Auckland twice, the second occasion being the relegation playoff game at the end of the season. These wins and the closely contested games with Manawatu and Counties Manukau indicated the team could develop further in the coming seasons. The experience of the union's two Black Ferns, Lesley Elder and Renee Wickliffe, were influential in the performances.

Loose forward Christie Yule led a team which contained several newcomers, some still in their teens. Regular starters among the forwards included Kate Henwood, Kendra Reynolds, Amanda Aldridge and Lily Florence. Fullback Sapphire Tapsell was in her third season but still only 20 years of age and became the Volcanix top try-scorer. Tynealle Fitzgerald was a member of the NZ Under 18 Sevens team that won the Oceania Under 18 event in Sydney and the gold medal at the Youth Olympics in Argentina. 41-year-old Calli Perrott had last appeared in 2004.

Higher honours went to:
New Zealand: L. Elder, R. Wickliffe
New Zealand Sevens: M.G. Blyde, K.A. Brazier, R.M. Tui

BAY OF PLENTY REPRESENTATIVES 2018

	Club	Games for Union	Points for Union
Amanda Aldridge	Rangiuru	12	0
Lesley Elder	Rangataua	10	20
Tynealle Fitzgerald	Rangiuru	4	0
Lily Florence	Whakarewarewa	20	0
Kate Henwood	Rangataua	20	0
Kororia Heyblom	Rangiuru	4	0
Renee Holmes	Rangataua	4	4
Baye Jacob	Rangiuru	18	5
Tracey Lemon	Rangataua	1	0
Rawinia Luka	Rangiuru	4	0
Mystery McLean Kora	Rangiuru	13	25
Emily Magee	Rotoiti	5	10
Bree Meyer	Rangataua	2	0
Te Rina Mohi	Whakarewarewa	3	0
Angel Mulu	Rangiuru	5	5
Calli Perrott	Rangiuru	20	0
Polly Playle	Rotoiti	13	10
Tania-Rose Raharuhi	Whakarewarewa	14	0
Kendra Reynolds	Rangiuru	26	5
Olivia Richardson	Rangataua	4	0
Hana Tapiata	Whakarewarewa	15	10
Sapphire Tapsell	Rangiuru	20	51
Jade Tuilaepa	Rangataua	10	15
Braxton Walker	Rangiuru	7	0
Mikyla Wardlaw	Waimana	12	0
Renee Wickliffe	Rangataua	6	46
Ereti Williams	Rangiuru	20	15
Ora Williams	Rotoiti	11	30
Christie Yule	Rangiuru	19	10

INDIVIDUAL SCORING

	Tries	Con	PG	DG	Points
Wickliffe	4	7	4	–	46
Tapsell	5	4	1	–	36
Elder	4	–	–	–	20
O. Williams	3	–	–	–	15
Magee	2	–	–	–	10
Playle	2	–	–	–	10
Tuilaepa	2	–	–	–	10
Yule	2	–	–	–	10
Jacob	1	–	–	–	5
Mulu	1	–	–	–	5
Reynolds	1	–	–	–	5
Holmes	–	2	–	–	4
Totals	**27**	**13**	**5**	**0**	**176**
Opposition scored	32	16	2	0	198

BAY OF PLENTY 2018	Canterbury	Waikato	Manawatu	Taranaki	Auckland	Counties Manukau	Auckland	TOTALS
S.N.K. Tapsell	15	15	15	15	15	15	15	7
M.A. McLean Kora	14	11	s	–	s	–	–	4
E.P. Magee	11	–	–	14	11	11	11	5
P–J.M. Playle	s	s	11	11	14	14	14	7
O.D. Richardson	s	–	–	s	–	s	s	4
T–R.N. Raharuhi	13	13	12	s	s	s	12	7
H.J. Tapiata	–	–	13	13	13	13	13	5
Te R.T. Mohi	–	–	–	s	s	–	s	3
K.F. Heyblom	12	s	–	–	–	–	–	2
R.W.M. Wickliffe	–	14	14	12	12	12	10	6
R.M.M. Holmes	10	12	s	–	–	10	–	4
O.P.R. Williams	–	10	10	10	10	9	–	5
J.U. Tuilaepa	9	9	9	9	9	–	9	6
B.B. Meyer	s	s	–	–	–	–	–	2
K.L. Reynolds	7	8	8	6	6	6	6	7
C.E. Yule (capt)	6	6	6	8	8	8	8	7
L-A.T. Elder	s	7	7	7	7	7	7	7
T.A. Fitzgerald	s	s	s	s	–	–	–	4
C.E. Perrott	5	s	s	s	s	s	–	6
A.V.H. Aldridge	s	5	5	5	5	5	5	7
M.A. Wardlaw	4	s	s	s	s	–	s	6
K.K. Henwood	8	4	4	4	4	4	4	7
T.M. Lemon	–	–	–	–	s	–	–	1
E.R.R. Williams	3	3	3	–	–	–	–	3
B.M.M. Walker	–	–	–	3	3	s	3	4
B.L. Jacob	1	1	s	–	1	1	1	6
A.J. Mulu	s	s	1	1	–	3	–	5
R.A.S. Luka	–	–	s	s	s	s	–	4
L.J. Florence	2	2	2	2	2	2	2	7

BAY OF PLENTY TEAM RECORD, 2018

Played 7 Won 3 Lost 4 Points for 176 Points against 198

Date	Opponent	Location	Score	Tries	Con	PG	DG	Referee
September 1	Canterbury (P)	Tauranga	5–55	Elder				M. Cogger-Orr
September 8	Waikato (P)	Matata	7–44	Tuilaepa	Holmes			N.P. Briant
September 15	Manawatu (P)	Palmerston North	10–22	Jacob	Holmes	Tapsell		M.I. Fraser
September 21	Taranaki (P/C)	Rotorua	73–0	Playle (2), Tapsell (2), Yule (2), Wickliffe (2), Magee (2), Reynolds, Mulu, O. Williams	Tapsell (4)			D.J. Waenga
September 28	Auckland (P)	Auckland	34–29	O. Williams, Tuilaepa, Wickliffe, Elder	Wickliffe (4)	Wickliffe (2)		R.M. Mahoney
October 6	Counties Manukau (P)	Pukekohe	22–26	Wickliffe, Tapsell, O. Williams	Wickliffe (2)	Wickliffe		M. Cogger-Orr
October 13	Auckland (relegation playoff)	Tauranga	25–22	Tapsell (2), Elder (2)	Wickliffe	Wickliffe		M.C.J. Winter

CANTERBURY

2018 Status: Premiership
NPC participation: 1999–
Coach: Kieran Kite
Assistant coaches: James Jowsey, Melissa Ruscoee
Home Ground: Rugby Park; Christchurch Stadium
(v Counties Manukau and Auckland)

RECORDS

Most appearances	89	*Stephanie Te Ohaere-Fox, 2004-18*
Most points	800	*Kendra Cocksedge, 2007-18*
Most tries	53	*Kendra Cocksedge, 2007-18*
Most points in a season	116	*Kendra Cocksedge, 2018*
Most tries in a season	10	*Kendra Cocksedge, 2018*
Most conversions in a season	27	*Kendra Cocksedge, 2018*
Most penalty goals in a season	11	*Kendra Cocksedge, 2014*
Most dropped goals in a season	1	*Charntay Poko, 2017*
Most points in a match	30	*Kendra Cocksedge, v Taranaki, 2013*
		v North Harbour, 2016
Most tries in a match	4	*Stephanie Mortimer v Waikato, 2004;*
		Kendra Cocksedge, v Taranaki, 2013
		v Auckland, 2018
Most conversions in a match	8	*Kendra Cocksedge v Hawke's Bay, 2012*
Most penalty goals in a match	5	*Kendra Cocksedge v Auckland, 2009*
		v Waikato, 2016
Highest team score	92	*v Taranaki, 2013*
Record victory (points ahead)	80	*92–12 v Taranaki, 2013*
Highest score conceded	70	*v Auckland, 2015*
Record defeat (points behind)	62	*8–70 v Auckland, 2015*

Canterbury again dominated the Farah Palmer Cup competition, defeating Counties Manukau comfortably in the final. The Stewart Trophy was successfully defended and the only glitch in the season was the narrow loss to Wellington in a high-scoring game in Wellington.

Experienced prop Stephanie Te Ohaere-Fox captained the team for the sixth season and her side could be regarded as a star team rather than a team of stars. Phillipa Love and Kendra Cocksedge were the union's only Black Ferns and no one was chosen for the national sevens squad. Fullback Olivia McGoverne was the team's player of the year but it was the efficiency of the team as a whole which produced the results and placed the team on the same level as the men in the Mitre 10 Cup. Becky Davidson and Sam Curtis were regular try scorers on the wings. Flanker Greer O'Rourke had a promising first season and Forne Burkin shows continued improvement. 18-year-old Georgia Ponsonby had played for Manawatu the previous year.

Halfback Kendra Cocksedge continues to rewrite the records with her points-scoring as a tryscorer and goalkicker. Her four tries against Auckland was followed up with 27 points in the final including converting all seven tries.

Lucy Anderson was a late replacement for the Black Ferns tour but not chosen in the playing squads.

CANTERBURY REPRESENTATIVES 2018

	Club	Games for Union	Points for Union		Club	Games for Union	Points for Union
Lucy Anderson	Christchurch	37	60	Lucy Jenkins	Christchurch	16	10
Alana Bremner	Lincoln Univ	32	10	Phillipa Love	Christchurch	28	45
Chelsea Bremner	Lincoln Univ	16	5	Olivia McGoverne	Canterbury Univ	27	72
Grace Brooker	HSOB	15	50	Greer O'Rourke	Canterbury Univ	7	5
Forne Burkin	Lincoln Univ	8	5	Nina Poletti	Christchurch	15	10
Kendra Cocksedge	Canterbury Univ	75	800	Georgia Ponsonby	Lincoln Univ	8	0
Sam Curtis	Christchurch	20	70	Melanie Puckett	Lincoln Univ	10	20
Taylor Curtis	Christchurch	11	0	Cassie Siataga	Linwood	16	14
Becky Davidson	Lincoln Univ	16	60	Grace Steinmetz	Lincoln Univ	1	0
Terauoriwa Gapper	Canterbury Univ	14	15	Kaylee Tavendale	Christchurch	17	0
Catriona Greenslade	Lincoln Univ	12	0	Stephanie Te Ohaere-Fox	Christchurch	89	85
Jess Hansen	Canterbury Univ	29	20	Charna Thompson	Christchurch	12	5
Dianne Hiini	Christchurch	26	5	Estelle Uren	Christchurch	37	55

INDIVIDUAL SCORING

	Tries	Con	PG	DG	Points		Tries	Con	PG	DG	Points
Cocksedge	10	27	4	–	116	Siataga	1	1	–	–	7
Davidson	8	–	–	–	40	Burkin	1	–	–	–	5
S. Curtis	7	–	–	–	35	Hansen	1	–	–	–	5
Brooker	5	–	–	–	25	O'Rourke	1	–	–	–	5
Anderson	3	–	–	–	15	Thompson	1	–	–	–	5
McGoverne	3	–	–	–	15	Uren	1	–	–	–	5
A. Bremner	2	–	–	–	10						
Jenkins	2	–	–	–	10	**Totals**	**52**	**28**	**4**	**0**	**328**
Love	2	–	–	–	10						
Puckett	2	–	–	–	10	Opposition scored	24	11	1	0	145
Te Ohaere-Fox	2	–	–	–	10						

CANTERBURY 2018	Bay of Plenty	Wellington	Waikato	Manawatu	Counties Manukau	Auckland	Manawatu	Counties Manukau	TOTALS
O.B. McGoverne	15	15	15	15	15	15	15	15	8
M.C. Puckett	14	–	–	s	s	s	s	–	5
B.L. Davidson	s	14	14	14	14	14	14	14	8
G.L. Steinmetz	–	s	–	–	–	–	–	–	1
S.G.B. Curtis	11	11	s	11	11	11	11	11	8
T.R.B. Curtis	s	–	s	s	–	s	–	s	5
G.E. Brooker	13	13	11	13	13	13	13	13	8
T. Gapper	–	s	13	–	s	–	s	s	5
L.E. Anderson	12	12	12	12	12	12	12	12	8
D.J.M. Hiini	10	10	10	s	s	s	s	s	8
C.M.T. Siataga	s	s	s	10	10	10	10	10	8
K.M. Cocksedge	9	9	9	9	9	9	9	9	8
G.R.A. Ponsonby	8	8	8	s	s	8	8	s	8
C.J. Thompson	–	s	–	–	–	–	–	–	1
C.J. Greenslade	s	s	s	8	8	s	s	8	8
L.V.M. Jenkins	7	7	6	s	s	s	6	s	8
G.R. O'Rourke	–	s	7	7	7	7	7	7	7
E.D. Uren	6	6	4	4	4	4	4	4	8
A.J. Bremner	5	5	5	5	5	5	5	5	8
C.J. Bremner	4	–	s	s	s	s	s	s	7
K.V. Tavendale	s	4	–	–	–	s	s	–	4
S.A. Te Ohaere-Fox (capt)	3	3	3	3	3	3	3	3	8
P.E.A. Love	1	1	1	1	1	–	1	1	7
N.J.N. Poletti	s	–	s	s	s	1	s	s	7
F.K. Burkin	2	2	2	6	6	6	2	6	8
J.E. Hansen	s	s	s	2	2	2	–	2	7

CANTERBURY TEAM RECORD, 2018

Played 8 Won 7 Lost 1 Points for 328 Points against 145

Date	Opponent	Location	Score	Tries	Con	PG	DG	Referee
September 1	Bay of Plenty (P)	Tauranga	55–5	Cocksedge (2), McGoverne (2), Jenkins, Puckett, Uren, Love, S. Curtis	Cocksedge (5)			M. Cogger-Orr
September 8	Wellington (P/C)	Porirua	38–43	Davidson (2), Brooker (2), Cocksedge, Thompson	Cocksedge (4)			R.M. Mahoney
September 15	Waikato (P, ST)	Christchurch	28–10	Davidson (2), Te Ohaere-Fox, S. Curtis	Cocksedge	Cocksedge (2)		Lara West *Australia*
September 23	Manawatu (P)	Palmerston North	48–12	Davidson (2), Love, Hansen, Te Ohaere-Fox, Brooker, A. Bremner, Anderson	Cocksedge (3), Siataga			M. Cogger-Orr
September 30	Counties Manukau (P, ST)	Christchurch	39–22	McGoverne, Anderson, S. Curtis, Davidson, Brooker, Cocksedge, Puckett	Cocksedge (2)			C. Paul
October 6	Auckland (P, ST)	Christchurch	37–12	Cocksedge (4), Davidson, Burkin	Cocksedge (2)	Cocksedge		B.J. Andrew
October 13	Manawatu (semi-final)	Christchurch	31–12	S. Curtis (2), A. Bremner, Siataga, Jenkins	Cocksedge (3)			J.D. Munro
October 20	Counties (final)	Christchurch	52–29	Cocksedge (2), S. Curtis (2), O'Rourke, Brooker, Anderson	Cocksedge (7)	Cocksedge		R.M. Mahoney

ST *Stewart Trophy*

COUNTIES MANUKAU HEAT

2018 Status: Premiership
NPC participation: 1999–2005, 2013–
Coach: Jeremy Clark
Home grounds: Navigation Homes Stadium, Pukekohe;
Massey Park, Papakura

RECORDS

Most appearances	45	*Arihiana Marino-Tauhinu 2013-18*
Most points	211	*Arihiana Marino-Tauhinu 2013-18*
Most tries	26	*Te Kura Ngata-Aerengamate, 2013-18*
Most points in a season	78	*Hazel Tubic, 2017*
Most tries in a season	10	*Renee Wickliffe, 2015*
Most conversions in a season	28	*Hazel Tubic 2017*
Most penalty goals in a season	8	*Hazel Tubic, 2013*
Most dropped goals in a season	0	
Most points in a match	27	*Hazel Tubic v Taranaki, 2013*
Most tries in a match	4	*Renee Wickliffe v Otago, 2015*
		Portia Woodman v Wellington 2016
Most conversions in a match	7	*Hazel Tubic v Taranaki, 2013*
Most penalty goals in a match	4	*Hazel Tubic v Auckland, 2013*
Highest team score	84	*v North Harbour, 2017*
Record victory (points ahead)	77	*84-7 v North Harbour, 2017*
Highest score conceded	65	*v Auckland B, 2005*
Record defeat (points behind)	65	*0–65 v Auckland B, 2005*

The Heat finished in third place after the round-robin and defeated second-placed Waikato in a semi-final but were no match for Canterbury in the final. Arihiana Marino-Tauhinu, in her fifth year as captain, led the team well and had in front of her among the forwards experienced Black Ferns in Justine Lavea, Aroha Savage, Aotearoa Matau, Leilani Perese and Te Kura Ngata-Aerengamate. Prop Matau was the top try scorer with eight tries. The solid pack wore down most opponents.

Higher honours went to:
New Zealand: T. Ngata-Aerengamate, L. Perese, A. Savage
New Zealand Sevens: P.L. Woodman

COUNTIES MANUKAU REPRESENTATIVES 2018

	Club	Games for Union	Points for Union		Club	Games for Union	Points for Union
Glory Aiono	Manurewa	6	0	Te Kura Ngata-Aerengamate	Ardmore Marist	42	130
Aleasha Brider	Manurewa	3	0	Leilani Perese	Manurewa	21	20
Stacey Brown	Manurewa	32	10	Feofa'aki Piliu	Ardmore Marist	8	15
Waikohika Flesher	Manurewa	7	10	Hinewai Pomare	Manurewa	28	20
Grace Gago	Manurewa	12	0	Aroha Savage	Manurewa	29	59
Emily Kitson	Ardmore Marist	11	5	Lauryn Steed	Ardmore Marist	15	10
Justine Lavea	Ardmore Marist	25	25	Lavinia Tauhalaliku	Manurewa	5	5
Timara Leaf	Manurewa	24	15	Amiria Te Iringa	Manurewa	5	0
Georgina Lidgard	Manurewa	12	0	Harono Te Iringa	Manurewa	16	10
Larissa Lima E Silva	Ardmore Marist	14	0	Shyanne Thompson	Waiuku	3	0
Anastasia Mamea	Manurewa	7	20	Shonte To'a	Ardmore Marist	5	2
Arihiana Marino-Tauhinu	Manurewa	45	211	Lanulangi Veainu	Ardmore Marist	15	50
Aotearoa Matau	Ardmore Marist	36	90	Azania Watene	Ardmore Marist	28	20
Victoria Meki	Ardmore Marist	27	15	Kararaina Wira-Kohu	Manurewa	4	5

INDIVIDUAL SCORING

	Tries	Con	PG	DG	Points		Tries	Con	PG	DG	Points
Marino-Tauhinu	1	16	2	–	43	Steed	1	–	–	–	5
Matau	8	–	–	–	40	H. Te Iringa	1	–	–	–	5
Savage	4	2	–	–	24	Veainu	1	–	–	–	5
Mamea	4	–	–	–	20	Watene	1	–	–	–	5
Meki	3	–	–	–	15	Tauhalaliku	1	–	–	–	5
Piliu	3	–	–	–	15	Wira–Kohu	1	–	–	–	5
Flesher	2	–	–	–	10	To'a	–	1	–	–	2
Lavea	2	–	–	–	10						
Ngata-Aerengamate	2	–	–	–	10	**Totals**	**37**	**19**	**2**	**0**	**229**
Brown	1	–	–	–	5						
Perese	1	–	–	–	5	Opposition scored	31	19	3	0	202

COUNTIES MANUKAU 2018

	Waikato	Manawatu	Auckland	Otago	Canterbury	Bay of Plenty	Waikato	Canterbury	TOTALS
E.F. Kitson	s	15	15	–	15	15	15	15	7
A.O.R. Watene	14	14	14	14	14	14	14	14	8
S. Thompson	–	–	–	s	–	s	–	s	3
W. Flesher	11	11	11	15	11	11	–	s	7
L. Tauhalaliku	s	–	s	–	s	–	11	11	5
F. Piliu	13	13	13	13	13	13	13	13	8
K. Wira-Kohu	12	s	–	s	12	–	–	–	4
L. Lima E Silva	–	12	12	12	7	–	s	7	6
L. Veainu	–	–	–	s	–	–	–	–	1
A.V. Brider	–	–	–	–	–	s	12	12	3
T.R. Leaf	10	–	10	10	10	12	10	10	7
S. To'a	15	10	–	11	s	10	–	–	5
A.A.H. Marino-Tauhinu (capt)	9	9	9	9	9	9	9	9	8
A. Savage	–	8	8	8	–	8	8	8	6
J. Lavea	8	7	7	7	8	7	7	6	8
S.J. Brown	7	6	6	6	6	–	–	s	6
A. Te Iringa	–	s	s	–	–	–	–	–	2
H. Te Iringa	4	5	5	5	5	5	5	5	8
A. Mamea	5	–	s	s	s	4	4	s	7
G. Aiono	s	–	–	s	4	6	6	4	6
G. Lidgard	s	4	s	4	s	s	s	s	8
A.K. Matau	3	3	3	3	3	3	3	3	8
L.R.R. Perese	1	1	1	–	–	s	s	1	6
L. Steed	s	s	s	1	1	1	1	s	8
H. Pomare	s	–	–	s	s	–	–	–	3
T.R. Ngata-Aerengamate	2	s	2	2	2	–	–	2	6
G.L.F. Gago	s	–	s	s	s	2	s	–	6
V. Meki	6	2	4	–	–	s	2	s	6

COUNTIES MANUKAU TEAM RECORD, 2018

Played 8　Won 5　Lost 3　Points for 229　Points against 202

Date	Opponent	Location	Score	Tries	Con	PG	DG	Referee
September 1	Waikato (P)	Taupiri	27–33	Mamea (2), Watene, Lavea, Meki	To'a			B.J. Andrew
September 8	Manawatu (P)	Papakura	31–22	Meki (2), Matau (2), Ngata-Aerengamate	Marino-Tauhinu (3)			Amber Hibbard *Australia*
September 15	Auckland (P)	Pukekohe	31–12	Piliu (2), Matau, Flesher	Marino-Tauhinu (4)	Marino-Tauhinu		H.G. Reed
September 22	Otago (P/C)	Dunedin	39–8	Steed, Te Iringa, Flesher, Brown, Wira-Kohu, Savage, Piliu	Marino-Tauhinu (2)			B.E. Pickerill
September 30	Canterbury (P, ST)	Christchurch	22–39	Matau (2), Lavea, Veainu	Marino-Tauhinu			C. Paul
October 6	Bay of Plenty (P)	Pukekohe	26–22	Savage (2), Matau (2)	Marino-Tauhinu (3)			M. Cogger-Orr
October 13	Waikato (semi-final)	Hamilton	24–14	Marino-Tauhinu, Matau, Savage	Marino-Tauhinu (3)	Marino-Tauhinu		B.J. Andrew
October 20	Canterbury (final)	Christchurch	29–52	Mamea (2), Ngata-Aerengamate, Perese, Tauhalaliku	Savage (2)			R.M. Mahoney

ST *Stewart Trophy*

HAWKE'S BAY TUI

2018 Status: Championship
NPC participation: 1999–2012, 2014–2015, 2017–
Coach: Stephen Woods
Home grounds: Tremain Field, Park Island, Napier;
McLean Park (v North Harbour)

RECORDS

Most appearances	69	*Chanel Huddleston, 2001–18*
Most points	192	*Nerina Hawkins, 1999–2004*
Most tries	21	*Deidre Hakopa, 1999–2009*
Most points in a season	61	*Nerina Hawkins, 2003*
Most tries in a season	9	*Deidre Hakopa, 2003*
Most conversions in a season	16	*Nerina Hawkins, 2003*
Most penalty goals in a season	8	*Nerina Hawkins, 2003*
Most dropped goals in a season	0	
Most points in a match	25	*Deidre Hakopa v Southland, 2003*
Most tries in a match	5	*Deidre Hakopa v Southland, 2003*
Most conversions in a match	7	*Nerina Hawkins v Poverty Bay, 2000*
Most penalty goals in a match	4	*Nerina Hawkins v Auckland, 2003*
Highest team score	100	*v Southland, 2003*
Record victory (points ahead)	95	*100–5 v Southland, 2003*
Highest score conceded	93	*v Auckland, 2014*
Record defeat (points behind)	93	*0–93 v Auckland, 2014*

The Hawke's Bay Tuis showed much improved form on 2017. The Cup opener against Wellington was the Tuis first win over that opponent since 2006, and the season ended with a Championship semi-final defeat to Otago.

There was quite a significant change in playing personnel as a dozen of last year's team was not involved. Two significant arrivals were former Black Fern Emma Jensen who commuted from Auckland to play for her home province, and Hanna Brough arrived from Counties Manukau. In addition, record appearance holder Chanel Huddleston was available again having last appeared in 2014.

Hooker Jessie Taueki was a very good striker in the scrums winning a number of tightheads while lock Hanna Brough was very effective in the lineout and an influential figure in the engine room. Laurae Blake was the best of the loose forwards with Gemma Woods and Niamh Jefferson not far behind. The experience of Chanel Huddleston was valuable in the forward exchanges and versatile enough to make one appearance at centre.

As expected, the halfback-first five-eighth combination of Emma Jensen and Krysten Cottrell was all class, it being a shame Cottrell missed the last two matches due to injury. In the midfield both Natasha Greville and Te Maari MacGregor were always dangerous, and MacGregor missing the semi-final due to injury was a blow. Wing Tori Iosefo was very hard to stop, making the most of her opportunities to score six tries in just five matches.

Higher honours went to:
New Zealand: K. Cottrell

HAWKE'S BAY REPRESENTATIVES 2018

	Club	Games for Union	Points for Union
Davina Atkin (nee Winiata)	Napier Technical	12	0
Hailey Baker	Taradale	7	0
Kaitlin Bates	Taradale	5	0
Laurae Blake	Clive	28	5
Hanna Brough	Hastings R&S	5	10
Kathleen Brown	Napier Technical	9	5
Natalie Cotton	Taradale	45	15
Krysten Cottrell (nee Duffill)	Taradale	24	64
Natasha Greville	Taradale	11	30
Kara Huata	Clive	5	0
Chanel Huddleston	Napier Technical	69	50
Rebekah Hurae	Clive	18	0
Tori Iosefo	Napier Technical	5	30
Niamh Jefferson	Clive	12	10
Emma Jensen	Hastings R&S	7	14
Lara Kendrick	Clive	3	0
Helen McGregor	Taradale	31	5
Te Maari MacGregor	Clive	45	94
Rawinia Mason	Napier Technical	8	0
Whitney Olsen	Taradale	2	0
Danielle Pomare-Mackay	Clive	7	0
Felicity Powdrell	Taradale	18	20
Jennifer Simati	Napier Technical	5	0
Jessie Taueki (nee Carter)	Clive	25	0
Jasmine Taukamo-Apiata	Taradale	3	0
Shaylee Tipiwai	Clive	33	45
Yarnisae Whaitiri	Clive	12	5
Amy Williams	Clive	62	121
Gemma Woods	Taradale	49	40

INDIVIDUAL SCORING

	Tries	Con	PG	DG	Points
Cottrell	3	11	5	–	52
Iosefo	6	–	–	–	30
Greville	5	–	–	–	25
Tipiwai	4	–	–	–	20
MacGregor	3	–	–	–	15
Powdrell	3	–	–	–	15
Jensen	–	4	2	–	14
Brough	2	–	–	–	10
Cotton	2	–	–	–	10
Jefferson	2	–	–	–	10
Huddleston	1	–	–	–	5
Woods	1	–	–	–	5
Totals	**32**	**15**	**7**	**0**	**211**
Opposition scored	24	9	1	0	141

HAWKE'S BAY 2018	Wellington	Otago	Taranaki	North Harbour	Tasman	Manawatu	Otago	TOTALS
S.T. Tipiwai	15	15	15	15	15	15	15	**7**
F.R. Powdrell	14	14	11	14	14	14	14	**7**
K.B. Bates	–	–	14	s	s	s	s	**5**
T.P.L.A. Iosefo	11	–	–	11	11	11	11	**5**
D.J. Pomare-Mackay	–	11	–	–	s	–	–	**2**
N.D.D. Greville	13	13	s	s	12	12	12	**7**
Te M.T. MacGregor	s	s	13	13	13	13	–	**6**
A.L. Williams (capt)	12	12	12	12	–	10	10	**6**
K.J. Cottrell	10	10	10	10	10	–	–	**5**
E.M. Jensen	9	9	9	9	9	9	9	**7**
H.R.E. Baker	–	s	–	–	s	–	–	**2**
G.L. Woods	8	8	8	5	8	–	8	**6**
K.M.T. Brown	s	s	s	8	–	–	s	**5**
C.A. Huddleston	7	7	6	7	–	–	13	**5**
N.W. Jefferson	s	s	7	s	7	7	7	**7**
L.M.A. Blake	6	6	s	6	6	6	6	**7**
J.R. Taukamo-Apiata	–	–	s	s	–	–	–	**2**
R.P. Mason	5	5	s	s	s	8	s	**7**
R.K. Hurae	4	4	5	s	5	5	5	**7**
H.L. Brough	–	s	4	4	4	–	4	**5**
L.S. Kendrick	–	–	–	–	s	4	s	**3**
W.A.M. Olsen	–	–	–	–	–	s	–	**1**
N.J. Cotton	3	3	3	3	3	3	3	**7**
K.T.I. Huata	1	1	–	–	1	1	1	**5**
J.L. Simati	s	s	1	1	s	–	–	**5**
Y.R. Whaitiri	–	–	–	–	–	s	–	**1**
J.M. Taueki	2	2	–	2	2	2	2	**6**
D.S. Atkin	–	s	2	s	–	–	s	**4**
H. McGregor	–	–	s	–	s	s	–	**3**

Woods captained the team v Tasman.

HAWKE'S BAY TEAM RECORD, 2018

Played 7   Won 4   Lost 3   Points for 211   Points against 141

Date	Opponent	Location	Score	Tries	Con	PG	DG	Referee
September 1	Wellington (C)	Napier	25–22	Greville, Cottrell, Iosefo	Cottrell (2)	Cottrell (2)		R.M. Mahoney
September 8	Otago (C)	Dunedin	12–31	Cotton, MacGregor	Cottrell			J.R. Nutbrown
September 15	Taranaki (C)	Inglewood	55–10	Cottrell (2), Tipiwai (2), Greville (2), Powdrell, Huddleston, Brough	Cottrell (5)			N.E.R. Hogan
September 22	North Harbour (C)	Napier	52–10	Iosefo (3), MacGregor (2), Greville (2), Tipiwai	Cottrell (3)	Cottrell (2)		D.J. Waenga
September 30	Tasman (C)	Napier	47–12	Jefferson (2), Iosefo (2), Brough, Powdrell, Woods	Jensen (3)	Cottrell, Jensen		B.J. Andrew
October 6	Manawatu (P/C)	Palmerston North	10–22	Cotton	Jensen	Jensen		C.J. Stone
October 13	Otago (semi-final)	Dunedin	10–34	Tipiwai, Powdrell				J.J. Doleman

MANAWATU CYCLONES

2018 Status: Premiership
NPC participation: 1999–
Coach: Fusi Feaunati
Assistant coach: Scott Lewis
Home grounds: Central Energy Trust Arena

RECORDS

Most appearances	75	Selica Winiata, 2002–18
Most points	426	Selica Winiata, 2002–18
Most tries	65	Selica Winiata, 2002–18
Most points in a season	110	Selica Winiata, 2012
Most tries in a season	14	Selica Winiata, 2012
Most conversions in a season	17	Selica Winiata, 2012
Most penalty goals in a season	8	Anika Tiplady, 2004
Most dropped goals in a season	2	Rebecca Hull, 2002
Most points in a match	38	Selica Winiata v Waikato, 2012
Most tries in a match	4	Catherine Doyle v Poverty Bay-East Coast, 2002; Selica Winiata v Waikato, 2012; Selica Winiata v Wellington, 2012
Most conversions in a match	9	Elizabeth Goulden v Hawke's Bay 2017
Most penalty goals in a match	4	Anika Tiplady v Bay of Plenty, 2004
Highest team score	86	v Hawke's Bay, 2017
Record victory (points ahead)	78	86-8 v Hawke's Bay, 2017
Highest score conceded	70	v Auckland, 2011
Record defeat (points behind)	65	5–70 v Auckland, 2011

Considering the union has only three clubs and 48 senior players it performed very well in 2018, the Cyclones achieving their highest ranking by finishing fourth in the premiership. Earlier in the year Manawatu won its fourth national sevens title in six years. In the opening round of the Farah Palmer Cup the shock win over perennial giants Auckland boosted confidence but the light forward pack was overpowered by the bigger forwards of the stronger metropolitan unions. Losing prop Sita Kuruyabaki early in the campaign lessened forward power. Selica Winiata scored her 100th first-class try during the game against Bay of Plenty. Suffering concussion late in the game resulted in the fullback missing the next three games.

Co-captain Nicole Dickins was the outstanding forward. Flanker Samantha Tipene was everywhere and her performance against Hawke's Bay was rewarded with two tries. Rachael Rakatau, sister of Black Ferns Sevens captain Sarah Goss, impressed in her first season.

Black Ferns halfback Kristina Sue directed the backline very well, her experience being most valuable. Corrineke Windle, Ruby Finau and Vaine Greig were a reliable trio and on one wing Lauren Balsillie continues to improve. Megan Gaffney had played 25 tests for Scotland 2011–17 before arriving in the city where her partner also played club rugby. Stephanie McKenzie took up rugby in 2017 after a career as a track cyclist. She had competed at the 2014 Commonwealth Games.

Talented schoolgirls Lucy Brown, Carys Dallinger, Kalyn Takitimu–Cook and Nicola Chase (all from Manukura) had their first taste of first–class rugby while Ashleigh Knight (Feilding HS) experienced her second season. Dallinger and Takitimu–Cook were members of the NZ Under 18 sevens team that won the gold medal at the Youth Olympics in Argentina, the pair also in the team that won the Oceania Under 18 sevens tournament in Sydney

Higher honours went to:
New Zealand: K. Sue, S. Winiata
New Zealand Sevens: S.L. Goss

MANAWATU REPRESENTATIVES 2018

	Club	Games for Union	Points for Union		Club	Games for Union	Points for Union
Lauren Balsillie	Feilding OB Oroua	22	57	Jayme Nuku	Kia Toa	23	0
Lucy Brown	Feilding OB Oroua	6	5	Samantha Olsen	Feilding OB Oroua	5	0
Nicola Chase	Feilding OB Oroua	4	5	Mahalia Polson	Kia Toa	18	0
Carys Dallinger	Feilding OB Oroua	3	0	Shanna Porima	Kia Toa	22	20
Nicole Dickins	Feilding OB Oroua	50	10	Rachael Rakatau	Feilding OB Oroua	6	0
Jessica Fagan-Pease	Kia Toa	12	5	Rikki-Lee Rawleigh	University	21	0
Ruby Finau	Kia Toa	8	5	Abbey Rivers	Kia Toa	3	0
Megan Gaffney	Kia Toa	5	10	Kristina Sue	Feilding OB Oroua	57	35
Vaine Greig	Feilding OB Oroua	12	25	Kaylyn Takitimu-Cook	Feilding OB Oroua	3	24
Sequita Hemmingway	Kia Toa	10	0	Kahli Tipene	Kia Toa	32	0
Ashleigh Knight	Feilding OB Oroua	5	0	Samantha Tipene	Kia Toa	30	25
Sita Kuruyabaki	Feilding OB Oroua	22	20	Sydnee Wilkins	University	4	0
Maggie Leota	Kia Toa	5	0	Corrineke Windle	Feilding OB Oroua	15	8
Marilyn Live	Kia Toa	15	5	Selica Winiata	Kia Toa	75	426
Stephanie McKenzie	University	1	0				

INDIVIDUAL SCORING

	Tries	Con	PG	DG	Points		Tries	Con	PG	DG	Points
Winiata	3	5	1	–	28	Chase	1	–	–	–	5
Takitimu-Cook	4	2	–	–	24	Finau	1	–	–	–	5
Balsillie	3	1	–	–	17	Live	1	–	–	–	5
Greig	3	–	–	–	15	Windle	–	–	1	–	3
S. Tipene	3	–	–	–	15						
Gaffney	2	–	–	–	10	**Totals**	**24**	**8**	**2**	**0**	**142**
Sue	2	–	–	–	10	Opposition scored	27	17	3	0	178
Brown	1	–	–	–	5						

MANAWATU 2018

	Auckland	Counties Manukau	Bay of Plenty	Canterbury	Waikato	Hawke's Bay	Canterbury	TOTALS
S.C. Winiata (co-capt)	15	15	10	–	–	–	15	4
C. Dallinger	s	–	15	15	–	–	–	3
S.L. Wilkins	–	–	–	s	15	15	14	4
K. Takitimu-Cook	14	–	14	13	–	–	–	3
M.E. Gaffney	11	14	s	14	14	–	–	5
L.N.Y. Balsillie	s	11	11	11	11	11	12	7
N. Chase	–	–	–	s	s	14	11	4
V.A.P. Greig	13	13	13	–	13	13	13	6
M. Leota	–	s	s	–	s	s	s	5
S.R. Finau	12	12	12	12	12	12	s	7
C.M. Windle	10	10	–	10	10	10	10	6
K.J. Sue	9	9	9	9	9	9	9	7
L. Brown	s	–	s	s	s	s	s	6
M. Live	8	8	8	1	1	1	1	7
N.H. Dickins (co-capt)	7	6	6	8	8	8	8	7
S.J. Tipene	6	7	7	7	7	7	7	7
S. Olsen	s	s	s	6	–	s	–	5
S.J.T. Porima	–	s	s	s	6	6	6	6
A. Rivers	–	s	–	–	s	s	s	3
R. Rakatau	5	–	5	5	s	s	s	6
J.K. Fagan-Pease	s	5	s	s	5	5	5	7
M.R. Polson	4	4	–	4	4	4	4	6
A.J. Knight	–	s	4	–	–	–	–	2
A. Kuruyabaki	3	3	–	–	–	–	–	2
K.M. Tipene	2	2	s	3	3	3	3	7
R-L. Rawleigh	1	–	1	s	–	s	s	5
S.M. Hemingway	s	1	3	s	s	s	s	7
J.R. Te O. Nuku	s	s	2	2	2	2	2	7
S. McKenzie	–	s	–	–	–	–	–	1

MANAWATU TEAM RECORD, 2018

Played 7   **Won 3**   **Lost 4**   **Points for 142**   **Points against 178**

Date	Opponent	Score	Location	Tries	Con	PG	DG	Referee
September 1	Auckland (P)	44–17	Pakuranga	Takitimu-Cook (3), Greig, S. Tipene, Sue, Live	Winiata (3)	Winiata		L.A. Jenner
September 18	Counties Manukau (P)	22–31	Papakura	Balsillie (2), Winiata, Gaffney	Winiata			Amber Hibbard *Australia*
September 15	Bay of Plenty (P)	22–10	Palmerston North	Winiata, Balsillie, Gaffney, Greig	Takitimu-Cook			M.I. Fraser
September 23	Canterbury (P)	12–48	Palmerston North	Finau, Takitimu-Cook	Takitimu-Cook			M. Cogger-Orr
September 29	Waikato (P)	8–31	Hamilton	Chase		Windle		M. Cogger-Orr
October 6	Hawke's Bay (P/C)	22–10	Palmerston North	S. Tipene (2), Sue, Greig	Balsillie			C.J. Stone
October 13	Canterbury (semi-final)	12–31	Christchurch	Brown, Winiata	Winiata			J.D. Munro

NORTH HARBOUR HIBISCUS

2018 Status: Championship
NPC participation: 1999–2005, 2016–
Coach: Moni Collins
Assistant coaches: Willie Walker, Duncan McGrory
Home grounds: QBE Stadium, Albany;
    Windsor Park, Mairangi Bay

RECORDS

Most appearances	23	*Joanne Cherrington 1999–2004*
Most points	76	*Sophie Fisher, 2017–18*
Most tries	7	*Pia Tapsell, 2016–18*
Most points in a season	52	*Sophie Fisher, 2018*
Most tries in a season	5	*Caitlyn Cox, 2017*
Most conversions in a season	14	*Sophie Fisher, 2018*
Most penalty goals in a season	7	*Rachel Howard, 2003*
Most dropped goals in a season	0	
Most points in a match	24	*Sophie Fisher v Taranaki, 2018*
Most tries in a match	2	*by ten players*
Most conversions in a match	7	*Sophie Fisher v Taranaki, 2018*
Most penalty goals in a match	3	*Rachel Howard v Auckland B, 2003*
Highest team score	59	*v Taranaki, 2018*
Record victory (points ahead)	59	*59–0 v Taranaki, 2018*
Highest score conceded	116	*v Auckland, 1999*
Record defeat (points behind)	116	*0–116 v Auckland, 1999*

Hibiscus enjoyed big wins over Taranaki and Tasman but suffered losses, some by large scores, to the other unions in the championship division. Centre Juliana Newman was the team's player of the year. 19-year-old lock forward Sophie Fisher, in her second season in the team, continues to improve and contributed 37 points with her accurate goalkicking. There were frequent changes in the team and only three players started every game — Stacey Tupe, Pia Tapsell and Sophie Fisher.

Higher honours went to:
New Zealand: C. Tofa

NORTH HARBOUR REPRESENTATIVES 2018

	Club	Games for Union	Points for Union		Club	Games for Union	Points for Union
Karina Christiansen	East Coast Bays	7	0	Jemma Palmer	East Coast Bays	18	5
Caitlyn Cox	East Coast Bays	11	30	Amy Robertshaw	Glenfield	10	10
Lydia Crossman	Glenfield	3	0	Pia Tapsell	East Coast Bays	20	35
Brooke Ellison	Glenfield	3	0	Jayjay Taylor	East Coast Bays	3	5
Florida Fatanitavake	Glenfield	10	10	Inga Timani	Glenfield	9	0
Sophie Fisher	East Coast Bays	14	76	Cristo Tofa	East Coast Bays	8	0
Katelyn Hilton	East Coast Bays	7	5	Stacey Tupe (nee Martin)	East Coast Bays	13	5
Billy-Jo Jones	East Coast Bays	16	0	Te Hine-ngaro Tuterangiwhiu	Glenfield	7	0
Shawn Lomu	Glenfield	1	0	Gloria Vegar	East Coast Bays	6	0
Kelsey Macdonald	East Coast Bays	6	5	Justine Vizirgianakis	Glenfield	16	5
Claudia McMeekin	East Coast Bays	16	32	Olivia Ward-Duin	East Coast Bays	17	5
Briar-Anne McNamara	Glenfield	15	22	Rona-Latisha Wharawhara	Glenfield	6	10
Finesa Makasini	Glenfield	6	5	Mikayla Whitehead	East Coast Bays	4	0
Heather Muir	East Coast Bays	5	0	Cheyenne Wikaira	East Coast Bays	11	0
Tearren Nanjan	Glenfield	4	0	Kate Williams	East Coast Bays	11	5
Juliana Newman	East Coast Bays	10	20	Rebecca Wood	East Coast Bays	11	5
Nikita Ngarongo-Porima	Glenfield	10	0				

INDIVIDUAL SCORING

	Tries	Con	PG	DG	Points		Tries	Con	PG	DG	Points
Fisher	3	14	3	–	52	Macdonald	1	–	–	–	5
Newman	4	–	–	–	20	Makasini	1	–	–	–	5
Tapsell	4	–	–	–	20	Taylor	1	–	–	–	5
McMeekin	3	–	–	–	15	Wood	1	–	–	–	5
Robertshaw	2	–	–	–	10						
Wharawhara	2	–	–	–	10	**Totals**	**24**	**14**	**3**	**0**	**157**
Cox	1	–	–	–	5	Opposition scored	35	18	3	0	220
Hilton	1	–	–	–	5						

NORTH HARBOUR 2018	Otago	Taranaki	Tasman	Hawke's Bay	Wellington	Waikato	Wellington	TOTALS
C. McMeekin	–	15	15	15	–	–	–	3
B. McNamara	–	–	–	–	–	15	15	2
K. Macdonald	15	11	14	–	14	S	S	6
J. Vizirgianakis	S	–	–	–	S	S	S	4
H.E. Muir	14	–	–	S	11	14	14	5
M.G. Whitehead	–	14	S	S	S	–	–	4
C.R. Cox	11	S	S	14	–	–	–	4
F.C. Fatanitavake	–	–	11	11	15	11	11	5
J.P. Newman	13	13	13	13	–	12	13	6
R-L.H. Wharawhara	12	S	12	12	12	–	S	6
S.A. Tupe	10	12	10	10	13	13	12	7
N-D.D. Ngarongo-Porima	S	10	–	–	10	10	10	5
G. Vegar	9	S	S	S	S	9	–	6
K.A. Hilton	S	9	9	9	9	S	9	7
L.J. Crossman	8	8	8	–	–	–	–	3
J. Palmer	S	S	S	–	8	S	8	6
K.R. Williams	7	7	7	7	–	7	7	6
P.H. Tapsell	6	6	6	8	7	8	6	7
T.A. Nanjan	–	–	–	S	6	S	S	4
R.J. Wood (capt)	5	5	–	–	–	5	–	3
K. Christiansen	S	S	5	6	5	6	4	7
J. Taylor	–	–	S	5	–	–	S	3
S.R. Fisher	4	4	4	4	4	4	5	7
B.M. Ellison	–	–	S	S	S	–	–	3
C. Wikaira	3	3	1	1	–	–	–	4
A. Timani	1	–	3	3	3	3	3	6
F.A. Makasini	S	S	–	S	S	S	S	6
O.Y. Ward-Duin	–	–	–	S	1	1	1	4
S. Lomu	–	–	–	–	S	–	–	1
A.G. Robertshaw	2	1	2	–	–	2	2	5
L.C.S. Tofa	–	2	–	–	–	–	–	1
B-J. Jones	S	S	S	–	S	S	S	6
Te H.U. Tuterangiwhiu	–	–	–	2	2	–	–	2

Tupe was captain in Wood's absence

NORTH HARBOUR TEAM RECORD, 2018

Played 7　Won 2　Lost 5　Points for 157　Points against 220

Date	Opponent	Location	Score	Tries	Con	PG	DG	Referee
September 1	Otago (C)	Dunedin	13–57	Makasini	Fisher	Fisher (2)		J.J. Doleman
September 8	Taranaki (C)	Inglewood	59–0	Fisher (2), McMeekin (2), Robertshaw, Wood, Newman, Cox, Wharawhara	Fisher (7)			C.J. Stone
September 16	Tasman (C)	Albany	51–14	Tapsell (2), Newman (2), Macdonald, Hilton, McMeekin, Fisher, Robertshaw	Fisher (3)			A.W.B. Mabey
September 22	Hawke's Bay (C)	Napier	10–52	Taylor, Wharawhara				B.J. Andrew
September 29	Wellington (C)	Mairangi Bay	10–50	Tapsell	Fisher	Fisher		L.A. Jenner
October 6	Waikato (P/C)	Albany	7–44	Newman	Fisher			L.A. Jenner
October 13	Wellington (semi-final)	Porirua	7–33	Tapsell	Fisher			M. Cogger-Orr

OTAGO SPIRIT

2018 Status: Championship
NPC participation: 1999–
Coach: Scott Manson
Assistant coaches: Karina Nafatali
Home grounds: Forsyth Barr Stadium;
University Oval (v North Harbour);
Logan Park (v Hawke's Bay)

RECORDS

Most appearances	53	*Greer Muir, 2011–18*
Most points	221	*Claire Richardson, 2002–12*
Most tries	25	*Carla Hohepa, 2006–09*
		Greer Muir, 2011–18
Most points in a season	70	*Kelly Brazier, 2012*
Most tries in a season	11	*Annaleah Rush, 1999*
Most conversions in a season	17	*Kelly Brazier, 2012*
Most penalty goals in a season	12	*Hannah Myers, 2000*
Most dropped goals in a season	0	
Most points in a match	45	*Kelly Brazier v Hawke's Bay, 2012*
Most tries in a match	8	*Annaleah Rush v Mid/South Canterbury, 1999*
Most conversions in a match	10	*Kelly Brazier v Hawke's Bay, 2012*
Most penalty goals in a match	5	*Anika Tiplady v Auckland, 2013*
Highest team score	85	*v Hawke's Bay, 2012*
Record victory (points ahead)	82	*82–0 v Mid/South Canterbury, 1999;*
		82–0 v Tasman 2017
Highest score conceded	86	*v Auckland, 2011*
Record defeat (points behind)	81	*5–86 v Auckland, 2011*

Otago Spirit produced improved results with the only losses being to Counties Manukau in the crossover game and twice to Wellington. Having been beaten finalists for two years Spirit will need to overcome Auckland Storm in 2019 in order to be promoted into the premiership division. Tegan Hollows led the team, she alternating positions between hooker and number eight. Sheree Hume, Greer Muir and Rosie Kelly were the only backs to start every game while of the forwards Morgan Henderson and Hollows started in each game. Rebecca Todd returned to the team after playing for Auckland Storm and Canterbury. Rosie Buchanan-Brown played for Tasman in 2017.

There were fine contributions from players based outside the union. Cheyenne Cunningham, Georgina McCullough and Henderson from Oamaru-based North Otago club and Southlanders Amy du Plessis, Cassandra Engler and Amy Rule. Engler and Kendall Buckingham, also from Southland, were in the NZ Sevens Development squad. Kilisitina Moata'ane was selected for the Black Ferns touring team to USA and France but forced to withdraw due to injury.

OTAGO REPRESENTATIVES 2018

	Club	Games for Union	Points for Union
Erin Adams	Green Island	1	0
Rosie Buchanan-Brown	University	6	5
Paige Church	Alhambra Union	11	0
Cheyenne Cunningham	North Otago	15	40
Jessica Dermody	University	4	0
Eilis Doyle	Alhambra Union	25	0
Amy du Plessis	Southland	4	10
Cassandra Engler	Southland	3	0
Islay Fowler	University	2	0
Julia Gorinski	University	30	10
Morgan Henderson	North Otago	16	15
Tegan Hollows	University	27	15
Patricia Hopcroft	University	7	0
Sheree Hume	Pirates	41	61
Rosie Kelly	University	8	43
Jessica Kendall	University	21	5
Georgina McCullough	North Otago	14	10
Georgia Mason	University	28	25
Gemma Millar	Pirates	5	0
Kilisitina Moata'ane	Pirates	30	65
Greer Muir	Pirates	53	125
Isla Pringle	University	13	10
Janelle Romanchuck	Alhambra Union	3	0
Amy Rule	Southland	6	0
Rachel Scott	Wakatipu	27	10
Kate Smith	University	21	5
Rebecca Todd	University	31	10
Morgan Walker	Pirates	12	0
Kiana Wereta	Alhambra Union	16	20
Zoe Whatarau	Alhambra Union	30	10
Sammy Wong	Pirates	9	5

INDIVIDUAL SCORING

	Tries	Con	PG	DG	Points
Kelly	2	15	1	–	43
Hume	5	1	1	–	30
Cunningham	5	–	–	–	25
Muir	5	–	–	–	25
Wereta	4	–	–	–	20
Hollows	3	–	–	–	15
Moata'ane	3	–	–	–	15
du Plessis	2	–	–	–	10
Pringle	2	–	–	–	10
Todd	2	–	–	–	10
Whatarau	2	–	–	–	10
Buchanan-Brown	1	–	–	–	5
Smith	1	–	–	–	5
Wong	1	–	–	–	5
Totals	**38**	**16**	**2**	**0**	**228**
Opposition scored	27	16	3	0	176

OTAGO 2018	North Harbour	Hawke's Bay	Wellington	Counties Manukau	Taranaki	Tasman	Hawke's Bay	Wellington	TOTALS
S.J. Hume	15	15	15	15	15	15	15	15	8
P.A. Hopcroft	14	9	9	11	–	14	14	14	7
K.M.P.Y. Wereta	s	14	14	14	–	s	11	11	7
C.L. Engler	11	11	11	–	–	–	–	–	3
C.B. Cunningham	s	s	s	s	14	11	s	s	8
A. du Plessis	–	–	s	s	11	–	–	s	4
G.K. McCullough	13	s	13	13	13	s	s	–	7
I.M. Fowler	s	13	–	–	–	–	–	–	2
K. Moata'ane	–	–	–	–	s	13	13	13	4
G.A. Muir	12	12	12	12	12	12	12	12	8
R.C. Kelly	10	10	10	10	10	10	10	10	8
S.L. Wong	9	–	s	s	s	s	s	s	7
R.M. Buchanan-Brown	–	s	–	9	9	9	9	9	6
G.E. Mason	7	7	7	–	–	–	–	7	4
Z.J.T. Whatarau	s	s	s	7	7	–	7	–	6
M.A. Henderson	6	6	6	6	6	7	8	8	8
R.M. Scott	s	s	s	s	–	–	–	–	4
G.A. Millar	–	–	–	s	–	–	–	s	2
J.A. Romanchuck	–	–	–	–	s	6	s	–	3
J.B. Kendall	5	5	s	4	5	5	5	5	8
J.F. Gorinski	4	4	4	5	–	s	6	6	7
K.E. Smith	s	s	5	s	4	4	4	4	8
J.N. Dermody	–	–	–	–	s	s	s	s	4
E.O. Doyle	3	3	3	–	3	–	3	3	6
A. Rule	s	–	s	3	–	3	s	s	6
I.R. Pringle	1	1	1	1	–	1	1	1	7
P.L.L. Church	–	s	–	s	1	s	–	–	4
E.S. Adams	–	–	–	–	s	–	–	–	1
T.J. Hollows (capt)	2	8	2	8	8	8	2	2	8
R.A. Todd	8	2	8	2	2	2	–	–	6
M.J. Walker	–	–	–	–	s	s	s	s	4

OTAGO TEAM RECORD, 2018

Played 8 Won 5 Lost 3 Points for 228 Points against 176

Date	Opponent	Location	Score	Tries	Con	PG	DG	Referee
September 1	North Harbour (C)	Dunedin	27–13	Muir, Hume, Cunningham, Wereta	Kelly, Hume	Hume		J.J. Doleman
September 8	Hawke's Bay (C)	Dunedin	31–12	Todd, Kelly, Wereta, Hume, Hollows	Kelly (3)			J.R. Nutbrown
September 15	Wellington (C)	Porirua	10–38	Wereta, du Plessis				T.N. Griffiths
September 22	Counties Manukau (P/C)	Dunedin	8–39	Todd		Kelly		B.E. Pickerill
September 29	Taranaki (C)	New Plymouth	65–0	Cunningham (3), Whatarau (2), du Plessis, Hume, Muir, Buchanan-Brown, Moata'ane, Smith	Kelly (5)			T.M.T. Cottrell
October 6	Tasman (C)	Blenheim	48–7	Hollows (2), Muir (2), Pringle, Kelly, Cunningham, Wong	Kelly (4)			N.E.R. Hogan
October 13	Hawke's Bay (semi-final)	Dunedin	34–10	Moata'ane (2), Hume (2), Pringle, Muir	Kelly (2)			J.J. Doleman
October 20	Wellington (final)	Porirua	5–57	Wereta				B.J. Andrew

TARANAKI WHIO

2018 Status: Championship
NPC participation: 2000–01, 2013, 2018
Coach: Matt Stone
Assistant coaches: Ben Siffleet
Home grounds: TET Stadium, Inglewood;
Yarrow Stadium, New Plymouth.

RECORDS

Most appearances	13	*Badinlee Munro-Smith, 2013–18*
Most points	20	*Michaela Blyde, 2013*
Most tries	4	*Michaela Blyde, 2013*
Most points in a season	20	*Michaela Blyde, 2013*
Most tries in a season	4	*Michaela Blyde, 2013*
Most conversions in a season	6	*Kate Broadmore, 2013*
Most penalty goals in a season	2	*Kate Broadmore, 2013*
Most dropped goals in a season	0	
Most points in a match	10	*Michaela Blyde v Manawatu, 2013*
Most tries in a match	2	*Michaela Blyde v Manawatu, 2013*
Most conversions in a match	2	*Kate Broadmore v Auckland, 2013*
Most penalty goals in a match	1	*Kate Broadmore v Otago, 2013;*
		v Wellington, 2013
Highest team score	14	*v Auckland, 2013*
Record victory (points ahead)	–	
Highest score conceded	118	*v Wellington, 2018*
Record defeat (points behind)	118	*0–118 v Wellington, 2018*

It will be a time to celebrate when Taranaki wins its first game in the national championship. The union entered a team after an absence of four years, last appearing in 2013 and, before then, back in 2000 and 2001, being combined with Wanganui in 2001. After 19 games the union has yet to register a victory. During 2015–17 Stratford club played in the Manawatu competition and three players represented the Cyclones. Taranaki took some hammerings in 2018 including a record defeat delivered by Wellington.

There were six survivors from the 2013 squad. Badinlee Munro-Smith appeared for Counties Manukau 2015–16. Utumalama Atonio played for Counties Manukau in 2017 and the centre became the Whio player of the year. Fullback Jessie Aitken-Fowell was one of the best among the backs and 17-year-old wing Elle Johns showed much promise. Captain Jalana Smith was the best forward. Team manager Patsy Matheson was a substitute in the last three games.

Higher honours went to:
New Zealand Sevens: Gayle Broughton

TARANAKI REPRESENTATIVES 2018

	Club	Games for Union	Points for Union		Club	Games for Union	Points for Union
Jessie Aitken-Fowell	Clifton	6	5	Elle Johns	Clifton	6	0
Marika Allen	Clifton	9	0	Natalie Jones	Coastal	5	0
Lisa Appert	Coastal	6	0	Victoria McCullough	Coastal	11	0
Utumalama Atonio	Coastal	5	5	Patsy Matheson	Southern	3	0
Casio Austin	Spotswood United	6	2	Tina Moeahu	Clifton	6	0
Leah Barnard	Bell Block	12	0	Badinlee Munro-Smith	Coastal	13	5
Kate Batchelor	Coastal	1	0	Danika Northcott-Weherua	Canterbury Univ[1]	1	0
Awhina Blackburn-Kingi	Clifton	5	5	Kate Parkinson	Spotswood United	6	0
Sharee Brown	Southern	6	0	Briana Poingdestre	Southern	6	0
Maree Dallinger	Clifton	6	0	Caterina Poletti	Clifton	1	0
Hineana Dando	Coastal	4	0	Karen Pullen	Southern	1	0
Freedom Edmonds	Clifton	5	0	Brooke Sim	Coastal	8	0
Atalya Fakavamoeanga	Coastal	2	0	Jalana Smith	Coastal	6	5
Natale Haupapa	Clifton	6	0	Kate Thomson	Southern	1	0
Nga Pera Hei Hei	Clifton	5	0	Kelsey Walsh-Tito	Spotswood United	2	0
Kayla Henry	Clifton	2	0				

[1] Canterbury RU

INDIVIDUAL SCORING

	Tries	Con	PG	DG	Points
Aitken-Fowell	1	–	–	–	5
Atonio	1	–	–	–	5
Blackburn-Kingi	1	–	–	–	5
Smith	1	–	–	–	5
Austin	–	1	–	–	2
Totals	**4**	**1**	**0**	**0**	**22**
Opposition scored	71	40	0	0	435

TARANAKI 2018	Tasman	North Harbour	Hawke's Bay	Bay of Plenty	Otago	Wellington	TOTALS
J.M. Aitken-Fowell	15	15	15	15	15	15	6
E. Johns	14	11	11	11	11	11	6
U. Atonio	11	–	13	13	13	13	5
K.P.T. Walsh-Tito	–	s	–	s	–	–	2
D. Northcott-Weherua	–	–	–	–	–	s	1
B.A. Sim	13	–	–	–	–	–	1
K. Henry	–	13	14	–	–	–	2
B.A. Poingdestre	s	12	s	s	s	s	6
B.C.R. Munro-Smith	12	s	10	10	10	10	6
K. Parkinson	10	10	12	12	12	12	6
T. Moeahu	9	9	s	14	14	14	6
C.Te O. Austin	s	14	9	9	9	9	6
K.L. Batchelor	s	–	–	–	–	–	1
K.G. Pullen	–	–	–	–	s	–	1
A.K. Fakavamoeanga	8	6	–	–	–	–	2
C. Poletti	–	8	–	–	–	–	1
N-A. Haupapa	3	s	8	8	8	8	6
J.R. Smith (capt)	7	7	7	7	7	7	6
A. Blackburn-Kingi	6	s	6	–	6	6	5
F.S. Edmonds	s	s	–	6	s	s	5
N.A.C. Jones	5	–	s	s	s	–	4
V.L. McCullough	–	5	5	5	5	5	5
S.E. Brown	4	4	4	4	4	4	6
P.J. Matheson	–	–	–	s	s	s	3
L. Barnard	s	3	3	3	3	3	6
N.P.S. Hei Hei	1	–	s	s	s	s	5
M.L. Dallinger	s	s	s	s	1	s	6
H.G.J. Dando	–	1	1	1	–	1	4
K.V. Thomson	–	–	–	–	–	s	1
M. Allen	2	2	2	s	2	–	5
L.C. Appert	s	s	s	2	s	2	6

TARANAKI TEAM RECORD, 2018

Played 6 Lost 6 Points for 22 Points against 435

Date	Opponent	Location	Score	Tries	Con	PG	DG	Referee
September 1	Tasman (C)	Motueka	12–65	Atonio, Smith	Austin			B.D. O'Keeffe
September 8	North Harbour (C)	Inglewood	0–59					C.J. Stone
September 15	Hawke's Bay (C)	Inglewood	10–55	Aitken-Fowell, Blackburn-Kingi				N.E.R. Hogan
September 21	Bay of Plenty (P/C)	Rotorua	0–73					D.J. Waenga
September 29	Otago (C)	New Plymouth	0–65					T.M.T. Cottrell
October 6	Wellington (C)	Porirua	0–118					M.I. Fraser

TASMAN MAKO

2018 Status: Championship
NPC participation: 2017–
Coach: Martyn O'Cain
Assistant coach: Mark Kelly
Home Grounds: Sports Park, Motueka; Trafalgar Park, Nelson; Lansdowne Park, Blenheim;

RECORDS

Most appearances	12	by six players
Most points	26	Hayley Hutana, 2018
Most tries	4	Wairakau Greig, 2017; Michelle Curry, 2017–18
Most points in a season	26	Hayley Hutana, 2018
Most tries in a season	4	Wairakau Greig, 2017
Most conversions in a season	9	Hayley Hutana, 2018
Most penalty goals in a season	1	Risi Pouri-Lane, 2017; Hayley Hutana, 2018
Most dropped goals in a season	0	
Most points in a match	15	Amelia Hammett v Taranaki, 2018
Most tries in a match	3	Amelia Hammett v Taranaki, 2018
Most conversions in a match	5	Hayley Hutana v Taranaki, 2018
Most penalty goals in a match	1	by two players
Highest team score	65	v Taranaki, 2018
Record victory (points ahead)	53	65–12 v Taranaki, 2018
Highest score conceded	88	v Wellington, 2018
Record defeat (points behind)	85	3–88 v Wellington, 2018

The 65–12 win over Taranaki in the first game was to be the only cause for celebration in 2018, the Mako being well beaten in the other five games. The union lost Rosie Buchanan-Brown to Otago but gained former Manawatu representatives Crystal Mayes and Hayley Hutana. Mayes, a Black Ferns Sevens representative, won the team's defender of the year award. Captain Jessica Foster-Lawrence was the player of the year while prop Anna Bradley was rookie of the year. Several teenagers were in the squad including 17-year-olds Hannah Beech, Sophie O'Cain and Jamie Paenga. Motueka High School student Risi Pouri-Lane captained the NZ Under 18 Sevens team to win the gold medal at the Youth Olympics in Argentina.

Higher honours went to:
New Zealand Sevens: R.I.R. Pouri-Lane

INDIVIDUAL SCORING

	Tries	Con	PG	DG	Points		Tries	Con	PG	DG	Points
Hutana	1	9	1	–	26	Mitchell	1	–	–	–	5
Curry	3	–	–	–	15	Salton	1	–	–	–	5
Hammett	3	–	–	–	15	T. Silcock	1	–	–	–	5
Beech	2	–	–	–	10						
Mayes	2	–	–	–	10	**Totals**	**16**	**9**	**1**	**0**	**101**
Bradley	1	–	–	–	5						
Kelly	1	–	–	–	5	Opposition scored	54	28	2	0	332

TASMAN REPRESENTATIVES 2018

	Club	Games for Union	Points for Union
Hannah Beech	Motueka HS	5	10
Anna Bradley	Waimea OB	6	5
Kelly Couper	Moutere	11	0
Michelle Curry	Marist	12	20
Jessica Foster-Lawrence	Waimea OB	12	7
Leti Fotumoala	Moutere	10	0
Tess Golding	Waimea OB	1	0
Amelia Hammett	Marist	5	15
Gina Healey	Wanderers	6	0
Hayley Hutana	Moutere	5	26
Hannah Kelly	Motueka HS	6	5
Staci Kohe	Marist	12	0
Crystal Mayes	Kia Toa[1]	5	10
Leah Miles	Waimea OB	3	0
Stephani Mitchell	Waimea OB	12	10
Louise Nalder	Waimea OB	5	0
Ashleigh Nathan	Moutere	3	5
Sophie O'Cain	Motueka HS	4	0
Jamie Paenga	Waimea OB	5	0
Demi Salton	Waimea OB	5	5
Erika Saunders	Motueka HS	5	0
Niska Scott	Moutere	9	0
Katie Silcock	Marist	1	0
Tamara Silcock	Marist	12	5
Kelly Stanford	Moutere	12	0
Jaunita Thomson	Waimea OB	5	0
Dana-Lee Wilson	Marist	8	5
Rheanna Wood	Motueka HS	5	0

[1] Manawatu RU

TASMAN 2018

	Taranaki	Auckland	North Harbour	Wellington	Hawke's Bay	Otago	TOTALS
C.A.M. Mayes	15	–	15	15	15	15	5
A. Hammett	14	15	–	s	11	11	5
M.A. Curry	s	14	14	14	14	14	6
H. Beech	11	11	11	11	–	s	5
T. Golding	–	s	–	–	–	–	1
H.S. Hutana	13	–	13	13	13	13	5
L.L. Fotumoala	–	13	s	s	s	s	5
D. Salton	12	s	–	s	s	s	5
S.E. Kohe	s	12	12	12	12	12	6
D.L. Wilson	10	–	–	10	10	–	3
S. O'Cain	s	10	10	–	–	10	4
H. Kelly	9	9	9	s	s	s	6
J. Paenga	–	s	s	9	9	9	5
N.M. Scott	8	8	8	8	–	–	4
K. Silcock	s	–	–	–	–	–	1
R. Wood	7	7	7	–	6	6	5
L. Miles	s	s	–	–	s	–	3
A. Nathan	–	–	s	7	–	–	2
J. E-M. Foster-Lawrence (capt)	6	6	6	6	8	8	6
T. Silcock	5	5	5	5	5	5	6
G. Healey	4	s	4	s	s	s	6
J. Thomson	–	4	s	4	4	4	5
S.L. Mitchell	3	3	3	2	2	2	6
L. Nalder	s	–	s	s	s	3	5
K.M. Couper	–	s	s	3	3	s	5
A. Bradley	1	1	1	1	1	1	6
E. Saunders	s	s	–	s	s	s	5
K.A. Stanford	2	2	2	s	7	7	6

TASMAN TEAM RECORD, 2018

Played 6 Won 1 Lost 5 Points for 101 Points against 332

Date	Opponent	Location	Score	Tries	Con	PG	DG	Referee
September 1	Taranaki (C)	Motueka	65–12	Hammett (3), Beech (2), Mayes (2), Kelly, Mitchell, T. Silcock, Curry	Hutana (5)			B.D. O'Keeffe
September 7	Auckland (P/C)	Auckland	0–86					L.A. Jenner
September 16	North Harbour (C)	Albany	14–51	Curry, Hutana	Hutana (2)			A.W.B. Mabey
September 23	Wellington (C)	Nelson	3–88			Hutana		N.E.R. Hogan
September 30	Hawke's Bay (C)	Napier	12–47	Curry, Salton	Hutana			B.J. Andrew
October 6	Otago (C)	Blenheim	7–48	Bradley	Hutana			N.E.R. Hogan

WAIKATO

2018 Status: Premiership
NPC participation: 1999–2005, 2012–
Coach: Wayne Maxwell
Assistant coach: James Semple
Home Grounds: Taupiri RFC, Taupiri;
FMG Stadium Waikato

RECORDS

Most appearances	44	*Victoria Edmonds, 2012–18*
Most points	291	*Chelsea Alley, 2012–18*
Most tries	19	*Honey Hireme, 2001–16*
Most points in a season	81	*Chelsea Alley, 2014*
Most tries in a season	11	*Stacey Waaka, 2014*
Most conversions in a season	21	*Chelsea Alley, 2014, 2018*
Most penalty goals in a season	12	*Chelsea Alley, 2013*
Most dropped goals in a season	1	*Emma Jensen, 2000*
Most points in a match	18	*C. Alley v Bay of Plenty, 2014*
Most tries in a match	3	*Jordon Webber v Manawatu, 2012;*
		Honey Hireme v Manawatu, 2014;
		Stacey Waaka v Canterbury, 2014;
		v Bay of Plenty 2015
Most conversions in a match	5	*C. Alley v Manawatu, 2014;*
		v Bay of Plenty, 2014
		v Auckland, 2018
Most penalty goals in a match	4	*Emma Jensen v Northland, 2000*
		Tenika Willison v North Harbour, 2016
Highest team score	48	*v Bay of Plenty, 2014*
Record victory (points ahead)	48	*48–0 v Bay of Plenty, 2014*
Highest score conceded	78	*v Auckland, 2002*
Record defeat (points behind)	78	*0–78 v Auckland, 2002*

Waikato finished second on the premiership ladder but lost to Counties Manukau in a semi-final. Sosoli Talawadua was the captain for the season but never started in a game, she being a regular second half substitute. However, the experienced Chelsea Alley was an astute on-field leader, an intelligent director of the backline and a reliable goalkicker. Alley was in fine form and was the team's player of the year. She started in all seven games as did wing Donna Fermanis, second five-eighth Ryleigh Hayes, halfback Ariana Bayler, lock Karli Faneva and three loose forwards Natalie Delamere, Ashlee Gaby-Sutherland and Kennedy Simon.

Fullback Calista Wihone, aged 17, was in her second year with the team and continues to show promise. Lonita Ngalu-Lavemei, also aged 17, impressed as a threequarter.

Higher honours went to:
New Zealand: C. Alley, S.J.A.K. Waaka
New Zealand Sevens: S.J. Baker, H.R. Harding, S.T. Kaka, T.L.R. Te Tamaki, S.J.A.K. Waaka, T.R. Willison

WAIKATO REPRESENTATIVES 2018

	Club	Games for Union	Points for Union
Chelsea Alley	University	32	291
Ariana Bayler	Hamilton OB	30	42
Natalie Delamere	University	20	20
Victoria Edmonds	University	44	10
Karli Faneva	Melville	11	25
Donna Fermanis	Hamilton OB	13	10
Ashlee Gaby-Sutherland	Melville	15	15
Ryleigh Hayes	Melville	15	32
Emma-Lee Heta	University	16	10
Grace Houpapa-Barrett	Melville	20	20
Tanya Kalounivale	Hamilton OB	12	5
Leomie Kloppers	Hamilton OB	7	0
Stacey Littleworth	University	1	0
Ana Marsters	Hamilton OB	15	36
Lena Mitchell	Hamilton OB	7	0
Toka Natua	University	22	10
Lonita Ngalu-Lavemei	Melville	6	15
Danielle Paenga	Melville	3	5
Rina Paraone	University	14	15
Kanyon Paul	Melville	10	0
Tyler Reid	Hamilton OB	7	5
Makaia Riki-Te Kanawa	Hamilton OB	21	25
Kennedy Simon	Hamilton OB	12	0
Awhina Tangen-Wainohu	Hamilton OB	4	5
Sosoli Talawadua	University	33	20
Esther Tilo	Melville	5	0
Awa Whitiora-Te Uira	University	2	0
Calista Wihone	University	13	30
Azusa Yama	Hamilton OB	5	0

INDIVIDUAL SCORING

	Tries	Con	PG	DG	Points
Alley	5	21	4	–	79
Hayes	4	1	–	–	22
Bayler	3	–	–	–	15
Faneva	3	–	–	–	15
Gaby-Sutherland	3	–	–	–	15
Ngalu-Lavemei	3	–	–	–	15
Wihone	3	–	–	–	15
Fermanis	1	–	–	–	5
Houpapa-Barrett	1	–	–	–	5
Kalounivale	1	–	–	–	5
Marsters	1	–	–	–	5
Paenga	1	–	–	–	5
Paraone	1	–	–	–	5
Reid	1	–	–	–	5
Talawadua	1	–	–	–	5
Tangen-Wainohu	1	–	–	–	5
Totals	**33**	**22**	**4**	**0**	**221**
Opposition scored	17	9	4	0	115

WAIKATO 2018

	Counties Manukau	Bay of Plenty	Canterbury	Auckland	Manawatu	North Harbour	Counties Manukau	TOTALS
M. Riki-Te Kanawa	15	15	15	s	s	–	–	5
C. Wihone	s	s	s	15	15	15	–	6
A. Whitiora-Te Uira	–	–	–	–	–	s	15	2
A. Marsters	14	14	14	14	–	–	14	5
D. Fermanis	11	11	11	11	11	11	11	7
R. Paraone	13	13	13	–	s	s	13	6
L. Ngalu-Lavemei	–	s	s	13	14	14	s	6
D. Paenga	–	–	–	s	13	13	–	3
R. Hayes	12	12	12	12	12	12	12	7
C.H. Alley	10	10	10	10	10	10	10	7
A.J. Bayler	9	9	9	9	9	9	9	7
K. Paul	s	s	s	s	s	s	s	7
N. Delamere	8	8	8	8	8	8	8	7
A. Gaby-Sutherland	7	7	7	7	6	6	6	7
K. Simon	6	6	6	6	7	7	7	7
E-L. Heta	s	s	s	s	s	s	s	7
L. Kloppers	5	5	–	–	–	–	–	2
L. Mitchell	s	s	s	s	s	s	s	7
V.R. Edmonds	–	–	5	5	5	5	5	5
K. Faneva	4	4	4	4	4	4	4	7
T. Reid	3	–	–	–	s	s	–	3
E. Tilo	s	s	s	s	–	–	s	5
T. Kalounivale	–	3	3	3	–	3	3	5
G. Houpapa-Barrett	1	1	1	–	1	–	2	5
A. Tangen-Wainohu	–	–	–	1	3	1	s	4
T.I. Natua	–	–	–	–	–	–	1	1
S. Littleworth	2	–	–	–	–	–	–	1
S.J. Talawadua (capt)	s	–	s	s	s	s	–	6
A. Yama	–	2	2	2	2	2	–	5

Alley was captain when Talawadua was not on the field.

WAIKATO TEAM RECORD, 2018

Played 7 Won 5 Lost 2 Points for 221 Points against 115

Date	Opponent	Location	Score	Tries	Con	PG	DG	Referee
September 1	Counties Manukau (P)	Taupiri	33–27	Hayes, Alley, Bayler, Paraone, Gaby-Sutherland	Alley (4)			B.J. Andrew
September 8	Bay of Plenty (P)	Matata	44–7	Hayes (2), Gaby-Sutherland, Houpapa-Barrett, Alley, Wihone	Alley (3), Hayes	Alley (2)		N.P. Briant
September 15	Canterbury (P, ST)	Christchurch	10–28	Faneva	Alley	Alley		Lara West *Australia*
September 22	Auckland (P)	Taupiri	45–14	Faneva, Ngalu-Lavemei, Tangen-Wainohu, Fermanis, Bayler, Alley, Wihone	Alley (5)			R.P. Kelly
September 29	Manawatu (P)	Hamilton	31–8	Faneva, Alley, Wihone, Ngalu-Lavemei	Alley (4)	Alley		M. Cogger-Orr
October 6	North Harbour (P/C)	Albany	44–7	Kalounivale, Gaby-Sutherland, Paenga, Alley, Hayes, Ngalu-Lavemei, Reid, Talawadua	Alley (2)			L.A. Jenner
October 13	Counties Manukau (semi-final)	Hamilton	14–24	Bayler, Marsters	Alley (2)			B.J. Andrew

ST *Steewart Trophy*

WELLINGTON PRIDE

2018 Status: Premiership
NPC participation: 1999–
Coach: Ross Bond
Assistant coaches: Brendan Reidy
Home ground: Porirua Park

RECORDS

Most appearances	58	Rebecca Liua'ana, 1999–2012
Most points	184	Elizabeth Goulden 2012–16
Most tries	29	Ayesha Leti-I'iga 2015–18
Most points in a season	118	Amanda Rasch, 2014–18
Most tries in a season	11	Ayesha Leti-I'iga, 2018
Most conversions in a season	21	Elizabeth Goulden 2015
Most penalty goals in a season	46	Amanda Rasch, 2018
Most dropped goals in a season	0	
Most points in a match	43	Amanda Rasch v Taranaki, 2018
Most tries in a match	4	Huia Paul v Otago, 2011; Helen Collins v Hawke's Bay, 2012
Most conversions in a match	14	Amanda Rasch v Taranaki, 2018
Most penalty goals in a match	5	Elizabeth Goulden v Taranaki, 2013
Highest team score	118	v Taranaki, 2018
Record victory (points ahead)	118	118–0 v Taranaki, 2018
Highest score conceded	65	v Auckland, 2012
Record defeat (points behind)	65	0–65 v Auckland, 2012

The Pride, after a narrow loss to Hawke's Bay, rampaged through the championship, setting several new records. It was the only team to defeat eventual premiership champions Canterbury. Scoring a record 449 points, including a record 69 tries, and 118 points against Taranaki, this was an exceptional season for the Pride. It was unfortunate that, due to the poor results of 2017, the team was playing in the championship division and we can only wonder how well the team would have performed had they met heavyweights Counties Manukau, Waikato and the other teams of the higher division.

Ayesha Leti-I'iga was the star performer, the 19-year-old wing scoring 11 tries and already has scored more tries for the union than any other player. For her club Oriental Rongotai she scored a hat-trick, or more, in nine of her 13 games and finished the club season with 41 tries. Her reward was selection for the Black Ferns tour to USA and France.

The season's form also saw Joanah Ngan-Woo, Jackie Patea-Fereti, Marcelle Parkes and Monica Tagoai in the Blacks Ferns touring party, the highest Pride representation for many years. Ngan-Woo was not included in the playing squad for any of the three tests.

Amanda Rasch set several points-scoring records. Her 43 points (3 tries, 14 conversions) against Taranaki and 118 points for the season bettered previous records in the national championship.

Higher honours went to:
New Zealand: A. Leti-I'iga, M. Parkes, J. Patea-Fereti, M. Tagoai
New Zealand Sevens: K.R. Whata-Simpkins

WELLINGTON REPRESENTATIVES 2018

	Club	Games for Union	Points for Union		Club	Games for Union	Points for Union
Ana-Maria Afuie	Marist St Pats	8	0	Alicia Print	Oriental Rongotai	28	15
Tyler Bentley	Hutt OB Marist	1	5	Amanda Rasch	Oriental Rongotai	19	147
Courtney Clarke	OB University	11	0	Bernadette Robertson	Oriental Rongotai	14	15
Dhys Faleafaga	Northern United	6	15	Mary-Lee Sa'u	Petone	4	0
Nina Foaese	Northern United	7	5	Rosie Stirling	Hutt OB Marist	16	0
Montana Heslop	OB University	1	5	Monica Tagoai	Marist St Pats	17	35
Isadora Laupola	Northern United	8	15	Elieta Taito	Petone	17	25
Ayesha Leti-I'iga	Oriental Rongotai	25	145	Brooke Tauaneai	Avalon	13	5
Sanita Levave	Northern United	46	25	Janet Taumoli	Oriental Rongotai	23	10
Fa'asua Makisi	Oriental Rongotai	34	15	Acacia Te Iwimate	Petone	50	62
Kiri Mei	Avalon	34	65	Sinead To'oala-Ryder	Marist St Pats	10	15
Sieni Mose-Samau	Petone	3	10	Timena Tuma'ai	Oriental Rongotai	22	40
Joanah Ngan-Woo	Oriental Rongotai	42	45	Angelica Uila	Petone	14	35
Marcelle Parkes	Marist St Pats	3	0	Rejieli Uluinayau	Oriental Rongotai	15	15
Jackie Patea-Fereti	Petone	56	80	Shaye-Moana Whareaorere	Northern United	2	0
Tina Paulo	Oriental Rongotai	4	0	Gina Williamson	OB University	31	5

INDIVIDUAL SCORING

	Tries	Con	PG	DG	Points		Tries	Con	PG	DG	Points
Rasch	4	46	2	–	118	Makisi	2	–	–	–	10
Leti-I'iga	11	–	–	–	55	Mose-Samau	2	–	–	–	10
Patea-Fereti	8	–	–	–	40	To'oala-Ryder	2	–	–	–	10
Tagoai	6	–	–	–	30	Bentley	1	–	–	–	5
Te Iwimate	3	3	–	–	21	Faleafaga	1	–	–	–	5
Uila	4	–	–	–	20	Foaese	1	–	–	–	5
Laupola	3	–	–	–	15	Heslop	1	–	–	–	5
Mei	3	–	–	–	15	Levave	1	–	–	–	5
Ngan-Woo	3	–	–	–	15	Taumoli	1	–	–	–	5
Print	3	–	–	–	15						
Robertson	3	–	–	–	15	**Totals**	**69**	**49**	**2**	**0**	**449**
Taito	3	–	–	–	15						
Tuma'ai	3	–	–	–	15	Opposition scored	14	8	4	0	98

WELLINGTON 2018

	Hawke's Bay	Canterbury	Otago	Tasman	North Harbour	Taranaki	North Harbour	Otago	TOTALS
R. Uluinayau	15	s	–	–	s	–	s	–	4
T.M.P. Tuma'ai	s	15	15	15	15	–	15	15	7
M.J. Parkes	14	s	–	–	–	–	s	–	3
M.F. Tagoai	13	14	14	14	14	14	14	14	8
S. Mose-Samau	11	–	–	s	–	15	–	–	3
A.A. Leti-I'iga	–	11	11	11	11	11	–	11	6
D. Faleafaga	–	–	–	–	–	s	11	s	3
F.A.R.M. Makisi	12	13	13	13	s	s	13	13	8
M.B.J. Robertson	–	s	s	s	13	13	s	s	7
T. Bentley	–	–	–	–	–	s	–	–	1
A.A. Rasch	10	12	12	12	12	12	12	12	8
A.M. Te Iwimate	9	10	10	10	10	10	10	10	8
A-M. Afuie	s	9	9	9	9	9	9	9	8
S-M.L. Whareaorere	–	–	s	–	s	–	–	–	2
Heslop	–	–	–	s	–	–	–	–	1
T. Paulo	8	8	8	–	–	–	–	–	3
J.S. Patea-Fereti (capt)	–	5	5	8	8	8	8	8	7
S. To'oala-Ryder	7	7	–	7	7	–	7	7	6
G.M. Williamson	s	–	7	–	–	7	–	s	4
K.R.W. Mei	6	6	–	–	–	s	s	–	4
N. Foaese	s	s	6	6	6	–	6	6	7
S.D. Levave	–	s	s	5	5	5	5	5	7
J.M.P. Ngan-Woo	5	4	4	4	4	6	4	4	8
C.E. Clarke	4	–	s	–	s	–	–	–	3
M-L. Sa'u	–	–	–	s	–	4	s	s	4
J. Taumoli	3	3	3	3	s	3	3	3	8
I.T. Laupola	s	s	s	s	3	s	s	s	8
A. Uila	1	1	1	1	–	1	1	1	7
E. Taito	s	–	–	–	–	1	s	s	4
B. Tauaneai	–	–	s	s	s	–	–	–	3
A. Print	2	2	2	2	s	2	2	2	8
R. Stirling	s	s	s	s	2	s	s	s	8

Te Iwimate was captain v Hawke's Bay

WELLINGTON TEAM RECORD, 2018

Played 8   Won 7   Lost 1   Points for 449   Points against 98

Date	Opponent	Location	Score	Tries	Con	PG	DG	Referee
September 1	Hawke's Bay (C)	Napier	22–25	Te Iwimate, Mei, Mose-Samau	Rasch (2)	Rasch		R.M. Mahoney
September 8	Canterbury (P/C)	Porirua	43–38	Leti-I'iga (2), Tagoai (2), Patea-Fereti (2), Mei	Rasch (4)			R.M. Mahoney
September 15	Otago (C)	Porirua	38–10	Leti-I'iga (2), Uila, Patea-Fereti, Robertson	Rasch (5)	Rasch		T.N. Griffiths
September 23	Tasman (C)	Nelson	88–3	Leti-I'iga (3), Print, Tagoai, Rasch, To'oala-Ryder, Te Iwimate, Uila, Ngan-Woo, Heslop, Patea-Fereti, Robertson, Laupola	Rasch (9)			N.E.R. Hogan
September 29	North Harbour (C)	Mairangi Bay	50–10	Leti-I'iga (2), Tuma'ai, Uila, Laupola, To'oala-Ryder, Print, Makisi	Rasch (5)			L.A. Jenner
October 6	Taranaki (C)	Porirua	118–0	Rasch (3), Leti-I'iga (2), Taito (2), Mose-Samau, Te Iwimate, Patea-Fereti, Print, Ngan-Woo, Robertson, Levave, Mei, Bentley, Faleafaga, Tagoai	Rasch (14)			M.I. Fraser
October 13	North Harbour (semi-final)	Porirua	33–7	Patea-Fereti (2), Foaese, Makisi, Taito	Te Iwimate (3), Rasch			M. Cogger-Orr
October 20	Otago (final)	Porirua	57–5	Tuma'ai (2), Tagoai (2), Uila, Ngan-Woo, Taumoli, Patea-Fereti, Laupola	Rasch (6)			B.J. Andrew

WOMEN'S FIRST-CLASS STATISTICS
to January 1, 2019

85 GAMES IN FIRST-CLASS RUGBY

	Career	Games		Career	Games
Emma Jensen	1999-2018	164	Selica Winiata	2001-18	111
Fiao'o Faamausili	1999-2018	164	Amiria Rule	1999-2014	98
Justine Lavea	2001-18	144	Karina Stowers	2004-17	95
Anna Richards	1990-2011	125	Linda Itunu	2003-18	92
Kendra Cocksedge	2007-18	123	Monalisa Codling	1998-2008	91
Stephanie Te Ohaere-Fox	2003-18	119	Victoria Heighway	1999-2009	90
Casey Robertson	1999-2014	118	Aleisha Nelson	2008-18	90
			Eloise Blackwell	2009-18	87

300 POINTS IN FIRST-CLASS RUGBY

	Career	Games	Tries	Con	PG	DG	Points
Kendra Cocksedge	2007-18	123	70	250	79	–	1087
Selica Winiata	2001-18	111	103	34	11	–	616
Emma Jensen	1999-2018	164	11	147	81	1	595
Hannah Porter	1999-2008	59	20	115	61	–	513
Tammi Wilson	1998-2001	45	40	92	24	1	459
Kelly Brazier	2005-17	75	35	84	27	–	424
Chelsea Alley	2011-18	61	22	74	34	–	360
Claire Richardson	2001-14	79	36	33	25	–	321
Fiao'o Faamausili	1999-2018	164	63	-	-	–	315
Hazel Tubic	2005-17	57	18	83	19	–	313

45 TRIES IN FIRST-CLASS RUGBY

	Tries	Games		Tries	Games
Selica Winiata	103	111	Dianne Kahura	53	35
Kendra Cocksedge	70	123	Victoria Grant	51	69
Fiao'o Faamausili	63	164	Louisa Wall	48	32
Vanessa Cootes	54	50	Carla Hohepa	45	44

MOST DROPPED GOALS IN FIRST-CLASS RUGBY

	DG	Games
Rebecca Mahoney (*nee* Hull)	4	69

100 POINTS IN A SEASON

	Teams	M	Tries	Con	PG	DG	Total
Kendra Cocksedge	Canterbury/NZ, 2018	13	13	45	6	–	173
Kendra Cocksedge	Canterbury/NZ, 2017	14	11	52	4	–	171
Tammi Wilson	Auckland/NZ, 1999	10	15	34	4	–	155
Kendra Cocksedge	Canterbury/NZ, 2016	12	11	32	12	–	155
Kendra Cocksedge	Canterbury/NZ, 2014	17	5	32	16	–	137
Tammi Wilson	Auckland/NZ, 2002	11	8	20	14	1	125
Amanda Rasch	Wellington, 2018	8	4	46	2	–	118
Selica Winiata	Manawatu/NZ, 2012	9	15	17	2	–	115
Hannah Myers	Auckland/NZ, 2003	7	6	25	9	–	107
Hannah Myers	Auckland/NZ, 2005	12	4	27	11	–	107

MOST TRIES IN A SEASON

	Teams	Tries	Games
Dianne Kahura	Auckland/NZ, 2002	19	11
Vanessa Cootes	New Zealand, 1996	18	3
Selica Winiata	Manawatu/NZ, 2016	18	11
Mele Hufanga	Auckland 2015	16	7
Portia Woodman	New Zealand, 2017	16	8
Tammi Wilson	Auckland/NZ, 1999	15	10
Selica Winiata	Manawatu/NZ, 2012	15	9
Selica Winiata	Manawatu/NZ, 2014	15	13

MOST POINTS IN A GAME

	Match	Tries	Con	PG	DG	Points
Vanessa Cootes	New Zealand v France, 1996	9	–	–	–	45
Kelly Brazier	Otago v Hawke's Bay, 2012	5	10	–	–	45
Amanda Rasch	Wellington v Taranaki, 2018	3	14	–	–	43
Annaleah Rush	Otago v Hanan Shield Unions, 1999	8	1	–	–	42
Portia Woodman	New Zealand v Hong Kong, 2017	8	–	–	–	40
Selica Winiata	Manawatu v Waikato, 2012	4	6	2	–	38
Tammi Wilson	New Zealand v USA, 1999	6	3	–	–	36
Christine Ross	New Zealand v France, 1996	2	12	–	–	34
Kelly Brazier	Otago v Manawatu, 2009	4	7	–	–	34
Tammi Wilson	Auckland v North Harbour, 1999	1	13	–	–	31
Kendra Cocksedge	New Zealand v Hong Kong, 2017	1	13	–	–	31
Ruahei Demant	Auckland v Tasman, 2018	3	8	–	–	31
Tammi Wilson	New Zealand v Germany, 1998	4	5	–	–	30
Kendra Cocksedge	Canterbury v Taranaki, 2013	4	5	–	–	30
Kendra Cocksedge	Canterbury v North Harbour, 2016	4	5	–	–	30

MOST TRIES IN A GAME

	Match	Tries
Vanessa Cootes	New Zealand v France, 1996	9
Annaleah Rush	Otago v Hanan Shield Unions, 1999	8
Portia Woodman	New Zealand v Hong Kong, 2017	8
Tammi Wilson	New Zealand v USA, 1999	6
Helen Reader	New Zealand v New South Wales, 1994	5
Vanessa Cootes	New Zealand v USA, 1996	5
Vanessa Cootes	New Zealand v USA, 1998	5
Vanessa Cootes	New Zealand v Germany, 2002	5
Deidre Hakopa	Hawke's Bay v Southland, 2003	5
Kelly Brazier	Otago v Hawke's Bay, 2012	5
Selica Winiata	New Zealand v Samoa, 2014	5
Kilisitina Moata'ane	Otago v Tasman, 2017	5

MOST CONVERSIONS IN A GAME

	Match	Con
Amanda Rasch	Wellington v Taranaki, 2018	14
Tammi Wilson	Auckland v North Harbour, 1999	13
Kendra Cocksedge	New Zealand v Hong Kong, 2017	13
Christine Ross	New Zealand v France, 1996	12
Kelly Brazier	Otago v Hawke's Bay, 2012	10

MOST PENALTY GOALS IN A GAME

	Match	PG
Annaleah Rush	Auckland v Wellington, 2001	6
Kendra Cocksedge	Canterbury v Auckland, 2009	5
Elizabeth Goulden	Wellington v Taranaki, 2013	5
Kendra Cocksedge	Canterbury v Waikato, 2016	5

HIGHEST TEAM SCORES

Score	Match	Result
134	New Zealand v Germany, 1998	134-6
121	New Zealand v Hong Kong, 2017	121-0
118	Wellington v Taranaki, 2018	118-0
117	New Zealand v Germany, 2002	117-0
116	Auckland v North Harbour, 1999	116-0
109	New Zealand v France, 1996	109-0
101	Auckland v Bay of Plenty 2015	101-0
100	Hawke's Bay v Southland, 2003	100-5

WOMEN'S RUGBY REFEREES 2018
by Chris Jansen

WOMEN'S RUGBY REFEREE SQUAD 2018

			Tests	HC	Nat[1]	FPC	Sevens	Total
B.J. Andrew	Manawatu	2015	–		–	14	2	16
M. Cogger-Orr	Auckland	2017				11	1	12
L. Collingwood	Waikato	2018					1	1
M. Dalley	Wellington	2018				–	2	2
L. Jenner	Counties Manukau	2017	–		–	9	4	13
R.M. Mahoney	Wairarapa Bush	2015	3	3	1	17	11	35

HC Heartland Championship   Nat[1] Tour fixture   FPC Farah Palmer Cup

REFEREE APPOINTMENTS 2018

Brittany Andrew

September	1	FPC	Waikato v Counties Manukau	Taupiri
	22	FPC	Hawke's Bay v North Harbour	Napier
	30	FPC	Hawke's Bay v Tasman	Napier
October	6	FPC	Canterbury v Auckland	Christchurch
	13	FPC s-f	Waikato v Counties Manukau	Hamilton
	20	FPC f	Wellington v Otago	Porirua

Maggie Cogger – Orr

January	13/14		National Sevens	Rotorua
September	1	FPC	Bay of Plenty v Canterbury	Tauranga
	23	FPC	Manawatu v Canterbury	Palmerston North
	29	FPC	Waikato v Manawatu	Hamilton
October	6	FPC	Counties Manukau v Bay of Plenty	Pukekohe
	13	FPC s-f	Wellington v North Harbour	Porirua

Larissa Collingwood

December	15/16		National Sevens	Tauranga

Monique Dalley

January	13/14		National Sevens	Rotorua
December	15/16		National Sevens	Tauranga

Lauren Jenner

January	13/14		National Sevens	Rotorua
April	5/6		World Rugby Women's Sevens Qualifiers	Hong Kong
September	1	FPC	Hawke's Bay v Wellington	Napier
	7	FPC	Auckland v Tasman	Auckland
	29	FPC	North Harbour v Wellington	Mairangi Bay
October	6	FPC	Tasman v Otago	Blenheim
November	29/30		Dubai World Rugby Women's Series	Dubai
December	15/16		National Sevens	Tauranga

Rebecca Mahoney

January	13/14		National Sevens	Rotorua
	26/28		Australia World Rugby Women's Sevens	Sydney
April	13–15		Commonwealth Games Rugby Sevens	Gold Coast
	21/22		Japan World Rugby Women's Sevens	Kitakyushu
May	12/13		Canada World Rugby Women's Sevens	Langford
July	20–22		Rugby World Cup Sevens	San Francisco
September	1	FPC	Hawke's Bay vs Wellington	Napier
	8	FPC	Wellington v Canterbury	Porirua
	15	HC	Thames Valley v King Country	Te Aroha
	28	FPC	Auckland v Bay of Plenty	Auckland
October	6	HC	Buller v Mid Canterbury	Westport
	13	HC	Poverty Bay v Buller	Gisborne
	20	FPC f	Canterbury v Counties Manukau	Christchurch
November	18		Ireland v USA	Dublin
	24		Wales v Canada	Cardiff

HC Heartland Championship
FPC Farah Palmer Cup

Two overseas referees controlled National Sevens fixtures:
Amy Perrett (Australia)
Madeline Putz-Skiba (Australia)

Two overseas referees controlled Farah Palmer Cup fixtures:
Amber Hibbard (Australia) Sep 8 Counties Manukau v Manawatu.
Lara West (Australia) Sep 15 Canterbury v Waikato.

INTERNATIONAL ASSISTANT REFEREES

Lee Jeffrey

August	25	New Zealand v Australia (TMO)	Auckland

Rebecca Mahoney

August	25	New Zealand v Australia	Auckland

(TMO) Television Match Official

INTERNATIONAL REFEREES
to 1 January, 2019

Beard, J.D.L. (Counties Manukau) 2014–16	10
Inwood, N.A. (Wanganui & Canterbury) 2002–14	32
Mahoney, R.M. (Wairarapa Bush) 2016–18	3
Mellor, K.E. (North Harbour) 2006	1

TWENTY-FIVE AND MORE FIRST-CLASS MATCHES
to 1 January, 2019

N.A. Inwood	2000–14	86	C.F. Gurr	2011–16	37
J.D.L. Beard	2012–16	50	R.M. Mahoney	2015–18	35
L. Jeffrey	2003–16	42			

WOMEN'S SEVENS RUGBY

The Black Ferns Sevens won three of the five tournaments of the 2017/18 HSBC Sevens Series but when the series concluded at Paris New Zealand trailed Australia by two series points. Finishing fifth at the first tournament of the series, at Dubai in December 2017, proved to be very costly. Australia, winners at Dubai, then inflicted a 31–0 win over the Ferns at Sydney in January. The team responded from the Sydney record defeat by winning every game of the seven tournaments during the rest of the year including the winning of gold medals at the Commonwealth Games at Gold Coast and the Rugby World Cup Sevens at San Francisco. To win both major events was remarkable.

A Development team took part in the Hokkaido Sevens in Japan and the Oceania Sevens in Fiji, being beaten by Australia in the final at both events. The Under 18 team won the Oceania tournament at Sydney then won the gold medal at the Youth Olympics in Argentina.

At the National Sevens, held in January, Manawatu won its fourth title in six years. This event is usually held early in the year but the union made the decision to bring the event forward and a second tournament was held in Tauranga in December, and again won by Manawatu. The December date allowed national squads more time to prepare for the Hamilton World Series event in Hamilton late in January 2019 and the Sydney event the following week.

Player	Team	Australia	C'wealth Games	Japan	Canada	France	RWC	USA	Dubai	TOTALS
Shakira Baker	Waikato	–	*	*	*	–	*	*	*	6
Michaela Blyde	Bay of Plenty	*	*	*	*	*	*	*	*	8
Kelly Brazier	Bay of Plenty	*	*	*	*	*	*	*	*	8
Gayle Broughton	Taranaki	*	*	*	–	*	*	–	*	6
Theresa Fitzpatrick	Auckland	*	*	*	*	*	*	*	*	8
Sarah Goss (capt)	Manawatu	*	*	*	*	*	*	*	*	8
Huia Harding	Waikato	–	–	*	–	–	–	–	–	1
Shiray Kaka (nee Tane)	Waikato	–	–	–	–	*	–	–	–	1
Tyla Nathan-Wong	Auckland	*	*	*	*	*	*	*	*	8
Risi Pouri-Lane	Tasman	–	–	–	–	–	–	–	*	1
Alena Saili	Southland	*	*	–	–	–	–	*	*	4
Terina Te Tamaki	Waikato	–	–	–	*	–	–	*	*	3
Ruby Tui	Bay of Plenty	*	–	–	*	*	*	*	*	6
Stacey Waaka	Waikato	*	*	*	*	*	*	–	*	7
Katarina Whata-Simpkins	Wellington	–	–	–	–	–	–	*	–	1
Niall Williams	Auckland	*	*	*	*	*	*	*	–	7
Tenika Willison	Waikato	*	*	*	*	*	*	–	–	6
Portia Woodman	Counties Manukau	*	*	*	*	*	*	*	–	7

Coach: Allan Bunting
Assistant coach: Cory Sweeney, Stu Ross
Manager: Jenelle Strickland (first four events); Strickland and Toni Kidwell (Paris); Strickland (RWC); Kidwell (last two events).
Strength & conditioning trainer: Bradley Anderson; Albert Chang (RWC).
Video analyst: Stu Ross.
Physiotherapist: Nicole Armstrong; Kate Niederer (Dubai).

INDIVIDUAL SCORING

	Tries	Con	Points
Woodman	58	–	290
Blyde	57	–	285
Nathan-Wong	8	110	260
Brazier	20	6	112
Goss	19	–	95
Broughton	18	–	90
Williams	15	–	75
Waaka	10	–	50
Willison	1	18	41
Tui	8	–	40
Baker	7	–	35
Fitzpatrick	6	–	30
Kaka	2	–	10
Saili	2	–	10
Pouri-Lane	1	–	5
Whata-Simpkins	–	2	4
Totals	**232**	**136**	**1432**
Opposition scored			307

Final points for 2017/18 World Rugby Sevens Series: Australia 92, New Zealand 90, France 68, Canada 60, USA 56, Russia 46, Spain 43, England 32, Fiji 31, Ireland 29, Japan 10, China 6, South Africa 3, Brazil 2, Wales 1, Papua New Guinea 1. The series was held over five tournaments from December 2017 to June 2018.

Previous winners: New Zealand 2013, 2014, 2015, 2017; Australia 2016.
World Rugby Sevens Series Cup championship titles (2012 to 1 January 2019): New Zealand 20, Australia 8, Canada 3, England 2.

NEW ZEALAND AT AUSTRALIA SEVENS
Allianz Stadium, Sydney   January 26–28, 2018

Date	Opponent	Result	Tries	Conversions
Jan 26	Japan	won 48–7	Woodman (4), Blyde (2), Tui, Waaka	Nathan-Wong (3), Willison
Jan 26	England	won 33–12	Woodman (3), Blyde (2)	Nathan-Wong (3), Willison
Jan 26	USA	won 31–0	Woodman (3), Blyde, Broughton	Nathan-Wong (3)
Jan 27	Ireland (Cup q-f)	won 36–0	Blyde (2), Woodman (2), Waaka, Broughton	Nathan-Wong (3)
Jan 27	Canada (Cup s-f)	won 26–0	Broughton, Woodman, Blyde, Brazier	Nathan-Wong (3)
Jan 28	Australia (Cup final)	lost 0–31		

NEW ZEALAND AT XXI COMMONWEALTH GAMES
Robina Stadium, Gold Coast, Australia April 13–15, 2018

Date	Opponent	Result	Tries	Conversions
Apr 13	Kenya	won 45–0	Woodman (3), Williams (2), Brazier, Broughton	Nathan-Wong (5)
Apr 13	South Africa	won 41–0	Woodman (2), Goss, Blyde, Broughton, Williams, Brazier	Nathan-Wong (3)
Apr 14	Canada	won 24–7	Blyde (2), Waaka, Woodman	Nathan-Wong (2)
Apr 15	England (s-f)	won 26–5	Goss, Blyde, Baker, Woodman	Nathan-Wong (3)
Apr 15	Australia (final)	won 17–12 (extra time)	Woodman, Blyde, Brazier	Willison

England defeated Canada 24–19 in the playoff for the bronze medal

NEW ZEALAND AT JAPAN SEVENS
Mikuni World Stadium, Kitakyushu April 21/22, 2018

Date	Opponent	Result	Tries	Conversions
Apr 21	Japan	won 38–5	Woodman (2), Blyde (2), Goss, Waaka	Nathan-Wong (4)
Apr 21	USA	won 31–12	Woodman, Williams, Blyde, Broughton, Baker	Willison (3)
Apr 21	France	won 38–7	Woodman (3), Broughton, Waaka, Baker	Nathan-Wong (3), Willison
Apr 22	China (Cup q-f)	won 50–0	Blyde (2), Brazier (2), Broughton, Baker, Goss, Willison	Nathan-Wong (3), Willison (2)
Apr 22	Australia (Cup s-f)	won 17–12	Broughton, Blyde, Nathan-Wong	Nathan-Wong
Apr 22	France (Cup final)	won 24–12	Blyde, Fitzpatrick, Woodman, Nathan-Wong	Nathan-Wong (2)

NEW ZEALAND AT CANADA SEVENS
Westhills Stadium, Langford, Victoria, British Columbia May 12/13, 2018

Date	Opponent	Result	Tries	Conversions
May 12	Brazil	won 51–0	Williams (2), Blyde (2), Woodman, Tui, Goss, Fitzpatrick, Brazier	Willison (2), Nathan-Wong
May 12	England	won 22–0	Blyde (2), Nathan-Wong, Williams	Nathan-Wong
May 12	Fiji	won 12–7	Williams, Blyde	Nathan-Wong
May 13	England (Cup q-f)	won 17–12	Woodman (3)	Nathan-Wong
May 13	USA (Cup s-f)	won 33–10	Blyde (2), Brazier, Goss, Woodman	Nathan-Wong (4)
May 13	Australia (Cup final)	won 46–0	Woodman (2), Williams (2), Brazier (2), Tui, Goss	Willison (2), Nathan-Wong

NEW ZEALAND AT FRANCE SEVENS
Stade Jean Bouin, Paris   June 8–10, 2018

Date	Opponent	Result	Tries	Conversions
June 8	England	won 24–12	Blyde (2), Woodman (2)	Willison (2)
June 8	Wales	won 54–7	Kaka (2), Williams (2), Brazier, Fitzpatrick, Waaka, Broughton	Nathan-Wong (5), Willison (2)
June 8	Ireland	won 17–0	Blyde (2), Williams	Nathan-Wong
June 9	Spain (Cup q-f)	won 38–0	Woodman (2), Broughton (2), Blyde, Brazier	Nathan-Wong (3), Willison
June 9	Canada (Cup s-f)	won 34–7	Nathan-Wong (2), Blyde, Woodman, Tui, Brazier	Nathan-Wong (2)
June 10	Australia (Cup final)	won 33–7	Blyde (2), Woodman (2), Goss	Nathan-Wong (3), Brazier

NEW ZEALAND AT RUGBY WORLD CUP SEVENS
AT&T Park, San Francisco, USA   July 20/21, 2018

Date	Opponent	Result	Tries	Conversions
July 20	Mexico	won 57–0	Goss (3), Blyde (2), Woodman (2), Brazier, Waaka	Nathan-Wong (6)
July 20	Ireland (q-f)	won 45–0	Blyde (3), Woodman (2), Williams, Waaka	Nathan-Wong (5)
July 21	USA (s-f)	won 26–21	Blyde, Tui, Broughton, Woodman	Nathan-Wong (3)
July 21	France (final)	won 29–0	Blyde (3), Woodman, Nathan-Wong	Nathan-Wong (2)

Australia defeated USA 24-12 for the bronze medal

NEW ZEALAND AT USA SEVENS
Infinity Park, Glendale, Colorado   October 20/21, 2018

Date	Opponent	Result	Tries	Conversions
Oct 20	China	won 45–0	Woodman (3), Brazier, Tui, Blyde, Saili	Nathan-Wong (3), Whata-Simpkins (2)
Oct 20	England	won 28–7	Woodman (2), Blyde, Fitzpatrick	Nathan-Wong (4)
Oct 20	USA	won 35–12	Brazier, Goss, Tui, Baker, Blyde	Nathan-Wong (4), Brazier
Oct 21	Ireland (Cup q-f)	won 34–7	Blyde (3), Brazier, Goss, Fitzpatrick	Nathan-Wong (2)
Oct 21	Canada (Cup s-f)	won 28–19	Woodman (2), Baker, Goss	Nathan-Wong (4)
Oct 21	USA (Cup final)	won 33–7	Woodman (3), Goss, Williams	Nathan-Wong (4)

NEW ZEALAND AT DUBAI SEVENS
The Sevens, Dubai   November 29/30, 2018

Date	Opponent	Result	Tries	Conversions
Nov 29	Kenya	won 34–7	Goss, Blyde, Brazier, Saili, Broughton, Pouri-Lane	Brazier (2)
Nov 29	Russia	won 29–12	Goss (2), Waaka (2), Broughton	Nathan-Wong (2)
Nov 29	Ireland	won 24–17	Blyde (2), Broughton, Tui	Brazier (2)
Nov 30	Russia (Cup q-)	won 31–0	Brazier (2), Blyde, Goss, Broughton	Nathan-Wong (3)
Nov 30	USA (Cup s-f)	won 22–0	Blyde (3), Baker	Nathan-Wong
Nov 30	Canada (Cup final)	won 26–14	Nathan-Wong (2), Fitzpatrick, Broughton	Nathan-Wong (3)

NEW ZEALAND SEVENS DEVELOPMENT TEAM

The Black Ferns Sevens Development team took part in two tournaments – in Japan and Fiji.

Squad: Shakira Baker (*Waikato*) 2; Kendall Buckingham (*Southland*) 1,2; Georgia Daals (*Wellington*) 1; Cassandra Engler (*Southland*) 1; Huia Harding (*Waikato*) 2; Talei Kidd (*Auckland*) 2; Natahlia Moors (*Auckland*) 1; Rina Paraone (*Waikato*) 1; Marcelle Parkes (*Wellington*) 1; Cheyelle Robins-Reti (*Waikato*) 2; Leanna Ryan (*Waikato*) 1,2; Kennedy Simon (*Waikato*) 2; Susana Sotutu (*Auckland*) 1,2; Grace Steinmetz (*Canterbury*) 1,2; Terina Te Tamaki (*Waikato*) 1,2; Rebekah Tufuga (*Manawatu*) 2; Janna Vaughan (*captain, Manawatu*) 1,2; Katarina Whata-Simpkins (*Wellington*) 1.

Coach: Kane Jury (in Japan); Crystal Kaua (in Fiji)
Assistant coach: Crystal Kaua (in Japan); Jimmy Sinclair (in Fiji)
Manager: Belinda Muller

RESULTS
1. **Hokkaido Sevens,** at Hokkaido Barbarians RFC, Jozankei, Sapporo, Hokkaido. September 23/24, 2018.
Pool Play: v Cook Islands won 27–0; v Hokkaido Barbarians Diana won 19–17; v USA won 17–7; *Quarter-final.* v Japan won 26–5
Semi-final: v Canada won 21–12
Final: v Australia lost 7–33

2. **Oceania Sevens,** at ANZ Stadium, Suva. November 9/10, 2018.
Pool Play: v New Caledonia won 45–8; v Cook Islands won 31–0; v Fiji won 27–0
Semi-final: v Papua New Guinea won 30–0
Final: v Australia lost 10–12

NEW ZEALAND UNDER 18 SEVENS TEAM

New Zealand was represented at the Oceania Under 18 Sevens Championship held in Australia during April 21–22. With a reduction in teams, due to unforeseen circumstances, the team played Australia and Fiji in a double round over two days, with the top two teams playing off in the final to enhance their opportunity to be selected to represent the Oceania region at the Youth Olympic Games in October. Games were played at St Ignatius College, Riverview in Sydney.

Squad: Carys Dallinger (*Manukura, Palmerston Nth*), Tiana Davison (*Sacred Heart C, New Plymouth*), Dhys Faleafaga (*St Mary's C, Wellington*), Tynealle Fitzgerald (*Rangiuru RFC, BoP*), Iritana Hohaia (*Opunake HS*), Jazmin Hotham (*capt, Hamilton GHS*), Ricshay Lemanu (*Papatoetoe HS*), Azalleyah Maaka (*Gisborne GHS*), Risaleaana Pouri-Lane (*Motueka HS*), Montessa Tairakena (*Hamilton GHS*), Kalyn Takitimu-Cook (*Manukura, Palm. Nth*), Arorangi Tauranga (*Hamilton GHS*), Hinemoa Watene (*Howick C*).

Coach: Victoria Grant
Assistant coach: Peter Nock
Manager: Tangi Waikari
Strength & conditioning coach: Michael Jacobs
Physiotherapist: Kate Niederer
Performance analyst: Jimmy Sinclair

RESULTS
Pool Play:
v **Australia won 26–17** Tairakena 2, Dallinger, Pouri-Lane tries; Pouri-Lane 3 conversions.
v **Fiji won 37–0** Tairakena 4, Lemanu 2, Maaka tries; Dallinger conversion.
v **Australia lost 15–17** Tairakena 2, Watene tries.
v **Fiji won 31–5** Dallinger, Hohaia, Hotham, Lemanu, Tairakena tries; Dallinger 3 conversions.
Final:
v **Australia won 21–7** Tairakena 2, Hohaia tries; Pouri-Lane 3 conversions

2018 YOUTH OLYMPIC GAMES

New Zealand was represented by the women's Under 18 squad at the Youth Olympic Games held in Argentina during October. Playing two games each day, October 13–15, the team was undefeated in pool play and won the gold after defeating France in the final. Games were played at Club Athletico San Isidro, sede la Boya, Buenos Aires.

Squad: Carys Dallinger (*Manukura, Palmerston North*), Tiana Davison (*Sacred Heart C, New Plymouth*), Tynealle Fitzgerald (*Rangiuru RFC, BoP*), Iritana Hohaia (*Opunake HS*), Azalleyah Maaka (*Gisborne GHS*), Mahina Paul (*St Kentigern C*), Risi Pouri-Lane (*capt, Motueka HS*), Kiani Tahere (*Te Wharekura o Mauao*), Montessa Tairakena (*Hamilton GHS*), Kalyn Takitimu-Cook (*Manukura, Palmerston Nth*), Arorangi Tauranga (*Hamilton GHS*), Hinemoa Watene (*Howick C*).

Coach: Jimmy Sinclair
Manager: Tangi Waikari
Strength & conditioning coach: Michael Jacobs
Physiotherapist: Kate Niederer

RESULTS
Pool Play:
v **Tunisia won 53–0** Hohaia 2, Davison, Maaka, Paul, Pouri-Lane, Tairakena, Takitimu-Cook, Tauranga tries; Pouri-Lane 2, Takitimu-Cook 2, conversions.
v **Colombia won 38–5** Dallinger, Fitzgerald, Hohaia, Pouri-Lane, Tairakena, Takitimu-Cook tries; Pouri-Lane 4 conversions.
v **France won 26–12** Tairakena 2, Pouri-Lane, Watene tries; Pouri-Lane 3 conversions.
v **Canada won 20–5** Tairakena 2, Maaka, Pouri-Lane tries.
v **Kazakhstan won 32–5** Tahere 2, Dallinger, Tairakena, Takitimu-Cook, Watene tries; Pouri-Lane conversion.
Final: v **France won 15–12** Hohaia, Tairakena, Paul tries.

SEVENS RECORDS
to January 1, 2019

BY NEW ZEALAND TEAMS

Most successive wins	44	2014–15
Most successive tournament wins	7	2014–15, 2018
Most successive appearances in finals	10	2013–15

Tournament records

Most points	293	Hong Kong 2000
Most tries	47	Hong Kong 2000
Most conversions	30	New Zealand 2001

Match records

Highest team score	83	v International Selection, Japan 2001
Record victory (points ahead)	83	83–0 v International Selection, Japan 2001
Highest score conceded	35	v Australia (final), Dubai 2013
Record defeat (points behind)	31	0–31 v Australia, Sydney 2018
Most tries	13	v International Selection, Japan 2001
Most conversions	10	v Tahiti, Fiji 2017

BY THE PLAYERS

Career records

Attended most tournaments	39	S.L. Goss
Most points	1200	P.L. Woodman
Most tries	240	P.L. Woodman
Most conversions	401	T.B. Nathan-Wong

Tournament records

Most points	70	P.L. Woodman, USA 2015
Most tries	14	P.L. Woodman, USA 2015
Most conversions	29	A.M. Richards, New Zealand 2001

Match records

Most points	25	M. Blyde, v Samoa, Noosa 2013 P.L. Woodman v France, Brazil 2015; P.L. Woodman v USA, USA 2015 M. Blyde v England, Canada 2017; T.R. Willison v Tahiti, Fiji 2017
Most tries	5	M. Blyde, v Samoa, Noosa 2013 P.L. Woodman v France, Brazil 2015; P.L. Woodman v USA, USA 2015 M. Blyde v England, Canada 2017
Most conversions	10	T.R. Willison v Tahiti, Fiji 2017

NEW ZEALAND SEVENS REPRESENTATIVES, 2000–18

	Tournaments
Alley, C.H. (*Waikato*) 2014	1
Aniseko, F. (*Auckland*) 2008	1
Baker, S.J. (*Wellington*) 2012 (*Manawatu*) 2013 (*Waikato*) 2016–17–	14
Bird, O.M. (*Canterbury*) 2013	1
Blyde, M.G. (*Taranaki*) 2013–14–15–16 (*Bay of Plenty*) 2017–18	26
Brazier, K.A. (*Otago*) 2013–14 (*Bay of Plenty*) 2015–16–17–18	29
Broughton, G.P. (*Taranaki*) 2014–15–16–17–18	21
Burgess, L.A. (*Taranaki*) 2012–13	2
Cocksedge, K.M. (*Canterbury*) 2008–12–13	3
Cootes, V. (*Waikato*) 2001	3
Drummond, J.A. (*Tasman*) 2017	2
Davis, M.F. (*Counties Manukau*) 2012	1
Ferguson, J. (*Hawke's Bay*) 2009	1
Fitzpatrick, T.M. (*Auckland*) 2016–17–18	17
Forbes, M.H. (*Tasman*) 2012	1
Goss, S.L. (*Manawatu*) 2012–13–14–15–16–17–18	39
Gould, L. (*Canterbury*) 2000 (*Wellington*) 2001 (*Bay of Plenty*) 2012	4
Grant, K.M. (*Canterbury*) 2014	1
Grant, V.E. (*Auckland*) 2008–09	2
Greig, V.A.P. (*Manawatu*) 2013	2
Halapua, C. (*Auckland*) 2012	1
Hansen, S. (*Wanganui*) 2000	1
Harding, H.R. (*Waikato*) 2018	1
Hira-Herangi, A.P. (*Waikato*) 2014	1
Hireme, A.H. (*Waikato*) 2013–14–15	11
Hohepa, C.G. (*Otago*) 2009 (*Waikato*) 2012–13–14–15	10
Hohepa, C.H. (*Waikato*) 2012	1
Holden, S.E. (*Manawatu*) 2000 (*Wellington*) 2001	2
Hurring, H.A. (*Otago*) 2013	2
Hutana, H.S. (*Manawatu*) 2013	2
Itunu, L.F. (*Auckland*) 2009–12–13–14	11
Kahura, D.M.T. (*Auckland*) 2000–01	4
Kaka, S.T. (nee Tane) (*Waikato*) 2013–14–15–16–18	11
Karanga, P. (*Manawatu*) 2001	1
Kurei, N. (*Bay of Plenty*) 2000	1
Lavea, J. (*Auckland*) 2009	1
Lavea, V.N.H. (*Auckland*) 2008	1
McAlister, K.M. (*Auckland*) 2012–13–14–15–16–17	20
McGregor, A. (*Auckland*) 2008–09	2

	Tournaments
Manuel, H.R. (*Auckland*) 2008–09–12–13–14–16	16
Mayes, C.A.M. (*Manawatu*) 2013–17	3
Morrow, M.L. (*Bay of Plenty*) 2014–15	3
Naoupo, T. (*Auckland*) 2001	3
Nathan-Wong, T.B. (*Auckland*) 2012–13–14–15–16–17–18	35
Ngawati, T.A. (*Auckland*) 2012	1
Paul, T. (*Bay of Plenty*) 2001	3
Porter, H.J. (nee Myers) (*Otago*) 2000–01 (*Auckland*) 2008–09	6
Pouri-Lane, R.I.R. (*Tasman*) 2018	1
Reti, T.C. (*Manawatu*) 2017	1
Richards, A.M. (*Auckland*) 2000–01	4
Robins-Reti, C.R.A. (*Waikato*) 2017	3
Ruscoe, M.J. (*Canterbury*) 2008	1
Rush, A.M. (*Auckland*) 2000–01	3
Saili, A.F. (*Southland*) 2017–18	11
Scanlan, C.R. (*Auckland*) 2014–15	3
Shelford, E.T. (*Bay of Plenty*) 2001	3
Shortland, S. (*Auckland*) 2000–01	4
Sue, K.J. (*Manawatu*) 2013	2
Sutorius, A.E. (*Wellington*) 2008	1
Tane, S.T. (*Waikato*) 2013–14–15–16	10
Tapsell, A.N.O. (*Canterbury*) 2013 (*Bay of Plenty*) 2015	5
Te Tamaki, T.K. (*Auckland*) 2008–09	2
Te Tamaki, T.L.R. (*Waikato*) 2016–17–18	11
Townsend, M.A. (*Manawatu*) 2008	1
Tubic, H.S. (*Counties Manukau*) 2012–13–14–15–16	15
Tufuga, R. (*Manawatu*) 2016–17	3
Tui, R.M. (*Canterbury*) 2012–13–14–15 16 17 18	29
Vaughan, J.M. (*Manawatu*) 2016	1
Waaka, S.J.A.K. (*Waikato*) 2016–17–18	11
Webber, J.B.M. (*Waikato*) 2014–15–16	10
Whata-Simpkins, K.R. (*Wellington*) 2014–15–16–17–18	18
Wickliffe, R.W.M. (*Counties Manukau*) 2009–13–16–17	7
Wikeepa, R. (*Waikato*) 2009	1
Williams, N.L.V. (*Auckland*) 2015–16–17–18	20
Willison, T.R. (*Waikato*) 2016–17–18	9
Wilson, T. (*Auckland*) 2000	1
Winiata, S.C. (*Manawatu*) 2008–09–13–14–15–16	15
Woodman, P.L. (*Auckland*) 2012–13–14–15– (*Counties Manukau*) 2016–17–18	35

NATIONAL SEVENS

Rotorua International Stadium   January 13/14, 2018

POOL

A   Waikato 25 Poverty Bay 5; Otago 17 Canterbury 7;
    Waikato 31 Otago 0; Canterbury 27 Poverty Bay 0;
    Waikato 17 Canterbury 0; Otago 33 Poverty Bay 0.

B   Manawatu 43 North Harbour 0; Wellington 15 Bay of Plenty 12;
    Manawatu 38 Wellington 5; Bay of Plenty 38 North Harbour 5;
    Bay of Plenty 19 Manawatu 12; Wellington 45 North Harbour 0.

C   Auckland 22 Southland 0; Counties Manukau 50 Hawke's Bay 7;
    Auckland 39 Hawke's Bay 0; Counties Manukau 36 Southland 5;
    Auckland 38 Counties Manukau 5; Hawke's Bay 28 Southland 12.

CUP CHAMPIONSHIP

Quarter-finals   Waikato 26 Canterbury 0; Counties Manukau 22 Bay of Plenty 21;
                       Auckland 33 Otago 0; Manawatu 22 Wellington 14.
Semi-finals   Waikato 24 Counties Manukau 0; Manawatu 14 Auckland 12.
Final   Manawatu 17 Waikato 15.
Play-off for 3rd/4th Auckland 24 Counties Manukau 0.

PLATE CHAMPIONSHIP

Semi-finals   Bay of Plenty 29 Canterbury 10; Wellington 33 Otago 0.
Final (5th/6th)   Bay of Plenty 36 Wellington 7.
Play-off for 7th/8th Otago 10 Canterbury 5.

BOWL CHAMPIONSHIP

Semi-finals   North Harbour 26 Hawke's Bay 12; Southland 15 Poverty Bay 14.
Final   Southland 25 North Harbour 0.
Play-off for 11th/12th Hawke's Bay 17 Poverty Bay 0.

Tournament referees: Maggie Cogger-Orr, Monique Dalley, Lauren Jenner, Rebecca Mahoney, Madeline Putz-Skiba (*Australia*).

Anna Richards Trophy (*Player of the Tournament*):
2013   Selica Winiata (*Manawatu*)
2014   Hazel Tubic (*Counties Manukau*)
2015   Kayla McAlister (*Auckland*)
2016   Katarina Whata-Simpkins (*Wellington*)
2017   Kelly Brazier (*Bay of Plenty*)
2018   (January) Tenika Willison (*Waikato*);
       (December) Sarah Goss (*Manawatu*).

NATIONAL SEVENS

Tauranga Domain December 15/16, 2018

POOL

A Auckland 24, Taranaki 0; Otago 24, Canterbury 12;
 Auckland 41, Otago 0; Canterbury 24, Taranaki 19;
 Auckland 24, Canterbury 5; Otago 26, Taranaki 17.

B Manawatu 27, North Harbour 5; Wellington 33, Counties Manukau 21;
 Manawatu 29, Wellington 12; Counties Manukau 31, North Harbour 14;
 Manawatu 31, Counties Manukau 12; Wellington 31, North Harbour 12.

C Waikato 32, Tasman 12; Bay of Plenty 22, Hawke's Bay 12;
 Waikato 50, Hawke's Bay 0; Bay of Plenty 26, Tasman 0;
 Bay of Plenty 24, Waikato 7; Tasman 14, Hawke's Bay 7.

CUP CHAMPIONSHIP

Quarter-finals Auckland 17, Canterbury 5; Waikato 26, Wellington 7;
 Bay of Plenty 19, Otago 12; Manawatu 21, Counties Manukau 0.
Semi-finals Waikato 19, Auckland 12; Manawatu 31, Bay of Plenty 5.
Final Manawatu 12, Waikato 7.
Play-off for 3rd/4th Auckland 14, Bay of Plenty 5.

PLATE CHAMPIONSHIP

Semi-finals Canterbury 24, Wellington 14; Counties Manukau 19, Otago 10.
Final (5th/6th) Canterbury 24, Counties Manukau 19.
Play-off for 7th/8th Wellington 31, Otago 17.

BOWL CHAMPIONSHIP

Semi-finals Tasman 26, Hawke's Bay 17; North Harbour 22, Taranaki 14.
Final Tasman 24, North Harbour 5.
Play-off for 11th/12th Hawke's Bay 17, Taranaki 14.

Tournament referees: Larissa Collingwood, Monique Dalley, Lauren Jenner, Amy Perrett (Australia)

TOURNAMENT TROPHY WINNERS

	Venue	Cup	Plate	Bowl
1998	Rotorua	Auckland		
1999	Palmerston North	Wellington		
2000	Palmerston North	Bay of Plenty		
2001	Palmerston North	Auckland		
2002	Palmerston North	Canterbury		
2013	Queenstown	Manawatu		
2014	Rotorua	Manawatu	Taranaki	Canterbury
2015	Rotorua	Auckland	Wellington	Otago
2016	Rotorua	Manawatu	Waikato	Tasman
2017	Rotorua	Counties Manukau	Bay of Plenty	Taranaki
2018	Rotorua (Jan)	Manawatu	Bay of Plenty	Southland
	Tauranga (Dec)	Manawatu	Canterbury	Tasman

PLAYING RECORD OF NEW ZEALAND SEVENS TEAMS

	Tournaments			Games				Points	
	Attended	Won	Runner-up	Played	Won	Draw	Lost	For	Against
2000	1	1	–	7	7	–	–	293	20
2001	3	3	–	15	15	–	–	661	17
2008	1	–	1	6	4	–	2	174	57
2009	1	–	1	6	5	–	1	177	37
2012	2	2	–	12	10	2	–	378	69
2013	6	3	1	36	30	–	6	958	279
2014	6	5	1	37	36	–	1	1102	262
2015	6	3	–	36	30	–	6	1011	402
2016	6	1	3	36	30	–	6	915	279
2017	7	5	–	41	39	–	2	1018	251
2018	8	7	1	45	44	–	1	1432	307
TOTALS	**47**	**30**	**8**	**277**	**250**	**2**	**25**	**7204**	**1980**

CHRONICLE OF EVENTS

JANUARY 2018

10 NZR Judicial Committee suspends four club players for possession, use, or attempted use of banned substances under NZ Sports Anti-Doping rules. All four, who were playing club rugby in 2017, plead guilty. Two are banned for four years, one for two years and one for 21 months, from various dates in 2017.

11 Lima Sopoaga announces he has signed for English club Wasps . . . Sky TV announces Rikki Swannell has been added to its roster of rugby play-by-play commentators, making her the first female in the role. She has been a play-by-play commentator for netball on Sky TV . . . Finalists for the Halberg Awards are announced and include: Sportswoman of the Year Portia Woodman; Sportsman of the Year Beauden Barrett; Team of the Year Black Ferns; Coach of the Year — Glenn Moore.

12 NZR releases its list of High Performance referees for 2018 and women are included for the first time: *Professional Squad* — Nick Briant, Mike Fraser, Glen Jackson, Jamie Nutbrown, Brendon Pickerill, Ben O'Keeffe, Paul Williams; *National Squad* who will officiate in the Mitre 10 Cup, Heartland Championship and Farah Palmer Cup — Tipene Cottrell, James Doleman, Natarsha Ganley (new), Tim Griffiths, Nick Hogan, Richard Kelly, Mike Lash, Damian MacPherson (new), Rebecca Mahoney (new), Angus Mabey, James Munro, Hugh Reed, Cameron Stone, Michael Winter, Nick Webster; *Wider Training Squad* of 12, including four women, who will officiate at the Jock Hobbs National Under 19 tournament.

18 The New Plymouth District Council receives an engineer's report on the main West (TSB) stand, housing 3300 covered seats, team changing sheds, corporate boxes, and Taranaki RU office, at Yarrow Stadium. It will either need strengthening work or be demolished. In November a preliminary inspection of the West Stand found it was earthquake prone and the Taranaki Rugby Union immediately vacated its office. In December the Chiefs transferred their scheduled 7 April home match at New Plymouth v Blues to Hamilton. Taranaki will still play their Ranfurly Shield/Mitre 10 Cup matches at Yarrow Stadium this year but with the West Stand out of action.

19 Liam Messam has signed for French club Toulon.

23 Highlanders announce they will play their home match v the Chiefs in Suva on 30 June. The match was originally to have been played at Invercargill. Instead a non-competition match will be played at Invercargill during the June Super Rugby break while the tests are on.

25 NZR launches an independent online and 0800 complaints management service to provide ready access for people to raise complaints about inappropriate conduct in rugby. Employment lawyer Steph Dyheberg has been appointed the independent manager of the complaints process. This was one of the recommendations of last year's Respect and Responsibility review . . . 18-year old Etene Nanai-Seturo of Counties Manukau is selected to debut in the All Blacks sevens team at Sydney. The NZ Warriors maintain he is signed to them, having signed a five-year contract when aged 15 to the end of 2019. Last year Nanai-Seturo had sent a resignation letter to the Warriors but not a request for a release from his contract.

29 The All Blacks from last year's end of year tour start training with their Super Rugby clubs but are still ineligible to play any pre-season games for another two weeks . . . SANZAAR releases its Super Rugby referee team for 2018. Because of the reduction of teams and matches this year, the number of referees has been reduced from 19 to 17. NZ has the largest representation with seven: Nick Briant, Mike Fraser, Glen Jackson, Jamie Nutbrown, Ben O'Keeffe, Brendon Pickerill and Paul Williams.

30   Hurricanes coach Chris Boyd announces he will leave the job after this year's competition to take up a three-year contract with English club Northampton as director of rugby . . . French club Lyon confirm the signing of Charlie Ngatai.
31   NZR will host this year's third Bledisloe Cup test at Yokohama, Japan on 27 October. A test against Japan in Tokyo the following Saturday on 3 November was announced last year . . . French club Bordeaux announces the signing the Seta Tamanivalu.

FEBRUARY

4   NZR General Manager of Rugby Neil Sorensen confirms the NZR Board has approved a change in qualification for All Blacks coaching eligibility. Any offshore-based NZ coach can now apply for the job. Previously, a candidate had to have coached at Super Rugby or Mitre Cup in the preceding 12 months or have at least three years' experience in those roles in the last five years.

7   NZR CEO Steve Tew confirms the All Blacks will be involved in four one-day assemblies and two three-day camps during the Super Rugby season. These are being held due to NZ teams starting Super Rugby one week later than the South African teams and therefore will only break six days before the All Blacks first test against France in June.

8   Glenn Moore is reappointed Black Ferns coach for 2018–19 . . . Halberg Awards: Crusaders' Mitch Hunt wins the Best Sporting Moment award chosen by the public, with his last-minute drop goal for the Crusaders in their win over the Highlanders; Steve Hansen receives the Sport NZ Leadership Award.

9   The Black Ferns Sevens contracted squad for 2018 is named. The list of 23 (20 fully contracted and 3 training contracts) includes six new players.

12   The Ministry of Business, Innovation and Employment releases its report of the economic impact and benefit to New Zealand generated by the 2017 British and Irish Lions tour: 25,760 visitors came to New Zealand for the matches, and with 56,260 domestic travellers, combined they contributed $194 million to New Zealand's GDP.

15   The NZ Secondary Schools Sports Council census for 2017 reveals that the highest participation sport was netball (28,445), followed by rugby union (26,951) and basketball (26,549) . . . Canterbury and the Crusaders have both bought a 1 per cent share in US Major League Rugby franchise team Seattle Seawolves.

16   NZR and NZ Warriors reach confidential agreement following mediation in the dispute over Etene Nanai-Seturo. They also have agreed on protocols should any future player be interested in changing codes between the two organisations while still under contract to either organisation . . . NZME and Sky TV have reached confidential settlement over NZME using rugby footage from Sky TV in brief highlights clips in NZME's online content. TVNZ, Fairfax and Mediaworks have earlier settled same claims with Sky TV. Sky TV had filed action in the High Court against all four organisations in October 2016.

19   A Te Awamutu club player is suspended from all rugby for four years, backdated to February 2017, for possession and use of banned steroid clenbuterol. The player pleaded guilty to the charge brought by Drug Free Sport NZ . . . Tonia Cawood is appointed Chairman of the Chiefs from Dallas Fisher who has stepped down from the role. She is the first woman chairman of a NZ Super Rugby club . . . Wellington announces the signing of former rep Thomas Waldrom from English club Exeter Chiefs. Waldrom left NZ in 2010 and played four tests for England.

23   Deb Robinson, current Black Ferns doctor and former All Blacks doctor, is appointed NZR's first woman representative on the World Rugby Council. In November last year World Rugby approved a 2017–2025 Women's Plan to accelerate women in rugby on and off the field, including gender balance to its highest levels of governance. The 11

Chronicle of Events

unions and six regional associations who have gained an extra vote have the right to send an additional representative to the World Rugby Council subject to that person being female. This will increase the number of people who may sit on the Council from 32 to 49, with the extra 17 all being women . . . NZR also releases the dates of the now six All Blacks assemblies to be held during Super Rugby: South Island foundation days in Christchurch for the Crusaders and Highlanders All Blacks on Mondays 12 March and 16 April; North Island foundation days for the Blues/Chiefs/Hurricanes All Blacks on Tuesday 20 March (Auckland) and Monday 23 April (Wellington) and three-day preparation camps for all on Sundays to Tuesdays 20–22 May (Auckland) and 27–29 May (Christchurch).

26 Canterbury report a loss of $21,819 for 2017.
27 Wyatt Crockett announces his retirement from international rugby, and after completing this Super Rugby season for the Crusaders will play for Tasman for two years . . . Hawke's Bay announces a profit of $15,334.
28 Jerome Kaino confirms a move to French club Toulouse and will leave after the Super Rugby season.

MARCH

1 NZR announces a record profit for 2017 of $33.4 million. Income was a record $257 million.
2 NZR announces a co-operation agreement with English club Harlequins. The two organisations will share in a number of projects relating to playing, coaching, team training and commercial opportunities.
7 Hurricanes confirm assistant coach John Plumtree will take over as head coach for 2019–2021 once Chris Boyd steps down after the 2018 campaign (see 30 Jan) . . . Manawatu announces a loss of $237,982.
9 NZR General Manager Neil Sorensen has resigned and will leave at the end of the month. He has been with the organisation for 17 years.
10 Club competitions in NZ start with opening rounds in Counties Manukau and Northland.
12 NZR and NZ Rugby Players Association announce a professional performance programme for the Black Ferns. A minimum 30 players will be contracted yearly with a guaranteed retainer (four tiers from $12,500 to $20,000); assembly fees ($2000 per week); a share of a Black Ferns Legacy Fund ($100,000 this year, $150,000 in 2019) based on experience-related criteria; each player in the 2017 World Cup-winning team will be offered a standalone role as a Rugby World Cup Legacy Ambassador to undertake promotional activity at a payment of $10,000; if a player becomes pregnant, NZR must be notified no later than the end of the first trimester. The player's contract will continue for two months after the first trimester, at which point the player can go on unpaid leave or into safe employment within the rugby network until such time as maternity leave is undertaken. If the player returns to the programme after having their child, the player will be entitled to have a support person of their choice to travel and stay with them to look after the infant while they are on assembly. The travel and accommodation cost of the support person is to be met by the Player Payment Pool (capped at $15,000 per year) until the infant is one year old.
16 The draws for the Mitre 10 Cup and Heartland Championship are released . . . NZR announces a change to its refereeing structure. Current NZR High Performance Coach Bryce Lawrence will head a new structure as National Referee Manager that will oversee both High Performance and Community Refereeing in NZ.

19	SANZAAR Game Manager Lyndon Bray issues a warning to all Super Rugby teams in the wake of the weekend's Highlanders v Crusaders match. Crusader's Jordan Taufua was awarded a try, and as Mitchell Hunt had the ball placed for the conversion attempt, Highlanders co-captain Ben Smith walked out to where the kick was to be taken, interrupted the conversion attempt, and asked referee Nick Briant to consult the TMO over Taufua's try. The officials were actually already engaged in conversation about reviewing the try when Ben Smith reached Nick Briant. The try was then referred to the TMO who ruled out the try. As the perception of the TV audience and ground attendance was that Smith had influenced the outcome, Lyndon Bray's warning to all teams is that it is outside the boundaries of good practice to approach the referee while a conversion is being attempted and will not be tolerated . . . Waitakiri Primary School in Canterbury inform parents they will not offer rugby as an option this year after a child suffered severe concussion last year whilst playing rugby.
21	The NZ men's and women's sevens teams for the Commonwealth Games are announced. There are no new caps in either team . . . Otago announces a profit of $58,986 . . . The 20th anniversary edition of *ESPN The Magazine* lists the dominant 20 sports teams of the last 20 years: 16 of the 20 are American franchise teams, the four non-American teams are: the 2002–03 Australian cricket team (2nd), the 2013–14 Real Madrid football team (11th), 2002 Brazil football team (13th), the 2015 All Blacks (17th).
25	Counties Manukau announces a loss of $179,987.
27	Northland announces a profit of $78,806 . . . Waikato record a profit of $532,182 and back into positive equity.
28	Sky TV announces it has been advised it is not the preferred bidder for the NZ rights to screen the 2019 World Cup. Within 30 minutes of the NZ Stock Exchange opening, Sky's share price drops 7 per cent . . . Bay of Plenty show a profit of $156,472 . . . North Harbour a profit of $49,375 . . . Wellington a profit of $204,000.
31	Buller celebrate their 125th jubilee.

APRIL

4	Taranaki announces a profit of $235,643.
5	A player registered to the Uawa club in East Coast receives a two-year ban backdated to 17 July last year for the use of clenbuterol, resulting from last year's investigation into the activity of NZ website Clenbuterol NZ.
9	NZR opens its first Official All Blacks Store, at Auckland Airport . . . The June test window will see NZ refereeing involvement in 15 of the 28 tests, with 10 referees involved in referee, assistant referee, and TMO duties . . . Tasman announces a profit of $69,249.
10	Hurricanes promote their upcoming derby match v Chiefs at Wellington as 'Taranaki Land War' on their Facebook and Twitter pages. After an hour the promotion is removed in response to angry posts on the social media platforms, and the Hurricanes make a public apology.
14	An article in *The New Zealand Herald* spotlights the current nature of Auckland club rugby. In 2017 the ethnic make-up of the club competitions in the province was 65 per cent Polynesian, 24 per cent Pakeha, 10 per cent Maori. In terms of population the 2013 census of the province recorded 60 per cent Pakeha, 14.6 per cent Polynesian.
16	Spark announces it has won the NZ broadcast rights to the 2019 Rugby World Cup, as well as the 2018 World Rugby Under 20 Championship and 2018 Rugby World Cup Sevens. The 2019 World Cup matches will be streamed live and on demand on TVs, mobiles, desktops, laptops and tablets. Advertisements will not run during live game

	time, and pricing details and options will be announced next year. Spark has reached agreement with TVNZ on free-to-air TV coverage, with TVNZ to screen seven games live, including the opening game and final.
17	Mike Anthony is appointed NZR Head of High Performance. He replaces Don Tricker who announced a move to San Diego baseball club in December. Anthony shifts from his NZR High Performance Player Development role.
18	English newspaper *The Guardian* claims England coach Eddie Jones will have the approval of the England RU if he wishes to select Hurricanes player Brad Shields for England's three-test tour to South Africa in June during the Super Rugby break. Shields has played for the Hurricanes since 2012 and his contract with them expires at the end of this year's Super Rugby competition when he will then join English club Wasps. Shields qualifies for England as both his parents were born in England.
19	NZR Annual Meeting: Sir Michael Jones is a new Elected member to the Board, defeating Dame Annette King in a vote to replace Glenn Wahlstrom. Farah Palmer has been re-elected as a Nominated member for the Maori representative place on the Board by the Appointments and Remuneration Committee. Dick Littlejohn is elected a Life Member.
20	NZR receives a formal request from Brad Shields for a release to be available to play for England in South Africa during the Super Rugby break in June.
23	Manawatu Cyclones rep Aroha Nuku receives a two-year ban following a failed drugs test, which showed use of methamphetamine, after the Manawatu Cyclones v Waikato match on 22 September last year. The ban is backdated to 22 September last year.
24	Despite the Blues having won only two of their eight games so far this year, lost their last 15 matches to NZ teams, and falling crowds, Blues CEO Michael Redman says coach Tana Umaga has his support and that of the Board . . . The Crusaders and the Highlanders will both play the French Barbarians during the June Super Rugby break, and the All Blacks Game of Three Halves match this year will be at Christchurch against Canterbury and Otago. The Black Ferns will play their two Laurie O'Reilly Memorial Trophy tests against Australia in Sydney and Auckland on the same nights as the Bledisloe Cup matches in those cities.
26	NZR signs a three-year partnership with NZ technology company VX Sport. VX Sport collects athletes' physical data via wearable devices.
27	Minister for Greater Christchurch Regeneration Megan Woods says a new roofed stadium will be built in Christchurch. The final design and costings will be subject to a business case. Christchurch City Council has $253 million budgeted towards it.
30	Southland announces a profit of $110,387.

MAY

1	Former referee Paul Honiss is appointed NZR High Performance Referee Coach. Matt Peters is appointed NZR National Referee Development Manager.
3	*The Sydney Morning Herald* reveals a leaked current SANZAAR discussion document — *SANZAAR 2030 Strategy* — canvasses five options for the future: contraction, retention, three alternatives of expansion.
6	*WalesOnline* reports that three more South African Super Rugby teams will leave Super Rugby and join the Guinness Pro14 competition (Ireland, Italy, Scotland, Wales with already two South African ex-Super Rugby teams — the Kings and the Cheetahs). The Sharks, the Lions and the Stormers will all join in time for the 2020–21 season.
7	SANZAAR issues a statement that South African teams leaving Super Rugby 'is unsubstantiated speculation and simply wrong' with all four members of SANZAAR

committed to future participation in Super Rugby and the Rugby Championship, and currently engaged in a detailed planning process for both competitions through to 2030.

9 NZ Under 20 squad is named for the World Championship in France. The 28-man squad contains two players who did not play at the Oceania Under 20 Championship — Caleb Clarke and Xavier Numia — while four players who played at the Oceania Championship — Suetana Asomua, Ciarahn Matoe, Carlos Price and Ngane Punivai — missed selection.

10 NZR grants temporary release for Brad Shields to be available for England selection during the Super Rugby break. Although not contractually obliged to do so — he is currently eligible for NZ (born in New Zealand and lived all his life here) as well as England (the birthplace of his parents) and his contract with NZR was for availability to only NZ teams — NZR took into consideration his long-standing service to the Hurricanes and his leaving to play for English club Wasps and granted the request . . . World Rugby launches tender process for hosting of the 2021 Women's World Cup. Unions have until 31 May to submit an expression of interest. Bid documents will be distributed to interested unions on 1 June and bid responses must be submitted by 10 August. The World Rugby Council will select the host on 14 November. The 2021 tournament will remain at 12 teams but will increase to a 35-day tournament (from 23 days) to give longer rest periods between games, and the addition of a quarter-final round. Squad sizes will increase by two to 30 players.

12 Rikki Swannell debuts with her play-by-play commentary on the Crusaders v Waratahs match for Sky TV (see 11 January).

16 The Black Ferns and Maori All Blacks will both play against USA national teams in Chicago on 3 November as part of a triple bill with the Ireland v Italy fixture . . . Blues announce Tana Umaga has been reappointed as Head Coach for 2019 . . . World Rugby Council annual meeting in Dublin, its first meeting with the increased membership (to 49 from 32) announced in November last year, although only 43 seats were filled. The 12 laws which have been trialled in the Northern Hemisphere since August and the Southern Hemisphere since January are approved into law with immediate effect, the major ones being: (1) Uncontested scrums must have eight players; (2) Penalties can be kicked to touch for a lineout after halftime and fulltime have elapsed; (3) Where multiple penalty infringements occur in a movement the non-offending team can choose the most advantageous; (4) Penalty try is worth 7 points — there will be no conversion attempt; (5) Referee no longer is to give a signal to the halfback to put the ball into a scrum; (6) At a scrum the hooker of the team putting the ball in must make a compulsory strike for the ball; (7) At a scrum the number eight can pick the ball up from under the feet of players in the second row; (8) Tackler must get up before playing the ball and then only play the ball from their side of the tackle gate; (9) The offside line at a ruck is created when at least one player is on his feet and over the ball which is on the ground; (10) The ball cannot be kicked in a ruck except raked backwards. NZR CEO Steve Tew also joins the Rugby World Cup Board.

18 Details of the report by PricewaterhouseCoopers commissioned last year by the Auckland Council into a brand-new downtown/waterfront stadium considers a rectangular football stadium with a retractable roof could be built in one of six possible locations for a cost of $1.5 billion. Seating would be 25,000 and expand to 55,000 for test matches. The report also looked at upgrading Eden Park as an alternative to a new downtown stadium, and the cost would be $700–800 million . . .

20 The All Blacks squad for the three tests against France in June is announced. The 33-man squad contains three new players in Shannon Frizell, Jordan Taufua and

Chronicle of Events

Te Toiroa Tahuriorangi. In addition, Liam Coltman (injury cover) and Akira Ioane (development) will also assemble. All Blacks captain Kieran Read is unavailable as he recovers from injury and Sam Whitelock will captain the side.

22 NZR announces that the Black Ferns will be officially capped from now on, and so far 193 players have played test rugby for the Black Ferns. Capping ceremonies will take place over the next three years to ensure all current and past representatives will receive a cap.

23 The first contracts offered to the Black Ferns are announced, with 28 players securing contracts. A further two contracted positions are still to be filled. In addition, 20 players will be identified to make up a wider training squad.

25 World Rugby announces the World Under-20 Championship will trial new laws to reduce the risk of head injury. The tackler must be bent at the waist when making a tackle. A high-tackle warning will be issued if the tackler is upright and there is clear and obvious head contact for either player. This can be called by any match official during the match or by the citing commissioner after the match. If a second warning is issued, the player will receive a one-match ban.

28 Tasman/Crusaders player Peter Samu signs for the Brumbies for 2019 and Rugby Australia has requested NZR provide a temporary release so he can be available for Australia during their test series v Ireland in the Super Rugby break. Born in Australia, Samu came to NZ in 2014 when signing for Tasman and is also eligible for NZ on residency.

31 Deadline ends for expressions of interest to host the 2021 Women's World Cup. Six unions confirm their interest by the end of day: New Zealand, Australia, England, France, Portugal, and Wales.

JUNE

1 Part one of the six-part documentary *All or Nothing: New Zealand All Blacks* debuts on Amazon.com streaming platform *Prime Video*. An Amazon film crew was given inside behind-the-scenes access following the All Blacks last year from the British and Irish Lions series through to the last Bledisloe Cup test.

2 NZR and Rugby Australia reach agreement on Pete Samu to be available for Australian selection during the Super Rugby break this month. Still signed to Tasman for this year's Mitre 10 Cup, he has also been released from his contract by Tasman.

4 Queen's Birthday Honours List: Officer of NZOM — Black Fern Fiao'o Faamausili; Member of NZOM — *Rugby Almanack* co-editor Clive Akers, former Black Fern Rochelle Martin, Sky TV commentator Grant Nisbett, and current Counties Manukau coach/former Black Ferns coach Darryl Suasua . . . Blues Chairman Tony Carter says he will stand down at the end of the Super Rugby season. With the team's current record 3–10 and not having made the playoffs since 2011, the organisation probably needs more rugby expertise at board level.

5 New Plymouth District Council informs Taranaki RU that their home ground Yarrow Stadium is closed for the foreseeable future with the West Stand also now declared closed due to the ground underneath having been now deemed an earthquake risk (also see 18 Jan).

8 First capping ceremony for the Black Ferns, at Auckland. The first 46 caps are handed out.

11 Luke Crawford is appointed to a new NZR role of Maori Advisor and Kaumatua to the Maori All Blacks.

12 SANZAAR releases the draw for next year's Super Rugby tournament. With no June test matches because of being a World Cup year, the tournament will run uninterrupted from 15 February to 6 July.

16	The All Blacks v France Test at Wellington is Sky TV commentator Grant Nisbett's 300th test match. His first test call was the 1984 All Blacks v France match at Christchurch.
18	Julian Savea confirms a move to French club Toulon.
19	Molenberg will sponsor the Black Ferns and Black Ferns Sevens teams for two years. The Molenberg logo will feature on their shorts.
25	Taranaki RU announce Yarrow Stadium will, after all, be used for their home games this year. The Southern and Northern terraces will be available to the public and the Stadium will operate on a reduced capacity of 14,000 with the East and West Stands both out of action.
26	Christchurch City Council announces it will bring forward to 2021, from 2023, $253 million in funding for a covered stadium. The cost will be about $500 million with the government contributing $220 million. Capacity will be about 30,000.
27	Sport and Recreation Minister Grant Robertson confirms the government will contribute financial support to New Zealand's bid to host the 2021 Women's World Cup... All Black captain Kieran Read plays his first match of the year — 40 minutes for Counties Manukau in their pre-season match against Tasman.
29	NZR announces a review of Secondary Schools Rugby to consider growth and retention of teenage participants. Schools, clubs and provincial unions will be consulted and submissions can be made by the public. An independent project team from across the rugby spectrum will carry out the process.

JULY

3	A young player is suspended from all rugby for four years, backdated to 1 August 2017, for the use of banned substance clenbuterol that he used while still at school in 2014.
6	The Maori All Blacks will play against Chile and Brazil, for the very first time, on their end of year tour in November... Crusaders home ground of AMI Stadium is renamed Wyatt Crockett Stadium just for tonight's match v Highlanders. Crockett becomes the first player to play 200 Super Rugby matches in the history of the competition.
10	The All Blacks Sevens and Black Ferns Sevens teams for the World Cup in San Francisco are named.
11	The Black Ferns will make a two-test tour of France in November and will also have a Game of Three Halves fixture against Bay of Plenty and Auckland next month as preparation for their two tests against Australia... The draw for the Farah Palmer Cup is released and will feature 12 teams, with Taranaki an additional team this year. Sixteen of the matches, including one semi-final and the final, will be screened live by Sky TV.
16	SANZAAR announces that the current protocols of the use of the TMO are 'clearly not working' and a review is needed by World Rugby. In SANZAAR's opinion the TMO interventions for foul play are taking away from the referee their ability to remain the key decision maker on the field. In the Reds v Sunwolves match at Brisbane on the weekend the TMO spotted a Sunwolves player striking a Reds player in a ruck (missed by the three officials on the park) and the referee was required to stop the game to review the incident. The offending player received a red card and the coaches of both teams were critical of the intervention.
17	Black Ferns squad for the two tests against Australia next month is announced. The 28-strong squad includes eight uncapped players — Krysten Cottrell, Ruahei Demant, Alena Saili, Monica Tagoai, Joanah Ngan-Woo, Marcelle Parkes, Leilani Perese and Cristo Tofa.

19 North Otago ban a spectator for five years for punching the referee at the end of a Citizens Shield semi-final match last weekend. The player also faces criminal charges in the Oamaru District Court.

24 NZR confirms the Jock Hobbs Memorial National Under 19 tournament will remain in Taupo for 2019–2021 . . . Three players receive two-year suspensions (backdated to 2017) for doping offences, including two first-class players Brandyn Laursen and Tukiterangi Raimona, as investigations continue into the operations of website Clenbuterol NZ and its supply of banned substances . . . NZR announces open trials for any aspiring male and female player to play sevens, known as the Ignite7 programme. The initiative invites 18 to 20 year olds from anywhere in the country, even if not currently involved in rugby, to make application if interested. From these, 48 men and 48 women will be selected to attend a four-day camp in November — the fourth day being a one-day tournament.

AUGUST

6 The All Blacks 33-man squad for the Rugby Championship is announced. Dropped from the squad that played France are Jeffrey Toomaga-Allen, Vaea Fifita, and Ngani Laumape while Jordan Taufua is missing through injury. In are Kieran Read, Dane Coles, Karl Tu'inukuafe and Jackson Hemopo — Tu'inukuafe and Hemopo both played against France through injuries in that squad. Liam Coltman and Ngani Laumape will assemble as injury cover.

7 NZR launches Mitre 10 Cup, Heartland Championship, Farah Palmer Cup competitions. Referees have been given guidelines for interpretation of foul play which will allow for intent of action to be considered: action is deliberate and dangerous and with force = red card; action is reckless but dangerous but with limited force = yellow card; action is unintentional and low level = penalty only. Teams with a maximum travel of six hours to an away game by road will travel by bus. If the journey is more than six hours by road, teams will travel by air. Previously, NZR had set the threshold at four hours.

9 Taranaki confirms the signing of former All Black Brendon Leonard who has returned from overseas.

10 The All Blacks defeat Otago 32–0 and Cantabrians 40–5 in their Game-of-Three-Halves hit-out in Christchurch. In the first half Otago defeated Cantabrians 28–12 . . . Deadline for submission of bids to World Rugby for hosting of the 2021 Women's World Cup. NZR has submitted its bid, which contains matches being played at Auckland, Albany and Whangarei, with the bid having the financial backing of the government.

11 The Black Ferns defeat Bay of Plenty 44–0 and Auckland 46–0 in their Game-of-Three-Halves hit-out in Tauranga. In the final half Auckland defeats Bay of Plenty 10–0 . . . AMI's sponsorship of AMI Stadium in Christchurch ends. The home ground of Canterbury and Crusaders will be known as Christchurch Stadium for the time being.

25 NZR hosts a women in rugby governance conference at Auckland with the 40 women serving in governance roles on NZR/Maori/Provincial Unions and Boards/Super Rugby boards to support the growth of women in governance and leadership roles across rugby in New Zealand . . . At Te Aroha in the opening Heartland Championship round, West Coast player Brad Houston suffers a heart attack early in the second half. He was given CPR for 45 minutes and taken to Waikato Hospital.

31 South Canterbury confirms plans for an upgrade of their home ground Alpine Energy Stadium into a multi-purpose facility at a cost of $3.6 million by 2020. Both fields will be regressed with a hybrid mixture of real and artificial grass for all, and a new two-

storey commercial complex is to replace the Eastern Stand . . . After an independent review of the Blues governance structure and 2018 Super Rugby campaign, Bolton Equities Limited, the largest shareholder (40 per cent) of the Blues, has agreed to sell its interest back to NZR who will take over the running on an interim basis. NZR and the other shareholders will look to find a new group of investors.

SEPTEMBER

2 The annual All Blacks To The Nation visit this year sees the squad split into five groups to visit the communities of Drury, New Plymouth, Invercargill, Nelson and Blenheim.

13 Blues announce the signing of Ma'a Nonu on a one-year deal for 2019. Nonu has been playing for French club Toulon since leaving after the 2015 World Cup . . . French newspaper *L'Equipe* reports Lyon have tabled an offer to Beauden Barrett of a reputed world record $1.5 million euros a season (NZ$2.6 million) to sign after next year's World Cup.

15 Rebecca Mahoney becomes the first woman to referee a men's NZ first-class fixture when she officiates the Thames Valley v King Country Heartland Championship match at Paeroa.

17 This week's round of matches in the Mitre 10 Cup and Farah Palmer Cup will mark the 125th anniversary of NZ women gaining the right to vote (legislation signed by the Governor on 19 September 1893 to vote in the 28 November election) with a Wahine Round celebrating the involvement of women in rugby. Five double-header Farah Palmer Cup and Mitre 10 Cup matches have been scheduled with four of the five Farah Palmer Cup matches being shown live on Sky TV. Referees will wear purple uniforms as an acknowledgement to the official colour of women's suffrage.

18 World Rugby and the IOC announce the qualifying process for the men's and women's sevens tournaments at the 2020 Tokyo Olympics: 12 countries will participate in each, with Japan as host having automatic entry. The other 11 spots will be filled in three stages. (1) The top four countries at the end of the 2018–19 World Rugby Sevens Series; (2) One winner from each of six regional qualifying tournaments; (3) The last remaining spot to come from an Olympic repechage event.

19 NZR releases its registered player numbers for 2018. Total number of 157,218 is up 1 per cent, including 27,838 female players (up 14.6 per cent), males 5 to12 number 69,123; males 13 to 20 number 33,780 (down 4.8 per cent), males 21 and over number 26,477 . . . The Ligue Nationale de Rugby, who run the French Top 14 club competition, announces that the salary cap for each club in the following three seasons (2019/20–2021/22) will be 1.3 million euros (NZ$19.8 million) per season.

20 NZR has appointed three directors to the seven-member Blues Board — Richard Dellabarca, John Hart, and Sam Lotu-liga.

22 Horowhenua Kapiti celebrates its 125th jubilee.

24–28 World Rugby meets in Sydney. Considered is a proposal to scrap the proposed July and November test windows from 2020 and have a 12-team tournament each year hosted on an alternating basis in the Northern and Southern Hemispheres, with four pools of three followed by semi-final and final. This would add meaning to tests instead of the plethora of friendlies.

OCTOBER

1 In the Hamilton District Court, Waikato winger Sevu Reece is discharged without conviction over a domestic violence incident on 1 July, to allow him to take up a contract with Irish province Connacht he had signed in May.

4 Connacht cancels its contract with Reece.

6	West Coast's home ground of Rugby Park, Greymouth is officially renamed John Sturgeon Park. Sturgeon served the West Coast RU on the Management Committee, including as Chairman, and a Life Member, and the NZRU on the Council, as President, and as All Blacks' manager. The venue has been West Coast's home ground since 1931.
8	Thames Valley wear a special charity jersey for their match against Horowhenua Kapiti. Afterwards the jerseys are sold on Trade Me and raise $19,340 for Goldfields school.
9	The All Blacks will select 51 players for the end of year tour. The main body of 32 will play Australia in Japan on 27 October and the three tests in Europe, while another 19 players will be selected solely for the test against Japan on 3 November. This will allow 22 of the 32-man squad to head to Europe straight after the 27 October test to prepare for the test against England on 10 November, instead of after the 3 November test.
10	West Coast are fined $4000 for fielding an ineligible player. In the first four rounds they recorded a player as a local when he did not meet that criteria. West Coast brought the breach to NZR's attention when they realised the error. Half of the $4000 fine is suspended for five years.
11	In the November test window, Brendon Pickerill, Glen Jackson (2), Ben O'Keeffe (2) and Paul Williams (2) will referee internationals, while Mike Fraser will be an assistant referee, and Aaron Paterson and Ben Skeen (2) will be TMOs.
12	NZR Appeal Council hears an appeal by nine Heartland Unions on the West Coast case. The Appeal Council uphold the original breach but change the penalty to a deduction of six competition points instead of the financial fine.
13	South Canterbury's home ground of Alpine Energy Stadium is renamed Matt Fetu Stadium for today's match against Thames Valley in honour of Fetu reaching 100 games for the province the previous Saturday at Oamaru.
15	NZR/Waikato issue a statement that a misconduct process against Reece has been completed. He had a one-match ban (last weekend v Otago) and the player has asked to be taken out of consideration for the Duane Monkley medal to Mitre 10 Cup player of the year (he was equal first with Luke Romano and Jack Debreczeni before the Otago match) . . . 51 players are announced for the All Blacks end of year tour, although 19 of them will only be required for the test against Japan and then return home. In the first 32 the only new cap is Dalton Papali'i. The selection of Matt Todd, currently playing Japan, required the approval of the NZR Board.
16	The Black Ferns squad is named for the end of year tour and includes six new caps in Joanah Ngan-Woo, Marcelle Parkes, Ayesha Leti-l'iga, Kilisitina Moata'ane, Nathalia Moors and Monica Tagoai.
22	The three finalists for World Rugby's Women's Sevens Player of the Year are all Black Ferns — Michaela Blyde, Portia Woodman, and captain Sarah Goss.
26	From over 500 applications, 96 athletes have been finalised to take part in the Red Bull Ignite7 event to uncover future sevens stars (see 24 July). They are split into four men's and four women's teams and the tournament at Waitakere will be screened live on Sky TV on 24 November.
27	A crowd of over 20,000 attends the Auckland v Canterbury Mitre 10 Cup Premiership final at Eden Park, as a result of the Auckland RU having announced free entry for the match . . . Karl Tu'inukuafe is a finalist for World Rugby's Breakthrough Player of the Year award.
29	NZR has appointed the Graeme Dingle Foundation as the official charity of the organisation and its national teams in a three-year agreement.

31 The full 38-man squads for our Super Rugby teams in 2019 are announced. There are 33 new fully contracted players across the five teams . . . The new All Blacks jersey is unveiled by adidas. It is 25 per cent lighter and has a white half collar. The jersey will be debuted against Japan on 3 November.

NOVEMBER

1 Taranaki confirm the earthquake-prone West and East Stands at Yarrow Stadium will both still be out of action when the 2019 Mitre 10 Cup competition starts in August. The Union is still considering a move to play at Inglewood's TET Stadium or Hawera's TSB Hub.

2 Beauden Barrett and Rieko Ioane are among the five finalists for World Rugby's Men's Player of the Year and Fiao'o Fa'amausili is one of five finalists for Women's Player of the Year.

5 NZR has appointed Richard Thomas as new Chief Commercial Officer, starting January. He replaces Nick Brown who has resigned.

7 The Mitre 10 Cup unions make their crossover match selections for 2019.

10 In the test against England, the All Blacks wear the RSA poppy on their sleeves in honour of the Centenary of Armistice Day tomorrow, which officially marked the end of World War One 100 years ago.

14 NZR releases the 2019 home test venues. Wellington will host the match v South Africa on 27 July while Auckland will host a double header by the Black Ferns and All Blacks against Australia on 17 August. As usual in a World Cup year, the Rugby Championship tournament is reduced . . . The Blues install Leon MacDonald as head coach for three years, replacing Tana Umaga. Umaga will become an assistant coach . . . World Rugby Executive Council awards the 2021 Women's World Cup to New Zealand.

17 Black Ferns captain Fiao'o Fa'amausili announces her retirement after the final test v France.

20 A 31-year-old Southland club player receives a two-year suspension for anti-doping violations, buying and using banned substances from website NZ Clenbuterol.

22 Australian company Gain Line Analytics ranks the Crusaders as the number one Australasian sporting team in an Australian or Australasian league over the past 25 years with their nine Super Rugby titles. The other 24 teams in the top 25 are Australian teams.

24 From the Red Bull Ignite7 talent search, three women's players — Isla Norman-Bell, Mererangi Paul, Kalyn Takitimu-Cook — and three men's players — William Warbrick, Chay Fihaki, Jacob Kneepkens — are picked to attend national development camps with the All Blacks Sevens and Black Ferns Sevens teams.

25 The All Blacks have added a test against Tonga to their programme for next year. It will be played at Hamilton on 7 September. It will be a 2.35pm kick-off . . . At the World Rugby Awards in Monaco, Michaela Blyde is Sevens Player of the Year, and DJ Forbes receives a Special Merit Award for his sevens career. Johnny Sexton (Ireland) is Men's Player of the Year; Jessy Tremouliere (France) is Women's Player of the Year. Ireland is Team of the Year and Joe Schmidt (Ireland) is Coach of the Year.

26 Considered a contender to be the next All Blacks coach, Joe Schmidt announces he will step down as Ireland coach after the 2019 World Cup and take a break from rugby.

DECEMBER

3 Ten of the 12 schools in the Auckland 1A First XV competition inform Saint Kentigern College they will not play Saint Kentigern in the 2019 competition. The 10 schools

are unhappy at Saint Kentigern's recruitment programme in which five established players from first XVs outside of the province have been recruited for next year. The 10 schools plus King's College last month signed a charter agreeing to a set of principles for future participation in the 1A competition, which Saint Kentigern has declined to sign, claiming they have abided by the rules set by College Sport Auckland, who run the 1A competition, which make no rules about recruitment from outside of Auckland.

4   The Black Ferns Sevens team wins the Lonsdale Cup, awarded annually since 1961 by the NZ Olympic Committee, for best achievement by a NZ team to an Olympic/Commonwealth Games sport.

6   The schools who participate in the North Island's Super Eight competition confirm they will boycott matches against Saint Kentigern also . . . At the request of Saint Kentigern College, College Sport Auckland announces it will set up an independent panel to investigate the saga.

10 Auckland announce a profit of $227,000 for 2018.

11 Five more club players have received bans of up to four years for purchasing prohibited substances from website Clenbuterol NZ in 2014–15.

13 Ben Smith announces he has signed for French club Pau after next year's World Cup . . . High Performance Sport NZ announces $36 million of funding for 2019. The All Blacks Sevens and Black Ferns Sevens will receive $900,000 and $1.2 million respectively, the same as 2018 . . . ASB Rugby Awards: Kendra Cocksedge wins the Kelvin R Tremain Memorial Trophy as player of the year; the Black Ferns Sevens are team of the year, and former All Black Waka Nathan is awarded the Steinlager Salver for outstanding contribution to rugby . . . French club Toulon announces the signing of Nehe Milner-Skudder after next year's World Cup.

14 All Blacks coach Steve Hansen confirms he will stand down after next year's World Cup.

18 In a newsletter sent to parents last week, Saint Kentigern announces it will review its policy on the offering of sports scholarships, with negative feedback from fee-paying parents being a factor in the decision.

20 Rebecca Mahoney will referee two of the Women's Six Nations Championship matches next year.

24 Three more club players receive bans up to four years for having purchased banned substances from NZ website Clenbuterol NZ. This brings to 19 the number of bans in 2018 from this investigation (see 9 Dec 2017).

31 New Year Honour's List: former Auckland and Blues team manager Rex Davy is made a Member of the NZ Order of Merit.

INTERNATIONAL RESULTS 2018

Date	Team 1	Score	Team 2	Score	Venue	Referee
Feb 03	Brazil	16	Chile	14	Santiago	P Deluca (*Argentina*)
Feb 09	Uruguay	27	Brazil	18	Sao Paulo	F Anselmi (*Argentina*)
Feb 10	United States	29	Canada	10	Sacramento	F Gonzalez (*Uruguay*)
Feb 17	United States	45	Chile	13	Fullerton	C Assmus (*Canada*)
Feb 17	Canada	45	Brazil	5	Fullerton	K Weaver (*USA*)
Feb 24	Uruguay	67	Chile	15	Santiago	H Platais (*Brazil*)
Feb 24	United States	43	Brazil	16	São José	F Gonzalez (*Uruguay*)
Mar 03	United States	61	Uruguay	19	Montevideo	F Anselmi (*Argentina*)
Mar 03	Canada	33	Chile	17	La Serena	P Deluca (*Argentina*)
Jun 02	Wales	22	South Africa	20	Washington	M Carley (*England*)
Jun 09	Scotland	48	Canada	10	Edmonton	S Kubo (*Japan*)
Jun 09	Wales	23	Argentina	10	San Juan	A Brace (*Ireland*)
Jun 09	Georgia	16	Tonga	15	Suva	B Pickerill (*NZ*)
Jun 09	Fiji	24	Samoa	22	Suva	M Fraser (*NZ*)
Jun 09	South Africa	42	England	39	Johannesburg	B O'Keeffe (*NZ*)
Jun 09	Australia	18	Ireland	9	Brisbane	M Van der Westhuizen (*SA*)
Jun 09	Japan	34	Italy	17	Oita	N Berry (*Australia*)
Jun 09	New Zealand	52	France	11	Auckland	L Pearce (*England*)
Jun 09	United States	60	Russia	13	Denver	F Anselmi (*Argentina*)
Jun 16	Russia	43	Canada	20	Ottawa	B Whitehouse (*Wales*)
Jun 16	Wales	30	Argentina	12	Santa Fe	J Peyper (*SA*)
Jun 16	Ireland	26	Australia	21	Melbourne	P Williams (*NZ*)
Jun 16	Italy	25	Japan	22	Kobe	N Briant (*NZ*)
Jun 16	United States	30	Scotland	29	Houston	W Barnes (*England*)
Jun 16	Tonga	28	Samoa	18	Suva	M Carley (*England*)
Jun 16	South Africa	23	England	12	Bloemfontein	R Poite (*France*)
Jun 16	New Zealand	26	France	13	Wellington	A Gardner (*Australia*)
Jun 16	Fiji	37	Georgia	15	Suva	J Garces (*France*)
Jun 23	Scotland	44	Argentina	15	Resistencia	M Raynal (*France*)
Jun 23	United States	42	Canada	17	Halifax	A Ruiz (*France*)
Jun 23	England	25	South Africa	10	Cape Town	G Jackson (*NZ*)
Jun 23	Tonga	27	Fiji	19	Suva	L Pearce (*England*)
Jun 23	Ireland	20	Australia	16	Sydney	P Gauzere (*France*)
Jun 23	Japan	28	Georgia	0	Aichi	N Owens (*Wales*)
Jun 23	New Zealand	49	France	14	Dunedin	J Lacey (*Ireland*)
Aug 18	New Zealand	38	Australia	13	Sydney	J Peyper (*SA*)
Aug 18	South Africa	34	Argentina	21	Durban	B O'Keeffe (*NZ*)

Aug 25	Argentina	32	South Africa	19	Mendoza	A Gardner (*Australia*)
Aug 25	New Zealand	40	Australia	12	Auckland	W Barnes (*England*)
Sep 08	Australia	23	South Africa	18	Brisbane	G Jackson (*NZ*)
Sep 08	New Zealand	46	Argentina	24	Nelson	P Gauzere (*France*)
Sep 15	Argentina	23	Australia	19	Gold Coast	J Lacey (*Ireland*)
Sep 15	South Africa	36	New Zealand	34	Wellington	N Owens (*Wales*)
Sep 29	New Zealand	35	Argentina	17	Buenos Aires	M Raynal (*France*)
Sep 29	South Africa	23	Australia	12	Port Elizabeth	J Garces (*France*)
Oct 06	Australia	45	Argentina	34	Salta	J Peyper (*SA*)
Oct 06	New Zealand	32	South Africa	30	Pretoria	A Gardner (*Australia*)
Oct 27	New Zealand	37	Australia	20	Yokohama	R Poite (*France*)
Nov 03	New Zealand	69	Japan	31	Tokyo	M Carley (*England*)
Nov 03	England	12	South Africa	11	London	A Gardner (*Australia*)
Nov 03	Wales	21	Scotland	10	Cardiff	M Raynal (*France*)
Nov 03	Ireland	54	Italy	7	Chicago	N Owens (*Wales*)
Nov 10	South Africa	29	France	26	Paris	N Owens (*Wales*)
Nov 10	New Zealand	16	England	15	London	J Garces (*France*)
Nov 10	United States	30	Samoa	29	San Sebastian	A Ruiz (*France*)
Nov 10	Wales	9	Australia	6	Cardiff	B O'Keeffe (*NZ*)
Nov 10	Ireland	28	Argentina	17	Dublin	N Berry (*Australia*)
Nov 10	Italy	28	Georgia	17	Florence	G Jackson (*NZ*)
Nov 10	Russia	47	Namibia	20	Krasnodar	R Rasivhenghe (*SA*)
Nov 10	Scotland	54	Fiji	17	Edinburgh	A Brace (*Ireland*)
Nov 17	Fiji	68	Uruguay	7	Gloucester	T Foley (*England*)
Nov 17	United States	31	Romania	5	Bucharest	C Maxwell-Keyes (*England*)
Nov 17	Australia	26	Italy	7	Padua	P Gauzere (*France*)
Nov 17	South Africa	26	Scotland	20	Edinburgh	R Poite (*France*)
Nov 17	Ireland	16	New Zealand	9	Dublin	W Barnes (*England*)
Nov 17	Georgia	27	Samoa	19	Tbilisi	K Dickson (*England*)
Nov 17	France	28	Argentina	13	Lille	G Jackson (*NZ*)
Nov 17	England	35	Japan	15	London	P Williams (*NZ*)
Nov 17	Spain	34	Namibia	13	Madrid	P Brousset (*France*)
Nov 17	Wales	74	Tonga	24	Cardiff	N Berry (*Australia*)
Nov 24	New Zealand	66	Italy	3	Rome	A Brace (*Ireland*)
Nov 24	Samoa	28	Spain	10	Madrid	F Murphy (*Ireland*)
Nov 24	Fiji	21	France	14	Paris	M Carley (*England*)
Nov 24	Uruguay	27	Romania	20	Bucharest	B Whitehouse (*Wales*)

Nov 24	Namibia	29	Portugal	23	Coimbra	M Adamson (*Scotland*)
Nov 24	Japan	32	Russia	27	Gloucester	J Garces (*France*)
Nov 24	Scotland	14	Argentina	9	Edinburgh	P Williams (*NZ*)
Nov 24	Wales	20	South Africa	11	Cardiff	L Pearce (*England*)
Nov 24	Georgia	20	Tonga	9	Tbilisi	M Raynal (*France*)
Nov 24	England	37	Australia	18	London	J Peyper (*SA*)
Nov 24	Ireland	57	United States	14	Dublin	B O'Keeffe (*NZ*)

SIX-NATIONS CHAMPIONSHIP

Feb 03	Ireland	15	France	13	Paris	N Owens (*Wales*)
Feb 03	Wales	34	Scotland	7	Cardiff	P Gauzere (*France*)
Feb 04	England	46	Italy	15	Rome	M Raynal (*France*)
Feb 10	England	12	Wales	6	London	J Garces (*France*)
Feb 10	Ireland	56	Italy	19	Dublin	R Poite (*France*)
Feb 11	Scotland	32	France	26	Edinburgh	J Lacey (*Ireland*)
Feb 23	France	34	Italy	17	Marseilles	W Barnes (*England*)
Feb 24	Ireland	37	Wales	27	Dublin	G Jackson (*NZ*)
Feb 24	Scotland	25	England	13	Edinburgh	N Owens (*Wales*)
Mar 10	France	22	England	16	Paris	J Peyper (*SA*)
Mar 10	Ireland	28	Scotland	8	Dublin	W Barnes (*England*)
Mar 11	Wales	38	Italy	14	Cardiff	J Garces (*France*)
Mar 17	Ireland	24	England	15	London	A Gardner (*Australia*)
Mar 17	Scotland	29	Italy	27	Rome	P Gauzere (*France*)
Mar 17	Wales	14	France	13	Cardiff	B O'Keeffe (*NZ*)

FINAL TABLE

	P	W	D	L	For	Against	Pts
Ireland	5	5	0	0	160	82	26
Wales	5	3	0	2	119	83	15
Scotland	5	3	0	2	101	128	13
France	5	2	0	3	108	94	11
England	5	2	0	3	102	92	10
Italy	5	0	0	5	92	203	1

RUGBY WORLD CUP QUALIFICATION MATCHES

EUROPE

Feb 10	Spain	20	Russia	13	Krasnodar	F Murphy (*Ireland*)
Feb 10	Georgia	47	Belgium	0	Kutaisi	M Mitrea (*Romania*)
Feb 10	Romania	85	Germany	6	Cluj	M Burlet (*Belgium*)
Feb 17	Georgia	64	Germany	0	Offenbach	C Evans (*Wales*)
Feb 17	Russia	48	Belgium	7	Krasnodar	I Attorrasagasti (*Spain*)
Feb 18	Spain	22	Romania	10	Madrid	T Charabas (*France*)
Mar 03	Romania	25	Russia	15	Bucharest	A Ruiz (*France*)
Mar 03	Georgia	23	Spain	10	Tbilisi	I Davies (*Wales*)
Mar 03	Belgium	69	Germany	15	Brussels	P Brousett (*France*)
Mar 10	Georgia	29	Russia	9	Krasnodar	A Woodthorpe (*England*)
Mar 10	Romania	62	Belgium	12	Buzau	S Grove-White (*Scotland*)
Mar 11	Spain	84	Germany	10	Madrid	M Mitrea (*Romania*)
Mar 18	Russia	57	Germany	3	Koln	I Tempest (*England*)
Mar 18	Belgium	18	Spain	10	Brussels	V Iordachescu (*Romania*)
Mar 18	Georgia	25	Romania	16	Tbilisi	L Cayre (*France*)

ASIA

Apr 28	South Korea	35	Malaysia	10	Kuala Lumpur	T Baker (*Hong Kong*)
May 05	Hong Kong	67	Malaysia	8	Kuala Lumpur	S Kubo (*Japan*)
May 12	Hong Kong	30	South Korea	21	Incheon	S Kubo (*Japan*)
May 19	South Korea	67	Malaysia	12	Incheon	S Copeman (*Hong Kong*)
May 26	Hong Kong	91	Malaysia	10	Hong Kong	S Kubo (*Japan*)
Jun 02	Hong Kong	39	South Korea	5	Hong Kong	S Kubo (*Japan*)

Africa

Jun 16	Zimbabwe	23	Morocco	23	Harare	Q Immelman (*SA*)
Jun 16	Namibia	55	Uganda	6	Windhoek	C Jadezweni (*SA*)
Jun 23	Kenya	28	Morocco	24	Casablanca	S Minery (*France*)
Jun 24	Namibia	118	Tunisia	0	Windhoek	Q Immelman (*SA*)
Jun 30	Namibia	67	Morocco	3	Casablanca	A Descottes (*France*)
Jun 30	Kenya	45	Zimbabwe	36	Nairobi	T Trainini (*France*)
Jul 07	Tunisia	18	Zimbabwe	14	Monastir	J Dufort (*France*)
Jul 07	Kenya	38	Uganda	22	Nairobi	Q Immelman (*SA*)
Aug 04	Uganda	67	Tunisia	12	Kampala	C Jadezweni (*SA*)
Aug 11	Namibia	58	Zimbabwe	28	Harare	E Seconds (*SA*)
Aug 11	Kenya	67	Tunisia	0	Nairobi	J Castaignede (*France*)

Aug 18	Zimbabwe	38	Uganda	18	Kampala	E Seconds (*SA*)
Aug 18	Uganda	47	Morocco	29	Kampala	R Rasivhenge (*SA*)
Aug 18	Tunisia	36	Morocco	13	Monastir	C Marchat (*France*)
Aug 18	Namibia	53	Kenya	28	Windhoek	C Jadezweni (*SA*)

Repechage & Play-offs

Jan 27	Uruguay	38	Canada	29	Vancouver	A Brace (*Ireland*)
Feb 03	Uruguay	32	Canada	31	Montevideo	L Pearce (*England*)
Jun 16	Germany	16	Portugal	13	Heidelberg	T Foley (*England*)
Jun 30	Samoa	66	Germany	15	Apia	J Garces (*France*)
Jul 01	Hong Kong	26	Cook Islands	3	Rarotonga	B Pickerill (*NZ*)
Jul 07	Hong Kong	51	Cook Islands	0	Hong Kong	D Murphy (*Australia*)
Jul 14	Samoa	40	Germany	28	Heidelberg	M Carley (*England*)
Nov 11	Germany	26	Hong Kong	9	Marseilles	P Gauzere (*France*)
Nov 11	Canada	65	Kenya	19	Marseilles	W Barnes (*England*)
Nov 17	Canada	29	Germany	10	Marseilles	L Pearce (*England*)
Nov 17	Hong Kong	42	Kenya	17	Marseilles	J Peyper (*SA*)
Nov 23	Germany	43	Kenya	6	Marseilles	A Gardner (*Australia*)
Nov 23	Canada	27	Hong Kong	10	Marseilles	R Poite (*France*)

THE FOREIGN LEGION
by John Lea

These New Zealand origin players were either contracted with professional overseas clubs for play in 2018/19 or commenced and completed an overseas contract during 2018 (denoted by *). Those no longer eligible for New Zealand have their country of allegiance shown in brackets.

AUSTRALIA
Super Rugby

ACT Brumbies:	Wharenui Hawera, Christian Lealifano (Australia), Chance Peni-Ataera, Toni Pulu (Niue), Peter Samu (Australia), Irae Simone, Henry Speight (Australia)*
Melbourne Rebels:	Jermaine Ainsley (Australia), Quade Cooper (Australia), Jack Debreczeni*, Tetera Faulkner (Australia), Michael Ruru, Jordan Uelese (Australia)
NSW Waratahs:	Lalakai Foketi, Sekope Kepu (Australia), Curtis Rona (Australia), JP Sauni
Queensland Reds:	Chris Feauai-Sautia (Australia), Karmichael Hunt (Australia), Adam Korczyk, Matt McGahan, Brandon Paenga-Amosa (Australia), Duncan Paia'aua (Australia), Caleb Timu (Australia), Lukhan Tui (Australia), Taniela Tupou (Australia)

NRC

Brisbane City:	Quade Cooper (Australia), Karmichael Hunt (Australia), Adam Korczyk, Brandon Paenga-Amosa (Australia), Tautalatasi Tasi, Lukhan Tui (Australia), Dillon Wihongi
Canberra Vikings:	Wharenui Hawera, Chance Peni-Ataera, Peter Samu (Australia), Irae Simone
Melbourne Rising:	Jermaine Ainsley (Australia), Anaru Rangi, Michael Ruru, Andrew Tuala (Samoa)
NSW Country Eagles:	Jaline Graham, Sekope Kepu (Australia), Afa Pakalani (Tonga)
Queensland Country:	Fred Burke, Chris Feauai-Sautia (Australia), Duncan Paia'aua (Australia), Caleb Timu (Australia), Taniela Tupou (Australia)
Sydney Rays:	Pama Fou (Australia), Curtis Rona (Australia), JP Sauni
Western Force:	Johan Bardoul, George Pisi (Samoa), Leon Power, Henry Stowers (Samoa), Jeremy Thrush

CANADA
Major League Rugby

Toronto Arrows	Sam Malcolm, Aaron McLelland

ENGLAND
Aviva Premiership

Bath:	Kahn Fotuali'i (Samoa), Paul Grant, Anthony Perenise (Samoa), Cooper Vuna (Australia), Jackson Willison, Jack Wilson (England), James Wilson
Bristol Bears:	John Afoa, Jake Heenan, Jack Lam (Samoa), Joe Latta, James Lay (Samoa), Jordan Lay (Samoa), Alapati Leuia (Samoa), Steven Luatua, Tusi Pisi (Samoa), Charles Piutau, Soane Tonga'uiha (Tonga)*, Chris Vui (Samoa)

Exeter Chiefs:	Tom Hendrickson, Thomas Waldrom (England)*
Gloucester:	Willie Heinz, Josh Hohneck, Tom Marshall, Jason Woodward (England)
Harlequins:	Elia Elia (Samoa), Jono Kitto*, Paul Lasike (USA), Matt Luamanu (Samoa), Francis Saili, Winston Stanley (Samoa), Matt Symons
Leicester Tigers:	Mike FitzGerald, Valentino Mapapalangi (Tonga), Brendon O'Connor, Telusa Veianu (Tonga)
London Wasps:	Ambrose Curtis, Jimmy Gopperth, Nathan Hughes (England), Brad Shields (England), Lima Sopoaga, Jacob Umaga
Newcastle Falcons:	Rodney Ah You (Ireland), Tevita Cavubati (Fiji), John Hardie (Scotland), Sinoti Sinoti (Samoa), Sonatane Takulua (Tonga)
Northampton Saints:	Piers Francis (England), Ben Franks, Teimana Harrison (England), Dylan Hartley (England), Ken Pisi (Samoa), Apisoloma Ratuniyarawa (Fiji), Ahsee Tuala (Samoa), Nafi Tuitavake (Tonga)
Sale Sharks:	Bryn Evans, Johnny Leota (Samoa), Denny Solomona (England)
Saracens:	Sean Maitland (Scotland), Hisa Sasagi (Samoa), Will Skelton (Australia), Mako Vunipola (England)
Worcester Warriors:	Michael Fatialofa, Bryce Heem, Ben Te'o (England)

RFU Championship

Bedford Blues:	Paul Tupai (Samoa)*
Cornish Pirates:	Jake Ashby (Netherlands), Don Koster, Jordan Payne, Marien Walker
Coventry:	Daniel Faleafa (Tonga), Jack Ram (Tonga)
Doncaster Knights:	Mike Mayhew, Kurt Morath (Tonga), Matt Talaese (Samoa)
Hartpury College:	Ollie Walker
Jersey Reds:	Adam Batt, Regan King, Uili Kolo'ofai (Tonga)*, Leroy Van Dam
London Irish:	Mike Coman, Blair Cowan (Scotland), Terrence Hepetema, TJ Ioane (Samoa), William Lloyd, Motu Matu'u (Samoa), Filo Paulo (Samoa), Asaeli Tikoirotuma (Fiji)*
London Scottish:	Mark Bright (England), Grayson Hart (Scotland), Chris Walker
Richmond:	Rob Kirby, Jordan Simpson-Hefft
Rotherham Titans:	Tom Burns, Eru Smith-Wano (Cook Islands)
Yorkshire Carnegie	Antonio Kirikiri, Fa'atiga Lemalu (Samoa), Nick Mayhew, Richard Mayhew, Daniel Temm, Myles Thoroughgood, Jade Te Rure, Jack Whetton*

FRANCE
Top 14

Agen:	Paul Ngauamo (Tonga), Jordan Puletua, Sam Vaka
Bordeaux Begles:	Ole Avei (Samoa), Luke Braid, Fa'asiu Fuatai*, Leroy Houston (Australia), Seta Tamanivalu, George Tilsley
Castres:	Paea Fa'anunu (Tonga), David Smith (Samoa), Alex Tulou (Samoa), Ma'ama Vaipulu (Tonga)

Clermont:	Peter Betham, (Australia), Fritz Lee, George Moala, Tim Nanai-Williams (Samoa), Isaia Toeava, Loni Uhila, John Ulugia
Grenoble:	Halani Aulika (Tonga), Dayna Edwards, Leva Fifita (Tonga), Nigel Hunt, Steven Setephano (Cook Islands), Nuku Swerling, Latu Talakai (Tonga), Alisona Taumalolo (Tonga)*, Taiasina Tu'ifua (Tonga), Edgar Tuinukuafe, Taleta Tupuola, Lolagi Visinia
La Rochelle:	Uini Atonio (France), Hikairo Forbes, Tawera Kerr-Barlow, Rene Ranger*, Victor Vito, Ihaia West
Lyon:	Toby Arnold, Cameron Mapusua, Charlie Ngatai, Rudi Wulf
Montpellier:	Aaron Cruden, Jarrad Hoeata, Nemani Nadolo (Fiji)
Pau:	Frank Halai, Jamie Mackintosh, Daniel Ramsey, Peter Saili, Colin Slade, Conrad Smith*, Benson Stanley, Tom Taylor
Perpignan:	Shahn Eru (Cook Islands), Michael Faleafa (Tonga), Manu Leiataua (Samoa), Genesis Mamea Lemalu (Samoa), Eric Sione, Tima Fainga'anuku*
Racing 92:	Dominic Bird, Census Johnston (Samoa), Casey Laulala*, Edwin Maka, Ope Peleseuma (Samoa), Joe Rokocoko, Ben Tameifuna (Tonga), Anthony Tuitavake, Virimi Vakatawa (France), Ben Volavola (Fiji)
Stade Francais:	Paul Alo-Emile (Samoa), Tony Ensor, Ziegfried Fisi'ihoi (Tonga), Paul Williams (Samoa)*
Toulon:	Brian Alainu'uese, Teariki Ben-Nicholas*, Malakai Fekitoa, Liam Messam, Filipo Nakosi (Fiji), Ma'a Nonu*, Julian Savea
Toulouse:	Pita Ahki, Carl Axtens, Piua Fa'asalele (Samoa), Charlie Faumuina, Jerome Kaino, Paul Perez (Samoa), Joe Tekori (Samoa)

Second Division

Aix en Provence:	Ed Fidow (Samoa), Poutasi Luafutu (Australia), Lachie Munro
Albi:	William Whetton
Aurillac:	Jack McPhee, Adrian Smith, Danny Tusitala (Samoa)*
Bayonne:	Matt Graham, Kade Poki*
Beziers:	Steve Fualau (Samoa)*, Lua Lokotui (Tonga)*
Biarritz:	Tyrone Elkington-McDonald, Adam Knight, Elvis Levi, Felipe Manu, Guy Millar, Joseph Penetito, Nemia Soqeta (Fiji)*
Brive:	So'otala Fa'aso'o, James Johnston (Samoa), Dominiko Waqaniburotu (Fiji)
Colomiers:	Jonny Fa'amatuainu (Tonga), Daniel Faleafa (Tonga), Randall Kamea, Chris Tuatara-Morrison
Massy:	Billy Ropiha, Matt Talaese (Samoa)*, Sasa Tofilau*, Jotham Wrampling*
Montauban:	Richard Haddon, Alex Luatua, Aviata Silago
Mont De Marsan:	Matt James*, Maselino Paulino (Samoa)
Nevers:	Fa'atoina Autagavaia (Samoa), Auvasa Faleali'i (Samoa), Zac Guildford
Oyonnax:	Ben Botica, Hika Elliot*, Rory Grice, Roimata Hansell-Pune, Vili Ma'afu (Tonga)*, Quentin MacDonald, Hoani Tui

Soyaux-Angouleme:	Dylan Hayes, Kimami Sitauti (Australia), Pingi Tala'apitaga
Vannes:	Sione Anga'aelangi (Tonga)*, Hugh Chalmers, Phil Kite (Tonga), Pat Leafa (Samoa), Ash Moeke, Albert Vulivuli (Fiji)

IRELAND
Guinness Pro 14

Connacht:	Bundee Aki (Ireland), Jarrad Butler, Naulia Dawai (Fiji)*, Tom McCartney, Stacey Ili (Samoa)*, Dominic Robertson-McCoy
Leinster:	Michael Bent (Ireland), Jamison Gibson-Park, James Lowe, Isa Nacewa (Fiji)*, Joseph Tomane (Australia)
Munster:	Tyler Bleyendaal, Joey Carbery (Ireland), Rhys Marshall, Alby Matthewson
Ulster:	Sean Reidy (Ireland), Henry Speight (Australia)*

ITALY
Guinness Pro 14

Benetton Treviso:	Dean Budd (Italy), Whetu Douglas*, Hame Faiva, Monty Ioane, Jayden Hayward (Italy), Nasi Manu (Tonga), Michael Tagicakibau (Fiji)*, Iliesa Ratuva Tavuyara (Fiji)
Zebre:	Josh Renton, Matu Tevi, Jimmy Tuivaiti (Italy)

JAPAN
Super Rugby

Sunwolves	Mark Abbott, Aisea Ai Valu (Japan), Jamie Booth, Phil Burleigh (Scotland), Jason Emery, Timothy Lafaele (Japan)*, Michael Leitch (Japan), Lomano Lemeki (Japan), Michael Little, Pauliasi Manu, Craig Millar, Hayden Parker, Sam Prattley, Dan Pryor, Kara Pryor, Rene Ranger, Robbie Robinson (Japan)*, Tom Rowe, Hendrix Tui (Japan)

Top League

Canon Eagles:	Israel Dagg, Blair Tweed
Coca Cola Red Sparks:	Mark Abbott, Johan Bardoul, Dan Hollinshead, Solomon King, Timothy Lafaele (Japan), James Marshall*, Daniel Peters, Joe Tupe, Will Tupou (Japan), Nathan Vella
Hino Red Dolphins:	Hayden Cripps (Japan), Joel Everson, Gillies Kaka, Nili Latu (Tonga), Pauliasi Manu, Liaki Moli, Augustine Pulu
Honda Heat:	John Akauola-Laula*, Josh Bekhuis, Baden Kerr, Lomano Lemeki (Japan), David Milo, Tetuhi Roberts, Tomasi Soqeta (Fiji), Shaun Treeby
Kobelco Steelers:	Nigel Ah Wong, Fraser Anderson (Tonga), Richard Buckman, Dan Carter, Nick Ealey, Andrew Ellis, Tom Franklin, Charlie Lawrence, Hayden Parker, Aidan Rodd, Toni Vaihu, Matt Vant Leven
Kubota Spears	Patrick Osborne (Fiji)

Munakata Sanix Blues:	Siliva Ahio, Sam Chongkit, Josh Gordon*, Karne Hesketh (Japan), Dan Pryor, Bryce Robbins (Japan), Andre Taylor
NEC Green Rockets:	Derek Carpenter (Japan), Stephen Donald, Maritino Nemani, George Risale, Amanaki Savieti, Sanaila Waqa
NTT Shining Arcs:	Brackin Karauria-Henry (Australia), Luteru Laulala, Hapakuki Moala-Liavaa. Leilua Murphy, Isaac Ross
Ricoh Black Rams:	Tim Bateman*, Colin Bourke, Mike Broadhurst (Japan), Elliot Dixon*, Josh Mau, Robbie Robinson (Japan), Jacob Skeen, Alex Woonton (Cook Islands)
Panasonic Wild Knights:	Asaeli Ai Valu (Japan), Ash Dixon, Digby Ioane (Australia), Craig Millar, Emerson Tamura-Paki, Matt Todd*, Tevita Tupou
Suntory Sun-Goliath:	Kosei Ono (Japan), Jordan Smiler (Australia), Hendrix Tui (Japan), Joe Wheeler
Toshiba Brave Lupus:	Johnny Fa'auli, Michael Harris (Australia), Richard Kahui, Michael Leitch (Japan), James Tucker
Toyota Industries Shuttles:	Scott Fuglistaller, Jono Hickey, Tevita Taufu'i (Tonga)
Toyota Verblitz:	Jamie Henry (Japan), Male Sa'u (Japan), Shneil Singh, Stephen Yates
Yamaha Jubilo:	Matt McGahan, Mose Tuiali'i

Top Challenge

Kamaishi Seawaves:	Scott Manson, Seilala Mapusua (Samoa), Dallas Tatana (Japan), Michael Toloke
Kintetsu Liners:	Iopu Iopu-Aso, Semi Masirewa, Luke Thompson (Japan)
Kurita Water Gush	Jacob Ellison (Japan), Ben Paltridge, Ash Parker (Japan)
Mitsubishi Dynaboars:	Albert Anae, Heiden Bedwell-Curtis*, Dan Hawkins, Tevita Lepolo, Michael Little, Alaia'sa Roland, Matt Vaega
NTT Docomo:	Marty Banks*, Gareth Evans*, Jamason Fa'anana-Schultz, Keepa Mewett

ROMANIA
Continental Shield

Timisoara Saracens:	Viliami Moala, Michael Stewart, Stephen Shennan (Romania), Jack Umaga (Romania)

SCOTLAND
Guinness Pro 14

Edinburgh:	Simon Berghan (Scotland), Phil Burleigh (Scotland)*, Simon Hickey, Mungo Mason (Scotland)
Glasgow:	Corey Flynn, Callum Gibbins, Nick Grigg (Scotland), Siosiua Halanukonuka (Tonga), Lelia Masaga, Samu Vunisa (Italy)

SPAIN
Supercopa

Alcobendas:	Brad Linkater (Spain), Lolohea Loco

El Salvador: Olajuwon Noa, Junior Nuu, Matthew Smith, Joshua Tafili, Jacob Wainwright
Santboiana: Paul Eti Slater, Afa Tauli (Spain)
VRAC Quesos: Brendan Asomua-Godman, Todd Doolan, Greg Dyer, Chris Eaton

UNITED STATES
Major League Rugby
Glendale Raptors: Mickey Bateman, Peter Dahl (USA)
Houston Sabercats: Mathew Faoagali
New Orleans Gold: Taylor Howden, Kane Thompson (Samoa)
Utah Warriors: Ara Elkington, Wineera Elkington, Jackson Kaka, Josh Reeves (Brazil), Fetu'u Vainikolo (Tonga)

WALES
Guinness Pro 14
Cardiff Blues: Gareth Anscombe (Wales), Tau Filise (Tonga)*, Willis Halaholo, Rey Lee-Lo (Samoa), Nick Williams
Dragons: Sam Beard*, Jacob Botica, Brandon Nansen (Samoa)
Ospreys: Ma'afu Fia (Tonga), Brendon Leonard*
Llanelli Scarlets: Kieron Fonotia (Samoa), Johnny McNicholl, Hadleigh Parkes (Wales), Blade Thomson

NEW ZEALAND ORIGIN AND FIRST-CLASS PLAYERS CAPPED OVERSEAS, 2018

Compiled by John Lea

Provincial Union and Year indicate most recent first-class play when applicable.

Player	Country	Provincial Union	Year
Jermaine Ainsley	Australia	Otago	–
Sekope Kepu	Australia	Counties Manukau	2007
Brandon Paenga-Amosa	Australia	Auckland	–
Duncan Paia'aua	Australia XV	Wellington	–
Matthew Philip	Australia XV	Southland	2016
Peter Samu	Australia	Crusaders	2018
Lukhan Tui	Australia	Auckland	–
Taniela Tupou	Australia	Auckland	–
Josh Reeves	Brazil	Canterbury	2018
Tyler Ardron	Canada	Bay of Plenty	2018
Hubert Buydens	Canada	Manawatu	2014
Jake Ilnicki	Canada	Manawatu	2016
Josh Larsen	Canada	Otago	2018
Evan Olmstead	Canada	Auckland	2018
Djustice Sears-Duru	Canada	North Otago	2014
Sam Anderson-Heather	Cook Islands	Otago	2018
Shahn Eru	Cook Islands	Bay of Plenty	2016
Marnus Hanley	Cook Islands	Waikato	2013
Te-Ara Henderson	Cook Islands	Wellington	–
James Iopu-Johnston	Cook Islands Sevens	Auckland	–
Reece Joyce	Cook Islands	Counties Manukau	–
Junior Kiria	Cook Islands Sevens	Auckland	–
Tai Marsters	Cook Islands	Counties Manukau	–
Greg Mullany	Cook Islands	Wairarapa Bush	2014
Matt Mullany	Cook Islands	Wellington	–
Junior Napara	Cook Islands Sevens	Auckland	–
Tuakana Paitai	Cook Islands	Waikato	–
James Pakoti	Cook Islands	Wairarapa Bush	2018
Francis Smith	Cook Islands	Tasman	2013
Gene Te Amo	Cook Islands	Counties Manukau	–
Brynn Uriarau	Cook Islands	Poverty Bay	2014
Christian Vainirere	Cook Islands	Mid Canterbury	2018

Player	Country	Provincial Union	Year
Eru Wano-Smith	Cook Islands	Bay of Plenty	2017
Joshua Brajkovic	Croatia	Auckland	–
Mario Ozich	Croatia	North Harbour	2016
Piers Francis	England XV	Blues	2017
Dylan Hartley	England	Bay of Plenty	–
James Haskell	England	Highlanders	2012
Nathan Hughes	England	Auckland	2013
Brad Shields	England	Hurricanes	2018
Denny Solomona	England	Auckland	–
Ben Te'o	England	Auckland	–
Mako Vunipola	England	Auckland	–
Tevita Cavubati	Fiji	Tasman	2014
Temo Mayanavanua	Fiji Warriors	Northland	2017
Sikeli Nabou	Fiji	Counties Manukau	2018
Nemani Nadolo	Fiji	Crusaders	2014
Nemani Nagusa	Fiji	Tasman	2012
Akapusi Qera	Fiji	Wanganui	2004
Apisoloma Ratuniyarawa	Fiji	North Harbour	2012
Peni Ravai	Fiji	Southland	2016
Ropate Rinakama	Fiji	Northland	2018
Tuapati Talemaitoga	Fiji	Southland	2014
Ben Volavola	Fiji	North Harbour	2017
Poasa Waqanibau	Fiji Warriors	Canterbury	2017
Dominiko Waqaniborotu	Fiji	Waikato	2010
Uini Atonio	France	Counties Manukau	2011
Virimi Vakatawa	France	Canterbury	–
Hagen Schulte	Germany	Buller	2015
Josh Dowsing	Hong Kong Dragons	Counties Manukau	2016
Ruan Du Plooy	Hong Kong Dragons	Waikato	2016
Nick Hewson	Hong Kong	Taranaki	–
Tau Koloamatangi	Hong Kong Dragons	Waikato	2016
Ben Rimene	Hong Kong	Waikato	–
Bundee Aki	Ireland	Counties Manukau	2014
Joey Carberry	Ireland	Auckland	–
Dean Budd	Italy	Northland	2011
Jayden Hayward	Italy	Taranaki	2012
Jimmy Tuivaiti	Italy	North Harbour	2014
Asaeli Ai Valu	Japan	Otago	–

NZ Origin and First-Class Players Capped Overseas, 2018

Player	Country	Provincial Union	Year
Jamie Henry	Japan	Auckland	–
Shota Horie	Japan	Otago	2012
Timothy Lafaele	Japan	Auckland	–
Michael Leitch	Japan	Chiefs	2017
Lomano Lemeki	Japan	Auckland	–
Robbie Robinson	Japan A	North Harbour	2014
Kaito Shigeno	Japan	Auckland	2015
Fumiaki Tanaka	Japan	Highlanders	2016
Hendrix Tui	Japan	Auckland	–
Will Tupou	Japan	Auckland	–
Willie Ambaka	Kenya	Manawatu	2017
Jake Ashby	Netherlands	Mid Canterbury	2014
Alex Barendregt	Netherlands	Wellington	2018
Josh Gascoigne	Netherlands	Waikato	2016
Liam McBride	Netherlands	Taranaki	2015
Leslie McIlroy-Taleni	Niue Sevens	Auckland	–
Cassius Paitai	Niue Sevens	Auckland	–
Willie Sionetali	Niue Sevens	Auckland	–
Keonte Tohilima	Niue Sevens	Auckland	–
David Robinson-Polkey	Philippines	Auckland	–
Paula Kinikinilau	Romania	Otago	2010
Steven Shennan	Romania	Auckland	–
Jack Umaga	Romania	Tasman	2010
Jake Ale	Samoa Sevens	King Country	2018
Paul Alo-Emile	Samoa	Waikato	2013
Thomas Alosio	Samoa Sevens	Wellington	2015
Donald Brighouse	Samoa	Otago	2018
Pele Cowley	Samoa	Waikato	2017
Elia Elia	Samoa	Canterbury	–
Piua Fa'asalele	Samoa	Wellington	–
Ed Fidow	Samoa	Auckland	–
Neria Fomai	Samoa Sevens	Southland	2017
Stacey Ili	Samoa	Hawkes Bay	2018
TJ Ioane	Samoa	Otago	2014
Darren Kellett-Moore	Samoa Sevens	Auckland	–
Jack Lam	Samoa	Waikato	2013
James Lay	Samoa	Bay of Plenty	2018
Jordan Lay	Samoa	Bay of Plenty	2017

Player	Country	Provincial Union	Year
Kane Leaupepe	Samoa	Bay of Plenty	2018
Rey Lee-Lo	Samoa	Hurricanes	2015
Manu Leiataua	Samoa	North Harbour	2013
Alapati Leuia	Samoa	Wellington	2014
D'Angelo Leuila	Samoa	Auckland	2018
Faifili Levave	Samoa	Hurricanes	2014
Matt Luamanu	Samoa	North Harbour	2012
Meli Matavao	Samoa	Otago	2018
Motu Matu'u	Samoa	Hurricanes	2015
Tim Nanai-Willliams	Samoa	Chiefs	2017
Brandon Nansen	Samoa	North Harbour	2017
Ben Nee Nee	Samoa	Auckland	2018
Della Neli	Samoa Sevens	Auckland	–
Ray Niuia	Samoa	Tasman	2018
Silao Nonu	Samoa Sevens	Auckland	–
Filo Paulo	Samoa	North Harbour	2012
Paul Perez	Samoa	Taranaki	2009
Iakopo Petelo-Mapu	Samoa	Bay of Plenty	–
Tusi Pisi	Samoa	Hurricanes	2013
Dwayne Polataivao	Samoa	Auckland	2015
Hisa Sasagi	Samoa	Otago	2018
Fa'alemiga Selesele	Samoa Sevens	Hawke's Bay	2017
Howard Sililoto	Samoa A	Counties Manukau	2018
Sinoti Sinoti	Samoa	Wellington	2013
Henry Stowers	Samoa A	Bay of Plenty	2017
Gafatasi Sua	Samoa	Counties Manukau	2018
Willie Talataina-Mu	Samoa A	Southland	2017
Jamie-Jerry Taulagi	Samoa	Hawke's Bay	2018
Joe Tekori	Samoa	Auckland	2007
Ahsee Tuala	Samoa	Counties Manukau	2014
Belgium Tuatagaloa	Samoa Sevens	Wellington	2014
Danny Tusitala	Samoa Sevens	Auckland	–
Josh Tyrell	Samoa	North Harbour	2017
Chris Vui	Samoa	North Harbour	2016
Simon Berghan	Scotland	Canterbury	–
Hugh Blake	Scotland Sevens	Bay of Plenty	2018
Nick Grigg	Scotland	Wellington	–
Sean Maitland	Scotland	Canterbury	2012
Mungo Mason	Scotland Sevens	Waikato	2016

NZ Origin and First-Class Players Capped Overseas, 2018

Player	Country	Provincial Union	Year
Byron McGuigan	Scotland	Bay of Plenty	2014
Nick McLennan	Scotland Sevens	Hawke's Bay	2012
Brad Linklater	Spain	Auckland	–
Dan Snee	Spain	Otago	2008
Afa Tauli	Spain	Manawatu	–
Eddie Aholelei	Tonga A	Auckland	–
Sione Anga'aelangi	Tonga	Counties Manukau	2016
Paea Fa'anunu	Tonga	Canterbury	2013
Tolu Fahamakioa	Tonga	Wellington	2018
James Faiva	Tonga	Counties Manukau	–
Daniel Faleafa	Tonga	Northland	2012
Michael Faleafa	Tonga	Northland	2017
Jethro Felemi	Tonga A	North Harbour	2016
Ma'afu Fia	Tonga	Manawatu	2015
Leva Fifita	Tonga	Waikato	2017
Sione Fifita	Tonga	Counties Manukau	2017
Irwin Finau	Tonga A	North Harbour	2014
Ziegfried Fisi'ihoi	Tonga	Chiefs	2017
Latiume Fosita	Tonga	Auckland	2018
Leon Fukofuka	Tonga	Auckland	2018
Kali Hala	Tonga	Counties Manukau	2018
Siosiua Halanukonuka	Tonga	Tasman	2017
Sione Ika	Tonga A	Hawke's Bay	–
Zane Kapeli	Tonga	Bay of Plenty	2018
Penikolo Latu	Tonga	Waikato	2016
Fotu Lokotui	Tonga	Counties Manukau	2018
Vili Lolohea	Tonga	Tasman	2017
Nasi Manu	Tonga	Highlanders	2015
Valentino Mapapalangi	Tonga	Manawatu	2016
Kurt Morath	Tonga	Taranaki	2008
Paul Ngauamo	Tonga	Canterbury	2011
Atieli Pakalani	Tonga	Auckland	2010
Siale Piutau	Tonga	Highlanders	2012
Jack Ram	Tonga Sevens	Northland	2017
George Taina	Tonga A	Auckland	–
Sonatane Takulua	Tonga	Northland	2014
Latu Talakai	Tonga	Waikato	2017
Ben Tameifuna	Tonga	Waikato	2015
Joe Tuineau	Tonga	Southland	2011
Nafi Tuitavake	Tonga	North Harbour	2015
Sam Ulufonua	Tonga	Hawke's Bay	2018
Latu Vaeno	Tonga	Taranaki	2018

Player	Country	Provincial Union	Year
Ma'ama Vaipulu	Tonga	Chiefs	2016
Cooper Vuna	Tonga	Auckland	–
Chris Baumann	United States	Wellington	2016
Devereaux Ferris	United States	Northland	–
Eric Fry	United States	Manawatu	2012
Tony Lamborn	United States	Southland	2018
Paul Lasike	United States	Auckland	–
Gannon Moore	United States	North Harbour	–
Gareth Anscombe	Wales	Auckland	2014
Hadleigh Parkes	Wales	Auckland	2014

OVERSEAS PLAYERS IN NEW ZEALAND FIRST-CLASS RUGBY 2018

For previously capped players the most recent year and level of selection are shown. Some players have since, or soon will, also become eligible for New Zealand.

Player	Country	Year	NZ Team in 2018
Robbie Abel	Australia	Uncapped	Auckland
Nigel Ah Wong	Australia	Uncapped	Counties Manukau
Tyler Campbell	Australia Schools	2015	Waikato
James Dargaville	Australia Under 20	2012	North Harbour
Jack Debreczeni	Australia Schools	2011	Northland
Sef Fa'agase	Australia XV	2016	Canterbury
Matthew Garland	Australia Schools	2009	Bay of Plenty
Junior Laloifi	Australia Sevens	2013	Manawatu
Tyrell Lomax	Australia Under 20	2016	Tasman
Guy Millar	Australia Schools	2010	Highlanders
Andrew Ready	Australia XV	2016	Southland
Faalelei Sione	Australia Under 20	2016	Manawatu
Toby Smith	Australia	2017	Waikato
Lucas Albornoz	Canada	2017	Northland
Reegan O'Gorman	Canada	2017	South Canterbury
Sergio de la Fuente	Chile	2017	Thames Valley
Heimona Potoru	Cook Islands Sevens	2015	Wairarapa Bush
Tom Crozier	England Students	2014	Bay of Plenty
Warwick Lahmert	England Sevens	2015	Taranaki
Jacob Umaga	England Under 20	2017	Auckland
Thomas Waldrom	England	2013	Wellington
Kaveni Dabonaise	Fiji Under 20	2015	Wanganui
Naulia Dawai	Fiji	2017	Otago
Alex Hodgman	Fiji Under 20	2012	Canterbury
Mitieli Kaloudigibeci	Fiji	Uncapped	Buller
Taniela Koroi	Fiji	2016	Auckland
Jone Macilai-Tori	Fiji	Uncapped	Crusaders
Tevita Nabura	Fiji Sevens	2017	Counties Manukau
Viliame Rarasea	Fiji Under 20	2014	Counties Manukau
Sevu Reece	Fiji	Uncapped	Waikato
Asaeli Sorovaki	Fiji Under 20	2015	Taranaki
Pita-Gus Sowakula	Fiji	Uncapped	Taranaki
Michael Tagicakibau	Fiji	2012	Manawatu

Player	Country	Year	NZ Team in 2018
Oliver Jager	Ireland Under 18	2013	Canterbury
Tim Bond	Japan A	2012	Waikato
Toni Pulu	Niue Sevens	2012	Chiefs
Jared Adams	Samoa Under 20	2015	Auckland
Michael Ala'alatoa	Samoa Under 20	2011	Manawatu
Moo Moo Falaniko	Samoa Under 20	2018	Wairarapa Bush
Jonathan Fa'auli	Samoa Under 20	2015	Chiefs
Mario Fepuleai	Samoa Under 20	2015	Auckland
Losi Filipo	Samoa Under 20	2017	Wellington
Greg Foe	Samoa	2016	Wellington
Josh Ioane	Samoa Under 20	2015	Otago
Tom Iosefo	Samoa Sevens	2017	Poverty Bay
Luteru Laulala	Samoa Under 20	2014	Counties Manukau
Orbyn Leger	Samoa Under 20	2015	Counties Manukau
Fa'atiga Lemalu	Samoa	2017	Auckland
Jeff Lepa	Samoa	2016	Buller
Valentine Meachen	Samoa A	2016	Bay of Plenty
Melani Nanai	Samoa Under 20	2012	Auckland
Savelio Ropati	Samoa Sevens	2017	Counties Manukau
James So'oialo	Samoa	2011	Horowhenua-Kapiti
Mike Tamoaieata	Samoa Under 20	2015	North Harbour
Galu Taufale	Samoa	2017	Wellington
Jordan Taufua	Samoa Under 20	2011	Crusaders
Jonathan Taumateine	Samoa Under 20	2015	Counties Manukau
Tanielu Tele'a	Samoa Under 20	2017	Auckland
Kane Thompson	Samoa	2015	Taranaki
Chase Tiatia	Samoa Under 20	2015	Bay of Plenty
Phil Burleigh	Scotland	2017	Canterbury
Murray Douglas	Scotland	Uncapped	Northland
Ross Geldenhuys	South Africa	Uncapped	Bay of Plenty
Dylan Nel	South Africa	Uncapped	Canterbury
Sosaia Fale	Tonga Under 20	2018	Waikato
Vaea Fifita	Tonga Under 18	2010	Wellington
Shannon Frizzell	Tonga Under 20	2014	Tasman
Billy Fukofuka	Tonga Under 20	2015	Southland
Kali Hala	Tonga	2017	Counties Manukau
Latu Vaeno	Tonga	2011	Taranaki
Mike Sosene-Feagai	United States	2016	Auckland
Henri Williams	Wales	Uncapped	Wanganui
Brian Matoramusha	Zimbabwe Under 20	2014	Mid Canterbury
Shepherd Mhembere	Zimbabwe Under 20	2014	Mid Canterbury

OFFSHORE NEW ZEALAND ORIGIN COACHES 2018

Country	Team	Coach
Australia	Waratahs	Daryl Gibson
Cook Islands	National	Stan Wright
Croatia	National	Milan Yelavich
England	Bath	Todd Blackadder
England	Bristol	Pat Lam
England	Northampton Saints	Chris Boyd
Estonia	National	Chris Budgen
Fiji	National	John McKee
France	La Rochelle	Jono Gibbes
France	Montpellier	Vern Cotter
France	Pau	Simon Mannix
France	Stade Francais	Greg Cooper
Georgia	National	Milton Haig
Ireland	Connacht	Kieran Keane
Ireland	National	Joe Schmidt
Italy	Benetton Treviso	Kieran Crowley
Japan	Coca Cola Red Sparks	Earl Va'a
Japan	Kobelco Steelers	Wayne Smith
Japan	NEC Green Rockets	Peter Russell
Japan	NTT Shining Arcs	Rob Penney
Japan	Pansonic Wild Knights	Robbie Deans
Japan	National & Sunwolves	Jamie Joseph
Kenya	National	Ian Snook
Korea	National Sevens	John Walters
Samoa	National	Steve Jackson
Samoa	National Sevens	Gordon Tietjens
Scotland	Glasgow	Dave Rennie
South Africa	Bulls also: England (national defence coach)	John Mitchell
Sri Lanka	National Sevens	Peter Woods
Tahiti	National	Romi Ropati
Wales	National	Warren Gatland
Wales	Scarlets	Wayne Pivac

ALL BLACKS
TEST MATCH RECORD

to January 1, 2019

Opponents	Played	Won	Lost	Drawn	For	Against
Argentina	28	27	–	1	1130	406
Australia	164	114	43	7	3490	2318
British Isles	41	30	7	4	700	399
Canada	5	5	–	–	313	54
England	41	33	7	1	985	575
Fiji	5	5	–	–	364	50
France	61	48	12	1	1596	801
Georgia	1	1	–	–	43	10
Ireland	31	28	2	1	871	375
Italy	14	14	–	–	820	131
Japan	4	4	–	–	351	61
Namibia	1	1	–	–	58	14
Pacific Islands	1	1	–	–	41	26
Portugal	1	1	–	–	108	13
Romania	2	2	–	–	99	14
Samoa	7	7	–	–	411	72
Scotland	31	29	–	2	922	349
South Africa	97	58	36	3	2011	1548
Tonga	5	5	–	–	326	35
United States	3	3	–	–	171	15
Wales	34	31	3	–	1070	374
World XV	3	2	1	–	94	69
	580	**449**	**111**	**20**	**15,974**	**7,709**

The All Blacks have won 77.41 per cent of all test matches.
This figure has increased in 17 out of the last 18 years.

COMPARATIVE FIGURES FOR NEW ZEALAND'S MAJOR RIVALS TO 1/1/19

	Played	Won	Win %
South Africa	491	305	62.12
France	754	405	53.71
England	727	400	55.02
Wales	717	374	52.16
Australia	631	320	50.71
Ireland	690	309	44.78
Scotland	687	296	43.09

ALL BLACK STATISTICS
to January 1, 2019

LEADING ALL BLACK APPEARANCES IN ALL MATCHES

R.H. McCaw	149	I.J. Clarke	83	M.W. Shaw	69
C.E. Meads	133	A.K. Hore	83	B.J. Lochore	68
K.F. Mealamu	133	J. Kaino	83	C.W. Dowd	67
S.B.T. Fitzpatrick	128	A.L. Smith	82	C.R. Jack	67
K.J. Read	119	S.C. McDowall	81	A.D. Oliver	67
T.D. Woodcock	118	J.F. Umaga	79	G.M. Somerville	67
A.M. Haden	117	G.J. Fox	78	I.J.A. Dagg	66
I.A. Kirkpatrick	113	R.W. Loe	78	G.A. Knight	66
B.G. Williams	113	A.J. Williams	78	A.J. Whetton	65
D.W. Carter	112	B.R. Smith	77	A.R. Sutherland	64
S.L. Whitelock	108	W.J. Whineray	77	T.J. Wright	64
O.T. Franks	106	B.A. Retallick	75	D.C. Howlett	63
I.D. Jones	105	W.K. Little	75	K.L. Skinner	63
M.A. Nonu	104	M.N. Jones	74	R. So'oialo	63
J.M. Muliaina	102	B.J. Barrett	74	M.R. Brewer	61
B.J. Robertson	102	J.T. Lomu	73	M.J. Brownlie	61
G.W. Whetton	101	P.A.T. Weepu	73	G.N.K. Mourie	61
Z.V. Brooke	100	W.W.V. Crockett	72	R.W. Norton	61
J.J. Kirwan	96	A.P. Mehrtens	72	T.C. Randell	61
C.G. Smith	94	M.G. Mexted	72	D. Young	61
D.B. Clarke	89	J.W. Wilson	71	C.M. Cullen	60
J.W. Marshall	88	R.M. Brooke	69	B.C. Thorn	60
S.M. Going	86	O.M. Brown	69	S.J. Cane	60
K.R. Tremain	86	F.E. Bunce	69	D.S. Coles	60
S.S. Wilson	85	J.T. Rokocoko	69		

LEADING POINTS-SCORERS IN ALL MATCHES FOR NEW ZEALAND

		Matches	Points
D.W. Carter	2003–15	112	1598
G.J. Fox	1985–93	78	1067
A.P. Mehrtens	1995–2004	72	994
D.B. Clarke	1956–64	89	781
BB.J. Barrett	2012–18	74	601
W.F. McCormick	1965–71	44	453
B.G. Williams	1970–78	113	401[t]
C.J. Spencer	1995–2004	44	383
W.J. Wallace	1903–08	51	379
A.R. Hewson	1979–84	34	357
J.F. Karam	1972–75	42	345
A.W. Cruden	2010–17	50	322
K.J. Crowley	1983–91	35	316
J.W. Wilson	1993–2001	71	299
M.F. Nicholls	1921–30	51	284
J.J. Kirwan	1984–94	96	275
R.G. Wilson	1976–80	25	272
C.M. Cullen	1996–2002	60	266
R.M. Deans	1983–85	19	252
J.A. Gallagher	1986–89	41	251

[t] *includes a penalty try*

LEADING TRY-SCORERS IN ALL MATCHES

		Matches	Tries
J.J. Kirwan	1984–94	96	67
B.G. Williams	1970–78	113	66†
C.M. Cullen	1996–2002	60	52
I.A. Kirkpatrick	1967–77	113	50
J.W. Wilson	1993–2001	71	50
S.S. Wilson	1976–83	85	50
D.C. Howlett	2000–07	63	49
T.J. Wright	1986–92	64	49t
J. Hunter	1905–08	36	48
J.T. Rokocoko	2003–10	69	47
B.G. Fraser	1979–84	55	46
S.J. Savea	2012–17	54	46
G.B. Batty	1972–77	56	45
J.T. Lomu	1994–2002	73	43
Z.V. Brooke	1987–97	100	42
M.J. Dick	1963–70	55	42

†includes a penalty try

MOST APPEARANCES IN INTERNATIONALS

R.H. McCaw	2001–15	148	J.T. Lomu	1994–2002	63
K.F. Mealamu	2002–15	132	R.M. Brooke	1992–99	62
T.D. Woodcock	2002–15	118	D.C. Howlett	2000–07	62
K.J. Read	2008–18	118	R. So'oialo	2002–09	62
D.W. Carter	2003–15	112	C.W. Dowd	1993–2000	60
S.L. Whitelock	2010–18	108	J.W. Wilson	1993–2001	60
O.T. Franks	2009–18	106	S.J. Cane	2012–18	60
M.A. Nonu	2003–15	103	D.S. Coles	2012–18	60
J.M. Muliaina	2003–11	100	A.D. Oliver	1997–2007	59
C.G. Smith	2004–15	94	B.C. Thorn	2003–11	59
S.B.T. Fitzpatrick	1986–97	92	Z.V. Brooke	1987–97	58
A.K. Hore	2002–13	83	G.W. Whetton	1981–91	58
A.L. Smith	2012–18	82	C.M. Cullen	1996–2002	58
J. Kaino	2004–17	81	B.T. Kelleher	1999–2007	57
J.W. Marshall	1995–2005	81	O.M. Brown	1992–98	56
I.D. Jones	1990–97	79	L.R. MacDonald	2000–08	56
A.J. Williams	2002–12	77	F.E. Bunce	1992–97	55
B.R. Smith	2009–18	76	M.N. Jones	1987–98	55
B.A. Retallick	2012–18	75	C.E. Meads	1957–71	55
J.F. Umaga	1997–2005	74	T.T.R. Perenara	2014–18	55
B.J. Barrett	2012–18	73	J.A. Kronfeld	1995–2000	54
W.W.V. Crockett	2009–17	71	S.J. Savea	2012–17	54
P.A.T. Weepu	2004–13	71	C.S. Jane	2008–14	53
A.P. Mehrtens	1995–2004	70	Q.J. Cowan	2004–11	51
J.T. Rokocoko	2003–10	68	T.C. Randell	1997–2002	51
C.R. Jack	2001–07	67	S.B. Williams	2010–18	51
I.J.A. Dagg	2010–17	66	W.K. Little	1990–98	50
G.M. Somerville	2000–08	66	R.D. Thorne	1999–2007	50
J.J. Kirwan	1984–94	63			

MOST POINTS FOR NEW ZEALAND IN INTERNATIONALS

	Matches	Tries	Con	PG	DG	Mark	Points
D.W. Carter	112	29	293	281	8	–	1598
A.P. Mehrtens	70	7	169	188	10	–	967
G.J. Fox	46	1	118	128	7	–	645
B.J. Barrett	73	32	138	51	2	–	595
A.W. Cruden	50	5	63	56	1	–	322
C.J. Spencer	35	14	49	41	–	–	291
D.C. Howlett	62	49	–	–	–	–	245
C.M. Cullen	58	46	3	–	–	–	236
J.W. Wilson	60	44	1	3	1	–	234
J.T. Rokocoko	68	46	–	–	–	–	230
S.J. Savea	54	46	–	–	–	–	230
D.B. Clarke	31	2	33	38	5	2	207
A.R. Hewson	19	4	22	43	4	–	201
J.T. Lomu	63	37	–	–	–	–	185
J.F. Umaga	74	37t	–	–	–	–	185
T.E. Brown	18	5	43	20	–	–	171
J.M. Muliaina	100	34	–	–	–	–	170
B.R. Smith	76	33	–	–	–	–	165
M.A. Nonu	103	31	–	–	–	–	155
C.L. McAlister	30	7	26	22	–	–	153
L.R. MacDonald	56	15t	25	7	–	–	146
S.W. Sivivatu	45	29	–	–	–	–	145
J.J. Kirwan	63	351	–	–	–	–	143
R.H. McCaw	148	28t	–	–	–	–	140
I.J.A. Dagg	66	26	1	2	–	–	138
C.G. Smith	94	26	–	–	–	–	130
K.J. Read	118	25	–	–	–	–	125
W.F. McCormick	16	–	23	24	1	–	121
J.W. Marshall	81	24	–	–	–	–	120
S.D. Culhane	6	1	32	15	–	–	114
R.E. Ioane	24	22	–	–	–	–	110
K.J. Crowley	19	5	5	23	2	–	105
N.J. Evans	16	5	30	6	–	–	103
P.A.T. Weepu	71	7	10	16	–	–	103

1 includes three tries at five points
t includes penalty try

MOST STARTS IN EACH POSITION FOR NEW ZEALAND IN INTERNATIONALS

Fullback	J.M. Muliaina	2003–11	83	No 8	K.J. Read	2009–18	109
Wing	J.T. Rokocoko	2003–10	66	Flanker	R.H. McCaw	2001–15	139
Centre	C.G. Smith	2004–15	90	Lock	S.L. Whitelock	2010–18	89
2nd five-eighth	M.A. Nonu	2003–15	81	Prop	T.D. Woodcock	2002–15	105
1st five-eighth	D.W. Carter	2004–15	94	Hooker	S.B.T. Fitzpatrick	1986–97	91
Halfback	A.L. Smith	2012–18	76	Substitute	K.F. Mealamu	2002–15	55

The player must have started the match in that position. Appearances as replacements are not included except in this case Mealamu.

MOST TRIES FOR NEW ZEALAND IN INTERNATIONALS

	Matches	Tries		Matches	Tries
D.C. Howlett	62	49	M.A. Nonu	103	31
C.M. Cullen	58	46	D.W. Carter	112	29
J.T. Rokocoko	68	46	S.W. Sivivatu	45	29
S.J. Savea	54	46	R.H. McCaw	148	28t
J.W. Wilson	60	44	C.G. Smith	94	26
J.T. Lomu	63	37	I.J.A. Dagg	66	26
J.F. Umaga	74	37t	K.J. Read	118	25
J.J. Kirwan	63	35	J.W. Marshall	81	24
J.M. Muliaina	100	34	R.E. Ioane	24	22
B.R. Smith	76	33	F.E. Bunce	55	20
B.J. Barrett	73	32			

t Includes one penalty try

MOST TRIES IN AN INTERNATIONAL

M.C.G. Ellis	v Japan, 1995	6	C.M. Cullen	v Scotland, 1996	4
J.W. Wilson	v Fiji, 1997	5	J.W. Wilson	v Samoa, 1999	4
D. McGregor	v England, 1905	4	J.M. Muliaina	v Canada, 2003	4
C.I. Green	v Fiji, 1987	4	S.W. Sivivatu	v Fiji, 2005	4
J.A. Gallagher	v Fiji, 1987	4	Z.R. Guildford	v Canada, 2011	4
J.J. Kirwan	v Wales, 1988	4	B.J. Barrett	v Australia, 2018	4
J.T. Lomu	v England, 1995	4	J.M. Barrett	v Italy, 2018	4

MOST PENALTY GOALS IN AN INTERNATIONAL

A.P. Mehrtens	v Australia, 1999	9	D.W. Carter	v Australia, 2007	7
A.P. Mehrtens	v France, 2000	9	P.A.T. Weepu	v Argentina, 2011	7
G.J. Fox	v W Samoa, 1993	7	B.J. Barrett	v BI Lions, 2017	7
A.P. Mehrtens	v South Africa, 1999	7			

MOST CONVERSIONS IN AN INTERNATIONAL

S.D. Culhane	v Japan, 1995	20	C.J. Spencer	v Argentina, 1997	10
N.J. Evans	v Portugal, 2007	14	D.W. Carter	v Canada, 2003	9
T.E. Brown	v Tonga, 2000	12	C.R. Slade	v Japan, 2011	9
L.R. MacDonald	v Tonga, 2003	12	G.J. Fox	v Italy, 1987	8
T.E. Brown	v Italy, 1999	11	G.J. Fox	v Wales, 1988	8
G.J. Fox	v Fiji, 1987	10	A.P. Mehrtens	v Italy, 2002	8

HIGHEST POINTS-SCORERS IN AN INTERNATIONAL

	Opponent	Tries	Con	PG	DG	Points
S.D. Culhane	Japan, 1995[1]	1	20	–	–	45
T.E. Brown	Italy, 1999	1	11	3	–	36
D.W. Carter	Lions, 2005	2	4	5	–	33
C.J. Spencer	Argentina, 1997[1]	2	10	1	–	33
A.P. Mehrtens	Ireland, 1997	1	5	6	–	33
N.J. Evans	Portugal, 2007	1	14	–	–	33
T.E. Brown	Tonga, 2000	1	12	1	–	32
M.C.G. Ellis	Japan, 1995	6	–	–	–	30
B.J. Barrett	Australia, 2018	4	5	–	–	30
T.E. Brown	Samoa, 2001	3	3	3	–	30
A.P. Mehrtens	Australia, 1999	–	1	9	–	29
A.P. Mehrtens	France, 2000	–	1	9	–	29
L.R. MacDonald	Tonga, 2003	1	12	–	–	29
D.W. Carter	Canada, 2007	3	7	–	–	29
A.P. Mehrtens	Canada, 1995[1]	1	7	3	–	28
D.W. Carter	Wales, 2010	2	4	3	–	27
A.R. Hewson	Australia, 1982	1	2	5	1	26
G.J. Fox	Fiji, 1987	–	10	2	–	26
D.W. Carter	Wales, 2005	2	5	2	–	26
D.W. Carter	England, 2006	1	3	5	–	26
T.E. Brown	Samoa, 1999[1]	–	7	4	–	26
B.J. Barrett	Wales, 2016	2	5	2	–	26
D.W. Carter	South Africa, 2006	–	2	7	–	25
G.J. Fox	Western Samoa, 1993	–	2	7	–	25
J.W. Wilson	Fiji, 1997	5	–	–	–	25
C.J. Spencer	South Africa, 1997	1	4	4	–	25
D.W. Carter	France, 2004	1	4	4	–	25
W.F. McCormick	Wales, 1969	–	3	5	1	24
B.J. Barrett	Samoa, 2017	2	7		–	24
D.S. McKenzie	France, 2018	2	7	–	–	24

[1] international debut

NEW ZEALAND INTERNATIONAL CAPTAINS

R.H. McCaw	2004–15	110	J. Collins	2006–07	3
S.B.T. Fitzpatrick	1992–97	51	R.R. King	1937	3
K.J. Read	2012–18	43	D.J. Graham	1964	3
W.J. Whineray	1958–65	30	D.S. Loveridge	1980	3
R.D. Thorne	2002–07	23	K.F. Mealamu	2008–11	3
T.C. Randell	1998–2002	22	J.M. Muliaina	2009	3
J.F. Umaga	2004–05	21	F.J. Oliver	1978	3
G.N.K. Mourie	1977–82	19	J. Richardson	1924	3
B.J. Lochore	1966–70	18	F. Roberts	1910	3
A.G. Dalton	1981–85	17	R.W. Roberts	1914	3
G.W. Whetton	1990–91	15	G.G. Aitken	1921	2
W.T. Shelford	1988–90	14	S.J. Cane	2015–16	2
D.E. Kirk	1986–87	11	R.H. Duff	1956	2
T.J. Blackadder	2000	10	J.L. Griffiths	1936	2
A.R. Leslie	1974–76	10	A. McDonald	1913	2
A.D. Oliver	2001	10	N.A. Mitchell	1938	2
I.A. Kirkpatrick	1972–73	9	M.J. O'Leary	1913	2
C.G. Porter	1925–30	7	A.R. Reid	1957	2
F.R. Allen	1946–49	6	K.L. Skinner	1952	2
R.R. Elvidge	1949–50	5	J.B. Smith	1949	2
R. So'oialo	2008–09	5	P.B. Vincent	1956	2
R.C. Stuart	1953–54	5	S.S. Wilson	1983	2
S.L. Whitelock	2017–18	5	J. Duncan	1903	1
M.J. Brownlie	1928	4	P.W. Henderson	1995	1
D. Gallaher	1905–06	4	A.K. Hore	2011	1
M.J.B. Hobbs	1985–86	4	C.R. Laidlaw	1968	1
J. Hunter	1907–08	4	H.T. Lilburne	1929	1
P. Johnstone	1950–51	4	R.M. McKenzie	1938	1
F.D. Kilby	1932–34	4	J.R. Page	1934	1
J.E. Manchester	1935–36	4	E.J. Roberts	1921	1
J.W. Marshall	1997	4	B.R. Smith	2017	1
C.E. Meads	1971	4	J.C. Spencer	1905	1
R.W. Norton	1977	4	W.A. Strang	1931	1
J.W. Stead	1904–08	4	K.R. Tremain	1968	1
I.J. Clarke	1955	3	L.C. Whitelock	2018	1

MOST TEST MATCH WINS

R.H. McCaw	131	A.J. Williams	65
K.F. Mealamu	114	B.J. Barrett	65
T.D. Woodcock	102	P.A.T. Weepu	62
K.J. Read	101	J.W. Marshall	61
D.W. Carter	99	I.J.A. Dagg	60
S.L. Whitelock	95	I.D. Jones	59
M.A. Nonu	91	J.F. Umaga	59
O.T. Franks	91	C.R. Jack	57
J.M. Muliaina	84	J.T. Rokocoko	55
C.G. Smith	84	G.M. Somerville	55
S.B.T. Fitzpatrick	74	R. So'oialo	53
A.L. Smith	71	D.S. Coles	53
A.K. Hore	70	S.J. Cane	53
J. Kaino	68	D.C. Howlett	51
B.A. Retallick	68	B.C. Thorn	51
B.R. Smith	68	G.W. Whetton	50
W.W.V. Crockett	66		

HIGHEST SCORES IN TEST MATCHES

Opponent	Home		Away		Opponent	Home		Away	
Argentina	93–8	(1997)	54–18	(2012)	Namibia	–	–	58–14	(2015)
Australia	51–20	(2014)	54–34	(2017)	Pacific Islands	41–26	(2004)	–	
British Isles	48–18	(2005)	–		Portugal	–	–	108–13	(2007)
Canada	79–15	(2011)	68–8	(2003)	Romania		–	85–8	(2007)
England	64–22	(1998)	45–29	(1995)	Samoa	101–14	(2008)	25–16	(2015)
Fiji	91–0	(2005)	–		Scotland	69–20	(2000)	51–15	(1993)
								51–22	(2012)
France	61–10	(2007)	62–13	(2015)	South Africa	57–0	(2017)	57-15	(2016)
Georgia	–	–	43–10	(2015)	Tonga	102–0	(2000)	91–7	(2003)
Ireland	66–28	(2010)	63–15	(1997)	USA		–	74–6	(2014)
Italy	70–6	(1987)	101–3	(1999)	Wales	55–3	(2003)	53–37	(2003)
Japan	83–7	(2011)	145–17	(1995)					

MOST POINTS BY AN ALL BLACK AGAINST AN OPPONENT

Opponent	In an International			In a Career	
Argentina	33	C.J. Spencer	1997	103	G.J. Fox
Australia	30	B.J. Barrett	2018	366	D.W. Carter
British Isles	33	D.W. Carter	2005	46	A.R. Hewson
Canada	29	D.W. Carter	2007	47	D.W. Carter
England	26	D.W. Carter	2006	178	D.W. Carter
Fiji	26	G.J. Fox	1987	29	C.M. Cullen
France	29	A.P. Mehrtens	2000	146	D.W. Carter
Georgia	15	S.J. Savea	2015	15	S.J. Savea
Ireland	33	A.P. Mehrtens	1997	81	A.P. Mehrtens
Italy	36	T.E. Brown	1999	53	D.W. Carter
Japan	45	S.D. Culhane	1995	45	S.D. Culhane
Namibia	18	B.J. Barrett	2015	18	B.J. Barrett
Pacific Islands	11	D.W. Carter	2004	11	D.W. Carter
Portugal	33	N.J. Evans	2007	33	N.J. Evans
Romania	17	N.J. Evans	2007	17	N.J. Evans
Samoa	30	T.E. Brown	2001	56	T.E. Brown
Scotland	23	A.P. Mehrtens	1995	108	A.P. Mehrtens
South Africa	25	C.J. Spencer	1997	255	D.W. Carter
	25	D.W. Carter	2006		
Tonga	32	T.E. Brown	2000	32	T.E. Brown
USA	14	J.P. Preston	1991	14	J.P. Preston
Wales	27	D.W. Carter	2010	162	D.W. Carter

WINNING PERCENTAGE
Minimum 30 test appearances

Name	Record	%	Name	Record	%
W.W.V. Crockett	66/71	93.0%	T.D. Woodcock	102/118	86.4
S.B. Williams	47/51	92.2	Q.J. Cowan	44/51	86.3
B.J. Franks	43/47	91.5	G.W. Whetton	50/58	86.2
I.J.A. Dagg	60/66	90.9	O.T. Franks	91/106	85.9
B.A. Retallick	68/75	90.7	A.G. Dalton	30/35	85.7
L. Romano	28/31	90.3	L.R. MacDonald	48/56	85.7
B.R. Smith	68/76	89.5	K.J. Read	101/118	85.6
C.G. Smith	84/94	89.4	R. So'oialo	53/62	85.5
B.J. Barrett	65/73	89.0	C.R. Jack	57/67	85.1
S.J. Savea	48/54	88.9	C.S. Jane	45/53	84.9
A.J. Whetton	31/35	88.6	A.R. Lienert-Brown	28/33	84.8
R.H. McCaw	131/148	88.5	A.J. Williams	65/77	84.4
D.S. Coles	53/60	88.3	A.K. Hore	70/83	84.3
S.J. Cane	53/60	88.3	J.M. Muliana	84/100	84.0
D.W. Carter	99/112	88.4	R.D. Thorne	42/50	84.0
L.J. Messam	38/43	88.4	J. Kaino	68/81	83.9
N.S. Tialata	38/43	88.4	G.M. Somerville	55/66	83.3
M.A. Nonu	91/103	88.3	I. Toeava	30/36	83.3
S.L. Whitelock	95/108	88.0	A.S. Savea	29/35	82.9
V.V.J. Vito	29/33	87.9	C.J. Taylor	34/41	82.9
J. Collins	42/48	87.5	G.J. Fox	38/46	82.6
T.T.R. Perenara	48/55	87.3	S.C. McDowall	38/46	82.6
P.A.T. Weepu	62/71	87.3	D.C. Howlett	51/62	82.3
A.J.D. Mauger	39/45	86.7	S.W. Sivivatu	37/45	82.2
T.J. Wright	26/30	86.7	J.T. Rokocoko	55/68	80.9
A.L. Smith	71/82	86.6	B.T. Kelleher	46/57	80.7
J.P.T. Moody	32/37	86.5	S.B.T. Fitzpatrick	74/92	80.4
R.S. Crotty	38/44	86.4	C.W. Dowd	48/60	80.0
K.F. Mealamu	114/132	86.4	C.J. Hayman	36/45	80.0
B.C. Thorn	51/59	86.4	C.L. McAlister	24/30	80.0

INTERNATIONAL COMPARISONS

MOST TRIES IN TEST MATCHES

	Tries	Tests	Average
New Zealand	**2088**	**580**	**3.60**
France	1733	754	2.30
Australia	1654	631	2.62
England	1624	727	2.23
Wales	1556	717	2.17
South Africa	1376	491	2.80

MOST POINTS IN TEST MATCHES

	Points	Tests	Average
New Zealand	**15,974**	**580**	**27.54**
France	13,759	754	18.18
Australia	13,274	631	21.04
England	12,450	727	17.12
Wales	12,304	717	17.16
South Africa	11,391	491	23.20

POINTS DIFFERENTIAL IN TEST MATCHES

	For	Against	Differential
New Zealand	**15,974**	**7,709**	**8,265**
South Africa	11,391	7,994	3,357
England	12,450	9,268	3,182
France	13,759	11,524	2,235
Australia	13,274	11,111	2,163
Wales	12,304	10,795	1,509

PLAYING RECORDS OF NEW ZEALAND TEAMS
1884–2018

Year	Description	Played	Won	Lost	Drawn	Points for	Points against
1884	in **New South Wales** and **New Zealand**	9	9	–	–	176	17
1893	in **New Zealand, New South Wales** and **Queensland**	11	10	1	–	175	48
1894	**New South Wales** in **New Zealand**	1	–	1	–	6	8
1896	**Queensland** in **New Zealand**	1	1	–	–	9	0
1897	in **New Zealand, New South Wales** and **Queensland**	11	9	2	–	238	83
1901	**New South Wales** in **New Zealand**	2	2	–	–	44	8
1903	in **Australia** and **New Zealand**	11	10	1	–	281	27
1904	**Great Britain** in **New Zealand**	1	1	–	–	9	3
1905	in **Australia** and **New Zealand**	7	4	1	2	89	30
	Australia in **New Zealand**	1	1	–	–	14	3
1905/06	in **the British Isles, France** and **North America**	35	34	1	–	976	59
1907	in **Australia**	8	6	1	1	115	53
1908	**Anglo-Welsh** in **New Zealand**	3	2	–	1	64	8
1910	in **Australia** and **New Zealand**	8	7	1	–	138	78
1913	**Australia** in **New Zealand**	4	3	1	–	79	52
	in **North America**	16	16	–	–	610	6
1914	in **Australia** and **New Zealand**	11	10	1	–	260	69
1920	in **Australia** and **New Zealand**	10	9	–	1	352	91
1921	**South Africa** and **New South Wales** in **New Zealand**	4	1	2	1	18	31
1922	in **Australia** and **New Zealand**	8	6	2	–	198	102
1923	**New South Wales** in **New Zealand**	3	3	–	–	91	26
1924/25	in **Australia, New Zealand, the British Isles, France** and **Canada**	38	36	2	–	981	180
1925	in **Australia** and **New Zealand**	8	6	2	–	132	67
	New South Wales in **New Zealand**	1	1	–	–	36	10
1926	in **Australia** and **New Zealand**	8	6	2	–	187	109
1928	in **South Africa** and **Australia**	23	17	5	1	397	153
	New South Wales in **New Zealand**	4	3	1	–	79	40
1929	in **Australia**	10	6	3	1	186	80
1930	**Great Britain** in **New Zealand**	5	4	1	–	87	40
1931	**Australia** in **New Zealand**	1	1	–	–	20	13
1932	in **Australia** and **New Zealand**	11	9	2	–	331	135
1934	in **Australia** and **New Zealand**	9	7	1	1	201	107
1935/36	in **the British Isles** and **Canada**	30	26	3	1	490	183
1936	**Australia** in **New Zealand**	3	3	–	–	65	32
1937	**South Africa** in **New Zealand**	3	1	2	–	25	37
1938	in **Australia**	9	9	–	–	279	73
1946	**Australia** in **New Zealand**	2	2	–	–	45	18
1947	in **Australia** and **New Zealand**	10	8	2	–	263	113
1949	in **South Africa**	25	14	7	4	241	157
	Australia in **New Zealand**	2	–	2	–	15	27

Playing Records of New Zealand Teams

Year	Tour	Played	Won	Lost	Drawn	Points for	Points against
1950	**British Isles** in **New Zealand**	4	3	–	1	34	20
1951	in **Australia** and **New Zealand**	13	13	–	–	375	86
1952	**Australia** in **New Zealand**	2	1	1	–	24	22
1953/54	in **the British Isles, France** and **North America**	36	30	4	2	598	152
1955	**Australia** in **New Zealand**	3	2	1	–	27	16
1956	**South Africa** in **New Zealand**	4	3	1	–	41	29
1957	in **Australia** and **New Zealand**	14	13	1	–	472	94
1958	**Australia** in **New Zealand**	3	2	1	–	45	17
1959	**British Isles** in **New Zealand**	4	3	1	–	57	42
1960	in **Australia** and **South Africa**	32	26	4	2	645	187
1961	**France** in **New Zealand**	3	3	–	–	50	12
1962	in **Australia**	10	9	1	–	426	49
	Australia in **New Zealand**	3	2	–	1	28	17
1963	**England** in **New Zealand**	2	2	–	–	30	17
1963/64	in **the British Isles, France** and **Canada**	36	34	1	1	613	159
1964	**Australia** in **New Zealand**	3	2	1	–	37	32
1965	**South Africa** in **New Zealand**	4	3	1	–	55	25
1966	**British Isles** in **New Zealand**	4	4	–	–	79	32
1967	**Australia** in **New Zealand**	1	1	–	–	29	9
	in **the British Isles, France** and **Canada**	17	16	–	1	370	135
1968	in **Australia** and **Fiji**	12	12	–	–	460	66
	France in **New Zealand**	3	3	–	–	40	24
1969	**Wales** in **New Zealand**	2	2	–	–	52	12
1970	in **Australia** and **South Africa**	26	23	3	–	789	234
1971	**British Isles** in **New Zealand**	4	1	2	1	42	48
1972	**Internal Tour**	9	9	–	–	355	88
	Australia in **New Zealand**	3	3	–	–	97	26
1972/73	in **the British Isles, France** and **North America**	32	25	5	2	640	266
1973	**Internal Tour** and **England** in **New Zealand**	5	2	3	–	88	83
1974	in **Australia** and **Fiji**	13	12	–	1	446	73
	in **Ireland, Wales** and **England**	8	7	–	1	127	50
1975	**Scotland** in **New Zealand**	1	1	–	–	24	–
1976	**Ireland** in **New Zealand**	1	1	–	–	11	3
	in **South Africa**	24	18	6	–	610	291
	in **Argentina** and **Uruguay**	9	9	–	–	321	72
1977	**British Isles** in **New Zealand**	4	3	1	–	54	41
	in **France** and **Italy**	9	8	1	–	216	86
1978	**Australia** in **New Zealand**	3	2	1	–	51	48
	in **the British Isles**	18	17	1	–	364	147
1979	**France** in **New Zealand**	2	1	1	–	42	33
	in **Australia**	2	1	1	–	41	15
	Argentina in **New Zealand**	2	2	–	–	33	15
1979	in **England** and **Scotland**	11	10	1	–	192	95
1980	in **Australia** and **Fiji**	16	12	3	1	507	126

		Played	Won	Lost	Drawn	Points for	Points against
	Fiji in **New Zealand**	1	1	–	–	33	–
	in **North America** and **Wales**	7	7	–	–	197	41
1981	**Scotland** in **New Zealand**	2	2	–	–	51	19
	South Africa in **New Zealand**	3	2	1	–	51	55
	in **Romania** and **France**	10	8	1	1	170	108
1982	**Australia** in **New Zealand**	3	2	1	–	72	53
1983	**British Isles** in **New Zealand**	4	4	–	–	78	26
	in **Australia**	1	1	–	–	18	8
	in **Scotland** and **England**	8	5	2	1	162	116
1984	**France** in **New Zealand**	2	2	–	–	41	27
	in **Australia**	14	13	1	–	600	117
	in **Fiji**	4	4	–	–	174	10
1985	**England** in **New Zealand**	2	2	–	–	60	28
	Australia in **New Zealand**	1	1	–	–	10	9
	in **Argentina**	7	6	–	1	263	87
1986	**France** in **New Zealand**	1	1	–	–	18	9
	Australia in **New Zealand**	3	1	2	–	34	47
	in **France**	8	7	1	–	218	87
1987	**World Cup**	6	6	–	–	298	52
	in **Australia**	1	1	–	–	30	16
	in **Japan**	5	5	–	–	408	16
1988	**Wales** in **New Zealand**	2	2	–	–	106	12
	in **Australia**	13	12	–	1	476	96
1989	**France** in **New Zealand**	2	2	–	–	59	37
	Argentina in **New Zealand**	2	2	–	–	109	21
	Australia in **New Zealand**	1	1	–	–	24	12
	in **Canada, Wales** and **Ireland**	14	14	–	–	454	122
1990	**Scotland** in **New Zealand**	2	2	–	–	52	34
	Australia in **New Zealand**	3	2	1	–	57	44
	in **France**	8	6	2	–	175	110
1991	in **Argentina**	9	9	–	–	358	80
	in **Australia**	1	–	1	–	12	21
	Australia in **New Zealand**	1	1	–	–	6	3
	World Cup	6	5	1	–	143	74
1992	**Centenary matches** in **New Zealand**	3	2	1	–	94	69
	Ireland in **New Zealand**	2	2	–	–	83	27
	in **Australia** and **South Africa**	16	13	3	–	567	252
1993	**British Isles** in **New Zealand**	3	2	1	–	57	51
	Australia in **New Zealand**	1	1	–	–	25	10
	Western Samoa in **New Zealand**	1	1	–	–	35	13
	in **England** and **Scotland**	13	12	1	–	386	156
1994	**France** in **New Zealand**	2	–	2	–	28	45
	South Africa in **New Zealand**	3	2	–	1	53	41
	in **Australia**	1	–	1	–	16	20
1995	**Canada** in **New Zealand**	1	1	–	–	73	7
	World Cup	6	5	1	–	327	119
	Australia in **New Zealand**	1	1	–	–	28	16

Playing Records of New Zealand Teams

		Played	Won	Lost	Drawn	Points for	Points against
	in **Australia**	1	1	–	–	34	23
	in **Italy** and **France**	8	7	1	–	339	126
1996	**Western Samoa, Scotland** in **NZ**	3	3	–	–	149	53
	Tri Nations	4	4	–	–	119	60
	in **South Africa1**	7	5	1	1	190	139
1997	**Fiji, Argentina, Australia1** in **NZ**	4	4	–	–	256	36
	Tri Nations	4	4	–	–	159	109
	in **British Isles**	9	8	–	1	395	119
1998	**England** in **New Zealand**	2	2	–	–	104	32
	Tri Nations	4	–	4	–	65	88
	in **Australia1**	1	–	1	–	14	19
1999	**Internal, Samoa, France** in **NZ**	3	3	–	–	147	31
	Tri Nations	4	3	1	–	103	61
	World Cup	6	4	2	–	255	111
2000	**Tonga, Scotland** in **New Zealand**	3	3	–	–	219	34
	Tri Nations	4	2	2	–	127	117
	in **France** and **Italy**	3	2	1	–	128	87
2001	**Samoa, Argentina, France** in **NZ**	3	3	–	–	154	37
	Tri Nations	4	2	2	–	79	70
	in **Ireland, Scotland** and **Argentina**	5	5	–	–	179	98
2002	**Italy, Ireland, Fiji** in **New Zealand**	4	4	–	–	187	42
	Tri Nations	4	3	1	–	97	65
	in **England, France** and **Wales**	3	1	1	1	91	68
2003	**England, Wales, France** in **New Zealand**	3	2	1	–	99	41
	Tri Nations	4	4	–	–	142	65
	World Cup	7	6	1	–	361	101
2004	**England, Argentina, Pacific Islands** in **New Zealand**	4	4	–	–	154	48
	Tri Nations	4	2	2	–	83	91
	in **Europe**	4	4	–	–	177	60
2005	**Fiji, Lions** in **New Zealand**	4	4	–	–	198	40
	Tri Nations	4	3	1	–	111	86
	in **Europe**	4	4	–	–	138	39
2006	**Ireland** in **New Zealand**						
	New Zealand in **Argentina**	3	3	–	–	86	59
	Tri Nations	6	5	1	–	179	112
	in **Europe**	4	4	–	–	156	44
2007	**France, Canada** in **New Zealand**	3	3	–	–	167	34
	Tri Nations	4	3	1	–	100	59
	World Cup	5	4	1	–	327	55
2008	**Ireland, England, Samoa** in **New Zealand**	4	4	–	–	203	57
	Tri Nations	6	4	2	–	152	106
	in **Hong Kong, United Kingdom** and **Ireland**	6	6	–	–	152	54
2009	**France, Italy** in **New Zealand**	3	2	1	–	63	43
	Tri Nations	6	3	3	–	141	131
	in **Japan** and **Europe**	6	5	1	–	147	80

Year	Description	Played	Won	Lost	Drawn	Points for	Points against
2010	**Ireland, Wales** in **New Zealand**	3	3	–	–	137	47
	Tri Nations	6	6	–	–	184	111
	in **Hong Kong, United Kingdom** and **Ireland**	5	4	1	–	174	88
2011	**Fiji** in **New Zealand**	1	1	–	–	60	14
	Tri Nations	4	2	2	–	95	64
	World Cup	7	7	–	–	301	72
2012	**Ireland** in **New Zealand**	3	3	–	–	124	29
	Rugby Championship and **Bledisloe Cup**	7	6	–	1	195	84
	In **Europe**	4	3	1	–	147	80
2013	**France** in **New Zealand**	3	3	–	–	77	22
	Rugby Championship and **Bledisloe Cup**	7	7	–	–	243	148
	In **Japan** and **Europe**	4	4	–	–	134	69
2014	**England** in **New Zealand**	3	3	–	–	84	55
	Rugby Championship and **Bledisloe Cup**	7	5	1	1	193	119
	In **USA** and **United Kingdom**	4	4	–	–	156	59
2015	In **Samoa**, **Rugby Championship** and **Bledisloe Cup**	5	4	1	–	151	94
	World Cup	7	7	–	–	290	97
2016	**Wales** in **New Zealand**	3	3	-	-	121	49
	Rugby Championship and **Bledisloe Cup**	7	7	-	-	299	94
	In **USA, Italy, Ireland** and **France**	4	3	1	-	142	78
2017	**Samoa, Lions** in **New Zealand**	4	2	1	1	144	54
	Rugby Championship and **Bledisloe Cup**	7	6	1	–	264	142
	In **England, France, Scotland** and **Wales**	5	5	–	–	152	98
2018	**France** in **New Zealand**	3	3	–	–	127	38
	Rugby Championship and **Bledisloe Cup**	7	6	1	–	262	152
	In **Japan, England, Ireland** and **Italy**	4	3	1	–	160	65
	TOTALS	1305	1102	164	39	35,770	12,909

[1] non Tri Nations

SURVIVING NEW ZEALAND REPRESENTATIVES

(over the age of 71 years as at 31 December, 2018)

	Born	Represented New Zealand
R.R. Elvidge	2 March, 1923	1946-49-50
R.A. Roper	11 August, 1923	1949-50
J.M. Tanner	11 January, 1927	1950-51-53-54
S.F. Hill	9 April, 1927	1955-56-57-58-59
W.A. McCaw	26 August, 1927	1951-53-54
C.P. Erceg	28 November, 1928	1951-52
M.S. Cockerill	8 December, 1928	1951
L.B. Steele	19 January, 1929	1951
K.F. Meates	20 February, 1930	1952
D. Young	1 April, 1930	1956-57-58-60-61-62-63-64
K. Davis	21 May, 1930	1952-53-54-55-58
E.S. Diack	22 July, 1930	1959
S.G. Bremner	2 August, 1930	1952-56-60
D.D. Wilson	30 January, 1931	1953-54
D.L. Ashby	15 February, 1931	1958
C.J. Loader	10 March, 1931	1953-54
D.N. McIntosh	1 April, 1931	1956-57
B.P.J. Molloy	12 August, 1931	1957
W.S.S. Freebairn	12 January, 1932	1953-54
L.J. Townsend	3 March, 1934	1955
I.N. MacEwan	1 May, 1934	1956-57-58-59-60-61-62
F.S. McAtamney	15 May, 1934	1956-57
W.D. Gillespie	6 August, 1934	1957-58-60
K.F. Laidlaw	9 August, 1934	1960
R.J. Boon	23 February, 1935	1960
R.J. Conway	22 April, 1935	1959-60-65
D.M. Connor	9 September, 1935	1961-62-63-64
J.R. Watt	29 December, 1935	1957-58-60-61-62
T.R. Lineen	5 January, 1936	1957-58-59-60
S.R. Nesbit	13 February, 1936	1960
J.F. McCullough	8 August, 1936	1959
A.J. Soper	7 September, 1936	1957
R.W. Caulton	10 January, 1937	1959-60-61-63-64
B.E. McPhail	26 January, 1937	1959
J.N. Creighton	10 March, 1937	1962
B.T. Thomas	21 July, 1937	1962-64
D.W. McKay	7 August, 1937	1961-62-63
A.H. Clarke	23 February, 1938	1958-59-60
S.T. Meads	12 July, 1938	1961-62-63-64-65-66
D.H. Cameron	17 November, 1938	1960
K.A. Nelson	26 November, 1938	1962-63-64
B.A. Watt	12 March, 1939	1962-63-64
N.W. Thimbleby	19 June, 1939	1970
W.M. Birtwistle	4 July, 1939	1965-67
E.W. Kirton	29 December, 1939	1963-64-67-68-69-70
D.W. Clark	22 February, 1940	1964
A.G.T. Jennings	15 June, 1940	1967
W.J. Nathan	8 July, 1940	1962-63-64-66-67

J. Major	8 August, 1940	1963-64-67
B.J. Lochore	3 September, 1940	1963-64-65-66-67-68-69-70-71
A.J. Stewart	11 October, 1940	1963-64
M.J. Dick	3 January, 1941	1963-64-65-66-67-69-70
D.A. Arnold	10 January, 1941	1963-64
J.F. Burns	17 February, 1941	1970
R.A. Guy	6 April, 1941	1971-72
M.C. Wills	11 October, 1941	1967
T.N. Wolfe	20 October, 1941	1961-62-63-68
T.J. Morris	3 January, 1942	1972-73
P.H. Clarke	23 January, 1942	1967
R.W. Norton	30 March, 1942	1971-72-73-74-75-76-77
B.L. Muller	11 June, 1942	1967-68-69-70-71
A.E. Smith	10 December, 1942	1967-69-70
W.L. Davis	15 December, 1942	1963-64-67-68-69-70
I.R. MacRae	6 April, 1943	1963-64-66-67-68-69-70
S.M. Going	19 August, 1943	1967-68-69-70-71-72-73-74-75-76-77
C.R. Laidlaw	16 November, 1943	1963-64-65-66-67-68-70
A.R. Sutherland	4 January, 1944	1968-70-71-72-73-76
R.A. Urlich	8 February, 1944	1970-72-73
P.A. Johns	16 March, 1944	1968
L.A. Clark	1 May, 1944	1972-73
W.D.R. Currey	2 June, 1944	1968
A.J. Wyllie	31 August, 1944	1970-71-72-73
A.R. Leslie	10 November, 1944	1974-75-76
S.C. Strahan	25 December, 1944	1967-68-70-72-73
R.J. Barber	14 January, 1945	1974
B.D.M. Furlong	10 March, 1945	1970
A.J. Kreft	27 March, 1945	1968
K.J. Tanner	25 April, 1945	1974-75-76
M.O. Knight	20 May, 1945	1968
I.M. Eliason	6 June, 1945	1972-73
G.F. Kember	15 November, 1945	1967-70
G.M. Crossman	30 November, 1945	1974-76
P.C. Harris	11 January, 1946	1976
L.W. Mains	16 February, 1946	1971-76
G.S. Thorne	25 February, 1946	1967-68-69-70
B. Holmes	7 April, 1946	1970-72-73
M.W. O'Callaghan	27 April, 1946	1968
I.A. Kirkpatrick	24 May, 1946	1967-68-69-70-71-72-73-74-75-76-77
G.J. Whiting	4 June, 1946	1972-73
S.E.G. Cron	7 July, 1946	1976
P.J. Whiting	6 August, 1946	1971-72-73-74-76
A.J. Gardiner	10 December, 1946	1974
O.G. Stephens	9 January, 1947	1968
H.H. Macdonald	11 January, 1947	1972-73-74-75-76
D.J. Robertson	6 February, 1947	1974-75-76-77
M. Sayers	1 May, 1947	1972-73
O.D. Bruce	23 May, 1947	1974-76-77-78
A.M. McNaughton	5 July, 1947	1971-72
J.E. Spiers	4 August, 1947	1976-79-80-81
M.G. Duncan	8 August, 1947	1971
K.A. Eveleigh	8 November, 1947	1974-76-77
D.A. Hales	22 November, 1947	1972-73
G.D. Rowlands	10 December, 1947	1976

NEW ZEALAND REPRESENTATIVES
1884–2018

Union affiliations are shown in parentheses, preceded by date of birth and, where applicable, date of death. A few of these dates have proved impossible to be traced and these are indicated with a question mark. War casualties are denoted by an asterisk. The numbers that follow each entry show the number of games played for New Zealand. These are followed in parentheses by the number of appearances in test matches, which are included in the total. Franchise team rather than Provincial teams have been used from 2013.

Abbott H.L. 1882–1971
(Taranaki) 1905–06 — 11 (1)
Adkins G.T.A. 1910–1976
(South Canterbury) 1935–36 — 10 (–)
Afeaki B.T.P. 1988–
(Chiefs) 2013 — 1 (1)
Afoa I.F. 1983–
(Auckland) 2005–06–08–09–10–11 — 38 (36)
Aitken G.G. 1898–1952
(Wellington) 1921 — 2 (2)
Alatini P.F. 1976–
(Otago) 1999–2001 — 20 (17)
Algar B. 1894–1989
(Wellington) 1920–21 — 6 (–)
Allan J. 1860–1934 (Otago) 1884 — 8 (–)
Allen F.R. 1920–2012
(Auckland) 1946–47–49 — 21 (6)
Allen L. 1870–1932
(Taranaki) 1896–97–1901 — 13 (–)
Allen M.R. 1967–
(Taranaki) 1993–95–96
(Manawatu) 1997 — 27 (8)
Allen N.H. 1958–1984
(Counties) 1980 — 9 (2)
Alley G.T. 1903–1986
(Southland) 1926
(Canterbury) 1928 — 19 (3)
Anderson A. 1961–
(Canterbury) 1983–84–85–87–88 — 25 (6)
Anderson B.L. 1960–
(Wairarapa Bush) 1986–87 — 3 (1)
Anderson E.J. 1931–2014
(Bay of Plenty) 1960 — 10 (–)
Anesi S.R. 1981–
(Waikato) 2005 — 1 (1)
Archer J.A. 1900–1979
(Southland) 1925 — 2 (–)
Archer W.R. 1930–2018
(Otago) 1955
(Southland) 1956–57 — 13 (4)
Argus W.G. 1921–2016
(Canterbury) 1946–47 — 10 (4)
Armit A.M. 1874–1899
(Otago) 1897 — 9 (–)
Armstrong A.L. 1878–1959
(Wairarapa) 1903 — 5 (–)
Arnold D.A. 1941–
(Canterbury) 1963–64 — 15 (4)
Arnold K.D. 1920–2006
(Waikato) 1947 — 8 (2)

Ashby D.L. 1931–
(Southland) 1958 — 1 (1)
Asher A.A. 1879–1965
(Auckland) 1903 — 11 (1)
Ashworth B.G. 1949–
(Auckland) 1978 — 7 (2)
Ashworth J.C. 1949–
(Canterbury) 1977–78–79–80–81
–82–83–84
(Hawke's Bay) 1985 — 52 (24)
Atiga B.A.C. 1983–
(Auckland) 2003 — 1 (1)
Atkinson H.J. 1888–1949
(West Coast) 1913 — 10 (1)
Aumua A.J. 1997–
(Wellington) 2017 — 2 (–)
Avery H.E. 1885–1961
(Wellington) 1910 — 6 (3)
Bachop G.T.M. 1967–
(Canterbury)
1987–88–89–90–91–92–94–95 — 54 (31)
Bachop S.J. 1966–
(Otago) 1992–93–94 — 18 (5)
Badeley C.E.O. 1896–1986
(Auckland) 1920–21–24 — 15 (2)
Badeley V.I.R. 1898–1971
(Auckland) 1922 — 5 (–)
Bagley K.P. 1931–1999
(Manawatu) 1953–54 — 20 (–)
Baird D.L. 1894–1943
(Southland) 1920 — 9 (–)
Baird J.A.S.* 1893–1917
(Otago) 1913 — 1 (1)
Balch W. 1871–1949
(Canterbury) 1894 — 1 (–)
Ball N. 1908–1986
(Wellington) 1931–32–35–36 — 22 (5)
Barber R.J. 1945–
(Southland) 1974 — 6 (–)
Barrell C.K. 1967–
(Canterbury) 1996–97 — 4 (–)
Barrett B.J. 1991–
(Taranaki) 2012
(Hurricanes) 2013–14–15–16–17–18 — 74 (73)
Barrett J. 1888–1971
(Auckland) 1913–14 — 3 (2)
Barrett J.M. 1997
(Hurricanes) 2017–18 — 9 (9)
Barrett S.K. 1993–
(Crusaders) 2016–17–18 — 31 (29)

Barry E.F. 1905–1993
(Wellington) 1932–34   10   (1)
Barry K.E. 1936–2014
(Thames Valley) 1962–63–64   23   (–)
Barry L.J. 1971–
(North Harbour) 1993–95   10   (1)
Bates S.P. 1980–
(Waikato) 2004   2   (1)
Batty G.B. 1951–
(Wellington) 1972–73–74–75
(Bay of Plenty) 1976–77   56   (15)
Batty W. 1905–1979
(Auckland) 1928–30–31   6   (4)
Bayly A. 1866–1907
(Taranaki) 1893–94–97   20   (–)
Bayly W. 1869–1950
(Taranaki) 1894   1   (–)
Beatty G.E. 1925–2004
(Taranaki) 1950   1   (1)
Bell J.R. 1900–1963
(Southland) 1923   1   (–)
Bell R.C. 1893–1960
(Otago) 1922   8   (–)
Bell R.H. 1925–2016
(Otago) 1951–52   9   (3)
Belliss E.A. 1894–1974
(Wanganui) 1920–21–22–23   20   (3)
Bennet R. 1879–1962
(Otago) 1905   1   (1)
Berghan T. 1914–1998
(Otago) 1938   6   (3)
Berry M.J. 1966–
(Wairarapa Bush) 1986
(Wellington) 1993   10   (1)
Berryman N.R. 1973–2015
(Northland) 1998   1   (1)
Best J.J. 1914–1994
(Marlborough) 1935–36   6   (–)
Bevan V.D. 1921–1996
(Wellington) 1947–49–50–53–54   25   (6)
Bird D.J. 1991–
(Crusaders) 2013–14
(Chiefs) 2017   3   (2)
Birtwistle W.M. 1939–
(Canterbury) 1965
(Waikato) 1967   12   (7)
Black J.E. 1951–
(Canterbury) 1976–77–78–79–80   26   (3)
Black N.W. 1925–2016
(Auckland) 1949   11   (1)
Black R.S.* 1893–1916
(Otago) 1914   6   (1)
Blackadder T.J. 1971–
(Canterbury) 1995–96–97–98–
99–2000   25   (12)
Blair B.A. 1979–
(Canterbury) 2001–02   6   (4)
Blair J.A. 1872–1911
(Wanganui) 1897   9   (–)
Blake A.W. 1922–2010
(Wairarapa) 1949   1   (1)

Blake J.M. 1902–1988
(Hawke's Bay) 1925–26   13   (–)
Bligh S. 1887–1955
(West Coast) 1910   5   (–)
Blowers A.F. 1975–
(Auckland) 1996–97–99   18   (11)
Bloxham K.C. 1954–2000
(Otago) 1980   2   (–)
Boe J.W. 1955–
(Waikato) 1981   2   (–)
Boggs E.G. 1922–2004
(Auckland) 1946–49   9   (2)
Bond J.G.P. 1920–1999
(Canterbury) 1949   1   (1)
Boon R.J. 1935–
(Taranaki) 1960   6   (–)
Booth E.E. 1876–1935
(Otago) 1905–06–07   24   (3)
Boric A.F. 1983–
(North Harbour) 2008–09–10–11   25   (24)
Boroevich K.G. 1960–
(King Country) 1983–84
(Wellington) 1986
(North Harbour) 1988   26   (3)
Botica F.M. 1963–
(North Harbour) 1986–87–88–89   27   (7)
Botting I.J. 1922–1980
(Otago) 1949   9   (–)
Bowden N.J.G. 1926–2009
(Taranaki) 1952   1   (1)
Bowers R.G. 1932–2000
(Wellington) 1953–54   15   (2)
Bowman A.W. 1915–1992
(Hawke's Bay) 1938   6   (3)
Bradanovich N.M. 1907–1961
(Otago) 1928   2   (–)
Braddon H.Y. 1863–1955
(Otago) 1884   7   (–)
Braid D.J. 1981–
(Auckland) 2002–03–08–10   6   (6)
Braid G.J. 1960–
(Bay of Plenty) 1983–84   13   (2)
Brake L.J. 1952–
(Bay of Plenty) 1976   5   (–)
Bremner S.G. 1930–
(Auckland) 1952
(Canterbury) 1956–60   18   (2)
Brewer M.R. 1964–
(Otago) 1986–87–88–89–90–91–92
(Canterbury) 1993–94–95   61   (32)
Bridge G.C. 1995–
(Crusaders) 2018   1   (1)
Briscoe K.C. 1936–2009
(Taranaki) 1959–60–62–63–64   43   (9)
Broadhurst J.P. 1987–
(Hurricanes) 2015–   1   (1)
Brooke R.M. 1966–
(Auckland) 1992–93–94–95–
96–97–98–99   69   (62)
Brooke Z.V. 1965–
(Auckland) 1987–88–89–90–
91–92–93–94–95–96–97   100   (58)

Brooke-Cowden M. 1963–
(Auckland) 1986–87   6   (3)
Brooker F.J. 1876–1939
(Canterbury) 1897   4   (–)
Broomhall S.R. 1976–
(Canterbury) 2002   4   (4)
Brown C. 1887–1966
(Taranaki) 1913–20   11   (2)
Brown H.M. 1910–1965
(Auckland) 1935–36   8   (–)
Brown H.W. 1904–1973
(Taranaki) 1924–25–26   20   (–)
Brown O.M. 1967–
(Auckland)
1990–92–93–94–95–96–97–98   69   (56)
Brown R.H. 1934–2014 (Taranaki)
1955–56–57–58–59–61–62   25   (16)
Brown T.E. 1975–
(Otago) 1999–2000–01   19   (18)
Brownlie C.J. 1895–1954
(Hawke's Bay) 1924–25–26–28   31   (3)
Brownlie J.L. 1899–1972
(Hawke's Bay) 1921   1   (–)
Brownlie M.J. 1896–1957
(Hawke's Bay) 1922–23–24–
25–26–28   61   (8)
Bruce J.A. 1887–1970
(Auckland) 1913–14   10   (2)
Bruce O.D. 1947–
(Canterbury) 1974–76–77–78   41   (14)
Bryers R.F. 1919–1987
(King Country) 1949   1   (1)
Buchan J.A.S. 1961–
(Canterbury) 1987   2   (–)
Budd A. 1880–1962
(South Canterbury) 1910   3   (–)
Budd T.A. 1922–1989
(Southland) 1946–49   2   (2)
Bullock-Douglas G.A.H. 1911–1958
(Wanganui) 1932–34   15   (5)
Bunce F.E. 1962–
(North Harbour) 1992–93–94–
95–96–97   69   (55)
Burgess G.A.J. 1954–
(Auckland) 1980–81   2   (1)
Burgess G.F. 1883–1961
(Southland) 1905   1   (1)
Burgess R.E. 1949–
(Manawatu) 1971–72–73   30   (7)
Burgoyne M.M. 1951–2016
(North Auckland) 1979   6   (–)
Burke P.S. 1927–2017
(Taranaki) 1951–55–57   12   (3)
Burns J.F. 1941–
(Canterbury)1970   9   (–)
Burns P.J. 1881–1943
(Canterbury) 1908–10–13   9   (5)
Burrows J.T. 1904–1991
(Canterbury) 1928   9   (–)
Burry H.C. 1930–2013
(Canterbury) 1960   11   (–)

Burt J.R. 1874–1933
(Otago) 1901   1   (–)
Bush R.G. 1909–96
(Otago) 1931   1   (1)
Bush W.K. TeP. 1949–
(Canterbury) 1974–75–76–77–
78–79   37   (12)
Butland H. 1872–1956
(West Coast) 1893–94   9   (–)
Butler V.C. 1907–1971
(Auckland) 1928   1   (–)
Buxton J.B. 1933–2007
(Canterbury) 1955–56   2   (2)
Cabot P.S. deQ. 1900–1998
(Otago) 1921   1   (–)
Cain M.J. 1885–1951
(Taranaki) 1913–14   24   (4)
Calcinai U.P. 1892–1963
(Wellington) 1922   5   (–)
Callesen J.A. 1950–
(Manawatu) 1974–75–76   18   (4)
Calnan J.J. 1876–1947
(Wellington) 1897   9   (–)
Cameron B.D. 1996
(Crusaders) 2018   1   (1)
Cameron D. 1887–1947
(Taranaki) 1908   3   (3)
Cameron D.H. 1938–
(Mid Canterbury) 1960   8   (–)
Cameron L.M. 1959–
(Manawatu) 1979–80–81   17   (5)
Cane S.J. 1992–
(Bay of Plenty) 2012
(Chiefs) 2013–14–15–16–17–18   61   (60)
Carleton S.R. 1904–1973
(Canterbury) 1928–29   21   (6)
Carrington K.R. 1950–
(Auckland) 1971–72   9   (3)
Carroll A.J. 1895–1974
(Manawatu) 1920–21   8   (–)
Carson W.N.* 1916–1944
(Auckland) 1938   3   (–)
Carter D.W. 1982–
(Canterbury) 2003–04–05–06–
07–08–09–10–11–12
(Crusaders) 2013–14–15   112   (112)
Carter G. 1854–1922
(Auckland) 1884   7   (–)
Carter M.P. 1968–
(Auckland) 1991–97–98   10   (7)
Cartwright S.C. 1954–
(Canterbury) 1976   7   (–)
Casey S.T. 1882–1960
(Otago) 1905–06–07–08   38   (8)
Cashmore A.R. 1973
(Auckland) 1996–97   2   (2)
Catley E.H. 1915–1975
(Waikato) 1946–47–49   21   (7)
Caughey T.H.C. 1911–1993
(Auckland) 1932–34–35–36–37   39   (9)

Caulton R.W. 1937–
(Wellington) 1959–60–61–63–64   50 (16)
Cherrington N.P. 1924–1979
(North Auckland) 1950–51   7 (1)
Christian D.L. 1923–1977
(Auckland) 1949   11 (1)
Clamp M. 1961–
(Wellington) 1984–85   15 (2)
Clark D.W. 1940–
(Otago) 1964   2 (2)
Clark F.L. 1902–1972
(Canterbury) 1928   4 (–)
Clark L.A. 1944–
(Otago) 1972–73   7 (–)
Clark W.H. 1929–2010
(Wellington) 1953–54–55–56   24 (9)
Clarke A.H. 1938–
(Auckland) 1958–59–60   14 (3)
Clarke D.B. 1933–2002
(Waikato) 1956–57–58–59–60–
61–62–63–64   89 (31)
Clarke E. 1968–
(Auckland) 1992–93–98   24 (10)
Clarke I.J. 1931–1997
(Waikato) 1953–54–55–56–57–
58–59–60–61–62–63–64   83 (24)
Clarke P.H. 1942–
(Marlborough) 1967   4 (–)
Clarke R.L. 1909–1972
(Taranaki) 1932   9 (2)
Cobden D.G.* 1914–1940
(Canterbury) 1937   1 (1)
Cockerill M.S. 1928–
(Taranaki) 1951   11 (3)
Cockroft E.A.P. 1890–1973
(South Canterbury) 1913–14   7 (3)
Cockroft S.G. 1864–1955
(Manawatu) 1893
(Hawke's Bay) 1894   12 (–)
Codlin B.W. 1956–
(Counties) 1980   13 (3)
Coffin P.H. 1964–
(King Country) 1996   3 (–)
Coles D.S. 1986–
(Wellington) 2012
(Hurricanes) 2013–14–15–16–17–18   60 (60)
Colling G.L. 1946–2003
(Otago) 1972–73   21 (–)
Collins A.H. 1906–1988
(Taranaki) 1932–34   15 (3)
Collins J. 1980–2015
(Wellington) 2001–03–04–
05–06–07   50 (48)
Collins J.L. 1939–2007
(Poverty Bay) 1964–65   3 (3)
Collins W.R. 1910–1993
(Hawke's Bay) 1935   7 (–)
Colman J.T.H. 1887–1965
(Taranaki) 1907–08   6 (4)
Coltman L.J. 1990–
(Highlanders) 2016–18   4 (4)

Conn S.B. 1953–
(Auckland) 1976–80   6 (–)
Connolly L.S. 1921–2005
(Southland) 1947   5 (–)
Connor D.M. 1935–
(Auckland) 1961–62–63–64   15 (12)
Conrad W.J.M. 1925–1972
(Waikato) 1949   10 (–)
Conway R.J. 1935–
(Otago) 1959–60
(Bay of Plenty) 1965   25 (10)
Cooke A.E. 1901–1977
(Auckland) 1924–25
(Hawke's Bay) 1926
(Wairarapa) 1928
(Wellington) 1930   44 (8)
Cooke A.E. 1870–1900
(Canterbury) 1894   1 (–)
Cooke R.J. 1880–1940
(Canterbury) 1903   10 (1)
Cooksley M.S.B. 1971–
(Counties) 1992–93
(Waikato) 1994–95–97–2001   23 (11)
Cooper G.J.L. 1965–
(Auckland) 1986
(Otago) 1992   7 (7)
Cooper M.J.A. 1966–
(Hawke's Bay) 1987
(Waikato) 1992–93–94–96   26 (8)
Corbett J. 1880–1945
(West Coast) 1905   16 (–)
Corkill T.G. 1901–1966
(Hawke's Bay) 1925   4 (–)
Corner M.M.N. 1908–1992
(Auckland) 1930–31–32–34–35–36   25 (6)
Cossey R.R. 1935–1986
(Counties) 1958   1 (1)
Cottrell A.I. 1907–1988
(Canterbury) 1929–30–31–32   22 (11)
Cottrell W.D. 1943–2013
(Canterbury) 1967–68–70–71   37 (9)
Couch M.B.R. 1925–1996
(Wairarapa) 1947–49   7 (3)
Coughlan T.D. 1934–2017
(South Canterbury) 1958   1 (1)
Cowan Q.J. 1982–
(Southland) 2004–05–06–08
–09–10–11   53 (51)
Creighton J.N. 1937–
(Canterbury) 1962   6 (1)
Cribb R.T. 1976–
(North Harbour) 2000–01   15 (15)
Crichton S. 1954–
(Wellington) 1983–84–85   7 (2)
Crockett W.W.V. 1983–
(Canterbury) 2009–11–12
(Crusaders) 2013–14–15–16–17   72 (71)
Cron S.E.G. 1946–
(Canterbury) 1976   6 (–)
Cross T. 1876–1930
(Canterbury) 1901
(Wellington) 1904–05   3 (2)

Crossman G.M. 1945–
(Bay of Plenty) 1974–76　　19　(–)
Crotty R.J. 1988–
(Crusaders) 2013–14–15–16–18　44　(44)
Crowley K.J. 1961–
(Taranaki) 1983–84–85–86–
87–90–91　　35　(19)
Crowley P.J.B. 1923–1981
(Auckland) 1949–50　　21　(6)
Cruden A.W. 1989–
(Manawatu) 2010–11–12
(Chiefs) 2013–14–16–17　　50　(50)
Culhane S.D. 1968–
(Southland) 1995–96　　9　(6)
Cullen C.M. 1976–
(Manawatu) 1996–97
(Wellington) 1998–99–2000–01–02　60　(58)
Cummings W. 1889–1955
(Canterbury) 1913–21　　3　(2)
Cundy R.T. 1901–1955
(Wairarapa) 1929　　6　(1)
Cunningham G.R. 1955–
(Auckland) 1979–80　　17　(5)
Cunningham W. 1874–1927
(Auckland) 1901–05–06–07–08　39　(9)
Cupples L.F. 1898–1972
(Bay of Plenty) 1922–23–24–25　29　(2)
Currey W.D.R. 1944–
(Taranaki) 1968　　7　(–)
Currie C.J. 1955–
(Canterbury) 1978　　4　(2)
Cuthill J.E. 1892–1970
(Otago) 1913　　16　(2)

Dagg I.J.A. 1988–
(Hawke's Bay) 2010–11–12
(Crusaders) 2013–14–15–16–17　66　(66)
Dalley W.C. 1901–1989
(Canterbury) 1924–25–26–28–29　35　(5)
Dalton A.G. 1951–
(Counties) 1977–78–79–80–81–
82–83–84–85　　58　(35)
Dalton D. 1913–1995
(Hawke's Bay) 1935–36–37–38　21　(9)
Dalton R.A. 1919–1997
(Wellington) 1947
(Otago) 1949　　20　(2)
Dalzell G.N. 1921–1989
(Canterbury) 1953–54　　22　(5)
D'Arcy A.E. 1870–1919
(Wairarapa) 1893–94　　7　(–)
Davie M.G. 1955–
(Canterbury) 1983　　5　(1)
Davies W.A. 1939–2008
(Auckland) 1960
(Otago) 1962　　17　(3)
Davis C.S. 1975–
(Manawatu) 1996　　2　(–)
Davis K. 1930–
(Auckland) 1952–53–54–55–58　25　(10)

Davis L.J. 1943–2008
(Canterbury) 1976–77　　16　(3)
Davis W.L. 1942–
(Hawke's Bay) 1963–64–67–
68–69–70　　53　(11)
Davy E. 1850–1935
(Wellington) 1884　　3　(–)
Deans I.B. 1960–
(Canterbury) 1987–88–89　　23　(10)
Deans R.G. 1884–1908
(Canterbury) 1905–06–08　　24　(5)
Deans R.M. 1959–
(Canterbury) 1983–84–85　　19　(5)
Delamore G.W. 1920–2008
(Wellington) 1949　　9　(1)
Delany M.P. 1982–
(Bay of Plenty) 2009　　2　(1)
de Malmanche A.P. 1984–
(Waikato) 2009–10　　5　(5)
Dermody C. 1980–
(Southland) 2006　　3　(3)
Devine S.J. 1976–
(Auckland) 2002–03　　10　(10)
Dewar H.* 1883–1915
(Taranaki) 1913　　16　(2)
Diack E.S. 1930–
(Otago) 1959　　1　(1)
Dick J. 1912–2002
(Auckland) 1937–38　　5　(3)
Dick M.J. 1941–
(Auckland) 1963–64–65–
66–67–69–70　　55　(15)
Dickinson G.R. 1903–1978
(Otago) 1922　　5　(–)
Dickson D.McK. 1900–1978
(Otago) 1925　　7　(–)
Dixon E.C. 1989–
(Highlanders) 2016　　3　(3)
Dixon M.J. 1929–2004
(Canterbury) 1953–54–56–57　28　(10)
Dobson R.L. 1923–1994
(Auckland) 1949　　1　(1)
Dodd E.H.* 1880–1918
(Wellington) 1901–05　　3　(1)
Donald A.J. 1957–
(Wanganui) 1981–83–84　　20　(7)
Donald J.G. 1898–1981
(Wairarapa) 1920–21–22–25　22　(2)
Donald Q. 1900–1965
(Wairarapa) 1923–24–25　　23　(4)
Donald S.R. 1983–
(Waikato) 2008–09–10–11　25　(23)
Donaldson M.W. 1955–
(Manawatu) 1977–78–79–80–81　35　(13)
Donnelly T.J.S. 1981–
(Otago) 2009–10　　15　(15)
Dougan J.P. 1946–2006
(Wellington) 1972–73　　12　(2)
Douglas J.B. 1890–1964
(Otago) 1913　　9　(–)

Dowd C.W. 1969–
(Auckland) 1993–94–95–96–
97–98–99–2000   67   (60)
Dowd G.W. 1963–
(North Harbour) 1992   8   (1)
Downing A.J.* 1886–1915
(Auckland) 1913–14   26   (5)
Drake J.A. 1959–2008
(Auckland) 1985–86–87   12   (8)
Drake W.A. 1879–1941
(Canterbury) 1901   1   (–)
Drummond M.D. 1994–
(Crusaders) 2017–18   2   (1)
Duff R.H. 1925–2006
(Canterbury) 1951–52–55–56   18   (11)
Duffie M.D. 1990
(Blues) 2017   2   (–)
Duggan R.J.L. 1972–
(Waikato) 1999   1   (1)
Dumbell J.T. 1859–1936
(Wellington) 1884   5   (–)
Duncan J. 1869–1953
(Otago) 1897–1901–03   10   (1)
Duncan M.G. 1947–
(Hawke's Bay) 1971   2   (2)
Duncan W.D. 1892–1961
(Otago) 1920–21   11   (3)
Dunn E.J. 1955–
(North Auckland) 1978–79–81   20   (2)
Dunn I.T.W. 1960–
(North Auckland) 1983–84   13   (3)
Dunn J.M. 1918–2003
(Auckland) 1946   1   (1)

Earl A.T. 1961–
(Canterbury)
1986–87–88–89–91–92   45   (14)
Eastgate B.P. 1927–2007
(Canterbury) 1952–53–54   17   (3)
Eaton J.J. 1982–
(Taranaki) 2005–06–08–09   17   (15)
Eckhold A.G. 1885–1931
(Otago) 1907   3   (–)
Eliason I.M. 1945–
(Taranaki) 1972–73   19   (–)
Elliot H.T.P. 1986–
(Hawke's Bay) 2008–10,12
(Chiefs) 2015   5   (4)
Elliott K.G. 1922–2006
(Wellington) 1946   2   (2)
Ellis A.M. 1984–
(Canterbury) 2006–07–08–
09–10–11
(Crusaders) 2015   28   (28)
Ellis M.C.G. 1971–
(Otago) 1992–93–95   21   (8)
Ellison T.E. 1983–
(Wellington) 2009
(Otago) 2012   5   (4)
Ellison T.R. 1867–1904
(Wellington) 1893   7   (–)

Elsom A.E.G. 1925–2010
(Canterbury) 1952–53–54–55   22   (6)
Elvidge R.R. 1923–
(Otago) 1946–49–50   19   (9)
Elvy W.L. 1901–1977
(Canterbury) 1925–26   12   (–)
Erceg C.P. 1928–
(Auckland) 1951–52   9   (4)
Evans B.R. 1984–
(Hawke's Bay) 2009   2   (2)
Evans C.E. 1896–1975
(Canterbury) 1921   1   (–)
Evans D.A. 1886–1940
(Hawke's Bay) 1910   4   (1)
Evans G.O. 1991–
(Hurricanes) 2018   1   (1)
Evans N.J. 1980–
(North Harbour) 2004
(Otago) 2005–06–07   16   (16)
Eveleigh K.A. 1947–
(Manawatu) 1974–76–77   30   (4)

Fanning A.H.N. 1890–1963
(Canterbury) 1913   1   (1)
Fanning B.J. 1874–1946
(Canterbury) 1903–04   9   (2)
Farrell C.P. 1956–
(Auckland) 1977   2   (2)
Faumuina C.C. 1986–
(Auckland) 2012
(Blues) 2013–14–15–16–17   50   (50)
Fawcett C.L. 1954–
(Auckland) 1976   13   (2)
Fea W.R. 1898–1988
(Otago) 1921   1   (1)
Feek G.E. 1975–
(Canterbury) 1999–2000–01   10   (10)
Fekitoa M.F. 1992–
(Highlanders) 2014–15–16–17   24   (24)
Fifita V.T.L. 1992–
(Hurricanes) 2017–18   10   (9)
Filipo R.A. 1979–
(Wellington) 2007–08   5   (4)
Finlay B.E.L. 1927–1982
(Manawatu) 1959   1   (1)
Finlay J. 1916–2001
(Manawatu) 1946   1   (1)
Finlay M.C. 1963–
(Manawatu) 1984   2   (–)
Finlayson I. 1899–1980
(North Auckland) 1925–26–
28–30   36   (6)
Fisher T. 1891–1968
(Buller) 1914   5   (–)
Fitzgerald C.J. 1899–1961
(Marlborough) 1922   5   (–)
Fitzgerald J.T. 1928–1993
(Wellington) 1952–53–54   17   (1)
Fitzpatrick B.B.J. 1931–2006
(Poverty Bay) 1951
(Wellington) 1953–54   22   (3)

Fitzpatrick S.B.T. 1963–
(Auckland) 1986–87–88–89–90
91–92–93–94–95–96–97   128 (92)
Flavell T.V. 1976–
(North Harbour) 2000–01
(Auckland) 2006–07   22 (22)
Fleming J.K. 1953–
(Wellington) 1978–79–80   35 (5)
Fletcher C.J.C. 1894–1973
(North Auckland) 1921   2 (1)
Flynn C.R. 1981–
(Canterbury) 2003–04–08–09–
10–11   17 (15)
Fogarty R. 1891–1980
(Taranaki) 1921   2 (2)
Ford B.R. 1951–
(Marlborough) 1977–78–79   20 (4)
Ford W.A. 1895–1959
(Canterbury) 1921–22–23   9 (–)
Forster S.T. 1969–
(Otago) 1993–94–95   12 (6)
Fox G.J. 1962–
(Auckland) 1984–85–86–87–
88–89–90–91–92–93   78 (46)
Francis A.R.H. 1882–1957
(Auckland) 1905–07–08–10   18 (10)
Francis W.C. 1894–1981
(Wellington) 1913–14   12 (5)
Franks B.J. 1984–
(Tasman) 2008–10–11–12
(Hurricanes) 2013–14–15   48 (47)
Franks O.T. 1987–
(Canterbury) 2009–10–11–12
(Crusaders) 2013–14–15–16–17–18   106 (106)
Fraser B.G. 1953–
(Wellington) 1979–80–81–82–83–84   55 (23)
Frazer H.F. 1915–2003
(Hawke's Bay) 1946–47–49   15 (5)
Freebairn W.S.S. 1932–
(Manawatu) 1953–54   14 (–)
Freitas D.F.E. 1901–1968
(West Coast) 1928   4 (–)
Frizell S.M. 1994–
(Highlanders) 2018   4 (4)
Fromont R.T. 1969–
(Auckland) 1993–95   10 (–)
Frost H. 1869–1954
(Canterbury) 1896   1 (–)
Fryer F.C. 1886–1958
(Canterbury) 1907–08   9 (4)
Fuller W.B. 1883–1957
(Canterbury) 1910   6 (2)
Furlong B.D.M. 1945–
(Hawke's Bay) 1970   11 (1)

Gage D.R. 1868–1916
(Wellington) 1893–96   8 (–)
Gallagher J.A. 1964–
(Wellington) 1986–87–88–89   41 (18)
Gallaher D.* 1873–1917
(Auckland) 1903–04–05–06   36 (6)

Gard P.C. 1947–1990
(North Otago) 1971–72   7 (1)
Gardiner A.J. 1946–
(Taranaki) 1974   11 (1)
Gardner J.H. 1870–1909
(South Canterbury) 1893   4 (–)
Gatland W.D. 1963–
(Waikato) 1988–89–90–91   17 (–)
Gear H.E. 1984–
(Wellington) 2008–10–11–12   15 (14)
Gear R.L. 1978–
(North Harbour) 2004
(Nelson Bays) 2005
(Tasman) 2006
(Canterbury) 2007   20 (19)
Geddes J.H. 1907–1990
(Southland) 1929   6 (1)
Geddes W.McK. 1893–1950
(Auckland) 1913   1 (1)
Gemmell B.McL. 1950–
(Auckland) 1974   6 (2)
Gemmell S.W. 1896–1970
(Hawke's Bay) 1923   1 (–)
George V.L. 1908–1996
(Southland) 1938   7 (3)
Gibbes J.B. 1977–
(Waikato) 2004–05   8 (8)
Gibson D.P.E. 1975–
(Canterbury) 1999–2000–02   19 (19)
Gilbert G.D.M. 1911–2002
(West Coast) 1935–36   27 (4)
Gillespie C.T. 1883–1964
(Wellington) 1913   1 (1)
Gillespie W.D. 1934–
(Otago) 1957–58–60   23 (1)
Gillett G.A. 1877–1956
(Canterbury) 1905–06
(Auckland) 1907–08   38 (8)
Gillies C.C. 1912–1996
(Otago) 1936   2 (1)
Gilray C.M. 1885–1974
(Otago) 1905   1 (1)
Given F.J. 1876–1921
(Otago) 1903   9 (–)
Glasgow F.T. 1880–1939
(Taranaki) 1905–06
(Southland) 1908   35 (6)
Glenn W.S. 1877–1953
(Taranaki) 1904–05–06   19 (2)
Glennie E. 1870–1908
(Canterbury) 1897   6 (–)
Goddard J.W. 1920–1996
(South Canterbury) 1949   8 (–)
Goddard M.P. 1921–1974
(South Canterbury) 1946–47–49   20 (5)
Going K.T. 1942–2008
(North Auckland) 1974   3 (–)
Going S.M. 1943–
(North Auckland) 1967–68–69–70–
71–72–73–74–75–76–77   86 (29)

Goldsmith J.A. 1969–
(Waikato) 1988   8 (–)
Good A. 1867–1938
(Taranaki) 1893   4 (–)
Good H.M. 1871–1941
(Taranaki) 1894   1 (–)
Goodhue E.J. 1995–
(Crusaders) 2017–18   8 (7)
Gordon S.B. 1967–
(Waikato) 1989–90–91–93   19 (2)
Gordon W.R. 1965–
(Waikato) 1990   3 (–)
Graham D.J. 1935–2017
(Canterbury) 1958–60–61–62–
63–64   53 (22)
Graham J.B. 1884–1941
(Otago) 1913–14   19 (3)
Graham M.G. 1931–2015
(New South Wales) 1960   1 (–)
Graham W.G. 1957–
(Otago) 1978–79   8 (1)
Granger K.W. 1951–
(Manawatu) 1976   6 (–)
Grant L.A. 1923–2002
(South Canterbury) 1947–49–51   23 (4)
Gray G.D. 1880–1961
(Canterbury) 1908–13   14 (3)
Gray K.F. 1938–1992
(Wellington) 1963–64–65–66–
67–68–69   50 (24)
Gray R. 1870–1951
(Wairarapa) 1893   2 (–)
Gray W.N. 1932–1993
(Bay of Plenty) 1955–56–57   11 (6)
Green C.I. 1961–
(Canterbury) 1983–84–85–86–87   39 (20)
Greene K.M. 1949–
(Waikato) 1976–77   8 (–)
Grenside B.A. 1899–1989
(Hawke's Bay) 1928–29   21 (6)
Griffiths J.L. 1912–2001
(Wellington) 1934–35–36–38   30 (7)
Gudsell K.E. 1924–2007
(Wanganui) 1949   6 (–)
Guildford Z.R. 1989–
(Hawke's Bay) 2009–10–11–12   10 (10)
Guy R.A. 1941–
(North Auckland) 1971–72   9 (4)

Haden A.M. 1950–
(Auckland) 1972–73–76–77–78–
79–80–81–82–83–84–85   117 (41)
Hadley S. 1904–1970
(Auckland) 1928   11 (4)
Hadley W.E. 1910–1992
(Auckland) 1934–35–36   25 (8)
Haig J.S. 1924–1996
(Otago) 1946   2 (2)
Haig L.S. 1922–1992
(Otago) 1950–51–53–54   29 (9)
Halai F. 1988–
(Blues) 2013   1 (1)
Hales D.A. 1947–
(Canterbury) 1972–73   27 (4)
Hames K.S. 1988–
(Chiefs) 2016–17   10 (9)
Hamilton D.C. 1883–1925
(Southland) 1908   1 (1)
Hamilton S.E. 1980–
(Canterbury) 2006   2 (2)
Hammett M.G. 1972–
(Canterbury) 1999–2000–01–
02–03   30 (29)
Hammond I.A. 1925–1998
(Marlborough) 1951–52   8 (1)
Handcock R.A. 1874–1956
(Auckland) 1897   8 (–)
Hardcastle W.R. 1874–1944
(Wellington) 1897   7 (–)
Harding S. 1980–
(Otago) 2002   1 (1)
Harper E.T.* 1877–1918
(Canterbury) 1904–05–06   11 (2)
Harper G. 1867–1937
(Nelson) 1893   3 (–)
Harris J.H.* 1903–1944
(Canterbury) 1925   8 (–)
Harris N.P. 1992–
(Chiefs) 2014–16–17–18   22 (20)
Harris P.C. 1946–
(Manawatu) 1976   4 (1)
Harris W.A. 1876–1950
(Otago) 1897   9 (–)
Hart A.H. 1897–1965
(Taranaki) 1924–25   17 (1)
Hart G.F.* 1909–1944
(Canterbury) 1930–31–32–34–
35–36   35 (11)
Harvey B.A. 1959–
(Wairarapa Bush) 1986   1 (1)
Harvey I.H. 1903–1966
(Wairarapa) 1924–25–26–28   18 (1)
Harvey L.R. 1919–1993
(Otago) 1949–50   22 (8)
Harvey P. 1880–1949
(Canterbury) 1904   1 (1)
Hasell E.W. 1889–1966
(Canterbury) 1913–20   7 (2)
Havili D.K. 1994–
(Crusaders) 2017   5 (3)
Hay-MacKenzie W.E. 1874–1946
(Auckland) 1901   2 (–)
Hayman C.J. 1979–
(Otago) 2001–02–04–05–06–07   46 (45)
Hayward H.O. 1883–1970
(Auckland) 1908   1 (1)
Hazlett E.J. 1938–2014
(Southland) 1966–67   12 (6)
Hazlett W.E. 1905–1978
(Southland) 1926–28–30   26 (8)
Heeps T.R. 1938–2002
(Wellington) 1962   10 (5)

Heke W.R. (played as W. Rika) 1894–1989
(North Auckland) 1929   6   (3)
Helmore G.H.N. 1862–1922
(Canterbury) 1884   7   (–)
Hemara B.S. 1957–
(Manawatu) 1985   3   (–)
Hemi R.C. 1933–2000
(Waikato) 1953–54–55–56–57–59–60   46   (16)
Hemopo J.N. 1993–
(Highlanders) 2018   3   (3)
Henderson P. 1926–2014
(Wanganui) 1949–50   19   (7)
Henderson P.W. 1964–
(Otago) 1989–90–91
(Southland) 1992–93–95   25   (7)
Hendrie J.M. 1951–
(Western Australia) 1970   1   (–)
Herewini M.A. 1940–2014
(Auckland) 1962–63–64–65–66–67   32   (10)
Herrold M. 1869–1949
(Auckland) 1893   2   (–)
Hewett D.N. 1971–
(Canterbury) 2001–02–03   24   (22)
Hewett J.A. 1968–
(Auckland) 1991   1   (1)
Hewitt N.J. 1968–
(Hawke's Bay) 1993
(Southland) 1995–96–97–98   23   (9)
Hewson A.R. 1954–
(Wellington) 1979–81–82–83–84   34   (19)
Hickey P.H. 1899–1942
(Taranaki) 1922   2   (–)
Higginson G. 1954–
(Canterbury) 1980–81
(Hawke's Bay) 1982–83   20   (6)
Hill D.W. 1978–
(Waikato) 2001–06   3   (1)
Hill S.F. 1927–
(Canterbury) 1955–56–57–58–59   19   (11)
Hines G.R. 1960–
(Waikato) 1980   12   (1)
Hobbs F.G. 1920–1985
(Canterbury) 1947   6   (–)
Hobbs M.J.B. 1960–2012
(Canterbury) 1983–84–85–86   39   (21)
Hoeata J.M.R.A. 1982–
(Taranaki) 2011   3   (3)
Hoeft C.H. 1974–
(Otago) 1998–99–2000–01–03   31   (30)
Hogan J. 1881–1945
(Wanganui) 1907   2   (–)
Holah M.R. 1976–
(Waikato) 2001–02–03–04–05–06   39   (36)
Holden A.W. 1907–1970
(Otago) 1928   3   (–)
Holder E.C. 1908–1974
(Buller) 1932–34   10   (1)
Holmes B. 1946–
(North Auckland) 1970–72–73   31   (–)

Hook L.S. 1905–1979
(Auckland) 1928–29   12   (3)
Hooper J.A. 1913–1976
(Canterbury) 1937–38   7   (3)
Hopa A.R. 1971–1998
(Waikato) 1997   4   (–)
Hopkinson A.E. 1941–1999
(Canterbury) 1967–68–69–70   35   (9)
Hore A.K. 1978–
(Taranaki) 2002–04–05–06–07–08–09–10–11–12
(Highlanders) 2013   83   (83)
Hore J. 1907–1979 (Otago)
1928–30–32–34–35–36   45   (10)
Horsley R.H. 1932–2007
(Wellington) 1960
(Manawatu) 1963   31   (3)
Hotop J. 1929–2015
(Canterbury) 1952–55   3   (3)
Howarth S.P. 1968–
(Auckland) 1993–94   10   (4)
Howden J. 1900–1978
(Southland) 1928   1   (–)
Howlett D.C. 1978–
(Auckland) 2000–01–02–03–04–05–06–07   63   (62)
Hughes A.M. 1924–2005
(Auckland) 1947–49–50   7   (6)
Hughes D.J. 1869–1951
(Taranaki) 1894   1   (–)
Hughes E. 1881–1928
(Southland) 1907–08
(Wellington) 1921   9   (6)
Hullena L.C. 1965–
(Wellington) 1990–91   9   (–)
Humphreys G.W. 1870–1933
(Canterbury) 1894   1   (–)
Humphries A.L. 1874–1953
(Taranaki) 1897–1901–03   15   (–)
Hunt D. 1995–
(Highlanders) 2017–18   2   (1)
Hunter B.A. 1950–
(Otago) 1970–71   10   (3)
Hunter J. 1879–1962
(Taranaki) 1905–06–07–08   36   (11)
Hurst I.A. 1951–
(Canterbury) 1972–73–74   32   (5)

Ieremia A. 1970–
(Wellington) 1994–95–96–97–99–2000   40   (30)
Ifwersen K.D. 1893–1967
(Auckland) 1921   1   (1)
Innes C.R. 1969–
(Auckland) 1989–90–91   30   (17)
Innes G.D. 1910–1992
(Canterbury) 1932   7   (1)
Ioane A.L. 1995–
(Blues) 2017   1   (–)
Ioane R.E. 1997–
(Blues) 2016–17–18   24   (24)

Irvine I.B. 1929–2013
(North Auckland) 1952   1   (1)
Irvine J.G. 1888–1939
(Otago) 1914   10   (3)
Irvine W.R. 1898–1952
(Hawke's Bay) 1923–24–25–26
(Wairarapa) 1930   41   (5)
Irwin M.W. 1935–2018
(Otago) 1955–56–58–59–60   25   (7)
Ivimey F.E.B. 1880–1961
(Otago) 1910   1   (–)

Jack C.R. 1978–
(Canterbury) 2001–02–03–04–05
(Tasman) 2006–07   68   (67)
Jackson E.S. 1914–1975
(Hawke's Bay) 1936–37–38   11   (6)
Jacob H. 1894–1955
(Horowhenua) 1920   8   (–)
Jacob J.P. LeG. 1877–1909
(Southland) 1901   2   (–)
Jaffray J.L. 1950–
(Otago) 1972–75–76–77–78
(South Canterbury) 1979   23   (7)
Jaffray M.W.R. 1949–
(Otago) 1976   4   (–)
Jane C.S. 1983–
(Wellington) 2008–09–10–11–12
(Hurricanes) 2013–14   55   (53)
Jarden R.A. 1929–1977
(Wellington) 1951–52–53–54–
55–56   37   (16)
Jefferd A.C.R. 1953–
(East Coast) 1980–81   5   (3)
Jennings A.G.T. 1940–
(Bay of Plenty) 1967   6   (–)
Jervis F.M. 1870–1952
(Auckland) 1893   10   (–)
Jessep E.M. 1904–1983
(Wellington) 1931–32   8   (2)
Johns P.A. 1944–
(Wanganui) 1968   6   (–)
Johnson L.M. 1897–1983
(Wellington) 1925–28–30   25   (4)
Johnston D. 1903–1938
(Taranaki) 1925   2   (–)
Johnston W. 1881–1951
(Otago) 1905–07   27   (3)
Johnstone B.R. 1950–
(Auckland) 1976–77–78–79–80   45   (13)
Johnstone C.R. 1980–
(Canterbury) 2005   3   (3)
Johnstone P. 1922–1997
(Otago) 1949–50–51   26   (9)
Jones I.D. 1967–
(North Auckland) 1989–90–91–92–93
(North Harbour) 1994–95–96–
97–98–99   105   (79)
Jones M.G. 1942–1975
(North Auckland) 1973   5   (1)

Jones M.N. 1965–
(Auckland) 1987–88–89–90–91–
92–93–94–95–96–97–98   74   (55)
Jones P.F.H. 1932–1994
(North Auckland) 1953–54–55–
56–58–59–60   37   (11)
Joseph H.T. 1949–
(Canterbury) 1971   2   (2)
Joseph J.W. 1969–
(Otago) 1992–93–94–95   30   (20)

Kahui R.D. 1985–
(Waikato) 2008–10–11   18   (17)
Kaino J. 1983–
(Auckland) 2004–06–08–09–10–11
(Blues) 2014–15–16–17   83   (81)
Kane G.N. 1952–
(Waikato) 1974   7   (–)
Karam J.F. 1951–
(Wellington) 1972–73–74
(Horowhenua) 1975   42   (10)
Katene T. 1929–1992
(Wellington) 1955   1   (1)
Keane K.J. 1953–
(Canterbury) 1979   6   (–)
Kearney J.C. 1920–1998
(Otago) 1947–49   22   (4)
Kelleher B.T. 1976–
(Otago) 1999–2000–01–02–03–04
(Waikato) 2004–05–06–07   58   (57)
Kelly J.W. 1926–2002
(Auckland) 1949–53–54   16   (2)
Kember G.F. 1945–
(Wellington) 1967–70   19   (1)
Kenny D.J. 1961–
(Otago) 1986   3   (–)
Kerr A. 1871–1936
(Canterbury) 1896   1   (–)
Kerr-Barlow T.N.J. 1990–
(Waikato) 2012
(Chiefs) 2013–14–15–16–17   29   (27)
Ketels R.C. 1954–
(Counties) 1979–80–81   16   (5)
Kiernan H.A.D. 1876–1947
(Auckland) 1903   8   (1)
Kilby F.D. 1906–1985
(Wellington) 1928–32–34   18   (4)
Killeen B.A. 1911–1993
(Auckland) 1936   2   (1)
King R.M. 1980–
(Waikato) 2002   1   (1)
King R.R. 1909–1988
(West Coast) 1934–35–36–37–38   42   (13)
Kingstone C.N. 1895–1960
(Taranaki) 1921   3   (3)
Kirk D.E. 1961–
(Otago) 1983–84
(Auckland) 1985–86–87   34   (17)
Kirkpatrick A. 1898–1971
(Hawke's Bay) 1925–26   12   (–)

Kirkpatrick I.A. 1946–
(Canterbury) 1967-68-69
(Poverty Bay) 1970-71-72-73-
74-75-76-77   113   (39)
Kirton E.W. 1939–
(Otago) 1963-64-67-68-69-70   49   (13)
Kirwan J.J. 1964–
(Auckland) 1984-85-86-87-88-
89-90-91-92-93-94   96   (63)
Kivell A.L. 1897–1988
(Taranaki) 1929   5   (2)
Knight A. 1906–1990
(Auckland) 1926-28-34   14   (1)
Knight G.A. 1951–
(Manawatu) 1977-78-79-80-81-
82-83-84-85-86   66   (36)
Knight L.A.G. 1901–1973
(Auckland) 1925   5   (–)
Knight L.G. 1949–
(Auckland) 1974
(Poverty Bay) 1976-77   35   (6)
Knight M.O. 1945–
(Counties) 1968   8   (–)
Koteka T.T. 1956–
(Waikato) 1981-82   6   (2)
Kreft A.J. 1945–
(Otago) 1968   4   (1)
Kronfeld J.A. 1971–
(Otago) 1995-96-97-98-99-2000   56   (54)
Kururangi R. 1957–
(Counties) 1978   8   (–)

Laidlaw C.R. 1943–
(Otago) 1963-64-65-66-67
(Canterbury) 1968 (Otago) 1970   57   (20)
Laidlaw K.F. 1934–
(Southland) 1960   17   (3)
Lam P.R. 1968–
(Auckland) 1992   1   (–)
Lambert K.K. 1952–
(Manawatu) 1972-73-74-76-77   40   (11)
Lambie J.T. 1870–1905
(Taranaki) 1893-94   12   (–)
Lambourn A. 1910–1999
(Wellington) 1934-35-36-37-38   40   (10)
Larsen B.P. 1969–
(North Harbour) 1992-93-
94-95-96   40   (17)
Latimer T.D. 1986–
(Bay of Plenty) 2009   6   (5)
Laulala C.D.E. 1982–
(Canterbury) 2004-06   3   (2)
Laulala N.E. 1991–
(Crusaders) 2015-17-18   17   (17)
Laumape K.H. 1993–
(Hurricanes) 2017-18   12   (10)
Lauaki S.T. 1981–2017
(Waikato) 2005-07-08   17   (17)
Law A.D. 1904–1961
(Manawatu) 1925   4   (–)

Lawson G.P. 1899–1985
(South Canterbury) 1925   2   (–)
Lecky J.G. 1863–1917
(Auckland) 1884   7   (–)
Lee D.D. 1976–
(Otago) 2002   2   (2)
Leeson J. 1909–1960
(Waikato) 1934   5   (–)
LeLievre J.M. 1933–2016
(Canterbury) 1962-63-64   25   (1)
Lendrum R.N. 1948–
(Counties) 1973   3   (1)
Leonard B.G. 1985–
(Waikato) 2007-09   14   (13)
Leslie A.R. 1944–
(Wellington) 1974-75-76   34   (10)
Levien H.J. 1935–2008
(Otago) 1957   8   (–)
Leys E.T. 1907–1989
(Wellington) 1929   5   (1)
Lienert-Brown A.R. 1995–
(Chiefs) 2016-17-18   34   (33)
Lilburne H.T. 1908–1976
(Canterbury) 1928-29-30
(Wellington) 1931-32-34   40   (10)
Lindsay D.F. 1906–1978
(Otago) 1928   14   (3)
Lindsay W.G. 1879–1965
(Southland) 1914   4   (–)
Lineen T.R. 1936–
(Auckland) 1957-58-59-60   35   (12)
Lister T.N. 1943–2017
(South Canterbury) 1968-69-
70-71   26   (8)
Little P.F. 1934–1993
(Auckland) 1961-62-63-64   29   (10)
Little W.K. 1969–
(North Harbour) 1989-90-91-92-
93-94-95-96-97-98   75   (50)
Loader C.J. 1931–
(Wellington) 1953-54   16   (4)
Lochore B.J. 1940–
(Wairarapa) 1963-64-65-66-67-
68-69-70
(Wairarapa Bush) 1971   68   (25)
Lockington T.M. 1913–2001
(Auckland) 1936   1   (–)
Loe R.W. 1960–
(Waikato) 1986-87-88-89-90-91-92
(Canterbury) 1994-95   78   (49)
Lomas A.R. 1894–1975
(Auckland) 1925-26   15   (–)
Lomax T.S. 1996–
(Highlanders) 2018   1   (1)
Lomu J.T. 1975–2015
(Counties Manukau) 1994-95-96-
97-98-99
(Wellington) 2000-01-02   73   (63)
Long A.T. 1879–1960
(Auckland) 1903   10   (1)

Loveday J.K. 1949–
(Manawatu) 1978   7 (–)
Loveridge D.S. 1952–
(Taranaki) 1978–79–80–81–82–
83–85   54 (24)
Loveridge G. 1890–1970
(Taranaki) 1913–14   11 (–)
Lowen K.R. 1976–
(Waikato) 2002   1 (1)
Luatua D.S. 1991
(Blues) 2013–14.16   15 (15)
Lucas F.W. 1902–1957
(Auckland) 1923–24–25–28–30   41 (7)
Lunn W.A. 1926–1996
(Otago) 1949   2 (2)
Lynch T.W. 1892–1950
(South Canterbury) 1913–14   23 (4)
Lynch T.W. 1927–2006
(Canterbury) 1951   10 (3)

Maber G. 1869–1894
(Wellington) 1894   1 (–)
McAlister C.L. 1983–
(North Harbour) 2005–06–
07–09   31 (30)
McAtamney F.S. 1934–
(Otago) 1956–57   9 (1)
McCahill B.J. 1964–
(Auckland) 1987–88–89–90–91   32 (10)
McCarthy P. 1893–1976
(Canterbury) 1923   1 (–)
McCashin T.M. 1944–2017
(Wellington) 1968   7 (–)
McCaw R.H. 1980–
(Canterbury) 2001–02–03–04–05–06–
07–08–09–10–11–12
(Crusaders) 2013–14–15   149 (148)
McCaw W.A. 1927–
(Southland) 1951–53–54   32 (5)
McCleary B.V. 1897–1978
(Canterbury) 1924–25   12 (–)
McClymont W.G. 1905–1970
(Otago) 1928   3 (–)
McCool M.J. 1951–
(Wairarapa Bush) 1979   2 (1)
McCormick A.G. 1899–1969
(Canterbury) 1925   1 (–)
McCormick J. 1923–2006
(Hawke's Bay) 1947   3 (–)
McCormick W.F. 1939–2018
(Canterbury) 1965–67–68–
69–70–71   44 (16)
McCullough J.F. 1936–
(Taranaki) 1959   3 (3)
McDonald A. 1883–1967
(Otago) 1905–06–07–08–13   41 (8)
Macdonald A.J. 1981–
(Auckland) 2005   2 (2)
Macdonald H.H. 1947–
(Canterbury) 1972–73–74
(North Auckland) 1975–76   48 (12)

MacDonald L.R. 1977–
(Canterbury) 2000–01–02–03–
05–06–07–08   56 (56)
McDonnell P. 1874–1950
(Wanganui) 1896   1 (–)
McDonnell J.M. 1973–
(Otago) 2002   8 (8)
McDowall S.C. 1961–
(Auckland) 1985–86–87–88
(Bay of Plenty) 1989
(Auckland) 1989–90–91–92   81 (46)
McEldowney J.T. 1947–2012
(Taranaki) 1976–77   10 (2)
MacEwan I.N. 1934–
(Wellington) 1956–57–58–59–
60–61–62   52 (20)
McGahan P.W. 1964–
(North Harbour) 1990–91   6 (–)
McGrattan B. 1959–
(Wellington) 1983–84–85–86   23 (6)
McGregor A.A. 1953–
(Southland) 1978   3 (–)
McGregor A.J. 1889–1963
(Auckland) 1913   11 (2)
McGregor D. 1881–1947
(Canterbury) 1903
(Wellington) 1904–05–06   31 (4)
McGregor N.P. 1901–1973
(Canterbury) 1924–25–28   27 (2)
McGregor R.W. 1874–1925
(Auckland) 1901–03–04   10 (2)
McHugh M.J. 1917–2010
(Auckland) 1946–49   14 (3)
MacIntosh C.N. 1869–1918
(South Canterbury) 1893   4 (–)
McIntosh D.N. 1931–
(Wellington) 1956–57   13 (4)
McKay D.W. 1937–
(Auckland) 1961–62–63   12 (5)
Mackay J.D. 1905–1985
(Wellington) 1928   2 (–)
McKechnie B.J. 1953–
(Southland) 1977–78–79–81   26 (10)
McKellar G.F. 1884–1960
(Wellington) 1910   5 (3)
McKenzie D.S. 1995–
(Chiefs) 2016–17–18   23 (23)
MacKenzie R.H. 1869–1940
(Auckland) 1893   2 (–)
MacKenzie R.H.C. 1904–1993
(Wellington) 1928   2 (–)
McKenzie R.J. 1892–1968
(Wellington) 1913
(Auckland) 1914   20 (4)
MacKenzie R.M. 1909–2000
(Manawatu) 1934–35–36–37–38   35 (9)
McKenzie W. 1871–1943
(Wairarapa) 1893
(Wellington) 1894–96–97   20 (–)
Mackintosh J.L. 1985–
(Southland) 2008   2 (1)

Mackrell W.H.C. 1881–1917
(Auckland) 1905–06 — 7 (1)
Macky J.V. 1887–1951
(Auckland) 1913 — 1 (1)
McLachlan J.S. 1949–
(Auckland) 1974 — 8 (1)
McLaren H.C. 1926–1992
(Waikato) 1952 — 1 (1)
McLean A.L. 1898–1964
(Bay of Plenty) 1921–23 — 3 (2)
McLean C. 1892–1965
(Buller) 1920 — 5 (–)
McLean H.F. 1907–1997
(Wellington) 1930–32
(Auckland) 1934–35–36 — 29 (9)
McLean J.K. 1923–2005
(King Country) 1947
(Auckland) 1949 — 5 (2)
McLean R.J. 1960–
(Wairarapa Bush) 1987 — 2 (–)
McLeod B.E. 1940–1996
(Counties) 1964–65–66–67–68–69–70 — 46 (24)
McLeod S.J. 1973–
(Waikato) 1996–97–98 — 17 (10)
McMeeking D.T.M. 1896–1976
(Otago) 1923 — 2 (–)
McMinn A.F. 1880–1919
(Wairarapa) 1903
(Manawatu) 1905 — 10 (2)
McMinn F.A. 1874–1947
(Manawatu) 1904 — 1 (1)
McMullen R.F. 1933–2004
(Auckland) 1957–58–59–60 — 29 (11)
McNab J.A. 1895–1979
(Hawke's Bay) 1925 — 1 (–)
McNab J.R. 1924–2009
(Otago) 1949–50 — 17 (6)
McNaughton A.M. 1947–
(Bay of Plenty) 1971–72 — 9 (3)
McNeece J.* 1885–1917
(Southland) 1913–14 — 11 (5)
McNicol A.L.R. 1944–2017
(Wanganui) 1973 — 5 (–)
McPhail B.E. 1937–
(Canterbury) 1959 — 2 (2)
MacPherson D.G. 1882–1956
(Otago) 1905 — 1 (1)
Macpherson G. 1962–
(Otago) 1986 — 1 (1)
MacRae I.R. 1943–
(Hawke's Bay) 1963–64–66–67–68–69–70 — 45 (17)
McRae J.A. 1914–1977
(Southland) 1946 — 2 (2)
McRobie N. 1873–1929
(Southland) 1896 — 1 (–)
McWilliams R.G. 1901–1984
(Auckland) 1928–29–30 — 27 (10)
Maguire J.R. 1886–1966
(Auckland) 1910 — 6 (3)

Mahoney A. 1908–1979
(Bush) 1929–34–35–36 — 26 (4)
Mains L.W. 1946–
(Otago) 1971–76 — 15 (4)
Major J. 1940–
(Taranaki) 1963–64–67 — 24 (1)
Maka I. 1975–
(Otago) 1998 — 4 (4)
Maling T.S. 1975–
(Otago) 2001–02–04 — 13 (11)
Manchester J.E. 1908–1983
(Canterbury) 1932–34–35–36 — 36 (9)
Mannix S.J. 1971–
(Wellington) 1990–91–94 — 9 (1)
Markham P.F. 1891–1953
(Wellington) 1921 — 1 (–)
Marshall J.W. 1973–
(Canterbury) 1995–96–97–98–99–2000–01–02–03–04–05 — 88 (81)
Masaga L.T.C. 1986–
(Counties Manukau) 2009 — 1 (1)
Masoe M.C. 1979–
(Taranaki) 2005
(Wellington) 2006–07 — 20 (20)
Mason D.F. 1923–1981
(Wellington) 1947 — 6 (1)
Masters F.H. 1893–1980
(Taranaki) 1922 — 4 (–)
Masters R.R. 1900–1967
(Canterbury) 1923–24–25 — 31 (4)
Mataira H.K. 1910–1979
(Hawke's Bay) 1934 — 5 (1)
Matheson J.D. 1948–
(Otago) 1972 — 13 (5)
Mathewson A.S. 1985–
(Wellington) 2008–10 — 5 (4)
Mathieson R.G. 1899–1966
(Otago) 1922 — 4 (–)
Matson J.T.F. 1973
(Canterbury) 1995–96 — 5 (–)
Mattson H.A. 1900–1980
(Auckland) 1925 — 6 (–)
Mauger A.J.D. 1980–
(Canterbury) 2001–02–03–04–05–06–07 — 46 (45)
Mauger N.K. 1978–
(Canterbury) 2001 — 2 (–)
Max D.S. 1906–1972
(Nelson) 1931–32–34 — 8 (3)
Maxwell N.M.C. 1976–
(Canterbury) 1999–2000–01–02–04 — 36 (36)
Mayerhofler M.A. 1972–
(Canterbury) 1998 — 6 (6)
Meads C.E. 1936–2017
(King Country) 1957–58–59–60–61–62–63–64–65–66–67–68–69–70–71 — 133 (55)
Meads S.T. 1938–
(King Country) 1961–62–63–64–65–66 — 30 (15)

Mealamu K.F. 1979–
(Auckland) 2002–03–04–05–
06–07–08–09–10–11–12
(Blues) 2013–14–15   133 (132)
Meates K.F. 1930–
(Canterbury) 1952   2 (2)
Meates W.A. 1923–2003
(Otago) 1949–50   20 (7)
Meeuws K.J. 1974–
(Otago) 1998–99–2000–01–02–04
(Auckland) 2003   45 (42)
Mehrtens A.P. 1973–
(Canterbury) 1995–96–97–98–
99–2000–01–02–04   72 (70)
Mehrtens G.M. 1907–1954
(Canterbury) 1928   3 (–)
Messam L.J. 1984–
(Waikato) 2008–09–10–11–12
(Chiefs) 2013–14–15   45 (43)
Metcalfe T.C. 1909–1969
(Southland) 1931–32   7 (2)
Mexted G.G. 1927–2009
(Wellington) 1950–51   5 (1)
Mexted M.G. 1953–
(Wellington) 1979–80–81–82–
83–84–85   72 (34)
Mika B.M. 1981–
(Auckland) 2002   3 (3)
Mika D.G. 1972–2018
(Auckland) 1999   8 (7)
Mill J.J. 1899–1950
(Hawke's Bay) 1923–24–25–26
(Wairarapa) 1930   33 (4)
Miller P.C. 1975–
(Otago) 2001   2 (–)
Miller T.J. 1974–
(Waikato) 1997   4 (–)
Milliken H.M. 1914–1993
(Canterbury) 1938   7 (3)
Mills H.P. 1873–1905
(Taranaki) 1897   8 (–)
Mills J.G. 1960–
(Auckland) 1984   2 (–)
Millton E.B. 1861–1942
(Canterbury) 1884   7 (–)
Millton W.V. 1858–1887
(Canterbury) 1884   8 (–)
Milner H.P. 1946–1996
(Wanganui) 1970   16 (1)
Milner-Skudder N.R. 1990–
(Hurricanes) 2015,17–18   13 (13)
Mitchell J.E.P. 1964–
(Waikato) 1993   6 (–)
Mitchell N.A. 1913–1981
(Southland) 1935–36–37
(Otago) 1938   32 (8)
Mitchell T.W. 1950–
(Canterbury) 1974–76   17 (1)
Mitchell W.J. 1890–1959
(Canterbury) 1910   5 (2)

Mitchinson F.E. 1884–1978
(Wellington) 1907–08–10–13   31 (11)
Moala G. 1990
(Blues) 2015–16   4 (4)
Moffitt J.E. 1889–1964
(Wellington) 1920–21   12 (3)
Moli A. 1995–
(Chiefs) 2017   1 (–)
Molloy B.P.J. 1931–
(Canterbury) 1957   5 (–)
Moody J.P.T. 1988–
(Crusaders) 2014–15–16–17–18   37 (37)
Moore G.J.T. 1923–1991
(Otago) 1949   1 (1)
Moreton R.C. 1942–2016
(Canterbury) 1962–64–65   12 (7)
Morgan H.D. 1902–1969
(Otago) 1923   1 (–)
Morgan J.E. 1945–2002
(North Auckland) 1974–76   22 (5)
Morris T.J. 1942–
(Nelson Bays) 1972–73   23 (3)
Morrison T.C. 1913–1985
(South Canterbury) 1938   5 (3)
Morrison T.G. 1951–
(Otago) 1973   5 (1)
Morrissey B.L. 1952–
(Waikato) 1981   3 (–)
Morrissey P.J. 1939–2013
(Canterbury) 1962   3 (3)
Mourie G.N.K. 1952–
(Taranaki) 1976–77–78–79–80–
81–82   61 (21)
Mo'unga R. 1994–
(Crusaders) 2017–18   10 (9)
Mowlem J. 1870–1951
(Manawatu) 1893   4 (–)
Muliaina J.M. 1980–
(Auckland) 2003–04–05
(Waikato) 2006–07–08–09–10–11   102 (100)
Muller B.L. 1942–
(Taranaki) 1967–68–69–70–71   35 (14)
Mumm W.J. 1922–1993
(Buller) 1949   1 (1)
Munro H.G. 1896–1974
(Otago) 1924–25   9 (–)
Murdoch K. 1943–2018
(Otago) 1970–72   27 (3)
Murdoch P.H. 1941–1995
(Auckland) 1964–65   5 (5)
Murray F.S.M. 1871–1952
(Auckland) 1893–97   20 (–)
Murray H.V. 1888–1971
(Canterbury) 1913–14   22 (4)
Murray P.C. 1884–1968
(Wanganui) 1908   1 (1)
Myers R.G. 1950–
(Waikato) 1977–78   5 (1)
Mynott H.J. 1876–1924
(Taranaki) 1905–06–07–10   39 (8)

Naholo W.R. 1991
(Highlanders) 2015–16–17–18   27 (26)
Nathan W.J. 1940–
(Auckland) 1962–63–64–66–67   37 (14)
Nelson K.A. 1938–
(Otago) 1962–63–64   18 (2)
Nepia G. 1905–1986
(Hawke's Bay) 1924–25
(East Coast) 1929–30   46 (9)
Nesbit S.R. 1936–
(Auckland) 1960   13 (2)
Neville W.R. 1954–
(North Auckland) 1981   4 (–)
Newby C.A. 1979–
(North Harbour) 2004–06   3 (3)
Newton F. 1881–1955
(Canterbury) 1905–06   19 (3)
Ngatai C.J. 1990–
(Chiefs) 2015   1 (1)
Nicholls H.E. 1900–1978
(Wellington) 1921–22–23   7 (1)
Nicholls H.G. 1897–1977
(Wellington) 1923   1 (–)
Nicholls M.F. 1901–1972
(Wellington) 1921–22–24–25–26–
28–30   51 (10)
Nicholson G.W. 1878–1968
(Auckland) 1903–04–05–06–07   39 (4)
Nonu M.A. 1982–
(Wellington) 2003–04–05–06–07–08–
09–10–11–12
(Highlanders) 2013
(Blues) 2014
(Hurricanes) 2015   104 (103)
Norton R.W. 1942–
(Canterbury) 1971–72–73–74–
75–76–77   61 (27)

O'Brien A.J. 1897–1969
(Auckland) 1922   3 (–)
O'Brien J. 1871–1946
(Wellington) 1901   1 (–)
O'Brien J.G. 1889–1958
(Auckland) 1914–20   12 (1)
O'Callaghan M.W. 1946–
(Manawatu) 1968   3 (3)
O'Callaghan T.R. 1925–2004
(Wellington) 1949   1 (1)
O'Connor T.B. 1860–1936
(Auckland) 1884   7 (–)
O'Dea R.J. 1930–1986
(Thames Valley) 1953–54   5 (–)
O'Donnell D.H. 1921–1992
(Wellington) 1949   1 (1)
O'Donnell J.M. 1860–1942
(Otago) 1884   7 (–)
O'Dowda B.C. 1874–1954
(Taranaki) 1901   2 (–)
O'Halloran J.D. 1972–
(Wellington) 2000   1 (1)

O'Leary M.J. 1883–1963
(Auckland) 1910–13   8 (4)
O'Neill K.J. 1982–
(Waikato) 2008   1 (1)
Old G.H. 1956–
(Manawatu) 1980–81–82–83   17 (3)
Oliphant R. 1870–1956
(Wellington) 1893
(Auckland) 1896   3 (–)
Oliver A.D. 1975–
(Otago) 1996–97–98–99–2000
01–03–04–05–06–07   67 (59)
Oliver C.J. 1905–1977
(Canterbury) 1928–29–34–35–36   33 (7)
Oliver D.J. 1907–1990
(Wellington) 1930   3 (2)
Oliver D.O. 1930–1997
(Otago) 1953–54   20 (2)
Oliver F.J. 1948–2014
(Southland) 1976–77
(Otago) 1978–79
(Manawatu) 1980–81   43 (17)
Orchard S.A. 1875–1947
(Canterbury) 1896–97   8 (–)
Ormond J. 1891–1970
(Hawke's Bay) 1923   1 (–)
Orr R.W. 1923–2011
(Otago) 1949   1 (1)
Osborne B.M. 1971–
(North Harbour) 1995–96–
97–99   29 (19)
Osborne W.M. 1955–
(Wanganui) 1975–76–77–78–
80–82   48 (16)
O'Sullivan J.M. 1883–1960
(Taranaki) 1905–07   29 (5)
O'Sullivan T.P.A. 1936–1997
(Taranaki) 1960–61–62   16 (4)

Paewai L. 1906–1970
(Hawke's Bay) 1923–24   8 (–)
Page J.R. 1908–1985
(Wellington) 1931–32–34–35   18 (6)
Page M.L. 1902–1987
(Canterbury) 1928   1 (–)
Palmer B.P. 1901–1932
(Auckland) 1928–29–32   18 (3)
Papali'i D.R. 1997
(Blues) 2018   2 (2)
Parker J.H. 1897–1980
(Canterbury) 1924–25   21 (3)
Parkhill A.A. 1912–1986
(Otago) 1937–38   10 (6)
Parkinson R.M. 1948–2009
(Poverty Bay) 1972–73   20 (7)
Parsons J.W. 1986–
(Blues) 2014.16   2 (2)
Paterson A.M. 1885–1933
(Otago) 1908–10   9 (5)
Paton H. 1881–1964
(Otago) 1907–10   8 (2)

Pauling T.G. 1873–1927
(Wellington) 1896–97   9   (–)
Pene A.R.B. 1967–
(Otago) 1992–93–94   26   (15)
Pepper C.S.* 1911–1943
(Auckland) 1935–36   17   (–)
Perenara T.T.R. 1992–
(Hurricanes) 2014–15–16–17–18   56   (55)
Perry A. 1899–1977
(Otago) 1923   1   (–)
Perry R.G. 1953–
(Mid Canterbury) 1980   1   (–)
Perry T.G. 1988–
(Crusaders) 2017–18   8   (6)
Petersen L.C. 1897–1961
(Canterbury) 1921–22–23   8   (–)
Phillips W.J. 1914–1982
(King Country) 1937–38   7   (3)
Philpott S. 1965–
(Canterbury) 1988–90–91   14   (2)
Pickering E.A.R. 1936–2016
(Waikato) 1957–58–59–60   21   (3)
Pierce M.J. 1957–
(Wellington) 1984–85–86–87–
88–89–90   54   (26)
Piutau S.T. 1991–
(Blues) 2013–14–15   17   (17)
Pokere S.T. 1958–
(Southland) 1981–82–83
(Auckland) 1984–85   39   (18)
Pollock H.R. 1909–1984
(Wellington) 1932–36   8   (5)
Porteous H.G. 1875–1951
(Otago) 1903   3   (–)
Porter C.G. 1899–1976
(Wellington) 1923–24–25–26–
28–29–30   41   (7)
Potaka W.P. ca 1903–1967
(Wanganui) 1923   2   (–)
Preston J.P. 1967–
(Canterbury) 1991–92
(Wellington) 1993–96–97   27   (10)
Pringle A. 1899–1973
(Wellington) 1923   1   (–)
Pringle W.P. 1869–1945
(Wellington) 1893   5   (–)
Procter A.C. 1906–1989
(Otago) 1932   4   (1)
Proctor M.P. 1992–
(Hurricanes) 2018   1   (1)
Pulu A.W. 1990–
(Chiefs) 2014   2   (2)
Purdue C.A. 1874–1941
(Southland) 1901–05   3   (1)
Purdue E. 1879–1939
(Southland) 1905   1   (1)
Purdue G.B. 1909–1981
(Southland) 1931–32   7   (4)
Purvis G.H. 1960–
(Waikato) 1989–90–91–92–93   28   (2)

Purvis N.A. 1953–2008
(Otago) 1976   12   (1)
Quaid C.E. 1908–1984
(Otago) 1938   4   (2)
Ralph C.S. 1977–
(Auckland) 1998
(Canterbury) 2001–02–03   16   (14)
Ranby R.M. 1977–
(Waikato) 2001   1   (1)
Randell T.C. 1974–
(Otago) 1995–96–97–98–99–
2000–01–02   61   (51)
Randle R.Q. 1974–
(Waikato) 2001   2   (–)
Ranger R.M.N. 1986–
(Northland) 2010
(Blues) 2013   6   (6)
Rangi R.E. 1941–1988
(Auckland) 1964–65–66   10   (10)
Rankin J.G. 1914–1989
(Canterbury) 1936–37   4   (3)
Rawlinson G.P. 1978–
(North Harbour) 2006–07   4   (4)
Read K.J. 1985–
(Canterbury) 2008–09–10–11–12
(Crusaders) 2013–14–15–16–17–18   119 (118)
Reedy W.J. 1880–1939
(Wellington) 1908   2   (2)
Reid A.R. 1929–1994
(Waikato) 1951–52–56–57   17   (5)
Reid H.R. 1958–
(Bay of Plenty) 1980–81–83–
84–85–86   40   (9)
Reid K.H. 1904–1972
(Wairarapa) 1929   5   (2)
Reid S.T. 1912–2003
(Hawke's Bay) 1935–36–37   27   (9)
Reihana B.T. 1976–
(Waikato) 2000   2   (2)
Reside W.B. 1905–1985
(Wairarapa) 1929   6   (1)
Retallick B.A. 1991–
(Hawke's Bay/Bay of Plenty) 2012
(Chiefs) 2013–14–15–16–17–18   75   (75)
Rhind P.K. 1915–1996
(Canterbury) 1946   2   (2)
Richardson J. 1899–1994
(Otago) 1921–22
(Southland) 1923–24–25   42   (7)
Rickit H.A. 1951–
(Waikato) 1981   2   (2)
Ridge M.J. 1969–
(Auckland) 1989   6   (–)
Ridland A.J.* 1882–1918
(Southland) 1910   6   (3)
Riechelmann C.C. 1972–
(Auckland) 1997   10   (6)
Righton L.S. 1898–1972
(Auckland) 1923–25   9   (–)

Roberts E.J. 1891–1972
(Wellington) 1913–14–20–21   26   (5)
Roberts F. 1882–1956
(Wellington) 1905–06–07–08–10   52   (12)
Roberts H. 1862–1949
(Wellington) 1884   7   (–)
Roberts R.W. 1889–1973
(Taranaki) 1913–14   23   (5)
Roberts W. 1871–1937
(Wellington) 1896–97   8   (–)
Robertson B.J. 1952–
(Counties) 1972–73–74–76–
77–78–79–80–81   102   (34)
Robertson D.J. 1947–
(Otago) 1974–75–76–77   30   (10)
Robertson G.S. 1859–1920
(Otago) 1884   8   (–)
Robertson S.M. 1974–
(Canterbury) 1998–99–
2000–01–02   23   (23)
Robilliard A.C.C. 1903–1990
(Canterbury) 1924–25–26–28   27   (4)
Robins B.G. 1958–
(Taranaki) 1985   4   (–)
Robinson A.G. 1956–
(North Auckland) 1983   4   (–)
Robinson C.E. 1927–1983
(Southland) 1951–52   11   (5)
Robinson J.T. 1906–1968
(Canterbury) 1928   3   (–)
Robinson K.J. 1976–
(Waikato) 2002–04–06–07   12   (12)
Robinson M.D. 1975–
(North Harbour) 1997–98–2001   8   (3)
Robinson M.P. 1974–
(Canterbury) 2000–02   9   (9)
Rokocoko J.T. 1983–
(Auckland) 2003–04–05–06–07–
08–09–10   69   (68)
Rollerson D.L. 1953–2017
(Manawatu) 1976–80–81   24   (8)
Romano L. 1986–
(Canterbury) 2012
(Crusaders) 2013–14–15–16–17   32   (31)
Roper R.A. 1923–
(Taranaki) 1949–50   5   (5)
Ross I.B. 1984–
(Canterbury) 2009   8   (8)
Ross J.C. 1949–
(Mid Canterbury) 1981   5   (–)
Rowlands G.D. 1947–
(Bay of Plenty) 1976   4   (–)
Rowley H.C.B. 1924–1956
(Wanganui) 1949   1   (1)
Rush E.J. 1965–
(North Harbour) 1992–93–95–96   29   (9)
Rush X.J. 1977–
(Auckland) 1998–2004   8   (8)
Rushbrook C.A. 1907–1987
(Wellington) 1928   10   (–)

Rutledge L.M. 1952–
(Southland) 1978–79–80   31   (13)
Ryan E. 1891–1965
(Wellington) 1921   1   (–)
Ryan J. 1887–1957
(Wellington) 1910–14   15   (4)
Ryan J.A.C. 1983–
(Otago) 2005–06   9   (9)
Ryan P.J. 1950–1985
(Hawke's Bay) 1976   5   (–)
Ryan T. 1863–1927
(Auckland) 1884   9   (–)

Sadler B.S. 1914–2007
(Wellington) 1935–36   19   (5)
Saili F. 1991–
(Blues) 2013   2   (2)
Salmon J.L.B. 1959–
(Wellington) 1980–81   7   (3)
Sapsford H.P. 1949–2009
(Otago) 1976   7   (–)
Savage L.T. 1928–2013
(Canterbury) 1949   12   (3)
Savea A.S. 1993–
(Hurricanes) 2016–17–18   37   (35)
Savea S.J. 1990–
(Wellington) 2012
(Hurricanes) 2013–14–15–16–17   54   (54)
Saxton C.K. 1913–2001
(South Canterbury) 1938   7   (3)
Sayers M. 1947–
(Wellington) 1972–73   15   (–)
Schuler K.J. 1967–
(Manawatu) 1989–90
(North Harbour) 1992–95   13   (4)
Schuster N.J. 1964–
(Wellington) 1987–88–89   26   (10)
Schwalger J.E. 1983–
(Wellington) 2007–08   2   (2)
Scott R.W.H. 1921–2012
(Auckland) 1946–47–49–50–
53–54   52   (17)
Scott S.J. 1955–1994
(Canterbury) 1980   4   (–)
Scown A.I. 1948–
(Taranaki) 1972–73   17   (5)
Scrimshaw G. 1902–1971
(Canterbury) 1928   11   (1)
Seear G.A. 1952–2018
(Otago) 1976–77–78–79   34   (12)
Seeling C.E. 1883–1956
(Auckland) 1904–05–06–07–08   39   (11)
Sellars G.M.V.* 1886–1917
(Auckland) 1913   15   (2)
Senio K. 1978–
(Bay of Plenty) 2005   1   (1)
Seymour D.J. 1967–
(Canterbury) 1992   3   (–)
Shannon H.G. 1869–1912
(Manawatu) 1893   6   (–)

Shaw M.W. 1956–
(Manawatu) 1980–81–82–83–84–85
(Hawke's Bay) 1986 69 (30)
Shearer J.D. 1896–1963
(Wellington) 1920 5 (–)
Shearer S.D. 1890–1973
(Wellington) 1921–22 8 (–)
Sheen T.R. 1905–1979
(Auckland) 1926–28 8 (–)
Shelford F.N.K. 1955–
(Bay of Plenty) 1981–84–85
(Hawke's Bay) 1983 22 (4)
Shelford W.T. 1957–
(North Harbour) 1985–86–87–88–
89–90 48 (22)
Sherlock K. 1961–
(Auckland) 1985 3 (–)
Siddells S.K. 1897–1979
(Wellington) 1921 1 (1)
Simon H.J. 1911–1979
(Otago) 1937 3 (3)
Simonsson P.L.J. 1967–
(Wellington) 1987 2 (–)
Simpson J.G. 1922–2010
(Auckland) 1947–49–50 30 (9)
Simpson V.L.J. 1960–
(Canterbury) 1985 4 (2)
Sims G.S. 1951–
(Otago) 1972 1 (1)
Sinclair R.G.B. 1896–1932
(Otago) 1923 2 (–)
Sivivatu S.W. 1982–
(Waikato) 2005–06–07–08–09–11 46 (45)
Skeen J.R. 1928–2001
(Auckland) 1952 1 (1)
Skinner K.L. 1927–2014
(Otago) 1949–50–51–52–53–54
(Counties) 1956 63 (20)
Skudder G.R. 1948–
(Waikato) 1969–72–73 14 (1)
Slade C.R. 1987–
(Canterbury) 2010–11
(Highlanders) 2013
(Crusaders) 2014–15 21 (21)
Slater G.L. 1971–
(Taranaki) 1997–2000 6 (3)
Sloane P.H. 1948–
(North Auckland) 1973–76–79 16 (1)
Smith A.E. 1942–
(Taranaki) 1967–69–70 18 (3)
Smith A.L. 1998–
(Manawatu) 2012
(Highlanders) 2013–14–15–16–17–18 82 (82)
Smith B.R. 1986–
(Otago) 2009–11–12
(Highlanders) 2013–14–15–16–17–18 77 (76)
Smith B.W. 1959–
(Waikato) 1983–84 10 (3)
Smith C.G. 1981–
(Wellington) 2004–05–06–07–08–
09–10–11–12
(Hurricanes) 2013–14–15 94 (94)

Smith C.H. 1909–1976
(Otago) 1934 2 (–)
Smith G.W. 1874–1954
(Auckland) 1897–1901–05 39 (2)
Smith I.S.T. 1941–2017
(Otago) 1963–64
(North Otago) 1965–66 24 (9)
Smith J.B. 1922–1974
(North Auckland) 1946–47–49 9 (4)
Smith P. 1924–1954
(North Auckland) 1947 3 (–)
Smith R.M. 1929–2002
(Canterbury) 1955 1 (1)
Smith W.E. 1881–1945
(Nelson) 1905 1 (1)
Smith W.R. 1957–
(Canterbury) 1980–82–83–84–85 35 (17)
Smyth B.F. 1891–1972
(Canterbury) 1922 3 (–)
Snodgrass W.F. 1898–1976
(Nelson) 1923–28 3 (–)
Snow E.M. 1898–1974
(Nelson) 1928–29 16 (3)
Solomon D. 1913–1997
(Auckland) 1935–36 8 (–)
Solomon F. 1906–1991
(Auckland) 1931–32 9 (3)
Somerville G.M. 1977–
(Canterbury) 2000–01–02–03–
04–05–06–07–08 67 (66)
Sonntag W.T.C. 1894–1988
(Otago) 1929 8 (3)
So'oialo, R. 1979–
(Wellington) 2002–03–04–05–
06–07–08–09 63 (62)
Soper A.J. 1936–
(Southland) 1957 8 (–)
Sopoaga L.Z. 1991
(Highlanders) 2015–16–17 18 (16)
Souter R. 1905–1976
(Otago) 1929 4 (–)
Speight C.R.B. 1870–1935
(Auckland) 1893 7 (–)
Speight M.W. 1962–
(North Auckland) 1986 5 (1)
Spencer C.J. 1975–
(Auckland) 1995–96–97–
98–2000–02–03–04 44 (35)
Spencer G. 1878–1950
(Wellington) 1907 5 (–)
Spencer J.C. 1880–1936
(Wellington) 1903–05–07 6 (2)
Spiers J.E. 1947–
(Counties) 1976–79–80–81 28 (5)
Spillane A.P. 1888–1974
(South Canterbury) 1913 2 (2)
Squire L.I.J. 1991–
(Highlanders) 2016–17–18 24 (23)
Stalker J. 1881–1931
(Otago) 1903 6 (–)
Stanley B.J. 1984–
(Auckland) 2010 3 (3)

Stanley J.C. 1975–
(Auckland) 1997   3   (–)
Stanley J.T. 1957–
(Auckland) 1986–87–88–89–90–91   49   (27)
Stapleton E.T. 1930–2005
(New South Wales) 1960   1   (–)
Stead J.W. 1877–1958
(Southland) 1903–04–05–06–08   42   (7)
Steel A.G. 1941–2018
(Canterbury) 1966–67–68   23   (9)
Steel J. 1898–1941 (West Coast)
1920–21–22–23–24–25   38   (6)
Steele L.B. 1929–
(Wellington) 1951   9   (3)
Steere E.R.G. 1908–1967
(Hawke's Bay) 1928–29–30–31–32   21   (6)
Steinmetz P.C. 1977–
(Wellington) 2002   1   (1)
Stensness L. 1970–
(Auckland) 1993–97   14   (8)
Stephens O.G. 1947–
(Wellington) 1968   1   (1)
Stevens I.N. 1948–
(Wellington) 1972–73–74–76   33   (3)
Stevenson D.R.L. 1903–1962
(Otago) 1926   4   (–)
Stewart A.J. 1940–
(Canterbury) 1963
(South Canterbury) 1964   26   (8)
Stewart D.T. 1872–1931
(South Canterbury) 1894   1   (–)
Stewart E.B. 1901–1979
(Otago) 1923   1   (–)
Stewart J.D. 1889–1973
(Auckland) 1913   2   (2)
Stewart K.W. 1953–
(Southland) 1972–73–74–75–
76–79–81   55   (13)
Stewart R.T. 1904–1982
(South Canterbury) 1923–24–25–
26–28 (Canterbury) 1930   39   (5)
Stewart V.E. 1948–
(Canterbury) 1976–79   12   (–)
Stohr L. 1889–1973
(Taranaki) 1910–13   15   (3)
Stokes E.J.T. 1950–
(Bay of Plenty) 1976   5   (–)
Stone A.M. 1960–
(Waikato) 1981–83–84
(Bay of Plenty) 1986   23   (9)
Storey P.W. 1897–1975
(South Canterbury) 1920–21   12   (2)
Strachan A.D. 1966–
(Auckland) 1992
(North Harbour) 1993–95   17   (11)
Strahan S.C. 1944–
(Manawatu) 1967–68–70–72–73   45   (17)
Strang W.A. 1906–1989
(South Canterbury) 1928–30–31   17   (5)
Stringfellow J.C. 1905–1959
(Wairarapa) 1929   7   (2)

Stuart A.J. 1858–1923
(Wellington) 1893   7   (–)
Stuart K.C. 1928–2005
(Canterbury) 1955   1   (1)
Stuart R.C. 1920–2005
(Canterbury) 1949–53–54   27   (7)
Stuart R.L. 1948–
(Hawke's Bay) 1977   6   (1)
Sullivan J.L. 1915–1990
(Taranaki) 1936–37–38   9   (6)
Surman J.F. 1866–1925
(Auckland) 1896   1   (–)
Surridge S.D. 1970–
(Canterbury) 1997   3   (–)
Sutherland A.R. 1944–
(Marlborough)
1968–70–71–72–73–76   64   (10)
Svenson K.S. 1898–1955
(Buller) 1922
(Wellington) 1924–25–26   34   (4)
Swain J.P. 1902–1960
(Hawke's Bay) 1928   16   (4)
Swindley J.T. 1876–1918
(Wellington) 1894   1   (–)

Ta'avao–Matau A.W.F. 1990
(Chiefs) 2018   3   (3)
Tahuriorangi T.T.H. 1995
(Chiefs) 2018   3   (3)
Taiaroa J.G. 1862–1907
(Otago) 1884   9   (–)
Taituha P. 1901–1958
(Wanganui) 1923   2   (–)
Tamanivalu S. 1992–
(Chiefs) 2016–17   5   (3)
Tanner J.M. 1927–
(Auckland) 1950–51–53–54   24   (5)
Tanner K.J. 1945–
(Canterbury) 1974–75–76   27   (7)
Taumoepeau S. 1979–
(Auckland) 2004–05   4   (3)
Taylor C.J. 1989
(Crusaders) 2015–16–1718   41   (41)
Taylor G.L. 1970–
(North Auckland) 1992–96   6   (1)
Taylor H.M. 1889–1955
(Canterbury) 1913–14   23   (5)
Taylor J.M. 1913–1979
(Otago) 1937–38   9   (6)
Taylor K.J. 1957–
(Hawke's Bay) 1980   1   (–)
Taylor M.B. 1956–
(Waikato) 1976–79–80   30   (7)
Taylor N.M. 1951–
(Bay of Plenty) 1976–77–78
(Hawke's Bay) 1982   27   (9)
Taylor R.* 1889–1917
(Taranaki) 1913   2   (2)
Taylor T.J. 1989–
(Crusaders) 2013   3   (3)

Taylor W.T. 1960–
(Canterbury) 1983–84–85–86–
87–88   40 (24)
Tetzlaff P.L. 1920–2009
(Auckland) 1947   7 (2)
Thimbleby N.W. 1939–
(Hawke's Bay) 1970   13 (1)
Thomas B.T. 1937– 2018
(Auckland) 1962
(Wellington) 1964   4 (4)
Thomas L.A. 1897–1971
(Wellington) 1925   3 (–)
Thompson B.A. 1947–2006
(Canterbury) 1979   8 (–)
Thomson A.J. 1982–
(Otago) 2008–09–10–11–12   31 (29)
Thomson H.D. 1881–1939
(Wanganui) 1905–06
(Wellington) 1908   15 (1)
Thorn B.C. 1975–
(Canterbury) 2003–09–10–11
(Tasman) 2008   60 (59)
Thorne G.S. 1946–
(Auckland) 1967–68–69–70   39 (10)
Thorne R.D. 1975–
(Canterbury) 1999–2000–01–02–03–
04–06–07   51 (50)
Thornton N.H. 1918–1998
(Auckland) 1947–49   19 (3)
Thrush J.I. 1985–
(Hurricanes) 2013–14–15   12 (12)
Tialata N.S. 1982–
(Wellington) 2005–06–07–08–
09–10   44 (43)
Tiatia F.I. 1971–
(Wellington) 2000   2 (2)
Tilyard F.J. 1896–1954
(Wellington) 1923   1 (–)
Tilyard J.T. 1889–1966
(Wellington) 1913–20   10 (1)
Timu J.K.R. 1969–
(Otago) 1989–90–91–92–93–94   50 (26)
Tindill E.W.T. 1910–2010
(Wellington) 1935–36–38   17 (1)
Tiopira H. 1871–1930
(Hawke's Bay) 1893   8 (–)
Todd M.B. 1988–
(Crusaders) 2013,15–16–17–18   17 (17)
Toeava I. 1986–
(Auckland) 2005–06–07–08–
09–10–11   37 (36)
Tonu'u O.F.J. 1970–
(Auckland) 1996–97–98   8 (5)
To'omaga–Allen J.L. 1990–
(Hurricanes) 2013–17   3 (1)
Townsend L.J. 1934–
(Otago) 1955   2 (2)
Tregaskis C.D. 1965–
(Wellington) 1991   4 (–)

Tremain K.R. 1938–1992
(Canterbury) 1959
(Auckland) 1960
(Canterbury) 1961
(Hawke's Bay) 1962–63–64–65–
66–67–68   86 (38)
Trevathan D. 1912–1986
(Otago) 1937   3 (3)
Tuck J.M. 1907–1967
(Waikato) 1929   6 (3)
Tuiali'i M.M. 1981–
(Auckland) 2004–05–06   10 (9)
Tuigamala V.L. 1969–
(Auckland) 1989–90–91–92–93   39 (19)
Tu'inukuafe G.Z.K. 1993
(Chiefs) 2018   13 (13)
Tuipulotu P.T. 1993–
(Blues) 2014–16–17–18   23 (21)
Tuitavake A.S.M. 1982–
(North Harbour) 2008   7 (6)
Tuitupou S. 1982–
(Auckland) 2004–06   9 (9)
Tunnicliff R.G. 1894–1973
(Buller) 1923   1 (–)
Turnbull J.S. 1898–1947
(Otago) 1921   1 (–)
Turner R.S. 1968–
(North Harbour) 1992   2 (2)
Turtill H.S.* 1880–1918
(Canterbury) 1905   1 (1)
Tu'ungafasi A.O.H.M. 1992–
(Blues) 2016–17–18   28 (26)
Twigden T.M. 1952–
(Auckland) 1979–80   15 (2)
Tyler G.A. 1879–1942
(Auckland) 1903–04–05–06   36 (7)

Udy D.K. 1874–1935
(Wairarapa) 1901–03   9 (1)
Udy H. 1860–1933
(Wellington) 1884   8 (–)
Umaga J.F. 1973–
(Wellington) 1997–99–2000–01–
02–03–04–05   79 (74)
Urbahn R.J. 1934–1984
(Taranaki) 1959–60   15 (3)
Urlich R.A. 1944–
(Auckland) 1970–72–73   35 (2)
Uttley I.N. 1941–2015
(Wellington) 1963   2 (2)

Valli G.T. 1954–
(Southland) 1980   1 (–)
Vanisi O.K. 1972–
(Wellington) 1999   1 (–)
Vidiri J. 1973–
(Counties Manukau) 1998   2 (2)
Vincent P.B. 1926–1983
(Canterbury) 1956   2 (2)
Vito V.V.J. 1987–
(Wellington) 2010–11–12
(Hurricanes) 2013–14–15   33 (33)

Vodanovich I.M.H. 1930–1995
(Wellington) 1955   3   (3)
Vorrath F.H. 1908–1972
(Otago) 1935–36   12   (–)

Waldrom S.L. 1980–
(Taranaki) 2008   1   (–)
Wallace W.J. 1878–1972
(Wellington) 1903–04–05–06–
07–08   51   (11)
Waller D.A.G. 1974–
(Wellington) 2001   3   (1)
Walsh P.T. 1936–2007
(Counties) 1955–56–57–58–59–
63–64   27   (13)
Walter J. 1904–1966
(Taranaki) 1925   7   (–)
Warbrick J.A. 1862–1903
(Auckland) 1884   7   (–)
Ward E.P. 1899–1958
(Taranaki) 1928   10   (–)
Ward F.G. 1900–1990
(Otago) 1921   1   (–)
Ward R.H. 1915–2000
(Southland) 1936–37   4   (3)
Waterman A.C. 1903–1997
(North Auckland) 1929   7   (2)
Watkins E.L. 1880–1949
(Wellington) 1905   1   (1)
Watson J.D. 1872–1958
(Taranaki) 1896   1   (–)
Watson W.D. 1869–1953
(Wairarapa) 1893–96   3   (–)
Watt B.A. 1939–
(Canterbury) 1962–63–64   29   (8)
Watt J.M. 1914–1988
(Otago) 1936   2   (2)
Watt J.R. 1935–
(Southland) 1957
(Wellington) 1958–60–61–62   42   (9)
Watts M.G. 1955–
(Taranaki) 1979–80   13   (5)
Webb D.S. 1934–1987
(North Auckland) 1959   1   (1)
Webb P.P. 1854–1920
(Wellington) 1884   8   (–)
Weber B.M. 1991
(Chiefs) 2015   1   (1)
Webster T.R.D. 1920–1972
(Southland) 1947   4   (–)
Weepu P.A.T. 1983–
(Wellington) 2004–05–06–07–08–
09–10–11–12
(Blues) 2013   73   (71)
Wells J. 1908–1994
(Wellington) 1936   3   (2)
Wells W.J.G. 1867–1911
(Taranaki) 1897   7   (–)
Wesney A.W.* 1915–1941
(Southland) 1938   3   (–)

West A.H. 1893–1934
(Taranaki) 1920–21–23–24–25   24   (2)
Weston L.H. 1892–1963
(Auckland) 1914   1   (–)
Whetton A.J. 1959–
(Auckland) 1984–85–86–87–88–
89–90–91   65   (35)
Whetton G.W. 1959–
(Auckland) 1981–82–83–84–85–
86–87–88–89–90–91   101   (58)
Whineray W.J. 1935–2012
(Canterbury) 1957
(Waikato) 1958
(Auckland) 1959–60–61–62–63–
64–65   77   (32)
White A. 1894–1968
(Southland) 1921–22–23–24–25   38   (4)
White H.L. 1929–2016
(Auckland) 1953–54–55   16   (4)
White R.A. 1925–2012
(Poverty Bay) 1949–50–51–52–
53–54–55–56   55   (23)
White R.M. 1917–1980
(Wellington) 1946–47   10   (4)
Whitelock G.B. 1986–
(Canterbury) 2009   1   (1)
Whitelock L.C. 1991–
(Crusaders) 2013–17–18   8   (7)
Whitelock S.L. 1988–
(Canterbury) 2010–11–12
(Crusaders) 2013–14–15–16–17–18   108 (108)
Whiting G.J. 1946–
(King Country) 1972–73   31   (6)
Whiting P.J. 1946–
(Auckland) 1971–72–73–74–76   56   (20)
Wickes C.D. 1962–
(Manawatu) 1980   1   (–)
Wightman D.R. 1929–2012
(Auckland) 1951   4   (–)
Williams A.J. 1981–
(Auckland) 2002–03–04–05–06–07–
08–11–12   78   (77)
Williams A.L. 1898–1972
(Otago) 1922–23   9   (–)
Williams B.G. 1950–
(Auckland) 1970–71–72–73–74–
75–76–77–78   113   (38)
Williams C.W. 1916–1998
(Canterbury) 1938   4   (–)
Williams G.C. 1945–2018
(Wellington) 1967–68   18   (5)
Williams P. 1884–1976
(Otago) 1913   9   (1)
Williams R.N. 1909–2001
(Hawke's Bay) 1932   1   (–)
Williams R.O. 1963–
(North Harbour) 1988–89   10   (–)
Williams S. 1985–
(Canterbury) 2010–1–12
(Chiefs) 2014–15
(Blues) 2017–18   51   (51)

Williment M. 1940–1994
(Wellington) 1964–65–66–67   9 (9)
Willis R.K. 1975–
(Waikato) 1998–99–2002   12 (12)
Willis T.E. 1979–
(Otago) 2001–02   7 (5)
Willocks C. 1919–1991
(Otago) 1946–47–49   22 (5)
Willoughby S. de L.P. 1904–1985
(Wairarapa) 1928   4 (–)
Wills M.C. 1941–
(Taranaki) 1967   5 (–)
Wilson A. 1874–1932
(Auckland) 1897   8 (–)
Wilson A.L. 1927–2009
(Southland) 1951   7 (–)
Wilson B.W. 1956–
(Otago) 1977–78–79   12 (8)
Wilson D.D. 1931–
(Canterbury) 1953–54   14 (2)
Wilson F.R.* 1885–1916
(Auckland) 1910   2 (–)
Wilson H.B. 1957–
(Counties) 1983   3 (–)
Wilson H.C. 1868–1945
(Wellington) 1893   7 (–)
Wilson H.W. 1924–2004
(Otago) 1949–50–51   13 (5)
Wilson J.W. 1973–
(Otago) 1993–94–95–96–97–98–
99–2001   71 (60)
Wilson N.A. 1886–1953
(Wellington) 1908–10–13–14   21 (10)
Wilson N.L. 1922–2001
(Otago) 1949–51   20 (3)
Wilson R.G. 1953–
(Canterbury) 1976–78–79–80   25 (2)
Wilson R.J. 1861–1944
(Canterbury) 1884   6 (–)
Wilson S.S. 1954–
(Wellington)
1976–77–78–79–80–81–82–83   85 (34)
Wilson V.W. 1899–1978
(Auckland) 1920   7 (–)
Wise G.D. 1904–1971
(Otago) 1925   7 (–)
Witcombe D.J.C. 1978–
(Auckland) 2005   5 (5)
Wolfe T.N. 1941–
(Wellington) 1961–62
(Taranaki) 1963–68   14 (6)

Wood M.E. 1876–1956
(Wellington) 1901
(Canterbury) 1903
(Auckland) 1904   12 (2)
Woodcock T.D. 1981–
(North Harbour) 2002–04–05–06–
07–08–09–10–11–12
(Highlanders) 2013
(Blues) 2014–15   118 (118)
Woodman F.A. 1958–
(North Auckland) 1980–81   14 (3)
Woodman T.B.K. 1960–
(North Auckland) 1984   6 (–)
Woods C.A. 1929–
(Southland) 1953–54   14 (–)
Wright A.H. 1914–1990
(Wellington) 1938   4 (–)
Wright D.H. 1902–1966
(Auckland) 1925   7 (–)
Wright T.J. 1963–
(Auckland) 1986–87–88–89–90–
91–92   64 (30)
Wright W.A. 1905–1971
(Auckland) 1926   1 (–)
Wrigley E. 1886–1958
(Wairarapa) 1905   1 (1)
Wulf R.N. 1984–
(North Harbour) 2008   4 (4)
Wylie J.T. 1887–1956
(Auckland) 1913   12 (2)
Wyllie A.J. 1944–
(Canterbury) 1970–71–72–73   40 (11)
Wyllie T. 1954–
(Wellington) 1980   1 (–)
Wynyard J.G.* 1914–1942
(Waikato) 1935–36–38   13 (–)
Wynyard W.T. 1867–1938
(Wellington) 1893   7 (–)

Yates V.M. 1939–2008
(North Auckland) 1961–62   9 (3)
Young D. 1930–
(Canterbury) 1956–57–58–60–
61–62–63–64   61 (22)
Young F.B. 1874–1946
(Wellington) 1896   1 (–)

NZR ANNUAL AWARDS

Since 1994 the NZRU has hosted, at the end of each year, an annual awards function to honour players, personalities and teams. With the exception of the Tom French Cup all trophies were new. The Tom French Cup had been presented in 1949 by Mr J. Morris of Sydney, following the New Zealand Maori tour of Australia, in honour of the team's coach Mr T.A. French. The trophy has been awarded to the outstanding Maori player each season.

PLAYER OF THE YEAR
Kelvin Tremain Memorial Trophy
1994 Zinzan Brooke (*Auckland*)
1995 Jonah Lomu (*Counties*)
1996 Sean Fitzpatrick (*Auckland*)
1997 Jeff Wilson (*Otago*)
1998 Josh Kronfeld (*Otago*)
1999 Andrew Mehrtens (*Canterbury*)
2000 Tana Umaga (*Wellington*)
2001 Todd Blackadder (*Canterbury*)
2002 Chris Jack (*Canterbury*)
2003 Richard McCaw (*Canterbury*)
2004 Daniel Carter (*Canterbury*)
2005 Daniel Carter (*Canterbury*)
2006 Richard McCaw (*Canterbury*)
2007 Daniel Braid (*Auckland*)
2008 Andrew Hore (*Taranaki*)
2009 Richard McCaw (*Canterbury*)
2010 Kieran Read (*Canterbury*)
2011 Jerome Kaino (*Auckland*)
2012 Richie McCaw (*Canterbury*)
2013 Kieran Read (*Canterbury*)
2014 Brodie Retallick (*Waikato*)
2015 Ma'a Nonu (*Wellington*)
2016 Beauden Barrett (*Taranaki*)
2017 Samuel Whitelock (*Canterbury*)
2018 Kendra Cocksedge (*Canterbury*)

SUPER RUGBY PLAYER OF THE YEAR
1996 Joeli Vidiri (*Blues*)
1997 Christian Cullen (*Hurricanes*)
1998 Andrew Mehrtens (*Crusaders*)
1999 Byron Kelleher (*Highlanders*)
2000 Scott Robertson (*Crusaders*)
2001 Deon Muir (*Chiefs*)
2002 Chris Jack (*Crusaders*)
2003 Carlos Spencer (*Blues*)
2004 Daniel Carter (*Crusaders*)
2005 Rico Gear (*Crusaders*)
2006 Daniel Carter (*Crusaders*)
2007 James Cowan (*Highlanders*)
2008 Andrew Hore (*Hurricanes*)
2009 Mils Muliaina (*Chiefs*)
2010 Alby Mathewson (*Blues*)
2011 Wyatt Crockett (*Crusaders*)

2012 Conrad Smith (*Hurricanes*)
2013 Ben Smith (*Highlanders*)
2014 Jerome Kaino (*Blues*)
2015 Lima Sopoaga (*Highlanders*)
2016 Beauden Barrett (*Hurricanes*)
2017 Samuel Whitelock (*Crusaders*)
2018 Richie Mo'unga (*Crusaders*)

TEAM OF THE YEAR
2000 New Zealand Under 21
2001 Canterbury
2002 New Zealand Sevens
2003 All Blacks
2004 Canterbury
2005 All Blacks
2006 All Blacks
2007 Auckland
2008 All Blacks
2009 Canterbury
2010 Black Ferns
2011 All Blacks
2012 All Blacks
2013 All Blacks
2014 All Blacks
2015 All Blacks
2016 All Blacks
2017 Black Ferns

NEW ZEALAND TEAM OF THE YEAR
2018 Black Ferns Sevens

NATIONAL TEAM OF THE YEAR
2018 Crusaders

PREMIER DIVISION PLAYER OF THE YEAR
Duane Monkley Medal
from 2017

2006	Richard Kahui (*Waikato*)
2007	Isa Nacewa (*Auckland*)
2008	Jamie Mackintosh (*Southland*)
2009	Mike Delany (*Bay of Plenty*)
2010	Robbie Fruean (*Canterbury*)
2011	Aaron Cruden (*Manawatu*)
2012	Robbie Fruean (*Canterbury*)
2013	Andy Ellis (*Canterbury*)
2014	Seta Tamanivalu (*Taranaki*)
2015	George Moala (*Auckland*)
2016	Jordie Barrett (*Canterbury*)
2017	Jack Goodhue (*Northland*)
2018	Luke Romano (*Canterbury*)

HEARTLAND CHAMPIONSHIP PLAYER OF THE YEAR

2006	Scott Leighton (*Poverty Bay*)
2007	Ross Hay (*North Otago*)
2008	Cameron Crowley (*Wanganui*)
2009	Asaeli Tikoirotuma (*Wanganui*)
2010	Peter Rowe (*Wanganui*)
2011	Jon Smyth (*Wanganui*)
2012	Peter Rowe (*Wanganui*)
2013	Jon Dampney (*Mid Canterbury*)
2014	James Lash (*Buller*)
2015	Lindsay Horrocks (*Wanganui*)
2016	Te Rangatira Waitokia (*Wanganui*)
2017	Scott Cameron (*Horowhenua Kapiti*)
2018	Brett Ranga (*Thames Valley*)

MAORI PLAYER OF THE YEAR
Tom French Cup

1949	Johnny Smith (*North Auckland*)
1950	Manahi Paewai (*North Auckland*)
1951	Percy Erceg (*Auckland*)
1952	Keith Davis (*Auckland*)
1953	Keith Davis (*Auckland*)
1954	Keith Davis (*Auckland*)
1955	Pat Walsh (*South Auckland*)
1956	Bill Gray (*Bay of Plenty*)
1957	Muru Walters (*North Auckland*)
1958	Pat Walsh (*Counties*)
1959	Bill Wordley (*King Country*)
1960	Mac Herewini (*Auckland*)
1961	Victor Yates (*North Auckland*)
1962	Waka Nathan (*Auckland*)
1963	Mac Herewini (*Auckland*)
1964	Ron Rangi (*Auckland*)
1965	Ron Rangi (*Auckland*)
1966	Waka Nathan (*Auckland*)
1967	Sid Going (*North Auckland*)
1968	Sid Going (*North Auckland*)
1969	Sid Going (*North Auckland*)
1970	Sid Going (*North Auckland*)
1971	Sid Going (*North Auckland*)
1972	Sid Going (*North Auckland*)
1973	Tane Norton (*Canterbury*)
1974	Tane Norton (*Canterbury*)
1975	Bill Bush (*Canterbury*)
1976	Kent Lambert (*Manawatu*)
1977	Bill Osborne (*Wanganui*)
1978	Eddie Dunn (*North Auckland*)
1979	Vance Stewart (*Canterbury*)
1980	Hika Reid (*Bay of Plenty*)
1981	Frank Shelford (*Bay of Plenty*)
1982	Steven Pokere (*Southland*)
1983	Hika Reid (*Bay of Plenty*)
1984	Michael Clamp (*Wellington*)
1985	Wayne Shelford (*North Harbour*)
1986	Frano Botica (*North Harbour*)
1987	Wayne Shelford (*North Harbour*)
1988	Wayne Shelford (*North Harbour*)
1989	Wayne Shelford (*North Harbour*)
1990	Steve McDowell (*Auckland*)
1991	John Timu (*Otago*)
1992	Zinzan Brooke (*Auckland*)
1993	Arran Pene (*Otago*)
1994	Zinzan Brooke (*Auckland*)
1995	Robin Brooke (*Auckland*)
1996	Errol Brain (*Counties Manukau*)
1997	Mark Mayerhofler (*Canterbury*)
1998	Tony Brown (*Otago*)
1999	Norman Maxwell (*Canterbury*)
2000	Daryl Gibson (*Canterbury*)
2001	Caleb Ralph (*Canterbury*)
2002	Carlos Spencer (*Auckland*)
2003	Carlos Spencer (*Auckland*)
2004	Carl Hayman (*Otago*)
2005	Rico Gear (*Nelson Bays*)
2006	Carl Hayman (*Otago*)
2007	Daniel Braid (*Auckland*)
2008	Piri Weepu (*Wellington*)
2009	Zac Guildford (*Hawke's Bay*)
2010	Hosea Gear (*Wellington*)
2011	Piri Weepu (*Wellington*)
2012	Liam Messam (*Waikato*)
2013	Liam Messam (*Waikato*)
2014	Aaron Smith (*Manawatu*)
2015	Nehe Milner-Skudder (*Manawatu*)
2016	Dane Coles (*Wellington*)
2017	Rieko Ioane (*Auckland*)
2018	Codie Taylor (*Canterbury*)

NZ RUGBY PLAYERS' ASSN KIRK AWARD
2016 Justin Collins (*Northland*)
2017 DJ Forbes (*Counties Manukau*)
2018 Fiao'o Faamausili (*Auckland*)
 Keven Mealamu (*Auckland*)

AGE GRADE PLAYER OF THE YEAR
1994 Taine Randell (*Otago*)
1995 Anton Oliver (*Otago*)
1996 Andrew Blowers (*Auckland*)
1997 Norman Maxwell (*Northland*)
1998 Doug Howlett (*Auckland*)
1999 Samiu Vahafolau (*Auckland*)
2000 Ben Blair (*Canterbury*)
2001 Under 21
 Richard McCaw (*Canterbury*)
 Under 19
 Sam Tuitupou (*Auckland*)
2002 Luke McAlister (*North Harbour*)
2003 Ben Atiga (*Auckland*)
2004 Jerome Kaino (*Auckland*)
2005 Isaia Toeava (*Auckland*)
2006 Michael Paterson (*Canterbury*)
2007 Zac Guildford (*Hawke's Bay*)
2008 Zac Guildford (*Hawke's Bay*)
2009 Aaron Cruden (*Manawatu*)
2010 Liaki Moli (*Auckland*)
2011 Sam Cane (*Bay of Plenty*)
2012 Jason Emery (*Manawatu*)
2013 Ardie Savea (*Wellington*)
2014 Damian McKenzie (*Waikato*)
2015 Akira Ioane (*Auckland*)
2016 Jordie Barrett (*Canterbury*)
2017 Asafo Aumua (*Wellington*)
2018 Tom Christie (*Canterbury*)

SEVENS PLAYER OF THE YEAR
Richard Crawshaw Memorial Trophy from 1998
1994 Eric Rush (*North Harbour*)
1995 Jonah Lomu (*Counties*)
1996 Christian Cullen (*Manawatu*)
1997 Caleb Ralph (*Bay of Plenty*)
1998 Rico Gear (*Auckland*)
1999 Orene Ai'i (*Auckland*)
2000 Karl Te Nana (*North Harbour*)
2001 Karl Te Nana (*North Harbour*)
2002 Chris Masoe (*Taranaki*)
2003 Eric Rush (*North Harbour*)
2004 Liam Messam (*Waikato*)
2005 Amasio Valence (*Hawke's Bay*)
2006 Tafai Ioasa (*Hawke's Bay*)
2007 D.J. Forbes (*Auckland*)
2008 D.J. Forbes (*Counties Manukau*)
2009 Zar Lawrence (*Bay of Plenty*)
2010 Kurt Baker (*Taranaki*)
2011 Tim Mikkelson (*Waikato*)
2012 Tomasi Cama (*Manawatu*)
2013 Kurt Baker (*Taranaki*)
2014 DJ Forbes (*Counties Manukau*)
2015 Scott Curry (*Bay of Plenty*)
2016 Rieko Ioane (*Auckland*)
2017 DJ Forbes (*Counties Manukau*)
2018 Scott Curry (*Bay of Plenty*)

WOMEN'S PLAYER OF THE YEAR
1994 Anna Richards (*Auckland*)
1995 Rochelle Martin (*Wellington*)
1996 Vanessa Cootes (*Waikato*)
1997 Louisa Wall (*Auckland*)
1998 Farah Palmer (*Otago*)
1999 Suzanne Shortland (*Auckland*)
2000 Fiona King (*Otago*)
2001 Annaleah Rush (*Auckland*)
2002 Monique Hirovanaa (*Auckland*)
2003 Monalisa Codling (*Auckland*)
2004 Stephanie Mortimer (*Canterbury*)
2005 Melissa Ruscoe (*Canterbury*)
2006 Amiria Marsh (*Canterbury*)
2007 Victoria Heighway (*Auckland*)
2008 Victoria Grant (*Auckland*)
2009 Victoria Heighway (*Auckland*)
2010 Carla Hohepa (*Otago*)
2011 Fiao'o Faamausili (*Auckland*)
2012 Rawinia Everitt (*Auckland*)
2013 Kelly Brazier (*Otago*)
2014 Rawinia Everitt (*Counties Manukau*)
2015 Kendra Cocksedge (*Canterbury*)
2016 Selica Winiata (*Manawatu*)
2017 Sarah Goss (*Manawatu*)
2018 Kendra Cocksedge (*Canterbury*)

FARAH PALMER CUP PLAYER OF THE YEAR
Fiao'o Faamausili Medal
2017 Hazel Tubic (*Counties Manukau*)
2018 Kendra Cocksedge (*Canterbury*)

WOMEN'S SEVENS PLAYER OF THE YEAR

2013 Portia Woodman (*Auckland*)
2014 Sarah Goss (*Manawatu*)
2015 Tyla Nathan-Wong (*Auckland*)
2016 Sarah Goss (*Manawatu*)
2017 Ruby Tui (*Canterbury*)
2018 Michaela Blyde (*Bay of Plenty*)

COACH OF THE YEAR

1994 Brad Meurant (*North Harbour*)
1995 Graham Henry (*Auckland*)
1996 John Hart (*All Blacks*)
2001 Colin Cooper (*New Zealand Under 21*)
2002 Robbie Deans (*Crusaders*)
2003 Wayne Pivac (*Auckland*)
2004 Vern Cotter (*Bay of Plenty*)
2005 Graham Henry (*All Blacks*)
2006 Graham Henry (*All Blacks*)
2007 Peter Russell (*Hawke's Bay*)
2008 Graham Henry (*All Blacks*)
2009 Dave Rennie (*New Zealand Under 20*)
2010 Gordon Tietjens (*New Zealand Sevens*)
2011 Graham Henry (*All Blacks*)
2012 Steve Hansen (*All Blacks*)
2013 Steve Hansen (*All Blacks*)
2014 Steve Hansen (*All Blacks*)
2015 Steve Hansen (*All Blacks*)
2016 Steve Hansen (*All Blacks*)
2017 Glenn Moore (*Black Ferns*)

NEW ZEALAND COACH OF THE YEAR

2018 Clark Laidlaw (*All Blacks Sevens*)

NATIONAL COACH OF THE YEAR

2018 Alama Ieremia (*Auckland*)

REFEREE OF THE YEAR

1994 Colin Hawke (*South Canterbury*)
1995 Paddy O'Brien (*Southland*)
1996 Paddy O'Brien (*Southland*)
1997 Steve Walsh jnr (*North Harbour*)★
1998 Paddy O'Brien (*Southland*)
1999 Colin Hawke (*South Canterbury*)
2000 Colin Hawke (*South Canterbury*)
2001 Kelvin Deaker (*Hawke's Bay*)
2002 Paddy O'Brien (*Southland*)
2003 Paddy O'Brien (*Southland*)
2004 Paddy O'Brien (*Southland*)
2005 Paul Honiss (*Waikato*)
2006 Paul Honiss (*Waikato*)
2007 Steve Walsh (*North Harbour*)
2008 Bryce Lawrence (*Bay of Plenty*)
2009 Bryce Lawrence (*Bay of Plenty*)
2010 Bryce Lawrence (*Bay of Plenty*)
2011 Bryce Lawrence (*Bay of Plenty*)
2012 Glen Jackson (*Bay of Plenty*)
2013 Chris Pollock (*Hawke's Bay*)
2014 Glen Jackson (*Bay of Plenty*)
2015 Glen Jackson (*Bay of Plenty*)
2016 Glen Jackson (*Bay of Plenty*)
2017 Ben O'Keeffe (*Wellington*)
2018 Glen Jackson (*Bay of Plenty*)

★ for the Outstanding Referee Performance (Canterbury v Auckland round robin match)

STEINLAGER SALVER
For outstanding service to rugby

1999 Colin Meads
2000 Zinzan Brooke★
2001 Sir Terry McLean
2002 Fred Allen
2003 Sir Brian Lochore
2004 Peter Bush
2005 Richie Guy
2006 Stan Hill
2007 Ron Don
2008 Tane Norton
2009 John Graham
2010 Keith Quinn
2011 Jock Hobbs
2012 Ray Harper
2013 Graham Mourie
2014 Dick Littlejohn
2015 Mike Eagle
2016 Gavin Service
2017 Wayne Smith
2018 Waka Nathan

★ celebrating 25 years of the NPC

VOLUNTEER OF THE YEAR
**Charles Monro Memorial Trophy
from 2009**

2002	John George (*Taranaki*)
2003	Ru Rangi (*Wellington*)
2004	Adelle Wakely (*Hawke's Bay*)
2005	Daphne Boden (*Hawke's Bay*)
2006	Jason Martin (*Otago*)
2007	Robbie Ball (*Northland*)
2008	Ken Swain (*Horowhenua Kapiti*)
2009	Blair Crawford (*Otago*)
2010	Hilton Williams (*Horowhenua Kapiti*)
2011	Andy MacDonald (*Canterbury*)
2012	Ray Watson (*Bay of Plenty*)
2013	Rob Jones (*Manawatu*)
2014	Dean File (*Horowhenua Kapiti*)
2015	Tania Karaitiana and Vio Ugone (*Wellington*)
2016	Gary Donovan (*Auckland*)
2017	Sid Tatana (*Wairarapa Bush*)
2018	Irene Eruera-Taiapa (*Horowhenua Kapiti*)

SKY FANS TRY OF THE YEAR

2013	Selica Winiata (*Black Ferns*)
2014	Malakai Fekitoa (*Highlanders*)
2015	Samu Kubunavanua (*Wanganui*)
2016	Isaiah Punivai (*Christ's College*)
2017	Portia Woodman (*Black Ferns*)
2018	Chris Hala'ufia (*St Peter's College*)

OBITUARIES

NEW ZEALAND REPRESENTATIVES

William Roberts 'Robin' Archer *(Otago and Southland)* played in four tests, the first two against Australia in 1955 and the first and third against South Africa in 1956. He was the leading first five-eighth of his era and would have played in all four tests of the Springbok series had he not been injured in each game. He toured Australia with the 1957 team but Ross Brown became the preferred player in his position although Archer had the honour of captaining the All Blacks against New England.

Born in Invercargill on 19 September 1930 Robin Archer was a member of the Gore High School first fifteen 1946-48 and then headed to Otago University where he gained a Batchelor of Science degree. He represented South Island Colts in 1951 and made his debut for Otago two years later. Following sound appearances for NZ Universities in 1954 he came into the national spotlight when playing for the Rest of New Zealand against a shadow All Blacks side and later for a New Zealand XV against the NZ Maori team. South Island and All Blacks honours followed in 1955.

Returning to Southland in 1956 he commenced an outstanding career with the union and captained the side, he being joined in the Southland backline by younger brother Wattie in 1957, the pair playing 52 games together for the union until 1963. Wattie was equally as talented as Robin but, sadly, developed motor neurone disease and forced to retire. Robin's 1963 season was interrupted by injuries and he did not appear in 1964. However, the illness of his brother motivated Robin to return in 1965 and his presence in the Southland side inspired the team. Although losing to the touring Springboks Southland didn't lose any provincial games in which Robin played including a drawn Ranfurly Shield challenge against Taranaki. In 1966, Robin's final season in rep rugby, the backline general guided Southland to a 14-8 win over the touring Lions. Wattie, after several years of declining health, died in 1971, aged 36.

Despite being in All Blacks trial teams until 1961 and playing the best rugby of his career during the 1958-60 period Robin never regained the All Black jersey. He led Southland to a 26-8 victory over the 1958 Wallabies and a 23-6 win in a successful Ranfurly Shield challenge against Taranaki in 1959 and early in 1960 captained three trial teams but missed selection for the South African tour. On his 1960 form for Southland the *Almanack* commented that Archer 'clearly showed that he should have been with the New Zealand touring side; right from the Trials he stood out as a versatile attacker and solid defender; it was the best season of his career.'

Robin Archer had two periods as Southland coach 1973-75 and 1980-81and also selector and coach of the Eastern Southland sub-union team for several years. He was a successful businessman in the family building firm and took a keen interest in the racing industry, breeding and racing thoroughbreds and being a regular attendee at the Melbourne Cup between 1979 and 2010. In 2000 he was made a life member of the NZ Thoroughbred Breeders' Association. Archer moved from Southland to Christchurch in 1989 and then to Auckland in 2011.

Robin Archer's first-class record:

For	Matches	Tries	DG	Points
Otago (Univ) 1953(8), 1954(9) (Pirate) 1955(7)	24	2	–	6
Southland (Gore Pioneer) 1956(3), 1957(12), 1958(10), 1959(13), 1960(12), 1961(13), 1962(7), 1963(4), 1965(7), 1966(10)	91	7	–	21
Centurions Club 1961	1	1	–	3
South Island Colts 1951	1	–	–	0

New Zealand Universities 1954	3	–	1	3
New Zealand Trials 1956, 1957(2), 1958, 1959(2), 1960(3), 1961	10	2	–	6
White XV 1957	1	–	–	0
South Island XV 1956	1	1	–	3
South Island 1955, 1957, 1959	3	–	–	0
Rest of New Zealand 1954, 1955	2	–	–	0
New Zealand XV 1954, 1955	2	–	–	0
NEW ZEALAND 1955(2), 1956(2), 1957(9)	13	5	–	15
TOTALS	**152**	**18**	**1**	**57**

At Auckland, 9 March 2018, aged 87.

Mark William Irwin *(Otago, Poverty Bay and Bay of Plenty)* was one of those All Blacks from the 1950s and 60s who might have wondered what heights their rugby careers might have reached had they been born a generation or two later. Irwin certainly had the physical attributes, at 1.85m and 100kg, in an age where weight training for rugby players was not encouraged, which would have made him ideal for professional rugby. Had the game been the only thing in his life he might well have been rated among New Zealand's greatest props. But it is highly unlikely that in later life Irwin ever regretted playing when he did. For as with many of his All Black contemporaries Irwin was an achiever outside rugby, either in business or, as in Irwin's case, the higher professions. For more than 50 years Irwin was one of Rotorua's most prominent medical practitioners and anaesthetists.

Irwin entered top rugby aged only 18, unusually young for a prop, having been singled out as an exceptional prospect at Wanganui Collegiate School, where he had played in the first XV in 1950-52. With his size and natural strength Irwin on the tighthead side was an effective scrummager.

Yet Irwin never quite achieved the rugby fame for which he seemed destined. Though his representative career stretched over a decade from 1953 to 1962 he finished short of 100 first-class games and for his main provincial union, Otago, he had only 24 games. Injuries and his medical studies limited his appearances, as did a decision in 1956, after he had suffered rib injuries in the first test against South Africa in Dunedin, to concentrate on rowing, at which he was also accomplished. He came close to representing New Zealand in two sports for he was in the eight nominated for the 1956 Melbourne Olympic Games, only for the crew to be rejected in the final selection.

But Irwin still had a creditable rugby career with plenty of major honours. He was among the youngest ever All Black trialists, certainly for a prop, when in 1953 he played for South Island B and in 1954 he made the first of his five appearances for South Island. And when he was fit and available he was a regular selection for New Zealand Universities, including their match against the 1959 Lions.

He made his All Blacks debut in 1955, aged only 20, in the first two tests against Australia, and played the first test against the 1956 Springboks, becoming one of several injury casualties in that stormy series. His replacement for the second test, another young Otago prop Frank McAtamney, also received a torrid time from the tough Springboks, Jappie Bekker and Chris Koch, leading to the now legendary return for the last two tests of Kevin Skinner.

Irwin regained his All Black spot for the second test against Australia in 1958 and also appeared in two of the tests against the 1959 British Lions. He toured South Africa in 1960 and played the first test but a slight slump in form and involvement in a car crash saw him miss the last three tests, even though he had become available for at least two of them. The South Africans especially did not regret his absence as he was regarded by them as the best All Black scrummager, an area where the All Blacks on that tour often struggled.

By 1960 Irwin had qualified as a doctor and practising medicine soon became his priority. But in each of the 1961 and 1962 seasons he represented Poverty Bay and Bay of Plenty and in 1961 he appeared in two national trials. *(Obituary contributed by Lindsay Knight).*

Mark Irwin's first-class record:

For	Matches	Tries	Points
Otago (Univ) 1953(4), 1955(3), 1956(4), 1957, 1958(7), 1959(5)	24	1	3
Poverty Bay (HSOB) 1961	5	–	0
Bay of Plenty (Rotorua HSOB) 1962	3	–	0
Otago B 1955	3	–	0
Centurions Club 1959	1	–	0
South Island Universities 1955, 1958, 1959	3	–	0
New Zealand Universities 1954(3), 1955, 1958, 1959(3)	8	–	0
South Island B 1953	1	–	0
South Island 1954, 1955, 1956, 1958, 1959	5	–	0
New Zealand Trials 1953, 1956, 1959(2), 1960, 1961(2)	7	–	0
Rest of New Zealand 1955, 1956	2	–	0
New Zealand XV 1955, 1956(2), 1958	4	1	3
NEW ZEALAND 1955(2), 1956, 1958, 1959(2), 1960(19)	25	–	0
TOTALS	**91**	**2**	**6**

At Rotorua, 30 June 2018, aged 83.

William Fergus McCormick *(Canterbury)* was an outstanding All Black fullback from 1965 to 1971, but his legendary status in New Zealand rugby was due perhaps more to his exploits for Canterbury for whom between 1958 and 1975 he played a phenomenal 222 games. Only 1.71m tall, Fergie McCormick would have been too short for a modern-day fullback. But in his era he was an imposing figure and with his pocket battleship build became renowned for his fearless tackling. He was also one of the first running fullbacks, possessing surprising speed which was ideally suited for broken play attacks when in the 1960s restricted kicking into touch rules were introduced.

McCormick entered first-class rugby in 1958 as a teenaged first five-eighths in a Canterbury B match against Mid Canterbury but shifted to fullback in 1959, where in only his second game he made a big impression, especially with his tackling, when Canterbury beat the 1959 British Lions. That was the beginning of his long tenure as Canterbury's fullback and as early as 1960 he was acclaimed as one of the country's best, becoming a regular selection for South Island sides, for whom he made 10 appearances, and in national trials.

But despite his consistent provincial performances, McCormick had trouble winning national selection. The early to mid 1960s was the era of the goal-kicking colossus, Don Clarke, and even when injuries affected Clarke in 1964 and caused his retirement a year later McCormick faced the stiff competition of Wellington's Mick Williment to be his fullback successor. Only in 1965, in the fourth test against the touring Springboks, did McCormick make his All Black debut when Williment was spelled, having suffered a knock playing against the tourists for New Zealand Universities. That seemed to be McCormick's only international chance for in 1966, against the British Lions and in the Jubilee one-off test against Australia in 1967, Williment, a superior goal-kicker, returned.

But for the 1967 tour of Britain and France Williment was suddenly overlooked and McCormick chosen as the only specialist fullback. Though 28, and seemingly near the end of his career, McCormick was one of the stars of the tour, not just for his defence, which won comparisons with George Nepia of the 1920s, and attacking play, but more surprisingly for his goal-kicking.

McCormick was unchallenged as the All Blacks fullback for the next three seasons and in 1969, in the second test against Wales, he scored 24 points which at the time was an individual world test record. His goal-kicking success was unexpected for even in club rugby, as a stalwart of Christchurch's Linwood club, he kicked only occasionally.

On the 1970 tour of South Africa McCormick played with his usual zest and pugnacity, but had indifferent patches with his kicking and was involved in controversy for a tackle on a Springbok wing Syd Nomis. Physically and mentally battered, he was left out of the fourth test. He returned for the first test against the 1971 Lions touring side, but had another off-day with his kicking and struggled with the tactical kicking of the Lions fly-half Barry John. That ended his All Black career, though in hindsight his international departure might have been premature. The Lions were delighted McCormick was no longer an opponent and subsequently in 1971 and later seasons he showed many glimpses of the form when he was at his peak, particularly his vintage 1969 season.

He continued playing for Canterbury until he was 36, scoring the province's winning try against the 1975 Scotland tourists. That was one of four international wins he secured with Canterbury and he also played in Ranfurly Shield wins in 1969 and 1972. Despite his moderate goal-kicking ability, McCormick was the first New Zealand player to exceed 2000 first-class points.

McCormick came from a notable sporting family and was close to being part of three generations of All Blacks. His father, Archie, was an All Black on a 1925 tour of Australia and his son, Andrew, played for New Zealand XVs, before playing and captaining Japan. Daughter Jessica represented the Canterbury women's rugby team. Fergie represented the South Island in softball and his mother, Helen, was a national hockey representative. *(Obituary contributed by Lindsay Knight).*

Fergie McCormick's first-class record:

For	Matches	Tries	Con	PG	DG	Points
Canterbury (Linwood) 1959(11), 1960(17), 1961(13), 1962(18), 1963(11), 1964(13), 1965(11), 1966(15), 1967(12), 1968(11), 1969(13), 1970(4), 1971(14), 1972(16), 1973(15), 1974(16), 1975(10)	220	38	269	204	7	1294
Canterbury B 1958, 1959	2	–	–	1	–	3
Evergreens Club 1962, 1974	2	–	5	2	–	16
Barbarians Club 1964, 1973(2), 1977	4	1	3	6	–	27
WJ Whineray's XV 1966	1	–	4	–	–	8
Cantabrians Club 1973	1	–	3	–	–	6
Harlequins Club 1975	1	–	4	1	–	11
Centurions Club 1978	1	1	–	–	–	4
Tongan Invitation XV 1973 (in Tonga)	2	1	6	2	–	22
South Island 1960, 1961, 1962, 1963, 1964, 1965, 1966, 1967, 1968, 1969	10	1	10	12	1	62

New Zealand Trials 1961, 1962(2), 1963(4), 1965, 1966, 1967(2), 1968, 1969, 1970(2), 1971(2), 1973	18	5	32	16	–	127
Rest of New Zealand 1960, 1966	2	–	2	5	–	19
New Zealand XV 1960, 1965	2	–	5	1	–	13
NEW ZEALAND 1965, 1967(12), 1968(13), 1969(2), 1970(15), 1971	44	10	114	64	1	453
TOTALS	**310**	**57**	**457**	**314**	**9**	**2065**

At Christchurch, 10 April 2018, aged 78.

Tiumalumanaia **Dylan Gabriel Mika** (*Auckland*) was one of only a handful of players to play Test rugby for both the All Blacks and Manu Samoa.

He first gained prominence in the 1991 NZ Schools side, a team that included seven future All Blacks, out of Auckland's St Peter's College. He skippered the Auckland Colts in 1993 before cracking an Auckland side that was laden with quality loose forwards. Indeed, he had to work hard to even make his Marist club side when the likes of Pat Lam and Zinzan Brooke were available. But Mika was a mainstay — if not always a front-liner — of the great Auckland and Blues sides of 1995-97.

He had already played two Tests for Manu Samoa in 1994-95, coming off the bench in the win over Wales and starting against Australia in 1994.

A rangy, athletic loose forward, equally at home in the No. 8 or No. 6 jersey, Mika was also an adept lineout operator and could even slot in at lock if required.

Former All Blacks coach John Hart kept a close eye on Mika's progress while he was serving his three-year stand-down from international rugby, and promoted him to the 1996 NZ Barbarians.

By 1999, Mika was at the Chiefs, and used that franchise, appearing in all 11 games, scoring three tries, as a launching pad into the All Blacks. Seven of his eight games were Tests, having debuted against New Zealand A in Christchurch to become All Black number 982. Mika's sole All Blacks try came in the 101-3 defeat of Italy at the Rugby World Cup in Huddersfield.

By the end of the 2000 season, and at just 28, he was lost to New Zealand rugby, taking up a contract in Japan with Coca-Cola. His playing days ended in 2004.

Mika soon proved himself an astute businessman, taking up a senior role at Glengarry Wines and was latterly the CEO of the Samoa Water company.

He was invited to join the NZ Barbarians club in 2014 and swiftly made his way up the ranks, serving as vice-president at his sudden death. A quiet achiever, Mika had a vast array of contacts and networks he tapped into to help his many friends inside and outside of rugby.

Mika had diabetes from his early 20s and one wonders how much of his potential, like his old mate Jonah Lomu, was stymied by illness. The mothers of Mika, Lam and Tongan international Gus Leger were all Fepulea'i sisters, making the rugby trio first cousins.

His funeral, held at Eden Park, brought rugby people from far and wide. Among the speakers were John Hart, Tana Umaga, Sir Bryan Williams and the CEO of the Samoan Rugby Union, Vincent Fepulea'i.

Mika would have taken pride at the manner in which his old First XV clinched the Auckland and national titles just months later, using his memory as inspiration.

Mika's younger brother Anthony, also a loose forward, played one Test match for Manu Samoa, versus Scotland, in 2000. He is survived by his wife Tracy and young daughter Marley.

(Obituary contributed by Campbell Burnes.)

Dylan Mika's first-class record:

For	Matches	Tries	Points
Auckland (Marist) 1994(5), 1995(14), 1996(13), 1997(11), 1998(2), 1999, 2000(9)	55	19	95
Blues 1996(5), 1997(14), 1998(2), 2000(3)	24	4	20
Chiefs 1999	11	3	15
North Otago Invitation XV 1996	1	–	0
Counties Manukau Invitation XV 1997	1	2	10
Crusaders Invitation XV 1996	1	–	0
New Zealand Barbarians 1996	1	–	0
NEW ZEALAND 1999	8	1	5
TOTALS	**102**	**29**	**145**

At Auckland, 20 March 2018, aged 45.

Keith Murdoch *(Otago, Hawke's Bay and Auckland)* was one of the most powerful forwards to ever wear the All Blacks' jersey yet he appeared in only three tests, the most memorable being against Wales, at Cardiff, in 1972 when he scored a try which, with Joe Karam's five penalty goals, gave New Zealand a narrow 19-16 victory. Sadly, that was the last seen of the 29-year-old, 1.83m, 110kg prop forward. Following an incident with a security guard in the Angel Hotel several hours after the game British administrators placed immense pressure on tour management to send Murdoch home. He never arrived home, choosing to live in outback Australia for the rest of his life.

Keith Murdoch was born on 9 September 1943 and educated at Ravensbourne Primary School and King Edward Technical College. He represented Otago in the fourth and fifth grades and Under-20 grade and in 1964 the 20-year-old played in all 11 of Otago's games appearing at prop and lock. The *Almanack* included Murdoch among its five promising players of the year. He moved to Hawke's Bay in 1965 and appeared in his first All Blacks trial but then moved on to Auckland before returning to Dunedin in 1967. He travelled about a lot until 1969 when he gave a full season to the Otago team and impressed with his strength in the scrums and mobility about the field.

Murdoch was selected for the 1970 tour to South Africa but injuries and illness restricted him to nine tour games including the fourth test. He had a full season with Otago in 1971 but did not meet the touring Lions despite being chosen for the first and third tests. Injury was given as the reason for his withdrawals. In May 1972 Murdoch was in outstanding form during the All Blacks internal tour, he being rested for only one of the nine games. The NZRFU were asked to send representatives to New Caledonia for a fixture at Noumea between a South Pacific Invitation XV and France. All Blacks Keith Murdoch, Phil Gard and Richie Guy were sent over which suggests that the union had no concerns about Murdoch's behaviour at this time. Murdoch suffered a rib injury in the match but he returned to the Otago team in August and played in the third test against Australia at Auckland.

The *Almanack* included Murdoch among its five players of the 1972 season, commenting that Murdoch 'reached the peak of his career to that date during the 1972 season in New Zealand and was a first choice as the outstanding prop forward in the country.... Murdoch maintained his outstanding form on the 1972 tour [UK] in nine of the first 13 matches, and scored a magnificent try in the international against Wales at Cardiff Arms Park, surely the peak of ambition. The tragedy of subsequent events is to be deplored, and does not affect Keith Murdoch's standing as an outstanding prop forward, and one hopes more will be seen of him on the rugby field.'

Keith Murdoch's first-class record:

For	Matches	Tries	Points
Otago (Zingari Richmond) 1964(11), 1967, 1969(13), 1971(11), 1972(7)	43	5	16
Hawke's Bay (Napier Marist) 1965	6	1	3
Auckland (Ponsonby) 1966	2	–	0
Cantabrians Club 1972	1	–	0
South Pacific Invitation XV (v France at Noumea) 1972	1	–	0
South Island 1969, 1971	2	–	0
New Zealand Trials 1965, 1970(2), 1971(2), 1972	6	–	0
NEW ZEALAND 1970(9), 1972(18)	27	6	20
TOTALS	**88**	**12**	**39**

At Carnarvon, Western Australia, 27 February 2018, aged 74.

Poinisitia Teleisia 'Tia' Paasi *(Wellington)* was a strong 99kg prop who could play in both tighthead and loosehead positions and appeared for the Black Ferns in 2001 as a substitute in both tests against England, at Rotorua and Albany. She retired in 2004 but returned to club rugby in 2007 and recalled to the Black Ferns for the two tests against Australia, the 38 year-old being a substitute at Wanganui and gaining a starting position in the second test, played at Porirua Park.

Tia Paasi was active in club rugby for 21 seasons and with clubs not fielding a women's team on a regular basis during the pioneering days of women's rugby she was compelled to play for several clubs and appeared for Poneke, Petone, Wainuiomata and Marist St Pats. However, she played for Johnsonville for 10 years and represented Wellington from 1997 but it wasn't until the establishment of the national provincial competition in 1999 that first-class status was given to provincial rugby. Paasi played in each of Wellington's games during 2000-02 but injury restricted her appearances in 2003. She played for a World XV against the Black Ferns at Eden Park and then retired.

A shortage of players in her club team in 2007 gave her the incentive to play again and she enjoyed a full season with Wellington and a return to the Black Ferns. In 2011 the 41-year-old had her last season in representative rugby.

After her death from illness in early 2018 the Wellington union introduced the Tia Paasi Memorial Cup for the women's senior championship.

Tia Paasi's first-class record:

For	Matches	Tries	Points
Wellington (Johnsonville) 1999, 2000(6), 2001(7), 2002(7), 2003(2), 2007(5), 2008(5), 2009(6) (Marist St Pats) 2011(6)	45	4	20
World XV (v New Zealand) 2003	1	–	0
NEW ZEALAND 2001(2), 2007(2)	4	–	0
TOTALS	**50**	**4**	**20**

At Wellington, 3 March 2018, aged 48.

Gary Alan Seear *(Otago)* commenced his All Black career in 1976 as the junior lock on the tour of South Africa but it soon became apparent that his mobility and lean frame was better suited as a No. 8. While he was an excellent lineout jumper he wasn't as robust as his locking competitors yet his versatility suited the selectors and he was a reserve during the 1977 test series against the Lions but did not take the field. Playing at No. 8 he made his test debut in France in November and in the second test surprised followers by kicking a long-range penalty goal. During 1978 he retained his position during the three-test series against Australia and on the northern tour when Ireland, Wales, England and Scotland were defeated. 1979 was to be his last year in the jersey. In July France was beaten in the first test but then followed two test defeats, France winning the second test, at Auckland, then the Wallabies took possession of the Bledisloe Cup when defeating the All Blacks in Sydney. Seear scored two tries and one penalty goal in his 12 tests.

Gary Seear was born in Dunedin on 19 February 1952 and commenced playing rugby with Southern club when aged eight. At Bayfield High School he was in the first fifteen 1968-69 and the following year went straight into the Southern club senior team. Late in the 1971 season the lanky 19-year-old made his debut for Otago and became a regular the next season. He was chosen in the NZ Under-21 (Colts) team in 1972 and NZ Under-23 (Juniors) in 1973, the Juniors making history with a shock 14-10 win over the All Blacks at Dunedin. Seear was appointed captain of the 1974 NZ Juniors team he contributing a try in the first game, a 55-31 win over Japan.

Apart from 1976, when on the South Africa tour, Seear rarely missed a game for Otago from 1972 through to 1979. Not chosen for the All Blacks northern tour at the end of the 1979 season Seear and his wife went to Italy for 18 months where he played for first division club Fracasso San Dona for two seasons.

Back with Otago in 1981 Seear played in an All Blacks trial and made his sixth appearance for South Island in the annual inter-island fixture. During the season he played his one hundredth game for Otago. He did not support the Springboks tour and made himself unavailable for Otago when that union played the tourists. 1982 was his final season in first-class rugby and he was unavailable for several of Otago's games during August.

Gary Seear's first-class record:

For	Matches	Tries	Con	PG	Points
Otago (Southern) 1971(3), 1972(14), 1973(15), 1974(9), 1975(16), 1977(13), 1978(11), 1981(14), 1982(9)	115	10	–	1	43
Cantabrians Club 1973	1	1	–	–	4
Nelson Bays Invitation XV 1975	1	–	–	–	0
Zingari Richmond Invitation XV 1978	3	1	–	–	4
New Zealand Colts 1972	1	–	–	–	0
New Zealand Juniors 1973(7), 1974(6)	13	3	–	–	12
South Island 1973, 1974, 1975, 1977, 1979, 1981	6	–	–	–	0
New Zealand Trials 1972, 1973, 1974(2), 1975, 1976, 1977, 1978, 1979, 1981	10	3	–	–	12
NEW ZEALAND 1976(11), 1977(6), 1978(13), 1979(4)	34	9	2	2	46
TOTALS	**184**	**27**	**2**	**3**	**121**

At Christchurch, 8 February 2018, aged 65.

Anthony Gordon 'Tony' Steel *(Canterbury)* was developing into a prolific try-scoring All Blacks wing until cruelly struck down with injury in 1968. Having scored 20 tries in just 23 games, including seven in his nine tests, the speedster suffered a niggle in a Achilles tendon but the treatment, intended to repair the strain, resulted in completely burning the tissue and terminating his promising career. He made his debut in 1966, when aged 24, playing in all four tests against the Lions, scoring in three of the tests. The following year two tries against Australia in the jubilee test was followed with the tour to Britain where his tries in the final two games, against East Wales and Barbarians Club, preserved the great team's unbeaten tour record. He played in the tests against France and Scotland and in 1968 appeared in both tests on the Australian tour. He was never in a losing All Blacks team.

Born at Greymouth on 31 July 1941 Tony Steel received his early education at Grey Main Primary School before the family moved to Christchurch when he was aged nine. After attending Waltham Primary School he moved on to Christchurch Boys' High School in 1955 and had three years in the first fifteen 1957-59.

In 1964 Steel played in three first-class games for Canterbury B and early the following season appeared in the South Island trial before promotion to the Canterbury A team. Having established himself as a regular wing tries soon followed, he scoring eight in his final three games including two hat-tricks. During 1966 he was the highest try-scorer in the country with 17 in 16 games the tally included four for Canterbury against Buller. His blistering pace took him past hopeful tacklers. Not surprising considering he was the national 100 yards and 220 yards champion in both 1965 and 1966.

On returning from the 1968 All Blacks' tour of Australia Steel was chosen for the first test against France but was forced to withdraw because of injury. Careless treatment by a physiotherapist resulted in permanent damage to his leg and he never played first-class rugby again.

A schoolteacher, he was at Christchurch BHS 1966-68 then moved to Brisbane Grammar 1968-74. He coached Brisbane's West club and was a Queensland selector in 1974. Back in New Zealand in 1974 he was at Kelston BHS 1974-77, deputy principal at Tauranga Boys' College 1977-79 and, finally, principal at Hamilton Boys' High School 1980-90. He entered politics and was MP for Hamilton East 1990-93 and a further term 1996-2000.

Tony Steel's first-class record:

For	Matches	Tries	DG	Points
Canterbury (HSOB) 1965(12), 1966(10), 1967(10), 1968(2)	34	31	1	96
Canterbury B (HSOB) 1964	3	4	–	12
South Island 1967	1	–	–	0
New Zealand Trials 1965, 1966, 1967(2)	4	3	–	9
Rest of New Zealand 1966	1	–	–	0
NEW ZEALAND 1966(4), 1967(12), 1968(7)	23	20	–	60
TOTALS	**66**	**58**	**1**	**177**

At Hamilton, 4 May 2018, aged 76.

Graham Charles Williams *(Wellington)* over a first-class career spanning 13 seasons between 1964 and 1976, was always rated among the front rank of New Zealand loose forwards. But surprisingly his tenure as an All Black was relatively brief, confined to the 1967 and 1968 seasons when still in his early 20s he seemed on the verge of a long, illustrious international career. He toured Britain and France in 1967, and with Waka Nathan injured and unavailable for much of the tour with a broken jaw, played in all four internationals. He then toured Australia a few months later in 1968, playing in the second test and in one match, against Tasmania, he scored five tries. In his 18 All Blacks matches on those two tours he scored 16 tries.

Among his loose forward contemporaries were Ian Kirkpatrick, Tom Lister and Alex Wyllie, and of this group he appeared the best suited to what has since evolved as an open-side flanker, back of the lineout exponent. But Williams was never again an All Black after 1968 and never once played for the All Blacks at home. He was perhaps unfortunate that it was not until the mid-1970s that New Zealand began to make more use of players of similar physique to Williams as open-side specialists.

Even by the standards of the 1960s and 70s Williams was not big, barely 1.83m and about 90kg. But he always played with an uncompromising commitment and even when playing in some moderate Wellington packs never spared a battle-scarred body. In one match against Auckland in 1974 he played on despite a severed ear.

Williams was introduced to the Wellington representative side in his first year out of Rongotai College. Wellington coach Bill Freeman had intended nursing the 19-year old in his debut season but Williams, with his determination and high work rate, quickly made himself an automatic selection. Williams gave Wellington exemplary service and became a legend in that union. His 173 games for Wellington, many as captain, is a record which still stands and that tally would have been higher had he not been injured during the 1973 representative season. He played in Wellington's 1965-66 wins over the Springboks and the Lions, and ended many Ranfurly Shield disappointments by being in the side which in 1974 won the shield from South Canterbury.

The lack of recognition he received after 1968 did not entirely reflect a harsh assessment of his abilities. He probably would have gone on the 1970 tour of South Africa but was unavailable because he could not be spared from his family business. He might also have made the 1971 series against the Lions but dropped out of calculations when he was in a Wellington side hammered 47-9 by the tourists. His last major appearance at national level was in the 1972 inter-island match.

Williams served the game as an administrator and coach. In 1993-94 he was a Wellington assistant coach and was forward coach for John Hart's New Zealand Colts sides in the early 90s. He became a Wellington life member in 2008 and was union president in 2006. *(Obituary contributed by Lindsay Knight).*

Graham Williams' first-class record:

For	Matches	Tries	Con	PG	Points
Wellington (Wellington) 1964(17), 1965(14), 1966(16), 1967(13), 1968(6), 1969(14), 1970(19), 1971(13), 1972(13), 1974(16), 1975(16), 1976(16)	173	54	3	1	182
Wellington XV 1964	1	–	–	–	0
Wellington Invitation XV 1967	1	–	–	–	0
Centurions Club 1978	1	–	–	–	0
New Zealand Juniors Trial 1967	1	–	–	–	0

New Zealand Juniors 1965, 1966(2), 1967	4	–	–	–	0
North Island 1970	1	–	–	–	0
New Zealand Trials 1965, 1966, 1967(2), 1968, 1969, 1971(2), 1972	9	2	–	–	6
NEW ZEALAND 1967(9), 1968(9)	18	16	1	–	50
TOTALS	**209**	**72**	**4**	**1**	**238**

At Wellington, 25 January 2018, aged 72.

PROVINCIAL REPRESENTATIVES

John Anthony Anderson *(Wellington B)* scored five tries in his three first-class games for Wellington B in 1968. He later became chairman of the NZ Cricket Board, chief executive of the National Bank (1989-2003) and ANZ Bank (NZ) 2003-05. He was knighted in 1995 for services to business management, banking and the community. At Wellington, 13 November 2018, aged 73.

Ramon Franklyn 'Ray' Bell *(Bay of Plenty)* made one appearance, against Thames Valley, in 1952. He was president of Bay of Plenty union 1997-98 and made a life member in 2002. At Manurewa, 4 December 2018, aged 90.

Bruce Donald Bowie *(Wairarapa Bush)* was a flanker from Puketoi club playing 57 games for his union 1989-97. At Pongaroa, 28 February 2018, aged 54.

Ross Alexander Brown *(Wellington)* made two first-class appearances for Wellington B in 1964. At Lower Hutt, 17 January 2018

Alan Francis Bullick *(Hawke's Bay and Waikato)* played nine games for Hawke's Bay 1946-47 and seven for Waikato 1948-50. He represented NZ Services in Britain 1945-46 and took part in trials for selection for the NZ Army 'Kiwis' team and later had four All Blacks trials 1947-50. At Cambridge, 16 March 2018, aged 95.

Brian Finlay Burkhart *(Otago)* made only two appearances for Otago, one in 1956 and the other the following year. The dental student was number eight for the NZ Universities team that defeated the 1956 Springboks. At Hamilton, 17 November 2018, aged 85.

Charles Frederick 'Roger' Burt *(King Country)* was from the Marokopa club and made one appearance for his union in 1952. At Te Kuiti, 1 October 2018, aged 91.

Kevin William 'Pat' Carter *(Bay of Plenty and Manawatu)* made five appearances for Bay of Plenty 1951-52 followed by seven for Manawatu 1953-54. At Hamilton, 5 June 2018, aged 87.

Michael James Clare *(Hawke's Bay)* played one first-class game for Hawke's Bay B in 1964, against Bush. At Taradale, 10 February 2018, aged 80.

Gary Austin Condon *(Hawke's Bay)* was a loose forward during Hawke's Bay's Ranfurly Shield era, he playing 63 games for the union 1965-71. A police constable, he represented NZ Services in 1966. At Napier, 9 October 2018, aged 73.

William Barry Cross *(Nelson and Golden Bay-Motueka)* played once for Nelson in 1959 and once for Golden Bay-Motueka in 1962. Member of the Horowhenua RU management committee 1969-92, treasurer 1991-95, executive officer 1999-2002, president 2003-04, life member, patron from 2011. At Levin, 22 June 2018, aged 81.

Bruno Julio Dalliessi *(Marlborough)* played 79 games 1957-66. NZ amateur heavyweight boxing champion 1955 and 1957. Was mayor of Picton in 1966 when in his last year playing for Marlborough. At Blenheim, 23 August 2018, aged 83.

James Vulavou 'Jimi' Damu *(Auckland)* played only five games for Auckland 1985-87 but he had nine first-class games for Auckland B 1984-89. A wing he played four tests for Fiji and participated at the 1987 RWC. At Auckland, 9 October 2018, aged 56.

Thomas Patrick 'Paddy' Donovan *(Hawke's Bay)* played two games for the Bay in 1955 and a further two in 1959. A prominent boxer he competed at the 1956 and 1964 Olympics and 1958 and 1962 Commonwealth Games. At Napier, 11 March 2018, aged 81.

Gregory Ronald Fuller *(Counties, Nelson Bays and Hawke's Bay)* had 12 games for Counties 1968-70, one appearance for Nelson Bays in 1971 and two for Hawke's Bay in 1972. At Hastings, 4 March 2018, aged 68.

John Phillip Gallagher *(North Otago and South Canterbury)* had a career of 67 first-class games, firstly for North Otago 1947-51 (26 games) then for South Canterbury 1951-55 (28 games). A lock forward he represented South Island 1953-54-55. At Timaru, 25 September 2018, aged 92.

Kevin John 'Jack' Handley *(Thames Valley)* played 110 games for his union during a period of 11 seasons 1979-89, the wing scoring 19 tries. At Paeroa, 30 May 2018, aged 58.

Kerry Charles Hanna *(Bay of Plenty)* was a midfield back appearing in four games during 1975 and a further two in 1977. At Papamoa, 10 September 2018, aged 63.

Mose Matamauroa Harvey *(Poverty Bay)* made one appearance in 1962. Earlier, the five-eighth had appeared for Tai Tokerau 1957-58-59 when in the Auckland region. At Gisborne, 11 February 2018, aged 82.

George Parata Hicks *(Bay of Plenty)* was a lock playing seven games 1970-72. At Welcome Bay, Tauranga, 3 December 2018, aged 71.

Ruruarau Heitia Hiha *(Hawke's Bay and East Coast)* played 19 games for Hawke's Bay 1954-57 then one appearance for East Coast in 1958 and a further six in 1961. Returning to Napier, he played a further 14 games for the Bay in 1963. A lock he represented NZ Maori 1954-56. In 2017 he was honoured with the ONZM for services to Maori. At Hastings, 22 August 2018, aged 85.

Zane Samuel Hiko *(Mid Canterbury)* was halfback in 11 games during 2007. He died 14 November 2018 when he got into difficulties while diving off Mahia Peninsula. He was aged 36.

Eric Arthur Hogge *(Hawke's Bay)* played at lock in 41 games for his union 1956-62. He won a national junior surf lifesaving title in 1952 and in 1956 was awarded the Royal Humane Society's bronze medal for a rescue off Napier's Marine Parade. At Napier, 25 May 2018, aged 84.

Obituaries

Barry Humphrey *(Golden Bay-Motueka)* appeared in two games, as a threequarter, in 1955. At Tauranga, 14 June 2018.

Huia Ralph Hutton *(Wellington)* played three games for Wellington A in 1968 and also nine first-class games for Wellington B 1968-70 and two for Wellington Colts 1966-67. At Palmerston North, 10 April 2018, aged 72.

Donald Melville Ineson *(South Canterbury)* played 25 games 1988-90. He was a lock from Mackenzie club. Died in a police incident near Darfield, 25 November 2018, aged 56.

Frank Whanau Pani Jones *(Hawke's Bay)* played 27 games 1961-67 and represented Tai Rawhiti in 1961. At Ruapekapeka, Whangarei, 9 January 2018, aged 78.

Russell Raata Kemp *(North Auckland)* was a prop playing 23 games for his union 1975-76. He coached North Auckland in 1990. Died 10 January 2018, aged 71.

Melanie Leanne 'Piwi' King *(Bay of Plenty)* played five games for the Bay of Plenty Volcanix in 2001. She died in a work place accident at a Kawerau sawmill, 5 October 2018, aged 39.

Max Bayley Mabin *(Nelson)* made one appearance in 1946, he also making a first-class appearance for the Nelson Colts team, against Centurions club. At Napier, 18 March 2018, aged 92.

James Ronald 'Jim' McCaa *(Golden Bay-Motueka)* played eight games, at lock, 1961-62. At Nelson, 20 March 2018, aged 83.

Leigh Warwick 'Mac' McCallion *(Counties)* was prominent in Counties teams 1973-80, playing 46 games. He captained the NZ Maori team in 1978 and on the 1979 tour of Australia, Fiji, Samoa and Tonga. Earlier, the soldier served in the Vietnam War and represented NZ Services in 1971. Counties coach 1995-99, Blues assistant coach 1996-99 and Fiji RU director of coaching 2002-03. At Papakura, 14 March 2018, aged 67.

Trevor John McGrath *(Nelson Bays)* was a flanker playing 11 games 1980-84. At Stoke, 16 October 2018, aged 59.

Kevyn George Male *(Auckland)* played 18 games for Auckland 1964-70 and was vice-captain of the 1964 NZ Colts team in Australia. At Auckland, 4 December 2018, aged 75.

Nehemiah Samson 'Miah' Melsom *(Waikato)* played 13 games for NZ Maori 1978-82, the loose forward appearing in 110 games for his union 1977-84. He played a total of 133 first-class games. At Ngaruawahia, 6 June 2018, aged 65.

Henry Graeme Albert Mitchell *(Manawatu and Bush)* made one appearance for Manawatu, at lock, in 1958 and one game for Bush in 1963. Both games were against Wellington. At Palmerston North, 25 December 2018, aged 79.

Ereatara 'Eri' Mohi *(Bay of Plenty)* played once for his union in 1970 and once for NZ Maori the same season. A hooker, he represented Northern Maori 1970-71 in the annual Prince of Wales Cup fixture. At Rotorua, 11 May 2018, aged 72.

Stuart Noel Morton *(Otago and West Coast)* made four appearances for Otago in 1956 followed by 24 for West Coast 1960-62. At Alexandra, 8 June 2018, aged 88.

Marc Nathan Morunga *(King Country and Waikato)* was a lock playing 48 games for King Country 2000-04 and seven for Waikato 2005-06. Drowned at Lake Wanaka, 29 January 2018, aged 39.

Kevin John Murray *(Thames Valley)* played eight games for his union 1974-75. At Hamilton, 18 February 2018, aged 69.

Barry Robert Neale *(Hawke's Bay and Wellington)* was halfback for Hawke's Bay in 65 games 1958-59, 62-65 and for Wellington in five games 1960-61. At Napier, 11 November 2018, aged 80.

Murray Graham Niven *(Wellington)* was a halfback playing two first-class games for Wellington Colts 1969-70 and once for Wellington B in 1976. At Palmerston North, 6 March 2018, aged 68.

Hohepa Justyn 'Hepa' Paewai *(Hawke's Bay)* was halfback during the Bay's Ranfurly Shield era he playing in 64 games for his union 1966-77. Represented NZ Maori in 1969 and was Hawke's Bay selector-coach 1997. At Okawa, 22 February 2018, aged 70.

Ernest William Pauling *(Golden Bay-Motueka)* made one appearance in 1958, against Nelson. At Brightwater, 12 June 2018, aged 85.

Byron Quigan *(Bush and Manawatu)* played seven games for Bush 1970 followed by four for Manawatu 1975-76. At New Plymouth, 29 May 2018, aged 67.

Douglas Edward Allen Reeves *(Hawke's Bay and Canterbury)* made four appearances for the Bay in 1945 followed by 12 for Canterbury 1949-50. He represented South Island in 1949. At Whangarei, 17 July 2018, aged 91.

Laurie Richardson *(Manawatu)* was a long-serving hooker for his union appearing in 88 games 1949-59. He represented North Island in 1951. At Mt Maunganui, 1 June 2018, aged 89.

Haki 'Jack' Ririnui *(Bay of Plenty)* was a lock playing eight games for his union 1949-52. At Tauranga, 29 June 2018, aged 91.

James Nepia Ritchie *(King Country)* played 27 games for his union 2012-16. Died in a car accident on 4 February 2018, Te Kuiti, aged 31.

Huru 'Sonny' Rutene *(Poverty Bay)* had a long career of 90 games spanning 14 seasons for Poverty Bay 1955-68 and represented NZ Maori 1959-60. The five-eighth played a total of 116 first-class games. At Patutahi, Gisborne, 15 December 2018.

Herbert John Schuler *(Thames Valley)* was a lock in 16 games 1951-58. He was the father of All Black Kevin and Thames Valley representatives John and Paul. At Te Aroha West, 16 August 2018, aged 89.

Douglas Antony Scrimgeour *(Hawke's Bay)* played nine games for his union 1958-59. He was the father of NZ Sevens representative Owen. At Otaki, 24 September 2018, aged 89.

John Dennis Sherlock *(Auckland)* was a regular lock in NZ Universities teams 1967-71 playing 25 games. He played 15 games for his union 1970-71. At Auckland, 5 August 2018, aged 72.

Leslie Ernest Simmons *(Wellington and Bay of Plenty)* played 10 games for Wellington 1949-50 and also first-class appearances for Wellington XV and the B team. In 1951 he played twice for Bay of Plenty. At Tauranga, 8 June 2018, aged 80.

James Clifford 'Jim' Simpson *(Otago, Wellington and Horowhenua)* played 13 games for Otago 1972-73 and then three first-class games for Wellington B 1976-77 and, finally, 12 appearances for Horowhenua 1978-81. At Otaki, 24 February 2018, aged 70.

Spencer James 'Jim' Speedy *(Bush)* was from Weber club playing 15 games for his union 1956-61 and for Wairarapa-Bush in 1956 and 1959. The 19-year-old prop opposed experienced Springbok prop Chris Koch in 1956. At Feilding, 12 August 2018, aged 81.

Donald George Sturgeon *(Golden Bay-Motueka)* played 40 games at five-eighth 1955-62. His brother Neil also appeared for the union and sons George and Graham played for Nelson Bays. At Motueka, 17 May 2018, aged 85.

Martin Joseph 'Joe' Syron *(Buller)* made 62 appearances for his union 1961-73, mainly at prop. He was the Buller coach in 1986. At Greymouth, 21 August 2017, aged 80.

Edward Te Rangihiwinui 'Hiwi' Tauroa *(Manawatu, Taranaki and Auckland)* was a fullback appearing for Manawatu in 10 games 1950-51, one first-class game for Auckland B in 1952 and three games for Taranaki 1953-55. He represented NZ Universities 1951 and NZ Maori 1951-54. Later principal of Wesley College 1968-74 and Tuakau College 1974-79. Counties coach 1976-79. He was Race Conciliator 1979-86 and in 1994 made a Companion of the Order of St Michael and St George (CMG) for services to the community. At Hokianga, 11 December 2018, aged 91.

Barney John Te Kani *(NZ Defence Force)* played four games for the Defence Force in 2015. At Burnham, 3 January 2018, aged 28.

Robert John 'Bob' 'Tommo' Thompson *(Bay of Plenty)* played once for Bay of Plenty in 1968, the hooker then appearing in the annual Prince of Wales Cup after which he was chosen for NZ Maori for the game against Manawatu. He moved to Perth and represented Western Australia against the touring All Blacks in 1970 and in 1971 was the first player from Western Australia to be selected for Australia, he making his test debut against the touring Springboks. He toured with the Wallabies to France later that year and to Fiji and New Zealand in 1972. At Rotorua, 18 November 2018, aged 71.

Colin Roderick Twigley *(Poverty Bay and Taranaki)* played seven games for Poverty Bay in 1964 and two for Taranaki in 1967. At New Plymouth, 6 May 2018, aged 73.

Isaia Vuki *(Poverty Bay)* was a loan player from Whakatane 2016-17 scoring 103 points in his 16 appearances. At Nadi, Fiji, 4 March 2018, aged 24.

Edward John 'Eddie' Watts *(Hawke's Bay)* played six games in 1959. He was the union's chairman 1981-84 and made a life member in 1992. At Hastings, 15 May 2018, aged 82.

Donald Richard Wills *(Golden Bay-Motueka)* made two appearances in 1957 and a further two in 1959. He died 1 January 2018.

Andrew March Wilson *(Wellington)* was a first five-eighth for Wellington B in five first-class games. At Wellington, 5 June 2018, aged 64.

DISTINGUISHED OPPONENTS

Angus William 'Gus' Black *(Scotland and British Isles)* toured New Zealand with the 1950 Lions. The halfback played in eight games including the first two tests. At Dunfermline, 14 February 2018, aged 92.

Daniel Sarel 'Darius' Botha *(South Africa)* played on the wing in seven games, including the first test, during the 1981 Springboks tour of New Zealand. He died on 12 February 2018, aged 62.

Gertjie Steenkamp Brynard *(South Africa)* played on the wing in 16 games during the 1965 Springboks tour and appeared in all four tests, he scoring two tries in the 19-16 win at Christchurch. At Hermanus, Western Cape, 1 December 2018, aged 80.

Wynand Jacobus Mans *(South Africa)* played at centre and wing in 12 games during the 1965 Springboks tour of New Zealand but did not appear in the test series. At Hermanus, Western Cape, 6 December 2018, aged 76.

Sydney Harold Nomis *(South Africa)* played seven tour games at centre during the 1965 Springboks tour of New Zealand but did not oppose the All Blacks until the 1970 test series when he played in all four tests on the wing and scored a try in the first. At Johannesburg, 16 June 2018, aged 76.

Sir Nicholas Shehadie *(Australia)* was a regular in Wallaby teams from 1947 until 1958 and opposed the All Blacks in 10 tests in 1947, 1949, 1951, 1952, 1955 and 1957. Playing at lock or prop he visited New Zealand with Wallaby teams in 1949, 1952 and 1955. At Sydney, 11February 2018, aged 91.

Claude Brian 'Stack' Stevens *(England and British Isles)* played 25 tests for England 1969-75 including two against New Zealand. The first was at Twickenham in January 1973 and in September the prop scored a try in England's upset 16-10 win over the All Blacks at Eden Park. In 1971 he was a mid-tour replacement during the Lions tour and played in six games. He died on 10 October 2017, aged 77.

Clive Anthony Ulyate *(South Africa)* played 11 games, including the first three tests, during the 1956 Springbok tour of New Zealand. He was a first five-eighth. At Virginia, Free State, 18 March 2018, aged 84.

FIRST-CLASS REFEREES

Douglas Peter Cameron *(Manawatu)* was halfback for his union in one game in 1954. As a referee in Manawatu he controlled nine home games between 1959 and 1965. At Palmerston North, 18 March 2018, aged 89.

Samuel Hamish Grant *(Manawatu)* controlled six of Manawatu's home games between 1965 and 1973. At Palmerston North, 9 April 2018, aged 89.

Kelvyn Ross Kendrew *(North Otago)* controlled two games in 1975. The next year he moved to Fiji where he continued refereeing. At Wellington, 1 May 2018, aged 79.

Noel Scott *(Bay of Plenty, Wairarapa and Wairarapa Bush)* had eight games 1963-67 when with Bay of Plenty before moving to Masterton to become foundation principal of Makoura College. He had a further eight first-class appointments with Wairarapa RRA 1968-71. His major appointment was British Isles against Manawatu-Horowhenua in 1966. Later MP for Tongariro 1984-90. Awarded QSO 2002 for public services. At Tauranga, 25 February 2018, aged 88.

AMENDMENTS

to 2018 edition

Page 38	attendance was 38,931
Page 39	attendance was 48,906
Page 43	Ardie Savea (sub Cane 57m), not the reverse.
Page 61	attendance was 29,620
Page 64	attendance was 38,690
Page 82	Damien Scott was from Otago, not Auckland.
Page 97	v Bulls. Moulds, not Moala, scored a try.
Page 102	v Rebels. Score should read 27-14, not 27-13.
Page 106	v Reds, was played at Brisbane, not Melbourne.
	v Stormers. J. Savea, not A. Savea, scored a try.
Page 110/111	Opposing teams scored 345 points, not 376.
Page 113	Ash Dixon shared captaincy duties with Ben Smith, not Christie.
Page 116	v Sunwolves, was played at Invercargill, not Dunedin.
	v Blues (April 8) score should read 26-20. Total points against was 347, not 387.
Page 117	Reds v Sharks. J-L du Preez was a try scorer, not du Plessis.
	Hurricanes v Sunwolves. Kin, not Kim, was a try scorer.
Page 118	Hurricanes v Rebels. Referee N. Berry is from Australia, not South Africa.
	Cheetahs v Bulls. Jenkins, not Jordaan, was a try scorer.
Page 119	Lions v Reds. Paia'aua, not Perese, was a try scorer.
Page 120	Blues v Bulls. Moulds, not Moala, was a try scorer.
Page 121	Force v Kings. de Wet, not Cronje, kicked a penalty goal.
Page 123	Lions v Force. M. Fraser (NZ) was the referee, not A. Gardner.
	Hurricanes v Stormers. J. Savea, not A. Savea, was a try scorer.
Page 128	Force v Waratahs. Grant kicked 2 conversions and Lance 1 conversion.
Page 238	v Counties Manukau. Sweeney kicked 3 conversions and Christie 1 conversion.
	v Bay of Plenty. Score should read 32-36.
Page 273	Jackson was also referee on March 31, Highlanders v Rebels at Dunedin.
Page 275	Ringrose was also referee on October 14, Thames Valley v Poverty Bay at Te Aroha.
Page 359	Tangen-Wainohu's career games should read 13 and Woods' 43 games.
Page 379	v Canterbury (semi-final). Hayes scored 1 try, not 2.

to 2017 edition

Page 169	S.B. Malcolm was a sub v Bay of Plenty.

to 2015 edition

Page 20	James W. Parsons was born at Palmerston North, not Auckland.